THE
EMIGRATION
GROUP

LICENSED BY

MIGRATION AGENT

D0230167

Living & Working in AUSTRALIA

• A Survival Handbook •

David Hampshire

First published 1988
Eighth edition 2013

Survival Books Limited
Office 169, 3 Edgar Buildings, George Street, Bath, BA1 2FJ, UK
+44 (0)1935-700060, info@survivalbooks.net
www.survivalbooks.net

British Library Cataloguing in Publication Data.
A CIP record for this book is available from the British Library.
ISBN: 978-1-907339-07-3

Also available as ePUB/Kindle (ISBN: 978-1-909282-61-2)

Printer in Singapore by International Press Softcom Limited

Acknowledgements

My sincere thanks to all those who contributed to the successful publication of this, the eighth edition of Living and Working in Australia, in particular Sarah Bowyer of the Emigration Group for unravelling the mysteries of the visa system; Leo Lacey for research; Peter Read for editing and updating; Di Bruce-Kidman for research, photo selection, DTP and cover design; David Woodworth for final proofing; and Jim Watson for the cartoons and maps. Also a big thank you to the many people who contributed to this and previous editions, including Alan Allebone, Ruth Barringham, Eugene Benham, James Burton, Graeme Chesters, Graeme Dargi, John Holmes, Adèle Jekgan, Nassem Mohammed, Yolande Pierce-Holmes, Vera Poole, Dianne Rodgers, Joanna Styles, Ian Wallace and anyone else I've omitted to mention.

Finally, special thanks to all the photographers (see page 365) – the unsung heroes – whose beautiful images add colour and bring Australia to life. And, last but not least, the publisher would like to thank the Emigration Group for their continuing support

REVIEWS

Reader (Amazon)

"This book is highly recommended to serious people who are look for Immigrating to Canada. This book is very useful since you will know exactly what all u must do and what all u must not do when you are in Canada. It gives u an OUTLINE of Jobs and many other things which u must know when you want to settle in Canada. A MUST TO READ FOR IMMIGRANTS"

Living France Magazine

"If I were to move to France, I would like David Hampshire to be with me, holding my hand every step of the way. This being impractical, I would have to settle for second best and take his books with me instead!"

Reader (Amazon)

"I read most of the books available on this subject before migrating to Australia, so I feel confident enough to say that although this guide is sometimes exhausting... if you pick out the information which is relevant to you the information is golden."

The Riviera Reporter

"Let's say it at once. David Hampshire's Living and Working in France is the best handbook ever produced for visitors and foreign residents in this country; indeed, my discussion with locals showed that it has much to teach even those born and bred in l'Hexagone. It is Hampshire's meticulous detail which lifts his work way beyond the range of other books with similar titles. This book is absolutely indispensable."

ICI (Switzerland) AG

"We would like to congratulate you on this work: it is really super! We hand it out to our expatriates and they read it with great interest and pleasure."

Reader (Amazon)

"I have been travelling to Spain for more than seven years and thought I knew everything - David has done his homework well - Excellent book and very informative! Buy it!"

American Citizens Abroad

"It's everything you always wanted to ask but didn't for fear of the contemptuous put down – The best English language guide – Its pages are stuffed with practical information on everyday subjects and are designed to complement the traditional guidebook."

Reader (Amazon)

"A must for all future expats. I invested in several books but this is the only one you need. Every issue and concern is covered, every daft question you have but are frightened to ask is answered honestly without pulling any punches. Highly recommended."

France in Print

"Covers every conceivable question that might be asked concerning everyday life – I know of no other book that could take the place of this one."

Swiss News

"Rarely has a 'survival guide' contained such useful advice – This book dispels doubts for first time travellers, yet is also useful for seasoned globetrotters – In a word, if you're planning to move to the US or go there for a long term stay, then buy this book both for general reading and as a ready reference."

Important Note

Australia is a vast country with many faces and numerous ethnic groups, religions and customs, and continuously changing rules and regulations, particularly with regard to immigration, social security, health services, education and taxes (a change of government can have far-reaching consequences). Each state and territory also has different laws and regulations, encompassing a wide range of subjects. I cannot recommend too strongly that you check with an official and reliable source (not always the same) before making any major decisions or taking an irreversible course of action. However, don't believe everything you're told or read – even, dare I say it – herein!

Useful addresses, websites and references to other sources of information have been included in all chapters and in **Appendices A, B** and **C** to help you obtain further information and verify details with official sources. Important points have been emphasised, in boxes or bold print, some of which it would be expensive, or even dangerous, to disregard. **Ignore them at your peril or cost!**

Unless specifically stated, the reference to any company, organisation or product in this book doesn't constitute an endorsement or recommendation. None of the businesses, products or individuals recommended in this book have paid to be mentioned (apart from the sponsor).

Contents

Author's Notes

- All times are shown using am (ante meridiem) for before noon and pm (post meridiem) for after noon. Most Australians don't use the 24-hour clock. All times are local, so check the time difference when making international telephone calls (see **Time Difference** on page 326).
- All prices are in Australian dollars unless otherwise noted. Prices should be taken as estimates only, although they were mostly correct at the time of publication. (See 💻 www.xe.com to make currency conversions.)
- His/he/him also means her/she/her – please forgive me ladies. This is done to make life easier for both the reader and the author, and isn't intended to be sexist.
- Spelling is (or should be) British English and not American English.
- Warnings and important points are printed in **bold** type.
- The following symbols are used in this book: ☎ (telephone), 💻 (Internet) and ✉ (email).
- Lists of **Useful Addresses, Further Reading** and **Useful Websites** are contained in **Appendices A, B** and **C** respectively.
- Maps are contained inside the back cover (states) and in **Appendix D** (communications).

Pinnacles, Fraser Island

Introduction

Whether you're already living or working in Australia or just thinking about it – this is THE BOOK for you. Forget about those glossy guide books, excellent though they are for tourists; this amazing book was written especially with you in mind and is worth its weight in snags. Furthermore, this fully revised and updated 8th edition is printed in colour. *Living and Working in Australia* is designed to meet the needs of anyone wishing to know the essentials of Australian life – however long your intended stay, you'll find the information contained in this book invaluable.

General information isn't difficult to find in Australia, but reliable and up-to-date information specifically intended for foreigners living and working in Australia isn't so easy to find, least of all in one volume. Our aim in publishing this book is to help fill this void and provide the comprehensive, practical information necessary for a relatively trouble-free life. You may have visited Australia as a tourist, but living and working there is a different matter altogether. Adjusting to a different environment and culture and making a home in any foreign country can be a traumatic and stressful experience – and Australia is no exception.

Living and Working in Australia is a comprehensive handbook on a wide range of everyday subjects and represents the most up-to-date source of general information available to foreigners in Australia. It isn't, however, simply a monologue of dry facts and figures, but a practical and entertaining look at life.

Adjusting to life in a new country is a continuous process, and although this book will help reduce your 'beginner's' phase and minimise the frustrations, it doesn't contain all the answers (most of us don't even know the right questions to ask!). What it will do, is help you make informed decisions and calculated judgements, instead of uneducated guesses and costly mistakes. **Most importantly, it will save you time, trouble and money, and repay your investment many times over!**

Although you may find some of the information a bit daunting, don't be discouraged. Most problems occur only once and fade into insignificance after a short time (as you face the next half a dozen!). Most foreigners in Australia would agree that, all things considered, they love living there. A period spent in Australia is a wonderful way to enrich your life, broaden your horizons, and with any luck (and some hard yakka), also please your bank manager. I trust *Living and Working in Australia* will help you avoid the pitfalls of life in Australia and smooth your way to a happy and rewarding future in your new home.

Good luck!

David Hampshire
October 2012

1.
FINDING A JOB

Not surprisingly, Australia is a popular destination among prospective migrants; few countries offer such an attractive lifestyle, high standard of living, and good business and employment prospects. Australia has a labour force of around 10m and a relatively low unemployment rate (around 5 per cent). However, if you don't automatically qualify to live or work in Australia, e.g. as a citizen or resident of New Zealand, obtaining a visa is likely to be more difficult than finding a job. Australia is no longer the fabled 'land of opportunity' or ' the lucky country' – at least not for the type of migrant it previously welcomed. As former Prime Minister Bob Hawke famously declared, Australia would become 'the clever country' through the importation of highly educated and skilled workers, with the emphasis on science and innovation.

In the early years of the 21st century, the UK was the largest source of 'skilled migrants' (see **Chapter 3**) with around 15 per cent of the total. Migrant quotas have risen considerably after a low of just 85,000 in 2001-02, to 158,630 in 2007-08, 185,000 in 2011-12 and 190,000 in 2012-13 (the last two are target levels). Australian embassies and consulates receive enquiries from around a million people a year, of whom over 400,000 make applications. Of those accepted in recent years, around a third have relatives in Australia, while the vast majority of the remainder are professionals or skilled workers or people with business skills.

The Australian government provides a wealth of resources for jobseekers (🖳 http://australia.gov.au/people/jobseekers) and Australian states also have websites that provide information for those wishing to live, work or invest in Australia, such as 🖳 www.liveinvictoria.vic.gov.au and www.business.nsw.gov.au.

ECONOMY

Australia has a prosperous market economy which is dominated by its service sector – including tourism, education and financial services (around 70 per cent of GDP) – with the mining (and mining-related) sector representing almost 20 per cent of GDP. Rich in natural resources, Australia is also a major exporter of agricultural products, particularly wheat and wool. Manufacturing accounts for around 10 per cent of GDP.

Although agriculture and natural resources constitute only 3 and 5 per cent of GDP respectively, they contribute substantially to export performance, although mining accounts for the bulk of exports and is the driving force behind economic growth. The country is a major exporter of bauxite, coal, copper, diamonds, food products, (natural) gas, gold, grain, iron, lead, meat, mineral sands, opals, silver, tin, tungsten, uranium, wool and zinc. Its largest export markets are Japan, China, South Korea, India and the US.

In the last few decades, Australia has gone from boom to bust and back again, the prosperous '80s being followed by the worst recession since the Great Depression of the '30s – a recession which hit Australia earlier than most other developed countries. There followed a period of sustained growth until the onset of the worldwide recession in

2008, although Australia was one of only a few countries to avoid recession. Historically, from 1959 until 2012, Australia's GDP Growth Rate averaged 0.89 per cent, reaching an all time high of 4.5 per cent in March 1976 and a record low of -2 per cent in June 1974.

GDP growth was around 3 per cent in 2011 and 1.3 per cent in the first quarter of 2012. In April 2012, the International Monetary Fund (IMF) predicted that Australia would be the best performing major advanced economy in the world over the next two years, while the Australian Government Department of the Treasury anticipated growth of 3 per cent in 2012 and 3.5 per cent in 2013, although these forecasts have generally now been cut by around 0.5 per cent. Inflation was around 1.6 per cent in March 2012 and the base interest rate 3.5 per cent in August 2012.

EMPLOYMENT PROSPECTS

In the 20th century Australia's economic success was based on its abundant agricultural and (later) mineral and fuels resources. However, while these sectors remain important, Australia has increasingly become a knowledge-based economy. Many factors have contributed to this development: the pace of technological and social change; the influx of highly-educated and trained migrants; advances in transport making travel cheaper and faster; the influence of the internet which has accelerated the exchange of ideas; and broader access to higher education.

If you want a good job in Australia, you must usually be well qualified and speak fluent English – if you're an independent migrant, you won't be accepted without these skills. Unemployment is high among non-English speaking adult migrants, particularly those from the Indian subcontinent, the Middle East and North Africa, who came to Australia under the Family Reunion Program (although two-thirds have professional qualifications), many of whom believe that they were better off before coming to Australia.

Most states publish data on current job prospects, indicating occupations with a shortage of experienced workers. However, it's important to obtain the latest information concerning jobs (official information sometimes lags behind the situation 'on the ground'); if possible, try to secure a position before your arrival. It's advantageous to make a fact-finding visit to Australia to check your job prospects first hand, although this may not be feasible; a research trip can also help you judge more accurately whether you're likely to enjoy the Australian way of life. This may also help you find a prospective employer willing to sponsor you, which makes the task of obtaining a visa much easier.

If you plan to arrive in Australia without a job, you should have a detailed plan for finding employment on arrival and try to make some contacts in advance. You shouldn't plan on obtaining immediate employment unless you have a firm job offer or special qualifications and experience for which there's a strong local demand, for example in IT or medicine.

The Australian job market changed dramatically in the '90s, during which most new jobs shifted from construction, finance and manufacturing to the communications, property and service industries, e.g. retailing and computing. In fact, Australia has undergone an economic revolution, during which many sacred cows have gone to the wall, including the power of the unions, protectionism, state ownership and the welfare state.

There has been huge job growth in the white-collar services sector in recent years, particularly in property and business support services, which now employ some 80 per cent of the sector's workforce and are responsible for 25 per cent of export earnings. Agriculture (including fishing, forestry, horses, horticulture and the service industries to agriculture and agribusiness) has also created some 20,000 jobs in the last decade or so. Retailing is the largest source of jobs in Australia, with over 1m workers; property and business services are the second-largest, and manufacturing the third, although its share of national employment has fallen to around 10 per cent. In the last decade most new jobs have been created in Queensland and Western Australia due to the booming mining sectors in these states, although there are also mining jobs in other states.

Australian manufacturers and the labour market were relatively slow to embrace new technology and to adjust to the rapidly changing world economy, although there's now an intensive government drive to rectify this. Many companies used to depend on (declining) assistance through export incentives, production bounties and import tariffs rather than aiming to eradicate restrictive working practices, improve productivity and reduce costs. Australian productivity is lower than that of the US and many other Western countries. Like most developed countries, Australia has found it increasingly difficult to compete with cheap imports from countries (e.g. in Asia) where labour costs are much lower.

The information technology age has spawned a new class of casual, low paid, low skilled, part-time workers, and one of the trade unions' main fears is that new technology will create an 'underclass' and dump thousands of people on the job scrap heap. Although there was major job-shedding by banks and utility companies in the mid-'90s, in recent years economic growth has led to greater employment. Indeed, while new technology is blamed for putting people out of work in some industries, it's credited with creating jobs overall. Australia's job market, like that of most developed countries, was transformed in the '90s and it's important for workers in the 21st century to keep their skills up to date in order to stay ahead of the pack.

There are currently shortages of skilled workers in many sectors, including medicine, where there's a particular need for doctors and nurses in regional areas.

Although it isn't as easy to find work as it was a few years previously, there's a steady demand for skilled workers in most regions and a shortage in some areas, which has been exacerbated by a sharp reduction in apprenticeships and training in recent years. If you have a choice, compare the job or business opportunities in all states and territories before deciding where to live, as job prospects vary considerably from city to city and state to state, as does the culture, lifestyle and weather. Some states (notably South Australia) have a shortage of skilled workers and sometimes offer incentives to migrants such as job-matching schemes, low-interest loans and subsidised accommodation. It's also easier to qualify for immigration if you're willing to settle outside the major cities in a designated 'low-growth' area, and in recent years job prospects have improved faster in regional centres than in state capitals.

Job Outlook is an initiative of the Department of Education, Employment and Workplace Relations (DEEWR), which maintains the Job Outlook website (💻 http://joboutlook.gov.au/pages/alpha.aspx#a), which provides data on employment characteristics, trends and prospects for occupations. For each occupation, Job Outlook has links to vacancies on the Australia JobSearch website (💻 http://jobsearch.gov.au/default.aspx).

Workforce

The jobs lost in the last decade or so have generally been well-paid skilled and semi-skilled manufacturing jobs, which have often been replaced by low-paid, part-time or temporary jobs with few benefits (over 2m workers, or around 40 per cent of the workforce, are estimated to be currently part-time or casual). Labour experts believe that the era of secure, full-time employment with comprehensive employee benefits and lifetime guarantees has gone forever (not just in Australia, but worldwide).

Today, employees must be flexible, with diverse and up-to-date skills, constantly renewed through further education and training. Australia has a highly mobile labour force (around a quarter of the workforce changes jobs each year), particularly among the young, and even managers and executives often need to change careers or move to another city to stay in work. An increasing number of people are 'tele-working' (working from home via the internet and telephone), either from choice or because their employers have closed offices to reduce costs. There are over half a million full or part-time home-based workers in Australia – which is growing much faster than the rate of overall employment – and it's estimated that home workers will comprise around 25 per cent of the workforce in the next decade.

Australia's workforce often lacks the skills and knowledge necessary in today's high-tech marketplace, which is why it has streamlined its migrant Skilled Occupations List (see 🖳 www.immi.gov.au/skilled/sol) and is planning to overhaul the country's education and training sector in order to provide the skills required by the current, emerging and future labour market (see 🖳 www.skillsaustralia.gov.au).

Women

Male chauvinism is alive and positively thriving in Australia, where women employees also face the additional hazard of sexual harassment (see **Discrimination** on page 52. Some 55 per cent of Australian women work, and they comprise around 45 per cent of the total workforce, including 35 per cent of full-time employees and 75 per cent of part-time workers (half of employed women work part-time). A woman doing the same or broadly similar work to a man and employed by the same employer is legally entitled to the same pay and terms of employment as a man ('equal pay for work of equal value'). However, as in most developed countries, although there's no official discrimination, in practice it's commonplace.

Despite equal pay legislation, enshrined in the Sex Discrimination Act of 1984, women have found it impossible to close the pay gap between themselves and men. Women are disadvantaged in terms of pay scales at all levels of employment in all industries and professions, and most employers pay only lip service to equal pay. According to the Australian Council of Trade Unions, women receive an average of around 15-20 per cent (higher in professional jobs) less than men for doing the same work, called the 'gender pay gap'.

Women's only advantage is probably that unemployment is lower among women than among men. Careers in which women predominate, such as librarianship, nursery and primary school teaching, nursing, and speech and occupational therapy, are poorly paid compared with those where men dominate. The concentration of women in part-time work is also widening the gap between male and female earnings.

In recent years, women have been moving into male-dominated professions in increasing numbers, including accountancy, auditing and mathematics. However, although more women are breaking into the professions, they don't usually reach the top, where the 'old boy' network thrives. The main discrimination among women professionals isn't in salary or title but in promotion opportunities, as many companies and organisations are loath to elevate women to important positions, ostensibly because of fears that they may leave and start a family or at least take long breaks from work – only around 20 per cent of men take leave from work for family reasons,

compared with some 40 per cent of women. Employers are (not surprisingly) wary of female employees becoming pregnant, as after one year's employment they're entitled to 12 months' (unpaid) maternity leave, after which they have the right to return to the same job with the same pay.

This invisible barrier is known as the 'glass ceiling'. The saying 'the best man for the job is often a woman' is seldom acknowledged by Australian employers, most of whom prefer male candidates. Although the glass ceiling is less of an obstacle to success than previously (cracks have been appearing in recent years), men are four times more likely than women to be managers and administrators. Women are rare among the directors of major companies and fewer than 5 per cent of Australia's top 200 companies have a female CEO and only one in twelve board members are women. Most successful businesswomen are forced to put their career before their family (most don't have children) and personal life, and most female executives work over 50 hours a week.

☑ **SURVIVAL TIP**

Self-employment is the best bet for women who want to get to the top and has increased steadily during the last decade, despite the fact that banks and other financial institutions are usually reluctant to lend women money.

Industrial Relations

Industrial relations have historically been poor in Australia, with a constant cycle of confrontation between workers, management and the government. However, there has been a huge reduction in strikes during the last two decades due, among other things, to legislation. The deal between unions and employers instigated by the Labor Party when it came to power in the early '80s was followed by the Workplace Relations Act of 1996 and the 2005 Amendment, which allowed any party affected by a strike to 'apply' for its cessation (previously, this could be done only if Australian industry as a whole was significantly affected). The WorkChoices programme introduced in 2006 and the Fair Work Act 2009 (see 🖳 www.fwa.gov.au) also helped reduce tension between workers and employers.

Instead of higher wages, workers now tend to be given better working conditions and benefits, which has helped put a brake on runaway inflation and strengthened the economy, though inevitably at some cost to employee protection, working hours and wages. According to the Australian Bureau of Statistics, since the Workplace Relations Act was passed there has been an average annual number of 61 working days lost per 1,000 employees due to disputes, while in the decade before the Act the average was 174.

Unemployment

Australia generally has more problems with labour shortages than with unemployment, although unemployment has risen from a 30-year low in 2007 to 5.1 per cent in mid-2010, where it remained in mid-2012. The rate varied from 3.4 per cent in the ACT to 7.3 per cent in Tasmania, with NSW being right on the average. However, many commentators consider the real unemployment figure to be much higher, as many people in 'employment' are in low-paid, part-time jobs (around 1m people are reckoned to be under-employed).

Unemployment is much higher in rural areas (which is why most migrants head for the cities), among unskilled and semi-skilled workers, and in the younger and older age groups (most long-term unemployed are aged under 25 or over 45). Age discrimination is widespread in Australia, although it's illegal to specify age limits in job advertisements in some states; however, employers are beginning to discover that older people are generally more reliable, which has made it easier for them to find jobs.

Unemployment is, not surprisingly, much higher than average among migrants who don't speak fluent English. In recent years, many migrants who have been unable to find a job have experienced great hardship, as they cannot claim social security benefits during their first two years in the country. Would-be working holidaymakers also no longer find it easy to find jobs, as unemployed young Australians are snapping up the low-paid temporary and casual jobs which were once the preserve of the itinerant 'backpacker'. In the last few years, the government has introduced a number of job creation schemes, such as Jobsearch and Newstart, in an effort to boost employment, particularly among the young and the long-term unemployed.

The Australian Bureau of Statistics (💻 www.abs.gov.au) publishes job figures and employment forecasts.

SALARY

It can be difficult to determine the salary you should command in Australia, as salaries aren't always stated in job advertisements, except for public sector employees who are paid according to fixed salary bands. Salaries may vary considerably for the same job in different parts of the country. In general, wages are highest in NSW (particularly Sydney, which has the highest cost of living) and Canberra, and lowest in Queensland and South Australia. However, salary variations aren't uniform across Australia and those living in areas with a low cost of living can sometimes earn as much as those in cities with a much higher cost of living.

Australia has a similar cost of living to most Western European countries and higher than the US. However, although Australians have traditionally been highly paid, some analysts believe that Australia's future may be low-tech, low-pay. In recent years, salary growth hasn't kept pace with inflation (Queensland and WA have had the highest salary growth in recent years).

Australia has a federal minimum wage which increased to $15.96 per hour on 1st July 2012 ($606.40 for a 38-hour week), although most job sectors are bound by workplace agreements (see page 39).

Overtime rates are usually one and a half times the normal hourly rate, but can be twice the normal rate for weekend work. The task of setting the minimum wage is the responsibility of the Minimum Wage Panel of Fair Work Australia (💻 www.fwa.gov.au/index.cfm?pagename=minnatorders).

Many analysts believe that the relatively high federal minimum wage is partly responsible for unemployment, although it's undercut by employers hiring part-time and casual workers; many employers, particularly restaurant owners, pay below the legal rate of pay. Many people think that there should be a lower federal minimum wage for unskilled workers, who are currently priced out of jobs.

Government surveys of average weekly earnings are published regularly for a wide range of trades and professions, both nationally and for individual states and cities. The Fair Work website (💻 www.fairwork.gov.au/awards/pages/default.aspx) provides information about rates of pay (awards) for most industries.

Real wages for many workers have fallen over the last decade and many families receive social security payments (e.g. a 'family payment') to top up their income. Government employees earn more on average than employees in the private sector – an average of over $60,000 per year for federal government employees and almost as much for local government workers – and receive larger wage increases. The highest paid private-sector jobs are generally in finance, insurance and mining, while the lowest are in catering, retailing and tourism. As in most other countries, the self-employed are generally the worst off, with an average salary of just over $40,000. Under a scheme called 'leave loading', full-time employees are paid an extra 17.5 per cent of their normal wage when they're on holiday (usually paid in December).

Not surprisingly, the highest average salaries are in Sydney, followed by Canberra, Melbourne, Perth, Brisbane and Adelaide; bottom of the table is the inappropriately named Gold Coast. There are allowances (called 'tropical loading' or 'remote area allowances') for work in remote parts of the Northern Territory and Western Australia (above the Tropic of Capricorn).

Salaries are usually negotiable and it's up to you to ensure that you receive a level of salary and benefits commensurate with your qualifications and experience (in other words, as much as you can get!). If you have friends

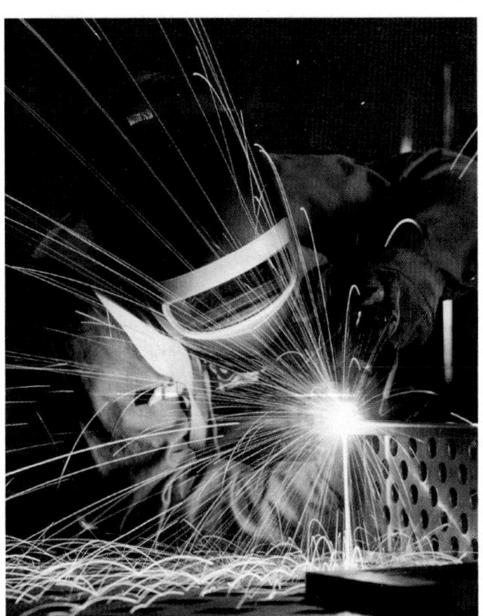

or acquaintances working in Australia or who have worked there, ask them what an average or good salary is for your trade or profession.

Salaries paid by some foreign companies (e.g. American or Japanese companies) may be higher on average than those paid by Australian companies, particularly for executives and managers imported from overseas. Pay increases are often linked to improved productivity and performance, and pay generally rises in line with inflation. A deal between workers, management and the government in recent years generally heralded the end of massive pay rises for workers in return for better working conditions and fringe benefits. However, women have fallen behind in the pay stakes, particularly those employed in part-time and temporary jobs, where wage growth has been minimal.

Fringe Benefits

For many employees, notably executives and senior managers, their 'salary' is much more than what they receive in their weekly or monthly pay packets. Many companies offer a number of fringe benefits (or perks) for executives and managers, which may even continue into retirement. These include children's private education, company cars available for private use, expense accounts and private health insurance. However, such benefits have declined considerably since the introduction of fringe benefit tax (FBT – see page 239), which is levied at 46.5 per cent on the taxable value of employee fringe benefits. There has also been a tax crackdown on executive pay packages, particularly 'salary sacrifice' schemes, where executives sacrifice part of their pay in return for higher superannuation payments and other benefits.

The most common forms of fringe benefit are allowances for living away from home, subsidised company restaurants or canteens, and superannuation (which is compulsory), all of which are covered by union awards and aren't liable to FBT. Under the mandatory Superannuation Guarantee (introduced in 1992), employers must pay a percentage of their employees salary into a superannuation fund (see page 216). Most employees consider fringe benefits to be important, particularly childcare on business premises, company cars, 'flexi-days', income protection insurance, health and life insurance, staff discounts and superannuation. The opportunity to work overtime is also seen as an important 'fringe benefit' by most hourly paid workers, many of whom earn around a quarter of their wages from overtime.

Check whether a quoted salary is salary only or a total salary package, including for example superannuation and a company car.

QUALIFICATIONS

The most important qualification for working in Australia is the ability to speak English fluently (see **Language** on page 34). If English isn't your mother tongue, but you have a degree or a certificate from a recognised educational establishment in an English-speaking country, this usually presents no problems. However, applicants from non-English speaking countries or backgrounds must usually pass an English test and possibly also an occupational English examination, where the pass mark depends on your profession or trade. The failure rate is high.

Once you've overcome this hurdle, you should establish whether your trade or professional qualifications and experience are recognised in Australia. While you may be well qualified in your own country, you may need to pass professional examinations or trade tests to satisfy Australian standards (foreign-trained doctors went on hunger-strike some years ago claiming that they were denied the right to practise by discriminatory qualification tests). If you aren't experienced, Australian employers expect your studies to be in a relevant discipline and to have included work experience.

The points system, on which most immigration is based, depends to a large extent on the skills and qualifications of applicants. Points are awarded for skill levels based on your current or previous employment and whether your qualifications are adequate, including occupational training.

Theoretically, qualifications recognised by professional and trade bodies overseas are recognised in Australia. However, recognition varies with the country and in some cases foreign qualifications aren't recognised by Australian employers or professional and trade associations. All academic qualifications should also be recognised, although they may be given less prominence than equivalent Australian qualifications, depending on the country and the educational institution where they were obtained.

To work in Australia as a licensed tradesman you must have your qualifications assessed by a Vocational Training Board or similar state organisation; you may also need to obtain a licence (or pass an examination) to work in some professions, states or trades. Trades Recognition Australia (💻 www.deewr.gov.au/skills/programs/skillsassess/tra/pages/default.aspx) assesses migrants' experience, qualifications and skills against comparable standards in Australia. For example, the metal and electrical trades have a system whereby overseas-trained tradesmen can be awarded an Australian Recognised Tradesman's Certificate.

The recognition of professional qualifications is usually the responsibility of the relevant professional body, which migrants are normally required to join to practise in Australia. However, a favourable assessment isn't a guarantee that you'll be professionally recognised or be able to gain employment in your field of expertise, as some professional bodies require overseas practitioners to pass examinations conducted or supervised by themselves. In some cases, it's necessary for foreign professionals to work under the supervision of a registered professional Australian for a period, e.g. a year, or to undertake further training. Medical practitioners must have studied medicine in Australia or New Zealand to work in some states, and until recently foreign doctors couldn't work for Medicare (the state healthcare scheme – see page 196). This was reviewed in 2004 – as a result of a shortage of medical staff in parts of Australia – and it's estimated that some 30 per cent of practising doctors in Australia have trained wholly or partly overseas.

The Australian government no longer lists the skills and qualifications necessary for occupations. However, you can check the qualifications required for a particular job in the *Australian Standard Classification of Occupations* (ASCO) dictionary, available for reference at Australian High Commission offices and other Australian government offices overseas, and at offices of the Department of Immigration and Multicultural and Indigenous Affairs in Australia or on the website of the Australian Bureau of Statistics (💻 www.abs.gov.au). Additional information can be obtained from the government's Australian Education International (AEI) service (☎ 1300-615262 or +61-3-5454 5245 from abroad, 💻 https://aei.gov.au/services-and-resources/services/assessment-of-overseas-qualifications/our-assessments/pages/default.aspx).

Whatever kind of job you're looking for, whether temporary or permanent, part- or fulltime, always take proof of your qualifications, training and experience to an interview, plus copies of references and an up-to-date curriculum vitae.

When leaving a job in Australia, you should ask for a written reference (one isn't usually provided automatically), particularly if you intend to look for further work in Australia or you think your work experience will help you to obtain employment overseas.

GOVERNMENT EMPLOYMENT SERVICE

In Australia, the government authority in charge of employment at federal level

is the Department of Human Services/ DHS (💻 www.humanservices.gov.au), whose offices provide a range of customer services. These include education, training and youth affairs; employment; health and family services; primary industries and energy; and social security. DHS offices also provide advice and information regarding the government's Jobs, Education and Training (JET) programme; registration and acceptance of new applicants for income support and employment assistance; self-help job-finding facilities, including computer access to a national job vacancies database; and services for disadvantaged groups, including migrants, those with disabilities, single parents and young people.

If you're a newly-arrived migrant and need help finding employment, your local DHS office should be your first port of call. DHS can help you find a job, arrange for recognition of your skills and qualifications, and help you access certain courses.

The Department of Human Services has a comprehensive website (💻 www.humanservices.gov.au), which provides the latest information about DHS services, and also has a multilingual phone service (☎ 131202).

PRIVATE EMPLOYMENT AGENCIES

Private employment agencies abound in all major cities and towns in Australia and find work for some 100,000 people annually, although nearly two-thirds of jobs are for casual work. Many large companies engage agents and consultants to recruit employees, particularly executives, managers, professionals and temporary staff.

There are four main types of private agency in Australia: personnel consultants, labour hire contractors, student employment agencies and 'employment agencies' (see below).

Personnel consultants (head-hunters) handle mostly executive, managerial and professional positions, although there's some overlap with employment agencies. Labour hire contractors handle jobs for skilled, semi-skilled and unskilled manual workers, and tend to be located in industrial areas rather than the main streets of major cities.

The largest number of agencies simply come under the generic term 'employment agencies'. Some specialise in particular fields or industries: accounting; agriculture; au pairs and nannies; banking; care work; computing, engineering and technical; hospitality; industrial and manual; legal; medical and nursing; mining; outback jobs; resort work; sales; secretarial; and tourism. Others deal with a range of industries and professions. Some agencies deal exclusively with temporary workers in a variety of occupations, including baby-sitters, chauffeurs, cleaners, cooks, gardeners, hairdressers, housekeepers, industrial workers, labourers, office staff and security guards. Care, nanny and nursing agencies are common. Many agencies find both permanent and temporary positions.

Agencies are usually prohibited from charging a fee to job applicants, as they receive their fees from clients, although in some states they may charge a registration fee. For permanent staff, the fee paid by the employer is a percentage of the annual salary (e.g. 10 per cent); for temporary staff, agencies are paid a percentage of the hourly rate paid by employers. If you take a temporary job through an agency, you're paid by the agency, usually weekly or fortnightly, which may include paid public and annual holidays after a qualifying period. Always obtain a contract and ensure that you know exactly how much you'll be paid and when, and the conditions regarding the termination of a job.

Agencies must deduct income tax from gross pay and you're required to give an agency your tax file number when starting work, otherwise they must deduct tax at the highest rate.

Salaries vary considerably according to the type of job, but most secretarial jobs pay between $20 and $30 per hour. You usually receive extra pay (loading) for weekend and night work.

Employment agencies earn a great deal of money from finding people jobs so, provided you have something to offer their clients, they'll be keen to help you (if you're an experienced accountant, nurse or secretary you may get trampled in the rush). If they cannot help you, they'll usually tell you immediately and won't waste your time.

When visiting employment agencies, you should dress appropriately for the type of job you're seeking, and take your bank details (if you want to get paid!), curriculum vitae (CV), passport (with a visa if applicable), references and tax file number (TFN). Office staff may be given a typing or literacy test (if applicable) – some agencies have in-house training programmes for secretarial staff. You should register with a number of agencies to maximise your chances of finding work. Keep in close contact (ring in every day if necessary) and try to provide a telephone number and/or email address where you can be reached.

There's a plethora of employment agencies in Australia, many operating nationally with offices in all major cities, while others operate in one or two cities only. Among the larger agencies operating nationwide or in most major cities are Accountancy Placements, ADIA, BDS Challenge International, Catalyst Recruitment Systems, Centastaff, Dial-an-Angel, Drake Personnel, Extrastaff (formerly Brook Street), Forstaff, IPA Personnel, Julia Ross Personnel, Kelly Services, Key People, Manpower, Mitier Personnel, Select Appointments, Templine and Western Staff Services. Check the *Yellow Pages* for local offices of these and other agencies. If you're travelling around Australia and plan to work in a number of major cities, you may find it advantageous to work for an agency with offices nationwide.

To find local agencies, look in the *Yellow Pages* under 'Employment Agencies' and in local newspapers. Employment agencies are increasingly using the internet to advertise job vacancies (*see* **The Internet** on page 30), which speeds up the response and processing of job applications. Many Australian agencies employing temporary staff advertise overseas in publications (see **Appendix B**) targeted at those with working holiday visas.

CONTRACT JOBS

Contract or freelance jobs are available through specialist employment agencies in Australia. Contracts are usually full-time and for a fixed period, although they may be open-ended. In recent years, many companies have been moving from full-time employees to contract workers and contracting out jobs such as building maintenance, catering, cleaning, computer programming, construction, and even parts of the manufacturing process. However, the Independent Contractors' Act 2006 overrides all state and territory laws, and allows independent contractors the right to choose the form of working arrangement that best suits their needs so that they can no longer be deemed to be employees. Penalties now apply to any employer who tries to disguise an offer of employment as an independent contracting arrangement. For information see the government website (💻 www.innovation.gov.au/smallbusiness/independentcontractors) or contact the Independent contractors hotline (☎ 1300-667850 or +61-2-6213 6000 from abroad).

Many contract positions are for specialists, in fields such as accountancy, computing, electronics, engineering and mining, although there's also a strong market in providing catering, cleaning and maintenance services. Rates vary considerably, e.g. from around $20 per hour for a clerk to $100 or more for a computer or mining specialist. Contractors may work at home or on a client's or contract company's premises. There used to be a lucrative market in contract jobs in Australia, particularly for information technology specialists, although the recession has put paid to many jobs. Consultant companies (also called bodyshops) specialise in supplying contract staff to major companies. The usual visa regulations apply (see **Chapter 3**) to contract workers, unless you're employed to work outside Australia.

An organisation that may be of interest to contractors in Australia is Independent Contractors of Australia (✉ contact@contractworld.com.au, 💻 www.contractworld.com.au).

PART-TIME JOBS

A part-time job is generally defined as one for less than 20 hours per week. Part-time jobs are available in most industries and professions in Australia and are most common in cafés, factories, offices, pubs, restaurants and shops. In the last decade the number of part-time workers in Australia has risen considerably, particularly among women, and now totals over 3m – around 30 per cent of the workforce. Over 75 per cent of part-time jobs in larger workplaces (with a minimum of 20 staff) are in the accommodation, catering and hospitality, education, health and community service, and retail sectors. Part-time jobs apply to all levels (from executives to clerks) and all businesses; many people turn to part-time work for family, health or lifestyle reasons.

Part-time workers are usually paid on an hourly basis and don't have the same rights as full-time workers, but pay awards normally contain provisions to protect part-time workers' rights. They don't, however, usually receive annual leave, maternity leave, sick pay, or other entitlements of full-time workers, although the balance is being redressed in various industries. Part-time workers are now paid the same rate (pro rata) as full-time employees.

TEMPORARY & CASUAL JOBS

Temporary and casual jobs differ from part-time jobs in that they're usually for a limited (fixed) period, e.g. from a day to a few months, or even intermittent. Casual work usually refers to labouring jobs, whereas a temporary job can be in almost any field.

Most Australian companies employ temporary or casual staff at some time (around 50 per cent on a regular basis), particularly in clerical positions when staff are sick or on holiday, for special projects and in busy periods.

The temporary job market was hit hard during the recession but there has been a huge increase in demand in the last few years, particularly in the major cities. Overall, around 20 per cent of employees identify themselves as casual workers. Downsizing and the cost of making full-time employees redundant (and unfair dismissal claims) have led many companies to employ an army of temporary employees, which is often cheaper and more efficient than employing full-time staff.

Many people choose 'careers' in temporary and contract work, which provides them with maximum flexibility when it comes to holidays, time off, travel and working hours. Although there's less security than with a full-time job and you don't usually receive any benefits, you're generally compensated by a higher hourly rate of pay. Temporary work also provides an opportunity to try your hand at a range of jobs or industries, which would otherwise be impossible. The easiest way to find temporary work in the major cities is through an agency; provided you have a marketable skill (e.g. accountancy, computing or nursing), it's relatively easy to find well paid work. Rates range from around $20 per hour for clerical staff to over $100 for IT

professionals. Casual workers are usually employed on a daily, first-come-first-served basis. The work often entails hard labouring and is therefore usually better suited to men. Pay for casual work is usually low and is usually paid in cash, although this is illegal.

A good source of temporary work is notice boards in shopping malls, e.g. those provided by Coles and Woolworths, where employers can advertise free of charge.

Working Holidaymakers

Temporary or casual work is often undertaken by foreigners with working holiday visas, which permit you to work for any employer for up to three months. It isn't easy to find work in many areas, however, and you often need to hustle to get a job and may require experience or qualifications. It's important to ensure that you have sufficient funds to tide you over until you can find work. You should be prepared to splash out on some smart clothes if a job requires them.

During university holiday periods there's stiff competition from students, therefore if you're planning to work in a major city you should try to get there before the local students break for their holidays. Most holiday jobs are available in the fast food, agriculture, hospitality and retailing sectors. Recruiting is often done a few months before holiday periods, e.g. companies hire in August to October for the summer period of December to February.

The easiest work to find is on farms, usually picking fruit or vegetables (see **Farm Work** below), but well known department and chain stores are generally the best employers. Avoid jobs offering unpaid 'trial' periods, which is illegal and is usually simply a ploy to get you to work for nothing. You should also avoid door-to-door selling requiring advance payment (e.g. $200) for sample kits (selling them is how some companies make their money) and jobs which only pay commission.

> ☑ **SURVIVAL TIP**
>
> **You usually have better job prospects if you plan to stay put for a number of months rather than just a few weeks.**

Visitors to Australia with working holiday visas may be interested in the Visitoz Scheme, which is a work placement scheme designed particularly with working holiday visa holders in mind. Those who are accepted are guaranteed jobs and on-the-spot training during their stay in Australia. Jobs offered are mainly outdoors in the agricultural or rural hospitality industries, although there are jobs available in education, healthcare and maintenance. For more information contact the Visitoz Scheme (☎ 07-4168 6106, 💻 www.visitoz.org).

Good sources of information for working holidaymakers include TNT's *Australia & New Zealand Travel Planner* (see **Appendix B**), which contain advice on finding casual and temporary work. The British Universities North America Club (BUNAC, UK, ☎ 020-7251 3472, 💻 www.bunac.org/uk) has a 'Work Australia' programme that helps graduates with working holiday visas to find temporary work. There are a number of websites that provide employment contacts for working holidaymakers, including 💻 www.nextstepaustralia.com/portal/find-work-in-australia-49.html and http://workstay.com.au.

You may be entitled to a tax rebate when you leave Australia, although claiming it may be more trouble than it's worth.

Farm Work

One of the most common forms of temporary work in Australia is fruit and vegetable picking, which can be done somewhere in Australia throughout the year (many people manage to stay in work all year). Pay varies considerably (from excellent to poor) and is either an hourly rate or, more often, piece work, where the more you pick the more you earn. Doing piece work you can earn around $700 per week, although you need to work between 50 and 80 hours and possibly every day. You should expect to earn from around $15 to $20 per hour for most harvesting jobs. Always establish your conditions, working hours and pay in advance, as there are unscrupulous employers around who will happily take advantage of you given half a chance.

Farming is a rough and ready experience and involves hard, often dirty work – definitely not for softies. You must usually have a tent or vehicle to sleep in; some employers provide basic accommodation and food (there may be a charge), but it's usually terrible and it's better to provide your own. It pays to have your own transport, as farms are generally in remote areas. Large farms are sometimes targeted by immigration officials, resulting in the deportation of illegal workers.

There are harvest labour offices in many country areas. A useful contact is Outbackpackers (www.outbackpackers.com), which specialise in finding farm work for those with a working holiday visa.

Wages & Tax

Employers or agencies require your tax file number (see page 236) and when you leave an employer you should receive a group certificate (for tax purposes). If you don't provide a tax file number, your employer must deduct tax at the highest tax rate (45 per cent). If you earn over $450 per month, your employer must pay 9 per cent of your salary into a superannuation fund.

This is rolled over from employer to employer until you reach retirement age, but if it amounts to less than $500 it's usually paid to you in cash. Many employers illegally pay temporary staff in cash without making any deductions for tax or superannuation.

JOB HUNTING

When looking for a job in Australia (or anywhere for that matter), you shouldn't put all your eggs in one basket, as the more job applications you make the better your chances of success. Contact as many prospective employers and employment agencies as possible, by writing to them, telephoning them or calling on them in person. It's important to find out how employees are normally recruited. For example, the recruitment of executives and senior managers in Australia is usually handled by consultants, who advertise in the Australian national press (and also overseas) and interview all applicants before presenting clients with a shortlist. At the other end of the scale, manual jobs requiring no previous experience may be advertised in local newspapers or in shop windows, where the first suitable applicant may be offered the job on the spot.

Your method of job hunting obviously depends on your circumstances, experience, qualifications and the sort of job you're seeking, and may include the following:

- visiting an 'Australia Needs Skills' expo (www.immi.gov.au/skillevents) in the UK; these are held in London (and possibly other cities) and all attendees must register (see website).
- checking employment sites and job boards via the internet (see below), which are increasingly being used by Australian agencies and head hunters. The Department of Employment, Education and Workplace Relations (DEEWR) maintains a regularly updated site with a list of most employment websites (www.deewr.gov.au). University students can use the Gradlink site, established by the Graduate Careers Council of Australia (www.graduatecareers.com.au).
- contacting private recruitment consultants and employment agencies;
- obtaining copies of Australian daily newspapers or viewing then online (see www.newspapers.com.au and www.onlinenewspapers.com/australi.htm), most of which contain 'positions vacant' sections (the Saturday editions are the best), including job advertisements dedicated to particular industries or professions

on certain days. Most local and national newspapers are available in the reading rooms of local libraries in Australia, so you don't usually need to buy them. Jobs are also advertised in industry and trade newspapers and magazines. Australian newspapers are available in some countries from international news agencies. In the UK, single copies of the major Australian newspapers can be purchased from Smyth International Media Representatives (UK, ☎ 020-8446 6400, 💻 www.smyth-international.com).

- networking – getting together with like-minded people to discuss business – is a popular way of making contacts in Australia. It can be particularly successful for executives, managers and professionals when job hunting.
- if you have a professional qualification that's recognised in Australia, it may be worthwhile contacting an Australian professional organisation for information and advice (addresses are obtainable from Australian chambers of commerce overseas). Membership of the organisation may be obligatory to work in Australia. All associations publish journals containing 'positions vacant' advertisements, where members can also offer their services to prospective employers. Information about specific professions, trades and industries, particularly job opportunities in individual states, cities or areas, can be obtained from local chambers of commerce in Australia.
- applying to international and national recruiting agencies acting for Australian companies. Agencies mainly recruit executives and key managerial and technical staff, and some have offices overseas, e.g. in the UK.
- applying to foreign multi-national companies with offices or subsidiaries in Australia and making written applications directly to Australian companies. You can obtain a list of companies working in a particular field from trade directories, copies of which are available at reference libraries in Australia (they can also be consulted at Australian embassies and consulates and chambers of commerce overseas).
- placing an advertisement in the 'situations wanted' section of a national newspaper in Australia or a local newspaper in the area where you wish to work. If you're a member of a recognised profession or trade, you could place an advertisement in a newspaper or magazine dedicated to your profession or a particular industry.
- asking acquaintances, friends and relatives working in Australia whether they know of an employer looking for someone with your experience and qualifications;
- if you're already in Australia, contacting or joining expatriate groups, professional organisations, social clubs and societies, particularly your country's chamber of commerce;
- applying in person to Australian companies (see **Personal Applications** below).

The Internet

The internet has rapidly become the number one resource for finding employment, both in Australia and elsewhere. Websites include mainstream (High Street) and internet-only employment agencies (temporary, contract and full-time); professional headhunters; job boards where employers and jobseekers can place ads; companies advertising vacancies on their own websites; and Commonwealth and state government sites. The main resources include:

- Job boards which include: 💻 http://adage.com.au, www.careerone.com.au, http://employment.byron.com.au, http://mycareer.com.au, www.positionsvacant.com.au and www.seek.com.au.
- 💻 http://jobsearch.gov.au – a government-run website (one of the largest and most comprehensive) with daily additions; it incorporates both 'Find a Job' pages (💻 http://jobsearch.gov.au/findajob/maplvl1.aspx) and an excellent list of job board links (💻 http://jobsearch.gov.au/keylinks/pages/jobboards.aspx).
- 💻 www.australia.gov.au/australian_government_jobs – for government positions; www.job-directory.com.au and www.lgnet.com.au/jobs/jobs_fs.html – local government job directories. There are also state government job sites such as 💻 http://jobs.nsw.gov.au, www.careers.vic.gov.au and www.jobs.wa.gov.au.

Other Useful Websites

- www.anglopacific.co.uk/jobs_abroad.htm
- www.australianworkforce.com.au
- www.bluecollar.com.au
- www.drakemedox.com.au
- www.graduatejobsnet.com.au
- www.jobnet.com.au
- http://jobs.com.au
- www.jobseeker.com.au
- www.linkrecruitment.com.au
- www.michaelpage.com.au
- www.reed.co.uk/jobs/australia
- www.workingdownunder.co.uk
- www.workingin-australia.com

Written Applications

When writing for a job, address your letter to the personnel director or manager (try to obtain his name) and include your CV. Writing for jobs from overseas is usually a hit-and-miss affair and it's probably the least successful method of securing employment. If you're applying from overseas and are planning to visit Australia, you should tell prospective employers when you'll be available for interview and should arrange as many interviews as you can fit into your timetable. Visiting Australia for an interview will convince prospective employers of your commitment, but companies may wish to see a copy of your visa before interviewing you.

Personal Applications

Your best chance of obtaining some jobs (particularly temporary jobs) in Australia is to apply in person, when success is often simply a matter of being in the right place at the right time. Many companies don't advertise but rely on attracting workers by word of mouth and via their own vacancy boards. Always leave your name, telephone number and email address with a prospective employer, which is particularly important if a job could become vacant at short notice.

SELF-EMPLOYMENT & RUNNING A BUSINESS

Anyone who's an Australian citizen or a permanent resident can work in a self-employed capacity in Australia, which includes setting up a co-operative, franchise, partnership, private limited company or sole proprietorship. There are numerous opportunities for entrepreneurs in Australia, where everyone has equal opportunity and is judged on his merits. Although new businesses have a high failure rate within the first few years, working for yourself is still the best way to become (and remain) rich in Australia.

Much of the fall in unemployment in the last decade has been due to self-employment or jobs created by small companies. Some 20 per cent of working Australians run their own businesses. Redundancy and the difficulty of finding full-time employment is often the spur for those aged over 45 to start a business; around 20 per cent of redundant (retrenched) employees turn to self-employment.

However, if you're planning to enter Australia as a skilled migrant, you must be under 45, have considerable financial resources and pass a points test. In recent years, skilled migrants have each brought in over $500,000

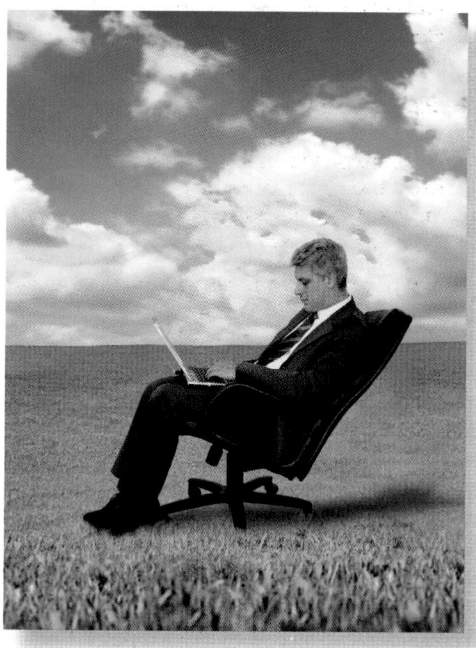

and created an average of seven jobs; you should regard these figures as a minimum requirement. There's also a considerable amount of red tape for those wishing to start a business in Australia; although it isn't as restrictive as in many other countries, the average small businessman spends as much as four hours per week on government paperwork. For many people, starting a business is one of the quickest routes to bankruptcy known to mankind. In fact, many people who start businesses would be better off investing in lottery tickets! If you're going to work for yourself, you must be prepared to fail (despite your best efforts), as almost two out of three new businesses fail within three to five years.

Research

The key to starting or buying a successful business is research, research and yet more research (plus innovation, service and value). Bear in mind that choosing the location for a retail business is of paramount importance. Always thoroughly investigate an existing or proposed business (including the catchment area, competition, history and location) before investing a cent. Generally speaking, it isn't wise to run a business in a field in which you have no experience, although obviously this isn't always possible (and some businesses require little experience, specialist knowledge or training). When experience or training is necessary, it's often better to work for someone else in the same line of business to gain experience rather than jump in at the deep end. Assistance (including hands-on training) from the seller can be made part of a purchase contract.

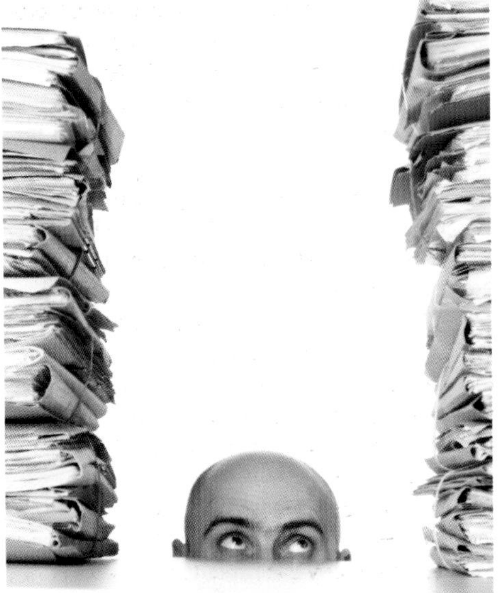

Business Structure

There are four main types of business structure to choose from in Australia: a limited company, a partnership, a franchise and a sole proprietorship, which can be public or private (proprietary). Because of the ever-changing and complex Australian tax laws, you should consult a tax expert before deciding on the best business structure. Although franchises have a higher success rate than other startup businesses, it can take years to make a profit (often the only people to get rich are the franchise companies!). A *Franchisees Guide* can be obtained from The Franchise Council of Australia (☎ 1300-669030 or +61-3-9508 0888 from abroad, 💻 www.franchise.org.au). Further information can be obtained from 💻 www.franchise.edu.au.

Buying a Business

It may be better to buy an established business than to start a business from scratch, as it gives you an immediate client/customer base and cash flow. However, you must thoroughly investigate the financial status, turnover and value of a business (always obtain an independent valuation). It's important to engage an accountant and lawyer at the earliest opportunity. A lawyer should be acting solely for you and not for any other parties in a transaction, and shouldn't be receiving commission from anyone involved. Take care, as there are crooks around who prey on innocent foreigners!

Businesses for sale are advertised in specialist magazines, e.g. *Business for Sale* directory (💻 www.businessforsale.com.au) and some daily newspapers. There are also business migration agents in Australia and overseas who can help you buy a company in Australia, although their fees can be high. The purchase of a business must be conditional on obtaining licences, loans and other necessary funding, permits, visas and anything else that's important to its success.

 Caution

Australia isn't a place for amateur entrepreneurs, particularly those who don't do their homework and are unfamiliar with the Australian way of doing business.

Finance & Cash Flow

Most people are far too optimistic about the prospects for a new business, overestimating income levels (it often takes years to make a profit) and under-estimating startup costs. Be realistic or even pessimistic when estimating your income; overestimate the costs and underestimate the revenue (then reduce it by a further 50 per cent!). While hoping for the best, you should plan for the worst and have sufficient funds to last until you're established and profitable. New projects are rarely completed within budget.

Australian banks are wary of lending to new businesses, especially those run by new immigrants. If you wish to borrow money for a business venture in Australia, you should carefully consider how and where you plan to raise it. Under-capitalisation is the main reason for small business failures and isn't helped by cash-flow problems caused by late payers.

Grants & Incentives

The Australian government encourages successful business people and investors to apply for residence in Australia, although applicants are generally required to invest at least $500,000 in a business. Business migration schemes provide prospective migrants with a link to professional and commercial advisors. Compare your business prospects in all states and territories, which compete to attract foreign investors and business people with incentives such as cash grants, free advice, loan guarantees and tax rebates. Some state governments publish lists of business opportunities for migrants.

For information about government-backed finance, contact Austrade, formerly the Australian Trade Commission (☎ 132878, 💻 www.austrade.gov.au – a list of office addresses can be found on their website).

Information & Professional Advice

A wealth of free advice and information for budding entrepreneurs is available from Australian chambers of commerce, embassies and high commissions, federal government and state agencies, local councils, professional associations and trade unions. The Australian Securities and Investments Commission (☎ 1300-300630 or +61-3-5177 3988 from abroad, 💻 www.asic.gov.au) also provides a wealth of information available from its regional offices and via its website.

The Office of Small Business (💻 www.business.gov.au) is a government agency with offices in all major cities, offering free advice and assistance to those planning to start a business. It publishes an abundance of information, particularly concerning raising finance for a new business. The Department of Human Services (see **Government Employment Services** on page 24) publishes various booklets about starting and running a business. There are Business Enterprise Centres (BECs) in some states and territories (e.g. NSW and the Australian Capital Territory), where you can obtain free advice and support on a wide range of business-related subjects.

Most international firms of accountants have offices in major cities in Australia and are an invaluable source of information (in English and other languages) on a wide range of subjects, including company law, forming a company, social security and taxation. Many publish free books about doing business in Australia. Information about starting a small business in Australia can also be obtained from the Department of Fair Trading (☎ 133220, 💻 www.fairtrading.[state initials].gov.au – e.g. 💻 www.fairtrading.nsw.gov.au for the New South Wales office). Australia's major banks operate small business centres which provide free banking, financial and other advice to new businesses, and the Australian Tax Office publishes a number of helpful booklets, including *How to Keep Your Business Records*.

There are many state and local government agencies and departments providing information and advice about starting and running a business. All states operate business advisory, development, industry, investment and technology corporations or departments. One of the best places to start is your local chamber of commerce, which is a mine of information about every aspect of business and relocation to particular towns or areas (many produce relocation and business information packages). Public libraries are also an excellent source of information about starting a business.

LANGUAGE

Surprisingly, an estimated one million migrants cannot speak English fluently, a huge number in a country of only around 23m people, and some 3m residents (around 15 per cent of the population) speak a language other than English at home. Sydney is Australia's most multicultural city (closely followed by Melbourne), where some 30 per cent of the population don't speak English at home (the figure is over 50 per cent in some suburbs). Sydney and Melbourne are home to around 65 per cent of all non-English speaking migrants, who together speak a total of some 250 foreign languages. Many migrants predominantly use their mother tongue on a day-to-day basis and have only a smattering of English. Australia's failure to train migrants in English is handicapping them in respect of economic, political and social life, and ghettos are emerging where Australian-born children don't speak fluent English.

Nevertheless, if you're planning to live or work in Australia, you'll need to read, speak and write English well enough to deal with government officials, find your way around the country, shop, and understand and hold conversations with the people you meet. Independent migrants from non-English speaking backgrounds need to take an English test. Your chance of obtaining a good job (or any job) in Australia is greatly diminished if you don't speak English fluently, and many immigrants from non-English speaking backgrounds are unemployed because their lack of English would endanger other employees and reduce workplace efficiency.

▲ Caution

English proficiency is also important if you have a job requiring a lot of contact with others or which involves speaking on the telephone or dealing with other foreigners, many of whom speak their own 'dialect' of English.

It's particularly important for students (unless they're studying English) to have a high standard of English, as they must be able to follow lectures and take part in discussions in the course of their studies. These may require a technical or specialised vocabulary. For this reason, most universities and colleges won't accept students who aren't fluent in English and many require a formal qualification or require students to take a written test. Whether you speak British English, American English or some other variety is irrelevant; although some foreigners have a problem understanding the natives (even Americans and Britons occasionally have problems understanding Australians).

Australian English is similar to British English but has its own colourful vernacular, called 'strine' (from the way 'Australian' is pronounced with a heavy Australian accent), thrown in for good measure. Strine (also called Ozspeak) is Australia's greatest creative product and is full of abbreviations, hyperbole, profanities, vulgar expressions and word-play. Strine is the language of a rebellious subculture and has its origins in the Cockney (London) and Irish slang of the early convicts. The use of strine varies with the state or region and the 'class' of person. The use of expletives is widespread; many are a sign of familiarity and even affection ('bloody' is in everyday use and is no longer considered a swear word in Australia). Absurd comparisons are frequently used for emphasis such as 'as busy as a bricklayer in Beirut' (i.e. idle), 'as useful as a wether at a ram sale' (useless) and 'as straight as a dog's hind leg' (bent). The Australian language also includes many words adopted from Aboriginal languages (see below).

Australians often cannot decide whether to use American or British spelling (program/

programme, labor/labour, etc.) and consequently misspellings abound. Many words have a completely different meaning in Australia and other English-speaking countries, such as crook (ill), game (brave), globe (light bulb), knock (criticise), ringer (top performer), shout (round of drinks) and tube (can of beer). Almost any word of more than two syllables is abbreviated, often with the addition of an o at the end of it, as in derro (derelict), garbo (dustman), reffo (refugee) and rego (car registration), or an ie or y, as in Aussie (Australian), barbie (barbecue), blowie (blowfly), brickie (bricklayer), chrissy (Christmas), cossie (swimming costume), footy (football), mozzie (mosquito), postie (postperson), tinny (can of beer) and truckie (truck driver).

There are slight regional variations in the Australian accent, although foreigners usually find it difficult to detect them. Accents are broader in isolated country areas than among middle-class city dwellers, many of whom are of British ancestry.

Many books have been written about Australian vernacular speech, including the *Australian Phrasebook* (Lonely Planet), *The Dinkum Dictionary* by Leni Johannsen (Viking O'Neil) and *The Dinkum Aussie Dictionary* by Richard Beckett (Child and Henry). The standard Australian English dictionary is the *Macquarie Dictionary* (compiled by the Macquarie University, Sydney), the bible of Aussie English (2,500 pages!).

An excellent book for newcomers wishing to learn more about Australia's language (containing an extensive glossary of 'strine'), culture and customs is our sister publication, *Culture Wise Australia*.

Aboriginal Languages

Australian Aboriginal (literally meaning 'indigenous') society has the longest unbroken cultural history in the world, dating back around 60,000 years. When the First Fleet arrived in Australia in 1788 there were estimated to be around 250 Australian languages (all believed to have evolved from a single language family) comprising some 700 dialects. Of the original 250 or so languages, only around 20 survive today, which are spoken regularly and taught in schools. Kriol, spoken mostly in northern Australia, is the most widely used Aboriginal language and the native language of many young Aboriginals. It contains many English words but the meanings are often different and the spelling is phonetic.

2. EMPLOYMENT CONDITIONS

Employment conditions in Australia are among the best in the developed world and are regulated in most fields of employment at federal or state level, where legislation covers such matters as annual and special leave, discrimination, occupational health and safety, redundancy procedures and payment, and workers' compensation. However, conditions were eroded in the period 1996-2007 by the Liberal conservative) Party.

In 2005, the government amended the Work Place Relations Act, 1996 and introduced the WorkChoices law, which came into force in March 2006, WorkChoices was the most comprehensive reform of workplace relations in Australia in almost a century and was ostensibly designed to 'protect' workers and to encourage more family-friendly working arrangements, it included provisions for young people, women, outworkers and people from a non-English speaking or indigenous background. In effect, however, it made employment (and dismissal) more 'flexible' and employment less secure, and was, not surprisingly, bitterly opposed by workers, unions and the Australian Labor Party.

The Labor Party, which was elected in 2007, made abolishing WorkChoices one of its priorities, and it was replaced on 1st July 2009 by Fair Work Australia (💻 www.fwa.gov.au) created under the Fair Work Act 2009. Fair Work Australia is the national workplace relations tribunal and assumed the functions of the Australian Industrial Relations Commission (💻 www.airc.gov.au) and the Australian Industrial Registry (both date back to 1904) and the Australian Fair Pay Commission (established in 2005) and some of the functions of the Workplace Authority (established in 2007). It also incorporates the Office of the Fair Work Ombudsman (💻 www.fairwork.gov.au), which promotes harmonious, productive and cooperative workplace relations and has a strong focus on advice and education for employers and employees, as well as a strong inspectorate service.

Fair Work Australia is an independent body with the power to carry out a range of functions, including: providing a safety net of minimum conditions, including minimum wages, in awards; facilitating good faith bargaining and the making of enterprise agreements; granting remedies for unfair dismissal; regulating the taking of industrial action; resolving a range of collective and individual workplace disputes through conciliation, mediation and, in some cases, arbitration; functions in connection with workplace determinations, equal remuneration, transfer of business, general workplace protections, right of entry and stand down. Critics say that Fair Work Australia has swung the pendulum too far the other way and that legislation now favours workers and discriminates against employers.

Information about workplace relations is also available from the Department of Education, Employment and Workplace Relations (💻 www.deewr.gov.au). On 1st

November 2009, Safe Work Australia (🖳 http://safeworkaustralia.gov.au) began operating as an independent statutory agency with primary responsibility to improve occupational health and safety and workers' compensation arrangements across Australia.

Most states also have their own employment regulations, for example in New South Wales they are the responsibility of NSW Industrial Relations (☏ 131628, 🖳 www.industrialrelations.nsw.gov.au).

NATIONAL EMPLOYMENT STANDARDS (NES)

Since 1st January 2010, employers and employees in the national workplace system have been covered by the new National Employment Standards (NES), which apply to all employees covered by the national workplace relations system (although only certain entitlements apply to casual employees). Under the NES, employees have certain minimum conditions, which together with pay rates in modern awards (see below) and minimum wage orders, make up the safety net that cannot be altered to the disadvantage of an employee. In addition to the NES, generally an employee's terms and conditions of employment come from a modern award, agreement, award and agreement based transitional instruments, minimum wage orders, transitional minimum wage instruments, state and federal laws.

The NES are set out in the Fair Work Act 2009 and comprise the following ten minimum standards of employment and entitlements:

- **Maximum weekly hours of work:** 38 hours per week, plus reasonable additional hours.
- **Requests for flexible working arrangements:** allows parents or carers of a child under school age or of a child under 18 with a disability, to request a change in working arrangements to assist with the child's care.
- **Parental leave and related entitlements:** up to 12 months unpaid leave for each employee, plus a right to request an additional 12 months unpaid leave, plus other forms of maternity, paternity and adoption related leave.
- **Annual leave:** four weeks paid leave per year, plus an additional week for certain shift workers.
- **Personal/carer's leave and compassionate leave:** ten days paid personal/carer's leave, two days unpaid carer's leave as required, and two days compassionate leave (unpaid for casuals) as required.
- **Community service leave:** unpaid leave for voluntary emergency activities and leave for jury service, with an entitlement to be paid for up to ten days for jury service.
- **Long service leave (LSL):** a transitional entitlement for certain employees who had certain LSL entitlements before 1st January 2010, pending the development of a uniform national long service leave standard.
- **Public Holidays:** a paid day off on a public holiday, except where reasonably requested to work.
- **Notice of termination and redundancy pay:** up to four weeks notice of termination (five weeks if the employee is aged over 45 and has at least two years of continuous service) and up to 16 weeks redundancy pay, both based on length of service.

- **Provision of a Fair Work Information Statement:** employers must provide this statement to all new employees. It contains information about the NES, modern awards, agreement-making, the right to freedom of association, termination of employment, individual flexibility arrangements, rights of entry, transfer of business, and the respective roles of Fair Work Australia and the Fair Work Ombudsman.

An employer and an employee cannot make an agreement with entitlements that are less than the NES, and employers who contravene its provisions face fines of up to $6,600 for an individual and $33,000 for a corporation.

Two NES entitlements apply to all full- and part-time employees, whether or not they're covered by the national workplace relations system: parental leave and related entitlements (this also applies to casual employees who have been employed for at least 12 months by an employer on a regular and systematic basis and with an expectation of ongoing employment) and notice of termination.

State employment agreements continue to apply until terminated by Fair Work Australia or replaced with an enterprise agreement or workplace determination made under the Fair Work Act. Employees under state employment agreements must receive conditions that are at least equal to the minimum entitlements in the NES and the base rates of pay in an applicable state award (while operative), or the relevant modern award or, if there's none, the national minimum wage.

WORKPLACE AGREEMENTS

In certain industries, agreements are made between employers and all employees (usually via a union) with regard to minimum conditions of employment. These may apply at national, regional or local level. These agreements include awards and enterprise agreements, described below. Employees in Australia are also protected by a comprehensive federal social security (welfare) system, which includes family payments, pensions, and sickness and disability allowances (see **Chapter 13**).

Terms in awards, agreements, transitional awards, enterprise agreements and employment contracts cannot exclude or provide for an entitlement less than those provided for in the NES (see above).

Awards

Employment conditions and wages in Australia are decided in negotiations between unions and employers, subject to the approval of Fair Work Australia (💻 www.fwa.gov.au). The result of this process is termed the 'award' for a particular job or industry. An award specifies minimum wages and 'penalty' rates of pay (for overtime and unsociable hours) and regulates such matters as holiday entitlement, redundancy and termination of employment, sick leave and working hours.

An award is an enforceable document containing the minimum terms and conditions of employment in addition to any legislated minimum terms. In general, an award applies to employees in a particular industry or occupation and is used as the benchmark for assessing related enterprise agreements. Fair Work Australia (FWA) is responsible for making and varying awards in the national workplace relations system.

Awards in the national workplace relations system include two main types:

- **modern awards:** these replaced many existing awards and came into effect on 1st January 2010;
- **federal awards created before 27 March 2006:** these have either been reviewed or are in the process of being reviewed to see if they should be replaced by a relevant modern award.

In 2010, a third category of awards became part of the national workplace relations system – state awards covering employees of non-constitutional corporations (generally sole traders and partnerships). These awards entered the national system due to the referral of industrial powers to the commonwealth by most states.

If an employee doesn't have an award or agreement that covers them, then they'll generally be covered by the national minimum wage (see **Salary & Benefits** below).

You can find out about existing awards via the Fair Work Australia website (💻 www.fwa.gov.au/index.cfm?pagename=awardsfind).

Modern Awards

Modern awards are awards created under the new national workplace relations system, which have covered most workplaces since 1st January 2010, which together with the NES (above) and the national minimum wage, form a new safety net for employees in the national workplace relations system. The introduction of modern awards means that there have been changes to minimum terms and conditions for many employees, which vary by state, industry and employer.

The first modern awards were created as part of an extensive review conducted by FWA's predecessor, the Australian Industrial Relations Commission (AIRC), which reviewed over 1,500 pre-reform awards and subsequently created 122 modern awards which came into effect on 1st January 2010. In many of these awards transitional provisions apply to phase in any changes in wages, loading and penalties over a five-year period.

The award modernisation process involved the review of two types of awards:

- **pre-reform awards:** federal awards created before 27th March 2006, covering employers that are the commonwealth, constitutional corporations or carrying on an activity in a territory in Australia;
- **notional agreements preserving state awards:** state awards created before 27th March 2006 covering employers that are constitutional corporations.

Modern awards mustn't include any terms and conditions that are less favourable than the National Employment Standards (effective from 1st January 2010).

> **Employees under state awards must receive conditions that are at least equal to the minimum entitlements in the NES and the national minimum wage.**

Fair Work Australia publishes a list of modern awards on its website (💻 www.fwa.gov.au/index.cfm?pagename=awardsmodernlist).

Enterprise Agreements

Enterprise agreements are agreements made at an enterprise level between employers and employees regarding the terms and conditions of employment. Fair Work Australia can assist in the process of making such agreements, deal with disputes arising under the terms of agreements, and assess and approve agreements.

An enterprise agreement is made between one or more employers and employees and, in the case of greenfields agreements (see below), one or more relevant employee organisations (unions). Awards (see above) cover a whole industry or occupation and only provide a safety net of minimum pay rates and employment conditions, while enterprise agreements can be tailored to meet the needs of particular enterprises.

An enterprise agreement can include a broad range of matters such as rates of pay; employment conditions, e.g. hours of work, meal breaks and overtime: consultative mechanisms; dispute resolution procedures; and deductions from wages for any purpose authorised by an employee. They cannot, however, include unlawful content, such as discriminatory or objectionable terms.

There are three types of enterprise agreements:

- **single-enterprise agreements:** involving a single employer or one or more employers (such as in a joint venture) co-operating in what's essentially a single enterprise (such employers are known as single interest employers);
- **multi-enterprise agreements:** involving two or more employers that aren't all single interest employers;
- **greenfields agreements:** involving a genuinely new enterprise that one or more employers are establishing or propose to establish and who haven't yet employed persons necessary for the normal conduct of the enterprise. Such agreements may be

either a single-enterprise agreement or a multi-enterprise agreement.

CONTRACTS

Under Australian law, a contract of employment exists as soon as an employee proves his acceptance of an employer's terms and conditions of employment, e.g. by starting work, after which both employer and employee are bound by the terms offered and agreed. A contract isn't always in writing (it can be oral and 'sealed' by a handshake), although a company must provide employees who are normally employed in Australia with a contract containing certain important terms of employment and additional notes, e.g. regarding discipline and grievance procedures. You should receive a contract even for part-time and temporary jobs, although you won't normally receive one for casual work such as fruit picking (but you should get written confirmation of your wages and hours).

A contract (which may be called a 'statement of terms and conditions' or an 'offer letter') may consist of a simple sheet of paper or can be a comprehensive multi-page document, e.g. from a multi-national company. A contract for a temporary position must state the period of the contract and should guarantee you compensation in the event that employment is terminated without notice.

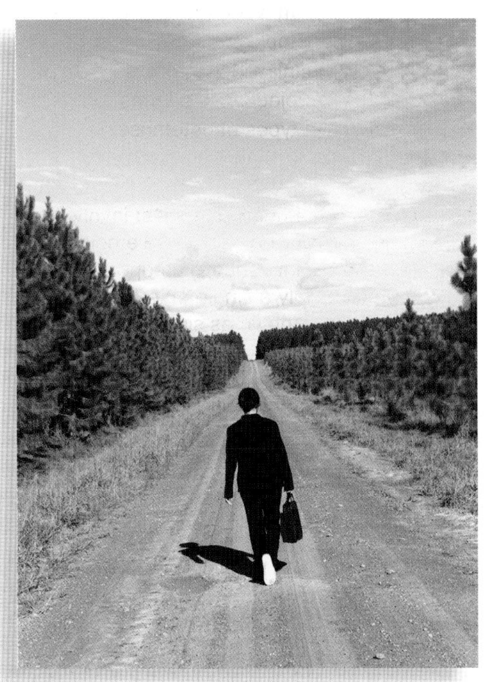

Any special arrangements you've made with an employer should also be contained in the contract. If there are no agreed terms under one or more of the above headings, this may be stated in the contract. If all or any of the above particulars are contained in a collective agreement, an employer may refer employees to a copy of this. Similarly, there may be references to other documents, such as the rules relating to flexible working hours and company holidays, sick pay and superannuation scheme conditions, wage regulation orders, and work rules or handbooks.

If you require a visa to work in Australia, your contract may contain a clause stating that the contract is subject to a visa being granted by the authorities. Your employment is usually subject to satisfactory references being received from your previous employer(s) and/or character references. If you're a school leaver or student, a reference may be required from the head teacher or principal of your last school, college or university.

For certain jobs, a pre-employment medical examination is required (see **Medical Examination** on page 49) and periodic examinations may be a condition of employment, e.g. where good health is necessary for the safe performance of your duties.

Before signing a contract of employment, you should obtain a copy of any general employment conditions (see below) or documents referred to in the contract and ensure that you understand them. There are usually no hidden surprises or traps for the unwary in an Australian contract of employment, although as with any contract you should know exactly what it contains before signing it. If your knowledge of English is poor, you should ask someone to explain anything you don't understand in simple English (Australian companies rarely provide foreigners with contracts in a language other than English).

TERMS OF EMPLOYMENT

Your terms of employment will include some or all of the topics listed on the following pages.

Relocation & Travel Expenses

Your travel and relocation expenses to Australia (or to a new job in another region of Australia) depend on your agreement with your employer and are usually detailed in your contract or your employer's general terms. If you're hired from outside Australia, your air ticket (or other travel) to Australia may be booked and paid for by your employer. You can usually also claim incidental travel costs, e.g. to and from airports.

Australian employers may also pay your relocation expenses to Australia up to a specified amount. This may be a percentage of your salary or as a set allowance, or cover only specific expenses, such as estate agent's, legal and removal fees. The allowance should be sufficient to move the contents of an average house.

Companies may ask you to obtain two or three removal estimates when they're liable for the total cost of removal. If you don't want to bring your furniture to Australia or have only a few belongings to ship, you may be given an allowance to purchase furniture locally (check with your employer). Generally, you're required to organise and pay for the removal yourself. Your employer usually reimburses the equivalent amount in Australian dollars after you've paid the bill, although it may be possible to get him to pay the bill directly or make an advance payment.

If you change jobs within Australia, your new employer may pay your relocation expenses when it's necessary for you to move home. Don't forget to ask, as he may not offer to pay (it may depend on how keen he is to employ you).

Salary & Benefits

Your salary is stated in your contract, and cost of living increases, overtime rates, piece and bonus rates, planned increases and salary reviews must also be included; only general points, such as the payment of your salary into a bank or other account and the date of salary payments, are usually included in an employer's standard terms.

Most employees are covered by a base rate of pay in a modern award, pre-modern award or an agreement. If nothing else applies to you, then you may be covered by the national minimum wage. Your pay rate depends on such things as your age, job classification and what 'instrument' you're covered by. You may also be entitled to other allowances or loadings, depending on the applicable instruments, what you do and the nature of your employment, e.g. if you're a casual you generally receive a casual loading.

You should receive an itemised pay statement (or wage slip), either with your salary, if it's paid weekly or fortnightly in cash, or separately when your salary is paid monthly into a bank account.

Always ensure that you receive a pay slip containing the legally required information, as it's almost impossible to dispute pay claims without one.

Salaries in Australia are generally reviewed annually, although the salaries of professional employees (or all employees in some businesses) may be reviewed every six months. The salaries of new employees may also be reviewed after six months. A percentage of your annual salary increase is usually to compensate for a rise in the cost of living, although some employees receive pay rises below the annual rate of inflation. Annual increases may be negotiated separately by employees on individual contracts, by an independent pay review board or by a union (or unions), when an industry is covered by an award (see above and **Contract Jobs** on page 26). The federal minimum wage from the age of 20 was $15.96 per hour (equivalent to ($606.40 per week for 38 hours) in July 2012, which is set by the Minimum Wage Panel of Fair Work Australia. Lower minimum wages apply to those aged 16 to 19.

When discussing your salary with a prospective employer, always take into account the total salary package, including bonuses, commission and fringe benefits such as a company car or a low-interest home loan, as well as fringe benefit tax (see page 239).

Commission & Bonuses

Your salary may include commission or bonus payments, calculated on your individual performance (e.g. based on your sales) or the company's performance as a whole, which may be paid regularly (e.g. monthly or annually) or irregularly. Some employers pay employees a bonus (in addition to any award holiday bonus) at the end of the year, although this isn't normal practice in Australia. When a bonus is paid, it may be stated in your contract, in which case it's obligatory. If applicable, an annual bonus is usually paid pro rata if you don't work a full calendar year, e.g. in your first and last years of employment with a company. In industry, particularly in small firms, blue-collar workers are often paid bonus or 'piece-work' rates based on their individual productivity. If you're employed on a contract basis for a fixed period, you may be paid an end-of-contract bonus.

Profit-sharing schemes aren't common in Australia, although performance-related bonuses or commissions are common in the banking industry. In some companies, directors and key employees may be offered share options at a discount well below the market price.

Expenses

Expenses paid by your employer are usually listed in your employment conditions. These may include travel costs from your home to your place of work, e.g. a bus or rail season ticket or the equivalent in cash (paid monthly with your salary). Companies without a company restaurant or canteen may pay employees a lunch allowance or provide luncheon vouchers. Claimable expenses for travel on company business or for training courses may be detailed in your employer's general terms or listed in a separate document. Most companies pay a per-kilometre allowance to staff authorised to use their cars on company business (you must ensure that business use is covered by your insurance).

Company Cars

Some employees (e.g. sales reps) are provided with a company car, and many Australian employers give senior employees such as directors and senior managers a car as a fringe benefit. Most companies provide cars under a lease arrangement, which means that employees must pay fringe benefit tax (FBT – see page 239) on the value of a company car that's used privately. If a company car is provided, check whether you're permitted to use it privately and whether, if you leave the company, you're responsible for the balance of the finance. Many companies allow employees to buy second-hand company cars at favourable prices. If you're provided with a company car, you usually receive details regarding its use and your obligations on starting employment. If you lose your licence (e.g. through drunk driving) and are unable to fulfil the requirements of your job, your employment may be terminated and you may not be entitled to compensation.

Acceptance of Gifts

With the exception of those in the public sector, employees are normally allowed to accept gifts of a limited value from customers or suppliers, e.g. bottles of wine or spirits or other small gifts at Christmas. Generally, any small gifts given and received openly and 'above board' aren't considered a bribe or unlawful. Nevertheless, you should declare any gifts received to your immediate superior, who will decide what's to be done with them. Some bosses pool gifts and divide them among all employees. (If you accept a real bribe, make sure it's a big one and that you have a secret bank account!)

Education & Training

The education and training provided by your employer may be stated in your standard terms. It's in your interest to investigate courses of study, lectures and seminars which you feel will be of direct benefit to you and your employer. Most employers give reasonable consideration to a request to attend a course during working hours, provided you don't make it a full-time occupation. It's compulsory for companies to provide appropriate and adequate health and safety training for all employees. Australian employers are notoriously lax in providing employee training and education, and only around half the workforce benefit from it. To encourage employers to improve the quantity and quality of their training programmes, there's an Industry Training Levy and employers must pay a penalty when specified minimum training levels aren't met.

If you need to improve your English, language classes may be paid by your employer. If it's necessary to learn a language other than English in order to perform your job, the cost of language study should also be paid by your employer. An allowance may be paid for personal education or hobbies which aren't work related or of direct benefit to your employer. In addition to relevant education and training, employers must also provide the essential tools and equipment for a job, although this is open to interpretation.

Working Hours

Since 1st January 2010, maximum weekly hours form part of the National Employment Standards (NES) and replace the maximum ordinary hours of work entitlements under the Australian Fair Pay and Conditions Standard (called the 'standard'). The NES sets out the maximum weekly hours for employees and also the circumstances in which an employee may refuse a request or requirement to work additional hours (overtime) if the hours are unreasonable.

An employer must not request or require an employee to work more than 38 hours a week for full-time employees or the lesser of 38 hours and the employee's ordinary hours of work in a week for employees who don't work full-time. When calculating the number of hours an employee has worked per week, any authorised leave (such as personal leave) should be included. Your working hours in Australia may differ from those in your previous country of residence and vary according to your profession and where you work. A national 38-hour working week was introduced in 1981 and reinforced by the Fair Work Act 2009, and the usual working week is 35 to 40 hours for most wage earners, but overtime is normally available and many employees work up to ten hours a week overtime.

Almost a third of full-time employees in Australia work over 48 hours per week.

Most employees work a five-day week, although over 25 per cent of men work weekends and some 20 per cent work shifts. In the last decade, many companies have switched from eight-hour to 12-hour shifts, which means working only 11 or 12 days per month or ten days every three weeks. Twelve-hour shifts are common in some industries (e.g. mining), where the advantage for employers is that they incur no overtime

payments. Employees also gain, as they earn around the same as previously (when they worked overtime) and have much more leisure time. Most workers prefer 12-hour shifts after having tried them, although there's a safety risk, particularly in factories, where it's estimated that there's double the risk of accidents due to fatigue. The Australian government is encouraging employers to adopt 'family-friendly practices' whereby employees enjoy more flexible working and leave arrangements (see below). Hourly paid workers are usually paid overtime (see below) for extra hours and higher (penalty) rates for night, shift and weekend work. In contrast, executives, managers and professionals often work over 50 hours per week without extra pay, but are more highly rewarded in their basic salary. Twelve-hour days aren't uncommon among managerial and professional staff. In fact, the higher you climb the ladder of success, the harder you're expected to work (burn-out is common among managers and executives).

A standard working day (without overtime) for a blue-collar worker is from 7 or 8am to 3.30 or 4.30pm, while working hours in most offices and shops are from 8.30 or 9.30am until 4.30 or 5.30pm, with an hour's break for lunch.

Tea or coffee breaks may be scheduled at set times mid-morning and mid-afternoon, particularly in factories (employers usually provide free tea and coffee). Long business lunches (two hours or more) are becoming less common, although it's still customary to find employees finishing their lunch late in the afternoon on Thursdays and Fridays.

Your working hours may not be increased above the hours stated in your employment terms without compensation or overtime being paid. Similarly, if you have a guaranteed working week, your hours cannot be reduced (i.e. short-time working) or changed without your agreement, unless there's a clause – sometimes referred to as a 'mobility clause' – in your contract. Some employers operate a system of flexible working hours and may also permit employees to job-share or work part of the time at home.

Around a third of Australian workers (usually blue-collar) are required to sign on or clock in and out of work; employees caught cheating may be summarily dismissed.

Mining Jobs (etc.)

Bear in mind that mining jobs usually operate on a 'fly in, fly out' (FIFO) basis, where mines operate 24-7 and workers do 10 or 12-hour shifts, seven days a week – two weeks on and two weeks off. Wages are good but are reduced when workers are back in their home base. Working conditions are harsh (HOT, dirty, dangerous, etc.) and living conditions extremely basic, and there's also little to do except drink on your time off. If you live locally, costs can be very high, not just for accommodation, but food and all supplies, which must be trucked or flown in. Not a job for the fainthearted.

Flexi-time & Flexible Working Arrangements

Many Australian companies operate flexi-time working hours or a system of 'rostered days off' (RDO). The conditions and rules relating to flexi-time and RDO schemes vary depending on the employer (they're most common in public service); they're more likely to apply to those in administrative, managerial and professional occupations and are standard in construction/labour contracts. At their peak, RDOs applied to almost a third of wage and salary earners. But RDOs were usually taken on a Monday or Friday to provide a long weekend, which proved disruptive to companies' operations. In recent years employers have therefore been cutting back on RDOs, e.g. from 12 to 6 per year, converting them to additional holiday, swapping them for superannuation payments or replacing them with time off in lieu on different days of the week.

Under the NES, eligible employees have a right to request flexible working arrangements to assist them to care for their child. An employee who's a parent or has responsibility for the care of a child, may request a change in their working arrangements such as a change in their hours of work (e.g. reduction in hours worked, changes to start/finish times); a change in patterns of work, e.g. working 'split-shifts' or job sharing arrangements; or a change in the work location (e.g. working from home or another location). In order to be eligible to make a request for flexible working arrangements an employee must have completed at least 12 months continuous service with their employer prior to making the request.

Overtime

The opportunity to work overtime is seen as a lucrative benefit by most blue-collar workers, many of whom earn around a quarter of their wages from overtime. In some industries there's an ingrained 'overtime culture', although for many workers overtime is a matter of economic necessity. Of the 10m people in employment, a third regularly work over 48 hours per week. Overtime (penalty rates) is generally paid at time-and-a-half for the first three hours and double-time thereafter (and on Sundays and Public Holidays), or as detailed in the award for the trade or industry (workers in some industries receive 2.5 times the normal rate for Sundays). Overtime may be paid at only the standard rate – more likely in non-union workplaces, where workers are three times more likely to have a standard working week longer than 38 hours.

In order to reduce overtime costs, many companies have been extending the normal working week and changing to 12-hour shifts. Many awards stipulate that employees work longer hours at ordinary time (e.g. up to 50 hours a week) in return for higher wages and bonuses. Shift workers have some special entitlements, conditions and general workplace protections under national workplace relations laws.

Some companies pay overtime only when work is urgent and officially approved, and many prefer salaried (i.e. monthly paid) employees to take time off in lieu of payment or expect them to work unpaid overtime. Up to half of all overtime worked is unpaid.

Holidays & Leave

This section covers annual and Public Holidays, and also time off for other reasons, e.g. for pregnancy, illness and compassionate reasons.

Annual Holidays

All permanent employees in Australia are entitled to at least four weeks' annual holiday and many receive up to six weeks, depending on the award for their trade or industry. Some employers offer four weeks in the first year of employment and six weeks thereafter or after a certain number of years service; employees in some industries and professions receive as many as nine weeks paid annual holiday. Eligible shift workers are entitled to an additional week's paid annual leave for each year of service. Under the NES, an employee's entitlement to annual leave accrues progressively during a year of service according to their ordinary hours of work and accumulates year to year. In some industries and professions (e.g. teaching), employees are required to take paid holidays at certain times.

Under a scheme called holiday or leave 'loading', most full-time employees are paid an extra 17.5 per cent of their normal wage when they take their annual holidays, although some companies pay leave loading only to employees below a certain salary level, e.g. $50,000.

Holidays must usually be taken in the year in which they're earned, although many companies allow employees to carry outstanding annual holiday over to the following year. Employers may also allow employees to take their total annual holiday in one block, rather than split it into periods throughout the year. Holiday entitlement is calculated on a pro rata basis (per completed calendar month of service) if you don't work a full calendar year. Part-time staff may also be entitled to paid holidays on a pro rata basis.

Before starting a job, check that any planned holidays will be approved by your new employer. This is particularly important if they fall within your probationary period, when holidays may not be permitted. Holidays may usually be taken only with your manager's permission and in many companies must be booked up to a year in advance.

If you resign or are given notice, most employers pay you in lieu of any outstanding holiday, although this isn't an entitlement and you may be obliged to take the holiday at your employer's convenience.

Public Holidays

The number of statutory Public Holidays in Australia varies from state to state between 10 and 12. There are eight national Public Holidays (see table) plus state Public Holidays, the number and dates of which vary according to the state or territory. All states celebrate Labor Day, although the date varies from state to state. Some companies and industries also have their own 'holidays', such as a company outing or a union picnic day. Banks, businesses, schools and most shops are closed on Public Holidays. The days shown in the table below are national Public Holidays.

Public holidays can also include any other days or part days, declared under state or territory law. For example, state or regional Public Holidays that apply only in a particular state, such as Labour Day and the Melbourne Cup Day in Victoria.

If a business is closed on a public holiday or if full-time or part-time employees take the day off, an employer must pay them at their base rate for the ordinary hours they would have otherwise worked. The base rate of pay doesn't include any incentive-based payments and bonuses, loadings, monetary allowances, overtime or penalty rates. Part-time and casual employees who don't normally work on the day on which the public holiday falls, don't receive payment.

If a public holiday falls on a weekend, there's usually a substitute holiday on the following Monday. Some companies close during Christmas and New Year, e.g. from 25th December until 1st January inclusive. To compensate for this shutdown and perhaps other extra holidays during the year, employees may be required to work extra hours throughout the year or to take it as part of their annual holiday entitlement. Part-time staff may be paid for a public holiday only when it falls on a day when they would normally be working.

National Public Holidays

Date	Holiday
1st January	New Year's Day
January	Australia Day (the date varies from state to state but is usually on the Monday following 26th January)
March/April	Good Friday (the date changes each year)
March/April	Easter Monday (the Monday after Good Friday)
25th April	Anzac Day (in memory of those who died in the two World Wars)
Second Monday in June	Queen's birthday (except in Western Australia, which celebrates the Queen's birthday in September)
25th December	Christmas Day
26th December	Boxing Day (called Proclamation Day in South Australia)

You aren't required to work on Public Holidays unless it's stated in your contract. When it's necessary to work on Public Holidays, you normally receive the same or a higher rate of pay than is paid for working on a Sunday (e.g. double, and often triple, the normal rate) and/or time off in lieu. When a job involves working at weekends and on Public Holidays (e.g. shift work), you usually receive a penalty rate or are paid a shift allowance.

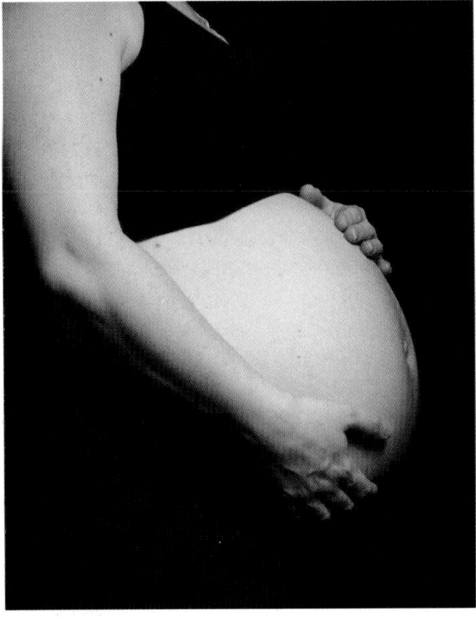

Pregnancy & Confinement

The government introduced a national Paid Parental Leave scheme from 1st January 2011, which provides eligible working parents with 18 weeks of parental leave pay at the national minimum wage (currently $606.40 per week before tax). For more information, see 💻 www.familyassist.gov.au. Employees can also take up to 12 months unpaid parental leave on the birth of a child or the adoption of a child under five years of age (maternity, paternity or adoption leave). A woman has the right to return to her job, or a job with the same status and pay, within 12 months of giving birth.

In addition to the above, time off work for sickness in connection with a pregnancy is usually given without question, but it may not be paid unless authorised by a doctor if it exceeds your annual sick leave allocation (see below).

Personal Leave

Personal leave – often referred to as sick leave – can be taken by an employee when they are sick or injured or to care for an immediate family or household member who's sick, injured or in an emergency. The definition of immediate family member is a spouse, de facto partner, child, parent, grandparent, grandchild or sibling of the employee or a child, parent, grandparent, grandchild or sibling of a spouse or a de facto partner.

Full-time employees receive ten days paid personal leave per year and part-time employees receive a pro-rata amount based on their hours of work. Casual employees don't receive any paid personal leave but can take up to two days unpaid carer's leave as needed.

At the completion of 12 months continuous service, a full-time employee will have accrued ten days (two weeks) personal leave. The personal leave accrues progressively, which means that it continues to accumulate each time an employee works; for example after six months of continuous service you'll have accrued five days (one week) of personal leave. Personal leave doesn't expire and any unused leave carries over from year to year. Paid personal leave continues accruing during all periods that count as service, which means it continues to add up while you're on paid annual leave and paid personal leave. It doesn't, however, accrue when you're on unpaid leave (e.g. unpaid parental leave or leave without pay granted by the employer) or during an unauthorised absence such as unprotected industrial action.

When you've run out of paid personal leave, you can take two days unpaid carer's leave on each occasion. Unpaid carer's leave is also available to casual employees and is available for the same purpose as paid carer's leave, i.e. to care for an immediate family or household member who's sick, injured or in an emergency.

Some employers operate an occupational sick pay (OSP) scheme, whereby you receive your full salary for a number of months (depending on your length of service) in the event of sickness or after an accident. OSP may be provided by your employer as part of a company pension scheme.

> ☑ **SURVIVAL TIP**
> **You're required to notify your employer as soon as possible of sickness or an accident that prevents you from working, i.e. within a few hours of your normal starting time, and keep your employer informed about your illness and when you expect to return to work.**

Other Leave

In addition to annual and personal leave, employees are also entitled to compassionate and personal/carer's leave, which may be paid or unpaid. These include:

- ten days paid personal/carer's leave per year;
- two days unpaid carer's leave (when needed);
- two days paid compassionate leave (when needed);
- 12 months unpaid parental leave.

Annual leave and paid personal/carer's leave accumulates over time. Minimum entitlements to parental leave under the NES apply to all employees in Australia, including those covered by state industrial laws. However, if state laws are more generous than the NES rules, then these will apply. Part-time employees also usually receive the minimum entitlements on a pro rata basis.

In addition, employees are allowed, by law, to take time off work under certain circumstances, as follows:

- An expectant mother is entitled to 'reasonable' unpaid time off for ante-natal care.
- A trade union official is entitled to paid time off for trade union duties and training for such duties. Employees may also be paid to attend union meetings during working hours. Similarly, a safety representative is allowed paid time off in connection with his safety duties.
- All employees are allowed time off for public duties such as service as a juror or court witness, councillor or school governor, or as a member of a statutory tribunal or authority, although your employer isn't usually required to pay you.
- Parents are usually permitted to leave work for up to an hour at any time to look after children.
- If you're made redundant, you're entitled to take one day off each week to look for a new job or to arrange training in connection with a new job.

Beyond these statutory rights, whether or not you're paid for time off work for compassionate reasons (e.g. a funeral) or time lost through unavoidable circumstances (e.g. public transport strikes or car breakdowns) depends on your employer, on whether you're paid weekly or monthly (e.g. with an hourly rate of pay), and whether you're required to punch a clock. The attitude to paid time off may also depend on your status and position. Executives and managers (who often work much longer hours than officially required) generally have much more leeway regarding time off than blue-collar workers. The conditions for 'special' leave should be detailed in your standard employment terms.

After 10 or 15 years' continuous service with an employer, you may be entitled to up to six months' leave on full or half pay. Some employers also permit unpaid career breaks (sabbaticals) of up to three years.

Medical Examination

Many Australian companies require prospective employees to have a pre-employment medical examination, which is performed by a company doctor (or a doctor nominated by the employer). An offer of employment is usually subject to your being given a clean bill of health. This may be required for employees over a certain age (e.g. 40 years) or for everyone in certain jobs, e.g. where good health is of paramount importance for safety reasons. Thereafter, a medical examination may be required periodically (e.g. every year or two) or when requested by your employer.

Medical examinations may be required as a condition of membership of a company health, life insurance or pension scheme. Some companies insist on key employees having regular health screening, particularly senior managers and executives.

Accident & Other Insurance

All employers in Australia are required to have occupational accident insurance (called workers' compensation insurance or WorkCover) for employees working on their premises, whether in a factory, office, residential accommodation, shop or warehouse. Schemes, many of which operate at a loss, are financed by a levy on salaries.

Insurance provision notwithstanding, employees must obey all safety regulations such as those relating to smoking, the use of safety equipment and clothing, the securing of long hair or ties, and the wearing of jewellery. However, unless an employee is grossly negligent and recklessly ignores safety rules and regulations, he's invariably deemed to be entitled to compensation.

A worker is paid compensation (commonly called 'compo') if he's injured or sick as the result of an accident in the workplace or when travelling to or from work or on company business. Compensation covers medical and other expenses and loss of earnings, and a worker's dependants are entitled to compensation if he's killed on the job. Australians tend to claim compo for the slightest injury at work. However, although bogus claims are endemic, particularly concerning the effects of work-related stress, making a claim for compo often carries a stigma and many workers try to avoid claiming (particularly those on contracts).

Occupational health and safety is dealt with by both federal and state governments, and at the federal level is determined by the National Occupational Health and Safety Commission. The conditions of payment and the amount of compensation payable are laid down in various state acts, although in some states Workers' Compensation Boards decide individual claims. If a claim is rejected, a worker can take his case to his union and it's decided by a workers' compensation commission.

Other insurance provided by your employer should be detailed in your employment conditions. This may include free life and health insurance, which may cover travel overseas on company business. Some companies provide free membership of a private health insurance scheme, although this may apply only to executives, managers and 'key' personnel. Where applicable, check whether health insurance includes your family. Companies may also operate a contributory group health insurance scheme, offering reduced subscriptions for employees. For information about social security 'insurance', see **Chapter 13**.

On 1st November 2009, Safe Work Australia (www.safeworkaustralia.gov.au) began operating as an independent statutory agency with primary responsibility to improve occupational health and safety and workers' compensation arrangements across Australia.

Union Membership

Trade unions have been active in Australia since the mid-19th century, when many professional 'agitators' were deported from the UK and Ireland. However, there has been a steady decline in union membership in the last few decades and in 2012 it stood at 1.8m or around 18 per cent of the workforce (down from 26 per cent in 1986). About four in ten (40 per cent) public servants and teachers belong to a trade union, while in the private sector it's less than 15 per cent.

Under the Workplace Relations Act, all employees have the right to belong or not to belong to a trade union. Employees can also join an enterprise association, which is a union where the majority of members are employees performing work in the same enterprise.

Unions earned themselves a terrible reputation during the '60s and '70s, when the country and the economy were frequently crippled by strikes. In the last decade there were a series of confrontations between the Liberal/National coalition government and the unions after the government brought in tougher 'anti-union' laws in an attempt to end 'outdated' restrictive work practices (and the resulting low productivity), which are rampant in industries with strong unions such as mining and the docks. These laws included anti-strike provisions and harsh sanctions against some strikers, and they led to bitter disputes between unions and employers. These changes were reversed by the Labor government elected in 2007.

Today, there are over 200 trade unions in Australia, many of which are affiliated to the Australian Council of Trade Unions (☎ 1300-362233 or 03-9664 7333, 💻 www.actu.asn.au). In the last few decades the unions have been losing ground and have largely failed to recruit young workers, women, small-business employees and those in growth industries. Some 60 per cent of workers believe that unions are no longer relevant to them and a survey as far back as 1997 found that non-union members are more likely to be satisfied at work, have more positive attitudes to management and feel more secure than those in unions.

The Workplace Relations Act, 1996 largely abolished compulsory union membership, and employers aren't allowed to discriminate against an employee because he belongs (or wishes to belong) to a trade union. Nevertheless, despite their reduced membership, unions have a great deal of influence, particularly in companies and industries which previously had 'closed shop' agreements, where all employees had to join a union. Large companies with over 100 employees have the highest rates of unionisation and small businesses with fewer than ten employees the lowest.

Whether you're better off as a member of a trade union depends largely on the industry in which you're employed, although there are general benefits to be gained from union membership. In addition to negotiating fair pay and safer working conditions for members, unions offer members legal and medical assistance in work-related disputes. In most industries that recognise trade unions, members' pay and conditions are decided by collective bargaining between employers and trade unions.

Changing Jobs & Confidentiality

If you disclose any confidential company information, either in Australia or overseas (particularly to competitors), you may be

liable to instant dismissal and may also have legal action taken against you. You may not take any secrets or confidential information (e.g. customer mailing lists) from a previous employer, but you may use any contacts, know-how, knowledge and skills acquired during his employ. If you make any inventions while an employee, they remain your property unless you sell or license them to your employer, they were made as part of your 'normal duties', or you were specifically employed to invent, e.g. in research and development.

Your contract may contain a clause defining the sort of information that the employer considers to be confidential, such as customer and supplier relationships and details of business plans. You may not compete against a former employer if there's a valid, binding restraint clause in your contract. However, if there's a confidentiality or restraint clause in your contract that's unfair (e.g. inhibits you from changing jobs), it's probably invalid in law and therefore unenforceable. If you're in doubt, consult a solicitor about your rights.

If you're a key employee, you may have a legal binding contract preventing you from joining a competitor or starting a company in the same line of business as your employer, and (in particular) from enticing former colleagues to join your company. However, such a clause is usually valid for a limited period, e.g. a year.

Part-time Job Restrictions

Restrictions on part-time employment for an employer other than your regular employer may be detailed in your employment conditions. Many Australian companies don't allow full-time employees to work part-time (i.e.

moonlight) for another employer, particularly one in the same line of business. You may, however, be permitted to take a part-time teaching job or similar employment (you can also write a book!).

Discrimination

It's illegal under the Racial Discrimination Act, 1975 and Sex Discrimination Act, 1984 for an employer to discriminate against an employee (or job candidate) because of his or her sex (unless a person's sex is an essential qualification for a job), marital status, ethnic or national origin, nationality, race, skin colour or sexual orientation. It's also illegal to discriminate against an employee because he does or doesn't wish to join a trade union. A woman doing the same or broadly similar work to a man or work of equal value is legally entitled to the same salary and other terms of employment as a man (see **Working Women** on page 20). Discrimination applies to appointment, dismissal, promotion, selection and training. Some companies have a policy of employing disabled applicants whenever possible ('positive discrimination').

 **Caution**

It's difficult to prove discrimination on the grounds of sex and almost impossible on the grounds of race or skin colour, although it's acknowledged that discrimination is widespread.

If you're subjected to sexual harassment (which can happen to both women and men) you should report it to your supervisor or manager, as many companies have internal procedures to deal with such matters. However, if you don't receive satisfaction, you can report it to your union (if applicable) or the police and take legal advice. The Human Rights and Equal Opportunities Commission (HREOC, ☎ 02-9284 9600, 💻 www.hreoc.gov.au) handles sexual harassment and discrimination cases in the utmost confidence and can advise you whether you have legal grounds for a complaint (which must be submitted in writing). HREOC's national office is in Sydney and it has regional offices throughout the country (listed on their website). They also have a local 'complaints infoline' (☎ 1300-656419).

Victims of discrimination who win compensation payments are often left frustrated and empty-handed. Rulings by the HREOC aren't legally enforceable and compensation ordered by it is rarely paid without victims being forced to take further legal action (many just give up). To combat this sense of frustration, since April 2000 the Federal Court has ruled in around 15 per cent of cases which the HREOC hadn't been able to. Rulings made by the Federal Court on discrimination are legally enforceable and, as a result, employers are now increasingly aware of their liability.

The government has also introduced educational campaigns and workplace training in an attempt to combat discrimination in the workplace, and change the general opinion that Australia's discrimination laws are a sham. If you have a grievance or complaint against a colleague or your boss, there may be an official procedure to be followed in order to obtain redress. If an official grievance procedure exists, it's usually detailed in your general employment terms.

Dismissal & Redundancy

The Labor government has brought in a new Fair Dismissal Code for Small Businesses under the Fair Work Act 2009. Under the new law, an employee of a small business (defined as having fewer than 15 employees) can make a claim for unfair dismissal after they have been employed for at least 12 months. To dismiss someone fairly after 12 months an employer must comply with the new code. For businesses with more than 15 employees a claim can be made after six months employment.

Most large and medium-size companies have comprehensive grievance and disciplinary procedures, which must usually be followed before an employee can be suspended or dismissed. In some cases employees may be suspended with or without pay for certain misdemeanours, e.g. for breaches of contract, usually with pay pending an investigation into an alleged offence or impropriety.

Disciplinary procedures usually include both oral and written warnings, e.g. first oral warning, second oral warning, first written warning, second written warning, interview with board, etc., and official records must be kept by the employer. These procedures are to protect employees from unfair dismissal and to ensure that dismissed employees cannot (successfully) sue their employer.

It's illegal to dismiss employees on grounds other than those detailed in government and union agreements. In cases where employment was terminated on unjustified grounds, there may be a review by an industrial court, and wrongful dismissal can result in a claim for damages. However, employees dismissed for 'serious misconduct' such as disobedience of management decisions, fraud or any other illegal activity aren't entitled to notice or benefits.

If you believe that you've been unfairly dismissed, you can take your case to Fair Work Australia (💻 www.fwa.gov.au/index.cfm?pagename=dismissalsclaim). Note that claims must be made within 14 days of the dismissal coming into effect and there's a lodgement fee of $64.20.

Probationary & Notice Periods

For most jobs there's a probationary period, which may vary from two weeks for weekly paid employees to 13 weeks for permanent employees. Your notice period normally depends on your method of salary payment, your employer, your profession and your length of service, and is detailed in your contract or the employer's standard terms of employment. Probationary and notice periods apply equally to employers and employees. The notice period for weekly paid workers is usually as follows:

Notice Period

Length of Service	Notice Period
Less than 1 year	1 week
1 to 3 years	2 weeks
3 to 5 years	3 weeks
Over 5 years	4 weeks

Most monthly paid employees have a one-month (or four-week) notice period, which takes effect after any probationary period.

Employees over 45 with more than two years' service are entitled to an extra week's notice or pay in lieu of notice. The notice period may be longer for executive or key employees, e.g. three or six months, or may be extended after a number of years' service (in which case it's noted in your employment conditions). If an employer doesn't give you the required notice in writing, he's liable to pay you in full for the period of official notice.

If you resign, you must usually do so in writing. If you resign or are given notice, your company may not require you to work your notice period, particularly if you're joining a competitor or your boss feels that you may be a disruptive influence. However, if he doesn't want you to work your notice, he must pay you in full for the notice period, plus any outstanding overtime or holiday entitlement.

If an employer goes bankrupt and cannot pay you, you may terminate your employment without notice, but your employer cannot legally do this. Other valid reasons for an employee not to give notice are assault or abuse of him or a colleague by the employer and failure to pay or persistent delay in paying his wages. Nevertheless, employees can usually leave a job for any reason without giving notice and the chances of an employer having any legal rights worth enforcing are negligible, although you may lose any bonuses

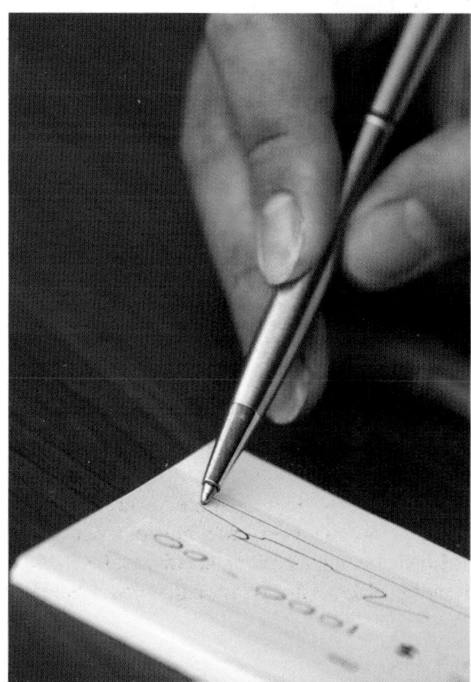

or other monies owed to you, plus any chance of receiving a reference.

Redundancy Pay

Redundancy (called retrenchment in Australia) has become a common occurrence in the last decade or so. It's defined as a situation 'where an employer has made a definite decision that he no longer wishes the job that an employee has been doing to be done by anyone, and this isn't due to the ordinary and customary turnover of labour'. Retrenched workers are entitled to severance pay in accordance with the Termination Change and Redundancy (TCR) case in 1984. The amount of severance pay (in terms of normal weeks' pay) for those employed under federal awards depends on the length of service of an employee, as shown in the table below. (Severance pay in Australia is below the average paid in most other western countries.)

Severance Pay

Length of Service	Severance Pay (weeks)
Less than 1 year	0 weeks
1 to 2 years	4 weeks
2 to 3 years	6 weeks
3 to 4 years	7 weeks
4 ot 5 years	8 weeks
5 to 6 years	10 weeks
6 to 7 years	11 weeks
7 to 8 years	13 weeks
8 to 9 years	14 weeks
9 to 10 weeks	16 weeks
Over 10 years	12 weeks*

* discounted by long-service leave

Employees aged over 45 with more than two years' service are entitled to an extra week's notice or pay in lieu of notice.

Severance pay is higher in some states, e.g. up to 16 weeks in New South Wales plus an extra 25 per cent (total 20 weeks) for those aged 45 and over. Many awards allow for three or four weeks' pay for each year of service when an employee takes forced redundancy.

Severance pay may not exceed the amount an employee would have earned had he remained in employment until his normal retirement date. If an employee receives a superannuation payment (see page 216), the amount is generally deducted from the severance pay to which he's entitled.

The average severance pay for executives is around six months' salary, although some executives, managers and key personnel have a clause in their contract whereby they receive a generous 'golden handshake' when they're made redundant, e.g. after a takeover.

When an employee has been notified of his redundancy, he's allowed to take a day off each week with pay to look for another job. Employers must contact a Department of Human Services (www.humanservices.gov.au) office and inform them of the number of proposed redundancies, the category of employees affected, and the period over which the redundancies will be made. Some companies provide 'outplacement' consultancy or agency services for employees who are made redundant. This includes advice and counselling on job prospects, investment (for employees fortunate enough to receive large redundancy payments), job hunting, retirement, retraining, setting up in business and state benefits. Redundant employees are entitled to a 'statement of employment' (reference). It's also possible for employees to take voluntary redundancy or early retirement and receive an early pension, e.g. in the event of ill health.

Australia has no unemployment benefit scheme, although the unemployed receive social security payments under the Jobsearch and Newstart schemes.

Retirement

There's no statutory retirement age in Australia. Your employment contract may be valid only until the official state retirement age, which is 65 for both men and women from 1st July 2013, although in many large companies retirement is possible from the age of 55. From 1st July 2017, the qualifying age for the state (age) pension will increase from 65 to 65.5 years for both men and women, after which it will increase by six months every two years, until reaching 67 on 1st July 2023.

If you wish to continue working after you've reached retirement age, you may need to negotiate a new contract of employment. If your employer has a compulsory retirement age, he isn't required to give you notice when you reach it. Many companies present employees with a gift on reaching retirement age (e.g. the key to your ball and chain), the value of which usually depends on your number of years' service.

REFERENCES

Employers in Australia aren't legally obliged to provide employees with a written reference or 'statement of employment', except in the case of redundancy. However, if you leave an employer on good terms, he'll usually provide a written reference on request. If your employer refuses to give you a written reference or gives you an unwarranted 'bad' reference, you should ask your immediate boss or a colleague instead.

In Australia, prospective employers may contact your previous employer (or employers) directly for a reference, either orally or in writing. This can be bad news for employees, as you have no idea what has been said about you and whether it's true or false. However, an employer cannot (legally) maliciously defame you, although should he do so orally, it's almost impossible to sue him successfully.

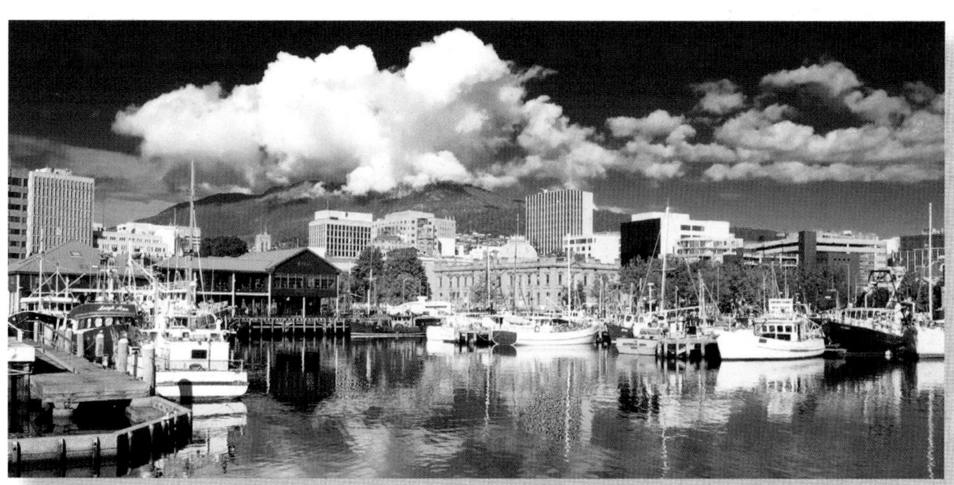

Hobart, TAS

Sichtvermerke/Visas/Visas

IMMIGRATION
ARRIVED
-6 AUG 2005
ADELAIDE AIRPORT
088K
AUSTRALIA

346 MALABA 346
KENYA KENYA
10. 1. 2003
IMMIGRATION OFFICER
346-346-346-346-346-346-346

177
EXIT
KENYA
04. 1. 2003
MALABA

3. PERMITS & VISAS

With the exception of New Zealanders, anyone wishing to enter Australia for any purpose requires a visa (see below). New Zealanders receive a Special Category Visa (SCV) on arrival and nothing is stamped in their passports; there are no formalities and they can live and work in Australia for as long as they wish.

Australia is a nation of migrants and only the Aboriginals represent the indigenous population (some 2 per cent); everyone else is an immigrant or descended from an immigrant. After the Second World War, Australia instituted a mass immigration policy ('populate or perish') and accepted virtually anybody who applied, even providing assisted passages whereby migrants paid only a small sum (e.g. £10 in the UK) towards their fare to Australia. However, immigration policy has altered dramatically since then and Australia's entry qualifications for independent migrants (those without family in Australia) are now among the most stringent in the world.

In the '60s, Australia accepted around 140,000 migrants a year, peaking at 172,000 in 1988, but in the '90s the quota was reduced considerably, although a review of immigration policy found that it was too low, particularly regarding skilied migrants, and could stifle economic growth. For the year 2012-13, the migration programme provides for a total of 190,000 places, comprising 129,250 places for skilled migrants (over two-thirds of the total), 60,185 places for the family stream and 565 special eligibility places. Additionally, in the year 2009-10, 36,519 New Zealanders came to Australia as permanent and long term arrivals, who were excluded from the quotas.

The Australian Government has recently made comprehensive changes to the points based skilled migration program, effective from 1st July 2012. These changes include the introduction of three new visas and the closure of some visas to new applicants, and are to ensure that the skilled migration programme remain responsive to changes in the Australian labour market. See www.awpa.gov.au for information.

▲ Caution

Before making any plans to live or work in (or even travel to) Australia, you must ensure that you have the appropriate visa, without which you'll be refused permission to enter the country and sent back to your home country at your own expense.

IMMIGRATION ISSUES

Immigration can be a sensitive subject in Australia, where many people are against large-scale immigration, although evidence shows that it provides significant benefits for the country and stimulates economic growth. Migrants bring $billions into Australia each year and migration is the country's third-largest foreign currency earner, after tourism and agriculture, to say nothing of the wealth created by migrants.

Over-crowding and over-population in the major cities, and damage to Australia's culture and environment are among the arguments frequently cited by those opposed to large-

scale immigration. Despite its vast size, Australia has a relatively small population (22.6m) but is nevertheless considered by many Australians to be over-populated due to its lack of productive land, shortage of water and generally overcrowded cities.

Many Australians feel that migrants are a strain on the economy and take jobs away from native Australians. The ethnic background of migrants is also a thorny issue, and although race and ethnic origin aren't officially immigration criteria, almost half of Australians believe that the country accepts too many Asians, and some would also like fewer migrants from the Middle East.

There's a huge unsatisfied demand for emigration to Australia, which is more difficult than, for example, emigrating to Canada or the USA (the regulations are designed to keep people out rather than let them in). It's becoming increasingly difficult to obtain a visa as an independent migrant and it's also more difficult (or impossible) for immigrants who don't speak fluent English. Australian missions receive over one million enquiries a year and over 400,000 applications, of which around a quarter are accepted for migration.

The information in this chapter is intended as a guide only, as the rules and regulations change frequently, as well as sometimes being ambiguous, confusing and vague. It's important to check the latest regulations with an Australian mission or immigration consultant (such as **The Emigration Group** – see inside covers) before making a visa application. Note that if you use a migration agent, you should use one who's registered with the Office of the Migration Agents Registration Authority (🖳 www.mara.gov.au).

The Department of Immigration and Citizenship (DIAC) provides a wealth of information about visas and life in Australia on its website (🖳 www.immi.gov.au) and also operates ImmiTV on YouTube (🖳 www.youtube.com/immitv), has a Facebook page (🖳 www.facebook.com/departmentofimmigrationandcitizenship) and a migration blog (🖳 http://migrationblog.immi.gov.au).

VISAS

With the exception of New Zealanders, anyone wishing to enter Australia must obtain a visa before arrival in the country. The type of visa issued depends on the reason for your planned trip, which may be anything from a few weeks' holiday or a short business trip to permanent residence. Note the following general points:

- There are three main categories of visas: visitor, temporary residence, and residence (described in detail in this chapter).
- Multiple-entry visas are issued to those who need to visit Australia frequently over a long period, such as businessmen, entertainers, the parents of children living there and sportsmen.
- There are fees for almost all visas, some of which are very high (see page 77).
- The processing of visa applications in some categories can take a considerable time in some countries due to the large number of applications to be processed, and approval can take anything from a few weeks to a number of years. Processing time standards are shown on the DIAC website (🖳 www.immi.gov.au/about/charters/client-servicescharter/standards/2.1.htm).

Information about visas, charges and forms can be obtained from offices of the Department of Immigration and Citizenship (DIAC) in Australia (🖳 www.immi.gov.au) and Australian missions overseas. General information about visa applications is contained in *Making and Processing Visa Applications* (form 1025i).

Applications

It's important to obtain and complete the correct form, pay the correct fee and satisfy other requirements such as being inside or outside Australia, as necessary. For most visas where an application is made overseas, you **mustn't** be in Australia when a decision is made and for visa applications made in Australia, you **must** be in Australia when the decision is made. However, many applications can now be made online which causes further confusion – see 🖳 www.immi.gov.au for guidance on how to choose and apply for the appropriate visa. If you make a visa application in Australia, you must ensure that you have a visa to return before leaving the country; otherwise, if your application is refused you may have no right of review. If you apply for a visa in Australia, you're usually granted a bridging visa to remain within the law if your current visa expires while a decision is being made.

You must be careful to indicate the visa class under which you wish to be considered, as your application cannot be considered under any class other than the one noted on your application form. There are different application forms for different visa classes, a full list of which can be found on the DIAC website (🖳 www.immi.gov.au). Applications must be sent or delivered to the correct DIAC office for the visa class in which you're applying, with all the relevant documentation and the fee.

Now, however, that many applications can be lodged online (see 🖳 www.immi.gov.au) for information). If your application is approved the electronic visa system may not require you to have a visa label (as previously) inserted in your passport to confirm your immigration status (see 🖳 www.immi.gov.au/visas/about-your-visa.htm), which is dependent on your country of nationality (see your approval letter).

Family members who apply at the same time can usually apply on the same form and pay just one fee (a child born after an application is made, but before it's decided, is included in the parents' application). In certain circumstances, a spouse or dependent child can be added to an application.

If you change your passport after a visa application is granted, you must advise the DIAC of your new passport details so that they can update their records.

If a visa is refused, the DIAC will send or give you a notification refusal letter indicating the reason(s) for the refusal, and – if applicable – your right to seek a review by the Migration Review Tribunal (MRT) and the time limit for doing so.

 **Caution**

If you plan to travel to or from Australia while a visa application is being considered (assuming this is possible), you should inform the DIAC, as a visa will be refused if you're in the 'wrong place' when a decision is made. If you're in Australia and planning a trip abroad, you must apply for a bridging visa that allows you to return (see 🖳 www.immi.gov.au/allforms/pdf/1024i.pdf).

Extensions & Restrictions

If your visa expires while you're in Australia and you haven't applied for an extension, you're committing a criminal offence and can be fined, given a suspended prison sentence of up to six months or even deported. If you're deported, you're usually barred from entering Australia for one to three years, while those deported for criminal or security reasons are permanently excluded. If a visa is granted subject to certain conditions, e.g. restrictions on work or study, you must abide by those conditions or your visa can be cancelled. If you wish to change your visa status, e.g. from a visitor to a student, you must seek advice from a local DIAC office in Australia, as your visa may have a 'no further stay' condition.

VISITORS

If you're planning a holiday visit or a business trip to Australia, you must apply for a visa (only holders of New Zealand passports are exempt). Depending on which passport you hold, you'll be eligible for either an Electronic

Travel Authority (ETA), an eVisitor or a tourist visa, each of which is described below.

If you're already in Australia and hold a valid ETA (visitor, subclass 976), an eVisitor, an e676 tourist visa or a paper lodged tourist visa (Subclass 676) granted for a stay of three months or less, you can apply to extend your stay in Australia up to a maximum of six months.

Visitors aren't permitted to engage in any type of employment or formal study and your passport must be valid for the period of your proposed stay in Australia.

For further details, see the DIAC website (💻 www.immi.gov.au/e_visa/visitors.htm).

Electronic Travel Authority (ETA)

The Electronic Travel Authority (ETA) allows people to visit Australia for short term tourism or business purposes of up to three months. It's designed to fast-track passengers at airports through immigration and customs processing, and has substantially reduced the time taken to process passengers. An ETA is valid for 12 months and allows holders to spend up to three months at a time in Australia during its 12-month validity period or a maximum of six months in a 12-month period, and can be issued immediately online.

To be eligible to apply for an ETA, you must be outside Australia and hold a citizen passport of an ETA eligible country, which include: Andorra, Austria, Belgium, Brunei*, Canada*, Denmark, Finland, France, Germany, Greece, Hong Kong (SAR)*, Iceland, Ireland, Italy, Japan*, Liechtenstein, Luxembourg, Malaysia*, Malta, Monaco, the Netherlands, Norway, Portugal, Republic of San Marino, Singapore*, South Korea*, Spain, Sweden, Switzerland, Taiwan, the UK (British Citizen), UK (British National – Overseas), the USA* and the Vatican City. Nationals of the above listed countries can apply for an ETA through a travel agent, airline, specialist service provider or an Australian visa office outside Australia. Nationals of countries listed above marked with an asterisk can also apply for an ETA online.

An ETA (or eVisitor visa) cannot be extended, but it's possible to obtain an extension for a visitor's visa (see below) under certain circumstances, although you must apply before your visa expires and must have a good reason. **Visitors aren't permitted to engage in any type of employment or formal study.** They may, however, undertake non-formal study involving short-term courses of up to three months, which are recreational or 'personal-enrichment' in nature and aren't subsidised by any government.

IMPORTANT

European passport holders who are eligible to apply for an ETA through a travel agent, airline, specialist service provider or an Australian visa office outside Australia, should apply for an eVisitor visa (see below) if they're applying online.

The fee varies depending on the provider, but an ETA costs $20 from the website of the Department of Immigration and Citizenship (see 💻 www.eta.immi.gov.au). You should print a copy of the ETA and keep it with you, although it's unlikely that you'll be asked to produce it.

eVisitor

The eVisitor allows visitors to travel to Australia for short term business or tourism purposes for up to three months. The main difference between eVisitor applications (see 💻 www.immi.gov.au/e_visa/evisitor.htm) and the Electronic Travel Authority/ETA (see above) is that the eVisitor is free and available to passport holders from European Union countries and a number of other European countries.

To be eligible to apply for an eVisitor you must be outside Australia and hold a citizen passport of an eVisitor eligible country: Andorra, Austria, Belgium, Bulgaria, Cyprus, Czech Republic, Denmark, Estonia, Finland, France, Germany, Greece, Hungary, Iceland, Ireland, Italy, Latvia, Liechtenstein, Lithuania, Luxembourg, Malta, Monaco, the Netherlands, Norway, Poland, Portugal, Romania, Republic of San Marino, the Slovak Republic, Slovenia, Spain, Sweden, Switzerland, the UK (British Citizen) and the Vatican City.

You can stay in Australia for up to three months on each visit within a 12-month period from the date of grant, although an eVisitor isn't designed to allow repeated extended stays. If you want to spend long periods in Australia for tourism or business purposes, you may want to consider applying for a tourist visa (see below) or an alternate visa that suits your purposes.

Tourist Visas

Tourist visas (subclass 676) allow people to visit Australia for holiday, sightseeing, social or recreational reasons, to visit relatives, friends or for other short-term non-work purpose, including study for less than three months. They are available for stays of three, six or 12 months, unlike ETAs and eVisitor permits (see above), which allow a maximum stay of just three months.

A tourist visa is normally valid for three to six months but parents of an Australian citizen can obtain a visitor's visa for 12 months (see **Sponsored Family Visitor Visa** below). Those who travel to Australia for medical treatment or medical consultations are granted a visitor's visa for three to twelve months. The period of stay and number of entries granted will depend on the purpose of your visit and your personal circumstances.

If you're applying for a long-stay visitor's visa, you must be able to show that you have access to adequate funds, although the amount is lower if you'll be staying with friends or family in Australia. If applicable, ensure that your visa allows multiple entries within its period of validity, when it should be marked 'multiple travel'.

A tourist visa costs $115 and $290 for a further stay visa lodged in Australia. Applications can be made online.

Sponsored Family Visitor Visa

The sponsored family visitor visa (subclass 679) allows you to travel to Australia to take a holiday or visit your family there (but isn't for business or medical treatment). You must have an eligible relative in Australia or an eligible Australian government official willing to sponsor you, who must provide a guarantee that you'll leave Australia before the visa expires.

The visa allows you to visit Australia once (not multiple entries) and usually allows a stay of up to three or six months, but in certain circumstances a stay of 12 months may be granted. The visa costs $125. Applications cannot be made online.

Business Visitors

Business visitors require either a temporary business entry (short stay) or a temporary business entry (long stay) visa, depending on the length of their proposed stay. Business visitors from eligible countries can visit Australia for up to three months with an ETA or eVisitor (see above). In addition to a standard ETA, an ETA business long validity (subclass 956) is available (fee $110).

If you don't qualify for an ETA or eVisitor, you require a short-stay business visa (subclass 456 or 459).

A business visa (subclass 459) requires an approved Australian sponsor and permits a business visit for up to three months, including attending a conference, negotiation or an exploratory business visit, e.g. to look for business opportunities, assess business conditions, act as a consultant, attend meetings and sign contracts. The fee is $140 for a 456 visa and $145 for a 459 visa.

Australia is a member of the APEC (Asia-Pacific Economic Cooperation) Business Travel Card scheme, which is designed to cut through the red tape of business travel. The card allows accredited business people to obtain multiple, short-term business visitor entry to participating countries, which saves cardholders the time and effort involved in applying for individual

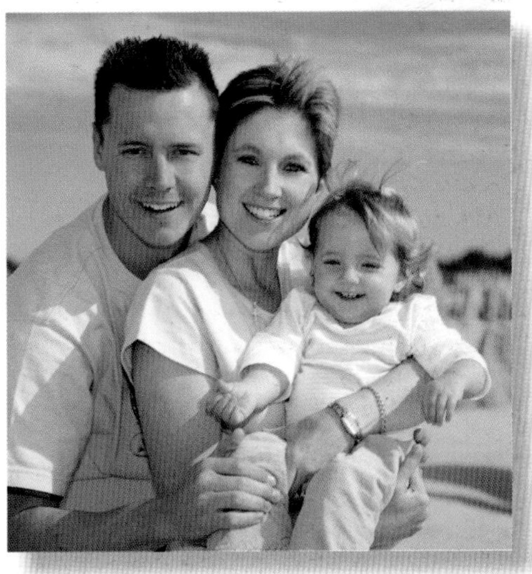

visas or entry permits. Cardholders can stay at least two or three months on each visit and cards (fee $200) are valid for multiple entry to participating countries for a period of three years. For further information and a list of participating countries, see 💻 www.immi.gov.au/skilled/business/apec.

Medical Treatment

A visitor's visa is required if you're coming to Australia for medical treatment. Two visas are available: for a short stay of up to three months (subclass 675) and for visits from three to twelve months (subclass 685). Medical treatment includes either elective or emergency treatment. You must:

- provide documentary evidence that you can pay for medical treatment;
- make arrangements for hospital accommodation and treatment in advance;
- receive significant benefit from such treatment in Australia;
- not pose a public health risk, e.g. due to a contagious disease.

If you're applying for an extension of stay for medical treatment, you must meet the above criteria and present evidence that:

- arrangements have been made with a doctor and/or hospital to provide you with medical and/or hospital care, i.e. a firm appointment for treatment must have been made;
- arrangements have been made to pay the full unsubsidised cost of treatment and you can demonstrate you have the means to pay;
- if treatment is in a public hospital, the state or territory medical authorities must have agreed to your admission and treatment.

If the purpose of your intended stay in Australia is to provide comfort and support to a person seeking medical treatment, you should also apply for a medical treatment visa.

There's no fee for a short stay medical treatment visa issued outside Australia, while a long-stay visa costs $60; however, both visas cost $245 when issued in Australia.

For more information about visas for medical treatment, see 💻 www.immi.gov.au/visitors/medical-treatment.

TEMPORARY RESIDENTS

Australia's temporary residence programme is designed to allow overseas people to come to Australia for specific purposes that benefit Australia. The programme consists of three categories:

- skilled;
- social and cultural;
- international relations.

Temporary residents are required to pay taxes on income earned in Australia, but don't have access to social welfare benefits or national public health cover. Visa holders must maintain adequate arrangements for health insurance during their stay in Australia.

Applications for certain temporary residence visas, can be made online (💻 www.immi.gov.au), while other temporary residence applications are made using form 147 *Application for a Temporary Residence Visa (non-business)*. Applicants may be required to have a medical examination and chest X-ray before a visa is granted, although this isn't usual when the intended stay is for 12 months or less. Some types of temporary residence visa require a fee and most require sponsorship.

Applicants are expected to stay for the full period of their planned stay. In most cases, temporary residents are granted a multiple entry visa for the period of their approved stay.

Temporary Workers

Certain categories of skilled workers and professionals are permitted to enter Australia for a fixed period (e.g. the duration of a contract) of up to four years to take up employment. There are no set quotas for most temporary workers, who may be engaged in a wide range of occupations and include academic staff; domestic staff; entertainers; executive, professional and technical people; foreign government officials; media and film staff; occupational trainees; religious personnel; retirees; sportsmen/women and working holidaymakers. Requirements for some of these categories of worker are detailed below. Students must also obtain a temporary residence visa (see page 66).

Applications for employer sponsored temporary residence visas (see 💻 www.immi.gov.au/skilled/skilled-workers/sbs) are granted provided the eligibility requirements for the sponsor and employee are satisfied, which include:

- the prospective employer provides sponsorship (see below);
- the position is full time;
- the position offers equivalent terms and conditions of employment (this requirement is designed to prevent skilled overseas workers being exploited and also to ensure that skilled overseas workers aren't used to 'undercut' local conditions of employment and salaries);
- the Temporary Skilled Migration Income Threshold is met, which ensures that temporary residents have sufficient pay to support themselves in Australia;
- the employment of a temporary resident isn't a substitute for training Australian or permanent residents for such a position;
- the position isn't for an unskilled or semiskilled job (a list of eligible occupations is provided on the DIAC website).

If you receive a temporary residence visa permitting you to work in Australia and your spouse is named on the application as your dependant, he or she's also permitted to work in Australia.

A temporary residence visa isn't automatically renewable and no change of job or sponsor is allowed after entry into Australia unless a further nomination application by a new sponsor is accepted by the DIAC. Applications can be made online at 💻 www.immi.gov.au.

Sponsorship

Many temporary residents must be sponsored or require a nomination, written invitation or a sponsor's undertaking to support an application, e.g. by a prospective employer or organisation (as shown in the table below). If sponsorship is required, a fee is payable.

Temporary workers seeking to work in Australia for a period of between one day and four years must be sponsored by their prospective employer. All stages of an employer sponsored 457 visa can now be lodged on-line. The sponsor must lodge a *Sponsorship for Entry to Australia for Temporary Residents* form and must have a satisfactory record of training staff and employing local labour. A sponsor must provide equivalent terms and conditions of employment, pay travel costs to enable sponsored employees to leave Australia, and employees must be employed in the nominated occupation and at the applicable salary rate.

There are three steps before a visa can be considered:

- The employer must be approved as an eligible sponsor.
- The position must be in an eligible nominated occupation.
- The nominated person must be eligible.

Business People

The Temporary Business Entry (Long Stay) visa caters for business visits to Australia of between one day and four years and is used by employers to sponsor overseas workers to work in Australia on a temporary basis to fill nominated skilled positions. Employers can be Australian or overseas businesses.

Cultural & Social Activities

The cultural and social activities visa class applies to entertainers, media and film staff, religious workers, sports people and others, as outlined below.

Entertainers

People involved in a wide range of social and cultural events and activities may be eligible for a visa, depending on the availability of Australians to fill the positions. You may not change your employer or change the times or places of engagements in Australia without permission.

Media & Film Staff

This visa applies to correspondents and other professional media staff members posted to Australia by overseas news organisations, and photographers and film and TV crews making documentaries or commercials for overseas consumption. You cannot change your employer without permission.

Religious Workers

For religious workers, including ministers, priests and spiritual leaders, visiting to serve the spiritual needs of people of their faith in Australia.

Sports People

Amateur or professional sports people coming to Australia to engage in competition with Australian residents and to improve general

Temporary Visas

Number	Visa Type	Sponsorship
405	Investor Retirement	Yes
411	Exchange	No
415	Foreign Government Agency	Yes (1)
416	Special Program	No
417	Working Holiday	No
418	Educational/Research	Yes (1)
419	Visiting Academic	No
420/421	Cultural & Social Activities	Yes (1)
422	Medical Practitioner	Yes
423	Media and Film Staff	Yes (1)
426	Domestic Worker (Diplomatic/Consular)	No
427	Domestic Worker (Overseas Executive)	Yes (3)
428	Religious Worker	Yes
442	Occupational Trainee	No
456	Business Entry (Short Stay)	No
457	Business Entry (Long Stay)	Yes

NOTE: There is a fee for the above visas

sporting standards through high calibre competition and training. Sponsorship or letters of invitation are necessary, depending on the activity and length of stay in Australia. Holders must sign a declaration that on arrival in Australia they will have a return or onward ticket and sufficient funds to support themselves (and any family members accompanying them) for the duration of their stay. You cannot change your employer without permission.

Others

People coming to Australia under approved programmes to broaden their work experience and skills (generally youth exchanges or a 'gap' year between secondary and higher education) may be eligible for a visa. This includes young people coming to Australia under a Churchill Fellowship to broaden their experience and understanding of the country, generally in the context of a youth exchange programme, or to take part in a community-based programme of cultural enrichment or community benefit. You may not change your employer or occupation without permission and are permitted to stay in Australia for a maximum of 12 months.

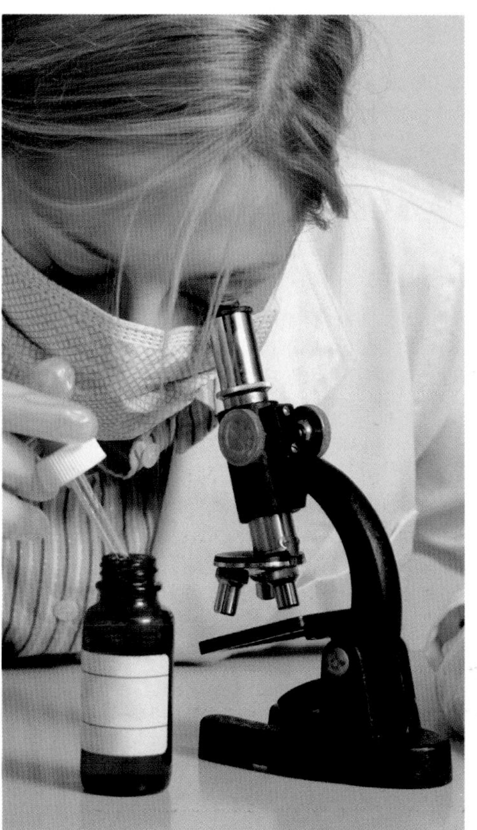

Domestic Workers

A domestic worker's visa class applies to domestic staff for diplomats and consular staff posted to Australia, for whom written approval is required from the Department of Foreign Affairs and Trade (DFAT), and domestic staff of certain holders of a Temporary Business Entry (Long Stay) visa. A visa may be granted only if it can be shown that the entry of domestic staff is necessary for the proper discharge of the executive's representational duties.

Domestic workers may not change employers or remain in Australia after the permanent departure of their employer.

Foreign Government Officials

Foreign government officials who are to conduct official business on behalf of their government for up to three months, when the officials don't have diplomatic or official status in Australia.

Occupational Trainees

People undergoing training in Australia compatible with their employment history. The training should be to upgrade existing skills and be readily usable on return to the applicant's home country. Holders may not work in Australia other than in connection with their course of training.

Visiting Academics

People whose presence in Australia will contribute to the sharing of research knowledge. You may not receive a salary from the host institution in Australia.

Retirees

The investor retirement visa (subclass 405) is designed for self-funded retirees with no dependants who want to reside in Australia during their retirement years. The visa is temporary and doesn't lead to Australian permanent residence or citizenship. You can apply for an investor retirement visa if you meet the following conditions:

- You're aged 55 or older;
- are sponsored by an Australian state or territory government agency (other than the ACT);
- have no dependants other than a spouse;
- if you're married or in a *de facto* relationship, your partner must have no dependants;
- have minimum assets legally owned and lawfully acquired by you (or you and your spouse), available for transfer to Australia and be invested in the state or territory in which you've been sponsored; the amount depends on where you intend to live in Australia and is generally between $500,000 and $750,000;
- have a minimum annual income (e.g. a pension) that can be accessed by you or you and your spouse; the amount depends on where you intend to live in Australia and is generally between $50,000 and $65,000 per year;
- have evidence that you and your spouse (if applicable) have adequate health insurance for the period of your intended stay in Australia;
- have no intention of working full time in Australia (you and your spouse are permitted to work only up to 20 hours per week while in Australia);
- meet the health requirements and be of good character.

The visa is initially issued for four years and before your visa expires you can apply for another four-year visa. The investor retirement visa is only temporary and doesn't lead to permanent residence or citizenship, and confers no right to Medicare or social security benefits.

The DIAC website (🖳 www.immi.gov.au) has a full list of the areas of Australia currently deemed to be regional/low population growth areas, which attract lower financial requirements for this visa.

An investment retirement visa application costs a reasonable $280, although there's a second visa application fee of $11,295 per person!

Australian Values Statement

Since 15th October 2007, applicants aged 18 years and over are required to sign a values statement, when applying for certain visas. The statement requires applicants to confirm that they will respect the Australian way of life and obey the laws of Australia.

Students

Although in effect a form of temporary residence visa, student visas are covered by their own eligibility rules. Foreign students require a student visa (costing $535), which is issued after acceptance on a course and payment of at least half the first year's annual fees. There are seven types of student visa:

- **Independent ELICOS:** For overseas students studying English for Overseas Students.
- **Schools:** For students at primary or secondary school.
- **Vocation Education and Training:** For certificate and diploma students.
- **Higher Education:** For students studying for a bachelor degree or a graduate certificate or diploma.
- **Post Graduate Research:** Masters research degree or a doctorate.
- **Non-award Foundation Studies/Other:** For students on courses that don't lead to a degree or other formal award.
- **AusAID or defence Sponsored**.

To be eligible for a student visa, you must be accepted for full-time study on a registered course. Courses that qualify for a student visa include tertiary level studies at universities or colleges; courses at Technical and Further Education (TAFE) colleges; English-language courses; occupational or religious training; business study or training, e.g. secretarial and business courses; short courses at universities or colleges of advanced education; and study exchange arrangements between Australian and overseas educational establishments.

Students must have the financial resources to meet tuition fees (scholarships are available), return fares to Australia and day-to-day living expenses for the first year of their course – estimated to be from $20,000 to $25,000 or more per year for a single person, depending on what and where you're studying. Students should also have Overseas Student Health Cover (OSCH) or alternative private health insurance. Your assessment level is determined by your nationality and course of study.

You and members of your family unit must not work unless you have been granted permission to do so after commencing study in Australia. See the DIAC website for information about the number of hours you and family members can work when (or if) permission is granted.

In order to retain a student visa, there are certain conditions that must be met, which include having a satisfactory course attendance and academic results' record.

Information about student visas is provided at 💻 www.immi.gov.au/students/students/chooser.

Working Holidaymakers

The working holiday visa is the largest visa category for temporary residents and accounts for around 45 per cent of the total. Concerns have been voiced in Australia over jobs being taken from Australians by working holidaymakers; however, the farming industry, particularly fruit and vegetable picking, relies to a large extent on working holidaymakers to harvest crops, and many working holidaymakers also work in the hospitality sector. Statistics show that those on working holiday visas inject some $2bn a year into the economy and many businesses in the tourist industry would be hard hit without them. There's no cap on the number of working holiday visas issued.

Note that in recent years there have been reports of working holidaymakers finding it increasingly difficult to find work, particularly on the east coast, therefore make sure that you have sufficient 'emergency' funds.

Eligibility

Working holiday visas are available to single people and childless couples between the ages of 18 and 30, their purpose being to allow young people the opportunity to visit

Australia and supplement their travels through casual employment. There are two classes of working holiday visa: subclass 417, which applies to nationals of Belgium, Canada, Cyprus, Denmark, Estonia, Finland, France, Germany, Hong Kong (SAR), Ireland, Italy, Japan, Korea, Malta, the Netherlands, Norway, Sweden, Taiwan and the UK; and subclass 462 (the work and holiday visa), which applies to nationals from Argentina, Bangladesh, Chile, Indonesia, Iran, Malaysia, Thailand, Turkey and the US.

Applicants must satisfy the following criteria:

- The prime purpose of your visit must be a temporary stay in Australia and you must have no intention of becoming a permanent resident.
- Employment must be incidental to your holiday and to supplement the money that you bring with you.
- Employment mustn't have been arranged in advance except on a private basis and on your own initiative.
- You must have a reasonable prospect of obtaining temporary employment.

- You must have reasonable funds to support yourself for some of your time in Australia and pay for your return air fare. The minimum amount required for British travellers is around £2,000, although it isn't necessary to have a return ticket at the time of your entry into Australia. It helps to have relatives or friends in Australia who can provide extra funds, if necessary.
- You must meet 'normal' character requirements and health standards.
- You mustn't work full time for more than six months with one employer (you may train or study for up to four months).
- You mustn't remain in Australia for longer than 12 months and must leave Australia when your working holiday visa has expired (although you can apply for a second working holiday visa – see below).

Applications can be made in person, by post or online (preferred), and can be made inside or outside Australia. You should apply for a working holiday visa at least four weeks before your intended departure date, and, if you're applying by post, should send documents by recorded delivery. The application fee for a working holiday visa is $280.

If your application is approved, your visa is valid for 12 months from the date of your first entry into Australia, during which period there's no limit on the number of times you can leave and re-enter Australia.

You can apply for a second working holiday visa (subclass 417 – fee $280) when you've completed three months' seasonal work in Australia on your first working holiday visa. If you successfully apply for a second working holiday visa while in Australia, you're allowed to remain for 24 months from the date you entered the country on your first working holiday visa.

MIGRANT VISAS

Applying for a visa as a migrant (i.e. for permanent residence) is confusing, difficult, expensive and time consuming – factors which have spawned a wealth of migration consultants and keep thousands of civil servants in employment.

> **▲ Caution**
>
> The Australian government is constantly changing the rules and sometimes introduces retrospective changes which apply to applications already lodged but not processed. However, even when new requirements have been announced, they may not be introduced for many months or even years, and could even be rejected by the upper house (Senate) of the Australian parliament after being passed by the lower house. Before making an application, check the latest regulations and criteria for visa applications.

To be accepted for migration to Australia you must meet the personal and occupational requirements of the category for which you're applying and be of good health and character. The Australian migration programme (often spelled program) is divided into two main categories: migration and humanitarian migration (see below). Migration is split into the following 'streams':

- **Family migration** – where migrants can be 'sponsored' by a relative who's an Australian citizen, a permanent resident or an eligible New Zealand citizen.
- **Skilled migration** – for people with particular business or work skills or 'outstanding talents', with a separate quota for states or territories with particular skill shortages.
- **Special eligibility migration** – covering former citizens or residents wishing to return to Australia, and also certain New Zealanders (not covered in detail in this book).

The Department of Immigration and Citizenship provides an enquiry service (☎ 131881, 🖳 www.immi.gov.au) for further information. The form 1126i (*Migrating to Australia*) contains general information about migration and the various categories. There are different forms for the different visa classes (there's also the facility to lodge an application online for some

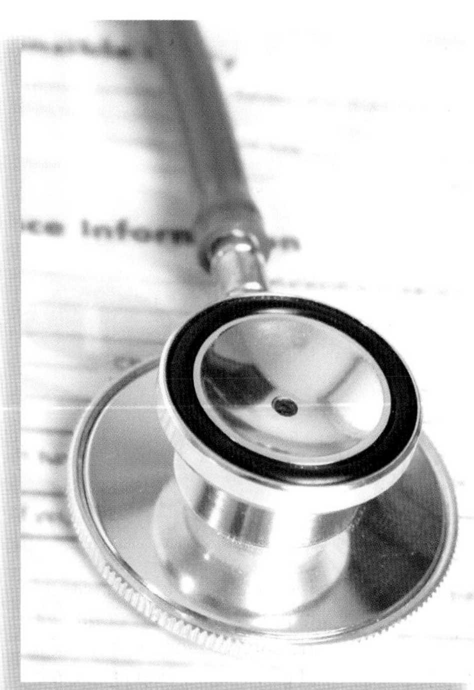

visa classes). There's a fee for the printed forms and the information package or you can download them free from the DIAC website (see above). You may telephone the DIAC and enquire about the progress of your application (although this can delay the processing), but detailed enquiries must be made by email, quoting your DIAC file number.

Never make any firm plans or arrangements (such as booking flights, selling your home or resigning your job) in the expectation that your visa application will be granted. Even when an application appears to be going smoothly, it can be delayed due to processing priorities or even be rejected at the last minute, e.g. on health grounds.

Application fees for migrant visas are high (see **Fees** on page 77) and aren't refundable, therefore you should ensure that you have a very good chance of being accepted before making an application.

Waiting Period

The processing time for migration applications varies depending on the country where you're applying, the number of applicants and your migrant category; for example, skilled migrants are given priority. In certain circumstances, e.g. for compassionate reasons, an application can be expedited, although no guarantees are provided. It can take a long time to receive a migrant visa – you should be prepared for a lot of questions and demands for additional paperwork from immigration officials – and a two-year waiting period has been introduced in recent years before most migrants can claim social security benefits, which has caused some unemployed migrants to become destitute.

However, if you're really keen to go and you meet the criteria for the category of visa for which you're applying (see below), you'll usually receive your visa in the end. On the other hand, if your application is queued or affected by processing priorities, could be delayed indefinitely.

Quotas

The Australian migration year runs from 1st July to 30th June (the same as the Australian financial year) and each year the federal government announces the quotas for the coming year, although these aren't set in stone. All applications for categories where a quota (or capping) applies are processed on a 'first come, first served' basis. When a cap is reached for the current immigration year, the granting of visas is suspended, although processing continues and applicants are granted visas when the new immigration year commences (and a new quota is allocated). The quotas for 2012-13 are shown in the table below:

Migrant Visa Quotas 2012-13

Stream	Quota
Family	60,185
Skilled	129,250
Special Eligibility	565
Total	190,000

Migration planning figures can never be exact, as some categories (particularly within the skilled stream) are demand-driven and there's no upper limit placed on the number of migrants who can qualify – if you meet the criteria you're accepted. On the other hand, quotas may be reassessed and reduced or increased when the demand for workers falls or increases.

Health & Character Checks

Applicants for migration visas must pass health and character checks before they're granted a visa. Medical and police certificates are valid for 12 months, therefore you're required to make your initial entry into Australia within 12 months of your medical or police clearance date, whichever occurs first.

Medical Examination

All applicants (and their family members) for permanent or long-term temporary residence (over 12 months), plus short-term temporary applicants if their health is of 'special significance', are required to undergo a medical examination. This includes an X-ray for those aged 11 or older, an HIV/AIDS test for those aged 15 or over, and TB screening for those aged 11 or over (and for those under 11 if it's suspected that they have or have had TB). Hepatitis B screening is compulsory if the applicant is pregnant, a child for adoption or an unaccompanied refugee minor. Pregnancy must be declared by prospective migrants. A long-term or serious illness or condition suffered by you or a dependent could void your application, e.g. if you have a child who requires special schooling.

Results of the examination are sent to the Department of Health in Australia and can take around six weeks to be assessed. Your case officer will provide you with instructions. Medical examinations carried out in the UK are forwarded to the health department online by an authorised panel doctor.

Police Check

One of the requirements for immigrants is that they are 'of good character'. You may be required to provide a police check for each country you've resided in for 12 months or more in the last ten years or since the age of 16.

The procedure for obtaining a police certificate varies from country to country. In the

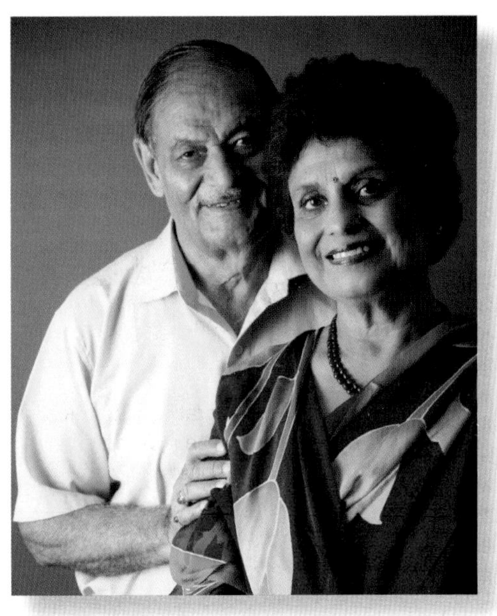

UK, forms and instructions for an ACPO Police Certificate are available from 💻 www.acro.police.uk/police_certificates.aspx. In Australia, a national police check (fee $42) can be obtained from the Australian Federal Police (☎ 02-6140 6502, 💻 www.afp.gov.au).

If you have a criminal record it could jeopardise your application, as stringent efforts have been made in recent years to prevent the entry of convicted criminals and other 'undesirables'. For information, see 💻 www.immi.gov.au/allforms/character-requirements.

Application Procedure

All application forms must be completed in English and you must provide originals or certified copies of all documents requested (see below).

Documentation & Interviews

You must usually provide copies of documents such as birth and marriage certificates, educational and trade qualifications, and employer references. Copies must be certified by a legal professional, a Justice of the Peace or other person authorised to witness statutory declarations (e.g. a Commissioner for Declarations in Australia), who must state that the copy is true to the original. Original documents mustn't be sent unless specifically requested.

Additional information concerning your application can be provided at any time (and is taken into account) before a decision is made, and you must keep the DIAC informed of any changes to the information provided. If you provide incorrect information or documents, your application or visa can be cancelled.

It's rare for applicants (particularly Britons) to be required to attend an interview with the Department of Immigration and Citizenship about a migration application.

Validity

If you're accepted for immigration you may not be required to have a visa label placed in your passport (e.g. UK nationals) to confirm your immigration. Note, however, that this depends on your country of nationality – see your approval letter from the DIAC for further guidance.

You must usually arrive in Australia within nine or ten months of the date stamped in your passport, known as the 'initial entry date' (explained in your grant letter from the DIAC). If you don't enter Australia by this date, the visa becomes invalid and you'll need to re-apply for migration. When you enter Australia before the initial entry date, you have used (or validated) your migrant visa, and by so doing will have become a permanent resident (if applicable).

Note that permanent foreign residents of Australia don't enjoy the same rights as Australian citizens with regard to their freedom to leave and enter Australia.

Leaving & Returning to Australia

If you migrated to Australia before 1987, you'll have been issued with either an Authority to Return (ATR) or a Return Endorsement (RE), which are valid provided you haven't been out of Australia for longer than three years and you haven't become a citizen. However, if you migrated to Australia in 1987 or later, your initial visa gives you permission to leave and return to Australia freely during only the three to five years after your first entry. After this time, if you choose not to apply for Australian citizenship, you must obtain a 'resident return visa' (RRV) before leaving the country, which allows a permanent resident to leave and return to Australia within a period of either three months or five years. Whether the visa is granted depends on how long you've spent in Australia during the previous five years.

An RRV cannot be extended and you must apply for a new one if required; the amount of time you've spent outside Australia in the five years immediately before your application determines whether you're eligible for a new RRV, and, if so, what type. For example, if you've lived in Australia for at least two years within the last five, you're probably eligible for an RRV which gives you the right to remain outside Australia for up to five years. If you aren't eligible for a five-year RRV, you may be eligible for a three-month RRV. If you choose to return to Australia just before your RRV expires, you're obliged to remain there for at least 12 months before you're eligible for another RRV. If you need to leave because of an emergency during this period, you're allowed to do so only once.

Sponsorship

Applicants in the family category need to be sponsored by a relative, who must be aged at least 18 and an Australian resident. Some family-sponsored classes require that the sponsor is 'settled', which is generally accepted to be the case after two years' continual residence. In spouse and parent classes, a minor child can act as a sponsor under certain circumstances. Your sponsor must undertake to assist you financially and with accommodation during your first two years in Australia, plus, if necessary, attendance at English-language classes.

Family migrants aren't usually eligible to receive unemployment benefit or other welfare benefits for a period of two years or longer, therefore sponsors must be prepared to accept the consequent costs.

FAMILY MIGRATION

There are the following classes of family migrant:

- **Partner** (subclass 309 Provisional, subclass 100 Permanent): This visa allows you to

enter Australia on the basis of your married or de facto relationship with your partner, who must provide sponsorship for you.

- **Dependent Child** (subclass 101): A natural or adopted child (usually aged under 18) of the sponsor who's dependent on the sponsor. A child who's married or engaged to be married isn't eligible.
- **Adoption** (subclass 102): A child aged under 18 coming to Australia for adoption, where the adoption is supported by the appropriate state or territory welfare authorities in Australia, or a child under 18 who was adopted by Australian citizens or permanent residents while they were resident overseas.
- **Parent** (subclass 103): A parent of the sponsor. Parents must meet the 'balance of family' criteria outlined on the DIAC website (www.immi.gov.au). There's a surfeit of applicants in this visa class and a low annual quota, and most parents must wait years before they obtain a visa.
- **Contributory Parent** (subclass 143 – Migrant): A parent of the sponsor who's willing to provide a ten-year assurance of support (see below) and a $10,000 bond for the primary applicant and $4,000 for each other adult applicant. Balance of family requirements are similar to the parent subclass (see above). More visas are available for this subclass (143) than for subclass 103, but the second instalment fee is $42,220 (forty two thousand two hundred and twenty!), compared with $1,795 for subclass 103. There are other parent visas – see the DIAC website (www.immi.gov.au) for information.
- **Orphan Relative** (subclass 117): An orphan under 18 who's unmarried and a relative of the sponsor.
- **Carer** (subclass 116): A relative capable of providing substantial and continuing help to an Australian citizen, permanent resident or eligible New Zealand citizen living in Australia, who's in need of such help in cases where this cannot be provided by a relative in Australia or by local community, hospital, nursing or welfare services.
- **Aged dependent Relative** (subclass 114): A single, widowed or divorced relative who's old enough to be granted an old age pension under the Social Security Act, 1991 and has been financially dependent on the sponsor for a 'reasonable' period. The sponsor is expected to have lived in Australia for at least two years before lodging the application.
- **Remaining Relative** (subclass 115): Those with a brother, sister, parent (or step equivalent) who's an Australian citizen, permanent resident or eligible New Zealand citizen usually resident in Australia. You and your spouse must have no brothers, sisters, children, parents (or step equivalent) other than those in Australia.
- **Prospective Marriage** (subclass 300 – Temporary): A prospective spouse planning to marry a sponsor receives a temporary visa to stay in Australia for up to nine months. You must marry your sponsor and apply to remain permanently within this period, after which you're granted a two-year provisional (temporary) visa if all the requirements are met. If you're still married at the end of the two-year period, you're granted a permanent visa.

Assurance of Support

In certain family migration visa subclasses (see below), an assurance of support (AOS) is mandatory and must be given before a visa is granted. The person giving the AOS is known as the 'assurer' and the migrant the 'assuree'.

An AOS is a legal commitment by the assurer to repay the Australian government if certain welfare benefits are paid to the assuree, which, depending on the type of visa the migrant is granted, can be for a period of two or ten years. Where applicable, a refundable bond is payable (a bond isn't required for orphan relatives).

The bond is $5,000 for the main applicant or $7,000 for a couple for a two-year AOS, and $10,000 for the main applicant or $14,000 for a couple for a ten-year AOS; the bond is refundable after two or ten years (as applicable), along with the accrued interest. The AOS system is administered by the Department of Human Services (www.humanservices.gov.au). An AOS is mandatory for the following categories of family migration:

- Aged Dependent Relative
- Aged Parent
- Carer
- Contributory Aged Parent
- Contributory Parent
- Parent
- Remaining Relative

Other visa subclasses may require an AOS if an applicant is assessed as liable to become a drain on Australia's welfare system. Skilled visas with family sponsorship lodged after 1st September 2007 no longer require an AOS.

For more information about assurances of support, see Fact Sheet 34, *Assurance of Support*, or the DIAC website (www.immi.gov.au/media/fact-sheets/34aos.htm).

SKILLED MIGRATION

The skilled migration category applies to people who are highly skilled, under 50 years of age (when invited to apply), have a high level of English and can quickly make a contribution to the Australian economy. There are two categories of General Skilled visas: permanent and provisional. If you're unable to meet the requirements for a permanent visa, a provisional or temporary visa can provide a route to permanent status (see **Temporary Workers** on page 62).

On 1st July 2012, a new online application system called SkillSelect (see www.immi.gov.au/skills/skillselect) was introduced, which changed the way people apply for migration to Australia. Now instead of applying for a skilled migration visa, applicants record their details – known as an 'Expression of Interest' (EOI) – via an online system. Prospective migrants can then be found and nominated for skilled visas by Australian employers or state and territory governments, or they could be invited by the Australian government to lodge a visa application.

DIAC continue to process applications that are employer sponsored as a priority followed by state sponsored and those on the skilled occupations list (SOL).

The DIAC announced a number of changes in recent years to ensure that the skilled migration programme responds to changes in the Australian labour market. A new Skilled Occupations List (SOL) came into effect on 1st July 2012, which includes managerial, professional, technical and trade occupations, called the Consolidated Sponsored Occupation List (CSOL), consisting of Schedule 1 (skilled occupations list) and Schedule 2 (consolidated sponsored occupations list). For a General Skilled Migration Visa, if you aren't nominated by a state or territory government, you must nominate an occupation from Schedule 1 of the SOL. If you're nominated by a State or Territory Government – each state has their own eligibility requirements – you must nominate an occupation from either Schedule 1 or Schedule 2.

Detailed information about the recent changes in the general skilled migration programme is available from www.immi.gov.au/skilled/general-skilled-migration/whats-new.htm.

Basic Visa Requirements

The basic requirements for a skilled migration visa are listed below; if you're unable to satisfy these it isn't worthwhile applying for a skilled migration visa.

- **Invitation to apply:** You can only apply if you have been invited to do so.

- **Age:** You must be under 50 years of age when invited to apply.
- **English ability**: The threshold English Language is Competent English, which is a minimum score of 6 in each of the four components of the International English Language Testing System (IELTS). You may also meet the threshold English language requirement if you hold a valid passport of the UK, USA, Canada, Republic of Ireland or New Zealand.
- **Nominated occupation:** When you register your EOI you must nominate a skilled occupation on the Skilled Occupation Lists (see above) which best fits your skills and experience.
- **Qualify under the points test:** See below.

Before submitting an EOI, you must have had your skills assessed as suitable for your nominated occupation by the required assessing authority and taken an English Language test (see **Points Test** below).

Skilled Migration Visa Classes

There are a number of visas and 'schemes' related to the skilled migration programme, each with their own guidelines, which include those listed below and the Business Skills programme and Employer Nomination Scheme (see below).

- **Skilled Independent (subclass** 189): Those who meet the basic requirements and pass the points test (see below) for this visa subclass don't need to be sponsored by family or a state or territorial government.
- **Skilled Sponsored** (subclass 190): You must satisfy the application requirements, be able to pass the points test and have been nominated by a state or territory agency.
- **Skilled Regional Nominated or Sponsored** (subclass 489 – provisional): You must satisfy the application requirements, be able to pass the points test and be sponsored by an eligible relative living in a designated area or nominated by a participating state or territory government, and must live, work or study in regional Australia or the designated area. This visa is valid for four years.

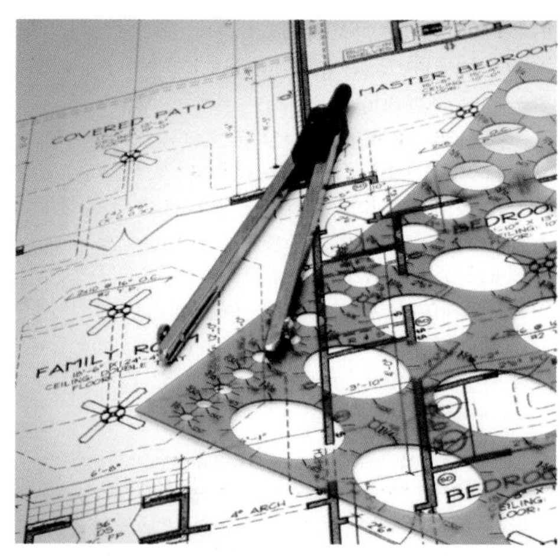

- **Skilled Recognised Graduate Visa** (subclass 476 – temporary): for graduates of a recognised university. You must be aged under 31 when you make your application and have completed an eligible Engineering qualification at a listed university. This visa isn't points tested and is valid for 18 months; you can apply for a permanent skilled visa during this period.

For further details about skilled migration, refer to Booklet 6, *General Skilled Migration* (see 💻 www.immi.gov.au/allforms/booklets/books6.htm) and booklet 11, *Skill Select* (see www.immi.gov.au/allforms/booklets/1406.pdf), and the latest updates in this ever-changing field on the DIAC website (💻 www.immi.gov.au/skilled/general-skilled-migration/whats-new.htm).

Points Test

A points test applies to certain categories of skilled migrants. The test aims to ensure that the principal applicant has the skills and other attributes necessary to allow him to quickly enter the Australian workforce and support himself and his family without relying on the Australian government. Only one spouse is assessed and either partner can be considered a principal applicant for the points test, therefore couples should choose the partner with the best prospects of scoring sufficient points.

Depending on the visa class applied under, points may be earned for skill; age; ability in English and a designated language; educational qualifications; related work experience; Australian qualifications and partner skills; whether you've studied and lived in certain parts of Australia; and whether you have state/territory government or designated area sponsorship.

The pass mark for the new SkillSelect visa subclasses 189, 190 and 489 is currently 60 points and is subject to change. Intending migrants first need to submit an expression of interest (EOI – see above) and be invited to make an application for these visas.

IMPORTANT

The points test is constantly under review and is subject to change. The ability to meet the points test pass mark doesn't guarantee an invitation to apply, as SkillSelect ranks a prospective migrant's score against other EOIs. The highest ranking migrants across a broad range of occupations may be invited to apply for a skilled visa.

Reports are published on the DIAC website regarding the number of applications that have been selected in each round and the points score attained (by state and occupation).

For further information see Booklet 6, *General Skilled Migration*, and www.immi.gov.au/skilled/general-skilled-migration/pdf/points-tested-migration-fact-sheet.pdf, which explains the points test and how points are allocated.

Employer Nomination Scheme

There are two permanent employer sponsored visa categories: The Employer Nomination Scheme (subclass 186) and the Regional Sponsored Migration Scheme (subclass 187), each of which is comprised of three streams:

- **Direct entry:** Applicant is outside of Australia and hasn't previously held a 457 temporary employer sponsored visa.
- **Temporary Residence Transition:** Applies to 457 visa holders who have worked for an Australian employer for at least the last two years in the nominated occupation, and the employer wishes to offer them a permanent position in the same occupation.
- **Agreement:** An applicant sponsored by an employer via a tailored and negotiated labour agreement or regional migration agreement.

Applications must now be lodged online. Booklet 5 (*Employer Sponsored Migration*) – see www.immi.gov.au/allforms/booklets/1131.pdf – provides details on the eligibility requirements for employers, employees and family members. These include the nature of the position and terms and conditions of employment, including salary, length of contract, nominated occupation, age requirements, English language ability, work experience, qualifications, skill assessment and licensing requirements, as applicable.

BUSINESS MIGRATION

Australia's Business Innovation and Investment programme encourages successful business people to settle in Australia and use their proven skills to develop business activity in Australia. The programme is designed to increase entrepreneurial talent and diversify business expertise in Australia. It targets migrants that have a demonstrated history of success in innovation and business and are able to make a significant contribution to the national innovation system and to the Australian economy. There are a number of visas available, including Business Innovation, Investment and Business Talent. An Expression of Interest (EOI – see **Skilled Migration** above) must be lodged for all visas after which you'll be considered for a visa application.

Business Innovation & Investment Visa

The Business Innovation and Investment visa (Subclass 188) has two streams: Business Innovation and Investor.

The Business Innovation stream is for those who have run their own business and wish to start a business venture in Australia. The basic criteria are that their current business must meet certain turnover requirements and the applicants must prove that they meet the required figure for total value of assets that will be available for transfer to Australia. There's also a points score of 65 that must be met, with points awarded for age, English language ability, qualifications, experience in business or investments, net personal and business assets, business turnover and innovation.

The Investor stream is for those who can demonstrate success in investments or running a qualifying business. If you apply for the Investor stream, you (or your partner, or you and your partner combined) must meet the following criteria:

- have a net value of at least $2.25m for the two fiscal years immediately before you're invited to apply;
- have an overall successful record of eligible investment or qualifying business activity with no involvement in unacceptable activities;
- have a high level of management skill in relation to eligible investments and/or qualifying business activity;
- have at least three years' experience of direct involvement in managing one or more qualifying businesses or eligible investments;
- make your government-approved designated investment of $1.5m before a visa can be granted;
- have a genuine and realistic commitment to continuing your business and investment activity in Australia after the original investment has matured.

In addition, you (or your partner, or you and your partner combined) must also have had one of the following:

- direct involvement, for at least one of the five fiscal years you're invited to apply, in managing your eligible investments that total at least $1.5m, or
- direct involvement, for at least one of the five fiscal years before you're invited to apply, in managing a qualifying business in which you owned at least 10 per cent of the total value of the business.

Both the above streams result in a provisional visa being issued and, provided the applicants meet the criteria for the visa, there's a defined route to apply for permanent residence.

Business Talent Visa

The Business Talent visa (subclass 132) has two streams – Significant Business History and Venture Capital Entrepreneur – both of which are permanent resident visas. It's targeted at

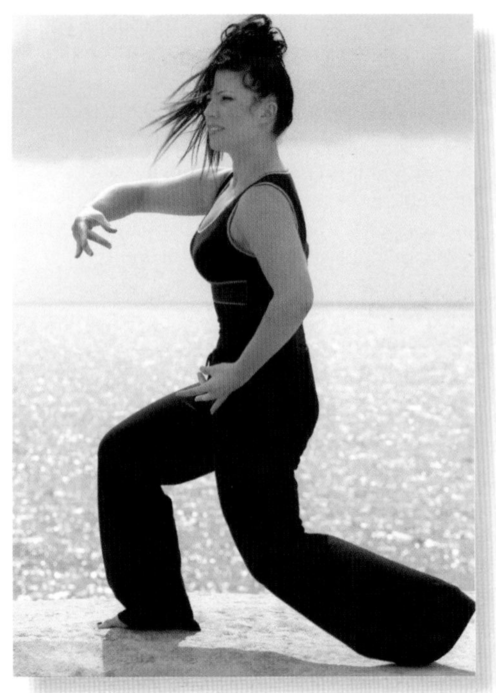

high calibre business people who are owners or part owners of an overseas business and have a genuine and realistic commitment to participate in the management of a new or existing business in Australia.

If you apply for the **Significant Business History** stream, you (or your partner, or you and your partner combined) must have the following:

- net assets of at least $400,000 (in a qualifying business) in at least two of the four fiscal years immediately before you're invited to apply;
- total assets of at least $1.5m that can be legally transferred to Australia within two years of the visa being granted;
- a total annual turnover of at least $3m (in one or more of your main businesses) in at least two of the four fiscal years immediately prior to being invited to apply;
- ownership of at least:
  - 51 per cent of a business with a turnover of less than $400,000 per annum, or
  - 30 per cent of a business with a turnover of more than $400,000 per annum, or
  - 10 per cent of a publicly-listed company

- an overall successful business career with no involvement in unacceptable business activities;

- a genuine desire to own and maintain a management role in a business in Australia.

Applicants for the **Venture Capital Entrepreneur** stream must have obtained at least $1m in funding from an Australian Venture capital firm for the start-up, product commercialisation or business development relating to a promising high value business idea.

For more information, see 💻 www.immi.gov.au/media/fact-sheets/27business.htm and www.immi.gov.au/allforms/booklets/books7.htm.

VISA FEES

There are fees for most visas and, although some are nominal, those for migrant visas can be high (see the table below). Fees, which are supposedly intended to cover the costs incurred by the Australian government in processing your application, aren't refunded if your application is unsuccessful, even if you're adversely affected by a change of rules while your application is being processed, such as an increase in the number of points required for a visa.

You should ensure that you have a very good chance of being accepted before making an application, otherwise you waste your application fee.

The fees shown below are examples of Australia's visa and migration fees – which sometimes vary depending on whether your application is lodged within or outside Australia, as indicated – and were applicable in July 2012 (fees are revised, but not necessarily increased, annually on 1st July). This information is intended as a guide only – for country-specific charges, contact an Australian mission or see the DIAC website (□ www.immi.gov.au/allforms/990i/visa-charges.htm).

Some visas require first and second instalments. Where applicable, the first instalment must be paid when an application is lodged and the second before the visa is granted.

Payment methods for fees vary depending on the type of application and where it's made. If you're making an internet application, you can pay by credit card. If you lodge your application in Australia, you can pay by credit card, by debit card in person, or by bank or money order made payable to DIAC. If you lodge your application outside Australia, check the acceptable methods of payment with the Australian mission where you plan to make your application. Details are provided on the DIAC website, alone with a currency converter that shows the visa fees in various currencies.

Visa Fees

Type of Application	Fee Outside Australia
ETA – visitor	$20
ETA – business (long validity)	$110
Business Visa (short stay)	$140
Working Holiday Visa	$280
Student Visa	$535
Medical Treatment Visa (up to three months stay)	NIL ($245 in Australia)
Medical Treatment Visa (over three months stay)	$60 ($245 in Australia)
Investment Retirement Visa	$280
Employer Nomination	$3,060
Family Migration (most subclasses)	$2,060
Provisional Business Migration	$4,065
Skilled Migration (independent & nominated)	$3,060

10
12

4. ARRIVAL

On arrival in Australia, your first task is to negotiate immigration and customs, which fortunately presents no problems for most people – provided they have a valid visa! With the exception of New Zealanders, everyone wishing to enter Australia requires a visa (see Chapter 3). If you arrive in Australia without one, you'll be refused entry. Australian customs and immigration officials are usually polite and efficient, although they may occasionally be a 'trifle over-zealous' in their attempts to deter smugglers and those planning to stay or work illegally. There are a number of tasks that should be completed on arrival, which are described in this chapter, along with suggestions for finding local help and information.

IMMIGRATION

All arrivals must complete an Incoming Passenger Card (IPC), distributed by airlines and shipping companies (one per person), on arrival. The IPC contains your personal details such as your address in Australia, name and passport number, and is used by immigration officials to record the reason for your visit. The card is also for customs and quarantine purposes, and contains questions concerning plants and animals and whether you've exceeded the duty-free allowances (see page 303). An IPC card also states that you must list every item of food you're carrying, even if it's only a small packet of sweets it must be declared on the card and customs will inspect it. It's far simpler not to take anything edible into Australia.

Duty Free

There's no need to buy your duty-free booze before arrival, as all of Australia's major airports have duty-free shops accessible to arriving passengers.

If you (or anyone over 12 months of age who's travelling with you) have stayed overnight or longer in a yellow fever infected country or area (e.g. Africa or South America) in the six days prior to your arrival in Australia, a yellow fever vaccination certificate is required.

When you disembark, you proceed to the Entry Control Point, where you present your passport and IPC. If you have an Electronic Travel Authority (ETA), there's no need to show it unless requested. You may be asked to verify the reason for your visit and provide evidence that you have sufficient funds for your trip and a return or onward ticket. Your IPC is returned to you and must be presented when you arrive at the customs checkpoint (see below).

Australia operates an Advanced Passenger Processing (APP) system at major airports (e.g. Sydney), where passengers can be cleared in the 'express' lane in as little as 20 seconds. It also allows passengers on certain flights (Air New Zealand, Cathay Pacific, Japan Airlines and Qantas) to complete their immigration and customs processing at check-in and be issued with an Express card, which is simply passed through an immigration card reader on arrival.

When you receive your visa from an Australian mission overseas, you usually get a stamp in your passport stating that the visa is valid 'subject to an entry permit on arrival'. This means that you must satisfy the immigration official that you won't infringe the terms of your visa. If you have a visitor's visa, you may be asked about your funds (or access to funds), although it's unlikely.

Generally, the onus is on you to prove that you're a genuine visitor and won't infringe the immigration laws. The immigration authorities aren't required to establish that you'll violate the immigration laws, and in cases where they believe that you plan to work illegally or overstay your visa, they can refuse you entry or restrict your entry to a shorter period than that permitted by your visa.

The treatment of foreigners by immigration officers varies, but young people in particular may be liable to close scrutiny, especially those travelling light and 'scruffily' dressed or coming from notorious drug areas such as certain Asian or South American countries. Like any other visitor, young people should carry evidence of their funds (or access to funds) and proof of why they're entering Australia and why they will need to leave, e.g. to return to work or study overseas.

Caution

Take care how you answer seemingly innocent questions from immigration officials (immigration officials never ask innocent questions), as you could find yourself being refused entry if you give incriminating answers.

Whatever the question, never imply that you may remain in Australia longer than the period permitted or for a purpose other than that for which you've been granted permission. For example, if you aren't permitted to work in Australia, you could be asked, "Would you like to work in Australia?" If you reply, "Yes", even if you have no intention of doing so, you could be refused entry.

When all is in order and the immigration official is satisfied, he'll stamp your passport with the official entry permit stating the period that you're permitted to remain in the country.

If you decide that this isn't long enough, some visas (e.g. visitor's visas) can be extended, but it's an expensive procedure and you'll need to convince the authorities that you should be granted an extension. You may find that it's easier to leave the country, e.g. by travelling to New Zealand or Indonesia, and apply for a new visa from there. If you have an ETA, it permits you to spend up to three months at a time in Australia during its 12-month validity period or a maximum of six months in a 12-month period.

CUSTOMS

After you've cleared immigration, you proceed to the luggage claim area to collect your bags. When you have all your bags go to the customs checkpoint and hand your IPC to a customs officer. All airports in Australia use a system of red and green 'channels'. Red means you have something to declare and green means you have nothing to declare, i.e. no more than the duty- or tax-free allowances, no goods to sell, and no prohibited or restricted goods. **If you're *certain* that you have nothing to declare, go through the 'green channel'; otherwise go through the red channel.**

Customs officers make random checks on people going through both red and green channels and there are stiff penalties for smuggling. If you're caught trying to smuggle any goods into Australia, they can be confiscated and, if you attempt to import prohibited items (see below), you may be liable to criminal charges and/or deportation. The bags of arriving passengers are scanned for prohibited items, particularly food items. It isn't uncommon for visitors to forget about a piece of fruit or other foodstuffs in their baggage, which will be confiscated.

When you enter Australia to take up temporary or permanent residence, you can usually import your belongings duty and tax-free. Personal and household goods that you've owned and used overseas for over 12 months can be imported free of duty and sales tax, although proof of length of ownership may be required, and this concession doesn't apply to alcohol, motor vehicles or tobacco products. Any goods not owned and used overseas for over 12 months may be subject to duty and tax at varying rates, depending on where you've come from, where you purchased the goods,

how long you've owned them, and whether duty and tax have already been paid in another country. If you need to pay duty or tax, it must be paid at the time goods are brought into the country. Payment may be made in cash, by travellers' cheque (in Australian dollars) or by credit or charge card.

There's no limit to the amount of Australian or foreign banknotes and coins that can be brought into Australia, but amounts of $10,000 or more (or the equivalent in foreign currency) must be declared on arrival. On the other hand, in accordance with the Anti-Money Laundering and Counter-Terrorism Financing Act 2006, travellers entering or leaving Australia must disclose to a customs or police officer, if asked, whether they're carrying Bearer Negotiable Instruments (BNIs) which include promissory notes, travellers' cheques, cheques, money orders and postal orders. This disclosure is made by completing a Cross Border Movement-Bearer Negotiable Instrument (CBM-BNI) form. This is in addition to declaring the amount of cash carried.

Australian Customs publishes a variety of information for travellers, including a booklet entitled *Customs Information for Travellers*, available from Australian customs offices (see **Appendix A** for a list). General enquiries should be directed to the Australian Customs Service (☎ 1300-363263 or +612-6275 6666 from abroad, 💻 www.customs.gov.au). For information regarding duty-free allowances (e.g. alcohol and tobacco), see page 303; the importation of motor vehicles, see page 169; and the importation of pets, see page 321.

Prohibited & Restricted Goods

There are strict laws prohibiting or restricting the entry of drugs, firearms, pornography, steroids, weapons and certain articles subject to quarantine. If you're carrying any goods which you think may fall into any of the following categories, you must declare them to customs on arrival in Australia.

Drugs & Other Substances

If you're carrying any prescribed 'drugs of dependence', including medicines containing amphetamines, barbiturates, hallucinogens, narcotics, tranquillisers or vaccines, you must declare them to customs on arrival. (Most airports employ 'sniffer' dogs to check baggage for drugs.)

If you're carry prescription drugs, it's wise to have a doctor's prescription with you. If you're uncertain about any drugs or medicines that you're carrying, check with the customs officer on your arrival.

The importation of anabolic steroids, androgenic substances, natural and manufactured growth hormones, and certain other pharmaceutical substances is prohibited unless written approval has been obtained from the Therapeutic Goods Administration (💻 www.tga.gov.au).

Penalties for drug offences in Australia are severe and can result in imprisonment (see **Crime** on page 313).

Firearms

Many firearms are prohibited in Australia, while others require a permit and safety testing. You should contact Australian Customs before you travel if you intend to import any firearms.

There are strict rules about carrying firearms and dangerous goods such as fireworks and flammable liquids in aircraft. If you wish to do so, contact your airline for advice before you travel.

Plants & Animals

Australia is free from many of the world's worst animal and vegetable diseases and from pests that afflict many other regions of the world, and it has strict quarantine regulations to ensure that

it remains that way. All food or goods of plant or animal origin must be declared on your Incoming Passenger Card. This includes the following:

- gifts and souvenirs made from plants or animals, or that contain plant or animal material (such as feathers, seeds or skin);
- any bottled, dried, fresh or cooked, packaged or tinned food products, e.g. beans, confectionery, eggs and egg products, herbal medicines, herbs and spices, honey and bee products, jams, meat and meat products, milk and dairy products, nuts, sauces, and teas and beverages;
- any food from meals you were served on an aircraft or ship;
- animal products, including bee products, bones, feathers, hair, hunting trophies, rawhide, shells, skins and hides, and wool (see also **Protected species** below);
- plants and plant products, including bamboo, cane and rattan items, fresh and dried flowers, pine cones, potpourri, seeds, straw objects such as corn dollies, wood carvings and wreaths;
- live animals, which can be imported only with a valid import permit.

There are also restrictions on taking fruit and vegetables (produced in Australia) between certain states.

If you have prohibited or unwanted items that you don't wish to declare, you can drop them in the quarantine bin on the way to collect your luggage. Declared goods won't automatically be confiscated and in most cases they're simply inspected by a quarantine officer and returned to you, although some items may require treatment (e.g. fumigation). Quarantine inspections have been strengthened in recent years and on the spot fines of up to $250 can be imposed for minor offences.

For further information contact the Australian Quarantine and Inspection Service (☎ 1800-020504 or +61-26272 3933 from abroad, 💻 www.daff.gov.au/aqis), which publishes information leaflets about what can and cannot be taken into Australia.

Protected species: Australia has laws which strictly regulate the import and export of wildlife and products made from the bones, feathers, shells, skins, etc. of protected species. Wildlife or any accessories, clothing, handbags, ornaments, shoes, souvenirs, trophies, etc. made from protected species are seized by customs on arrival. Travellers are particularly warned of restrictions on items made from alligators and crocodiles (including gavials and caimans), cats (jaguars, leopards, tigers, etc.), elephants (especially ivory and hide products), giant clam shells, hard corals (including black coral), lizards and monitors (goannas), orchids (including live orchids), rhinoceros, snakes, turtles, whales and zebras. Australia is a signatory to CITES (💻 www.cites.org), but may apply stricter standards,

Some overseas retailers provide certificates and other guarantees stating that their products are made from protected animals specially bred in captivity and legally farmed for by-products, such as their skins. Such certificates aren't recognised in Australia.

The only document recognised by Australian Customs is an import permit from The Department of the Environment and Water Resources (☎ 02-6274 1111, 💻 www.environment.gov.au). Import permits may be issued by this Department, provided that export approval has been obtained from the relevant wildlife authority in the country where you made the purchase, and when Australian wildlife import requirements have been met.

Telephones & CB Radios

The importation of cordless telephones and citizen band (CB) radios is prohibited unless they're approved by the Australian Spectrum Management Agency (SMA). Only importers authorised by the SMA and the Australian Telecommunications Authority (AUSTEL) who comply with strict conditions may bring cordless telephones into Australia. Approved cordless telephones must display an approval number and an AUSTEL 'permit to connect' authorisation number. Cellular mobile telephones and facsimile machines can be freely imported, although you should check that they'll work in Australia (see **Chapter 7**).

Visitors & Temporary Residents

In addition to the usual duty-free concessions (see page 303), visitors and temporary residents coming to Australia for a limited period may bring most articles into the country duty and tax free, provided customs is satisfied that they're for your personal use and will be taken out of Australia on your departure. Permitted articles include a caravan, motor vehicle, trailer, yacht or other craft (for up to 12 months, or longer under certain circumstances). However, you may be required to lodge a cash or bank security with customs to the value of the duty and tax otherwise payable. Customs determine the form of security acceptable in each case and, if you don't take the articles with you when you leave Australia, you must pay (or forfeit) the duty and tax assessed.

Before shipping any articles to Australia which you think will qualify for this concession, you should contact a customs office for advice (see **Appendix A**). This concession isn't available if you're migrating to Australia or a returning resident.

Migrants & Returning Residents

If you're coming to Australia to take up permanent residence for the first time or returning to resume permanent residence, you may import belongings, furniture and household articles that you've owned and used overseas for at least 12 months before your departure for Australia, duty and tax free. Migrants may also bring machinery, plant and other equipment to Australia duty and tax free, provided certain conditions are met. Commercial equipment imported tax and duty-free mustn't be hired, mortgaged, sold or otherwise disposed of during your first two years in Australia. Duty-free concessions don't apply to goods arriving in Australia as unaccompanied effects (see below).

Unaccompanied Effects

The Australian Customs Service is responsible for the clearance of all unaccompanied effects from overseas. Unaccompanied personal effects can be cleared by the owner, a nominee appointed by the owner or a customs broker (a list of brokers is published in the *Yellow Pages*). If you don't use a broker, you must contact the local state or territory customs office to arrange clearance and must produce your passport and complete an *Unaccompanied Effects Statement* (form B534).

Your effects can be cleared through customs before your arrival, provided you're arriving in Australia within six months of the arrival of your belongings. If you employ an international company (see **Moving House** on page 337), they usually handle the associated paperwork and customs clearance for you.

☑ SURVIVAL TIP

Household effects are inspected on arrival in Australia for possible illegal and quarantine risk items. A list of all the items you're importing is required if you pack the goods yourself.

Australian Customs publish an *Unaccompanied Effects* leaflet with further information.

EMBASSY REGISTRATION

Nationals of some countries are required to register with their local embassy or consulate as soon as possible after their arrival in Australia. Even if registration isn't compulsory, most embassies like to keep a record of their nationals resident in Australia (if only to help justify their existence) and it may help to expedite passport renewal or replacement, or notification in the event of an emergency.

FINDING HELP

One of the biggest difficulties facing new arrivals in Australia is how and where to obtain help with day-to-day problems – for example, finding a home, a school or insurance. This book was written in response to this need. However, in addition to the comprehensive information provided here you'll also require detailed local information. How successful you are at finding help depends on your employer, the town or area where you live (e.g. those who live and work in a major city are usually better served than those living in rural areas), your nationality and English proficiency, and even your sex.

Obtaining information isn't a problem, as there's a wealth of information available in Australia on every conceivable subject. The problem is sorting the truths from the half-truths, comparing the options available and making the right decisions. Much information isn't intended for foreigners and their particular needs. You may find that your acquaintances, colleagues and friends can help, as they're often able to proffer advice based on their own experiences and mistakes. But beware! Although they mean well, you're likely to receive as much irrelevant and conflicting information as helpful advice.

The Department of Immigration and Citizenship, which has at least one office in each state and territory (listed, along with telephone numbers, on its website, 💻 www.immi.gov.au), provides some basic post-arrival facilities and services, including English-language tuition for adult migrants, migrant community services, and a translating and interpreting service (see their website for details). There's also a wealth of settlement programmes for migrants run by individual states and territories. Contact your state or territory government (using the telephone directory) for details.

A limited number of hostels (in Melbourne and Sydney) and self-contained apartments are provided for immigrants with nowhere to stay on arrival, although they're drab, depressing places, mostly used by refugees. Government programmes for immigrants include an adult migrant English programme, a grant-in-aid scheme (mainly for refugees), migrant resource centres, telephone interpreter services, translation services and welfare assistance. Some states offer extra help to immigrants.

Sydney Harbour

Many people find their first few weeks or months in Australia stressful, so it helps if you're prepared for a turbulent time. There are over 30 migrant resource centres in major cities and towns, which provide settlement services for migrants and refugees. The British newspaper *Australian News* (see **Appendix B**) has a 'pen pals' page through which prospective migrants can make contact with recent migrants already in Australia, which helps ease the culture shock (see also 🖳 www.multiculturalaustralia.edu.au).

Telephone interpreter services are available 24 hours a day throughout the country for the cost of a local telephone call (131450). Operators speak several languages and can provide information about accommodation, education, health, insurance, legal and police matters, social welfare and a wide range of other topics. There are also translation units in Canberra, Melbourne and Sydney, and translations can be obtained via the telephone interpreter service (a fee may be charged for documents other than migrant settlement documents).

Citizens' Advice Bureaux (CABs), libraries, local council offices and tourist offices are excellent sources of information on a wide range of subjects. Some companies may have a department or staff whose job is to help new arrivals or they may contract this job out to a local company. If a woman lives in or near a major town, she's able to turn to many women's clubs and organisations for help (single men aren't so well served).

There are numerous expatriate associations, clubs and organisations in Australia's major cities and large towns (including 'settlers' or 'friendship' associations) for immigrants from most countries, providing detailed local information regarding all aspects of life in Australia, including health services, housing costs, schools, shopping and much more. Many organisations produce booklets, data sheets and newsletters, operate libraries, and organise a variety of social events, which may include day and evening classes ranging from cooking to English classes. For a list of local clubs, look under 'Clubs and Associations' in the *Yellow Pages*.

Most embassies and consulates provide information bulletin boards (accommodation, jobs, travel, etc.) and keep lists of social clubs and societies for their nationals. Many businesses (e.g. banks and building societies) produce books and leaflets containing useful information for newcomers, while libraries and bookshops usually have books about the local area (see also Appendix B).

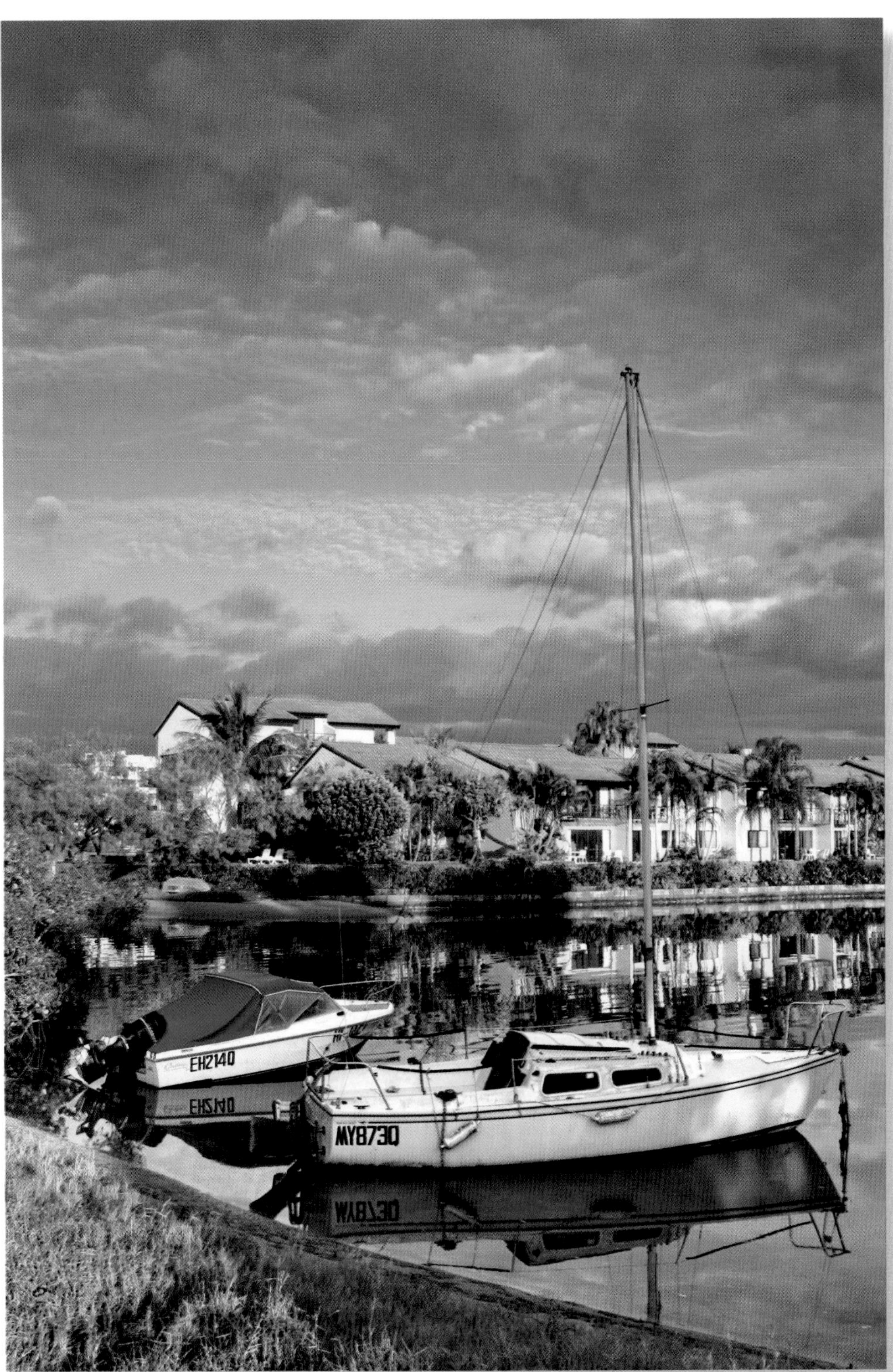

Noosaville, QLD

5. ACCOMMODATION

Australia is a highly urbanised society, some 70 per cent of the population living in the main cities situated on or near the coast, including Adelaide, Brisbane, Canberra, Darwin, Hobart, Melbourne, Perth and Sydney, all of which have particular characters and attractions. Only some 15 per cent of Australians live in rural areas. The vast majority of Australians live in detached bungalows on individual plots, although apartments are common in inner cities and coastal areas, and townhouses are popular in the suburbs.

The rate of home ownership in Australia is one of the highest in the world, and similar to the UK and the US at around 70 per cent, around half of whom own them outright. Most Australians expect to buy their own homes by the time they reach their 30s, although in recent years more people have been renting and many people under 35 have dropped out of the homeownership market altogether. In an attempt to reverse this trend, the government has introduced grants for first-time home buyers.

The cost of housing has skyrocketed in Australia in the last decade, particularly in the major cities (Australia is one of the world's best performing property markets). The OECD has warned on a number of occasions that Australia's house prices relative to incomes are far too high (seven to eight times average incomes). Housing affordability has rapidly deteriorated over the past decade for Australia's 500,000 key workers (e.g. nurses, teachers, police officers, fire-fighters and ambulance officers), with over 80 per cent of major city areas being too expensive for workers to buy a house in 2012, compared with around 50 per cent in 2002.

After fluctuating fortunes in the '80s and '90s, the Australian property market underwent a period of rapidly rising prices (aided by foreign investors), which although it cooled for a while in 2006-7, then surged ahead for a few years. In 2012, the market was stagnant or falling across the country, with a glut of properties (over 300,000) for sale. The National Housing Supply Council/ NHSC (www.nhsc.org.au/content/supply.html) stated in their 2011 State of Supply Report that the gap between supply and demand widened in 2009-10 from around 158,000 homes to some 187,000. Using 'medium' supply and demand scenarios, the council estimates that the gap will grow to about 329,000 dwellings by 2015.

Housing that's affordable, either to rent or buy is mostly located in outer suburban areas where there are fewer jobs and less public transport. This drives up the cost of living and for those or low or average incomes means that affordable housing does not equal affordable living.

The NHSC report makes clear that the housing shortage is primarily in NSW and Queensland. About 40 per cent of the shortage is in NSW, well ahead of the 32 per cent of Australians who live in that state, and a third in Queensland, despite only 20 per cent of Australians living there. The gap actually narrowed in Victoria, where it's 'just' 17,000 dwellings, and there's actually a small over-supply in South Australia. However,

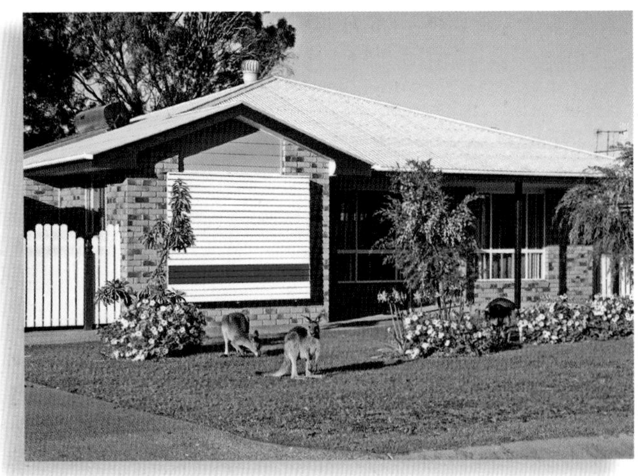

housing shortages are also a problem in the Northern Territory and the current shortage of 28,000 homes in Western Australia is expected to grow significantly when the next report is published.

The problem is exacerbated by the flood of foreign (non-resident) property investors who have been snapping up Australian property in recent years and fuelling the surge in prices, which has made it almost impossible for low-income residents to get on the housing ladder and forced up rents. In future, temporary residents will need permission to buy homes and if they decide to leave Australia they must sell their home, and foreign investors will also be limited to buying only new properties.

In most cities and regions of Australia there's a wealth of property for sale, but finding good, affordable rental accommodation isn't so easy, particularly in major cities such as Sydney and Melbourne. In Sydney, affordable rental property is in high demand and short supply, and rents are **very** high. Accommodation generally accounts for around 30 per cent of the average Australian family's budget, but can rise to over 50 per cent in the major cities and for low-income families. In some parts of Sydney caravan (trailer) parks have become the new suburbs for those who cannot afford to rent or buy a home – and even these are few and far between, with rents of $100 or more per week for a site. Not surprisingly, homelessness is a huge and growing problem in Australia.

MOVING HOUSE

Shipping your belongings to Australia usually takes two to three months from Europe or North America. Unless you plan well in advance, you'll almost certainly arrive in Australia before your belongings. A removal company (called a removalist in Australia) usually sends a representative to carry out an inspection and provide an estimate. You should obtain at least three written quotes before choosing a company (and don't increase the load later, as it isn't unknown for original estimates to escalate wildly). Some companies routinely increase the price after everything has been packed, ostensibly because more was included than was stated in the estimate.

If possible, always use an international removal company that's a member of an organisation such as the Association of International Removers (AIR), the International Federation of Furniture Removers (FIDI) or the Overseas Moving Network International (OMNI). Members usually subscribe to a payment guarantee scheme, whereby if a member company fails to fulfil its commitments to a customer, the removal is completed at the agreed price by another company or you receive a full refund. Removal companies will also pack your belongings and provide packing cases and containers, although this is much more expensive than doing it yourself (ask how they pack fragile and valuable items). Check whether the cost of insurance and packing cases and materials is included in a quote.

You can send your effects by full container load (FCL) or part load (groupage), which usually takes longer. FCL shipments are loaded into an individual container holding around 1,000ft^3 (28m^3), while a shipment of less than around 800ft^3 (22.5m^3) is cheaper to send as groupage. Obtain a separate quote for items that won't fit into a container. If the destination in Australia isn't within 30 miles (48km) of the port of arrival, you may need to pay an extra charge for door-to-door delivery and there may also be extra charges in Australia. Ask about possible extra charges in advance. Most international removers expect to be paid before your goods are shipped. The cost of moving your house contents from your previous country of residence to Australia may be paid for by your Australian employer.

Before shipping any household articles to Australia, check whether they're worth taking, e.g. many people take electrical apparatus that's incompatible and furniture which is unsuitable or simply isn't needed in their new home (see **Household Goods** on page 302). It isn't worthwhile taking cookers (which are usually provided), refrigerators, TVs (incompatible) or wardrobes (built-in in most homes). If you're moving from a country with a cold climate, bear in mind that furniture and furnishings must be suitable for a hot climate (unless you're heading for Tasmania). You should carefully consider the cost of packing and shipping large items to Australia, as it may be cheaper to sell them and buy new items on arrival. Good-quality furniture and antiques are worth taking, as are small electrical appliances if they operate on a 240V supply.

All containers are checked by customs on arrival, but because of the vast number arriving each day, it can take up to 14 days for a container to be checked. If you pack your belongings yourself, you must provide an inventory for Australian customs. If you do your own packing, use paper, wood or wool instead of straw, and don't include any prohibited or illegal items as customs and quarantine checks can be rigorous and penalties severe. On the day of the move, make sure there's room for the removal van or truck to park; if necessary get the police to cordon off an area outside your home. Give the shipping company a telephone number and an email address through which you can be contacted, and try to get a relative or friend to handle any problems in the country from which your belongings are being shipped.

Be sure to fully insure your household contents during removal with a well established insurance company – you aren't required to use the one recommended by the removal company, which may not provide the best cover. You should have an all-risks marine insurance policy from domicile to domicile, which is underwritten by a reputable insurance company. It's wise to make a photographic or video record of any valuables for insurance purposes. If you need to make a claim, be sure to read the small print, as all companies require you to make claims within a limited period. Your insurance cover may differ according to whether items were packed by you or by the shipper. Send a claim by registered post.

> ☑ **SURVIVAL TIP**
>
> **If you need to put your household effects into storage, it's imperative to have them fully insured, as warehouses have been known to burn down. Also don't forget to insure your home contents from the day you move in.**

Although most people wouldn't consider doing their own house move, if you have only personal effects to transport locally within Australia, you can hire a van by the hour, half-day or day (see **Car Hire** on page 172). Many removal companies sell packing boxes in various sizes and hire or sell removal equipment (trolleys, straps, etc.) for those who feel up to doing their own house move.

See also the checklists in **Chapter 20**.

TEMPORARY ACCOMMODATION

On arrival in Australia, you may find it necessary to stay in temporary accommodation for a few weeks (or even a few months) before moving into permanent accommodation or while waiting for your personal effects and furniture to arrive from overseas. In most large towns and cities, executive and holiday apartments (or apart-hotels) and motels are available, which are self-contained and fully furnished with their own bathrooms and kitchens (albeit small). They aren't a cheap option, but are better than staying in a hotel, particularly for families; generally the longer your stay, the lower the daily rate. Note, however, that there may be no room service (cleaning, linen change, etc.), although it may be offered as an (expensive) extra. Apart-hotels and motels also don't usually provide restaurants but may offer a breakfast service.

They're cheaper than hotels (e.g. 25 to 50 per cent less than a standard hotel double room), have over twice the space and are more convenient. Serviced apartments and aparthotels can usually be rented on a weekly basis, although some aren't rented for less than a month. The cost varies considerably depending on the location, season and the size of the property, from around $500 per week for a one-bedroom apartment up to $3,000 to $4,000 per month for a two-bedroom luxury apartment.

There are numerous apartment rental companies in Australia including Medina (💻 www.medina.com.au), Move and Stay (💻 www.moveandstay.com.au/brisbane-aparthotels-definition.php) and Corporate Housing (💻 www.corporatehousing.com.au). Many more can be found in particular cities and states via a search engine such as Google.

Single people and married couples (without children) may be able to find temporary accommodation in hostels and other budget accommodation (see **Chapter 15**).

AUSTRALIAN HOMES

There's a huge choice of homes in Australia, including mobile homes, apartments, townhouses and a wide range of 'standard' and architect-designed detached homes. Apartments (called units or home units) are common in inner cities and coastal areas, and townhouses (or row houses/homes) are common in cities and their suburbs. Villa units are low-rise properties separated by a garage or small garden (yard) and similar to a townhouse. Outside the major cities and in outer suburbs, most people have a home built to a standard or individual design on their own plot, although package deals which include a plot and a house, are common. There's usually a choice between modern and mock-period homes.

Over three-quarters of Australia's 9.5m homes are detached houses, some 15 per cent are apartments, and around 5 per cent are semi-detached or terraced houses/townhouses. The average size of new houses in Australia in 2012 was 243m² – the largest in the world – beating the US for which the current figure is 222m².

Around 80 per cent of houses in Australia have three bedrooms, 15 per cent four bedrooms, and just 5 per cent five bedrooms. Most have a back yard (garden) and a single or double lock up garage or carport. Houses may be made of brick, concrete, or timber (sometimes called weatherboard, which is wooden cladding, similar to North American clapboard). Purpose-built retirement homes and sheltered housing developments are popular throughout Australia, where there are some 2,500 retirement 'villages'.

For more information about Australia homes, see our sister publication *Buying a Home in Australia*.

RENTED ACCOMMODATION

Renting (rather than buying) a home is usually the best option for anyone who's staying in Australia for a few years or less, when buying isn't usually practical, as well as being the solution for those who don't want the expense and restrictions involved in buying and owning a home. If you're a migrant and intend to buy a property it's wise to rent for a period first, particularly if you're unsure where you'll be living or working. There's also the likelihood that you'll change jobs or states within your first few years in Australia or even decide to return home. Renting allows you to become familiar with a neighbourhood, the people and the weather before deciding whether you want to live somewhere permanently.

There's a strong rental market in the major cities, but renting isn't so popular in rural areas, where most people tend to buy. Some 70 per cent of Australian's own their homes and renters are sometimes made to feel like second-class citizens, as they have traditionally been people who couldn't afford to buy a home. Renting used to be regarded primarily as a temporary or transitional situation, but rising house prices have seen it become an increasingly permanent phenomenon; some 40 per cent of tenants rent for ten years or more, with many never being in a position to buy.

Rented accommodation has traditionally been in short supply in most major cities, particularly in Sydney, Brisbane and Melbourne, and the recent stagnation of the property purchase market has seen more people seeking rented accommodation, resulting in a further decline in availability and a leap in rents. Some landlords are cashing in by auctioning properties to let, where the highest bidder gets the rental! The majority of rental apartments have two bedrooms, with one- and three-bedroom apartments more difficult to find and homes with four or five bedrooms rare (apart from astronomically expensive houses).

Most rental properties have heating (although insulation is often poor) and some have air-conditioning. Carpets, curtains or blinds, light fittings, kitchen cupboards, hot water systems and stoves/ovens are generally included and most also include built-in wardrobes and a dishwasher. Fully furnished houses are sometimes available but aren't common.

There's a chronic shortage of rental properties in the major cities, where vacancies were at an all-time low in mid-2012 (an average of around 2 per cent) and rents have soared in recent years. If you're planning to rent for more than a few weeks, it's wise to investigate the rental market in your chosen area before arriving in Australia, e.g. by studying the advertisements in Australian newspapers and contacting agents (both of which can be done via the internet). Temporary accommodation (see above) can usually be arranged before arrival, but you shouldn't rent a property long term without inspecting it first; in fact, most estate agents don't allow you to and you must complete a pre-rental inspection report before you move in.

Furnished accommodation is naturally more expensive than unfurnished and is even more difficult to find. Some landlords don't allow pets or smokers, so check whether any restrictions apply in advance.

Despite its increasing popularity, renting in Australia is a precarious business. The majority of contracts are short term (often as little as six months), with no guarantee of renewal and no controls or limits on rent increases. Add to this the fact that you can be evicted at short notice at any time for any reason and you may decide to buy instead.

Finding a Rental Property

Your success or failure in finding a suitable rental property depends on many factors, not least the type of property you're looking for (a one-bedroom apartment is easier to find than a four-bedroom detached house), how much you want to pay and the area where you wish to live. Good rental accommodation is in short supply in all major cities.

In recent years, the demand for rental properties has been very high, coupled with a limited supply of new housing units, which has brought the average rental vacancy rates in Australia's capital cities to below 2 per cent in the last few years. There are sometimes 20 to 30 applicants for each vacant property in popular suburbs, particularly homes with three or more bedrooms, and you may have to take what you can get. Most people settle for something in the outer suburbs and commute to work. However, if you need to travel into a city centre (particularly Sydney) each day, you should be prepared to spend at least an hour or longer travelling each way from the outer suburbs.

There are a number of ways to find a rental property, including the following:

- Ask acquaintances, friends and relatives to spread the word. A lot of rental properties are found by word of mouth, particularly in the major cities, where it's difficult to find somewhere with a reasonable rent unless you have connections (many rental properties change tenants without coming onto the market).

Check the advertisements in local newspapers (see 🖳 www.newspapers.com.au). The best day for advertisements is Saturday.

- Visit letting agents and estate agents, who also act as letting agents (all cities and large towns have both – look under 'Real Estate Agents' in the *Yellow Pages*).
- Check websites such as 🖳 www.domain.com.au, www.realestate.com.au, www.realestateview.com.au and www.reiv.com.au, which list properties both for rent and for sale.
- Look for advertisements in shop windows and on notice boards in company offices, shopping centres, supermarkets, and universities and colleges.
- Check newsletters published by churches, clubs and expatriate organisations, and their notice boards.

To secure accommodation through advertisements in local newspapers, you must be quick off the mark, particularly in the cities. Buy newspapers as soon as they're published, and start telephoning 'at the crack of dawn'; even then you're likely to find a queue when you arrive to view a property. You must be available to inspect properties immediately and at any time. Some people will go to any lengths to secure a rental property, including offering to pay above the asking price (bidding wars sometimes break out), paying six months' rent in advance and signing a contract for two or three years.

Most properties in Australian cities are let through agents, whose main task is to vet prospective tenants. Always dress smartly when visiting properties or agents' offices in order to create a good impression. When registering with an agent, you need two forms of identification (e.g. a driving licence and passport), written references from your employer and/or previous landlord, and character references. Agents usually contact all referees and may ask why you left your previous accommodation. If you have a pet, you may need a reference from your previous landlord stating that it was clean and well behaved, but animals aren't usually permitted in rented apartments. You must complete a registration form and should ensure that it's correct in every detail, otherwise you may jeopardise your chances.

Single parents, students, the unemployed and young people have a tough time finding anywhere at an affordable price and, if you're on a low income or are unemployed, you must prove that you can pay the rent. Some people (e.g. Africans and Asians) may encounter discrimination, although it's illegal under the Federal Discrimination Act. If you pass muster, you may be given the keys to view a property on your own in return for a $50 deposit and proof of identity.

Costs & Payment

Rental costs vary considerably according to the size (number of bedrooms) and quality of a property, its age, the facilities provided, and – not least – the region, city and neighbourhood. Rents are lower in rural than urban areas and, as a general rule, the further a property is from a large city or town, public transport or other essential facilities, the cheaper it is. Average rents tend to be highest in Sydney, Melbourne and Darwin. Rents have skyrocketed in recent years, with increases of between 10 and 20 per cent in the major cities.

Australians have a simple basis for calculating the rental value of a property, the target for which is usually a gross (annual) rent equal to around 5 per cent of a property's value. Therefore the target rent for a unit with a value of $400,000 is around $20,000 per annum ($400 per week) or $10 per week for each $10,000 of value. Rents are usually higher when rental property is in short supply, e.g. in Sydney.

As a rough guide, average weekly rents for a two-bedroom apartment are from $200-400 and three-bedroom houses from $250-500.

The lowest rents apply to modest homes in the less expensive suburbs of Adelaide and Hobart, while the highest rents apply to the more popular areas in and around Sydney, Melbourne, Perth, Brisbane and Darwin. Average rents don't include properties in the central business district (CBD) of major cities or in exclusive residential areas, for which the sky's the limit: you can easily pay $1,000-2,000 per week for a swanky two-bedroom apartment in a smart suburb of Sydney.

Rents are controlled in some states, although this doesn't usually extend to new properties. Your contract may include details of when your rent is to be reviewed or increased, if applicable; the rent for a fixed-term tenancy can be increased only when provision for an increase is included in the lease contract. You must be given notice in writing of any rent increases and a rent tribunal can review excessive rent increases and the existing rent if services are reduced. It's best to pay your rent by cheque or standing order, for which you should (by law) receive a receipt from your landlord.

Fees & Bonds

An agent's fee of two weeks' rent for a one-year lease and one week's rent for a six-month lease are the legal maximum fees, but most agents charge less than this. Usually you must pay two to four week's rent in advance, depending on the type of property and the rental agreement, plus a bond (see below) against damages. Beware of hidden extras such as a fee for connecting the electricity, gas or telephone.

When renting property in Australia, a bond (deposit) must be paid in advance. The bond is usually equal to between two and six weeks' rent (it's usually higher for furnished than for unfurnished properties), and is unlimited in Queensland for properties with rents over $500 per week. See the Rental Agreements DIY website for more information (💻 www.rentalagreementsdiy.com.au/tenancy_laws_in_australia.php).

The bond is usually lodged with the state or territory rental authority, e.g. the Residential Tenancies Authority in Queensland or the Residential Tenancies Tribunal in South Australia, together with a copy of the inspection (condition) report. Information regarding rental bonds can be obtained from ☎ 133220.

Contracts

When you find a suitable house or apartment to rent, you should insist on a written contract with the owner or agent, called a tenancy agreement. In some states, such as NSW and Victoria, a standard form must be used by law, and in others there are usually minimum conditions which cannot be reduced by landlords. The tenancy agreement states the responsibilities of both parties. Although these are fairly balanced between landlord and tenant, you should read an agreement carefully before signing it. Apart from self-catering holiday accommodation (see page 250), renting a house or apartment usually requires a commitment of at least 6 or 12 months with an option to renew.

The owner is responsible for property tax (council rates) and unit service charges (in the case of a communal property), and the tenant for utility costs, unless otherwise agreed. If you rent a house with a garden and swimming pool, maintenance costs may be included in the rent. Tenants must take good care of a property, although the landlord is required to maintain it in a habitable condition and ensure that basic services such as water and sewerage are in order. If the landlord refuses to carry out urgent and necessary repairs within a reasonable period, you can arrange to have them done and send him the bill, although you mustn't deduct the cost from the rent. You may be required to have a smoke alarm in the property, e.g. in New South Wales.

> **Caution**
>
> If you wish to vacate a property before your lease expires, you're liable to pay the rent up to the end of your lease period, although you may be able to find someone to take over the lease and repay your bond (check with your agent or landlord whether this is possible).

If you give the landlord adequate notice of termination (usually 21 days), he should attempt to minimise his loss by advertising and re-letting the property. If you have an oral contract (termed a periodic tenancy), renewed on a weekly or monthly basis, a week's or a month's notice is sufficient.

Whether you have an oral or a written agreement, you cannot be evicted or forced to leave unless your landlord obtains an eviction order. In order to be evicted you must be in breach of your lease, e.g. by damaging the property, failing to pay the rent, refusing the landlord entry, renovating without permission or sub-letting. A landlord cannot remove your belongings, change the locks or cut off services in order to force you out. The landlord can terminate a fixed-term agreement by giving 60 days' notice. He may repossess a property for his own use or to sell it with vacant possession, and isn't required to state his reason for terminating a contract.

Most states have a Residential Tenancy Tribunal that handles complaints by landlords and tenants, and disputes over bonds, evictions, excessive rents and repairs, and there may be grounds for a tenant to appeal against termination, e.g. age, lack of alternative accommodation or poor health.

You can obtain advice regarding rental contracts from a Citizens' Advice Bureau, community legal centre, consumer affairs office, legal aid commission or tenants' advice centre. Most large cities also have a tenants' union hotline. The local Office of Fair Trading in many states publishes a *Renting Guide* or *Tenants' Rights Manual* (in NSW, see 💻 www.fairtrading.nsw.gov.au), and similar guides are available from estate agents.

Inspections

One of the most important tasks on moving into a rented house or apartment is to make an inventory of the contents and an inspection report on its condition. This includes the condition of fixtures and fittings, the state of furniture and carpets (if furnished), the cleanliness and state of the decoration, and anything missing or in need of repair. (A rental property should be spotless when you move in, as this is how your landlord will expect you to leave it when you move out.) An inventory is normally provided by your landlord or a letting agent and may include every single item in a furnished property (down to the number of teaspoons).

The inventory and inspection report must usually be completed within seven days of taking possession and you receive a copy which is signed by you and the agent or landlord. A copy is also lodged with the state or territory rental authority with the bond. The property is re-inspected when you leave and, if necessary, deductions are made from your bond for cleaning and repair, although there's no deduction for ordinary wear and tear.

Note the reading on your meters (electricity, gas and water as applicable) and check that you aren't overcharged on your first bill. Meters should be read by the relevant authorities before you move in, which you may need to organise yourself.

Shared Accommodation

Sharing a house or flat is an answer to high rents, particularly in major towns and cities, and is popular among students and the young. It usually involves sharing the bathroom, dining room, kitchen and living room of a house or apartment, and may even include sharing a bedroom. All bills are usually also shared (in addition to the rent), including electricity, gas and telephone, and in some cases food bills, as well as chores such as cooking and cleaning. As always when living with others, there are advantages and disadvantages to shared accommodation, and its success depends on the participants' ability to live together.

If you rent a property with the intention of sharing, make sure that it's permitted in your contract. The law regarding flat-sharing is complicated. It's possible for all sharers to be joint tenants with one tenancy agreement or individual tenants with individual tenancy agreements. However, it's simpler when one person is the tenant and sub-lets to the others. Whatever the arrangement, you should have a single rent book and pay the rent in a lump sum. It's usually the occupants' responsibility to replace flatmates who leave during the tenancy.

The cost of sharing a furnished apartment or house varies considerably according to its size, location and amenities. A rough guide is from $150 (single) to $175 (double) per week with your own bedroom, or up to $250 with your own bathroom. Sharing is particularly common in major cities, where many newspapers contain advertisements for flat-sharers, e.g. the *Sydney Morning Herald* and the *Melbourne Age*. (Note that the phrase 'broad minded girl/guy' in advertisements may be code for 'we are lesbian or homosexual'.) There are also agents in major cities who match sharers with similar interests and a number of websites that specialise in flat-sharing, which include 💻 http://au.easyroommate.com, www.flatmatefinders.com.au (Melbourne and Sydney only), www.flatmates.com.au and www.share-accommodation.net.

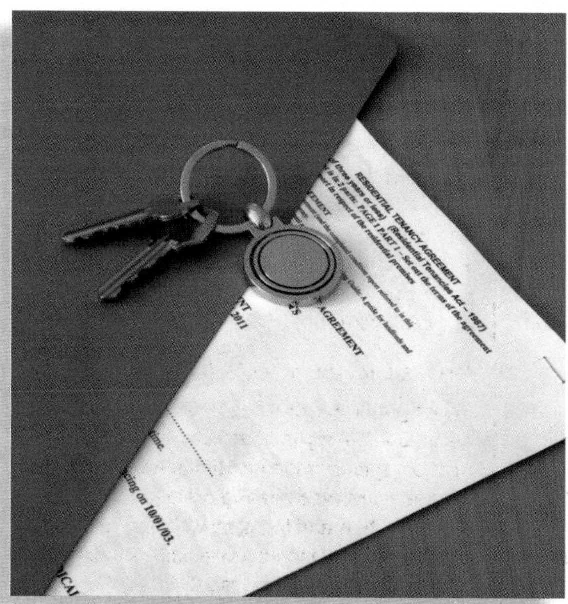

BUYING A HOME

Whether you choose to rent or buy a property in Australia will depend largely on how long you're planning to stay there. Buying a house or apartment has traditionally been a good long-term investment. However, you shouldn't expect to make a quick profit when buying property in Australia and should look upon it as an investment in your family's future happiness, rather than merely in financial terms. This is particularly true in the current uncertain property market.

Property values in Australian cities increased dramatically in the early years of the 21st century, but the market has slowed considerably in the last few years, with price falls in many areas. In 2012 it was a buyers' market, with prices in most areas stagnant. Some analysts believed that there has rarely been a better time to buy, with low interest rates, a flat market, and help from federal and state governments for first-time buyers.

Before making an irrevocable decision regarding buying a home in Australia, you should do extensive research, study the possible pitfalls and be prepared to rent for a period before buying.

This section contains a summary of information relevant to buying property in Australia; for further details refer to our sister publication, *Buying a Home in Australia*.

Restrictions

There are no restrictions on buying a home in Australia for Australian and New Zealand citizens, holders of permanent resident visas (including new migrants), and a foreigner purchasing a home with a spouse who's an Australian citizen.

However, unlike in many countries, where foreigners may buy property without any restrictions, Australia has strict regulations governing the purchase of real estate by non-residents. In many cases, foreigners must obtain approval from the Foreign Investment Review Board/FIRB (☎ 02-6263 2940, 💻 www.firb.gov.au) before they may buy real estate.

Foreigners with a temporary residence no longer require FIRB approval when buying:

- an established dwelling (not new) for their own residence;
- a new dwelling;
- a single block of vacant residential land (other acquisitions of vacant land will require notification and will normally be approved subject to development within 24 months).

Failure to obtain FIRB approval or meet FIRB requirements is a serious offence and can lead to prosecution and the possibility that you'll be unable to obtain a visa to visit or live in Australia in the future. In some cases, entry into Australia is refused.

Most non-residents need FIRB approval to buy real estate in Australia and you should obtain approval before committing themselves to a purchase. You may exchange contracts before you obtain permission, but one of the conditional clauses in the contract must state that the purchase is subject to FIRB approval.

You must complete form R3 (available from the FIRB directly and downloadable from the website listed above) and send it by post or fax (see above) together with the appropriate documentation, e.g. copy of passport, visa and information pages from the contract of sale. The FIRB is required to make a decision within 30 days of the application and to convey this to the interested parties within a further ten days.

First-time Buyers

A First Home Owner Grant (FHOG) of $7,000 was introduced in Australia on 1st July 2000. It was temporarily doubled to $14,000 in 2008 (called the First Home Owner Boost/FHOB) and to $21,000 for those buying a brand new property, although the FHOB ended on 30th September 2009.

In addition to the FHOG, there are a number of state based first home buyer benefits, which include grants and stamp duty concessions. For more information, see 💻 www.firsthome.gov.au or www.firsthomebuyers.net.au/?page_id=4.

Migrants with permanent residency (including New Zealanders) are also eligible for the grants.

Cost

Property prices vary considerably throughout the country and in the various suburbs of the major cities. Not surprisingly, the further you are from a town or city, the lower the cost of land and property. Properties in central and beach locations cost anywhere between two and four times as much as similar properties in less fashionable or convenient areas. Apartments are often as expensive as houses and townhouses (or even more so), as they're invariably located in city centres, whereas most houses are in suburbs or rural areas. For many buyers it's a choice between a small apartment in an inner city and a detached family home in the outer suburbs – in recent years the average 'Aussie battler' has had to move further and further into the outer suburbs of major cities in order to find affordable accommodation.

There's a high demand everywhere for waterfront properties, which have generally been an excellent investment, particularly in Sydney, whose 20 most expensive suburbs are all waterfront (harbour or ocean). Waterfront properties in Sydney can be astronomically expensive, and a reasonable two-bedroom apartment in an attractive building with water views costs over $1m (over 100 Sydney suburbs has an average property price of over $1m) and $2m homes are also commonplace in Sydney and Melbourne.

The average cost of a home (both houses and units) in the major cities of Australia in mid-2012 was around $503,000; the table below shows the average property selling prices in individual cities (source: 💻 www.rpdata.com).

Property Prices Mid-2012

City	Average Price	% Change Year on Year
Adelaide	$425,000	-2.4
Brisbane	$458,000	-4.96
Canberra	$581,000	+1.31
Darwin	$464,000	+0.24
Hobart	$331,000	-5.2
Melbourne	$578,000	-6.57
Perth	$554,000	-1.38
Sydney	$632,000	-1.97

A few kilometres can make a huge difference to the price of a property, with apartments in central areas costing up to $2,500 per square metre more than those in harbour-side developments a few kilometres further out. Land prices also reduce considerably from around 15km (9mi) outside a city and are at their lowest around 25km (16mi) from city centres. The cost of land varies from as little as $50,000-100,000 for a plot large enough for an average suburban house at least 25km from cities such as Adelaide, Hobart and Perth to over $500,000 for a similar plot within 15km (9mi) of central Sydney – if you can find one! Even the cost of building a home varies with the location as well as with the quality of materials used. For example, brick veneer costs from around $1,000 per m², depending on the location.

Property price indexes can be found on several websites including 💻 www.findmeahome.com.au, www.residex.com.au, www.rpdata.com and www.homepriceguide.com.au. There are also specialist property magazines such as *Australian Property Investor* (💻 www.australianpropertyinvestor.com) which monitor the latest so-called hotspots (the website 💻 www.hotspotting.com.au provides a similar service). You can find out the price of homes in any Sydney suburb through the *Sydney Morning Herald Home Price Guide*, which lists all the sales' results (both auction and private treaty) in Sydney suburbs for the last 12 months (it can be ordered online from Australian Property Monitors, 💻 www.apm.com.au). An online *Property Value Guide* is provided by the Commonwealth Bank of Australia (💻 www.commbank.com.au/propertyvalueguide).

You can also peruse property advertisements in a number of publications via the internet (e.g. 💻 www.sydneyproperty.com.au) and on a range of property websites, including 💻 www.domain.com au, www.myhome.com.au, www.realestate.com.au, www.realestateview.com.au and www.reiv.com.au.

Fees

The fees associated with buying a home in Australia are usually lower than in many other countries, the maximum being around 9 per cent and the minimum, with stamp duty discounts (see below) much lower. Total fees are usually between 4 and 5 per cent. Most fees are calculated as a percentage of the value of the property you're buying, therefore the more expensive a property, the higher the fees. Even removal costs are higher if you have a large house (unless you have a lot of empty rooms). If you're buying and selling, you must consider the cost of both transactions. Bear in mind that fees change regularly and, in the current slow market, there are calls to reduce or abolish some of them, particularly state taxes such as stamp duty.

- **Stamp duty:** Known as transfer duty in QLD and duty in TAS, stamp duty accounts for the largest slice of the fees involved in a property purchase and is payable on property transactions in all states, although rates and concessions (see below) vary considerably. Rates, which are calculating on a sliding scale in relation to the purchase price of a property, are published by state tax offices, whose websites include stamp duty calculators. Stamp duty must be paid within three months of purchase. There are many stamp duty calculators on the web (most of which give different figures!), e.g. 💻 www.stampdutycalculator.com.au. The table below shows the stamp duty levied by individual states on properties costing $250,000, $400,000, $500,000 and $750,000.

  All states offer discounts or concessions on stamp duty for first-home buyers, including new migrants, and some also offer discounts for the purchase of a principal home (you must usually live in the property for at least six months to qualify).

- **Land transfer registration fee**: Payable to the Land Titles Office for recording a change of owner, the land transfer registration fee is either a flat fee or a variable fee based on the price paid and varies considerably with the state. As a rough guide the fee is between 0.01 and 0.06 per cent of the purchase price (paid by the buyer).

- **Legal & conveyance fees**: These fees may vary according to the work involved and also vary from state to state, e.g. from around $550 in Adelaide, Perth and Hobart to around $1,750 in Brisbane for a property costing over $100,000. The fees in most states are within the $550 to $1,100 range or 0.5 to 2 per cent of the price (the seller pays a similar amount). Lawyers and conveyancers are generally free to set their own fees for conveyancing and should provide a written estimate of their fees in advance. In WA, however, conveyancers' (settlement agents) fees are set according to a fixed scale (see 💻 www.sasb.wa.gov.au for details). Always check what's included in the fee and whether a quoted fee is 'full and binding' or just an estimate. A low basic rate may be supplemented by much more expensive 'extras' (called disbursements) such as costs relating to title searches, debt certificates and courier charges.

- **Mortgage fees:** A range of fees is associated with mortgages, including a mortgage application or establishment fee, a valuation fee, legal fees, mortgage stamp duty, maintenance fees and a loan registration fee (for mortgage information, see page 234).

- **Inspection or survey fees:** Although it isn't compulsory to have a building inspection or a structural survey carried out, it's often wise, particularly when you're buying an old detached house. For a survey of a one-bedroom apartment you should expect to pay from around $400, for a two-bedroom apartment or house from $500 and for a four or five-bedroom house from around $750. Fees vary considerably and may depend

Stamp Duty Comparison

State	Purchase Price			
	$250,000	**$400,000**	**$500,000**	**$750,000**
ACT	$7,500	$15,000	$20,500	$34,875
NSW	$7,240	$13,490	$17,990	$29,240
NT	$7,857	$16,514	$23,929	$37,125
QLD	$6,575	$11,825	$15,525	$26,775
SA	$8,955	$16,330	$21,330	$35,080
TAS	$7,550	$13,550	$17,550	$27,550
VIC	$8,870	$16,370	$21,970	$40,070
WA	$6,935	$13,015	$17,765	$29,740

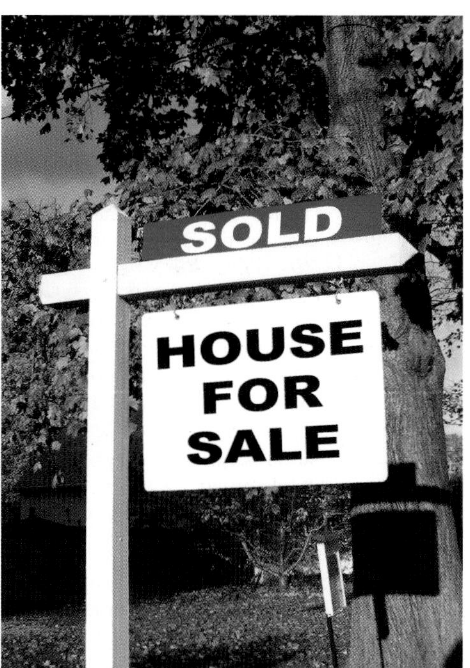

on exactly what's included or omitted from an inspection. A termite and pest inspection costs from around $150 to $250 and may be paid by the vendor or buyer, or shared. Strata inspections cost from around $200-250.

- **Building insurance** – It's invariably a condition of lenders that properties are fully insured against structural and other damage. It may be necessary to insure a property from the day you sign the purchase contract and you should allow for the cost of this in your budget (see **Building Insurance** on page 223).

You also usually need to pay utility connection (or reconnection) fees for electricity, gas, telephone and water supplies. Removal costs must also be taken into account, as must property running costs, which include a caretaker's or management fees if you leave a home empty or let it, maintenance fees for a community property, building and contents insurance (see page 223), property taxes (see page 242), and standing charges for utilities (electricity, gas, telephone, water). Annual running costs usually average around 2 to 3 per cent of the cost of a property.

If you buy a unit (flat or apartment) there are usually quarterly 'community' fees (usually called a levy) for services and maintenance, which you should be aware of as it can run into thousands of dollars a quarter, even for a modest flat.

ESTATE AGENTS

Most property in Australia is bought and sold through real estate agents, who sell property on commission for owners, although you may buy directly from a vendor. Their commission is usually from 2 to 4 per cent of the selling price, but may be higher (as a percentage) on cheaper properties. When buying property through an agent in Australia, always ensure that he's licensed. Estate agents must have professional indemnity insurance and sign a disclosure form (see below), while clients have access to a Tribunal and Complaints Fund. In 2007, the REIA introduced a 'National Principles of Conduct', designed to encourage better ethics among its members.

There's a multi-listing service in all states, whereby homes can be advertised in estate agents' offices throughout the state, which costs vendors nothing until their home is sold. However, some agents may only show you properties for which they have an exclusive listing (when they don't need to share the commission with anyone else), therefore you should specifically ask to see properties that are multi-listed.

Estate agents usually act for the seller and it's their job to obtain the highest price they can for a property, therefore don't expect impartial advice regarding what you should offer if you're a buyer. If an agent offers to make a considerable reduction on the advertised price, it probably means that the property is overpriced and has been on their books for a long time.

Among the largest chains of real estate agents in Australia are (in A-Z order), Century 21 (🖳 www.century21.com.au), Elders (🖳 www.eldersrealestate.com.au), First National (🖳 www.firstnational.com.au), LJ Hooker (🖳 www.ljhooker.com.au), McGrath (🖳 www.mcgrath.com.au), PRD Nationwide (🖳 www.prdnationwide.com.au), Rain & Horne (🖳 www.raineandhorne.com.au), Ray White (🖳 www.raywhite.com) and Remax (🖳 www.remax.com.au). In addition to the 'main street' agents there are also numerous internet only agents, including 🖳 www.domain.com.au, www.myhome.com.au, www.property.com.au, www.realestate.com.au and www.realestateview.com.au, which also list properties for rent.

The Real Estate Institute of Australia/REIA (🖳 www.reiaustralia.com.au) is the umbrella organisation for estate agents' associations, e.g. the Real Estate Institute of New South Wales. State Offices of Fair Trading also provide help and advice on choosing an estate agent and can tell you whether an agent is licensed.

Disclosure Form

Under Australian state law, estate agents are required to sign a disclosure form with a buyer before a purchase contract is drawn up. The form, known by different names in different states, e.g. a Disclosure Declaration in QLD and an Agency Agreement in NSW, includes information about the estate agent's relationship with the seller of the property (if any); details of their fees, commissions and any other remuneration that they will receive from the sale; and itemisation of the marketing and advertising costs for the sale. The form must be signed by the estate agent and the prospective buyer or vendor.

Contracts

Once a suitable property has been found and a price has been agreed between you and the vendor, both parties sign a contract of sale (also called an offer and acceptance). Contracts are published in standard form by the Law Society and the Real Estate Institute, although it's common for a lawyer or conveyancer to draw up a bespoke contract. Note that developers rarely allow anyone other than themselves to draw up a contract for the purchase of off-plan property. **You should never sign a contract without having it checked by a lawyer or conveyancer.** It's important to check that a property's particulars are complete in every detail and that the terms of sale are correct, including any changes made to the standard terms.

A government warning statement must be attached to the front of a contract of sale. The statement advises (in large, bold print) the buyer to obtain independent legal advice and an independent valuation of the property before signing the contract. It also lists the buyer's rights and explains the terms of the cooling-off period (see below). The buyer and estate agent must sign this statement in front of a witness. An example of a warning statement can be downloaded from the Queensland Government's Department of Fair Trading's website (🖳 www.fairtrading.qld.gov.au – go to 'Property transaction forms' and see 'PAMD Form 30c').

Contracts often contain conditional clauses, such as the sale being conditional on a clear survey, finance being obtained or approval for purchase from the Foreign Investment Review Board/FIRB (see **Restrictions** above).

Conditions usually apply to events out of the control of the vendor or buyer, although almost anything agreed between the buyer and vendor can be included in a contract. If any conditions aren't met, the contract can be suspended or declared null and void and the deposit returned. However, if you fail to go through with a purchase and aren't covered by a clause in the contract, you forfeit your deposit or may even be compelled to complete a purchase. If any fixtures or fittings, such as carpets, curtains or furniture, are included in the purchase price, you should have them listed in an addendum to the contract.

A 10 per cent deposit is payable when you sign the contract of sale and in some cases you must also pay a small holding deposit

(e.g. $1,000) as a sign of 'good faith'. Most states entitle you to a cooling-off period after a contract has been signed, unless the contract specifies otherwise. The amount of time varies with the state: in SA you have two working (business) days, in the ACT and VIC three working days, and in NSW, NT and QLD five. There's no cooling-off period in TAS or WA. Working days are non-bank holidays from Monday to Friday from 9am to 5pm, therefore if you sign a contract of sale in QLD on a Saturday, your cooling-off period is until 5pm on the following Friday.

☑ SURVIVAL TIP

During the cooling-off period, you have the right to withdraw from the purchase without losing your deposit, although you forfeit 0.25 per cent of the purchase price, known as the termination penalty. If you wish to withdraw from the purchase, you must notify the agent in writing within the cooling-off period. The agent or seller has 14 days to refund the 10 per cent deposit minus the termination penalty. Note that vendors sometimes refuse to sell unless a certificate waiving the cooling-off period is signed.

Buying at Auction

Buying property at auction is popular in Australia, where between 30 and 50 per cent of properties (usually in cities) are purchased under the auctioneer's hammer. Auctions have become increasingly popular in the last few years (they're most common in Melbourne and Sydney), as sellers can sell quickly and buyers can usually save money. If you have an eye for a bargain or enjoy the excitement of bidding, you may wish to consider buying a property at auction.

However, it's important to do your homework before buying at auction. In particular, you should ascertain the true market value of the property, arrange your finance, inspect the property thoroughly, check the conditions of purchase and carry out (or instruct your lawyer to do so on your behalf) checks on the property such as the title, registration, debts and planning developments for the area around the property (see **Conveyance** below).

Tips when buying at auction:

- do your research thoroughly – learn the area like the back of your hand;
- be selective – have a number of targets and move on if the price gets too high;
- find the TRUE market value;
- attend open homes to assess the level of interest;
- consider making a pre-auction offer (many vendors will accept a reasonable pre-auction offer);
- talk to your bank early if you need a mortgage;
- attend auctions as an observer before bidding;
- stick to your limit – but don't lose a property for the sake of a few thousand dollars;
- be prepared – arrive early – stay calm;
- bid late – wait until a property is 'on the market' (when the reserve has been met);
- don't worry about dummies, i.e. dummy bidding to drive the price up;
- go slow – ignore the recommended bid increase and go up slowly.

You also need to steel your nerves so that you don't get carried away and bid over your budget! If you're interested in an auction property, you could consider making a pre-auction bid of around 20 to 30 per cent less than its market value. Prices fetched at auction are notoriously unreliable, and sellers who are 'jittery' may (legally) agree to a deal before the auction, in which case you could have yourself a bargain.

You can engage a buyer's representative to find a house, bid for it at auction and negotiate the sale. Agents may charge as little as a few hundred dollars to bid at an auction or up to 3 per cent of the price if they also conduct searches (regarding title, etc.). However, this can save you a lot of money, time and trouble.

Auction contracts rarely include conditional clauses such as the purchase being subject to a favourable building inspection, which means buying at auction is riskier than a conventional purchase. In addition, cooling-off rights don't apply when buying at auction.

For auction results, see  www.homepriceguide.com.au/index.cfm?source=apm.

CONVEYANCE

Conveyance is the legal term for the process of buying and selling property (real estate) and transferring the deed of ownership, a legal document that conveys a property from the seller to the buyer. There are two main stages of conveyance: the first takes you up to the exchange of contracts; the second leads to the completion of the sale, when you become the new owner.

Conveyance in Australia is usually done by a lawyer (solicitor) or a conveyancer (also called a land broker, land agent or settlement agent), although you can also do it yourself. Irrespective of whether you employ a professional or do your own conveyance, the following should be done before a purchase:

- Verifying that a property belongs to the vendor or that he has legal authority to sell it.
- Checking for the existence of any clauses in the deeds restricting the use, development and possibly appearance of the property (known as restrictive covenants).
- Checking that there are no encumbrances or liens, e.g. mortgages or loans, against a property or any outstanding debts such as local taxes or utility bills – or that these are cancelled by the vendor before completion, i.e. a conditional clause to that effect is inserted into the contract.

▲ Caution

You must ensure that any debts against a property are cleared before you complete a purchase, as the new owner is liable for any debts on a property once it's sold.

- Enquiring about any planned developments that may affect the value of the property (like a new airport runway or motorway at the bottom of the garden).
- Ensuring that planning or building permits are in order (e.g. for water, electricity and sewerage connection). You should also check the drainage or sewerage service diagrams for a home.
- Ensuring that the property has a pest inspection certificate.
- Ensuring that legal title is obtained and arranging the necessary registration of ownership and payment of taxes such as stamp duty.

If you're buying a community property, the following checks should also be carried out:

- In the case of a Company Title property, verifying that the other owners approve of your purchase.
- Verifying that all community levies on the property are up to date and there are no debts.
- Finding out if there's any imminent community expenditure that requires a high one-off payment.
- Checking that your enjoyment of the property won't be adversely affected by any community by-laws.

Inventory

When moving into a property that you've purchased, you should check that the previous owners haven't absconded with anything that was included in the purchase price (and detailed in the contract), such as carpets, curtains, doors, fitted cupboards, kitchen appliances and light fittings, or have substituted inferior items. You should also note the reading on your meters (electricity, gas, water, etc.) and check that you aren't overcharged on your first bill. Meters should be read by the relevant authorities before you move in, which you may need to organise.

UTILITIES

Utilities is the collective name for electricity, gas and water supplies. Electricity and gas are used for cooking and heating in cities and towns throughout Australia, and it's common for homes to have both, although most new homes have electricity only. Many metropolitan households use gas for cooking and heating, and some 5 per cent of Australian homes use solar energy for heating water. In recent years, Australia has been hit by the increasing demands for power (particularly to run air-conditioners), sharply higher electricity costs and a chronic shortage of surface water. State governments are trying to encourage people to conserve energy (without much success) and to introduce new energy-efficient building standards.

Each state and territory has its own Energy Commission, which regulates local energy providers; Energy Commissions used to be owned and administered by local governments but are now mostly privatised. There are a number of electricity generating and electricity and gas distribution companies in most states, including the following (there's more choice in NSW, South Australia and Victoria):

- **Actew AgL** (💻 www.actewagl.com.au): based in the ACT, supplying electricity, gas and water.
- **Aurora energy** (💻 www.auroraenergy.com.au): Tasmania's electricity supplier, connected to nearly every household in Tasmania.
- **Australian Gas Limited** (AGL, 💻 www.agl.com.au): sells gas and electricity, and has 3m customers across Australia.
- **Energy Australia** (💻 http://energy.com.au): one of Australia's larger electricity and gas suppliers, providing energy to over 1.5m Australian homes and businesses. It currently operates in the ACT, NSW, SA and VIC.
- **Ergon Energy** (💻 www.ergon.com.au): Queensland's electricity supplier, also operating in the ACT, NSW and VIC.
- **ETSA Utilities** (💻 www.etsautilities.com.au): the South Australia electricity distributor.
- **Integral Energy** (💻 www.integral.com.au): the second-largest state-owned energy corporation in NSW, distributing electricity to over 2m people.
- **Power & Water** (💻 www.powerwater.com.au): the Northern Territory's major provider of electricity, sewerage and water services.
- **Western Power** (💻 www.westernpower.com.au): Western Australia's leading energy corporation.

The following is the key information relating to utilities in Australia; for further details, refer to our sister-publication *Buying a Home in Australia*.

- **Electricity:** The supply is 240/250 volts AC with a frequency of 50 Hertz (cycles). Plug configurations are unique to Australia and New Zealand, and light bulbs (globes) are of the bayonet, not screw, type.
- **Gas:** Mains (natural) gas is available in all main cities, although there may be no supply in older homes.
- **Heating & air-conditioning:** Central heating may not be installed in homes in eastern, northern or western Australia, as the climate doesn't usually warrant it (although Sydney can get quite cold in winter). Conversely, air-conditioning is considered a luxury in the south of the country but is a 'necessity' in the north and west.
- **Water:** Most homes in Australia have a water meter. Australian mains water is safe to drink, although it can taste awful.

> **▲ Caution**
>
> **Water**
>
> Australia is the world's driest continent and experiences some of the world's most prolonged droughts, resulting in severe water shortages (and consumption restrictions) in many areas.

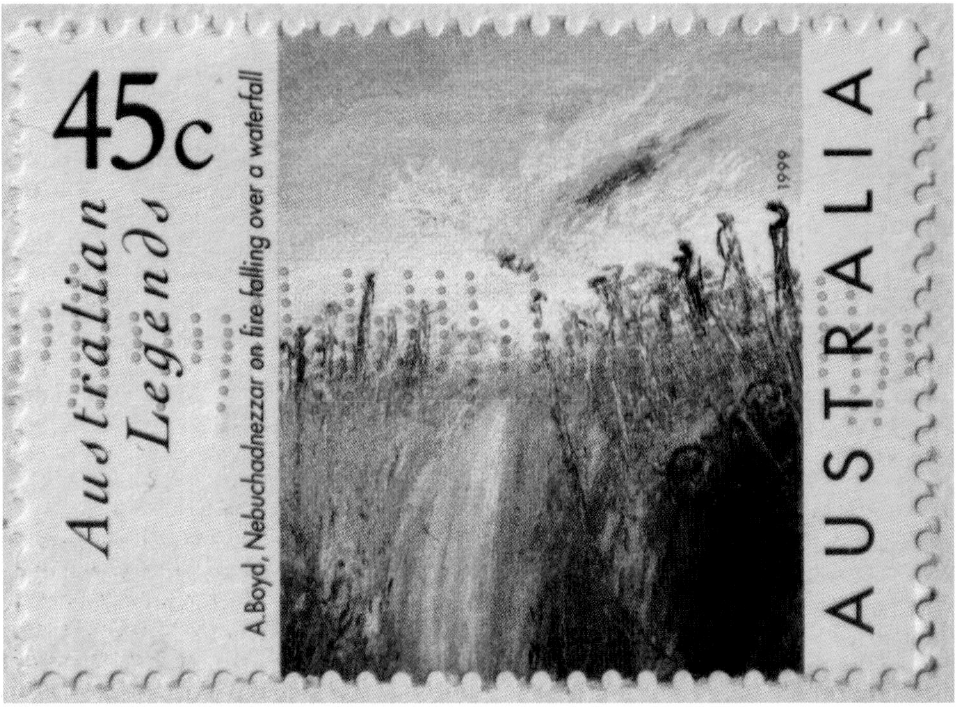
45c
Australian Legends
A.Boyd, Nebuchadnezzar on fire falling over a waterfall
1999
AUSTRALIA

AUSTRALIA
45c

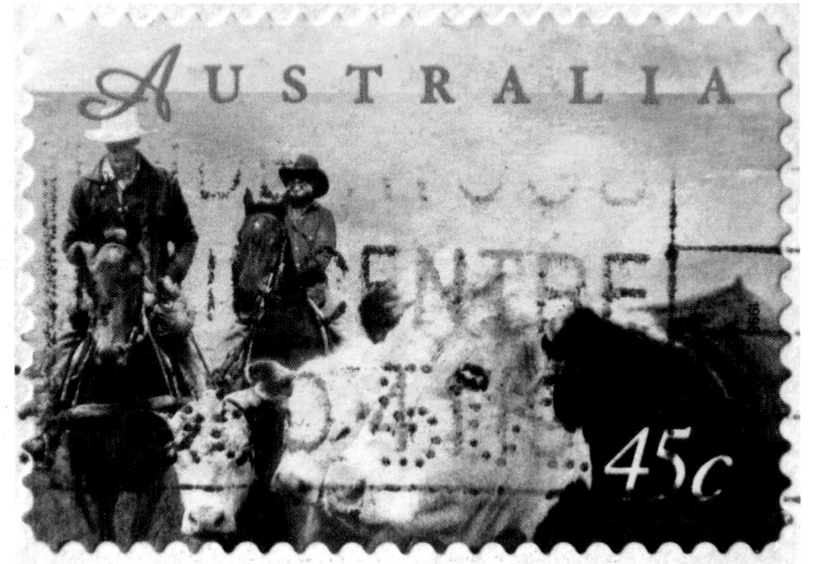

6.

POSTAL SERVICES

Australia Post (AP) handles over 5bn items of post per year (a large percentage of which is junk mail) and provides one of the best services in the world in terms of cost, reliability and speed. AP underwent deregulation in 1994, when parts of the business were opened to private competitors, but maintains a monopoly on letters weighing up to 250g. However, it has since gone from strength to strength and is a highly profitable and well run business.

There's a post office or AP agency in most main towns (a total of over 3,000), offering a wide range of services, most of which are described in this chapter. In rural and outback towns, post services are provided by an AP agency (e.g. a café/restaurant, general store or petrol station) licensed to provide most of the services offered by a main post office. Post offices provide a wide range of services, including 'faxpost', money orders (up to $5,000), passport applications, foreign currency, *poste restante* service, stamps and telegrams, gifts (e.g. at Christmas from AP shops or by mail-order), and stationery and office products (listed in a catalogue).

Stamps can be purchased at post offices, hotels, motels, newsagents, shops and from vending machines. Most machines issue fixed-value stamps, although new electronic machines print gummed postage 'labels' to the exact value required. No surcharge is levied by private stamp vendors in Australia.

AP produces a wealth of free brochures regarding postal rates and special services, most of which are available from any post office. A general *Post Charges* booklet contains details of most services and rates, and a comprehensive *Post Guide* ($50) is available for businesses. Information about AP's services is also available by phone (☏ 137678, Mon-Fri only) and via the internet (💻 www.auspost.com.au).

Private companies such as Mail Boxes Etc. (💻 www.mbe.com.au) also provide a wide range of postal services (e.g. post boxes), as well as business services, courier, fax and telephone. There's a thriving courier business in Australia, particularly in the major cities, where 24-hour domestic and international courier services are provided by many companies – in addition to AP – including Allied Express, Couriers Please, DHL, Fastway, FedEx and TNT.

BUSINESS HOURS

Post office business hours in Australia are usually from 9am to 5pm, Monday to Friday, although some post offices open on Saturday mornings, e.g. from 9am to noon. In major cities, general post offices may have slightly longer business hours, for example Sydney general post office (Martin Place) is open from 8.15am to 5.30pm, Monday to Friday and from 10am to 2pm on Saturdays. Post offices in major towns don't close at lunchtime. In country and outback areas, AP agencies generally have the same business hours as post offices, but may close for an hour for lunch or shut earlier in the afternoon. They may also open on Saturday mornings and have extended opening hours on some evenings.

LETTER POST

AP's letter handling system is generally efficient and reliable. If you send a letter with insufficient postage, it's usually delivered,

although the addressee is charged $1 plus the deficient postage (this also applies to parcels). If the post office is unable to deliver a letter, it's returned to the sender with a note stating the reason it couldn't be delivered.

Post Boxes & Deliveries

Post boxes in Australia are red with a white stripe and modern post boxes look like litter bins, although there are still some Victorian 'receiving pillars' around. In cities and large towns, there are express 'gold' post boxes (see **Express Service** below). Post boxes are scarce in rural areas and you may need to take your mail to a post office or agency.

In major towns and metropolitan areas, there are deliveries once a day, Monday to Friday, while in remote areas deliveries may be made just once or twice a week and they can be affected by the weather, as mail is usually delivered by air (in rural areas, mail is deposited in mailboxes situated at the perimeter of properties). Local post is usually delivered the next day and interstate post to major towns and cities in one to two days. However, deliveries to rural locations officially take two days in the same state and up to four days interstate. There are no weekend deliveries anywhere in Australia.

In the outback, post must usually be collected from a local post office or agency. You can also hire a post box (small, medium, large) or a 'locked bag' for large volumes of mail, e.g. for businesses. AP also provides a Mail2Day service, whereby you're informed when you have mail by email ($55 per year) or SMS ($89 per year).

Domestic Letters

For the standard domestic post service there's a single rate for 'small' letters and three rates for 'large' letters. Maximum limits for small letters are: size 130 x 240mm, thickness 5mm and weight 250g. Large letters must be rectangular, maximum size 260 x 360mm, thickness 20mm and weight 500g. The rates are as shown in the table below.

Parcel post rates apply to letters over 500g (see below). Domestic Christmas greeting cards posted in November and December are charged at a reduced rate of 55¢. Domestic post charges also apply to the Australian Antarctic Territories, Christmas Island (Indian Ocean), the Cocos (Keeling) Islands and Norfolk Island. Domestic post is sent by air between states or to remote areas within Australia.

Peel-and-stick (no licking) 60¢ stamps are available in booklets of 10 ($6), 100 ($60) and

Domestic Letter Rates

Size & Weight	Rate
Small letters (up to 250g)	$0.60 (priority $2.60, express $5.25)
Large letters	
– Up to 125g	$1.20
– 125 to 250g	$1.80 (express $6.65)
– 250 to 500g	$3.00

200 ($120). Pre-paid envelopes are available in various sizes.

Express Service

AP provides an express domestic letter post service with guaranteed next day delivery within states, between the capital city and provincial centres. Outside these areas, the fastest possible delivery is provided, but there are no guarantees. No paperwork or forms need be completed as items are sent in pre-paid envelopes or 'satchels'. There are three sizes of pre-paid envelope: DL window and C5 (both $5.25) and B4 ($6.65), which can be used for letters and documents up to 500g and 20mm thick. Express post satchels are available in three sizes (items can be any thickness): up to 500g ($9.55), up to 3kg ($13.05) and up to 5kg ($21.65). Items weighing 5 to 20kg or too large for an express satchel must be sent as express post parcels (see below). All types of envelopes and satchels are available in packs of ten.

Pre-paid envelopes and satchels can be handed in at post offices or posted in express 'gold' post boxes in cities and major towns. Items must be presented at a post office before close of business or the post closing time in some provincial centres. Items posted by 6pm (earlier in Perth and some provincial centres), Monday to Friday, are guaranteed next day delivery to Australia's capital cities and some provincial centres. The cost is refunded if items aren't delivered the next working day.

Express post must not be used to send cash, gold, jewellery, negotiable securities, precious stones or other valuables, which should be sent by registered post (see **Important Documents & Valuables** below).

State Abbreviations/Postcodes

State/Territory	Abbr.	First Digit
Australian Capital Territory	ACT	2
New South Wales	NSW	2
Northern Territory	NT	0
Queensland	QLD	4
South Australia	SA	5
Tasmania	TAS	7
Victoria	VIC	3
Western Australia	WA	6

Australian Addresses

The majority of mail in Australia is sorted by machine, which is facilitated by the use of full and correct postal addresses (omitting all punctuation). All items of post should have a four-digit postcode (zip code) after the town and state or territory. In major cities, codes indicate whether the town is a suburb of a major city, e.g. 2000 is the central business district (CBD) of Sydney and postcodes from 2001 to 2786 are suburbs. A post office box number (also referred to as a locked or private bag) should be prefixed by 'PO Box'. All addresses must contain the name of the state or territory, which are abbreviated as shown in the table above.

Postcodes are listed at the back of the *White Pages* or you can call 131317 for information. You can buy envelopes with pre-printed squares for the postcode. A typical Australian address is shown below:

Bruce & Sheila Kelly
99A Waltzing Matilda Street
Wooloowolloolulu
Sydney
NSW 2005

You should always put your address on the back of letters so that they can be returned if they cannot be delivered. Note that Australia's various islands, such as Norfolk and Christmas Islands and the Australian Antarctic Territory, all have their own unique postcodes.

International Letters

AP provides four services for international letters: airmail, economy airmail, express post international and seamail, detailed below. The fastest way to send post overseas via a post office is by EMS international courier, although this is an expensive option for letters. Delivery times for international mail are:

Parcels are usually delivered the next working day within the metropolitan area of capital cities and certain large towns in the same state, and within two working days to other locations in the same state. Interstate parcels are delivered within two to six working days, depending on the destination, although AP is unreliable regarding deliveries to rural locations.

AP provides an express domestic parcel service. There's guaranteed next day delivery between Australia's capital cities (except Darwin) and some other major towns; you can claim a refund if a parcel isn't delivered the next day. The service also operates within states between the capital city and provincial centres. Outside these areas, there are no delivery guarantees.

AP provides four services for international parcels: airmail, express courier international, express and sea post, which are also priced by both weight and zone.

Customs Declaration

Parcels sent to foreign addresses that are uninsured, weigh up to 2kg and have a value below $500, must be accompanied by a green *Customs/Douane* form CN22. (No customs form is required for letters.) For uninsured items weighing over 2kg or valued at over $500 you must also complete form CP72 (blue). For insured items you must complete form CP74 (red). Items valued at over $2,000 require a customs Export Declaration Number. Press firmly when completing customs forms, some of which have six copies!

Gifts sent to Australia with a value up to $1,000 are duty-free, except for alcohol and tobacco products; for gifts exceeding $1,000, duty is payable on the value in excess of $1,000. The value of packages that are part of a larger consignment are totalled for customs purposes.

Restrictions

There are restrictions on the sort of goods that can be posted in Australia (see below), and senders of all international parcels and satchels must sign a *Dangerous Goods Declaration*. A dangerous goods brochure, *Some Things Were Never Meant To Be Posted*, is available from post offices and lists what cannot be sent through the post. This includes anything that is alive, corrosive, explosive, flammable, oxidising, radioactive, or likely to deteriorate during its journey through the post (e.g. kippers). Many overseas countries have restrictions on certain items, such as alcohol and medicines.

A leaflet entitled *Packaging Hints* is available from post offices, describing how to pack goods for sending through the post.

'Postpak' packaging products, including boxes (or gift boxes), posting tubes and accessories, padded bags and tough bags are available from AP shops and stationery stores.

IMPORTANT DOCUMENTS & VALUABLES

The post office provides a number of services for the delivery of important documents and valuables:

Registered Post

If you're sending valuables, money or important documents, you should use registered post. You're obliged to use pre-paid envelopes for international post, but not for domestic post. Domestic pre-paid envelopes are available in two sizes: small or DLE (130 x 240mm, 5mm thick) and large or B4 (250 x 353mm, 20mm thick). Alternatively, domestic registered post labels for attaching to standard envelopes are available singly from $3.20 or in boxes of 50. International registered post is available only for letters and documents with the same size envelopes as the domestic service.

You receive a receipt for registered post, which must be signed for on delivery, although the signatory doesn't need to be the addressee. However, a person-to-person option is available, where a registered article must be signed for by the person to whom it's addressed.

Insurance

Domestic and international registered post is insured free for up to $50 against loss or damage. Additional insurance is available for domestic registered post for $9.60 for the first $100 insured and $2.50 for each additional $100, up to a maximum of $5,000. No insurance is available for international registered post but insurance up to $5,000 is available for Express Courier International services.

For insured international letters and parcels, customs forms CP74 (red) must be completed.

Delivery Confirmation

Delivery confirmation is available with registered post, insured items and, for some countries, parcel post. Delivery confirmation costs an additional $2.10 per article for domestic registered post ($5.80 for addressee confirmation); international delivery confirmation costs $3.70 per article plus postage. Proof of delivery must be requested at the time of posting. Signed evidence of delivery is returned to the sender, but not from a named individual.

BILL PAYMENT

AP operates the country's largest bill payment service, 'Postbillpay', at post offices, by phone (131816) and via the internet (💻 www.postbillpay.com.au). Some 160 organisations offer customers the option of paying their bills at post offices, including credit card companies; councils (for rates); electricity, gas, water and telephone companies; and insurance companies – some 25 per cent of consumer bills are paid at AP's retail outlets. AP handles over 175m financial transactions per year through its electronic retail network and provides one of the country's largest banking services (GiroPost).

CHANGE OF ADDRESS

When moving house within Australia, you should obtain a 'Mover's Kit' brochure from a post office containing a *Change of Address Request* form, a brochure describing the service, a moving home checklist and six postcards to inform your relatives and friends about your move (Australians don't have many friends). The change can be permanent or temporary and post can be forwarded, held at your local post office or collected from a nominated post office. Proof of identity must be provided when submitting the form and a minimum of three working days' notice is required. There's a fee of $17.50 for one month ($28.50 for 3 months) for individuals – there's no charge for certain pensioners and sickness beneficiaries – and $55 for one month ($147 for 3 months) for businesses. There's an additional charge for the redirection of parcels.

AP provides a 'priority address notification' service which saves time and effort in informing organisations of your address. Upon receipt of your *Change of Address* form, AP sends you a list of companies which you may wish to notify of your new address. If you're a customer of any of the companies listed on the form, simply tick the box beside the company's name and AP will inform them of your change of address free of charge.

AP provides a wide range of Moving Services – see their website for information (💻 www.movingservices.com.au).

If you're only going to be away from home temporarily, AP provide a mail holding service and a temporary redirection service.

7. TELECOMMUNICATIONS

Almost all Australian homes have a telephone and Australia also has one of the highest per capita rates of mobile phone ownership in the world. Due to its huge size, telecommunications in Australia have always been important and it employs the latest broadband cable, digital, fibre optic and satellite systems, although broadband services are often poor and relatively expensive. Under the National Broadband Network initiative (see 💻 www.nbn.gov.au), currently being rolled out across the country, some 93 per cent of homes and business should be connected to the internet via a fast and affordable fibre-optic cable network, with the remainder connected via fixed wireless or satellite.

The telecommunications industry is regulated by the Australian Communications & Media Authority/ACMA (💻 www.acma.gov.au – the website provides a number of useful factsheets about telephone services) and has its own ombudsman (☎ 1800-062058, 💻 www.tio.com.au). The ombudsman attempts to resolve complaints concerning telecommunications issues, but only after consumers have tried to settle them with the company or carrier concerned.

> ☑ **SURVIVAL TIP**
>
> **The general emergency telephone number throughout Australia is ☎ 000.**

TELEPHONE COMPANIES

The Australian telecommunications market was deregulated on 1st July 1997 and around 30 companies now operate in the country, although the market is still dominated by Telstra (💻 www.telstra.com.au), formerly Telecom Australia and privatised in 2006. Its main rival, Optus (💻 www.optus.com.au), established in 1992 and owned by Cable & Wireless, has around a third as many customers. Other major telecommunications companies include Gotalk (💻 www.gotalk.com.au) and Primus (💻 www.primus.com.au).

Customers in most regions and major cities can choose their carrier. To use a particular carrier, you must open an account with them and may either pre-select that company or dial an access code before an STD or overseas number. Local number portability (LNP), which allows users to switch between telephone companies without changing their number, has been introduced. However, if you sign up with a company you may have a prefix assigned to your telephone number and your calls will automatically go through your selected company when you dial. If you make a lot of international calls, it may be beneficial to sign up with a number of companies and 'cherry pick', using the one that offers the lowest rate to the country you're calling.

Since deregulation, international and long-distance telephone charges have been slashed by up to 70 per cent, the price of mobile telephone calls has fallen by 50 per cent and that of local calls by around 12 per cent. However, despite the increased competition, deregulation has failed to deliver all the expected benefits to consumers.

Before signing up with a telephone company, check the competition and compare rates.

You should continually monitor the market, as new deals are constantly being introduced and what was the best offer last month (or week) is unlikely to remain so for long. Many companies offer a range of services, which may include high speed access to online and interactive services such as the internet, local and long-distance telephone services and pay television (TV). This may be beneficial, as many companies offer attractive package deals if you buy two or more services, such as telephone and pay TV.

INSTALLATION & REGISTRATION

Before moving into a new home, check whether there's a telephone line and that the number of lines or telephone points is adequate (most homes already have telephone lines and points in a number of rooms). If a property has a cable system or other telephone network, you don't require a Telstra telephone line. However, if you move into a house or apartment where you aren't the first resident, a telephone line will almost certainly already be installed, although there's usually no telephone. If you're moving into a house or apartment without a telephone connection, e.g. a new house, you must usually apply to Telstra for a line to be connected.

To have a telephone line installed or reconnected, call in at any Telstra shop or contact the Telstra Customer Service Centre (132200). Telstra will arrange a suitable date and time with you to connect your telephone service. Your telephone should be connected within 2 to 20 working days, although if Telstra needs to extend its network to reach your home, connection will take longer.

It costs $59 to have an existing Telstra service reconnected and $299 for a new connection (more if Telstra extends the network when up to $1,540 is charged). The laying of underground cable, known as 'trenching', from your property to the Telstra network is your responsibility and should only be carried out by authorised cablers. Telstra can provide details of registered cablers in your area.

If you're moving house within the same exchange area and call-charging zone, you may retain your old number; otherwise your old number is typically re-allocated to the incoming customer at your old address.

When you register for a telephone line, you're required to provide details of your occupation, credit card and driving licence. Credit assessments are made for all customers and your billing period may depend on your credit assessment. Payment of a security bond may be required (e.g. $250 or $500), which is generally repaid after 12 months when you've established a satisfactory payment record.

USING THE TELEPHONE

Using the telephone in Australia is much the same as in any other country, with a few local eccentricities thrown in for good measure. In some remote areas, for example, there are manual exchanges where you must call the local operator to make a call. Some outback areas in the Northern Territory and Western Australia have radio telephones, where numbers are prefixed by R/T. Calls to R/T numbers can be made via the national network and radio telephone exchanges, although they're expensive. A radio telephone is like using a two-way radio and only one person can speak at a time; you need to say 'over' when you finish speaking and cannot interrupt the other person. Party lines (shared by two or more homes) are common in the outback.

Because of the huge time difference between Australia and many other countries, you should always check the local time when making international calls. If you have a problem obtaining a number, check that it's correct in the *White Pages* or by calling directory enquiries on 1223 (local and national) or 1225 (international). An information line, called Easy Info (12452), provides up to five information searches, e.g. addresses, telephone numbers and time zones, for a single call costing $2.50. For operator assistance dial 1234 (see **Operator-assisted Calls** below). *Yellow Pages* can also be accessed online (💻 www.yellowpages.com.au).

You can report line faults 24 hours a day to Telstra on 132203 (residential lines), 132999 (business lines) or 125111 (mobile phones). Telstra aims to repair telephone services within one working day in urban areas, two days in rural areas and three days in remote areas. If your health, life, safety or shelter may be at risk without a telephone, you can register for a priority repair service (24 hours, seven days a week).

If you suspect that your telephone is faulty, test the line with another telephone if you have one or test your telephone on another line, e.g. that of a friend or neighbour. A priority repair service is provided for non-commercial emergency and essential service organisations, and to individuals whose life, health, safety or shelter would be at risk without a telephone.

Codes & numbers

All Australian fixed line numbers have eight digits. The area codes for states and their capital cities are as shown below.

Telephone directories usually list the state code in brackets before the subscriber number, e.g. (02) 1234 5678. If you're using a service other than Telstra, you must dial the company's prefix unless you've preselected the company, in which case the prefix is automatically dialled when you make a call. Mobile telephone numbers have the prefix 04. When dialling a number within your own exchange area, dial only the number, e.g. if you live in New South Wales (NSW) and wish to dial another subscriber in NSW or the Australian Capital Territory (ACT). When dialling anywhere else, the area code must be dialled before the subscriber's number.

When dialling a number in Australia from overseas, dial the international access code of the country from which you're calling (e.g. 00), followed by Australia's international code (61), the area code without the first 0 (e.g. 2 for Sydney) and the subscriber's number. For example, to call Sydney 1234 5678 from the UK, you would dial 00-61-2-1234 5678.

International Calls

International links are provided by the Overseas Telecommunications Commission (OTC) using undersea cables and satellites (Australia has telephone connections with around 200 countries via Intelsat). All private telephones in Australia are on International Direct Dialling (IDD), allowing calls to be dialled direct to over 250 countries. To make an international call, dial 0011, the country code, the area code without the first zero, and the subscriber's number. Dial 0101 for the

State Telephone Codes

State/Territory	Capital	Code
Australian Capital Territory	Canberra	02
New South Wales	Sydney	02
Northern Territory	Darwin	08
Queensland	Brisbane	07
South Australia	Adelaide	08
Tasmania	Hobart	03
Victoria	Melbourne	03
Western Australia	Perth	08

international operator (0107 from payphones) to make credit card calls, non-IDD calls, person-to-person and reverse charge calls (which aren't accepted by all countries). Dial 1225 for international directory enquiries. The international code for most countries is listed at the back of the *White Pages* under 'Telstra 0011 International and Telstra Faxstream 0015 International', as well as the time difference.

You can purchase a huge variety of pre-paid calling cards in Australia, which can be used to make both national and international calls (some cards can also be used to access the internet). Over a billion are sold annually by gas stations, convenience stores, delis, highway rest areas and numerous other outlets, including online. The cost of international calls with calling cards varies considerably, e.g. from as little as 0.5¢ per minute, but you also need to check call connection costs. The only drawback is that you need to enter a lot of digits to make calls. Also bear in mind that calls from mobile and public phones with calling cards (and calls to mobile phones from land lines) are MUCH more expensive than calls made from land lines to land lines. To check which calling card is best for you, see www.ozphonecard.com.au or www.ozprepaidcards.com.au.

Free, Premium Rate & Reduced Rate Numbers

Toll-free numbers, called freecall in Australia, have a prefix of 1800. Numbers with the prefix 13 or 1300 are usually charged at the local call rate from anywhere in Australia, although some numbers are restricted to callers within a city or state (see www.1300numbers1800numbers.com.au). Note that mobile phone carriers charge a fee for both 1300 and 1800 calls.

 **Caution**

Premium Rate Numbers

Calls to numbers with the prefix 19 are charged at premium rate (e.g. $5 a minute). You can instruct Telstra (13-2200) to restrict access to 19 numbers on your phone line.

The 1901 prefix is specifically reserved for 'restricted services', where a user must register with the provider of the service; these may include services of a sexual nature, although this isn't the only definition of 'restricted'.

Operator-assisted Calls

There's an extra charge for operator-assisted calls (dial 1234), and the minimum charge period is three minutes. The following operator services are available:

- **Ring Back Price:** A call can be timed and the charge given at the end of the call. If you want to know the cost of a national or international call, dial 1222 before the number and the cost is given (for a fee) at the end of your call. Although useful when you aren't using your own telephone and must pay for a call, using 'ring back price' is expensive.
- **Particular Person Call:** You can make an international particular person call (called a personal or person-to-person call in most other countries), where you start paying for the call only when the person required comes on the line, although it may be cheaper to make a brief call to find out whether the person you wish to speak to is available.
- **Reverse Charge Call:** A collect, reverse charge or transferred call, is where the person called agrees to pay for it. This is useful when you've no change or a payphone won't accept your coins. Making a reverse charge international call is very expensive, as it's charged at the operator connected call rate. For reverse charge calls, dial 12550. These calls cannot be made to mobile phones.
- **Wake-up Call:** To book a wake-up or reminder call, dial 12454.

CALL RATES

All telephone companies offer a range of telephone plans, which seem to be primarily designed so that users cannot compare rates from different providers. In 2012, Telstra were offering Homeline Budget ($22.95 per month), Homeline Reach ($49.90) and HomeLine Ultimate ($89.90) plans.

Telstra aren't mentioned here because they are recommended – they are likely to be among the most expensive deals available – but so that you can compare them with other offers (good luck!).

If you make a lot of international calls, you'll need to shop around for a plan that offers the best rates (or use **Internet Telephony** – see page 121). The best deal may be a package that includes home, mobile, broadband internet and TV services. **Bear in mind that you must usually sign up for a minimum 12-month period.**

Optus offers similar prices and options to Telstra, which are just as obscurely worded and as difficult to understand. A typical Optus plan charges 30¢ per call for local and 13/1300 calls and 80¢ per call for national calls and calls to Australian mobiles. International calls to selected countries. e.g. Canada, Ireland, New Zealand, the UK and the US cost 18¢ per minute.

Most telephone companies offer the option to check your telephone use and cost at any time. To use this service, you must register online and log into your account on the company›s website.

TELEPHONE BILLS

Most residential customers are billed quarterly or bi-monthly for calls, line rental and telephone rental (if applicable). Business customers usually receive their bills monthly, although both business and residential customers may be able to choose to be billed monthly, bi-monthly or quarterly. Telstra provides a payment card which allows you to pay your account in advance instalments. Where applicable, the telephone connection fee is included in your first bill.

Bills are itemised and show local, national and international calls separately, calls to mobile telephones, Homelink 1800 calls, operator-connected calls, Telecard calls, line and equipment charges, and telephone information services. Telstra also provides email delivery of customer bills and a website where customers can check the status of their account. Optus has an all-in-one billing service with a single bill for all services.

Telstra bills can be paid at any post office, by post to Telstra (PO Box 9901 in all capital cities), at Telstra shops (cash, cheques, credit/charge/debit cards), with a Telstra payment card, by electronic telephone banking, via the internet and by telephone (with a credit/debit card). Telstra accepts American Express, Bankcard, Diners Club, MasterCard, Redicard and Visa credit cards. If you have any queries about your Telstra telephone bill, call the Telstra Customer Service Centre (132200 for residential services) between 8am and 5pm, Monday to Friday.

If you believe that your bill is wrong, you need only pay the amount that isn't in dispute while your query is being investigated. If you fail to pay your bill, a reminder or a disconnection notice is issued. If you still fail to pay, your service is disconnected and reconnection takes place only after payment of the account in full, plus a reconnection fee.

PUBLIC TELEPHONES

Australia has two major payphone operators, Telstra (including solar-powered public telephone boxes in outback areas) and TriTel (💻 www.tritel.com.au). Telstra have removed many of their payphones, due to their declining profit, ongoing maintenance and repair costs – and, not least – the widespread use of mobile phones. Payphones can, however, still be found in busy city streets, residential suburbs, towns and villages, transport terminals, along highways, in hotels, inside and outside post offices, pubs, restaurants, service stations, shopping centres, universities, and other private and public buildings.

Telstra Payphones are regulated at 50¢ a local call and some payphones also have the ability to send SMS messages at 20¢ a message. Some Telstra payphones, particularly in central city locations, also have a teletypewriter facility. Generally, Telstra payphones accept all coins except 5¢ plus Telstra Payphone cards. Local 1800 numbers are free and therefore a variety of calling cards and services, such as the Telstra PhoneAway Card, can be used free of charge. Telstra payphones can also be used to call +800 (dialled as 00111800 + 8 digits), and 1100 (Dial Before You Dig) numbers without payment.

TriTel operates payphones generally on lease sites, which are usually located in shopping centres. Most shopping centres, particularly newer ones, have TriTel payphones rather than Telstra payphones. TriTel payphones are charged at 50¢ per 15 minutes for a local call and for most 1800 calls. They accept all coins and TriTel payphone cards, which are sold at newsagents.

Payphones don't issue change for any unused (coin) credit, but whole unused coins are returned to the user, and remaining credit can be used for another call by pressing the 'follow on call' button. If the display flashes, you need to insert more coins until the flashing stops. All payphones can also call emergency services (000) free of charge. Note that payphones don't accept incoming calls and when making an international call, you should insert at least $5 in coins or a Phonecard (see below) with a minimum $5 credit.

There are also thousands of privately-operated payphones, e.g. in bars and restaurants, although these can be very expensive to use. Making non-local calls from hotels is usually very expensive, although free local calls can often be made from telephones in a hotel lobby.

The latest smart payphones accept a range of payment options, including coins, credit/debit cards, calling cards, account cards, Phonecards and reverse charge calls. Telephone company calling cards can be used to make calls from any tone telephone, which includes all payphones and most private telephones, although they cannot be used from mobile phones (the cost of calls is added to your normal telephone bill).

Phonecards are available in denominations of $5, $10, and $20 and are available from thousands of retail outlets nationally (displaying a 'Phonecard Sold Here' sign), including kiosks, newsagents, pharmacies and shops. An audible signal is given when a Phonecard is nearing the end of its value. Phonecards can store and automatically dial telephone numbers through the use of Autocall features.

Some phones accept only credit and debit cards (e.g. American Express, Diners Club, MasterCard and Visa), which are predominantly located in major airports and other transport hubs, and large shopping centres. To use a credit card telephone, swipe the magnetic strip of your card through the telephone's card reader, enter your PIN and dial when you hear the dialling tone.

▲ Caution

There's usually a high minimum charge when using a credit card payphone, so they should be used only in an 'emergency'.

SMS text messages can be sent from smart payphones, which also have a hearing aid coupler and volume control for those with hearing problems (☏ 1800-068424 for information). Many payphones have also been modified so that they can be used by people with various other kinds of disability, including those in wheelchairs or with poor sight. If you have difficulties, call the operator on 1234.

MOBILE TELEPHONES

The Australians love mobile phones and in 2012 there were as many mobile phones in use as people in Australia! Services are operated by Telstra (🖳 www.telstra.com.au), Optus (🖳 www.optus.com), Vodaphone (🖳 www.vodaphone.com.au) and Virgin (🖳 www.virgin.com.au). There are also a number of smaller companies such as TransACT (💻 www.transact.com.au) in the ACT and regional Victoria, and Southern Cross Telco (💻 www.sctelco.com.au).

The digital network covers some 99 per cent of the population, including all the major population centres and corridors, but only some 20 per cent of the country (all operators provide coverage maps). If you live or work in a remote area, you should ensure that a company's coverage includes that area.

In addition to services in the major metropolitan areas, Telstra mobile satellite and radio services provide mobile communications to the aeronautical, marine and remote land area markets. MobileSat allows you to plug a computer, fax machine or satellite navigation equipment into a terminal in an aircraft, boat or car and receive crystal clear communication wherever you are in Australia or up to 200km (124mi) off the coast. Australia subscribes to the GSM digital network, which allows the same telephone to be used in around 170 countries worldwide, including most of western Europe and parts of Asia, the Middle East, the Pacific, and central and South Africa (called international roaming).

Buying a mobile telephone is a minefield, as not only are there a number of networks to choose from (including 3G and 4G in some areas), but numerous contracts with different call charges, connection fees, insurance, monthly subscriptions and tariffs. Before buying a mobile, shop around and compare call rates, installation and connection charges, prices and features, and rental charges. If you're confused, eBay Australia has a mobile phone buying guide (💻 http://pages.ebay.com.au/buy/guides/mobile-phones-buying-guide).

Mobile phones are sold by specialist dealers, Telstra shops, and department and chain stores which have arrangements with service providers or networks to sell airtime contracts (along with telephones). Don't rely on getting good or impartial advice from retail staff, some of whom know little or nothing about telephones and networks (it's said that the difference between Clint Eastwood and a mobile phone seller is that Clint isn't a real cowboy). Retailers advertise in magazines and newspapers, where a wide range of special offers is promoted.

Calls to and from mobile telephones, including calls made from a fixed-line telephone, are much more expensive than calls between fixed-line telephones, and calls to 1800 numbers aren't free from mobile telephones.

If you choose a pre-paid phone without a contract, you can 'top up' your credit (up to $100 at a time) at post offices, department stores, supermarkets, convenience stores and mobile phone shops – you're given a receipt with an activation number on it – and there's no charge for receiving calls, as there is with some contracts (particularly for international and mobile-to-mobile calls).

Australia offers a wealth of options for those who don't wish to sign up to an expensive mobile phone contract and travellers who wish to make calls overseas from Australia and calls to Australia from overseas. If you have an overseas mobile phone (which must be unlocked) you can replace the SIM card with an Australian card and buy pre-paid credits as and when required. Pre-paid mobile services abound and include (in A-Z order) Boost mobile (💻 www.boost.com.au), Dodo (💻 www.dodo.com.au), Global Gossip (💻 www.globalgossip.com), Optus (💻 www.optus.com.au), Savvytel (💻 www.savvytel.com.au), Telstra PhoneAway (💻 www.telstra.com.au) and Virgin mobile (💻 www.virginmobile.com.au).

Free booklets, *Hold the phone – read this before you buy a mobile*, a general guide with advice on matters such as the different types of contract available, and *Mobile phone etiquette for Australia*, are available from the office of the telecommunications industry ombudsman (☏ 1800-062058, 💻 www.tio.com.au).

EMERGENCY NUMBERS

There's only one national emergency number in Australia – **000** – which is for ambulance, fire and police, as well as cave and mountain rescue services and the coastguard. Emergency calls are free from all telephones, including payphones. When you dial 000, the operator asks you which emergency service you require ("Emergency, which service please?") and you're immediately put through to that service. You must state clearly your name and location, and give a brief description of the emergency.

Lists of other '24-hour Emergency Numbers' and 'Personal Emergency & Help Services' are included at the front of the *White Pages* telephone directory and inside the front cover of the *Yellow Pages*. These include aviation search and rescue, chemist emergency prescriptions, child abuse, child protection, city missions, counselling for victims of crime, crime stoppers, crisis centre, customs 'coastwatch', dentists, distress call, doctors, domestic violence, drugs, electricity, gas, hospitals, kids' helpline, lifeline (see below), maritime rescue, Mindwise (mental health), poison information, rape line, state emergency service, translating and interpreting service, veterinary surgeons, water and youth line.

Lifeline (131114) provides a confidential, 24-hour counselling service in times of personal crisis throughout Australia for the cost of a local call.

See also **Emergencies** on page 195 and **Counselling** on page 206.

INTERNET

Australia is one of the highest (per capita) users of the internet in the world – in 2012 some 80 per cent of the population were online or used the web. A National Broadband Network (NBN, 💻 www.nbn.gov.au) is currently being built, although it isn't expected to be operational nationwide until 2021. When complete, the NBN is expected to connect some 93 per cent of homes and businesses to the internet via a fast and affordable fibre-optic cable network, with the remainder connected via fixed wireless or satellite.

Broadband connection and ADSL/DSL are popular and most of the population have access to it, although broadband speeds vary considerably and most people are unhappy with both the speed and cost. Australia rates lowly in international speed comparison tests and service is much slower and more expensive than most other industrialised countries. Around 20 companies provide broadband access, with monthly rates starting from around $40. Shop around as deals and conditions (e.g. a minimum one or two-year contract) vary considerably – compare the line speed and any restrictions on downloads (many deals have severe restrictions on the amount of data you can upload/download per month). Some of the best deals are for combined phone and internet packages.

There are internet service providers in all the major cities and many regional towns, and competition for customers is fierce. Major players include (in A-Z order) AAPT (💻 www.aapt.com.au), Big Pond (Telstra, 💻 www.bigpond.com), Dodo (💻 www.dodo.com.au), Grapevine (💻 www.grapevine.com.au), iinet (💻 www.iinet.com.au), Optus (💻 www.optus.com.au), Southern Cross Telco (💻 www.sctelco.com.au), TransACT (💻 www.transact.com.

au), Virgin (🖳 www.virginbroadband.com.au), Vodaphone (🖳 www.vodaphone.com.au) and Woosh (🖳 www.woosh.com).

Travellers are well-catered for in Australia, where internet cafés (from around $1.50 an hour) abound in the major cities and many convenience and other stores also provide internet access.

An excellent website for comparing broadband providers and internet plans is Broadband Guide (🖳 http://broadbandguide.com.au), which also provides a list of companies serving each region and town.

Internet Telephony

If you have a broadband internet connection, you can make long-distance and international phone 'calls' for free (or almost-free) to anyone with a broadband connection. Voice over internet protocol (VOIP) is the latest technology which is reshaping the telecoms landscape. The leading company in this field is Skype (🖳 www.skype.com) with some 700m registered users in 2012, while another major player is VOIP (🖳 www.voip.com). There are also other companies in the market.

All you need is access to a local broadband provider and a headset (costing as little as $15) or a special phone, and you're in business. Calls to other computers anywhere in the world are free, while calls to landlines are charged at a few cents a minute. The downside is that lines are prone to interference and sudden disconnections.

TELEGRAMS, TELEX & FAX

Australia Post closed its telegram (cable) service on 7th March 2011, although you can still send telegrams via companies such as iTelegram (🖳 www.itelegram.com) or Telegram Stop (🖳 www.telegramstop.com), but it's expensive.

Faxes can be sent from business offices, hotels and Telstra telephone centres in major towns and cities. Mobile telephone and portable computer users can use a portable fax, which allows fax transmissions to be made from virtually anywhere in Australia and overseas. International faxes can be transmitted to over 100 countries and to any fax machine in the world, provided IDD telephone access is available. When sending an international fax, dial 0015 (FaxStream Enhanced) instead of 0011, followed by the country code, area code and fax number. FaxStream Enhanced is a network of specially selected lines which provide optimum quality for international fax transmission.

Faxpost

Australia Post (see **Chapter 6**) provides a public fax and delivery service (FaxPost), which allows faxes to be sent to virtually anyone in Australia or overseas, irrespective of whether you or the recipient has a fax machine. FaxPost allows delivery of faxed documents to all major centres in Australia within two hours (or the same day) plus fast delivery overseas. To fax a document via FaxPost to someone in Australia without a fax machine, you fax the document to the Fax Centre Post Office nearest the addressee (there are around 2,000 throughout Australia); it's then delivered within two hours, the same day or by post, depending on your instructions.

Messages can be delivered to overseas addressees without a fax machine by courier messenger, often on the same day, or can be delivered next day by post. If you don't have a fax machine but the addressee does, you must deliver your document to the nearest Fax Centre, from where it's faxed to the addressee.

A document can also be sent to someone when neither party has a fax machine, in which case the document is delivered to the nearest Fax Centre and faxed to the Fax Centre Post Office nearest the addressee, from where it's delivered. The cost of receiving faxes (and sending domestic faxes) is $5 for the first page and $1.25 for each additional page, and for sending international faxes $10 for the first page and $2.50 for each additional page.

If you have a printer with a scanner feature, you can scan a document and send it as an email attachment – free of charge!

8. TELEVISION & RADIO

Australian television (TV) is among the best in the world, although over half the programmes are purchased from the UK and the US (most local content consists of current affairs, game shows, soaps and sport). However, 55 per cent of programmes broadcast between 6pm and midnight must be Australian produced plus 80 per cent of advertising between these hours.

The Australian Broadcasting Corporation (ABC, 💻 www.abc.net.au) — affectionately known as 'Aunty' after the British Broadcasting Corporation (BBC) on which it's modelled — is government-owned and operates both TV and radio stations throughout Australia. It's financed by the government and carries no advertising. Overall control of Australia's TV and radio services is by the Australian Communications and Media Authority (ACMA, 💻 www.acma.gov.au), which replace the Australian Broadcasting Authority (ABA) in 2005. No TV or radio licence is required.

TV programmes are listed in daily newspapers (Saturday editions also include Sunday programmes) and weekly guides such as *TV Week*, which is produced in separate editions for each state or territory (due to local time differences). Many Saturday and Sunday newspapers also contain free weekly TV and radio guides. However, few if any pay TV programmes are listed in most publications. Programmes can also be displayed via TV teletext or via the internet, e.g. 💻 www.yourtv.com.au. The time difference between the states (see page 326) means that nationwide programmes are broadcast at different times according to where you live in Australia.

TELEVISION

Free terrestrial (known as free-to-air) TV includes both government-owned and commercial stations. In addition, pay TV is provided (via cable) in most major cities, and satellite TV is also available in rural and outback areas.

Digital Television

Digital TV was introduced in early 2001 in Adelaide, Brisbane, Melbourne, Perth and Sydney, and in 2007 was available in all capital cities, many regional areas and some remote areas. The analogue TV signal will be 'switched off' between 2010 and 2013, depending on the state or territory. To find out if digital TV is available in your area, see 💻 www.digitalready.gov.au. Digital set-top TV boxes start from around $35 and HDTVs from around $170.

All new televisions sold in Australia are now High Definition (HD 1080P), therefore digital set top boxes are only required if you have an old analogue TV. Increasingly new televisions are, in many cases, also capable of receiving 3D television broadcasts and new TVs are provided with USBs and are capable of interconnecting with the internet, Skype, smart phones and similar devices.

Programmes

Australian TV is famous for its soaps, although some have terrible scripts and even worse 'acting'. The most popular Australian soaps include *Neighbours* and *Home and Away*, which are sold worldwide and are particularly popular in the UK. British comedy, drama and soaps are also popular in Australia, as are the 'better' American programmes. The choice of films on free-to-air (FTA) TV is usually terrible and you need to subscribe to pay TV to see the latest films (without ad breaks).

Australian TV isn't as paranoid about nudity as American TV, but you're unlikely to see any explicit sex (except perhaps on pay or satellite TV). News and current affairs programmes are popular, although news tends to be parochial and doesn't include much world news. There are good weather forecasts on all channels.

There's little good quality Australian produced comedy and drama, mainly because of lack of funds or small audiences.

The best Australian programmes are the so-called 'infotainment' shows, which show you how to revamp your garden, home, life, etc. for next to nothing.

Australian TV, particularly commercial stations, shows a surfeit of live sport, particularly at weekends. Coverage includes both local and international events, including American football, athletics, Australian rules football, baseball, basketball, cricket, motor racing, rugby, soccer, swimming and tennis. To protect significant sporting and cultural events from being bought by pay TV, the government introduced an 'anti-siphoning' list of events which should be televised free-to-air (FTA) to the general public. However, over half the events on the anti-siphoning list have never been shown at all on FTA TV and fewer than a third have been shown live on FTA. Pay TV companies are sometimes permitted to duplicate coverage of 'events' on the anti-siphoning list.

Standards & Equipment

The standards for TV reception in Australia aren't the same as in many other countries, as it uses the PAL-D system. TVs and video recorders manufactured for use in North America (NTSC standard) and for the European PAL B/G or PAL-I systems won't function in Australia. Some foreign TVs can be converted to Australia's PAL-D system, although it usually isn't worth the trouble and expense of shipping a TV (or VCR) to Australia.

The cost of a TV varies considerably according to its features, make, screen size and, not least, the retailer, although prices have tumbled in recent years (as they have around the world). A basic 19in LCD TV costs from around $170, a 32in LCD TV from $280 and a 55in LCD TV from $1,800. The latest Blu-Ray DVD players start at around $200. All the latest and most sophisticated entertainment systems are available in Australia. If you want a home theatre package it can cost anything from $500 to $5,000.

TV rental is offered by specialist national rental companies, such as Radio Rentals (💻 www.radio-rentals.com.au), who rent TVs by the day, week, month or even longer. However, it's always cheaper to buy than rent a TV, particularly over a long period. Radio Rentals also offer a 'rent try buy' scheme where you have the option to purchase a similar product to the one you're renting at the end of the 3-year rental term – for $1. Note, however, that you'll pay much, much more with this scheme that you would if you bought a TV outright (even if you borrowed the money).

Free-to-air Stations

There are five national terrestrial or free-to-air (FTA) networks in Australia: ABC, Seven, Nine, Ten and SBS. ABC (Australian Broadcasting Corporation) and SBS (Special Broadcasting Service) are government-owned, while Nine, Seven and Ten are commercial networks.

There are also FTA community television (CT – see 💻 www.communitytv.net.au) stations in the major cities, although these haven't really taken off. There are also a number of regional commercial stations (including NBN, Prime, Seven Network, Southern Cross, Ten Network and Win), Imparja Television (an Aboriginal commercial station), plus community, local and student TV.

Not all areas can receive all the national networks: most state capitals can receive between three and five, while in some remote areas ABC may be the only free-to-air station you can receive.

Australian Broadcasting Corporation (ABC)

ABC Television is a division of the Australian Broadcasting Corporation (💻 www.abc.net.au) established in 1956. Two ABC channels,

ABC1 and ABC2, are aired nationally; ABC2 is a digital-only channel that started broadcasting in 2005. The name of the local ABC station varies according to the state, e.g. it's called ABN in New South Wales (the N is for NSW) and ABV in Victoria, although it's usually found on channel two. There's also an ABC3 channel launched in 2009, which is a children's channel with programming from 6am to 9pm daily, targetting 6-15 year-olds. ABC24 (channel 24) is a 24-hour news channel launched in 2010, which provides the latest news every hour on the hour, interspersed with documentaries.

Being non-commercial, ABC holds the moral high ground with regard to quality programming (almost nothing American is aired!) and its output contains a large percentage of locally produced programmes with the emphasis on local and national news, current affairs, natural history (mostly about Australia) and sports coverage, as well as Australian arts and comedy programming. It also has a lot of British programming from the BBC, ITV and Channel 4. The ABC claims some 17 per cent of TV viewers (well behind the big 3 commercial stations) and is permitted to allocate 5 per cent of its viewing time to advertising future programmes and the sale of merchandise.

Commercial Television

Australia has three commercial networks: Nine, Seven and Ten, which are available in major cities and offer 24-hour programming. Seven Network has been the leading station for some years (with 29 per cent of viewers), although it's given a close run by Nine Network (27 per cent), with Ten bringing up the rear (21 per cent). Nine is unashamedly populist and produces game shows, lifestyle programmes, and news and current affairs programmes, but isn't so good at comedy and drama. Its other strength is sport, which dominates programming.

Seven Network is the second-highest rated network after Nine and is strong on comedy and drama, and more likely to show non-commercial programmes. Its most popular programmes include *Home and Away* and recent movies. Seven Network has weaker news and current affairs than Nine. Ten Network had given up trying to compete with Nine and Seven for the mainstream market and concentrates on screening popular American shows (*The Simpsons*, *Medium*) for the under 40s, although it has also had success with *Masterchef* and *Australian Idol*. It isn't strong on local programmes, although it did come up with *Neighbours* and *Heartbreak High*.

The quality of programmes on commercial TV varies from terrible to excellent. The competition to buy popular foreign (e.g. British and American) programmes and exclusive rights to sporting events is fierce, particularly with the increased competition from pay TV. It's hoped that this will result in the networks producing more of their own programmes, which, apart from being superior to a lot of the imported rubbish, are also a lucrative export product. Commercial TV networks currently produce just over half their programmes.

Advertisements on commercial TV are frequent and irritating, particularly when you're trying to watch a film or sport. Some sports events are ruined by commercial breaks, and advertisements are sometimes even screened during play at the bottom of the screen. Breaks tend to be more frequent and last longer than in many other countries and even exceed those on some American stations (where the advertisements seem to last longer than the programmes). The maximum

permitted advertising quota is an average of 13 minutes per hour, but when promotional slots and trailers are included it's much longer. Commercial stations are huge money-spinners and regularly change owners. Breakfast TV is popular on all commercial stations.

Imparja Television

Imparja Television (www.imparja.com) is an Aboriginal-owned and -run commercial TV station operating out of Alice Springs. It covers a third of the country, mainly in the Northern Territory, South Australia and western NSW. Broadcasts range from soap operas to programmes made especially for Aboriginal people.

Special Broadcasting Service (SBS)

The Special Broadcasting Service (www.sbs.com.au) is a government-sponsored, multicultural TV station, established in 1978 to provide multi-lingual radio and TV services that educate, entertain and inform all Australians and reflect Australia's multicultural society. SBS is available in all major cities and a number of regional areas, and attracts only some 5 per cent of viewers (there's now also an SBS2 station and plans for others).

It's similar to PBS in America, although it screens a large percentage of programmes in foreign languages with subtitles, in addition to English-language programmes. Although mainly funded by the government, it carries advertising. It's usually found on channel eight, although you need a special receiver in some areas.

SBS provides foreign 'culture' unavailable on other channels and excellent world news coverage, which is far superior to the more parochial output of ABC and the commercial stations. It also shows foreign sport (e.g. European soccer) that isn't found on commercial TV and is the traditional host channel of the (football) World Cup. It's sometimes criticised, however, as being insensitive to community needs and also shows a lot of 'trashy' foreign films.

Community Television

In 1993 the Australian Broadcasting Authority allocated licenses for a sixth television channel for non-profit community and educational use on a trial basis. Permanent licenses for Brisbane, Melbourne, Perth and Sydney were allocated in 2004, while trial licenses remain in effect in Adelaide, Lismore and Mount Gambier. The Australian Community Television Alliance (ACTA), established in March 2008, is the national representative organisation for community television.

There are community or local TV stations in all major cities including 31 Brisbane, Access 31 Perth, C31 Adelaide, C31 Melbourne, CTV Perth, TVS Sydney, LINCTV Lismore and Bushvision Mount Gambier. There's also student TV in some cities, such as RMITV in Melbourne, established by RMIT university students and the first community TV station to receive a test transmission permit.

Pay Television

Pay (or subscription) TV was introduced in Australia in 1995 and shouldn't be confused with pay-per-view, where subscribers pay on a per programme basis, e.g. for a live concert or sports event. With pay TV, viewers pay a monthly fee for a package of stations, delivered via cable or satellite (the same as Sky in the UK). Until recently there were two major pay TV operators in Australia, Foxtel and Austar, but in May 2012 Austar was acquired by Foxtel (www.foxtel.com.au), which is 50 per cent owned by Telstra. Foxtel is available to some 70 per cent of Australian homes and had 1.65m subscribers at the start of 2012.

Pay TV operators have been allowed to

broadcast advertisements since 1997, although advertising may not provide more than half of their income, which sometimes leads to advertisements occupying up to five minutes of every eight minutes of programming! However, some sports programmes and, occasionally, films are shown without interruptions.

If you want to watch live English Premiership soccer matches (or most other live sport), you'll need to subscribe to pay TV.

The installation of cables for pay TV in Australia was one of the largest and fastest such programmes undertaken anywhere in the world, and cable currently reaches over 3m homes, mostly in the major cities. Most homes in Brisbane, the Gold Coast, Melbourne and Sydney are cabled, plus parts of Adelaide and Perth. Cable is used to deliver FM radio, high-speed internet access, pay TV, telephone, and other interactive services such as community information systems. It also enables operators to offer pay-per-view films and other broadcasts on demand.

Unlike satellite and cable TV in Europe and North America, pay TV in Australia doesn't have sufficient big exclusive sports or entertainment specials to attract the average viewer (Australia's climate also means that many people have better things to do than watch TV). Foxtel is delivered by either cable (via the Telstra Cable network) or satellite, and is available to households in metro areas, including Sydney, Newcastle, Canberra, Melbourne, Brisbane, Gold Coast (cable only), Adelaide, Perth and Regional WA. You can check whether your home is covered by entering you postcode on their website (💻 www.foxtel.com.au/overview.htm).

Foxtel installation is free, with a monthly subscription fee of from $77 (family) to $132 (platinum HD), depending on the programme package. You can choose from a range of packages depending on your preferred viewing, e.g. sport or films. Subscriptions can be paid by cash at ANZ bank and post offices and by cheque, credit card, direct debit or money order. Foxtel's free iQHD service allows you to pause and rewind live TV and record two programs at the same time.

Although the major cities are dominated by Foxtel, the rest of the country is wide open and being exploited by small companies, such as TransACT (💻 www.transact.com.au) in the ACT and rural Victoria. You can also receive cable TV (and Foxtel programmes) via other providers such as Optus (💻 www.optuszoo.com.au/tvandvideo), which may be cheaper than Foxtel. You can compare pay TV providers via the internet (💻 http://youcompare.com.au/paytv). It may pay you to bundle your pay TV, broadband and phone services to get a better deal.

Pay TV subscribers usually receive free monthly programme guides, which may also be available from newsagents. However, most Australian newspapers and TV guides virtually ignore pay TV and don't list any programmes, while some list only selected channels.

DVDS

The purchase and hire of DVDs isn't as popular as it once was as nowadays it's possible to download and watch films via the internet – both legally and illegally – and many people now watch films via pay TV. However, there are still DVD shops in most towns and cities (and DVDs can also be rented by post), although they are a dying breed. Major rental chains include Blockbuster (💻 www.blockbuster.com.au), and the latest releases can also be purchased from stores such as J&B Hi-Fi (💻 www.jbhifi.com.au/dvd-movies-tv-shows), as well as from numerous online outlets. Most outlets also sell and hire (if applicable) computer games.

DVD rental shops usually open until 8 or 10pm, seven days a week. To rent a video or DVD you must usually be a member, which requires proof of address and verification of your signature. A parent is required to stand as a guarantor for those under 18.

> **☑ SURVIVAL TIP**
>
> **Some video shops have a children's membership scheme with deals for kids and cheap rental rates for children's films.**

The latest releases can be rented for around $10 per night, while older films can be rented for up to a week for as little as a few dollars. Rental outlets usually have special offers for film buffs such as a free old movie with each new release rented or seven old movies for a week for $10. You may also be able to hire the latest releases for a low fee on some nights (such as Tuesdays) for around $1.95.

Usually, you can hire up to three or four films at a time and must return them up to two hours before closing the following day. If you're late returning a film, you're charged an extra day's rental for each day overdue. DVDs can also be rented from some public libraries.

RADIO

Australian radio is regulated by the Australian Communications and Media Authority (ACMA). Radio reception is excellent in most parts of the country, including stereo radio, which is clear in all but the most remote areas. Radio is very popular, particularly among the young – three out of four teenagers listen daily. Local stations broadcast on the FM wave band in stereo or on the medium wave (MW) band. High-quality FM radio can also be received via cable or satellite, which provides dozens of stations. Last, but not least, you can receive hundreds of Australia radio stations via the internet, see 💻 www.australianliveradio.com.

The short wave (SW) band is useful for receiving foreign radio stations. Digital radio was introduced in 2001 and allows stations to transmit several channels of sound simultaneously, as well as text and pictures to a small screen attached to receivers.

There are literally hundreds of radio stations in Australia, including ABC, commercial, ethnic, community and university-based stations (operated on a shoe-string and run by volunteers). For a list of the major radio stations, see 💻 http://en.wikipedia.org/wiki/list_of_radio_stations_in_australia.

In the last few decades, dozens of public (community) radio stations have sprung up around Australia, supported by the government and various educational institutions. They often have a limited transmission range and cater for specific community groups within their areas, e.g. there are around 16 community stations in Sydney, which, although amateurish, are diverse and original.

ABC

The Australian Broadcasting Corporation (ABC) is government-funded and runs metropolitan radio stations in nine cities and 36 regional stations, including ABC Classic FM, Radio National and the Triple-J (JJJ) youth radio network. ABC metropolitan radio includes 702 Sydney and 774 Melbourne. It also operates the 24-hour Parliamentary & News Network, a parliamentary radio service broadcast to all capital cities except Darwin and Newcastle (lucky them!). The ABC is also responsible for Radio Australia, an international radio service broadcast via short wave and satellite (in English and eight other languages) to the Asia-Pacific region and worldwide, although services have been reduced in recent years and remain under threat from budget cuts.

ABC Radio National provides excellent news coverage (international news is sent by satellite from the BBC in London) and is broadcast nationwide on both AM and FM. However, in general, ABC stations aren't as popular as commercial stations and are regarded as the thinking person's radio stations. Triple-J is the one exception and is a good place to hear new music outside the main pop stream and plug into Australia's youth culture. There's no advertising on ABC radio stations.

Commercial Radio

Commercial radio stations are hugely popular in Australia and include large city stations with vast budgets and hundreds of thousands of listeners. The largest radio station networks in Australia are owned by Austereo, the Australian Radio Network and DMG Radio Australia.

The location of a station can be determined by its call sign, the first number of which is the same as a state or territory's postcode, e.g. 2UE is a Sydney station and 3CR is in Melbourne.

Stations provide a comprehensive service of consumer advice, education, local news and information, music and other entertainment, and traffic information. There are also 'talkback' stations (such as Melbourne's top-rated 3AW), which intersperse music with phone-in discussions. Many stations have star presenters whose 'fame' is often due to their outrageous and insulting behaviour towards their listeners (sports commentators can also be extremely rude about players' performances).

Stations cater for every musical taste, e.g. classical, easy listening, jazz, pop/rock, although pop stations are the most popular and cater mostly for mainstream tastes. Some stations even change their output, e.g. from easy listening to hard rock or vice versa, at the drop of a hat if their audience figures fall dramatically. Music is usually blended with news updates, traffic and weather reports, although some stations have taken to playing less music and telling jokes, which apparently receive a higher rating than music. Radio stations employ real comedians, not just DJs trying to raise a chuckle, with a down-to-earth sense of humour where anything goes and nothing is sacred.

As their name implies, commercial radio stations in Australia carry advertising, which is their main source of income.

Ethnic Radio

Australians can tune in to local radio broadcasts in over 50 languages, including Aboriginal radio in outback regions. One of these, the Special Broadcasting Service (SBS) was established in 1994 and like SBS TV (see above) broadcasts in many languages. It's available in all state and territory capital cities, plus some other cities.

BBC World Service

The BBC World Service (the insomniac's station) broadcasts worldwide, in English and around 35 other languages. The BBC World Service is the most famous and highly respected international radio service in the world, with regular listeners estimated at some 120m (give or take a few). Its main aims are to provide unbiased news, project British opinion, and reflect British culture, life and developments in science and industry. News bulletins, current affairs, political commentaries and topical magazine programmes form the bulk of its output, supported by drama, general entertainment, music and a comprehensive sports service. The BBC publishes a monthly magazine, *BBC On Air*, providing comprehensive information about BBC radio and TV programmes. A programme guide is available via the internet (💻 www.bbc.co.uk/worldservice/programmes).

9. EDUCATION

Australian educational institutions generally have a good international reputation, particularly universities and tertiary-level colleges, with some 250,000 foreign students in the Australian higher education sector. Australian schools provide a high standard of teaching and produce good academic results, and the country has a proud record of academic and scientific achievement.

Full-time education was introduced in Western Australia in 1871, other states following suit shortly afterwards, and is today compulsory between the ages of 6 and 17 in most states. Around 75 per cent of pupils complete 12 years of schooling, although this varies with the state or territory. Primary education lasts for six or seven years up to the age of 12 or 13 and secondary schooling for a further five or six years. Students are encouraged to remain at school until the completion of their 12th year (until the age of 18), although this may depend on the local job market. The government has cut unemployment benefits for young people in recent years to 'encourage' them to stay at school or take up training rather than searching for non-existent jobs. This has led to overcrowding in many high schools, where classes are bulging with students who don't want to be there.

Education in Australia is mainly the responsibility of state and territory governments, each of which has its own education system and provides most funding, supported by the federal government. States administer their own primary and secondary schools, and are also responsible for technical and further education. The federal government, through the Department of Education, Employment and Workplace Relations (💻 www.deewr.gov.au), is responsible for tertiary education and provides supplementary funding for schools and technical and further education. It's also responsible for education in the Australian territories of Christmas Island, the Cocos Islands and Norfolk Island.

Australian schools and universities rate highly in international surveys, with students doing particularly well in mathematics and science.

Illiteracy is a problem in Australia and is exacerbated by the thousands of migrant families who don't speak English or where English isn't spoken at home. Aboriginal children also have a low rate of literacy and are generally a few years behind other pupils.

There's no legal obligation for parents to educate their children at school and they may educate them themselves or employ private tutors (with the advent of the internet, it's possible for children to be educated almost exclusively at home). Parents educating their children at home don't require a teaching qualification, but must satisfy the local education authority that a child is receiving full-time education appropriate for his age and aptitude (the authorities may test your child). Information can be obtained from the Alternative Education Resources Group in most states.

Many schools have special programmes for children with learning difficulties and for gifted children, and there are also hospital schools, where children who need prolonged hospitalisation are educated, and special schools for blind and deaf children.

However, whenever possible, children with disabilities attend regular schools in which support is provided for them. Parents can obtain information from the Specific Learning Difficulties Association (💻 www.speld-sa.org.au).

The Australian term public school (or government school) refers to a 'free' (i.e. not fee-paying) school funded wholly from state and federal government budgets. However, in this book the term state school is used, to avoid confusion with the English term public school, which means a private school.

Australia has around 9,600 primary and secondary schools, some 27 per cent of which are private (mostly Catholic church schools with some Church of England and other parochial schools). Most state schools are co-educational (mixed) day schools, with the exception of a few secondary schools that accept boarders. It's generally considered that private schools are superior to state institutions and, although there's little difference between the best state and private schools, it's true that the worst-performing private schools are generally streets ahead of the worst state schools.

There are many books and magazines for parents who are able to choose between state and private education, including *Choosing a School* magazine (published in separate editions for Victoria and New South Wales), available from Universal Magazines (💻 www.universalmagazines.com.au). Information about education in individual states and territories is available from education departments, the website addresses of which are shown in the table above. Wikipedia (💻 http://en.wikipedia.org/wiki/education_in_australia) also provides an excellent overview of education across the country.

Education Department Websites

State/Territory	Website
ACT	www.det.act.gov.au
NSW	www.schools.nsw.edu.au
NT	www.det.nt.gov.au/education
QLD	http://education.qld.gov.au
SA	www.decs.sa.gov.au
TAS	www.education.tas.gov.au
VIC	www.education.vic.gov.au
WA	www.det.wa.edu.au

STATE SCHOOLS

Spending on state schools varies from state to state and is a hotly debated subject. Local businesses provide sponsorship and extra funding for schools, plus practical work experience, share resources such as computers and other equipment, and help in creating specialised science courses. In recent years, however, many primary schools have been forced to cut back on computer classes due to a lack of resources.

A large number of state schools are modern institutions, having been built in the last decade or so, particularly in the outer suburbs of capital cities. Nevertheless, budget restrictions have resulted in school closures and have driven more families to send their children to private schools. In the mid-'90s, there was an unprecedented exodus of students from state to private schools, making it difficult for governments to provide quality state education in some areas (a number of state schools were forced to close by falling enrolments).

In recent years, some state schools have been increasingly turning to 'voluntary' levies to raise funds (usually to pay for additional materials), as state and federal funding has been cut. In some states, 'free' state education is fast becoming a misnomer, with parents being forced to pay up to $6,000 per year (see **Parents & Citizens Committees** below and **Uniforms & Expenses** on page 135) and many families having to forego holidays and 'luxuries' to pay school fees.

The state school system has been in almost constant flux in the last few decades, during which there has been criticism of the quality of teacher selection and of training and teaching methods – added to which there's a shortage of teachers. Teachers' complaints include having to teach children with little or no English, falling pay compared with other professionals (although teachers are generally well paid), a lack of resources, long hours, low professional standing, large classes, a crowded curriculum, violence (bullying is rife in Australia) and discipline problems (corporal punishment is forbidden in state schools), and poor working conditions, e.g. teaching in portable classrooms in temperatures of over 40°C (104°F)!

State schools don't have canteens or restaurants, although school 'tuckshops' sell sandwiches, snacks and soft drinks at break and lunchtimes.

Education in Country & Remote Areas

Most children in state education attend schools near their homes, although in country areas a long journey may be involved, particularly to secondary school. Usually, primary and secondary schools are separate institutions, but in some country areas there are combined primary and secondary (area or central) schools. School buses may be provided for children in rural areas, while in remote outback regions children do their lessons by correspondence or via the 'school of the air', where lessons are given over the Flying Doctor radio network throughout Australia (both state and private schools participate in programmes). Correspondence lessons use video and audio tapes and are usually supervised by a member of the family and administered by a correspondence school in a state capital.

Young Australians living in rural and remote areas outside the public transport commuting distance of metropolitan centres face great difficulty when faced with the decision of what to do with their lives after leaving school. In order to train for a career or undertake further education, youths living in rural and remote areas must often leave home. However, the financial, emotional and social issues involved in relocating from home often prevent them from moving and realising their dreams.

The Country Education Foundation of Australia (CEFA, 💻 www.cef.org.au) is a national not-for-profit organisation whose mission is to ensure that as many young people as possible from rural Australia have the opportunity to pursue their chosen area of tertiary study or vocation. The CEFA assists rural and remote communities around the country to establish local Education Foundations which provide grants to local youth to assist them with their transition from high school into further education, training or vocations.

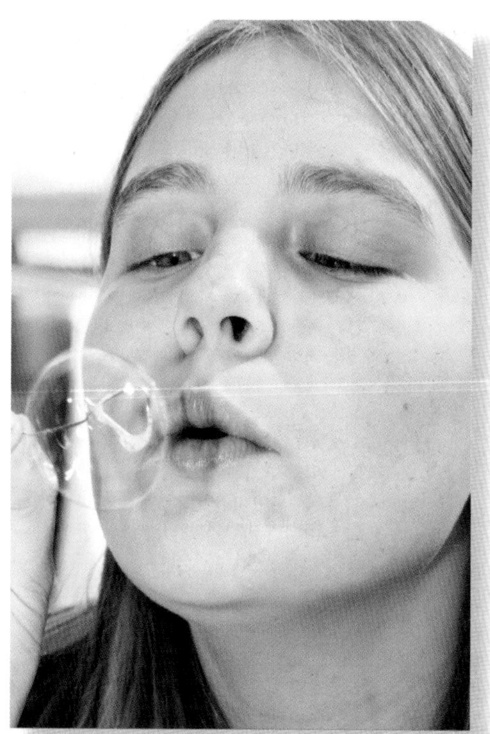

Parents' & Citizens' Associations

Parents play an important role in state education in Australia, where each school has a committee comprising parents, student representatives and teachers, called a Parents and Citizens (P&C) association or committee. Parents can influence decisions such as the design and wearing of uniforms, discipline, homework and even the curriculum. P&C associations (of which parents make up a third) also raise funds for school outings and equipment and assist in running certain aspects of the school such as administration, classroom assistance and school shops.

An enthusiastic and flourishing Parents and Citizens Association is usually a sign of a good school.

Curriculum & Homework

The state curriculum contains eight key learning areas: creative and practical arts; English; foreign languages; health and physical education; human society and the environment; mathematics; science; and technology. Although states and territories have a measure of autonomy in setting their own curricula, they must follow the guidelines laid down by the federal government, and the curriculum is broadly similar in all states, therefore children generally experience few problems when moving from one state to another.

Individual schools also have a degree of autonomy and can determine their own teaching and learning methods within the guidelines provided and offer options within the resources available. For example, some schools specialise in languages and place greater emphasis on foreign language study, with imaginative programmes and innovative teaching methods. Where necessary, students from non-English-speaking countries are given extra English classes, and English as a Second Language (ESL) programmes are provided in schools with significant numbers of children from non-English-speaking backgrounds.

Computer technology is an increasingly important part of teaching in Australian schools at all levels right across the curriculum. Some schools excel in their use of computers, although the ratio of computers to students is low in most state schools, many of which buy computers (and other equipment) with money raised by parents and sponsors.

Extra-curricular activities are common in Australia and include arts and crafts; camps and other excursions; social events such as discos and barbecues; and sports (an important feature of Australian school life). School bands, choirs, dance troupes, dramatic societies and orchestras are also common.

School homework varies considerably, some children doing too little, while others do more than is healthy; the amount is determined largely by individual teachers, although parental influence is important (parents' views are aired via P&C associations – see above).

Choosing a School

The quality of state schools, their teaching staff and the education provided varies considerably according to the state or territory, region, town, city, suburb and individual school. Children have the right to attend their local state school, although they may attend any other state school (in the state or territory where they live) where there's a vacancy. However, priority at any school goes to local children (see **Admissions** below).

It's important to research the best schools in a given area and to ensure that your child will be accepted at your chosen school before buying or renting a home. Some high schools (usually in the poorer and more disadvantaged areas) have discipline, drug and violence problems and have had to install video cameras and take other measures to identify offenders. Obviously, these schools are best avoided if at all possible.

Admissions

Enquiries about admission (enrolment) to a state school should be addressed directly to the headmaster or principal of the school of your choice well in advance of taking up residence in a new area. Most children go to the school nearest their home,

particularly at primary level. All children are guaranteed a place at their local state high school, but parents have the option of applying to up to four non-local high schools. Placement outside the local area depends on the availability of places and, if daily travel isn't feasible, accommodation at the school.

When visiting a school, you should take your child's certificates, references and reports from previous schools.

New pupils are assessed and admitted to the appropriate class for their age and educational level, and it's unusual for a child to be placed with children with more than a year's age difference.

Admission to a state primary school for foreign children is dependent on their parents securing a temporary residence visa (see **Temporary Residents** on page 62) or the child securing a visa sub-class 571 (for secondary exchange school students) – unless they're nationals of Papua New Guinea or certain South Pacific states. Secondary school-age children of any nationality may attend state schools, but non-Australians must pay full fees (called the Overseas Students' Charge), which vary from $5,000 to $13,000 annually.

Australia's academic year follows the calendar year from January to December. Starting ages for primary and secondary schools vary with the state or territory and there are at least six different school entry ages across Australia. In South Australia and the Northern Territory there's a continuous intake and children may begin school when they turn five years of age. However, in Western Australia children born after 30th June aren't eligible to start school until the year they turn seven, and in Victoria they must be aged five by 30th April of the year of enrolment. Such differences can cause problems when children move to a new state. All schools prefer children to start at the beginning of a term if possible, and most schools like parents to apply in October for children starting school the following year.

School Hours & Terms

All states have four terms of around ten weeks except Tasmania, which has three. Terms are separated by holidays lasting around two weeks, except the summer break, which is six or seven weeks. There may also be breaks for Public Holidays. The length and dates of school terms vary with the state or territory and are shown on the state and territory education websites. Holiday dates are also published by schools well in advance, thus giving parents plenty of time to schedule family holidays. Normally parents aren't permitted to withdraw children from classes during the school term, except for visits to a doctor or dentist, when the teacher should be informed in advance (if possible).

Classes start at around 9am and continue until 3 or 4pm, with breaks mid-morning and mid-afternoon as well as at lunchtime. Some children may need to work longer hours if they need extra tuition, for example in English. Many schools provide care and recreational facilities outside school hours for children whose parents are working, seeking work or studying, for which a fee is charged. Supervision may include before and after-school care and care during school holidays. Children being looked after may spend up to 25 hours a week in care, in addition to their normal school hours. Fees vary from almost nothing to $100 per week for one child, with higher fees for two or more children.

Uniforms & Equipment

Most state schools encourage pupils to wear uniforms and they're compulsory at some schools (although tracksuits or jeans may be permitted during winter). Uniforms are usually optional in primary schools. Uniforms can be expensive (with different uniforms for summer and winter), as each school usually has its own embroidered blazers, caps, jumpers and socks, which means that they must be specially made in small quantities. Uniforms can sometimes be purchased second-hand from school shops.

Hats are an integral part of school uniforms and are designed to protect pupils from the sun. High protection sunscreen is also provided free to pre-school and primary year one pupils in many states, and most schools have a 'hot

weather' policy where all children must wear sun hats (with a wide brim to protect the neck) at playtime. Students at some colleges are being encouraged to wear sunglasses with UV400 polycarbonate lenses to protect against eye cancer and other eye problems caused by the sun.

In addition to uniforms, parents can expect to pay for some or all of the following:

- additional clothing such as sportswear and gym shoes, and bags or satchels in which to carry them;
- transport to and from schools is usually free or subsidised (in rural areas state and private school students may share transportation, although there may be a fee);
- calculators, notebooks, pencils, pens, textbooks and writing paper, etc., and arts, crafts and manual work materials. Some states provide free books for primary school pupils and the cost may be subsidised for secondary school students. Many secondary schools operate a text book loan or rental scheme, whereby a refundable deposit is paid by each student at the beginning of secondary schooling. Text books can also be purchased second-hand.
- sports facilities and team matches and trips.

The estimated minimum cost of equipping a child is around $600 per year in primary school and around $3,000 per year in senior secondary school, but can be as high as $6,000. Parents are sometimes also asked to contribute to the cost of new books for school libraries.

Parents of children in the last two years (11 and 12) of secondary school can apply for a means-tested Austudy grant (see page 143).

Pre-school & Day Care

Attendance at a pre-school for children under five isn't compulsory in Australia and finding a pre-school or day care centre can be difficult, particularly in cities and urban areas. Finding one that's affordable can be even more of a problem. Attendance fees aren't usually charged in states where pre-schools are government-run, although there may be a 'voluntary' levy. However, federal government cuts have resulted in the closure of many non-profit, community-based, child-minding centres in recent years, and those that have remained open usually charge for attendance (and some have gone bust).

Fees at public day care centres may depend on the parents' income, better-off parents being asked to contribute more and low income parents exempt. State pre-schools, also called child-parent centres (or kindergarten for the year prior to primary school), are often incorporated within primary schools and open during school hours.

In commercially-run centres, fees are payable to private or voluntary organisations and, in city areas such as central Sydney, can easily be over $100 per day! Wages for childcare workers, rents and a shortage of places are pushing fees up much more quickly than overall consumer prices, and the cost and shortage of places is forcing many mothers out of the workforce, particularly those with a number of children of pre-school age.

Most pre-schools operate from 9am to 2.30pm, Monday to Friday. Programmes usually follow the free play approach, with the emphasis on social and emotional development through creative activity. Preschool doesn't generally provide formal education, although research has shown that children who attend pre-school are generally brighter and usually progress faster than those who don't. After one or two years in pre-school, a child is integrated into the local community and is well prepared for primary school. Preschool is highly recommended if your child's mother-tongue isn't English.

In Queensland, there's a compulsory preparatory (or 'prep') year for children who are age 5 by 30th June, which provide full-time (all day) education for all children prior to grade 1.

Primary School

Primary education in Australia is compulsory from the age of six – but begins at five in some states (see **Admissions** above) – and is almost always co-educational (mixed). Some primary schools also provide nursery or pre-school classes for children under the age of five (see above). Primary education lasts for six or seven years (school years 1 to 6 or 7) up to the age of 12 or 13, depending on the state or territory.

All primary schools must meet broad curriculum and standards' guidelines developed by the Board of Studies. The emphasis is on the development of basic language and literacy skills, simple arithmetic, moral and social education, health training and some creative activities. In later primary years, lessons include arts and crafts, English, health, mathematics, music, physical education, science, social studies (e.g. studies of society and environment), and technology and computer studies. Optional subjects may include community studies and foreign languages (called a 'language other than English' or LOTE), instruction on a musical instrument and religious instruction. In some states (e.g. Victoria) foreign languages are compulsory.

Swimming lessons are provided, usually at public swimming pools, as only around 30 per cent of state schools have their own pools. Sex education is also part of the curriculum, though schools can also develop their own programmes to suit local needs and priorities within government guidelines. The school day is usually between 9am and 3pm and is generally divided into three or four sessions; daily instruction lasts for around five hours and consists of 20- or 30-minute lessons.

Parent-teacher interviews are conducted once or twice a year and provide an opportunity for parents to discuss their child's progress. Children are continually assessed and parents periodically receive written reports, e.g. twice a year in Victoria. Under the state-wide literacy and numeracy standards initiative, pupils are assessed in years 3, 5 and 7. Assessment results are usually confidential and are used to identify pupils' needs, e.g. extra help with English.

Pupils in primary schools usually have one teacher for most (if not all) subjects. In large schools, pupils are graded according to age and are moved up each year irrespective of their level of achievement. In rural areas a primary 'school' may consist of no more than a couple of portable classrooms and two teachers teaching all subjects to 15 to 30 pupils of various ages.

Many new primary schools are designed on the 'open plan' concept, which allows two or more teachers to supervise up to 70 pupils (team teaching), although pupils are divided into small groups for separate activities, including individual study.

Children progress to a secondary (high) school at school year 7 or 8 (aged 12 or 13).

Secondary School

Secondary school (called high school in Australia) is for children aged from 12 or 13 to 17 or 18 (from school years 7 or 8 to year 12). The minimum school leaving age is 17 in most states and territories, where secondary school lasts for a maximum of five or six years. Most secondary students complete year 11 (age 17) and a large percentage stay on at school until year 12 (age 18). Completion of year 12 is usually necessary to attend an institution of higher education, such as a university or college of advanced education. Students may be able to leave school before the school leaving age, for example, in NSW those aged under 17 (the school leaving age) can leave school but must either enrol in a TAFE course, undertake an apprenticeship or be working more than 25 hours a week.

Years 11 and 12 are usually taken at separate colleges (also known as senior high schools), offering a range of subjects studied by adults as well as senior students – and sometimes also years 9 and 10. Secondary schools are usually co-educational, although there are some single-sex schools in capital cities. The most common state secondary school is the comprehensive or multi-purpose high school. In some states there are separate schools for agricultural, commercial and technical subjects, where general academic subjects are combined with practical training, and selective high and grammar schools for academically gifted students (competition for places is stiff). Some secondary schools are further classified as technology or language high schools, or as centres of excellence in certain subjects. At technical high schools, students learn a trade and go on to a TAFE college (see page 147).

Most secondary schools have modern facilities for teaching commercial subjects, home economics, manual crafts and other technical disciplines. Most states and territories also provide schools for outstandingly bright or gifted children, where admission is subject to a test and school reports. Agricultural high schools usually cater for boarders and some country state schools have hostels for children who are unable to travel to and from school daily.

Students in secondary schools generally have a different teacher for each subject, although variations may occur where open plan or more flexible teaching methods have been adopted. Moving up to the next year is generally automatic on completion of the previous year, although students may be grouped according to ability (streamed) in some subjects after an initial period in unstreamed classes. However, classes aren't streamed in academic or technically oriented subjects.

Curriculum

In most states, the first one or two years consist of a general programme that's followed by all students, although there may be some choice of lessons (electives). In the last two years, a basic core of subjects is retained and students are able to select additional subjects, although in some states students select a number of optional subjects from the start of high school.

The core subjects in all schools comprise the eight key learning areas of the arts, English, foreign languages (nowadays usually Chinese, Indonesian or Japanese), health, mathematics, science, social studies and the environment, and technology.

Examinations

Individual states and territories set their own examinations, although in most states (but no longer in NSW) students take the School Certificate (SC) at the age of 15 or 16 (at the end of year 10) and the Higher School Certificate (HSC) at the age of 17 or 18 (the end of year 12). Most states issue students with certificates after they've completed their compulsory education at the age of 17 (depending on the state), and the majority of students who leave at this age (or earlier) go on to do an apprenticeship or other trade training. The SC (replaced by a Junior or Achievement Certificate in some states) is based on school assessment as well as state-wide reference tests in English and mathematics.

The HSC (replaced by a Matriculation Certificate, Senior Certificate or the Tertiary Admission Examination/ Certificate of Education in some states) is based on an external examination held in October or November of school year 12, in addition to school assessment based on a student's last two years' work. In order not to disadvantage children who suffer from exam nerves and to reduce cramming and stress, more emphasis is placed on course work and continuous assessment than on the final examinations. In NSW, as part of a radical change in measuring performance in the final years of schooling, HSC students are assessed against a set of standards rather than against each other. Students receive detailed information about their performance in each subject, detailing the skills they've mastered.

The HSC (or equivalent) is necessary to gain entrance to an Australian university. However, a few universities (in NSW) have waived the HSC requirement if families can afford fees of at least $8,000 for a year at a private college undergoing a 'foundation' course.

A number of schools also offer the International Baccalaureate (IB) plus additional courses with state or TAFE accreditation. Senior high schools (see **Secondary School** on page 137) offer tertiary courses such as Open University or TAFE off-campus.

Leaving

Students aren't allowed to leave before age 17 (depending on the state) unless they have a guaranteed job or preferably an apprenticeship, and are encouraged to stay on until the end of year 12 (at age 18). However, students may be able to leave school before the minimum leaving age and enrol in a vocational course at a TAFE college (see page 147) or a private business college; completion of year 10 of secondary school is the minimum entry requirement for many TAFE courses.

Those who continue to year 12 have several options for further study, including TAFE institutions, higher education and other tertiary-level establishments. A student's eligibility for entry to higher education is assessed during or at the end of his final two years in secondary school. Most states use various combinations of school assessment and public examination.

PRIVATE SCHOOLS

Around 30 per cent of Australian children (over 35 per cent in years 11 and 12) attend private schools (officially referred to as independent schools), of which there are some 2,600 in Australia. These range from nursery (kindergarten) schools to secondary schools, from traditional-style schools to those offering 'alternative' methods of education such as Montessori and Rudolf Steiner schools. They include schools sponsored by churches and religious groups (parochial schools – see below), schools for students with learning difficulties or physical disabilities, and schools for gifted children.

In addition to mainstream parochial schools (see below), there are schools for religious and ethnic minorities, e.g. Muslim schools, where there's a strict code regarding the segregation of boys and girls. Most private schools are single-sex, although an increasing number have become co-educational in recent years. There are also boarding schools in Australia, although few schools accept boarders only. Children who board usually do so because they live too far from school to travel every day or because their parents work overseas.

The advantages of private schools are manifold, not least their academic record, which is generally much better than that of state schools. Although many private schools have resolutely embraced new technology (the use of computers and the internet to teach pupils is widespread), private schools tend to place the emphasis on traditional teaching, including consideration for others, good manners, hard work, responsibility and, not least, a sense of discipline (values which are sadly lacking in some state schools). They provide a broad-based education (aimed at developing a pupil's character) and generally offer a more varied approach to art, drama, music and sport, and a wider choice of academic subjects than state schools.

Their aim is more the development of children as individuals and the encouragement of their unique talents rather than imparting knowledge and skills on a 'production-line' basis. This is made possible by small classes (an average of around 15 to 20 pupils – as little as half that of many state schools), which allow teachers to provide pupils with individually tailored tuition. Don't, however, assume that all private schools are excellent or that they all offer a better education than state schools – which isn't true.

Many private schools are modelled on English schools and generally use the same terminology as them. For example, years are called forms, the first form of secondary school being equivalent to the state school year 7 or 8 at age 12 or 13, while final year students are referred to as sixth-formers. Some private primary schools are called preparatory (prep) schools – not to be confused with the pilot state prep school system.

There's no snobbery attached to attending a private school in Australia – what's important is a school's academic standing and how well your children perform. Some parents switch their children from the state to the private sector when they progress to secondary school.

Parochial Schools

The Catholic church operates by far the largest number of private schools in Australia, and there are relatively few other parochial schools (e.g. Anglican, Christian Community and Uniting Church). A total of some 650,000 children attend some 1,700 Catholic schools, or around two-thirds of all private school students and around 20 per cent of Australia's 3.3m school children. Most Catholic schools are part of a system administered by the Catholic Education Office (💻 www.ncec.catholic.edu.au), and their fees are usually lower than those of other private schools (see below) as most of their operating costs are met by the federal government. Clergy account for almost all teachers in Catholic schools, which (not surprisingly) devote an above average amount of time to religious subjects. Catholic secondary schools accept children from other religious backgrounds, but priority is given to Catholics.

Fees

Private schools are subsidised by the federal government on a 12-point sliding scale: wealthy schools are subsidised at the lowest level (1) and poor schools at the highest level (12). Students at most private schools receive more public funding than those in state schools and there's a certain amount of controversy over the public funding of schools attended by children of affluent parents. However, state funding in the most prestigious schools is minimal and the government saves a considerable sum by not funding private school students' education in state schools.

Private school fees vary considerably according to a variety of factors, including the age of students, the reputation and quality of the school, and its location (schools in major cities are usually the most expensive), but especially its denomination. At a parochial day school, fees vary from $2,000 to $4,000 per year at primary level, and $5,000 to $10,000 per year at secondary level. However, fees at non-denominational schools are up to $10,000 per year for primary schools and between $15,000 and $30,000 per year for 'elite' high schools (fees have risen considerably in recent years). Tuition fees at boarding schools can exceed $30,000 per year, with boarding charges an additional $10,000 to $15,000.

Some schools, particularly secondary schools, publish fees per term (usually four a year), while others are per school year. A school may offer reduced fees to parents with two or more children attending the school. In addition to the fees, some $2,500 must be added per year for books, computers, excursion charges, special equipment (e.g. for sports), uniforms and assorted surcharges, including 'building levies'.

Most private schools provide scholarships for bright or talented pupils, which vary in value from full fees to a small percentage. Scholarships are awarded as a result of competitive examination, individual talents or skills, and need.

Curriculum

Most private schools provide a similar curriculum to state schools and set the same examinations (see above). However, some private schools offer the International Baccalaureate (IB) examination, an internationally recognised university entrance qualification, which may be an important consideration if you plan to stay in Australia for a limited period.

Admissions

If possible, parents should apply at least one or two years in advance, which is generally considered to be the best time to book a place (obviously not possible for new migrants).

The best and most popular schools have a demanding selection procedure and long waiting lists (perhaps many years), and parents register a child for entry at birth (or even at conception!) at some schools. Don't rely on enrolling your child in a particular school and neglect the alternatives, particularly if your chosen school has a rigorous entrance examination. When applying, you're usually asked to send previous exam results, records and school reports.

Before enrolling your child in a private school, make sure that you understand the withdrawal conditions in the school contract.

HIGHER EDUCATION

Post-school education in Australia is generally divided into higher and further education. The states and territories are responsible for administering higher education (referred to as tertiary education in Australia), but the federal government provides the funding. Higher education is usually defined as courses of a standard equivalent to or higher than HSC (see **Examinations** on page 138) and usually refers only to first degree courses; further education (see page 146) generally embraces everything except first degree courses, although the distinction is often blurred. Higher education courses may be full-time, part-time or sandwich courses, which combine periods of full-time study with periods of full-time training and paid work in industry and commerce.

The Department of Education publishes a range of books for students and also has an excellent website (💻 www.goingtouni.gov.au). *The Good Universities Guide* by Dean Ashenden & Sandra Milligan (💻 www.thegoodguides.com.au) also makes interesting reading (although it has been criticised by some universities – no doubt those that were poorly rated!) and there's an associated online 'university rating' system (💻 www.gooduniguide.com.au). A higher education supplement is published in the Wednesday edition of *The Australian* newspaper.

Universities

Australia has one of the highest ratios of universities ('unis') to population in the world, and the number of students in higher education has increased considerably in the last decade, now totalling over 600,000. However, disadvantaged students (e.g. Aboriginals and Torres Strait Islanders, the disabled, those from non-English-speaking backgrounds, the poor and rural dwellers) are under-represented, particularly in elite institutions. Some leading unis draw less than 5 per cent of their students from those with low socio-economic status. However, a number are addressing the problem and some have increased the number of scholarships and changed the criteria from merit to need or income.

Many prospective students cannot afford the high fees, which have led to student protests in the form of occupations and sit-ins at university buildings. Universities have been struggling with funding cuts in recent years and many have been forced to axe places, cut research budgets and reduce the number of postgraduate courses.

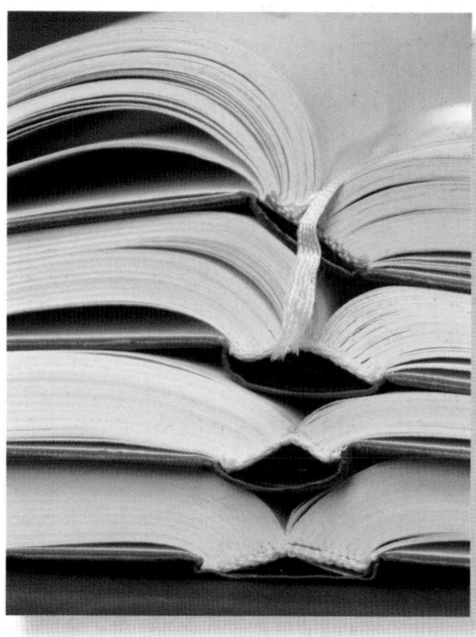

Australian universities are both teaching and research institutions, and many have world-renowned research programmes funded by industry in the applied science and technology fields. Degree level courses are offered by some 40 universities. The oldest universities are Sydney and Melbourne (established in the 1850s), which, along with the universities of Adelaide, Queensland, Tasmania and Western Australia, form the traditional 'sandstone' universities (the Australian equivalent of America's Ivy League). Degrees from the sandstone unis, 'corporate' universities (Monash and UNSW) and universities of technology (UTs) are the most highly rated.

Australian universities ranked in order of academic excellence are generally: ANU Canberra, Melbourne, Sydney UNSW, Queensland, Adelaide and University WA. In *The Time Higher Education* World University Ranking 2011-12 (💻 www.timeshighereducation.co.uk/world-university-rankings/2011-2012/top-400.html) of the world's top 400 universities, the highest ranked Australian universities were Melbourne and the ANU, in 37th and 38th places respectively.

Most older universities follow British or American traditions and offer a wide range of courses, although many have a multi-campus structure, each campus specialising in a particular discipline, e.g. an agricultural science college linked to the main campus.

The age of admission to university is usually 18 (although most admit exceptional students at a younger age) and courses are normally for three years, although some last for four. This is seen as a big advantage by foreign students from countries where courses last much longer, and helps Australian universities attract a large number of overseas students. Most Australian universities have between 10,000 and 30,000 students (the largest, Monash, has over 50,000), although they're usually dispersed over a number of campuses. Around a quarter of university students are 'mature' students aged over 30, two-thirds of whom are women.

Competition for students is fierce, and universities have resorted to innovative advertising to lure school-leavers; some have even lowered their entrance requirements to attract more students. Many universities deliberately over-enrol, partly in order to receive higher government grants, which has led to an increase in student-staff ratios and fears of a reduction in the quality of teaching. In order to compete with private colleges and other degree-level state institutions, many universities have introduced associate degree courses in fields such as applied science, dance, dental therapy, electrical and electronic engineering, and management.

Other Establishments

Australia also has a number of specialist higher education establishments, which include the Australian College of Physical Education (Sydney), the Australian Defence Force Academy (Canberra), the Australian Film, TV and Radio School (North Ryde, NSW), the Australian Institute of Music (Sydney), the Australian International Hotel School (Canberra), the Australian Maritime College (Launceston, Tasmania), the Christian Heritage College (Brisbane), Engineering Education Australia (distance education), the International College of Hotel Management (Adelaide), KvB Institute of Technology (Sydney), Macleay College (Sydney) and the National Institute of Dramatic Art (Sydney).

 **Caution**

Overseas students require a student visa (see page 66), which is issued after acceptance on a course and payment of at least half the first year's fees.

Overseas Students

All Australian universities accept overseas students – who comprise some 20 per cent of students – and many unis spend $millions on overseas marketing and student recruitment (the sandstone universities established their own overseas marketing arm in 1997). There are no quotas for foreign students, but all non-resident students must pay full fees (although grants and scholarships are available – see below). Overseas 'onshore' students, mostly from Asia, are a major source of income for universities, contributing over $16bn to the Australian economy in 2010-11. Many universities also have thousands of 'offshore' students at facilities in Asian countries and in New Zealand. Australian universities enrol some 100,000 foreign students per year and the number is expected to increase steadily. When students at secondary schools and private colleges are included, the total number of foreign students studying in Australia is well over 200,000.

Students must have the financial resources to meet day-to-day living expenses for the duration of their course, return fares to Australia and tuition fees (see below).

Foreign students must have an adequate knowledge of English (unless studying English!) and most must pass a foundation course before starting uni. If English isn't your mother tongue or the language in which you gained your entrance qualifications, you must take the Short Selection Test (SST). Private health insurance is required by all students, e.g. Medibank Private overseas student health cover.

Students must be attending full-time courses but are permitted to take part-time jobs of up to 20 hours per week to help cover their living costs.

In order to retain their visas, students must have satisfactory attendance and achievement records. If attendance or exam results are poor, a student may have his visa cancelled and be required to leave the country (failure to leave the country promptly can result in not being permitted re-entry for a minimum of three years). On completion of their courses, overseas students must leave Australia when their visas expire (a written undertaking must be made).

Fees & Expenses

Higher education tuition fees for Australian students were introduced in 1990 (prior to which tuition was free) under the Higher Education Contribution Scheme (HECS). Students' fees are determined by individual institutions but are subject to a legal maximum. Most institutions' charges are at or near the maximums, which depend on the subject(s) studied and are divided into three bands shown in the table below (for 2013).

Some students qualify for a 'Commonwealth-supported' place, whereby the government pays the majority of the cost of the course (averaging around 70 per cent). Resident students may be eligible for one of two government grants – a Youth Allowance or an Austudy Grant – or another grant or subsidy. Students can pay their tuition fees via a deferred payment arrangement known as the Higher Education Loan Programme (HELP). Further information about student grants, subsidies and loans

Student Contribution Fees 2013

Band	Range	Annual Fee Subjects
1	$0-5,868	education, clinical psychology, nursing, behavioural science, foreign languages, humanities, social studies, and visual and performing arts
2	$0-8,363	agriculture, built environment, computing, engineering, allied and other health, mathematics, science, statistics and surveying
3	$0-9,792	law, accounting, administration, commerce, dentistry, economics, medicine and veterinary science

can be obtained from Study Assist (http://studyassist.gov.au).

Overseas students must pay their full tuition fees in advance, which vary with the course and university between around $10,000 and $20,000 per year. Various scholarships are available which cover tuition fees and living costs or only tuition fees. Information can be obtained from Australian embassies and high commissions overseas and from www.studyinaustralia.gov.au.

In addition to tuition fees, students can expect to pay between $750 and $1,500 on text books, which are sold at a discount (under the Educational Textbook Subsidy Scheme) to students with proof that they're studying at an Australian educational institution. Books must be bought at a registered bookseller and you must take your current textbook list with you when you go to buy them. Textbooks can also be purchased second-hand and most universities have secondhand book shops.

Annual living costs for students (excluding course fees) are reckoned to be a minimum of $15,000 per year plus a further $7,500 for a spouse and $5,000 for each child (possibly less outside major cities). Many students find it difficult to survive and some choose an educational institution according to where they can more easily manage on their meagre resources (or where they can find part-time work), rather than the courses it offers or the quality of its teaching. Many students work part-time during terms and holidays to supplement their income, and around half live with their parents to save costs.

Qualifications & Admissions

Admission for Australian students is usually based on their results in the Higher School Certificate (HSC) or the equivalent taken in their final year of high school. However, some universities in NSW have waived the HSC requirement if families can afford fees of over $8,000 for a year at a private college doing a 'foundation' course. (This option has been available to overseas students for years).

University admission systems vary considerably and each state has its own method of ranking students for entry to universities within the state. For year 12 students the following systems are used:

- ACT & NSW – The University Admission Index (UAI) is used in these states.
- NT, SA, Tasmania & WA – These states give students a numerical 'score' called a Tertiary Entrance Rank (TER), based on exam results compared with a set of standards.
- Queensland – Queensland uses an Overall Position (OP) system, which ranks students on a scale of 1 to 25 (out-of-state students are ranked from 1 to 100).
- Victoria – Victoria uses the Equivalent National Tertiary Entrance Rank (ENTER).

All Australian universities accept students from other states, when a complicated system of converting marks is used. See www.goingtouni.gov.au for a table giving an indication of the minimum entrance requirements for each of Australia's universities. There are plans to introduce a nationwide system of university entrance marks, although it's expected to be some years before this is introduced (as with many things in Australia, most states think that their way of doing things is best).

Entrance requirements for mature students are usually different from those mentioned above, and most universities operate adult entry admission schemes, which allow applicants over a certain age admission on the basis of work experience and qualifications other than academic ones.

Generally, overseas students' qualifications which would admit them to a university in their own country are taken into consideration. Whatever your qualifications, each application is considered on its merits. All foreign students require a thorough knowledge of English, which is usually examined unless a certificate is provided. Australian universities accept the International Baccalaureate (IB) certificate as an entrance qualification, but an American high school diploma isn't usually sufficient.

Contact individual universities for detailed information or, for general information, the Department of Education, Employment and Workplace Relations (☏ 1300-363 079 in Australia, or +61-354-545 345 from overseas, 💻 www.deewr.gov.au).

To apply for a place at university, you should begin by writing to the Tertiary Admissions Centre (TAC) in the state of your choice. The deadline for applications is the end of September. Each state TAC allows you to make one application, on which you list a number of preferences. Acceptance depends on your qualifications (see above) and the number of available places on a course. You should make sure that you spread your preferences to include some courses on which you're almost 'certain' to gain acceptance. It's possible to change preferences once you know your score, e.g. if you score considerably higher or lower than anticipated. Alternatively, you can re-sit your exams or take a year off and re-apply the following year.

Terms & Courses

The university academic year follows the calendar year, courses taking place from February until November or December. The year commences with an orientation week (O-week), during which enrolment takes place for new students. The year is usually divided into two terms (semesters) of around 14 weeks, with a recess of around two weeks in the middle of each semester and a six-to eight-week summer break. However, most universities now offer summer semesters, which allow students to catch up on failed or missed subjects. Examinations are in November or December.

Students take a main subject plus one or two secondary subjects, concentrating on their main subject for the first one or two years. In some universities it's possible for students to design their own degree courses. Many students choose a sandwich course, which includes a period spent working in industry or commerce. Timetables may be flexible and usually include less than ten hours of classes a week in order to maximise reading and research time. Classes are usually very large, some lectures attracting as many as 500 students. Most courses are taught through lectures and tutorials, students being assessed on their work in assignments, essays, examinations (annual and final) and practical work.

Accommodation

After acceptance at university, students are usually advised to apply for a place in a hall of residence or other college accommodation, such as self-catering houses and apartments. However, such accommodation is limited and in high demand, and many universities don't provide student accommodation at all.

You should write as soon as possible after acceptance to the accommodation or housing officer, whose job is to help students find suitable accommodation. There's considerable demand for student accommodation (often from overseas students) in the major cities, particularly Sydney and Melbourne, and many universities are looking at ways of providing more student accommodation.

The cost of accommodation in halls of residence ranges from around $100 per week for self-catering to around $300 for full board. Overseas students are usually given priority for housing; you should investigate the availability and cost of local accommodation before accepting a place at a university. The Coordinating Committee for Overseas

Students also helps overseas students find accommodation.

A large number of students rent privately-owned apartments or houses, which are often shared with other students, although in some areas this kind of accommodation is difficult to find and expensive. The cost varies considerably depending on the city, town or suburb, but the following table can be used as a rough guide:

Cost of Student Accommodation

Type of Property	Weekly Rent
1-bed apt	$200-300
2-bed apt (per bedroom)	$150-200
2-3 bed house (per bedroom)	$150-250

See also **Cost of Living** on page 229.

Facilities

All universities have a huge variety of clubs, societies and organisations, many run by the students' association or union, which is the centre of social activities. Most campuses are members of the National Union of Students (NUS), which represents students at state and national levels; membership is compulsory for students!

Most universities also have excellent sports facilities, and all have bars and canteens. Clubs usually fall into the categories of cultural, department-based, political, recreational and sporting. During orientation week, most clubs and societies are represented and compete to sign up new members. Fees are payable, although there are a large number of benefits and facilities, many especifically for overseas students. All universities levy a student amenities or general service fee (anything from $100 to $500 per year), which helps finance the representative council, sports associations and the student union.

Degrees

A diploma is awarded to students who successfully complete a course of at least two years, either full-time or the equivalent period part-time. The most common degrees awarded in Australia are a Bachelor of Arts (BA) and a Bachelor of Science (BSc). Bachelor's degrees are given a classification, the highest of which is an 'honours' degree, which is granted to students who have undertaken an extra year of specialised study after a three-year course or who perform outstandingly in a four-year course.

The highest pass is a first class degree, which is quite rare. Second-class degrees are average, while a third-class degree is poor. The lowest classification is a 'pass'. Students can request special consideration and be given a second chance by sitting another exam; in some cases they're granted a 'conceded pass'.

Second (postgraduate) degrees are usually a Master of Arts (MA) or a Master of Science (MSc), which are awarded to Bachelors for a one-year course in a subject other than their undergraduate subjects. Students who do postgraduate work in the same subject(s) as their undergraduate work usually undertake a three-year Doctor of Philosophy (PhD) research programme. In addition to the above, qualifications include diploma, advanced diploma, graduate certificate and graduate diploma.

Under the Australia Qualifications Framework, a national system for the recognition of qualifications established in 1995, students can move more easily between private colleges, TAFE colleges (see below) and universities, and have their studies and experience classified.

FURTHER EDUCATION

Further education generally embraces everything except first degree courses taken at universities and colleges of higher education, although the distinction between further and higher education is sometimes blurred. Further education courses may be full-or part-time and are provided by a wide range of institutions, including the Adult Migrant Education Service; the Council of Adult Education; evening colleges; community colleges; technical colleges; technical and further education (TAFE) colleges (see below); vocational education and training (VET) courses; universities; the Workers' Education Association; and by numerous 'open learning'

institutions such as the Open Training and Education Network (OTEN).

Qualifications that can be earned through further education include the School Certificate (SC – most state but not NSW, where it was phased out in 2011), the Higher School Certificate (HSC), the International Baccalaureate (IB), trade certificates, Bachelor's and Master's degrees, Master of Business Administration (MBA) degrees, and a range of internationally recognised certificates and diplomas. Around 80 per cent of Australians take a further education course at some time during their lives.

Community colleges are found throughout Australia and are non-profit organisations with low course fees. They offer a huge range of courses including arts, humanities and science, business and computing, languages and communication, health and fitness, and lifestyle. Colleges work with local councils, schools and neighbourhood groups to organise, promote and offer lifelong learning. They cater for the educational needs of small business, parents, job seekers and busy city dwellers, and develop programs for adults with special needs in order to enrich their lives through learning.

There are many organisations that provide information about vocational education and training in Australia including Training (💻 http://training.gov.au), the official national register of information about training packages, qualifications, courses, units of competency and registered training organisations (RTOs).

Training.com (💻 www.training.com.au) provides a gateway to the vast range of vocational education and training information, products and services in Australia.

TAFE Colleges

By far the largest provider of further education courses in Australia is the string of over 200 Technical and Further Education (TAFE) colleges, which together number over a million students. TAFE colleges are state run and are similar throughout the country, many having a number of campuses and training centres (including some universities). Many courses have a strong vocational focus and are noted for their practical, hands-on emphasis. The majority of courses are at the certificate, diploma and advanced diploma levels, although some degree level courses are offered, and courses can be used as entry to a full-time degree course at university.

TAFE courses include pre-apprenticeships and apprenticeships, trade, post-trade and technician courses, plus commercial and general courses to certificate level. Courses are also used to supplement apprenticeships and on-the-job training. Most courses last around two years and can be undertaken on a part-time or full-time basis or combined with a job, when the employer allows time off to attend classes.

TAFE colleges offer hundreds of courses, including all major skills in a wide range of artistic, commercial, domestic and industrial occupations. Many courses are specifically designed for school-leavers to upgrade their skills and for adults wishing to get back into the workforce. Courses range from semi-skilled trade training to professional subjects and include correspondence courses and special programmes for disadvantaged groups. Courses for apprentices cover dozens of trades, including the automotive, building, electrical, electronics, farming, fashion, food, gardening, hairdressing, jewellery, metal, plumbing, printing, textiles and watchmaking industries, to name but a few. Pre-apprenticeship courses allow young people to undertake a substantial part of a trade course before taking up an apprenticeship in an 'advanced' discipline, such as electrical engineering.

Fees vary with the state or territory, each of which sets its own fees. The average cost of a full-time course in NSW is around $450 and for a diploma course around $1,500 per year; some states waive fees for school-leavers who enrol directly in TAFE courses on leaving school. There are concessionary rates (or no fees) for low-income earners. Resident students are also eligible for Austudy grants.

TAFE College (💻 www.tafe-college.org) is run by the AA Education network which provides information about study, work and travel in Australia and is aimed at overseas students. International students can work up to 20 hours per week while studying on a TAFE course and up to 40 hours per week during semester breaks.

A list of TAFE colleges can be found at 💻 www.australian-universities.com/colleges/list.php.

Open Universities Australia

Open Universities Australia (formerly Open Learning) was set up by the government to offer high quality tertiary education to all Australians. It's owned and operated by a consortium of seven Australian universities: Curtin University of Technology, Griffith University, Macquarie University, Monash University, RMIT University, Swinburne University of Technology and the University of South Australia.

There are no limits on the number of people who may enrol, no educational requirements and, usually, no requirement to attend on-campus or residential seminars. Students can study in any or all of the four study periods each year, beginning in March, June, September and December. Students have a choice of 700 individual units and 60 undergraduate, postgraduate and TAFE qualifications, and can take up to ten years to complete a course. All units can be studied at home, with the aid of CD-ROMs, on-line (internet) learning, and video and audio cassettes. For further information contact Open Universities Australia (☎ 1300-156176, 💻 www.open.edu.au).

Private Colleges

Vocational training is offered by private colleges, which are closely aligned to the industries for which they prepare students. Many private colleges offer training in courses such as business, computer studies, hospitality and secretarial skills. Prospective students should check whether a course has been accredited by the relevant body. Some institutions offer distance learning MBA courses for those who cannot (or don't wish to) study on a full- or part-time, locally taught basis. Around 40 business schools and professional organisations offer MBA courses in subjects such as banking, business administration, communications, economics, European languages, information systems, management, marketing, public relations, and social and political studies.

LANGUAGE SCHOOLS

If you don't speak English fluently (or you wish to learn another language) you can enrol on a language course. These are offered by numerous language schools in Australia. Obtaining a working knowledge or becoming fluent in English (or 'strine') while living in Australia is relatively easy, as you're constantly immersed in the English language and have the maximum opportunity to practise. However, if you wish to speak or write English idiomatically, you probably need to attend a language school or find a private tutor. Many thousands of foreign students (mostly from Asian countries) come to Australia each year to learn English, thus ensuring that English-language schools are big business. It's usually necessary to have a recognised qualification in English to be accepted at a college of higher or further education in Australia.

English-language courses are offered at all levels by foreign and international organisations, language schools, local associations and clubs, migrant education colleges, open learning institutions, private colleges, private teachers, universities, and technical and further education (TAFE) colleges. There are English-language schools in all cities and large towns in Australia, most of which are equipped with bookshops, computers, libraries and video studios.

Courses range from complete beginners, through specialised business or cultural courses, to university-level seminars leading to advanced diplomas. The Department of Immigration, Multicultural and Indigenous Affairs supports Settlement English courses for some migrants, and the cost may be funded by the department. Most language schools offer a variety of classes according to your current language ability, how many hours you wish to study per week, how much money you want to spend, and how quickly you wish (or are able) to learn. Language classes generally fall into the following categories: compact (10 to 20 hours per week), intensive (20 to 30 hours), and total immersion (30 to 40 hours or more).

Full-time, part-time and evening courses are offered by most schools, and many also offer residential courses or accommodation with local families (highly recommended to accelerate learning). Courses that include accommodation (often half-board, consisting of breakfast and an evening meal) usually represent good value.

Caution

Bear in mind that, if you need to find your own accommodation, particularly in Sydney or Melbourne, it can be difficult and very expensive.

Course fees vary considerably and are usually calculated on a weekly basis. Fees depend on the number of hours' tuition per week, the type of course, and the location and reputation of the school. Expect to pay up to $1,000 per week for an intensive course and around $500 per week for a compact course. Total immersion or executive courses, which are provided by many schools, can cost $3,000 or more per week, and not everyone is suited to learning at such a fast rate.

Apostles, VIC

trams, Melbourne

10. PUBLIC TRANSPORT

Public transport in Australia varies from region to region and town to town. In most cities and large towns services are good to excellent and relatively inexpensive, although some city suburbs and areas of the country are poorly served. Most Australian cities have a relatively small suburban rail network, only New South Wales (NSW) has an extensive rail network and many regions aren't served by trains at all; bus and rail services in most areas are severely curtailed on Sundays and in some cases on Saturdays also.

Poor public transport is one of the reasons most Australians are so attached to their cars – only Americans are more devoted motorists – although it isn't always essential to own a car, particularly if you live in a city where parking is often impossible. On the other hand, if you live in the country or a suburb off the main rail and bus routes, it's usually essential to have your own transport.

Bear in mind when travelling interstate that Australia is a huge country (as large as Europe or the US and over 30 times the size of the UK) with vast distances between capital cities. Flying saves you a lot of time and the loss of sleep associated with long-distance bus and train journeys, although you see nothing of Australia when flying around the country. Book early if you plan to travel long distance on Public Holidays or at the beginning or end of school holidays. Despite the vast distances involved in travelling in Australia, many Australians prefer to travel by car.

In cities, trains are much faster than buses, particularly during rush hours, even where new roads have been built. Most cities have an integrated public transport system, and tickets usually allow transfers between buses, ferries, trains and trams (as applicable), fares being calculated on a zone system. Buses and trams carry around 65 per cent of passengers in the major cities, where there's a range of daily, weekly, monthly, quarterly and annual tickets, plus discounted books of ten tickets offering savings on single fares. Many cities have free town centre (downtown) shuttle buses.

> ▲ **Caution**
>
> Passengers discovered travelling without a ticket can be heavily fined.

Students visiting or living in Australia should obtain an International Student Identity Card (ISIC), which offers a range of travel discounts (foreign students don't qualify for student discounts in NSW and Victoria, but they do in other states and territories). STA Travel (www.statravel.com.au) is the largest nationwide travel agency and can provide tickets for all domestic and international travel. A number of guides are available for disabled passengers, including the *Accessing City Rail* from City Rail, a guide to access for wheelchairs on trains, and *Easy Access Australia*, available from www.easyaccessaustralia.com.au.

CITY TRANSPORT SYSTEMS

Most Australian cities have an adequate or good public transport service consisting mainly

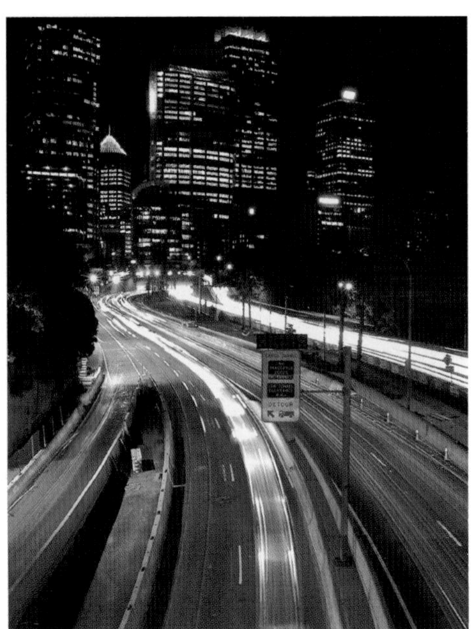

of buses and a limited suburban rail network, supported by a few ferries and, in Melbourne, an extensive tram network.

Brisbane

In Brisbane you can buy daily or weekly travel tickets through Translink (☎ 131230). Brisbane is divided into 23 zones, which stretch all the way from Noosa down to Coolangatta. You can buy a daily or weekly ticket for unlimited travel on any bus, train or ferry in the central zones (including the CityCats) or all 23 zones. For more information and fares, see 🖳 http://translink.com.au.

Melbourne

Melbourne has an inexpensive and efficient public transport network (called the 'Met'), consisting of buses, trains and trams, which has recently been privatised. A free *Get around on the Met* map is available (☎ 131638). Trams form the backbone of the public transport system and the city's network is one of the most extensive in the world and the only one remaining in Australia. The network covers 325km (202mi) and is served by some 750 trams operating up to 20km (12mi) outside the city centre. Tickets can be purchased at railway stations, on board buses and trams, and from retail outlets such as newsagents and cafés. An unpopular automated 'Metcard' ticketing system has recently been introduced. For more information about Melbourne's public transport, see 🖳 http://ptv.vic.gov.au.

Sydney

Australia's largest city has an integrated service that includes buses, ferries, suburban trains and City Rail's 'underground' system (a conventional railway that runs underground in the city centre). It also has a light railway (tram) network, which is being extended (the monorail was scrapped in 2012). Sydney has the most expensive public transport of any Australian city, but it's still relatively cheap by international standards. In 2000 (for the Sydney Olympics), Sydney received some much-needed transport improvements, including expanded rail and ferry lines and the Airport (rail) Line linking the airport to the city centre (Circular Quay).

You can buy a Sydney Pass for three, five or seven days which is valid for city buses, ferries and suburban trains (but not the Airport Line).

For more information about Sydney's public transport, see 🖳 www.131500.com.au.

TRAINS

In the mid-19th century, when the first Australian railways were built, the states were independent colonies and governed from London; consequently, Australia's rail network grew piecemeal without any consultation between states. When the Australian federation was formed in 1901, the six colonies all had different gauge lines from their neighbours! This resulted in passengers having to change trains at state borders, often in the middle of the night, a situation which stifled the development of rail travel until the early '60s, when a standard gauge (1,435mm) was introduced on some main lines. However, Australia still has three different railway gauges – 1,067mm, 1,435mm and 1,600mm – and, although the main interstate lines now use the standard gauge, it's only in the last few years that much thought has been given to expanding and updating the local rail network, which by European standards is antiquated and severely limited.

Rail Australia consists of four state-owned rail companies (Countrylink, Queensland Rail,

V/Line and Westrail) and the Great Southern Railway (GSR), which was created when the *Ghan*, *Indian Pacific* and *Overland* services were sold by the federal government in 1997. Some states (such as Victoria) have also since privatised their railways (trains in Melbourne are operated by Connex).

 **Caution**

Most Australian cities have only a sparse suburban rail network and many areas of the country aren't served by trains at all.

As in the US, the main task of Australian railways is to haul bulk minerals (particularly coal in NSW and Queensland), grain, petroleum products and other freight over long distances.

Australian trains are more comfortable, leisurely and sociable than buses, but slower (the average speed of Australian trains is around 65kph/40mph), more expensive and sometimes difficult to book. You need to reserve well in advance for the most popular long-distance trains, particularly during the peak holiday season.

Some trains have wheelchair access, including the V/Line Sprinter trains in Victoria and the Countrylink XPT (an abbreviation for Express Passenger Train) and Xplorer trains operating in NSW, Queensland and between Sydney and Melbourne (at speeds of up to 160kph/100mph).

Interstate Trains

Australia offers some of the most spectacular rail journeys in the world, although the unchanging scenery in some regions can begin to pall after a few hours (and interstate journeys can be VERY long) unless you're unnaturally keen on flat, red terrain. Interstate rail travel has been overtaken by the age of air travel and (apart from suburban services in the major cities) is mainly of interest to tourists and travellers with plenty of time on their hands. There's an interstate rail service serving all states except Tasmania. Trains don't stop at all intermediate stations, e.g. those within a few hours of major terminals.

Long-distance trains have evocative names such as the *Ghan* (Adelaide-Darwin), the *Great South Pacific Express* (Sydney-Brisbane-Cairns), *Indian Pacific* (Sydney-Adelaide-Perth), the *Prospector* (Perth-Kalgoorlie) and the *Spirit of the Outback* (Brisbane-Longreach). The *Indian Pacific* crosses Australia and takes its name from its route from the Indian Ocean (Perth) to the Pacific Ocean (Sydney), a journey of 4,348km (2,700mi) taking around 65 hours. It includes the longest stretch of straight track (478km/300mi) in the world, across the Nullabor Plain in Western Australia. The *Indian Pacific* is one of the world's longest passenger trains, with up to 25 carriages plus a bar and music room with piano, observation lounge and restaurant.

The *Great South Pacific Express* is 'the first five-star hotel on wheels' in Australia and the country's answer to Europe's Orient Express. Cars are transported on the *Queenslander*, the *Spirit of the Outback* and between Adelaide and Alice Springs, Melbourne and Perth, and on the Melbourne-Mildura goods line. The *Prospector* (Perth-Kalgoorlie) provides only first-class, air-conditioned accommodation and maintains the fastest average speed (around 110kph/68mph) of any train in Australia, taking 7.5 hours for the 655km (407mi) journey.

For more information about interstate trains, see 💻 www.railaustralia.com.au.

Accommodation

Interstate trains offer a range of accommodation which may include deluxe and first, holiday, economy and coach-class sleeping berths, and economy and first-class seats. Sleeping berths are available on overnight services (for a surcharge) and are well worth the extra charge on long journeys.

In first class there are 'twinette' cabins, which have seats that fold into two sleeping berths and share facilities with adjacent cabins. First-class single 'roomettes' have a private toilet and wash basin; first-class cabins have hot and cold water, a shower, a socket for an electric shaver, and a toilet and wash basin.

Deluxe cabins and family units are available on the *Ghan* and *Indian Pacific* trains, where meals are included with first-class sleeping berths. In Queensland, economy-class sleepers have three sleeping berths, and each carriage has communal showers and toilets. Where sleeping berths are unavailable there are reclining seats. Two-berth 'holiday-class' cabins are available on *The Ghan* and the *Indian Pacific* trains. Coach-class cars have reclining seats and, on trains to Alice Springs, Cairns and Perth, coach- and economy-class 'sitting' cars include showers. All long-distance trains are air-conditioned.

State Services

There are no regular passenger railways in Tasmania, although there's a freight rail service throughout the island and several steam railways for tourists, e.g. Ida Bay to Deep Hole. The main services in the other states are detailed below. A few small private railways serve mainly agricultural and industrial areas, e.g. the iron-ore mining developments in the northwest of Western Australia and an extensive tram network in Queensland connecting the sugar cane fields to the mills in sugar-producing areas.

State capital cities have more than one railway station, although long-distance trains always arrive and depart from the main interstate station, e.g. Central Station in Sydney and Spencer Street Station in Melbourne.

New South Wales

The NSW Countrylink network (🖳 www.countrylink.info) operates the most comprehensive state rail service in Australia using 'Xplorer' trains, on which seats must be booked. There are commuter trains between Sydney and Goulburn, Katoomba, Lithgow, Newcastle and Wollongong. For information ☎ 132232 between 6.30am and 10pm daily.

Sydney: Sydney has the most extensive suburban rail network in Australia, although even here many suburbs have no rail service. Most routes are served by old, mostly double-decker trains (Sydney was the first city in the world to introduce double-decker electric trains), on which seats can usually be reversed to face in either direction, but these are being replaced by 'ultra-modern' Tangara trains on which they cannot.

Yellow lines on platforms indicate where half-length, four-carriage trains stop (you must stand behind the yellow line). Doors open and close automatically, although the doors on old trains are rarely closed during hot weather, so keep clear of the doorways (or hold on tight).

Trains operate from around 5am until midnight – violence, although rare, has caused the cancellation of trains after midnight on some suburban routes. After dark there are 'Night Safe' areas (marked on the platform in blue) where you can wait for trains. After 8pm, only two carriages are in use (next to the guard's compartment, indicated by a blue light), and a help button is positioned near the door which can be used to alert the guard or driver.

Overcrowding on trains during rush hours is widespread. There's a need to increase capacity and/or the frequency of trains, although train operators have been cutting trains on some routes in recent years rather than increasing them. For information, see 🖳 www.cityrail.info.

Canberra: Australia's capital city is served by Countrylink trains (🖳 www.countrylink.info) from Sydney, taking around 4hrs 20mins to Canberra station (situated in Kingston, ACT). From Melbourne, you need to change to a coach at either Yass Junction or

Cootamundra, taking around nine hours to Canberra.

Northern Territory

Alice Springs: Alice (as it's known) is served by the *Ghan*, which departs from Adelaide at 12.20pm on Sundays and Wednesdays and arrives at 1.45 pm the following day. The return departs from Alice at 9.10am on Thursdays and 11.15am on Sundays and both arrive in Adelaide at 12.30pm the following day (although it's often early). The station in Alice is a 15-minute walk from the edge of the town (taxis meet trains).

Darwin: The Top End has recently joined the rail network, and the *Ghan* (see above) now travels as far as Darwin and is already heralded as one of the world's great rail journeys. For fares, see 💻 www.greatsouthernrail.com.au/site/the_ghan/fares.jsp.

Queensland

Queensland has the most extensive rail network of any Australian state, covering over 10,000km (6,200mi) of lines on narrow gauge tracks (trains in Queensland are slower than buses due to the narrow gauge, except tilt trains – see **Brisbane** below). All trains are operated by Queensland Rail (☎ 131617, 💻 www.qr.com.au), whose 'flagship' train (in which all passengers travel first class with sleeping berths) is the *Queenslander*, taking a leisurely 30 hours between Brisbane and Cairns. The *Westlander* operates from Brisbane to Charlesville (777km/482mi), taking 16 hours, and the *Inlander* links Townsville with Mount Isa. The only rail link from outside the state is from NSW (served by XPT trains), on which northbound trains run overnight and southbound trains during the day.

Seat or sleeper reservations are compulsory on long-distance trains, known as 'Traveltrains'. Most services are air-conditioned and provide sleeping cars and sitting cars with bar and meal services. Many trains stop at small stations on request and some trains are mixed freight and passenger trains (usually mainly freight with one passenger car). Vehicles can be transported on the *Queenslander* and the *Spirit of the Outback* (Brisbane-Longreach) services.

Local 'tourist' trains include the *Kuranda Scenic Railway* and the *Spirit of the Tropics*, designed for budget travellers and incorporating a non-stop disco car (Club Loco)! The vintage *Gulflander* train operates between Normanton and Croydon in the west of the state. There are plans for a regional rail line on the Sunshine Coast (the existing track is sited 20km/12mi inland from the heavily-populated coastal area).

'Sunshine' rail passes offer unlimited economy class travel on most routes (including the Brisbane suburban network). Ordinary one-way tickets allow unlimited stopovers and 14 days to reach your destination, while return tickets are valid for two months.

> **▲ Caution**
>
> Stop-offs must be stated when buying tickets and bookings made for all journeys. You can change your travel plans, but a re-booking fee may be charged.

Brisbane: There's a fast Citytrain service in Brisbane with seven lines, and an Airtrain (💻 www.airtrain.com.au) service connecting the airport to the city and the Gold Coast. The 640km (398mi) stretch between Brisbane and Rockhampton is electrified and served by modern 'tilt' trains (fast trains which run along narrow-gauge lines, sometimes at seemingly precarious angles – hence the name!).

South Australia

Adelaide: There's a small network of suburban trains in Adelaide operated by the State Transport Authority. Tickets must be purchased before entering platforms or boarding trains. Long-distance trains depart from the Adelaide Rail Passenger Terminal in Keswick, 2km southwest of the city centre. There's an overnight service to Melbourne taking around 12 hours and a day coach/train service taking 11 hours. The *Ghan* to Alice Springs (19 hours) departs at 12.20pm on Sundays and Wednesdays, and continues on to Darwin.

There are five weekly trains to Perth (none on Tuesdays and Thursdays) taking around 36 hours, possibly requiring a change of train at Port Pirie.

Victoria

The Victorian State Railway, the V/Line, was recently privatised and is now on lease to the British travel company National Express. V/Line operates all rail and associated coach routes within Victoria and 'high-speed' (XPT) services to Sydney (Melbourne-Sydney during the day and Sydney-Melbourne overnight) taking 13 hours. V/Line supersaver fares offer a 30 per cent discount when travelling off peak, i.e. on Tuesdays, Wednesdays and Thursdays, arriving in Melbourne after 9.30am and leaving Melbourne at any time except between 4 and 6pm. In recent years, new, air-conditioned, 'high-speed' Sprinter trains have been introduced on some routes. The Canberra Link involves taking a train to Wodonga on the border with NSW and a bus from there to Canberra. There are *Overland* daily night services to Adelaide taking 12 hours (change to the *Indian Pacific* in Adelaide for Perth).

Melbourne: The city centre 'City Loop' forms an underground railway around the centre of Melbourne. For information about suburban trains, see 💻 www.connexmelbourne.com.au.

Western Australia

The Indian Pacific (💻 www.railaustralia.com.au/indianpacific.php) takes 66 hours to travel from Perth to Sydney (4,352km) and runs twice a week in both directions, on Sundays and Wednesdays from Perth (departing at 11.55am) and Wednesdays and Saturdays from Sydney (departing at 2.55pm). For information and fares, see 💻 www.greatsouthernrail.com.au/site/indian_pacific/fares.jsp.

There are also suburban lines (operated by Westrail) between Perth and Armadale, Fremantle, Joondalup and Midland. The only other rail services in Western Australia are the Perth-Bunbury line and the Perth-Kalgoorlie route operated by the *Prospector*. Tickets should be purchased from vending machines at stations before boarding. Multi-ride tickets can be validated at stations. Seven-day advance purchase fares are available in the low season offering a 30 per cent discount. A car-train service is available between Adelaide and Perth.

For information about Perth local trains, see 💻 www.transperth.wa.gov.au.

Vintage trains

There are a number of 'vintage' trains in Australia, e.g. from Cairns to Kuranda, taking 90 minutes to cover the 33km (20mi), and there are vintage and tramway museums in all states where you can enjoy excursions on restored steam trains. These include the Ida Bay Railway in Tasmania, the NSW Railway Museum (at Thirlmere near Picton), and the *Puffing Billy* in the Dandenongs Ranges in Victoria. On the first Sunday of the month from March to November, a steam train leaves Sydney Central station for Thirlmere. The Hotham Valley Tourist Railway in WA operates Xplorer trains to various destinations, and restored locomotives operate on short excursions from Alice Springs. The Barossa Wine Train runs from Adelaide to the Barossa wine region on a day trip taking in wine tasting at three wineries.

General Information

The following is a summary of facilities available at Australian stations and on Australian trains:

> **Bicycles**
>
> **In most cities, bicycles can be transported on suburban trains free of charge or for a small fee during off-peak times, although it may not be permitted during peak periods. e.g. 6 to 9am and 3 to 7pm on weekdays, or a permit may be required.**

- **Food & drink:** Snacks are served on long-distance and in-state trains (such as XPT and Xplorer trains), and all interstate trains have dining cars offering both formal dining and light meals. There are also lounge and club cars on most services. Railway food is generally good and can be excellent on 'tourist' trains such as the *Ghan*, *Indian Pacific* and *Queenslander*. There are no bar facilities for economy passengers on some long-distance services (e.g. from Adelaide to Melbourne) and there may be a large fine (e.g. $100) for consuming your own alcohol! Taking your own picnic onto a train isn't prohibited but may be frowned upon. There are restaurants and snack bars at main stations, and food and drink machines are provided at many smaller stations.

- **Luggage:** Interstate train passengers are permitted up to 50kg (110lbs) of luggage (two items not exceeding 25kg/55lbs each and a maximum of 180cm/71in in circumference). Medium-size suitcases and hand luggage can be carried in compartments, but larger luggage should be booked in at the luggage desk not less than 30 minutes before departure. Booked luggage is carried in the luggage car and isn't accessible during the journey. There are also luggage storage spaces at the ends of passenger compartments. Luggage can be sent unaccompanied and can be insured. Many stations have left luggage offices, luggage lockers (from $2 for up to 24 hours) and luggage trolleys. When using a luggage locker, you need to insert the correct money to release the key. It's advisable to make a note the number of the locker in case you lose the key.
- **Smoking:** There's a smoking ban on all trains throughout Australia.
- **Telephones:** Public payphones (which accept Telecards) are available on long-distance train services.
- **Toilets:** Toilets are provided on trains on all but the shortest services, but shouldn't be used when a train is in a station.

Tickets

Rail tickets in Australia can be purchased from automatic ticket machines, newsagents (in major cities) and station ticket offices. Most interstate and main state trains have both first-class and standard (economy) seating, although there's little difference between seats on some trains, e.g. XPT trains operating in NSW, Queensland and Victoria. There's no first-class accommodation on the Perth-Bunbury line in Western Australia, most trains in outback Queensland and all suburban lines.

Many ticket offices in Sydney and other NSW towns are open only for a few hours per day during rush hours, although passengers can buy tickets from ticket machines at other times (see below). Many stations are unmanned for at least half the day during the week and all day at weekends. Tickets can be paid for with major credit cards (e.g. MasterCard and Visa) subject to a $10 minimum.

Fare evasion is endemic in Australia, particularly in the major cities, where an estimated 3 per cent of passengers travel without tickets (over 5,000 culprits were discovered in a three-week blitz on Sydney's city loop). Fare evaders face fines of up to $200 and Sydneysiders must pay up to $550!

Ticket Machines

Ticket machines have been introduced in recent years, although there have been a 'few' teething troubles, particularly in Melbourne (where the first machines ate your money, chewed up your tickets and stole your change!). You usually select your destination, choose the type of ticket (e.g. single or return), insert the fare (machines accept coins and notes) and, if you're lucky, a ticket is ejected with your change.

Whether you buy your ticket from a machine or at a ticket office, you must validate it (stamp it with the current date and time) in a separate machine, without which it's invalid; you must validate a multiple-ride ticket each time you travel.

In some cities you must insert your ticket in a ticket barrier with a green arrow (not a red cross) in the direction of the arrow shown on your ticket when leaving a station; a return ticket or multi-day pass is returned if you're on the outward journey, otherwise the ticket is retained by the machine.

Bookings

Bookings (reservations) are recommended (at least two months in advance) on all long-distance trains, many of which are fully booked months in advance in the summer season and during school holidays. There's no booking fee on major routes, on which bookings are accepted up to nine months in advance (six months on other long-distance routes). However, if a booking is altered or cancelled, there's a fee of $5 if you make the alteration or cancellation over 30 days prior to travel; 10 per cent of the fare if you make it less than 30 days prior to travel; and 20 per cent of the fare if it's within seven days of travel. There are no refunds for unused tickets after the departure time and date shown on the ticket. For bookings, call ☎ 132232. On some main routes there are discounts of up to 40 per cent for advance purchase tickets (e.g. seven days), although these aren't applied to the cheapest regular fares and therefore may not be the cheapest travel option.

Bookings can be made via Rail Australia's website (💻 www.railaustralia.com.au). Tickets can be booked for any journey throughout the country (apart from local suburban routes) and must be made and paid for at least seven days in advance. The outward journey must start on the date stamped on tickets, and journeys must be completed within the validity of the ticket. Journeys can usually be broken, except with discount fares. Bookings can be made through Thomas Cook offices in many countries.

Always check and double-check the departure (and arrival) time of a train (particularly in the outback when the next train may be a week next Thursday and be fully booked), especially when you need to make a flight connection. You may need to undertake part of your journey by air or bus to link with a connecting train. Schedules are liable to change at short notice, particularly at weekends and during holiday periods. Most long-distance trains operate throughout the year, but local and in-state trains may not run on Public Holidays, which vary with the state, e.g. many don't operate on holidays such as ANZAC Day (25th April). Christmas Day and Good Friday. It's also important to check that a train actually stops where you want to go, as long-distance trains usually make few stops.

Discounts

A variety of discounted tickets are available on Australian railways, including the following:

- **Advance purchase:** On some main routes there are discounts of up to 40 per cent for advance purchase tickets, e.g. seven days, although these aren't applied to the cheapest regular fares and may not be the cheapest travel option. Only a limited number of discounted seats may be available.
- **Children, students & pensioners:** Children under four travel free, unless they're occupying a separate seat or a sleeping berth on an interstate train (when the under-16 fare applies). Those aged from 4 to 15 travel at a discount (usually half-fare), as generally do students and pensioners, depending on the state where you're resident.
- **Low season discounts:** Low season is from 1st February to 30th June and the normal season from 1st July to 31st January. Low season fares are around 40 per cent lower than high season fares; standard fares fall between these two. Low season and standard fares are the same when travelling in economy-class and for travel on *Overland* trains between Adelaide and Melbourne.
- **Off-peak travel:** In major cities, off-peak suburban fares are available after 9am on weekdays and at any time on weekends, offering savings of up to 60 per cent on return journeys.

- **Season tickets:** There's a range of season tickets (weekly, quarterly and annual) for commuters, providing large discounts on standard fares, which may include travel on suburban buses, ferries, trains and trams, e.g. in Sydney. Weekly passes usually cost around eight times the single fare. A photograph is normally required for a season ticket.
- **Rail Passes:** Rail Australia offers rail passes for holiday travel, most of which are valid for three or six months unlimited travel on certain routes, although the East Coast Discovery Pass is only valid for a single journey on a fixed route. See http://passes.railaustralia.com.au for information and fares.
- **Standby fares** – Standby fares are available on some routes.

Further Information

For further information about Australian railways, contact Rail Australia (☎ 132147 in Australia, +61-08-8213 4592 from overseas, www.railaustralia.com.au). Rail Australia has agents in many countries, including Canada, Denmark, France, Germany, Hong Kong, Japan, Korea, the Netherlands, New Zealand, Singapore, South Africa, Sweden, the UK and the US. It publishes a brochure, *Australia By Rail*, which describes the long-distance routes and trains, or you can consult the information on their website.

> **☑ SURVIVAL TIP**
>
> **There are rail enquiry numbers in all states which can usually be reached by calling ☎ 13-2232, although it's often difficult to get through. It's usually easier to visit a rail information office or a station to obtain train information or use a website.**

BUSES & TRAMS

Buses are the cheapest form of public transport in Australia, both within cities and over long distances, and provide a far more comprehensive network than the railways, reaching almost every corner of Australia. There are comprehensive bus services in Australia's major cities and an extensive network of long-distance, interstate buses, usually referred to as coaches. Bus services in rural areas are less frequent.

Each city and region of Australia has its own bus companies providing town and country services. In large towns and cities, most bus services start and terminate at a central bus station, which is generally modern and clean. Most are equipped with luggage lockers or a left luggage office, shops, showers, a snack bar or restaurant, and toilets. They have little in common with the seedy places inhabited by drug addicts, drunks and assorted derelicts found in many other countries. Smoking is prohibited on all buses and trams in Australia.

If you need assistance, ask at the bus station information office. Modern city buses cater for wheelchair users by lowering or raising the boarding platform.

Most bus companies provide free timetables and route maps, and in some cities comprehensive timetables and maps are available which include all bus services operating within their boundaries. See also **Timetables & Maps** on page 163.

For information about trams, see page 162.

Long-distance Buses

Greyhound (☎ 131499, www.greyhound.com.au) is Australia's only national coach operator, formed in 2000 when McCaffertys bought Greyhound Pioneer Australia, although there are several regional operators. The main operator in the southern part of Western Australia is the state rail company, Westrail, while Tasmanian Redline Coaches (☎ 1300-360000, www.tasredline.com.au) provides express services throughout Tasmania.

Long-distance buses are generally cheaper, easier to book and faster than interstate trains, and there's a more comprehensive network. However, they're also less comfortable and more restrictive than trains. Long-distance buses are particularly popular among independent travellers (e.g. backpackers), 80 per cent of whom use them almost exclusively. Travelling by bus is around a third of the cost of travelling by air. There are numerous daily departures on the most popular routes, although some services operate only a few times per week and, in the Northern Territory, northern Queensland and northern parts of Western Australia, some routes are interrupted for weeks at a time during the wet season (November to May). There are also unsociable arrival hours on some long-distance routes.

Buses are usually equipped with air-conditioning, individual reading lights, panoramic windows, reclining seats, toilets, TV and videos with stereo sound, and water fountains. It's wise to get a seat near the front away from the toilet and on the left-hand side away from the lights of approaching traffic at night. Long-distance journeys are tiring and you shouldn't expect to get much (if any) sleep if you're travelling overnight. Frequent stops are made for drinks, food, showers and toilets. There are strict rules concerning what you can eat and drink on buses. No alcohol may be consumed (maximum fine around $500) and smoking is prohibited on all services. Long-distance buses don't cater for those in wheelchairs.

Routes & Fares

There's lively competition between the various regional long-distance bus companies, which helps reduce fares.

There's particularly fierce competition on the most popular routes, e.g. Melbourne-Sydney, where fares are from around $80, although off the main inter-city routes fares can be high. A 25 per cent discount is given for students and children on most services. Some companies offer discounts to backpackers on certain services, although the largest discounts are usually offered on last-minute bookings. Visitors can purchase bus passes overseas in many countries, although you may get a better deal in Australia. Bus passes aren't valid on some local services and a surcharge is usually payable on routes in remote areas. It's always cheaper to buy a through-ticket for a long journey, rather than separate tickets for short stretches, and most tickets allow unlimited stopovers.

Tickets

Long-distance bus tickets are similar to airline tickets, with destinations shown by a code, such as SYD for Sydney and MEL for Melbourne. When checking your luggage, make sure that the luggage code matches that of your destination (otherwise you may end up in Cairns and your luggage in Perth!).

Bookings can be made online, through travel agents or direct with bus companies. There are also many booking agents in major cities, including Youth Hostel Association (YHA) travel offices, some of which allow you to book tickets by telephone and pay with a credit card.

All bookings are non-refundable and non-transferable to other passengers, but can be transferred to another service up until the departure of the original service.

Tours

Numerous coach companies offer tours which include accommodation (e.g. bungalow, cabin, camping, hotel or motel) and most meals, ranging in duration from a few days to several months. On camping tours, meals are usually cooked by a travelling cook and prices include meals, sleeping bags, tents and other equipment. Passengers aren't required to erect tents. Some tour companies cater for backpackers and, although they usually offer a 'rough and ready' service, usually provide good value.

City & Country Buses

In most cities there are a number of local bus companies, sometimes operated by the local railway company or the state or city authorities. There's a comprehensive bus network in all Australian cities, and services are frequent but slow, although they are often the only option for getting to the suburbs. Major cities usually have an integrated public transport system, the same ticket being valid on buses, suburban trains, trams (Melbourne) and ferries (Sydney).

City buses on most routes operate from around 6am until 11pm or midnight (but possibly only until 7pm on Sundays). Buses run frequently during the weekday rush hours, e.g. every 10 or 15 minutes on the main routes. Outside rush hours there's usually a half-hour service on most routes during weekdays, although services are often severely restricted at weekends and on Public Holidays (there may be no service at

all on some routes on Sundays and Public Holidays).

In major cities there's usually an express bus service (called 'rockets' in some cities) operating between the outer suburbs and the CBD (express bus numbers are usually prefixed with an X). Night services operate in the major cities from around midnight until 6am, some of which have radio links with taxi operators, so that you can arrange to have a taxi meet you at your destination. There are free buses in most major cities covering a circular (loop) route within the city centre.

In stark contrast to the cities, in rural areas there's usually only one bus company and services are sparse and infrequent. In remote areas there may only be school buses, which usually carry other passengers but aren't obliged to.

It's usual to board a bus by the front door and disembark from the centre doors. You must normally ring a bell to inform the driver that you want him to stop at the next stop (a buzzer sounds in the cab) and stand by the centre door. When the bus stops, a green light is illuminated which signals that you must push the handle or press a button to open the door, which doesn't usually open automatically.

In most cities, bus stops have numbers, which are often quoted by people when giving directions (stops may be colour-coded). Buses also display their route number, although in some cities numbers may vary depending on whether they're running to or from the city centre. All bus companies publish route maps and there are comprehensive city guides in most cities and state bus directories in some states.

Tickets

In the major cities, journeys are based on a zone system whereby the bus network is divided into a number of concentric areas (the central business district and inner suburbs are usually designated zone 1). Tickets are valid for travel within a single zone or a number of zones, and may be colour-coded corresponding to the zones (and modes of transport) for which they're valid. Day Tripper tickets are valid all day with unlimited transfers.

Tickets can be purchased from bus stations, on board buses and trams, and from retail outlets such as newsagents and cafés in some cities. Automatic ticket machines are provided in some cities, but they may gobble your money and refuse to give you a ticket. You may not be able to buy a ticket from the driver on boarding a bus and may be refused boarding without one (except perhaps at weekends). Tickets must be validated in an on-board machine which stamps your ticket with the date and time of boarding, plus the time of expiry of the ticket. If you have a multi-ride ticket, you must validate it each time you travel.

All bus companies offer day passes and weekly, monthly and annual tickets for commuters. There are also off-peak tickets that allow you to travel at a reduced rate outside rush hours, e.g. between 9am and 3pm or 3.30pm, Monday to Friday and after 7pm until the last service, and at weekends. In most cities you can buy a book of ten tickets (e.g. a TravelTen in Sydney) at a saving of up to 40 per cent compared with buying single tickets. There are concessionary fares for children and pensioners, which are usually half the adult fare. There are fines of over $100 for anyone discovered travelling without a ticket.

A day 'rover' ticket is available in most cities and allows unlimited bus travel for a whole day; it may also include travel on other modes of city transport.

Trams

The Melbourne tram network (commencing with horse trams in 1884) remains a major form of public transport in the city – it's the largest network in the world, bigger than St Petersburg, Berlin, Moscow and Vienna – with 250km (155.3mi) of track, almost 500 trams, 30 routes and over 1,750 stops.

Not to be outdone, Sydney now has the Metro Light Rail (i.e. tram), which began operation in 1997 to link the Central Railway Station with the redeveloped inner-city areas of Darling Harbour, Ultimo and Pyrmont. It was extended in 2000 to serve the inner western suburb of Lilyfield (total length 7.2km/4.5mi) and there are proposed extensions to Dulwich Hill, the University of Sydney and the University of NSW. The State Government is also examining the feasibility of extending it from Central Station to Circular Quay and on to Barangaroo.

Adelaide had a tram network from 1878 until 1958 spanning most of its suburbs. Today there's only one remaining line connecting the CBD with the seaside suburb of Glenelg.

FERRIES

All of Australia's major cities are situated on the coast and most also have rivers and/or harbours, where ferry transport is a convenient way of getting around, particularly in Sydney. It's also the main way of getting to Tasmania form the mainland (mandatory if you want to take your car). There are also cruises and day trips in most major cities.

One of the first things you should do after boarding a ferry or boat is to study the safety procedures, i.e. what to do if it sinks! this is important in Australian waters, which may be home to crocodiles, jellyfish and sharks...

Sydney

Travelling by ferry is one of the joys of living in Sydney, where many people use them to commute to work. The city has eight main ferry routes and 33 ferry wharves, all served from the main Circular Quay ferry terminal. In addition to regular (slow) ferries, there's a catamaran (RiverCat) service from Circular Quay to Parramatta (via the Parramatta River) and a JetCat service to Manly.

Most ferries run from around 6am until midnight, although times vary with the route, and services are restricted at weekends, when ferries may not stop at all wharves. Most services run every 50 minutes during the day and more frequently during rush hours, e.g. every 15 or 20 minutes.

Regular commuters can buy a book of ten tickets (called a 'Ferry Ten') or weekly, quarterly and annual commuter tickets, which offer even greater savings and can be combined with other modes of public transport, such as buses and suburban trains.

Special tickets are available for trips to major attractions (such as Taronga Zoo), which include the return ferry trip from Circular Quay and the entrance fee, and are cheaper than buying separate tickets. Special ferries are also available to follow sailing races such as the famous Sydney-Hobart race, which starts on Boxing Day (26th December). For information, see 💻 www.sydneyferries.info.

Tasmania

The only regular maritime passenger service in Australia is the car ferry operating between Melbourne and Devonport on the north coast of Tasmania. It's served by the *Spirit of Tasmania* (💻 www.spiritoftasmania.com.au), a luxury 467-cabin ship of 31,356 tonnes, with a capacity of around 1,300 passengers plus vehicles. The trip is often rough, so poor sailors should take seasickness pills (or a plane). In fact, the ferry isn't much cheaper than flying and takes around 14 hours, compared with less than an hour by air from Melbourne to Hobart. Ferries run daily during the peak summer season (although there are seasonal variations). Departures are at 8pm or 9pm to Tasmania and at 9am or 8pm in the other direction. Cabins and hostel-style accommodation are available.

There are two fare rates, depending on the time of travel: off-peak (August to November, February to March and April to November) and peak (December to February and March to April). See the website for the exact fare rate periods. In mid-2012, a single fare was from around $130 (reclining seat – cabins extra). There are discounts for students and children. Vehicle transportation is heavily subsidised by the Tasmanian government and costs from $89 (vehicles less than 2m wide and up 5.3m in length) one way, all year round.

A ferry service also operates from Woodbridge on the south-east coast of Tasmania to Roberts Point on Bruny Island.

Other Ferries

Other regular ferry services in Australia include the following:

- **Brisbane:** A fast and efficient CityCat ferry service operates along and across the Brisbane River every 10 to 20 minutes from around 6am until 10.30pm, Monday to Saturday (operating hours are reduced on Sundays). There are also Inner City and Cross River ferries operated by Brisbane Ferries (www.brisbaneferries.com.au).
- **Darwin:** Harbour ferries make daily crossings to Mandorah on the Cox peninsula.
- **Fremantle:** Ferries operate from Fremantle to Rottnest Island.
- **Melbourne:** A leisure ferry service operates from Southgate (city) to Williamstown.
- **Perth:** There's a ferry service across the Swan River from Barrack Street jetty to Mends Street jetty.
- **Victoria:** Ferries operate between Cowes on Philip Island and Stony Point on the Mornington Peninsula, from Stony Point to Tankerton on French Island, and from Sorrento to Queenscliff.

TIMETABLES & MAPS

All public transport companies in Australia produce comprehensive guides, route maps and timetables, and many councils publish excellent guides and maps (available from council offices, libraries, newsagents and tourist centres), which include all bus, ferry and rail transport services operating within a city or region. Most transport companies use am (before noon) and pm (after noon) in timetables, rather than the 24-hour clock. When am and pm aren't indicated, the general practice is that times printed in light type are before noon and times printed in bold type are after noon. When travelling from east to west (or vice versa), bear in mind that there may be local time differences (see **Time Difference** on page 326).

Rail

The state rail authorities and the Great Southern Railway all publish free timetables, and Rail Australia publishes a summary of major interstate services (also available online). Suburban timetables are published separately, and leaflets are available regarding particular services from stations. The *Thomas Cook Overseas Timetable* is the nearest thing Australia has to an Australia-wide rail timetable. On interstate timetables, +1, +2 and +3 indicate that the train arrives one, two or three days after departure. However, bear in mind that rail timetables in Australia are often works of fiction and bear little relation to 'real' time.

Bus

Bus timetables may be for individual routes, all routes operated by a particular company, or all routes serving a city, town or region. Timetables include all local bus company services are often published by local councils and are available free (or for a nominal fee) from bus companies, libraries, tourist offices and travel agents.

TAXIS

There are two kinds of taxi in Australia: cabs (short for 'cabriolet') and radio taxis. The main difference from the passenger's point of view is that cabs (which are usually white or yellow) can be hailed in the street (or found at taxi ranks, railway stations, airports and hotels – there are courtesy telephones outside main hotels), whereas radio taxis can only be booked by telephone, although cabs can also be booked by telephone. Taxis can be 'officially' shared in some states, e.g. in Darwin there are 'multiride' taxis with 12 seats which pick up passengers en route. Wheelchair-accessible taxis are provided in most major cities. There are also water taxis in Sydney operating from Circular Quay to most areas on the harbour, which are a novel (but expensive) way of getting around the harbour. The fare depends on the time of day and the number of passengers.

Cabs for hire display a 'Vacant' or 'For Hire' sign or a light on the roof. Taxi drivers run a high risk of being mugged in some areas of major cities (e.g. Sydney), which has led to some suburbs being officially classified as 'no-go' areas (not just for taxi drivers!). Since 1997, taxis in Sydney have been fitted with a security screen between the passenger compartment and the driver, and a satellite tracking system is installed in taxis to monitor their position and speed (taxis in Melbourne are fitted with video cameras).

Taxis are relatively inexpensive in Australia, and rates vary little from city to city; you can calculate the fare using the taxi fare calculator website (💻 www.taxifare.com.au). Fares include a standing charge (flagfall) plus a fee per kilometre. There are a number of surcharges, including a charge when a cab is called by telephone and an extra charge when a toll (e.g. Sydney Harbour Bridge) is included in the journey. There's usually a surcharge for journeys late at night and at weekends (in some cities there are three daytime rates). There's usually also a small charge for luggage carried in the boot (trunk). Outside city limits you must pay a higher 'country' rate and possibly a surcharge (befouling fee) of 1 hour's waiting time (around $50) if you dirty a taxi! Many taxis accept credit cards for fares over around $5.

Tipping isn't necessary and, although most people round the fare up to the nearest dollar, drivers may actually round the fare down rather than give change and may even refuse tips. Australian taxi drivers are generally honest and helpful (unlike those in many other countries). Complaints about service or hire charges can be made to the local taxi licensing office. Make a note of the taxi's registration number and the date and time of the incident and, if you think you've been overcharged, obtain a receipt.

In addition to taxi services, many taxi companies operate chauffeur and courier services, and private hire (e.g. sightseeing or weddings), and sometimes provide contract and account services, e.g. to take children to and from school.

Caution

It's usually fairly easy to find a cab in a city late at night, as there are many 'night' cabs, although they can be difficult to find just after the pubs close because of the strict drink-driving laws in Australia (and between midnight and 6am on Sundays in major cities).

AIRLINE SERVICES

Australia's national airline is Qantas (Queensland and Northern Territory Aerial Service), formed in 1920 (only KLM is older) and privatised in 1995. It's one of the world's best and usually most profitable airlines, although it reported a $244m loss for the year to 30th June 2012 (almost the same as its profit the previous year), which led to the cancellation of 35 Boeing Dreamliner jets. Qantas (💻 www.qantas.com.au) has a fleet of around 200 aircraft and carries over 30m passengers a year (over 21m on domestic routes) to 120 destinations in 40 countries.

It has partnership agreements with several other international airlines, including American Airlines and British Airways, whereby partners can buy seats on Qantas flights and vice versa. There are Qantas Club lounges at all major airports in Australia and shared lounges in many other countries. Qantas has its own terminals at Australia's major airports, and caters for disabled passengers and those in wheelchairs. Qantas was one of the first airlines to fly the Airbus A380 (it has ordered 20).

Australia's newest international airline, V (Virgin) Australia (💻 www.vaustralia.com.au), took to the skies in February 2009 with an inaugural service between Sydney and Los Angeles (using Boeing 777 aircraft). V Australia also operates services to Los Angeles from Brisbane (April 2009) and Melbourne (December 2009), plus flights to Fiji, Johannesburg and Phuket (Thailand).

Australian airlines are strict about safety, and it's one of the safest places in the world to fly (Qantas is rated as one of the safest airlines in the world by IATA, who in 2000 also named Airservices Australia the world's best provider of air traffic control services). Smoking is prohibited on all flights operated by Australian airlines, both domestic and international, with a maximum $500 fine for offenders.

Domestic Flights

Air travel is the fastest way to get around Australia, and around 80 per cent of domestic long-distance trips are made by air. For many years, Qantas and Ansett monopolised the domestic flight market. The 'cooperation' between them meant that domestic air travel remained expensive for years. However, Ansett went bust in March 2002 and the regional airlines that it owned either went out of business or continued to operate only minor services. This had the effect of shaking up the market, and new airlines were formed which are took on Qantas, creating welcome competition.

Virgin Australia (💻 www.virginaustralia.com) – previously Virgin Blue – is Australia's second-largest airline and the largest by fleet size. It was the country's leading low-cost airline, serving over 30 destinations in Australia, New Zealand, Fiji, PNG, the Cook Islands and Vanuatu, but has since dropped out of the ultra-low fares sector. This has left Jetstar (💻 www.jetstar.com), a subsidiary of Qantas which flies to around 60 destinations, as the only major player in Australia's discount domestic sector, challenged only by the niche, low-cost carrier, Tiger Airways.

Tiger Airways (💻 www.tigerairways.com), a Singapore-based carrier, entered the low-cost fares market in 2004 and flies from Singapore to Perth and also has a limited number of domestic flights from Adelaide and Melbourne (but doesn't currently serve Brisbane or Sydney).

Regional Express (or Rex, 💻 www.regionalexpress.com.au), formed in 2002 and based in Wagga Wagga, is Australia's largest independent regional airline, It connects 29 metropolitan and regional centres across NSW, South Australia, Tasmania and Victoria. Other regional airlines include Airlines of South Australia, Skywest (Western Australia) and Sunstate (Queensland – a subsidiary of Qantas). Attempts by other small airlines (e.g.

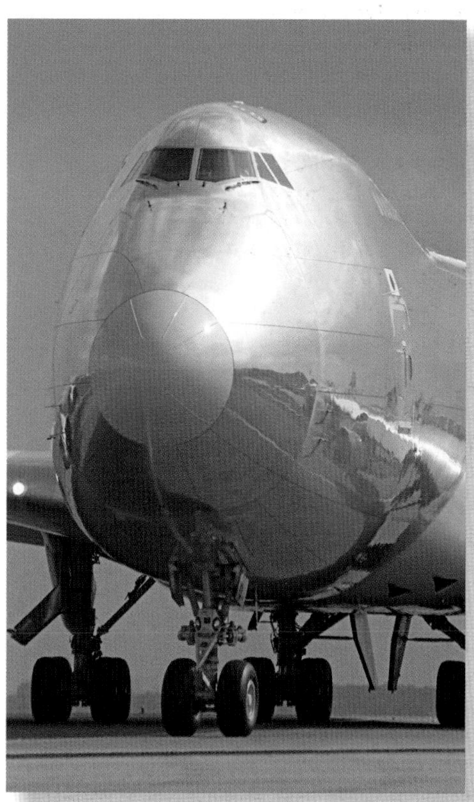

Compass and OzJet) to offer low-cost services have largely been unsuccessful.

Flying times between Sydney and other state capitals are: Canberra (236km/147mi) 30 minutes; Brisbane (746km/464mi) and Melbourne (708km/440mi) one hour 15 minutes; Adelaide (1,166km/725mi) and Hobart (1,039km/646mi) two hours; and Perth (3,284km/2,041mi) around five hours.

There are many flights each day between Australia's major cities (although some journeys require a number of stops), but on less travelled routes there are just one or two flights a week. You should always book a domestic flight as far in advance as possible, particularly during holiday periods (this also allows you to take maximum advantage of discount fares). Many regional and local airlines operate small aircraft, which are generally booked up well in advance and consequently don't offer discounts or low fares. Domestic airlines also offer a variety of air tours and excursion flights.

Domestic air travel is relatively expensive due to the long distances involved. Random discounting is common, although there are often conditions such as advance booking, flying at weekends only or between certain fixed dates. Apart from booking directly with airlines, you can book domestic flights via travel agents and online via a number of websites including 💻 www.flightcentre.com.au (who also have offices throughout Australia).

International Flights

Australia is served by around 50 international airlines operating scheduled passenger services. Check-in time is around two hours before departure (sometimes less for first and business class passengers).

International Fares

Australia's isolated location in the world means that international air travel is invariably expensive. Air fares are high from most countries, as there's a relatively low volume of traffic on most routes and little competition. The main exception is between the UK and Australia (the 'kangaroo route'), which is one of the most competitive in the world. Airlines regularly indulge in price wars, offering cut-price tickets on selected flights. The return fare from London to Sydney is around GB£600 in low season (April to June), rising to around GB£1,000 in high season (December and January), when fares vary little between airlines. Fares during the shoulder season (July to November and February to March) are usually between GB£700 and GB£800. Fares from London to Melbourne or Brisbane are usually higher than to Sydney.

Flights from the UK to Australia in the weeks immediately before Christmas are usually fully booked months in advance, and delaying your flight a few days until after the Christmas period can mean a considerable saving. If you fly to Australia from the UK at any time of year with British Airways, Qantas or Singapore Airlines, you usually pay between £100 and £200 more than with other airlines, but this may be worthwhile if you take advantage of these airlines' domestic deals within Australia, i.e. reduced domestic fares for those flying to and from Australia. Fares to Australia are higher if you break the journey, although most travellers find that it's worthwhile taking advantage of stopover deals and this helps to reduce jetlag.

Return fares from Australia to Europe are higher than when travelling in the opposite direction. The best deals are from Sydney, although bargains can be found from Melbourne and Perth (discount fares are advertised in the major daily newspapers). A 'departure tax' is incorporated into the ticket price for passengers aged 12 or over. Departing passengers must also complete an *Outgoing Passenger Card*.

Fares to the US haven't traditionally been as good value as to Europe, although excursion and promotional fares are available which are much lower than full fares. For years just two airlines, Qantas Airways and United Airlines, offered non-stop flights and consequently kept the fares high (as duopolies do on routes throughout the world). However, thanks to a landmark 'open skies' agreement between the US and Australia in 2008, Virgin (V Australia) has joined the fray and other airlines are expected to enter the market.

Asia and North America start at around GB£1,000 for four stops, depending on the season. From Europe you can also fly via South Africa or South America, although these options are much more expensive than the usual Asian or North American routes.

V Australia's entry into the market in February 2009 led to a dramatic drop in fares, with non-stop, round-trip economy tickets that previously averaged around $1,500 to $2,000 in 2008, falling below $1,000. Qantas responded by matching V Australia's low fares and by inaugurating the double-decker Airbus A380, the world's largest passenger jet, on its LAX route.

Regular tickets are valid for 12 months, so it may pay to buy your ticket well in advance of your trip. Many flights to North America make a stop in Auckland, Fiji, Honolulu or Tahiti (Papeete). An 'open-jaw' ticket (flying into one airport and out of another) may be no more expensive than an ordinary return.

Major airlines offer economy, business and first class fares. Full fare tickets allow you to change the date and time of travel at a moment's notice and offer a full refund should you decide not to travel. When buying apex and other discounted tickets, always make sure that you fully understand any ticket restrictions, e.g. some don't permit a change of flight (even for a fee).

If you're migrating to Australia, you should book as far ahead as possible – but never before you've received your visa!

Stopovers & round-the-world tickets: When travelling to Australia, you can travel one-stop or take advantage of a number of stopovers, e.g. in Asia, North America and the Pacific. Most return tickets from Europe include 'free' stopover options on outward and return journeys, usually in Asia or the Pacific. Round-the-world tickets to Australia from London via

Airports

The main airports in Australia are Adelaide, Brisbane, Cairns, Darwin, Melbourne, Perth, Port Hedland, Sydney and Townsville. Sydney and Melbourne are Australia's two largest international airports; Adelaide, Brisbane, Cairns, Darwin, Hobart, Perth and Townsville also have international airports. The capital, Canberra, doesn't have an international airport and is served only by domestic flights from other Australian cities (Sydney is only half an hour away by air). When minor airports and country landing strips are included, Australia has a total of over 400 'airports'.

Most of Australia's major airports are owned and controlled by the Federal Airports Corporation (FAC), although they're gradually being privatised. Most Australian airports are deserted much of the time and come to life for only a few hours a day, when international flights arrive and depart. Terminals may open for only a few hours before arrivals or departures and close for the day after the last flight has arrived or left. International terminals are usually separate from domestic terminals and the two may be located some distance apart. There are bus and taxi services from all major airports to local city centres.

outback road

11. MOTORING

Australians are devoted to their cars and (like Americans) rarely go anywhere without them. As a result, public transport provision, particularly in rural areas, is poor or non-existent and it's essential to have your own transport if you live anywhere other than in one of the main cities. Travelling inter-state involves vast distances (on the North American scale) and many Australians think nothing of driving hundreds of miles to visit relatives or friends for a few days or even a day out.

Almost 80 per cent of goods in Australia are transported by road and passenger travel is also dominated by road transport, with over 16.5m passenger vehicles (2011). Australian cities are often sprawling (particularly Sydney) and most people are inclined to use their cars rather than public transport. There are 'park and ride' facilities in cities to encourage commuters to use public transport, although they aren't widely used (encouraging car pooling is also a hard slog). However, despite the congestion – particularly during rush hours – driving in Australia is no worse than in most countries and better than many (e.g. the US), and once you get out of the cities it can even be a pleasure.

Australia has a relatively low road accident rate – similar to the UK and half that of the US – with around 1,300 fatalities per year (5.5 deaths per 100,000 motor vehicles or 1bn vehicle-km) and some 200,000 injuries. The death toll is falling and is now a third of what it was in the '70s, thanks to safer vehicles, the introduction of random breath testing and speed cameras, and a reduction in legal alcohol/blood levels. However, levels of alcohol (and drugs) among those involved in fatal accidents remain high. The risk of young males aged 17 to 25 dying on the roads is around three times that of other age groups, and they're five times more likely to die in a car accident than women of the same age. Public holiday periods are the most dangerous times to be on the roads.

Individual states and territories have jurisdiction over driving licences, the registration of motor vehicles and traffic rules, which vary with the state or territory. For specific information, obtain a copy of a state or territory's 'highway code' (it has various names, such as the *Road Users' Handbook* in New South Wales and *Your Keys To Driving* in Queensland).

If you're going to Australia for a short period, don't forget to take your car insurance policy, foreign licence, international driving permit (if applicable), no-claims discount certificate and records of membership of motoring organisations.

IMPORTING A VEHICLE

Before importing a vehicle into Australia you need to contact the Department of Transport and Regional Services (☏ 1800-815 272 or +61-2-6274 6013 from abroad, 💻 www.infrastructure.gov.au/vehicles/imports/index.aspx) to ensure that the vehicle meets Australia's safety requirements. If it does, there are three stages to importing a motor vehicle privately:

1. Obtain and complete an *Application for a Personally Imported Vehicle* (IO1) form the DTRS.

2. Pay customs duty (see below), goods and services tax (10 per cent) and, where applicable, luxury car tax (payable on vehicles valued above $59,133 in 2012-13) and obtain customs clearance at the port of entry.
3. Obtain quarantine clearance from the Australian Quarantine and Inspection Service (AQIS) after the vehicle has arrived at the port of entry (see below for details).

Vehicles manufactured before 1st January 1989 may be imported without restriction. Customs duty varies according to the vehicle's design and value and is subject to change. Contact a customs office before importing a vehicle to find out how much customs duty it will attract. Tourists and temporary residents can import a motor vehicle for a period of 12 months (longer under certain circumstances) without paying duty, provided the vehicle is subsequently exported from Australia.

The AQIS inspects all vehicles on arrival and sometimes requires them to be cleaned (usually steam cleaned) at your expense. This is to prevent the entry of diseases, insect pests and undesirable plant spores into Australia. To avoid this procedure (and the cost of cleaning), you should remove all soil and other matter from your vehicle (including the underside) before shipping it to Australia. See the AQIS website (www.daff.gov.au/aqis/import/vehicles-machinery/motor-vehicles) for information.

You must complete all customs clearance formalities at the port of entry. This is expedited if you have the following documents to hand: bill of sale, driving licence, insurance documents, log book, passport, registration papers and service record.

TECHNICAL INSPECTION

Vehicle inspection in Australia is done on a state basis and each state or territory sets its own laws regarding vehicle inspections, although all (with the exception of the self-governing territory of Norfolk Island) have some form of inspection, either periodically or before a transfer of ownership. There are usually two kinds of technical inspection: a comprehensive one (called a blue slip) and a relatively easy

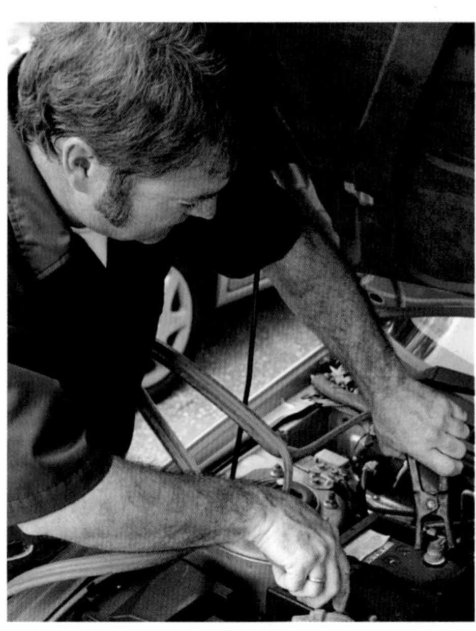

one, originally called a pink slip but nowadays white and called an e-safety check in NSW. In NSW, a pink slip is required for all cars over four years old (from the registration date) and annually thereafter, and is basically to ensure that a vehicle is roadworthy. The cost of a pink slip test is from around $30.

The blue slip is a thorough examination of a vehicle covering everything and is principally required for the importation of a vehicle (see page 169), but is also required when buying a vehicle from inter-state or when re-registering a vehicle that has been off the road for a considerable time. It can also be demanded by the police when they suspect a vehicle is in a dangerous condition.

In the state of Queensland, there's no legal requirement for a private vehicle's owner to have periodic vehicle inspections, e.g. when a vehicle is four or five year's old. The only time a vehicle inspection is mandatory is when a vehicle is being sold, when it must display a current Roadworthy Certificate (RWC) as an assurance to buyers that it meets minimum safety standards. Without an RWC, the vehicle can only be sold on an 'as-seen' basis, which doesn't permit it to be driven on public roads or registered until an RWC is obtained. Heavy goods vehicles (e.g. trucks) and public passenger vehicles (e.g. taxis, buses) have dedicated inspection schemes that must be complied with periodically, usually every 6 or 12 months.

In order to sell a car in Australia, you must have the car inspected within one month of the sale and present the inspection certificate to the buyer.

REGISTRATION

Vehicle registration (known colloquially as 'rego') must be renewed annually. In addition to road tax, the registration fee includes stamp duty (between 2 and 5 per cent of the vehicle's 'market' value depending on the state) and third party liability insurance, which is compulsory (the cost of which is fixed) in most states. Registration is the responsibility of states and territories, and fees vary depending on a car's unladen weight and use (private/ business). The following table shows '**typical**' annual rego fees for private cars in NSW:

Typical Rego Fees in NSW

Unladen Weight	Annual Fee
Up to 975kg	$245
976 to 1,154 kg	$274
1,155 to 1,504kg	$323
1,505 to 2,504kg	$461

Registration of a vehicle is made with the local state traffic authority, e.g. the Roads and Traffic Authority (RTA) in NSW – which now comes under Roads and Marine Services (see addresses in **Appendix A**). Payment of vehicle registration can be made at the traffic authority's office or at a post office, and a current registration label must be displayed behind your car windscreen; if you lose it, a replacement costs around $20. Motorists who don't pay their rego within a few weeks of the due date face a fine.

The following are required to register a vehicle:

- **Compliance plate** – Before a vehicle can be registered in Australia, it must be fitted with an Australian compliance plate, which indicates that it complies with Australian Design Rules (ADR); for details, see the Department of Transport and Regional Services (DOTARS) website (www.infrastructure.gov.au/vehicles/imports/index.aspx). A compliance plate is fitted automatically to a car manufactured in Australia; imported vehicles must be inspected by a state government motor vehicle registration authority. Before a vehicle can be tested, evidence must be shown that import duty and GST have been paid, as applicable.
- **Insurance** – It's necessary to have proof of third party (CTP) insurance (shown by a 'green slip' issued by an insurance company) to register a vehicle in Australia. You can choose the insurance company (shop around), which will send you the green slip and also notify the local state traffic authority.

Once you have completed the above steps and had you vehicle inspected (see **Technical Inspection** above), you can register it online (at the local state traffic authority's website), over the phone, via the post or in person at a motor registery or agency.

Number plates

Number (registration) plates are issued by state and territory authorities and must be displayed at the front and rear of cars and at the rear of motorcycles. The registration numbers must match those on the vehicle's registration papers. A vehicle may not be parked or driven on a public road without registration, and plates must be returned to the issuing authority when they expire. Each state or territory has unique coloured plates as shown below:

Number Plate Colours

State/Territory	Colour
ACT	Blue on white
NSW	Black on yellow
NT	Red on white
QLD	Green on white
SA	Green on yellow
TAS	Blue on white
VIC	Dark blue on white
WA	Black on yellow

There are also commercial, diplomatic, official and personalised registration plates with different colours. If you move to another state, you must re-register a vehicle.

Change of Ownership

If you buy a second-hand car, the previous owner must sign the back of the registration document, which you must take with the technical inspection certificate, if applicable, to the motor registry (the state government department concerned with the registration of motor vehicles, listed in the phone book). The change of ownership must be registered with the state authority and a registration transfer fee paid (between $20 and $30, depending on the state), plus stamp duty of around 2 to 5 per cent, depending on the state. When a vehicle is bought or sold, the CTP insurance transfers to the new owner until the registration expires.

Note that if you fail to re-register a vehicle within a reasonable period, the police may confiscate your number plates.

CAR HIRE

The car hire (rental) business is extremely competitive in Australia, with five multinational companies (Avis, Budget, Hertz, National and Thrifty) and a plethora of smaller companies. The major companies have offices in cities and towns throughout the country and at most major airports. Cars can be hired (rented) from garages and local car hire companies in most towns, which often have much lower rates than the nationals. Look in local newspapers and under 'Car Rentals' in the *Yellow Pages*. Shop around for the best rate. Airlines offer fly-drive deals on flights to or within Australia, which must be booked with the flight and don't necessarily represent good value.

As in most countries, the car hire business is a minefield for the unwary. You MUST always inspect a car thoroughly on collection, ensuing that EVERY scratch, dent and mark – even a small stone chip on the windscreen – is recorded (you receive a copy). When you return the car you must ensure that you receive written confirmation that the car was returned in good order. If you don't you could be charged for every little scratch – like the previous half a dozen drivers!

Hire companies often offer optional extras such as child seats and a roof rack, for which some charge a fee. All hire cars from national companies are covered for roadside breakdown assistance from a motoring organisation. You can also hire a 4WD vehicle, campervan or motorhome, minibus, prestige luxury car, sports car or a estate car (station wagon), and a choice of manual or automatic gearbox is often available. Performance cars' can be hired from a number of specialist rental companies, although if you want to test drive a car for a few days with a view to buying one, you may get a better deal from a garage. Vans and utility vehicles (pick-ups) are available by the hour, half-day or day. You can hire a campervan (motorhome), caravan or trailer from a number of companies (see below). Some companies also rent cars with hand controls for registered disabled drivers.

There's a wealth of companies in Australia hiring out old cars, sporting names such as 'Rent a Ruffy' and 'Rent a Wreck', typically from around $30 per day. However, you should be wary of hiring a very old car (cars from major hire companies aren't more than three years old and are usually less than a year old), as they could be dangerous. If you hire a car in an unroadworthy condition, you're responsible if you're stopped by the police or cause an accident. If you need a vehicle for a few months or longer, you may be better off buying one and selling it when you no longer need it.

The rates charged by the national companies in major cities are almost identical, daily rates averaging $50 to $60 for a small family car, $75 for a medium-size car and $100 for a large car. Four-wheel-drive vehicles cost from around $100 per day. Smaller local companies are usually cheaper, although you shouldn't automatically assume that this is so, as the major companies offer special deals, including standby, weekend (e.g. three days for the price of two), weekly and monthly rates. You may also be able to negotiate a lower rate if business is slow. In some areas where competition is fierce (such as Tasmania), rates are usually lower, particularly out of season.

Compulsory third party (CTP) insurance is usually included in basic rates, but collision damage waiver (CDW) isn't usually included. If you don't opt for CDW you must pay an excess, e.g. $300 to $1,500 (up to $4,000 in the Northern Territory!), if you have an accident. Personal accident insurance is available for an extra charge of around $2.50 per day. Stamp duty of 1 to 2 per cent is payable on all car rentals.

You should always check the kilometre restrictions, which may be only 100 to 300km (62 to 186mi) 'free' per day, after which you pay a charge (e.g. 25 cents) per km. In rural and outback areas, there's usually a flat daily charge, plus a charge per kilometre. Most companies restrict travel to sealed roads within 100 to 200km (62 to 124mi) of the hire outlet or within the state or territory where the car is rented (ACT rentals usually cover the whole of NSW). If you breach the rules regarding the operating area, your insurance is automatically cancelled.

Major companies usually quote different rates for 'metro' (city), country and 'remote' (outback) driving. Hire car insurance doesn't usually cover travel on dirt roads, with the exception of 4WD vehicles; even then insurance doesn't usually cover off-road travel, i.e. anything that isn't a maintained (sealed or dirt) road. The major companies offer one-way hire, which means you can hire a car at one branch and leave it at another. However, there are a number of conditions, e.g. the Northern Territory and Western Australia aren't always included, and it's expensive (around $200 extra). When returning a vehicle there's usually no point in filling it with petrol as you're invariably charged for a full tank anyway.

☑ SURVIVAL TIP

When comparing prices, take into account all the costs, insurance, taxes and surcharges, as what initially looks a bargain may not be when you include all the extras. If you're planning to travel in country areas or interstate, you should make sure that the hire includes membership of a local motoring organisation.

To hire a vehicle in Australia, you require a full national licence, which must have been held for a minimum of two or three years, or an International Driving Permit (valid for one year). You must usually be aged over 21, although some companies set the minimum age at 23 or 25 for certain vehicles, such as 4WDs. A major credit card is usually necessary for identification and the estimated costs (including a tank of petrol) must be paid in advance. Without a credit card, the estimated hire charge must be paid in advance plus a bond of around $200, which is returned, less any legitimate deductions.

BUYING A CAR

The cost of labour and parts for even the least expensive family cars is generally high in Australia, therefore it may pay to buy a car with a long or extended warranty. Popular, locally-manufactured cars are best if you don't want high repair bills, as spares and servicing for some German and Japanese cars are astronomical. Air-conditioning is standard on most cars in Australia and is essential for anyone who spends much time behind the wheel. It certainly isn't a luxury when you're stuck in a traffic jam in summer or on long-distance trips in the outback.

Information regarding the purchase of both new and used cars is published by Australian motoring organisations (see page 190) and is also available on their websites, e.g. NRMA (🖳 www.mynrma.com.au/motoring/buy-sell.htm). New and used car guides are published, including the *New Car Buyer's Guide*, the *Used Car Buyer's Guide* and Universal's *New 4WD Guide*.

New Cars

New cars generally cost around the same in Australia as in most European countries and up to twice as much as in the US, particularly imported cars, on which there's an import tariff. For example, a small hatchback costs from around $15,000 and a family car from around $30,000. A number of foreign manufacturers make or assemble cars in Australia, including Ford, Holden (General Motors), Mitsubishi, Nissan and Toyota, which comprise over 75 per cent of the new car market, although other Asian manufacturers are starting to establish a foothold. Ford and Holden models are among the most popular and consequently the cheapest for spares and repairs. Note, however, that local models are often different from those available in other countries, as manufacturers style their cars according to what the local market demands (Australians are proud of their cars, particularly 'classic' Holden models).

Used Cars

If you want a reliable old car, it's best to buy a Ford Falcon or Holden Commodore, which are engineered to survive Australia's rough outback roads, and have strong six-cylinder engines and relatively inexpensive parts that are easy to obtain. Second-hand parts for most older Australian-made cars can be picked up cheaply from car breakers' yards throughout the country. Estates and panel vans are popular among travellers, as you can put a mattress in the back. Imported cars (e.g. German and Japanese) are generally considered more reliable than Australian-built cars, although they're also much more expensive. Expect to pay from $1,000 for an old 'banger' (which should, however, be mechanically reliable) and from around $5,000 for a decent second-hand car that should last a number of years.

All used cars must be fitted with an immobiliser before transfer of ownership, if they don't already have one. It's important to contact the state Registry of Encumbered Vehicles/REV, who can tell you whether a car is under finance or has been stolen or if there are any outstanding fines (e.g. parking) against it – when you buy a car, you assume responsibility for any outstanding fines. In NSW there's a fee of $18 – see https://myrta.com/vehiclehistorycheck.

As an alternative to buying privately or from a dealer (see below), it's possible to buy at auction, although this isn't recommended unless you're an expert or advised by one. There are numerous companies who will do a pre-purchase car inspection, usually costing around $150.

Dealers

The Property Agents and Motor Dealers Act, 2000 came into effect on 1st July 2001, establishing trading standards for used car dealers, who are required to adhere to a code of conduct.

All dealers must display a 'statutory warranty', which guarantees that cars are free from serious defects and that any defects occurring during the warranty period will be repaired free of charge.

Warranty periods are three months or 5,000km for cars under ten years old or with under 160,000km on the clock, and one month or 1,000km for cars over ten years old or with more than 160,000km on the clock. Under the new law, buyers have a 'cooling off' period (until 5pm the next working day) and may take the car for a test drive and have it independently inspected. They also have the option of a 'complaint resolution process'. However, if you decide to use the 'cooling-off' period you must pay a deposit of up to $100, which is lost if you decide not to buy.

It's always best to buy a used car from a dealer who's licensed by the state business licensing authority, who's bound by the Auctioneers and Agents Act, and, preferably, who's a member of a motor traders association; the Motor Trades Association of Australia (MTAA) is the major national body and there are also state/territory associations. If there's any question about a car's authenticity or the dealer's right to sell it (e.g. it's stolen, still under finance or has been modified), a licensed dealer must rectify the problem.

When you buy from a car dealer, he'll usually help you with the paperwork and provide a technical inspection certificate and warranty, which is compulsory in most states. A dealer may also include free membership of a local motoring organisation. Always check carefully what's included or excluded from a used car warranty, as many contain a number of conditions, which, if you don't adhere to them, make the warranty void. However, if you buy a car in Sydney and break down in Perth the warranty won't be of much use!

A number of dealers in the major cities specialise in selling cars to travellers. Although they may operate from 'shabby' premises (they're generally known as car yards), most are honest, as their reputation depends upon it. Many offer to buy vehicles back at an agreed price (provided you don't wreck it), which is usually around half the purchase price. However, dealers may try to knock down the buy-back price by finding fault with the car, even when it has been agreed in writing. If this happens, you may get a better deal selling it privately (you should get around two-thirds of the price paid after six to nine months, provided you didn't pay too much). Obviously a buy-back deal is feasible only if you're returning to your starting point.

Buying Privately

Purchasing privately usually means you have less protection (such as a statutory warranty) than when buying through a dealer or at auction. However, to sell a car legally in Australia, the seller must have it inspected (see **Technical Inspection** on page 170) within a month of the sale and present the inspection certificate to the buyer. If you're buying privately, you should therefore only buy a car that has a valid 'pink slip'. It's obviously best to buy a car whose annual registration (see page 171) isn't about to expire. Stamp duty is payable as a percentage (between 2 and 5 per cent depending on the state) of the declared purchase price.

Car markets: Cheap cars can be purchased at car markets in most cities, where owners gather to sell their vehicles. For example, in Sydney you can buy or sell a vehicle at the Car Market at 110 Bourke Street, Woolloomooloo (☎ 1800 808188, 💻 www.carmarket.com.au), which is dedicated to travellers buying and selling cars and campervans. One of the advantages of buying direct from travellers is that they may include camping equipment, spares and other useful items in the price. You can also pick up cars registered in a state other than the one where it's being sold, which can be good buys, particularly if you plan to sell in the state where the vehicle is registered.

The best days for car advertisements in local newspapers are Wednesdays and Saturdays. You can also search for used cars on the internet via numerous sites such as 💻 www.carsguide.com.au, www.carsales.com.au and www.tradingpost.com.au. You can buy other state newspapers, although it's rarely worth travelling far to inspect a car unless it's a rare model or exceptional value. Deciphering used car advertisements can be difficult unless you speak 'Australian', e.g. a panel van is a van with no rear windows and only front seats, and a ute is a utility or pickup truck (an open-backed van).

DRIVING LICENCE

The minimum age for driving a car or motorcycle varies between 16 and 18 depending on the state or territory and all drivers must have a valid licence. There are heavy penalties in Australia for driving without a licence (or with an expired licence), including fines of between $300 and $4,000, a prison term of up to one year and a ban from driving for a period.

> **☑ SURVIVAL TIP**
>
> **Most foreign licences are valid for a year in Australia, although it's usually worthwhile obtaining an international driving permit, particularly if your national licence doesn't contain your photograph.**

If a foreign licence isn't written in English, an official translation must be obtained. This can be done in Australia by the local state Community Relations Commission or the Department of Immigration and Multicultural and Indigenous Affairs. Your driving licence, translation and passport must be carried when driving.

If you're a resident of Australia, you must have a licence issued by the state or territory where you're resident, and if you move to another state or territory you must obtain (not just apply for) a new licence and return your old licence within three months. The same applies to foreign licence holders coming to Australia as permanent residents.

The following licence classes apply throughout Australia (there are also special categories for industrial vehicles):

- **Category C:** The basic licence permits you to drive a car or van with a maximum of 12 seats (including the driver's) weighing less than 4.5 tonnes.
- **Category LR:** This licence is required to drive heavy goods vehicles and vehicles with more than 12 seats. You must have held a C licence for at least a year to qualify for an LR licence.
- **Category R-Date:** This type of licence is required to ride a motorcycle of up to 250cc.
- **Category R:** This licence entitles you to ride any motorcycle.

Each class of licence exists in three levels, distinguished by their colour: learner's licence (green); unrestricted licence (silver or gold); provisional licence (red) – for those ineligible for an unrestricted licence (see below). A silver licence is issued for one or three years after you first pass your test; after five years, you qualify for a gold licence, which is valid for a further five years. The cost of a driving licence varies with the state, e.g. in NSW it's $52 for one year, $122 for three years or $162 for five years.

Driving licences are valid until you're aged 80, but after reaching that age there are increasing requirements to retain your licence, possibly involving restrictions on where or when (e.g. daylight only) you may drive.

To obtain a driving licence, in most states you must:

- take an eyesight test and, in certain cases (e.g. sufferers from diabetes and epilepsy), pass a medical examination;
- pass a written road knowledge test (unless you hold a licence from an exempt country, which includes most EU countries, the US, Canada and Japan), costing $36;
- pass a driving test (unless you hold a licence from an exempt country). A driving test in NSW costs $40 for the written knowledge test and $50 for the practical driving test.

Take evidence of the above to the motor registry, along with:

- your foreign licence (with an English translation if necessary), which is photocopied and returned;
- proof of your identity, e.g. a passport and another document such as a credit card or an account card from a bank, building society or credit union;
- proof of your address;
- the fee, e.g. see www.rta.nsw.gov.au for a list of fees applicable in NSW.

If you fail the road knowledge test, you can take it again (e.g. on the next working day) and you're only asked the questions that you got wrong. If you hold a foreign licence and fail the Australian driving test, you can no longer drive in Australia until you pass it. You must first obtain a learner's licence, which allows you to drive while supervised by a licensed driver with a clean licence (i.e. no demerit points – see below) who has held a licence for at least seven years.

If you pass the test but have held a foreign driving licence for less than a year, you're eligible only for a provisional licence. This means that you must display 'P' plates on your vehicle at all times and are restricted to lower speeds (maximum 80kph/50mph), a reduced alcohol/blood level (0.02g per 100ml) and are permitted to accumulate a maximum of only three demerit points (see below) during the term of your licence.

If your last licence expired over five years ago, you may be required to return to learner's status. Learners must take a written road knowledge test before taking a practical driving test. They must display an 'L' plate until they've obtained a provisional or unrestricted licence. In some states, learner drivers must keep a logbook (teenagers are supervised by their parents) to prove that they've gained experience driving in a range of conditions and that their training period has extended to a year (a minimum three-month L-plate period applies in many states).

The state RTAs publish information about obtaining driving licences, e.g. *Licence to Drive*, and a *Guide to DART* (Driving Ability Road Test) in NSW, which are available from local motor registries.

Fines & Demerit points

Fines and 'demerit points' are issued for driving infringements depending on the severity of an offence. Demerit points range from one (e.g. failing to dip your headlamps) to six points (exceeding the speed limit by over 45kph/28mph), although most offences carry three demerit points. A list of the infringements and consequent demerit points varies from state to state and is detailed in a state's *Road User's Handbook*. If you accumulate a certain number of demerit points within a limited period (usually two years), your licence may be revoked. The number you need to accrue in order to be banned from driving depends on the type of licence you carry.

If you accumulate 12 points, your licence is usually cancelled for a minimum of three months. You should check with the RTA for the point limit of the type of licence you carry. Your licence can also be cancelled for up to five years (and you can be imprisoned) for serious offences, such as failing or refusing to take a breath test , failing to stop after an accident in which someone has been injured or killed, and exceeding the speed limit by over 45kph (28mph).

CAR INSURANCE

Car insurance is available from numerous Australian insurance companies. Foreign insurance policies aren't valid in Australia, and

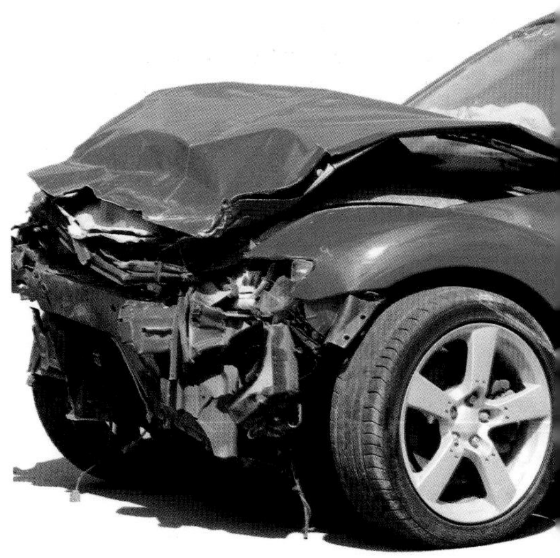

all vehicles operated there must be insured with an Australian company. Note that it can be difficult to insure some imported vehicles that aren't sold in Australia.

Four categories of car insurance are available: third party; third party property; third party, fire and theft; and comprehensive (explained below). Any insurance policy can include other drivers (either named or unnamed). Separate passenger insurance is usually unnecessary, as passengers are automatically covered by all Australian motor insurance policies. You must ensure that you state any previous accidents or driving offences when applying for car insurance or your insurer can refuse to pay out in the event of a claim.

Third Party

The minimum insurance cover required by law is third party, usually referred to as compulsory third party (CTP) or 'green slip', which is required in all states and territories.

CTP covers only bodily injury to third parties (including injuries caused by passengers) and doesn't cover damage done to third party property (including other vehicles), for which third party property insurance is required (see below). Under common law, compensation is paid for both economic loss (medical costs and loss of earnings) and non-economic loss (e.g. pain and suffering), if applicable.

Your 'green slip' must be produced when registering a vehicle. When a vehicle is bought or sold, the CTP transfers to the new owner until the registration expires. CTP is included in a car's annual registration fees (see page 171), but in the case of imported vehicles (which are exempt from the first year's rego insurance) it must be arranged independently.

> ☑ **SURVIVAL TIP**
>
> **Third party only insurance isn't recommended on its own, as you could be faced with a huge bill if you damage someone else's property.**

Third Party Property

Third party property (TPP) cover protects you against liability for damage caused to other people's property in an accident, e.g. if you damage another car or knock down a fence. TPP usually includes a provision of up to $3,000 for your own car if it's damaged by an uninsured driver (but you must be able to identify the driver).

Third Party, Fire & Theft

Known in some countries as 'part comprehensive', third party, fire and theft (TPF&T) cover includes third party cover (to people and property) and insurance against loss of or damage to your car and anything fitted to it caused by fire, lightning, explosion, theft or attempted theft. It usually also covers breakage of glass. The amount you can claim may be limited, e.g. to $5,000, unless otherwise agreed when you take out a policy. Bear in mind that it isn't unusual for a car to overheat and catch fire in Australia so, unless you're driving a worthless heap, it pays you to have TPF&T insurance (and to carry a fire extinguisher!). Note also that TPF&T may not cover all your belongings (e.g. if you're travelling around Australia in a campervan containing all your 'worldly possessions').

Comprehensive

Comprehensive insurance covers you for all the risks listed under CTP and TPP above, plus breakage of glass (e.g. windscreen replacement), medical expenses and theft of contents. It also usually includes damage due to natural hazards, e.g. storm damage, but not loss or damage due to fire and theft, which are subject to an additional premium. Extra cover may be included free or for an additional fee, e.g. the cost of hiring a car if yours is involved in an accident or stolen, legal assistance, no-claims discount protection, and extra cover for a car stereo system. Clothing and personal effects are usually included in comprehensive policies. Comprehensive insurance may also cover you against loss when your car is in a garage for servicing or repair.

Check a policy for any restrictions: for example, you may not be covered against theft if your car isn't garaged and locked overnight. Comprehensive insurance can be extended to include other vehicles that are loaned or rented to the policyholder, and generally covers you for third party risk when you're driving a car that doesn't belong to you. Most lenders insist on comprehensive insurance for leasing, contract hire and hire purchase agreements.

Premiums

The cost of CTP insurance (which is included in your annual registration fee – see page 171) is fixed in most states, but charges vary from state to state. The exception is NSW, where the cost can vary considerably, so shop around. Note that CTP and additional insurance premiums, such as comprehensive, are separate and must be paid in addition to CTP.

Other insurance premiums vary considerably according to a car's insurance class (although not all insurers place cars in the same class), which is calculated according to: the new cost, the cost of spare parts, and labour and repair times; the car's power; your age, occupation and sex (women drivers usually pay lower premiums as they have fewer accidents); what you use your car for, e.g. business or pleasure; the number of miles you cover per year (some policies offer reduced rates for those who do low mileage); your driving experience and driving record, e.g. demerit points or loss of licence; your accident record and no-claims discount (see below); who will drive the car besides the owner; your health (you may be required to pay an excess if you suffer from epilepsy or diabetes); where

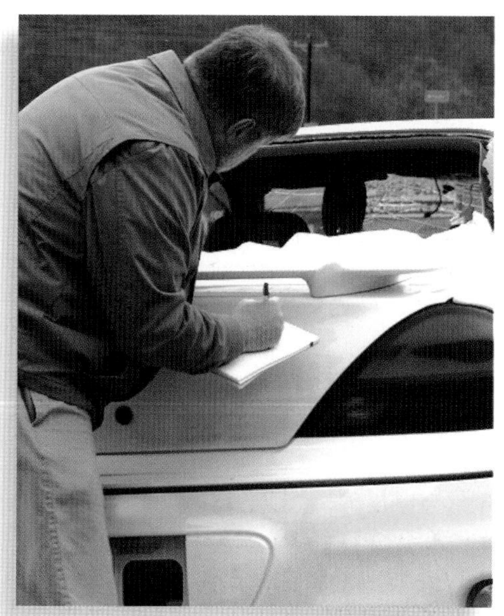

you live (see below) and whether your car is garaged overnight; and any extras you require, such as a protected no-claims discount.

Australian cities and states are divided into zones, and premiums are much higher for those living in inner cities than for those in outer suburbs and rural areas. Driving conditions are more hazardous in cities (owing to the high volume of traffic), and there's also usually a high risk of theft. Some insurers insist that a car (particularly a valuable or high-risk car) has an engine immobiliser and possibly also a tracking device.

For a small extra premium, most insurance companies provide cover for legal costs arising from road accidents (this is also available separately from Australian motoring organisations but is more expensive). If you cannot live without a car, ensure that your policy pays for car hire in the event of an accident or your car being stolen (or that you have separate 'uninsured loss' insurance to cover this). 'Mobility' insurance is available to pay for the cost of alternative transport after losing your licence for a motoring offence, medical revocation of your licence or being unable to drive due to injury.

Excess

With comprehensive insurance, you must usually pay an excess (deductible) when you make a claim. Drivers under 25, inexperienced drivers (holders of a licence for less than two years) and drivers with a bad accident record must usually pay a higher excess. You're usually also required to pay an excess, e.g. $50, if you make a claim on your windscreen cover (which normally covers all glass), but this doesn't affect your no-claims discount. You may be able to reduce the excess by paying a higher premium.

No-claims Discount

A foreign no-claims discount (or bonus) is usually valid in Australia, although some Australian insurance companies won't accept a no-claims discount earned overseas with a foreign insurance company. You must provide written evidence from your present or previous insurance company, not simply an insurance renewal notice. Some insurance companies offer an introductory discount.

The no-claims discount offered by Australia insurance companies is typically 20 per cent (after one year), 30 per cent (two years), 44 per cent (three years), 50 per cent (four years) and 60 per cent (five years), which is usually the maximum.

Some companies provide an additional no-claims discount for experienced motorists with a clean licence and an accident-free driving record, and you may get a further discount if you have other insurance (e.g. house) with the same insurer.

Normally, when you make a claim you lose two years' no-claims discount, even if the claim is for fire or theft, therefore it's sometimes cheaper to pay for minor repairs yourself. Damage to glass doesn't affect your no-claims discount, but you're usually required to pay the first $50 or $100 of a claim. Most insurance policies offer a protected no-claims discount policy or allow you to insure your no-claims discount. This means that you can usually make one 'at-fault' claim within a certain period (e.g. three years) or two claims within five years, for example, without losing any of your no-claims discount. If you're uninsured for longer than two years, you usually lose your entire no-claims discount.

If you insure two or more vehicles, you can claim a no-claims discount on only one vehicle, although you may be given a discount on the premium for the other vehicle(s).

MOTOR BREAKDOWN INSURANCE

Breakdown insurance for cars and motorcycles is available from Australian motoring organisations (see page 190), which also offer travel insurance for motoring holidays and other types of insurance.

RULES OF THE ROAD

Each state and territory has its own driving laws, although in general the variations are minor. The road rules detailed below apply in most states. However, it's essential to familiarise yourself with any local idiosyncrasies by obtaining a copy of a state or territory's 'highway code' (such as the *Road Users' Handbook* in NSW), available from the relevant local authority (the RTA in NSW) or motoring organisation. Handbooks contain advice for all road users, including motorcyclists, motorists and pedestrians. The NSW handbook is available in Arabic, Chinese, Croatian, English, Greek, Korean, Japanese, Serbian, Spanish, Turkish and Vietnamese. A *Heavy Vehicle Drivers' Handbook* and a *Motorcycle Riders' Handbook* are also published in NSW. The Australian Automobile Association (AAA) publishes a free booklet, *Motoring in Australia*, which contains sections in English, French, German, Japanese and Spanish.

Among the many strange habits of Australians is that of driving on the left-hand side of the road, which they inherited from the British. You may find this a shock if you come from a country where people drive on the right; however, it saves a lot of confusion if you do likewise. It may be helpful to have a reminder (e.g. 'think left!') on your car's dashboard. Take extra care when pulling out of junctions and one-way streets and at roundabouts. Remember to look first to the right when crossing the road on foot. If you're unused to driving on the left, you should be prepared for some disorientation (or even terror), although most people have few problems adjusting to it.

If you require spectacles or contact lenses to pass your sight test, you must always wear them when driving. It's wise to carry a spare pair of spectacles or contact lenses in your car.

> **☑ SURVIVAL TIP**
>
> **You're required by law to carry your driving licence (including an international driving permit if applicable) when driving in Australia.**

Drink & Drugs

You're no longer considered fit to drive in Australia when your blood contains between 0.02g and 0.05g of alcohol (depending on the state and other factors) per 100ml of blood. The limit for experienced drivers is 0.05g (some states are considering lowering it to 0.02g). In most states, the limit is 0.02g for drivers with a learner's or provisional licence; drivers under 25 who have held a licence for less than three years; anyone driving a bus, a car for hire or reward or a taxi; drivers of heavy goods vehicles; and anyone carrying a dangerous load. In some states, drivers with a learner's or provisional licence must not drive with any alcohol in their blood. Driving while under the influence of drugs is also illegal. If you're over the limit the police will confiscate your driving licence on the spot and you'll be fined and banned later.

Junctions

At crossroads and junctions (intersections) in Australia where no right of way is assigned, traffic coming from the right has priority (as in continental Europe). At major junctions, right of way is always indicated by a 'GIVE WAY' (yield) or a 'STOP' sign. There are also usually road markings. When faced with a stop sign, you must stop completely before pulling away, even if you can see that no traffic is approaching.

At a give way sign, you aren't required to stop, but must give priority to oncoming traffic. You must also give way to traffic on your right when joining a major road from a slip road. In towns in Queensland (i.e. in 60kph/37mph zones), motorists must give way to buses pulling out into traffic.

Lights

Headlights must be used when driving between sunset and sunrise or at any time when there's insufficient daylight to be able to see a person wearing dark clothing at a distance of 100m. It's illegal to drive on side (parking) lights in Australia, and headlights must usually be dipped (low beam) when driving in built-up areas where there's street lighting. Headlights must also be dipped within 200m of an approaching vehicle, immediately an oncoming vehicle has dipped its headlights and when travelling less than 200m behind another vehicle.

If you happen to be riding a camel on a road at night in Broome (WA), you must have a rear light!

Headlamp flashing has only one legal use – to warn another vehicle of your presence, although most people use it to give priority to another vehicle, e.g. when someone is waiting to pull out of a side road. It's illegal in some states to warn other vehicles that they're approaching a speed trap or police road block by flashing your lights (although many drivers do it).

Hazard warning lights (all indicators operating simultaneously) should be used to warn other drivers of an obstruction, e.g. an accident or traffic jam on a main road.

Overtaking

In Australia, the right-hand lane on a multi-lane highway is usually just for overtaking and you can be fined for hogging it, i.e. no keeping to the left when a lane is free. Motorists must indicate before overtaking and when moving back into an inside lane after overtaking, e.g. on a dual-carriageway or highway. Undertaking, i.e. overtaking on the inside, is permitted in some states.

Pedestrian Crossings

Always approach pedestrian crossings with caution and don't park or overtake another vehicle on the approach to a crossing (usually shown by zigzag lines or a large white diamond). At some crossings, a flashing amber light follows the red light, to warn you to give way to pedestrians before proceeding. Pedestrians have the legal right of way once they've stepped onto a crossing without traffic lights, and you must stop. Motorists who don't are liable to heavy penalties.

Where a road crosses a public footpath, e.g. at the entrance to a property or car park, motorists must give way to pedestrians.

Road Markings

White or yellow markings are painted on the road surface in towns and cities, e.g. arrows to indicate the direction traffic must go in a particular lane. White lines mark the separation of traffic lanes. Where there are no lane markings, you should keep to the left side of the road. In many cities, there are 'transit lanes' (indicated by roadside signs) for bicycles, buses, emergency vehicles, motorcycles and taxis during rush hours, e.g. 6 to 10am, Monday to Friday. A private vehicle may use these lanes only if it's carrying one or two passengers – e.g. in NSW a passenger vehicle

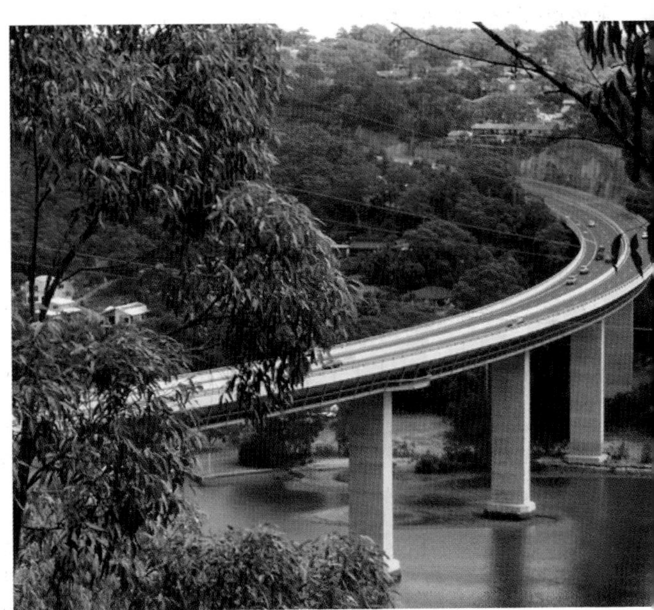

Woronora bridge, NSW

in a T2 lane must have at least one passenger and in a T3 lane at least two passengers – or if you intend to make a turn within 100m. There are also 'BUS ONLY' lanes in cities.

A solid single line or two solid lines between opposing lanes means no overtaking in either direction. A solid line to the left of the centre line, i.e. on your side of the road, means that overtaking is prohibited in your direction. You may overtake only when there's a single broken line in the middle of the road or double lines with a broken line on your side of the road. Double lines may be crossed when making a right turn in some states, but not in others, and U-turns are usually prohibited across any unbroken centre line even if it's combined with a broken line.

Roundabouts

There are many roundabouts (traffic circles) in Australia, which, although sometimes rather a free-for-all, speed up traffic considerably and are usually preferable to traffic lights, particularly outside rush hours (although some busy roundabouts also have traffic lights). On roundabouts, vehicles on the roundabout (i.e. coming from the right) have priority over those entering it. Traffic flows clockwise round roundabouts and not anti-clockwise, as in countries where traffic drives on the right. Some roundabouts have a filter lane which is reserved for traffic turning left. You should stay in the lane in which you entered the roundabout, follow the lane markings to leave and signal as you approach the exit you wish to take.

School Buses

You must drive slowly near school buses and give way to children crossing the road. When loading and unloading children, school buses have flashing orange lights at the front and rear, and may also display a 'GIVE WAY' sign at the rear. Lights remain flashing for around 30 seconds, after which the doors close and the bus moves off. When passing a stationary school bus, the maximum speed is 40kph.

Seatbelts

Seatbelts must be worn by all front and rear seat passengers when fitted. In all states, children aged from one to thirteen must use an approved child seat that meets the relevant Australian standard or a firmly adjusted adult seatbelt when available. A child must never travel in the front seat without using a child restraint or seatbelt, even when the back seat is full. If all available restraints in a car are in use, children may travel unrestrained (although this is extremely unwise).

> **If you're exempt from using a seatbelt for medical reasons, a safety belt exemption certificate is required from your doctor. More information can be obtained from motoring organisations and motor vehicle authorities.**

Signs

Speed limit signs are in kilometres per hour and not miles per hour, e.g. in NSW white rectangular signs indicate the speed limit in black numerals within a red circle. In addition to mandatory speed limits, there are often signs indicating advised limits, e.g. when approaching a sharp bend, which aren't compulsory. Apart from the international octagonal 'STOP' sign (white on red) and the triangular 'GIVE WAY' sign (black on white with a red border), most Australian road signs don't follow international standards; the different types of sign can usually be distinguished as follows:

- Warning signs telling you that there may be dangers ahead are usually diamond shaped with black or red diagrams (such as a kangaroo) on a yellow background.
- Regulatory signs giving instructions (in words) that must be obeyed are usually rectangular with black letters on a white background (some also have red markings).
- Highway signs giving information about the start, end and exits from highways are of various colours.
- Some parking signs are green on white. P1 on a parking sign means that you may park for one hour. If it isn't indicated by a sign, you can park for free.

In Melbourne, to accommodate the city's trams, a local rule applies at certain junctions. Where there's a 'RIGHT TURN FROM LEFT ONLY' sign accompanied by curved broken lines on the road surface, you must keep to the left lane and wait until you get a green light to make a right turn (known locally as a 'hook turn'). This will seem very odd to many people – for an illustration, see 💻 http://en.wikipedia.org/wiki/hook_turn.

Other types of sign include those used in rural areas to indicate where livestock can be expected on or near roads (you must slow or stop as required and can be fined for disobeying signs) and temporary signs used at road works. The most important signs are shown in a state or territory's road users' handbook. Signs may be emphasised by painted warnings on the road.

Speed limits

The following speed limits are in force for cars and motorcycles throughout Australia, unless indicated otherwise by a sign: 50kph (31mph) in residential areas; 60kph (37mph) in built-up areas and 100kph (62mph) on highways. In Western Australia the speed limit is 110kph (68mph) on country roads and highways, and in the Northern Territory there's no speed limit outside built-up areas, although speeds are severely limited on most roads by potholes and ruts. Learners and provisional licence holders and drivers towing a caravan, trailer or another vehicle are limited to 80kph (50mph), even when a higher limit is in force.

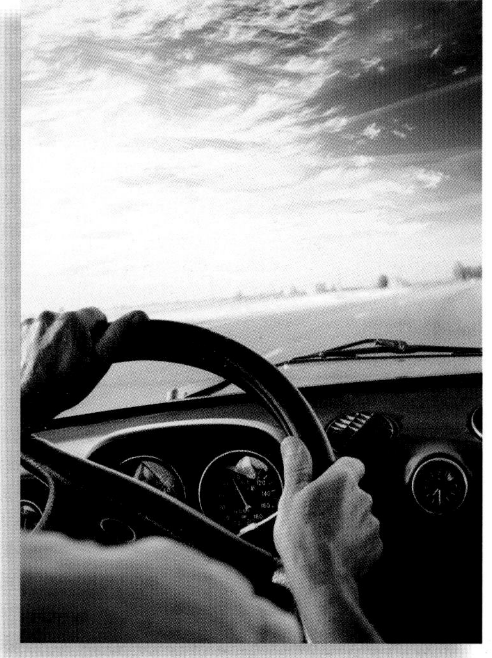

In some urban areas, there are zones with lower speed limits, including shared traffic zones, where pedestrians, bicycles and other vehicles may all use the road and the limit may be 10kph/6mph (so no running!); school zones, which have reduced speed limits on school days during school hours (e.g. 25kph/15mph or 40kph/25mph); and local traffic zones (40kph/25mph). However, after a court case and intervention by the federal Transport Minister, state governments were declared not to have the power to impose fines for 'speeders' in a 25kph/15mph speed limit school zone (after thousands had already been fined).

In some residential areas there are speed bumps (known as 'sleeping policemen' or 'traffic calmers' – although they certainly don't calm drivers!). They're sometimes indicated by warning signs and, if you fail to slow down, it's possible to damage your suspension or even turn your car over!

Speed limits are rigorously enforced in Australia and police employ radar units and speed cameras to identify speeders. Light planes and helicopters are used to spot speeding vehicles on interstate highways, where white lines may be painted on the road surface to help aerial police calculate speeds (by timing a vehicle between lines). Radar detectors are illegal in all states except Western Australia, and you can be fined up to around $1,200 for using one (it's also confiscated). However, they're in widespread use throughout Australia. If an oncoming vehicle flashes its headlights at you, it may be that the driver has spotted a radar trap and is warning you.

Marginal offences are usually dealt with by on-the-spot fines, which can run into $hundreds. You can also 'earn' demerit points on your licence and be disqualified from driving for a period.

Tram lines

In cities with tramways (e.g. Melbourne), tram lines are shown by yellow lines, which you should remain clear of unless you want a close encounter with a tram; continuous yellow lines may not be crossed, but broken lines may be crossed provided you don't obstruct a tram.

When a tram has started to cross a junction, it has right of way over all other vehicles. There are rules concerning the overtaking of trams; for example, you mustn't pass a tram when it stops to pick up or drop off passengers (unless there's a central island). Tram tracks can be slippery when wet, therefore cyclists and motorcyclists should take care.

AUSTRALIAN DRIVERS

Like motorists in all countries, Australians have their idiosyncrasies and customs (many of which run counter to the official rules of the road). Although they aren't considered to be among the best in the world, most Australians are good and careful drivers, who take their driving seriously. On the other hand, Australia has its fair share of seriously crazy drivers. Northern Territorians are reckoned to be Australia's worst drivers, particularly in traffic, and are scornfully referred to as 'bush motorists' as they tend not to bother with the niceties of roadcraft, such as indicating, keeping to lanes, and stopping at stop signs and red lights. Shooting (running) red lights is a common practice in Australian cities and the all-red period (when all vehicles are required to stop) has been increased to combat it.

Tempers are rising on Australia's overcrowded streets and in cities, particularly among truck drivers, and it's usually every man for himself, particularly in Sydney. Road rage ('invented' in California – where else?), where drivers blow their tops and attack or drive into other motorists, is becoming more common. It's often provoked by headlight flashing, obscene gestures, obstruction, tailgating and verbal abuse, so take care how you behave when driving in Australia.

Drinking and driving is still fairly commonplace, despite regular spot checks. The macho attitude among young male drivers in particular is a killer and the risk of young people aged 17 to 25 dying on the roads is around three times that of other age groups. However, the once appalling accident rate has fallen dramatically in recent decades through better driver training and education, improved roads, random breath testing, safer vehicles and stricter laws. Women generally have fewer accidents than men (particularly the under 25s) and are much less likely to drink and drive. However, young women drivers are increasingly showing aggressive driving behaviour normally associated only with men.

Don't be discouraged by the tailgaters and road hogs, as driving in Australia is less stressful than in many other countries and can even be enjoyable in country areas.

AUSTRALIAN ROADS

There are over 800,000km (500,000mi) of roads in Australia, varying in quality from eight-lane highways to rutted dirt tracks which are impossible to negotiate in anything other than a four-wheel-drive (4WD) vehicle. Only some 40 per cent of roads are sealed, although this includes the nearly 19,000km (12,000mi) of the National Highway System linking the capital cities plus Brisbane and Cairns in Queensland, and Hobart and Burnie in Tasmania.

Roads are usually classified as primary or secondary routes. Primary routes are the major roads that link the states and territories, together with those serving the principal centres of population and industry within them. Secondary routes include those which allow the carriage of produce from farms and mines, forest roads serving tourist resorts, and most

streets in towns and cities. Lighting is good on major urban roads and usually adequate on other urban roads.

Generally, the roads between major cities and state capitals are excellent, with dual-carriageways (divided highways) in metropolitan areas, particularly in the eastern coastal areas of Brisbane, Melbourne, Newcastle and Sydney, although it's generally felt that investment in roads hasn't kept pace with the continued growth of traffic, especially in metropolitan areas. In rural areas, where traffic density isn't high and there are vast distances between towns, roads may have only two lanes, and in the outback dirt roads are common.

☑ SURVIVAL TIP

You should swerve to avoid a kangaroo only when it's safe to do so, as many people kill themselves trying to avoid them.

Beware of kangaroos and other animals which stray onto country roads, particularly at dusk and dawn. An encounter with a big boomer can seriously damage your vehicle, not to mention the animal itself, which is why most car and truck owners who regularly use country roads fit their vehicles with 'roo bars' (the steel bars commonly seen on 4WD vehicles). Some cars are fitted with an alarm which emits a high-pitched noise to disperse kangaroos ('shu-roo').

Water buffalo are a problem in some northern parts of the country, and grazing cattle can also be a menace in country areas. Many Australians try to avoid travelling when it's dark due to the dangers posed by animals (most are nocturnal).

Tasmanian roads are fairly traffic-free (a few cars nose-to-tail represents a traffic jam) and driving there is relatively straightforward (except in winter). Take it easy when driving in inclement weather. Ice and snow are rare in most areas except the mountainous regions of NSW, Victoria and Tasmania, which, being farthest south experience the worst winter weather. Fog can also make driving extremely hazardous in winter in some regions.

Urban Roads

There are wide roads in most cities, particularly in the suburbs, where they're usually laid out on a grid system (except in Canberra and Sydney). Victoria's roads are the most crowded, followed by urban roads in NSW. Driving in Sydney is to be avoided if possible (finding somewhere to park can be a nightmare and can cost up to $15 an hour), while Melbourne isn't much better, in spite of the new Citylink toll system (see below).

Most major cities are choked during rush hours, and Sydney is congested at most times, although the Eastern Distributor and M5 and roads built for the 2000 Olympic Games have helped. Sydney Harbour bridge used to be an infamous bottleneck – a toll is charged when travelling south, which is now done electronically so that traffic no longer has to stop – and the harbour tunnel has also relieved some of the congestion. If you don't have an e-toll pass (see 💻 www.rta.nsw.gov.au/myrta/e-toll) then you must book a trip across the bridge (southbound only) via the internet or pay a fine (see also below).

Driving in Adelaide, Brisbane (with its new Gateway Bridge) and Perth is relatively easy, although rush hours should be avoided. Many Australian cities have tortuous one-way systems, and signposting in cities can be confusing and street names difficult to find.

Toll roads are – not surprisingly – unpopular with Australians and initially carried far fewer cars than was forecast. However, motorists have come round to using them, particularly as the alternatives are usually very slow. The major toll road operator in Australia is Roam (💻 www.roam.com.au), which operates a number of toll roads, bridges and tunnels in Sydney (Falcon Street Gateway, Sydney Harbour Bridge, Lane Cove and Cross City tunnels, the Eastern Distributor bypass, and the Hills M2, M4, M5 and Westlink M7 motorways), plus Citylink in Melbourne.

Most toll roads have no toll plazas or cash booths and drivers are charged electronically. You should obtain an e-TAG or e-PASS before using them or pay within 48 hours after your first trip (there's a fine of $100 if you don't pay the deferred toll). The e-TAG is for commuters and frequent travellers (and covers any toll road in Australia) and the e-PASS is for 'visitors' and infrequent travellers. You can obtain an application form from a post office or sign up online with Roam (💻 www.roam.com.au).

Rural Roads

Major roads in Australia are variously described as highways, expressways and freeways. The distinctions between these types of road are sometimes blurred, but in general freeways (as their name suggests) are toll-free roads, whereas tolls ($3.50 to $5) are payable at intervals on most highways and expressways.

Expressways usually have fewer junctions and traffic lights than highways, and neither expressways nor freeways allow bicycles. Highway and expressway numbers are sometimes prefixed with an M or an F (which doesn't indicate a freeway!). All major roads are sealed and many have three or four lanes in each direction.

Road numbers are rarely used in Australia and most people refer to roads by their names. Highway 1, which runs right around Australia, mostly hugging the coast, is known by various names in various parts of Australia, such as the Princes Highway between Sydney and Adelaide. It's the country's most dramatic road, some stretches being extremely picturesque, and it passes through many interesting towns.

The most direct route between Sydney and Melbourne is the busier inland Hume Highway (number 31). The most direct route between Melbourne and Adelaide is the Western Highway (number 8), but the Princes Highway (1) offers better views. The main roads between Sydney and Brisbane are the coastal Pacific Highway (1) and the inland New England Highway (15). The quickest route from Sydney to Adelaide is via the Great Western (32), Mid Western (24) and Stuart Highways (20).

On most highways, there are route markers (small shields by the roadside) every 5km (3mi) bearing the initial letter of the last or next major town above the distance in kilometres. There are emergency telephones every kilometre for use in the event of accidents and breakdowns. Some highways have a 'crawler' lane (for slow-moving vehicles) and escape lanes are common on steep downhill stretches to stop vehicles whose brakes fail.

National (i.e. interstate) highways are a federal government responsibility and have been funded from an excise levied on fuel since the early '80s, although it's claimed that far more fuel tax has been collected than is spent on the roads.

In some sparsely populated country areas ('back of Bourke') there are long stretches of main road with only one lane paved and wide unsealed shoulders. Even highways such as the Western Australia coastal road (see below) have stretches consisting of a single lane with dirt shoulders. Minor roads can be terrible, consisting mainly of dirt tracks.

☑ SURVIVAL TIP

Australia's vast distances and hot sun induce drowsiness in drivers and you should make frequent stops for refreshment and rests on a long journey.

There are plenty of roadside rest areas on main highways, and free coffee is provided at stops on some highways to help reduce driver fatigue. Drivers falling asleep at the wheel are a major cause of accidents on highways, particularly at night: as the sign says, 'Drowsy Drivers Die'!. It's always sensible to have company on long journeys.

Outback Roads

Many outback roads are made of dirt and are in varying stages of neglect, although in some outback areas of Western Australia there are sealed roads built privately by mining companies, and visitors may be allowed to use them with a permit. Signposting is virtually non-existent in the outback and can be a bit of a joke, e.g. 'Darwin 2,000km'.

There has, however, been a vast improvement in the outback road network in recent years, making it possible for the average motorist to explore the country by car (on main highways) without the need of a 4WD vehicle. However, high ground clearance is necessary on unsealed outback roads and four-wheel drive is often essential if you don't want to get stuck (although it isn't failsafe).

Outback driving can be hazardous for the inexperienced driver, and thorough preparation is essential. In bygone days it wasn't unusual to come across a vehicle in the outback containing the skeletons of its occupants, although (despite the horror stories) people rarely die in the outback nowadays.

Conditions vary from area to area and season to season. The best time to travel is during the cooler winter months between April and October. Many outback roads are deeply rutted and can be washed away by flash floods and remain impassable for weeks on end during the wet season (some roads in northern Australia are impassable from December until May). Dust can also be a problem during the heat of summer in central Australia (when air-conditioning is practically essential). You should keep a close eye on the temperature gauge in hot weather.

Road conditions and routes must be checked with the local authorities, in addition to weather forecasts and the availability of fuel. On some roads, motorists are required to complete a police destination card giving their expected time of arrival at the next town. It's sensible to carry a two-way UHF radio tuned to the local Royal Flying Doctor Service. Make sure that a vehicle is roadworthy and carry plenty of spares, including a first-aid kit, a plastic windscreen, two spare wheels, tools, a week's supply of food and water (20 litres per person in a number of containers), spare fuel (keep the tank topped up at all times), a workshop manual and maps.

If you break down, it's imperative to stay with your vehicle and wait for assistance. A motorist must (by law) aid someone who has broken down in the outback. As a last resort, burn a tyre, as property owners in the outback never ignore smoke.

On the outback roads of central and northern Australia, you're likely to come across road trains, which are multi-trailer, articulated lorries up to 50m in length and weighing over 100 tonnes, driven by maniacs who don't move over for anyone (except perhaps another road train). It's best to pull over if you see one coming towards you and let it pass. If you come up behind one and want to overtake it (if you can see for dust), allow at least a kilometre.

Many books are published for outback travellers, including *Explore Australia by 4WD* by Peter and Kim Wherrett (Five Mile Press), *The Driving Guide Series* (covering most of Australia's regions) by Ian Read (Cimino Publishing) and *Outback Australia* (Lonely Planet). The Flying Doctor also publishes a booklet, *Outback Travelling*, for visitors planning long-distance trips.

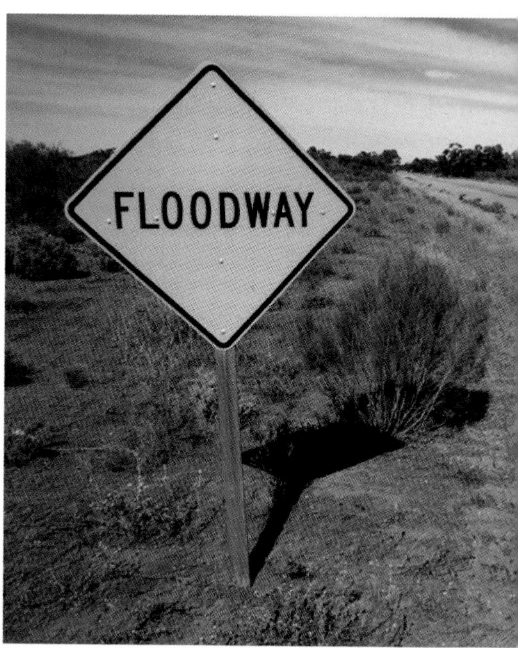

Information

Information about road conditions is provided by motoring organisations and state government roads departments, e.g. in Queensland the Main Roads Department publishes *Queensland Road Conditions*. Information about road conditions throughout Australia can be obtained from the National Roads' and Motorists' Association Limited (NRMA, ☎ 131122, 💻 www.mynrma.com.au). The telephone line provides recorded road reports for major highways, 24 hours a day.

TRAFFIC POLICE

Police in Australia don't need a reason to stop motorists and can make spot checks at any time and carry out random breath tests. Australian state police aggressively enforce all traffic regulations and use a variety of equipment and tactics to catch offenders.

Automatic cameras are installed at junctions to identify drivers shooting red lights, while radar units and hidden speed cameras are employed to identify speeders, and planes and helicopters are used to catch speeding vehicles on rural highways.

Never antagonise a police officer or make any wisecracks, as this is the fast lane to prosecution; remain courteous and obsequious and you may get away with a caution. Although you may have read about corrupt Australian police, don't even think about trying to bribe an officer unless you wish to be charged with a much more serious offence! When crossing a state border, your vehicle may be searched for drugs, guns, fresh fruit and vegetables (which may not be transported from one state to another, to prevent the spread of parasites), and pornography.

You must show your vehicle documents and give a police officer your name and address when requested, although you aren't required to answer questions before obtaining legal advice.

MOTORCYCLES

The minimum age for riding a motorcycle in Australia varies with the state or territory but is usually 17. You may obtain a licence before you reach the required age after passing a written road knowledge test. The following information is based on motorcycle licensing laws in NSW, which are similar to other states'.

A learner cannot ride a motorcycle with a maximum engine capacity above 250cc, with a power-to-weight ratio of no more than 150kw per tonne. An 'L' plate must be displayed on the back and you mustn't carry a passenger. In some areas, learners must complete a pre-provisional licence course before taking a road knowledge test. The course can be taken at 16 years and six months and allows a learner's licence to be issued at 16 years and nine months.

To obtain a provisional motorcycle licence (class R), you must take a riding test between three and six months after you receive your learner's licence. After passing the test, a 'P' (provisional) plate must be displayed on the back of the motorcycle for a year. If you've held a foreign motorcycle licence for less than a year you're eligible only for a provisional

licence, and if you fail the riding test you may be required to undertake further rider training.

Although Australia has an excellent climate for biking, it has declined in popularity in the last decade, and bikes are more a fashion statement nowadays than a transport option, many over-40s buying them only for leisure riding. Motorcyclists aren't particularly popular with motorists in Australia, where motorcycle gangs have given bikers a bad name.

The average price of a motorbike is $5,000-10,000, although top models can cost $50,000 or more. If you need a bike only for a relatively short period (e.g. a trip around Australia), some dealers offer buy-back options on secondhand bikes (see 💻 www.bikescape.com.au). There's a good market in second-hand bikes and you may be able to pick up a bargain from a departing visitor (the best time to buy a bike in May at the start of the Australian winter). You can buy bikes via a number of websites, including 💻 www.tradingpost.com.au and 💻 www.bikesales.com.au.

Motorcycles can be hired (rented), although rates are high and range from $50 per day for a scooter to over $300 per day for a big bike (there are discounts for longer rentals). A deposit (bond) of around $1,000-2,500 is payable by credit card and there's usually an insurance excess, e.g. up to $5,000. One-way rentals are possible with a drop-off fee, although it's usually cheaper to buy a second-hand bike and sell it when you no longer need it. Large capacity bikes are best for long-distance travel, although rentals usually have minimum age limits of 25 or 28.

It's essential to take spares and tools when on a long trip as well as plenty of drinking water, and travelling alone in the outback isn't recommended (see **Outback Roads** on page 186). Contact motorcycle clubs and motoring organisations for information about outback road conditions and the availability of fuel.

A helmet must be worn at all times (but remove it when going into a bank or they may think you're planning to rob it!). Otherwise, laws that apply to cars (see **Rules of the Road** on page 180) also apply to motorcycles. The NSW RTA publishes a *Motorcycle Riders' Handbook*.

ACCIDENTS

If you're involved in (or cause) an accident in Australia, which results in injury to a person or animal, or damage to any third party's vehicle or property, the procedure is as follows:

1. Stop immediately. If possible move your vehicle off the road and keep passengers and yourself off the road. **Failing to stop after an accident or failure to give particulars or report the accident to the police is a serious offence.**

2. Warn other drivers of any obstruction by switching on your hazard warning lights (particularly on highways) or by placing a warning triangle at the edge of the road at least 50m behind your car on secondary roads and 150m on a highway.

3. If anyone is injured, immediately telephone for an ambulance, the fire brigade (if someone is trapped or oil or chemicals are spilled) or the police (dial ☏ 000). Emergency telephones are provided on highways.

4. If damage worth over $500 or $1,000 (depending on the state) is caused to animals, property or vehicles, the nearest police station must be notified within 24 hours (if the police don't attend the scene). Calling the police to the scene of an accident may result in someone being fined or charged for a driving offence, although you aren't obliged to say anything (apart from giving your name and address). If you have an accident involving a domestic animal and are unable to find the owner, it must be reported to the police or the RSPCA.

> **☑ SURVIVAL TIP**
>
> **If you injure a wild animal, you should remove it from the road (care should be taken, as many Australian mammals carry their young in pouches), and notify the local Wildlife and Information Rescue Service (🖳 www.wires.org.au).**

5. Report the accident to your insurance company in writing as soon as possible, even if you don't plan to make a claim (but reserve your right to make a claim later). If you're injured and plan to make an insurance claim, you must obtain a doctor's report as soon as possible after the accident to verify your injuries (this is obviously done automatically if you're admitted to hospital).

FUEL

Most petrol (gas) stations stock four grades or types of fuel nowadays: 91 octane unleaded petrol containing 10 per cent ethanol (the least expensive), 91 octane petrol, 98 octane petrol (i.e. premium unleaded) and diesel. Specially treated petrol is sold in Sydney during the summer months in order to reduce pollution. Many petrol stations also sell two-stroke petrol for boats, lawn-mowers, mopeds, etc.

In mid-2012, fuel prices in urban areas were around $1.25-1.30 per litre for regular unleaded petrol and up to 5-10¢ a litre more for diesel and premium unleaded. Fuel prices vary from area to area, even within cities; in country and outback areas (where petrol stations are few and far between) and Tasmania, prices are around 10-15 cents per litre higher than in cities. Generally the more remote the area, the dearer the fuel.

Petrol is usually cheapest at supermarkets, which may also offer discounts to customers, e.g. if you have a current receipt for $30 or more, a participating petrol station may give you a discount of 4¢ a litre (which on special occasions may be increased to 8¢ cents a litre). You can check the lowest price in your area via the Motormouth website (💻 www.motormouth.com.au). Note that filling up on certain days, e.g. Tuesdays or Wednesdays, may also be cheaper and could save you $5 or $10 on a full tank.

Many cars in Australia have been converted to run on liquid petroleum gas (LPG) or propane, including most taxis and buses. Most petrol engines can be converted to use both petrol and LPG (they can be switched between them), although you lose around a third of your boot space to accommodate the gas tank. The advantage is that LPG costs from around 60 cents a litre, although there's a loss of power of around 15 per cent. All urban areas and most large country towns have LPG outlets.

The trading hours of petrol stations vary considerably. Most open from 7.30am to 6.30pm, Monday to Saturday, and on Sunday mornings. Many petrol stations in cities and on highways are open 24 hours a day. Some stations have automatic pumps accepting $5 and $10 bills, and possibly credit and debit cards (however, don't rely on finding any outside the major cities). Most petrol stations accept major credit and charge cards and Australian debit cards.

Most petrol stations provide additional services such as checking oil, water and tyre pressure, and cleaning windscreens. Some also have a car wash and most have a shop selling a wide range of motoring accessories and basic foodstuffs. Many petrol stations also have workshops and can usually do minor repairs on the spot. Most petrol stations also have toilets, although you may need to obtain a key to use it, and in rural areas they may also have a shower for customers' use.

MOTORING ORGANISATIONS

There are motoring organisations in all Australian states and territories, and some 75 per cent of Australian motorists are members of a motoring organisation, one of the highest rates in the world. The Australian Automobile Association/AAA (💻 www.aaa.asn.au) is the only national motoring organisation and operates as an umbrella organisation for motoring organisations in individual states and territories. It provides no services to individual motorists and any requests must be directed to local organisations. The largest of these is the National Roads and Motoring Association/NRMA (💻 www.nrma.com.au) in NSW, with some 2m members.

There are few essential differences between the basic services provided by Australian motoring organisations, although membership costs vary. The primary service of motoring organisations is to provide emergency assistance in the event of an accident or breakdown. Motoring organisations provide a fast and efficient breakdown service, usually arriving within an hour of notification.

Most organisations offer various membership packages providing different levels of service, which may include free public transport or a rental car, home start, legal advice, and towing and vehicle recovery. It's the vehicle that's covered (irrespective of the driver) and not the individual. The most expensive NRMA membership packages provide additional services, including emergency accommodation, passenger transport, a replacement car, and a towing service (up to a maximum cost of $3,000). The larger organisations offer both national and international accident or breakdown cover for no extra charge. All organisations charge a joining fee and an annual membership fee. For example, the NSW NRMA has a joining fee of around $55 and membership fees ranging from around $25.20 (club) to $177 (premium) per year. Fees are similar in other states and territories.

All organisations offer supplementary services, which may include accommodation guides, advice on weather and road conditions, car and household insurance (motoring organisations are among Australia's largest insurers), crash repair centres, driving schools, free publications, holiday centres, international camping cards, international driving permits, road maps and itineraries, technical advice, travel services and vehicle inspection. Some motoring organisations (e.g. the NRMA) are expanding into financial services, including cash management accounts, home loans and superannuation.

If you break down, call the local motoring organisation by telephoning a 24-hour number for assistance. Keep your membership card in your car (or wallet) and quote your membership number when calling for help. There are emergency telephones every kilometre on Australian highways for summoning help from motoring organisations.

Non-members can also get assistance, but it can be expensive. Members of foreign motoring organisations (affiliated to the AAA – such as the British AA and RAC organisations) who break down anywhere in Australia can obtain free breakdown assistance from Australian organisations, plus free maps and accommodation directories at members' rates (on production of your membership card). Most Australian organisations also have reciprocal arrangements with motoring organisations in other countries.

The AAA publishes a booklet called *Motoring in Australia*.

12. HEALTH

Australia is among the most advanced countries in the field of medicine and is noted for its highly trained medical staff and modern hospitals equipped with the latest high-tech apparatus. Two yardsticks widely used to measure the quality of a country's healthcare are the infant mortality rate (4.55 deaths for every 1,000 live births) and life expectancy (84.5 years for women, 79.5 for men), which are both among the 'best' in the world. (The life of expectancy of indigenous 'Aboriginal' Australians is around ten years lower, at 75 for women and 68 for men, although much improved.)

Healthcare services are provided by both government (including Commonwealth, state, territory and local governments) and private organisations. Australia has a national health service called Medicare (see below), which provides free or subsidised medical care and free hospital treatment in public hospitals for all permanent residents (plus certain visitors) irrespective of their age, health status or income. The public health system is supplemented by a wide variety of private clinics, hospitals and practitioners, plus a range of voluntary agencies and non-profit organisations.

The country spends around 10 per cent of its GDP on healthcare (compared with some 15 per cent in the US), which is around average for OECD countries. Despite the rising cost of modern medicine, costs have largely been contained in the last 15 years. Health facilities and doctors are unevenly distributed in Australia; however, the major cities and urban areas have a surplus of GPs, while in most country areas there's a shortage, particularly in the Northern Territory and Western Australia. Trying to persuade doctors to relocate from the cities to remote country and outback areas is a major problem, which the government is trying to overcome by importing doctors specifically to work in country areas. The Royal Flying Doctor Service provides medical services in remote country areas and evacuates urgent cases to hospital.

Recently, there has been a growing emphasis on preventive medicine and community care, including education programmes to promote a healthy lifestyle. Alternative medicine and natural remedies are popular in Australia, where acupuncture, chiropractic, homeopathy, naturopathy, osteopathy and physiotherapy thrive.

Voluntary euthanasia is a topical subject in Australia, particularly since the world's first voluntary euthanasia law was passed in 1995 in the Northern Territory. This was subsequently overturned in (1997) by the federal government after four people had been medically assisted to die. In most states patients can refuse life-sustaining treatment, but doctors cannot assist them to die (although in reality many doctors do 'assist' terminally-ill patients).

Health Risks

Australians are generally healthier than they were 20 years ago, due to a reduction in smoking and drinking and an improved diet, although their love affair with junk food and red meat is largely undiminished. The amount of exercise the average Australian gets isn't as high as many people would expect, given the country's famous love of sport and image as bronzed Amazonians. A relatively large number of people are overweight and around a quarter are classified as obese, although the percentage is much lower than the US and UK.

The biggest killers in Australia are heart disease, cancer, stroke and smoking-related illnesses. Other problems include alcoholism and drug addiction, although they are less prevalent than in many other Western countries (see **Drug & Alcohol** abuse on page 207). Diabetes is an increasing problem, but again it's less widespread than in many other Western countries. Air pollution can be a problem in the major cities.

You can safely drink the water in Australia, although the wine tastes much better and, taken in moderation, even does you good (if you believe the winemakers!). Water supplies are fluoridated in most parts of Australia in order to help prevent tooth decay.

Sun

Australia has the highest rate of skin cancer (melanoma) in the world. Although the incidence is reducing as people take heed of warnings, many people still die each year from skin cancer caused by overexposure to the sun. Other problems associated with too much sun include fungal infections, heat exhaustion, prickly heat, sunburn and sunstroke.

Even if you're used to a hot climate, you should limit your exposure to the sun and avoid it altogether during the hottest part of the day (usually between 10am and 3pm), wear protective clothing (including a hat) and use sunscreen. The government's slogan in the battle against skin cancer is 'Slip, Slop, Slap', i.e. slip on a shirt, slop on sunscreen and slap on a hat. This is backed by a 'SunSmart' campaign, which is particularly targeted at teenagers. It's important to use a sunscreen with a high protection factor, e.g. a pH 15+ broad-spectrum, water-resistant sunscreen (sunscreens with a protection factor of 50+ are now available). Medical experts recommend the wearing of good quality sunglasses, e.g. with UV400 polycarbonate lenses, to protect against eye cancer and other eye problems caused by the sun.

Those with fair skin should take extra care, as you can burn in just 15 minutes on a hot summer's day. Children are particularly vulnerable and should wear wide-brimmed hats in the sun and a T-shirt when swimming. Those who live the outdoor life (such as sportsmen) are especially at risk and should follow the example of Australian cricketers by wearing total-block zinc cream on exposed areas when spending a long time in the sun. Hikers should wear legionnaire or Arab-style hats with neck flaps.

Drink plenty of water when in the sun to prevent dehydration (in extreme heat you should drink a litre every hour), and avoid excessive alcohol consumption and overexertion, particularly if you're elderly.

Too much sun and too little protection also dry the skin and cause premature ageing, therefore care should be taken to replace the skin's natural oils (many Australian people in their 20s and 30s have the skin of people 20 or 30 years older).

Wildlife

Australia has some of the deadliest creatures in the world, including crocodiles, jellyfish, blue-ringed octopus, scorpions, sharks (see **Swimming** on page 284), a plethora of poisonous snakes (e.g. death adder, sea snakes and western taipan), venomous spiders (e.g. the funnel-web and red-back), and stonefish, many of which can deliver a fatal bite or sting. You're unlikely to have a close encounter with most of Australia's wildlife unless you venture into the bush or the sea off unprotected beaches, although poisonous snakes and spiders can be found in suburban parks, gardens and near watercourses. You should avoid undergrowth and country areas unless you're wearing protective clothing, i.e. not flip flops (thongs) or shorts, and try to avoid disturbing wildlife. Insects (e.g. mosquitoes, ticks and wasps) are also a problem in many areas, although they won't kill you. Children are taught at school to recognise dangerous wildlife.

The good news is that unless you're an adventurer and spend all your life in the sea or the outback, your chances of encountering any of Australia's most dangerous creatures is remote indeed.

Essential bedtime reading for acarophobes and agrizoophobes is *Dangerous Creatures of Australia* by Marty Robinson (New Holland).

IMMUNISATION

Children should have six sets of injections between the age of two months and four years in order to be fully immunised against diphtheria, hepatitis B, measles, mumps poliomyelitis, rubella, tetanus and whooping cough (A total of 27 vaccinations to cover 13 different infections are recommended in the first four years of life alone!) Children aged between 10 and 19 years also need booster shots for most of these diseases. Immunisations can be provided by your family doctor, an immunisation clinic, community health centres and some public hospitals. There's an Australian Child Immunisation Register (ACIR) where all immunisation details are recorded and which can be accessed by parents and authorities (☏ 1800-653809). There are also immunisation programmes for the elderly, e.g. against flu.

A large percentage of older children aren't fully immunised against diseases such as diphtheria, tetanus and whooping cough, resulting in many unnecessary deaths. Some parents are concerned about the side effects of vaccination, although these are insignificant (and mostly unproven) compared to the possible effects of the diseases themselves. In an attempt to 'encourage' parents to immunise their children, the government has introduced certain measures which include the requirement to have children immunised in order to receive family payments such as child care benefit.

There's also a maternity immunisation tax-free allowance (see 💻 www.humanservices.gov.au/customer/services/centrelink/maternity-immunisation-allowance), usually paid for children immunised between 18 to 24 months of age and between four and five years. As a result of such campaigns, nearly 90 per cent of children under 18 months are now fully immunised (in some states, such as NSW, the figure is nearer 100 per cent).

EMERGENCIES

The action to take in a medical 'emergency' depends on the degree of urgency. If you're unsure who to call, ask the telephone operator (☏ 1234) or call your local police station. They can tell you who to contact or even call the appropriate service for you. Whoever you call, you should give the approximate age of the patient and, if possible, specify the type of emergency.

> **☑ SURVIVAL TIP**
>
> **Keep a record of the telephone numbers of your ambulance service, dentist, doctor, local hospitals and clinics, and other emergency services, next to your telephone. A mobile telephone can be a lifesaver in a remote area or when you're alone and need help. Dial ☏ 000 for an ambulance in an emergency.**

Ambulances generally come with a paramedic and many are equipped with cardiac, oxygen and other emergency equipment (called intensive care ambulances). Ambulance services aren't covered by Medicare, although private health insurance may include ambulance costs. In Queensland, ambulance costs are paid for by a levy in domestic electricity bills.

There are air ambulances (helicopters) in some cities, and remote outback areas are served by the Royal Flying Doctor service, established as a non-profit organisation in 1927 and funded by the federal government and voluntary contributions. The service covers some 80 per cent of outback areas from 20 bases, ensuring that most people are less than two hours from medical help. Services include regular clinic visits to remote communities, visits by specialists and, in some areas, dental treatment. The service also offers advice on touring and emergency procedures; travellers in remote areas can rent a transceiver with emergency call buttons. For more information, contact the Royal Flying Doctor Service of Australia (☏ 02-8259 8100, 💻 www.flyingdoctor.net, ✉ enquiries@frdsno.com) or one of the regional offices listed on their website.

In minor 'emergencies' you should telephone your family doctor if you have one. Failing this you can ask the operator (☏ 1234) for the telephone number of a local doctor or hospital (or consult your telephone book). Police stations keep a list of doctors' and chemists' private telephone numbers in case of emergencies. In some cities and regions, there are private, 24-hour doctor services that make house calls (but check the cost before using them). If you have an emergency dental problem outside normal surgery hours, call a dentist providing an emergency service (listed in the *Yellow Pages*).

If you're physically capable, you can go to the Accident, Casualty or Emergency department of a public hospital, many of which provide a 24-hour service. Check in advance which local hospitals are equipped to deal with emergencies and the quickest route from your home. This information may be of vital importance in the event of an emergency, when a delay could mean the difference between life and death. Emergency cases, irrespective of nationality and the ability to pay, are never turned away in Australia, and treatment may be free if you're a national of a country with a reciprocal health agreement with Australia, which currently includes Finland, Ireland, Italy, Malta, the Netherlands, New Zealand, Norway, Sweden and the UK.

THE DISABLED

[illegible] strides in its provision [illegible] for the disabled in [illegible] now rates among [illegible] capital cities and [illegible] duce maps showing [illegible] aths and toilets for [illegible] ties; nationwide [illegible] *Access Australia* [illegible] asyaccessaustralia. [illegible] rovide a directory of [illegible] abilities and for older [illegible] ation is available from the National Information Communication Awareness Network (NICAN, ☏ 02-6241 1220, 💻 www.nican.com.au).

MEDICARE

Australia's national health service is called Medicare, which was established in 1984. It provides free treatment in public hospitals and free or subsidised treatment by doctors (including specialists). However, dental and optical (apart from eye tests) services are generally excluded (except in certain cases), as is the ambulance service. Medicare even covers 75 per cent of the cost of private treatment, therefore a private health insurance policy needs to cover only 25 per cent of costs.

As in many countries, the rising cost of healthcare and health insurance has created severe problems for Medicare, which is overworked, under-resourced and facing a funding crisis. It's also burdened by the increasing life expectancy of Australians (some

15 per cent of the population is aged 65 or older, a figure which is expected to double by the year 2050). In recent years, the cost of private health insurance, which usually supplements rather than replaces Medicare, has increased sharply and many people have cancelled their policies (thus adding to the burden on Medicare).

Before Medicare was introduced in 1984, some two-thirds of Australians had private cover, which has since fallen to less than a third. Many people believe that Australia now has a two-tier health system: a costly private health sector with all the 'bells and whistles' for those who can afford it and a neglected, second-rate public system for those who cannot.

Many public hospitals are cash-starved and cannot cope with the demand, with a shortage of nursing staff and doctors and a dearth of the best medical equipment. In recent years public hospitals have paid $millions to fly in locum medical staff, e.g. surgeons, obstetricians and anaesthetists, from New Zealand and interstate to cover shifts.

> **▲ Caution**
>
> Although most urgent (but not life-threatening) cases are admitted within 30 days, there are long waiting lists for elective surgery under Medicare, and non-urgent cases may have to wait up to a year for treatment.

It's generally agreed that vastly increased health expenditure is necessary if Medicare is to continue. With this in mind, the government introduced a Medicare Plus package, designed to protect the future of Medicare and address the shortage of doctors, nurses and other healthcare professionals, particularly in rural and regional Australia.

General information about Medicare in English is available from the Medicare Information Service (☎ 132011) and information in other languages is available from the Medicare Multilingual Telephone Information Service (☎ 131202). Medicare produces a comprehensive booklet *Welcome to Medicare* in a number of languages. The benefit system (see below) is constantly being revised. For more information and the latest developments, see the Medicare Australia website (💻 www.medicareaustralia.gov.au).

Eligibility

All permanent residents of Australia are eligible to join Medicare and restricted access is also granted to citizens of certain countries with which Australia has a reciprocal healthcare agreement (see above). If you're working in Australia, you're automatically covered by compulsory workers' compensation insurance against injury and illness as a result of an accident, Medicare eligibility is immediate upon application (and can even be backdated to your arrival in Australia) but new members may have to wait up to three months to receive refunds. Medical expenses incurred by men aged over 55 and women over 51 who have been sponsored in the family reunion migration category are the responsibility of their sponsor for ten years or until they reach retirement age.

Retirees

Foreign retirees with a temporary residence visa aren't covered by Medicare and must take out private health insurance. Permanent resident retirees who aren't in receipt of a social security or veterans' pension and whose income is below a certain amount can qualify for a range of free and concessionary health services. Retirees can apply for a Commonwealth Seniors Health Card (☎ 132300) and enjoy various benefits, including bulk-billed GP appointments (see **Bulk Billing** below) and reduced out-of-hospital medical expenses.

The proportion of eligible medical expenses covered by Medicare varies according to the type of service and the medical practitioner providing it.

Benefits

Medicare covers a percentage of set fees, as specified by the Medicare Benefits Schedule (MBS). These, known as 'schedule fees', are increased annually on 1st November at half the rate of inflation. In general terms, Medicare pays 85 per cent of the schedule fee for hospital outpatient treatment and 100 per cent of the schedule fee for inpatient services. Medicare normally provides 100 per cent cover for the following:

- doctors' consultation fees, including treatment by specialists when referred by a general practitioner (GP). However, when a doctor charges more than the schedule fee (as many do), patients must meet the additional cost or buy private insurance to cover it;
- most surgical and other therapeutic procedures performed by doctors;
- all treatment costs when you're treated as a Medicare patient in a public hospital;
- X-rays, pathology and other medical tests, examinations and certain surgical procedures (listed in the *Medicare Benefits Schedule*, available on the website of the Australian Department of Health and Ageing, 💻 www9.health.gov.au/mbs);
- eye tests performed by an optometrist;
- some surgical procedures performed at a hospital by dentists registered with Medicare and oral surgeons;
- specified items under the Cleft Lip and Palate Scheme.

Medicare provides only partial cover (usually 85 per cent) for medicines (see below); procedures and diagnostic tests performed by a general practitioner; referred services, e.g. those provided by consultant physicians, specialists, allied health professionals or dentists; non-referred services in the field of sports medicine or emergency medicine; contraceptives; immunisation; maternity care; psychiatric treatment; and services provided by optometrists.

Medicare doesn't cover dental examinations and treatment (although certain essential dental surgery is covered); ambulance services; home nursing; chiropody, occupational therapy, physiotherapy, podiatry, psychology, and speech and eye therapy; acupuncture (unless treatment is provided by a doctor); spectacles and contact lenses; hearing aids, prostheses and other appliances; medical and hospital costs incurred overseas; medical treatment that isn't necessary, including elective or cosmetic surgery; treatment arranged before arriving in Australia; accommodation and medical treatment in a private hospital or as a private patient in a public hospital; medical repatriation or funeral costs; or examinations for life insurance, membership of a friendly society or superannuation.

Medicare also doesn't cover situations where someone else is responsible for medical costs (e.g. a compensation insurer, an employer or a government authority).

If you receive treatment under Medicare for an injury or accident which is subject to compensation by a third party, such as an insurance company or workers' compensation fund, the insurer must reimburse Medicare for any benefits related to the injury before making any payments to you. You're usually required to indicate whether this is the position when making a claim.

Extended Medicare Safety Net (ESMN)

Those who require frequent treatment that isn't covered 100 per cent by Medicare are protected from high costs by the Extended Medicare Safety Net (EMSN). When you (or your family members) have made payments in a Medicare financial year (1st July to 30th June) amounting to a total of $598.80 for Commonwealth Concession Card holders (including those with a Pensioner Concession Card, a Health Care Card or a Commonwealth Seniors Card and those who receive Family Tax Benefits Part A) and $1,198 for everyone else, the safety net is triggered. Once the safety net has been reached, Medicare pays 80 per cent of the cost of the difference (gap) between the fee charged by a doctor and the Medicare rebate, e.g. if your GP charges $40 and Medicare covers $25, the gap payable by you is $15, but once you reach the safety net you'll pay only 20 per cent of the gap, i.e. $3.

It isn't necessary to register for the safety net as Medicare keeps a record of payments and the higher (100 per cent) benefits apply automatically as soon as the limit is reached. However, families (even when all members are listed on a Medicare Health card) need to complete a *Medicare Safety Net Registration Form* and take or send it to a Medicare customer service centre or register online. A family includes a spouse (or *de facto* spouse), children under 16 in your care and dependent full-time students under 25.

Further information and registration forms are available from Medicare Plus (☏ 1800-011163) and via the Medicare website (💻 www.medicareaustralia.gov.au)

Contributions

Medicare is funded by a 1.5 per cent levy on taxable income and by general taxation, deducted at source from employees' wages. In order to 'encourage' high earners to take out private health insurance, the government levies a Medicare surcharge of 1 to 1.5 per cent (in addition to the Medicare levy) on those without private health insurance that at least covers doctors' fees and hospital accommodation. The surcharge applies to single people earning over $84,000 a year and families earning over $168,000 a year (2012-13). The taxable threshold increases by $1,500 for the second and each subsequent dependent child. It may be cheaper to buy private health insurance than to pay the surcharge.

If you're self-employed, the levy is included in your annual income tax charge. Certain people are exempt from paying the levy, including defence force personnel without dependants, pensioners with a concession card (known as a Commonwealth Concession Card or a Commonwealth Seniors Health Card – see **Retirees** above), single people on low incomes and war veterans and widows. Couples and sole parents who earn less than a minimum amount are entitled to a reduction in their Medicare levy. The unemployed and dependants have automatic deductions made from their unemployment benefits or other allowances.

The cost of Medicare varies according to how old you are when you first become a member, with everyone paying more the older they are. It also increases annually in line with the cost of living. However, there are incentives to encourage people to take out private health insurance. If you're a new arrival to the country or when you reach the age of 18, you can take out insurance at the rate for your age and, if you do this before the 1st July (the start of the tax year), then your payments will stay at this rate (apart from annual cost of living increases) for the rest of your life. If you fail to take out insurance by the 1st July, you lose this benefit and must pay an annual age-related increase. For information, see 💻 www.privatehealth.gov.au/healthinsurance/incentivessurcharges.

Enrolment

Assuming you plan to stay in Australia for more than a few months, you should enrol in Medicare as soon as possible after you arrive – the government recommends you do this within 7-10 days after your arrival. However, it isn't absolutely necessary until you use the system, as you can join retrospectively, i.e. claim a refund of previous medical expenses after joining Medicare. You can apply in person at a Medicare office or you can call 132011 and have an application form sent to you. You're required to show proof of eligibility, e.g. your passport with a residence stamp if you're a permanent resident. Applicants must also provide details of their assets, income and residence.

Medicare card

You receive a plastic Medicare card (green and gold) by post around two to three weeks

after applying, which shows your Medicare membership number, the names of all dependants entitled to use the service and the expiry date of the card. Cards are valid for five years, although you must obtain a replacement card if your address or other details change, e.g. you have a baby. The card has a signature strip on the back and must be signed on receipt. If you receive treatment before you obtain your card, you must pay in full and claim a refund or delay payment until you receive your card. You must quote your Medicare number when making enquiries or a claim and use your Medicare card to:

- receive a cash benefit at a Medicare customer service centre;
- receive free or subsidised treatment from a doctor or optometrist who bulk bills Medicare (see below);
- obtain free or subsidised treatment in a public hospital;
- obtain free or subsidised prescriptions.

Bulk billing

Bulk billing (also called direct billing) is where a doctor (or optometrist) doesn't charge the patient, but the patient verifies his entitlement to benefits to the doctor, who bills Medicare directly. Most doctors bulk bill at least some of their patients, particularly pensioners and Commonwealth Seniors Health Card holders (see **Retirees** above). If your doctor bulk bills, you're asked to complete a form after treatment, of which you receive a copy. You don't need to pay anything and aren't required to make a claim to Medicare. However, doctors can bulk bill only if they charge the schedule fee (currently around $40 for a standard consultation – see www.health.gov.au).

☑ SURVIVAL TIP

If your doctor or optometrist doesn't bulk bill, he gives you a bill for his services. You can either pay the bill and claim a refund from Medicare or submit the bill to your local Medicare office with a claim form.

Claims

Bills can be submitted by post (addressed to Medicare, PO Box 9822 in your state's capital city) or in person with a completed claim form and the original bills or receipts for payments. You receive a cheque made out to the practitioner, which you give to him with your own payment for the balance (gap), if any.

If you've already paid for treatment and make a claim in person, you receive a refund in cash (although there's a limit to how much you can be paid in cash), by cheque or by direct payment into your bank account. Claims made by post are paid by cheque. Always take your Medicare card when attending a Medicare office.

Telephone claims (☎ 1300-360460) can by made by anyone living outside Adelaide, Brisbane, Melbourne, Perth and Sydney. These can be made at any time and don't require a form; you simply endorse your claim form with the information the telephone operator gives you and send it to Medicare. Electronic lodgement of Medicare claims was introduced in 2007 in an attempt to reduce delays in payments and improve access to Medicare for those living in rural and remote areas. The system enables members to use their Medicare cards in EFTPOS-style machines (like bank ATMs) and claims can also be made online for some consultations.

PRIVATE HEALTH SERVICES

Private health treatment functions both in conjunction with Medicare and independently of it, and most public hospitals admit private patients. In addition to specialist appointments and hospital treatment, people most commonly use private health services to obtain second opinions, health checks and screening, and for complementary medicine such as acupuncture, chiropractic, homeopathy, naturopathy, osteopathy and physiotherapy (which aren't usually covered by Medicare or, indeed, private health insurance). Private patients are usually free to choose their own doctor and hospital, and may be accommodated in a single, hotel-style room with an en suite bathroom, radio, room service, telephone and colour TV – at a correspondingly high cost!

With the deterioration of Medicare services and lengthening waiting lists, you're strongly recommended to consider having private health insurance (see page 219), which ensures you always receive the medical treatment you need, when you need it.

DOCTORS

There are excellent family doctors, who are generally referred to as general practitioners (GPs) in Australia. However, there's a glut of doctors in most cities and metropolitan areas and an acute shortage in rural areas, where the ratio of doctors to population is less than half the national average. Therefore in rural areas and the outback you may need to travel some distance to visit a doctor, although you may be served by the Royal Flying Doctor Service.

Your GP can provide advice and information on all aspects of health and medical care, including blood donations, home medical equipment, preventive medicine and counselling. If you're a Medicare patient, he should also be able to advise you about the range of benefits provided under Medicare (see above). Patients in Australia have no legal right to see their medical records.

It isn't necessary to be registered with a doctor in Australia, where you can choose to visit any doctor, either as a Medicare patient (provided the doctor is registered with Medicare) or a private patient. Many doctors in the suburbs of major cities work at public clinics and medical centres, where a number of doctors have a group practice and at least one is usually female (there's an unusually large percentage of women doctors in Australia). Clinics and medical centres usually have an in-house pharmacy, and medical tests, such as blood and urine analysis and X-rays, may also be conducted in-house.

In many towns there are also community health centres run by the local government which deliver health support services and advice, including health checks for babies and children, vaccination, health education and counselling.

Fees

If you wish to be treated as a Medicare patient, you must check whether a doctor charges the schedule fee for consultations and bulk bills Medicare (see **Bulk Billing** above) or whether he charges more and requires you to pay. Many doctors now charge more than the schedule fee, and in some areas you may have difficulty finding a doctor who doesn't, although pensioners and Commonwealth Seniors Health Card holders are usually exempt from additional fees. If you wish to see a GP privately, you (or your insurance company) must pay the full fee, which is at the doctor's discretion but is usually at least $50 for a routine consultation.

 **Caution**

The low remuneration paid to doctors by Medicare encourages doctors who charge the schedule fee to rush consultations (referred to as 'six-minute' or 'stop-watch' medicine).

If you're concerned that your doctor doesn't allow sufficient time for a thorough examination, you should change doctors, although you may need to choose one who charges a higher fee.

Surgery Hours

Surgery hours vary, but are typically from 8.30am to 6 or 7pm, Monday to Friday, with early closing one day per week, e.g. 5 or

5.30pm on Fridays. Evening surgeries may also be held one or two evenings a week. 'Emergency' surgeries may be held on Saturday mornings, e.g. from 8.30 to 11.30am or noon, when you can be treated without an appointment for urgent problems. Most doctors' surgeries have answering machines outside surgery hours, when a recorded message informs you of the name and telephone number of the doctor on call (or the deputising service).

Appointments

An appointment must be made to see a GP, usually one or two days in advance. If you're an urgent case (but not an emergency), your doctor will usually see you immediately, but you should still telephone in advance if possible. Surgeries are often overrun, however, and you may need to wait well past your appointment time to see a doctor. Australian doctors make house calls, although these can be expensive for private patients.

Specialists

Medicare patients must always be referred by a GP to a specialist, e.g. an eye specialist, gynaecologist or orthopaedic surgeon. If you want a second opinion on any health matter, you may ask to see a specialist, although your doctor may refuse to refer you – in which case you can obtain a second opinion from another GP, who may agree to refer you, or you can consult a specialist as a private patient. Patients with private health insurance may be free to make appointments directly with specialists, although most insurance companies prefer patients to be referred by GPs. Most specialists have long waiting lists for Medicare patients.

MEDICINES & CHEMISTS

Medicines (drugs) are obtained from chemists (pharmacies), which also provide free advice regarding minor ailments and recommend appropriate medicines. In some isolated areas, e.g. remote parts of Queensland, some doctors act as chemists and dispense a wide range of everyday medicines, including treatment for diabetes and contraceptive pills. Many medicines in Australia can be prescribed only by a doctor via an official prescription, which is written in a secret language decipherable only by doctors and chemists.

Some medicines sold freely in other countries require a doctor's prescription in Australia, while certain medicines that require a prescription in other countries are available over the counter in Australia. To obtain medicines prescribed by a doctor, simply take your prescription to any chemist. Your prescription may be filled immediately if it's available off the shelf or you may be asked to wait or come back later.

At least one chemist is open in most large towns during the evenings and on Sundays for the emergency dispensing of medicines, and there are 24-hour chemists in some cities. A roster is posted on the doors of chemists and published in local newspapers and guides. If you require medicine urgently when chemists are closed, you should contact your GP or a police station.

Most chemists also sell cleaning supplies, cosmetics, health foods, non-prescription medicines and toiletries. A health food shop sells diet foods, homeopathic medicines and eternal-life/virility/youth pills and elixirs, which are quite popular in Australia (even though their claims are often in the realms of fantasy). Unwanted medicines should be returned to a chemist or dispensing doctor.

> ☑ **SURVIVAL TIP**
>
> **You can obtain information and help about medicines from the Medicines Line (☎ 1300-888763, Monday to Friday, 9am-6pm EST) or visit the National Prescribing Service website (💻 www.nps.org.au).**

Charges

Medicare – via the Pharmaceutical Benefits Scheme (PBS) – subsidises the cost of around 1,700 'necessary and life-saving' medicines, although to benefit from the subsidy you must obtain a prescription from a doctor. PBS medicines are available to all Australian residents and to visitors from countries with which Australia has a reciprocal healthcare agreement. Proof of residence or nationality may be required. If you're eligible but unable to provide proof, you may be charged the full price for medicines, although you can obtain a refund at a Medicare customer service centre or by posting your claim (plus the receipt and your Medicare card or proof of eligibility) to Medicare, PO Box 9822 in a state or territory's capital city. If you're eligible, you pay a maximum of around $35.40 for each PBS medicine; if you qualify for a concession (see below), you pay only around $5.80. For more information, see 💻 www.medicareaustralia.gov.au/provider/pbs.

If medication isn't available under PBS (i.e. is non-prescription), you must pay the entire cost. The cost of non-prescription medicines varies considerably and, if you need medication regularly it's worth shopping around. If you have private health insurance, you may be able to reclaim the cost of prescriptions from your insurance company.

In recent years, the government has restricted the prescription of expensive medicines in order to control the escalating cost of pharmaceuticals. GPs must now prescribe the cheapest available brand of each type of medicine, and patients wishing to use a more expensive brand must pay a 'therapeutic premium' (the difference between the government subsidy and the actual cost).

It's possible to buy prescription (and other) medicines by post from a number of suppliers, including 💻 www.chemistdirect.com.au.

Concessions

Once you or your family (which includes your spouse or *de facto* spouse and children under 16 or dependent full-time students under 25) have spent a certain amount – $1,363.30 for 2012 (adjusted annually on 1st January) – on prescription medicines in a calendar year, you're entitled to receive all additional prescription medicines at the concessionary rate of around $5.80 per item for the remainder of the calendar year. All purchases must be recorded on a *Prescription Record* form by your chemist.

If you have a concession card (issued to low-income families, the unemployed and war widows), you pay the reduced rate per prescription until you've spent a total of $348 (2012), after which there's no charge for the remainder of the year.

Foreign Prescriptions

If you're visiting Australia, you may bring a maximum of four weeks' prescription medicines with you. The brand names for the same medicines vary considerably from country to country, therefore if you regularly take medication overseas you should ask your doctor for the generic name. If you wish to match medication prescribed overseas in Australia, you need a current prescription with the chemical name, the dosage, the manufacturer's name and the medication's trade name. This must be endorsed by an Australian-registered doctor before you can take it to an Australian chemist. Most foreign medicines have an equivalent in Australia, although particular brands may be difficult or impossible to obtain.

HOSPITALS & CLINICS

Most Australian towns have a hospital or clinic, shown by a sign of a white H on a blue background. Australia has a variety of public and private hospitals and clinics, and there are various kinds of public hospital. Major hospitals are called general hospitals and provide treatment and diagnosis for inpatients and outpatients. They may have an infectious diseases unit, maternity department, psychiatric and geriatric facilities, and rehabilitation and convalescent units, and cater for most forms of specialised treatment. Other types of public hospital include children's hospitals, day hospitals,

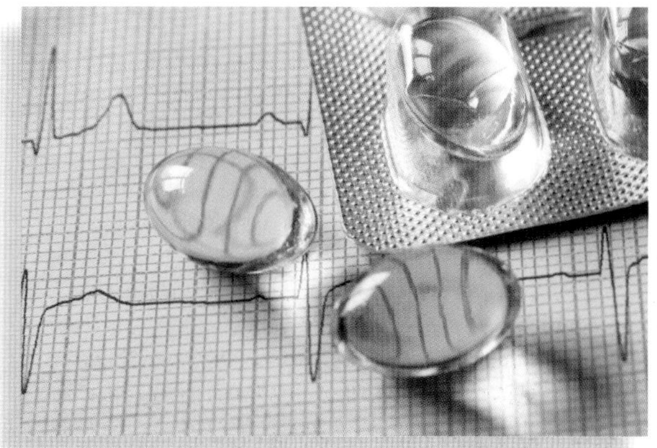

dental hospitals, district hospitals, psychiatric hospitals, teaching hospitals and veterans' hospitals.

Most of Australia's public hospitals are funded jointly by the federal government and state and territory governments, and administered by state and territory health departments, although some are operated by private companies under a contract.

Public Treatment

If you're eligible for Medicare, it pays for the full cost of accommodation and medical treatment performed by hospital-appointed doctors in public hospitals. Hospital bills for treatment under Medicare are always paid directly by Medicare. However, patients have no choice of doctors or hospital, nor of when they're admitted for treatment or surgery. Patients are usually accommodated in general wards or twin rooms. If you want a TV or a telephone, you must pay extra. When you visit a public hospital, you should take your Medicare card with you (if applicable). The staff may ask whether you wish to be treated under Medicare or as a private patient. Medicare patients also receive free X-rays and pathology tests in public hospitals, and free outpatient services in some hospitals.

In recent years, there has been a funding crisis in public hospitals in many states, some of which have chronic shortages of basic medical supplies. Some public hospitals also have a lack of diagnostic equipment, e.g. for brain scans. In some over-worked public hospitals, patients are left lying for hours in emergency departments and in corridors waiting for ward beds. Many public hospitals also suffer from a shortage of doctors and nurses, and are forced to recruit casual staff from locum doctor and nursing agencies. Fortunately, there's usually no shortage of life-saving equipment or medicines.

Private Treatment

Even private patients are subsidised by Medicare. If you're a private patient in a public or private hospital, Medicare pays 75 per cent of the schedule fee for medical services and the remaining 25 per cent is paid by your private health insurer, if you have one. When you leave hospital, you're generally asked to pay the difference (if any) between your health insurer's refund and the hospital fees, which you must then reclaim from your insurer.

If you don't have private health insurance, you're asked to pay the estimated costs at the time of admission. The average charge for a private bed is around $250 per day in a public hospital and over $600 per day in a private hospital, where costs have increased hugely in recent years. Patients in private hospitals are usually given one or two bills for the total cost of treatment, although some hospitals still prefer to charge separately for different treatments and care.

Private patients are usually accommodated in single rooms equipped with all the comforts of home, including en-suite bathroom, radio, room service, telephone and TV. If you're a private patient, you can choose the hospital and your attending doctor and surgeon, although if you want your own doctor to treat you in a public hospital there's a daily 'accommodation' charge.

CHILDBIRTH

Childbirth in Australia usually takes place in a hospital labour ward or birth centre (a small unit normally located in the grounds of a hospital), where a stay of up to five days is usual (although many women leave hospital within three days of giving birth). Public hospitals are under pressure to discharge mothers earlier, and even privately-insured mothers are being encouraged to cut their hospital stay in exchange for lower maternity (e.g. obstetrician) bills.

Few people in Australia choose to give birth at home and, if you wish to do so, you must find a doctor or midwife (see below) who's willing to attend you. Some doctors are opposed to home births in case there are complications requiring specialist equipment or staff. However, you can hire a private midwife to attend you at home throughout a pregnancy and after giving birth.

Medicare patients are usually unable to choose the hospital where they have a baby or their obstetrician. If you have a choice, find

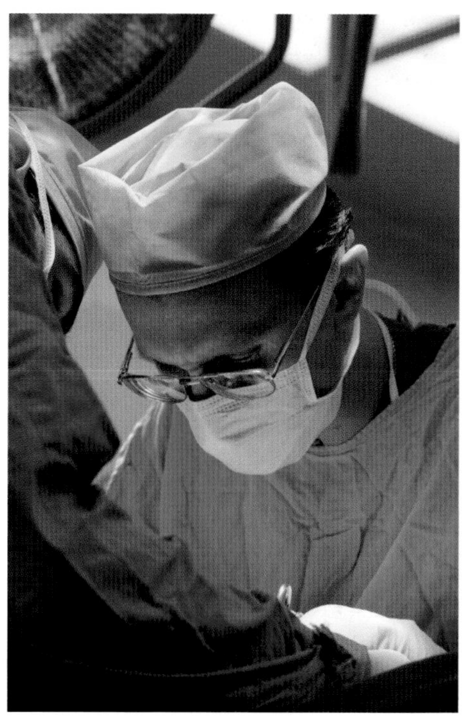

out as much as possible about local hospital methods and policies concerning childbirth, either directly or from friends or neighbours, before booking a bed.

The policy regarding a father's attendance at a birth varies with the hospital. A husband or partner doesn't have the right to be present with a woman during labour or childbirth; his presence is at the consultant's discretion.

Women who don't speak English often have problems and are generally dissatisfied with their hospital treatment during pregnancy; interpreters are rarely provided and information isn't usually published in foreign languages.

Antenatal classes must be paid for, although the cost is usually covered by private insurance. There are Maternal and Child Health Centres in some states (e.g. Victoria), funded by the state government or local councils. However, there's a dearth of services for new mothers in many areas and postnatal care may be patchy or even non-existent, new mothers being left to their own devices.

Births must be registered with the state or territory Registrar of Births, Deaths and Marriages within 60 days (even when a child is stillborn). When a birth takes place in a hospital, parents are given the relevant form to register the birth. In the case of home births, a form can be obtained from a hospital or from the Registrar of Births. A child born to an unmarried mother is usually registered in her name but can be registered in the father's name if both parents agree. The birth of a child to foreign parents may need to be reported to a consulate or embassy, e.g. to obtain a national birth certificate and passport for a child. If you need to obtain a copy of a birth certificate, the cheapest way is to apply to the registrar in the state or territory where the birth was registered.

Family planning associations provide free advice, counselling, instruction and other services.

DENTISTS

There are excellent dentists in cities and towns throughout Australia, although they're thin on the ground in rural areas. There are mobile dentists in some country regions, and in remote areas emergency dental services are provided by the Flying Doctor Service. There's no need to register with a dentist, and the best way to find a good one is to ask colleagues, friends or neighbours to recommend someone. Dentists are listed under 'Dental Surgeons' in the *Yellow Pages* and are permitted to advertise any special services they provide, such as emergency or 24-hour answering services, a dental hygienist, and evening or weekend surgeries. Many family dentists in Australia are qualified to perform treatment such as endodontics or periodontics, which are carried out by specialists in many other countries.

General dental services aren't funded by Medicare, although it pays for 75 per cent of in-hospital medical procedures performed by a Medicare-registered dentist or an oral surgeon. The cost of dental treatment has risen considerably in recent years, although charges vary with the area and the dentist. If you miss a dental appointment without giving 24 hours' notice, your dentist may charge you a standard fee. Most dentists accept payment by credit card (plus bearer bonds, diamonds, gold, etc.). Dental teaching hospitals in the major cities treat patients for lower fees than private dentists, although you may be something of a guinea pig.

Those with a concession card may be entitled to free general and emergency dental treatment under the Commonwealth Dental Health Program, although there are long waiting times for some treatment. Children in some states receive free school dental care. Information about dental charges can be obtained from the Australian Dental Association (☏ 02-9906 4412, 💻 www.ada.org.au).

OPTICIANS

There are three kinds of professional providing eye care in Australia. The most highly qualified is an ophthalmologist, who's a specialist physician trained in diagnosing and treating disorders of the eye. In addition to performing eye surgery and prescribing medicines, he may perform sight tests and prescribe spectacles and contact lenses. You may be referred to an ophthalmologist by an optometrist or your GP. Optometrists are licensed to examine eyes, prescribe corrective lenses, and dispense spectacles and contact lenses. They're also trained to detect eye diseases and may prescribe medicines and treatment. Medicare pays for 85 per cent of the cost of eye tests by optometrists, but not eye tests performed by ophthalmologists.

In Australian an optician isn't the same as an optometrist and may not examine eyes or prescribe lenses; opticians are licensed to fill prescriptions written by optometrists and ophthalmologists and to fit and adjust spectacles. There are opticians at optical retail chain stores in Australia, where you can have spectacles made within an hour. You aren't required to buy your spectacles or contact lenses from the optometrist who tests your sight, and he must give you your prescription at no extra charge.

As with doctors and dentists, there's no need to register with an optometrist or optician. You simply make an appointment with anyone of your choice, although it's sensible to ask colleagues, friends or neighbours if they can recommend someone. Opticians and optometrists are listed in the *Yellow Pages*, where they may advertise their services.

The eye care business is very competitive in Australia and, unless someone is highly recommended, you should shop around for the best deal. Prices for both spectacles and contact lenses vary considerably, so it's wise to compare costs (although make sure you're comparing like with like) before committing yourself to a large bill. Special offers are common, such as 'buy a new pair of spectacles and receive a spare pair free', but the cheapest products aren't necessarily the best value. Always ask about extra charges for adjustments, eye examinations, fittings, follow-up visits, lens-care kits and the cost of replacement lenses (if they're expensive, it may be worthwhile taking out insurance).

Many Australians wear contact lenses. Disposable (one-day) and extended-wear (e.g. one or three months) contact lenses are widely available, although most medical experts believe that extended-wear lenses should be approached with extreme caution, as they greatly increase the risk of potentially blinding eye infections. **Obtain advice from a doctor or eye specialist before buying them.**

Soft contact lenses or spectacles (frames and lenses) can be purchased in Australia from around $150 to $200 (usually inclusive of an eye examination).

It's advisable to have your eyes tested before your arrival in Australia and to bring a spare pair of spectacles or contact lenses with you – also bring a copy of your prescription in case you need to obtain a replacement in a hurry.

COUNSELLING

Counselling and assistance for health and social problems are available under Medicare and from many community groups and volunteer organisations, ranging from national associations to small local groups (including self-help groups). In times of need there's nearly always someone to turn to, and all services are strictly confidential.

Local authorities provide social workers to advise and support those requiring help within the community. If you need to find help locally, you can contact your council or voluntary services or a Citizens' Advice Bureau. A list of 24-hour emergency services (including many counselling services) is included at the front of both *White* and *Yellow Pages*, as are community help and welfare services and help for young people.

Many colleges and educational establishments provide a counselling service for students, and general hospitals have a psychiatrist on call 24 hours a day. Problems for which help is available are numerous and include alcoholism (e.g. Alcoholics Anonymous); obesity (e.g. Weight Watchers); drug, tobacco and gambling addiction; sexuality-related, marital and relationship problems; rape and battering; suicidal tendencies and other psychiatric disorders; and youth problems.

Trained counsellors provide advice and help for sufferers from various diseases (e.g. muscular dystrophy) and the disabled (e.g. the blind and deaf). They also help terminally ill patients (e.g. AIDS, multiple sclerosis, cancer and leukaemia sufferers) and their families come to terms with their situation. A number of voluntary organisations and local authorities run refuges for battered wives (and their children) or maltreated children, whose conditions have become intolerable (some provide 24-hour emergency telephone numbers).

If you or a member of your family are the victims of a violent crime, the police will usually put you in touch with a local victim support scheme.

In major towns, counselling may be available in your native language if you don't speak English. If you need help desperately, someone speaking your language can usually be found. Lifeline (☏ 131114) provides a confidential, 24-hour counselling service (e.g. for the desperate, lonely and suicidal) throughout Australia for the cost of a local call. There's also a Women's Information Service (☏ 1800-817227).

Many councils publish a directory of children's and family services.

DRUG & ALCOHOL ABUSE

Drug abuse is an increasingly serious problem in Australia, where it's estimated that heroin users alone spend $billions per year on the drug and it costs the country around $2bn annually to deal with its effects. The average drug abuser starts at just 14 and the average time between take-up and death is usually around ten years. Over 1,000 people die each year from drug abuse, heroin overdoses accounting for three-quarters of drug-related deaths. Cannabis or marijuana is the most widely taken drug, followed by amphetamines, ecstasy and hallucinogens. Cannabis is widely grown and smoked in Australia, where each state has its own laws regarding the use of drugs (see **Crime** on page 313).

The National Drug Strategy (💻 www.nationaldrugstrategy.gov.au), which is a cooperative venture between national, state and territorial governments and the non-government sector, works to improve the country's economic, health and social situation by preventing harmful drug use. Many other government and voluntary organisations provide drug advice and rehabilitation services, including residential facilities. There are government-run detoxification units in the major cities, where there are also voluntary groups providing counselling and support for drug users and their relatives and friends (see your local *White* or *Yellow Pages*). There's also a national Children's Help Line (1800-551800). If you can afford to pay for treatment, a number of private clinics and hospitals specialise in treating people for alcohol, drug and substance abuse, and other health problems.

Drunkenness and alcoholism are common in Australia, where it's estimated that over 6,000 Australians die each year of alcohol-related causes (including some 30 per cent of those who die on the roads); alcohol abuse is also a growing problem among children. Alcoholics Anonymous has self-help groups throughout Australia (see your telephone book for your local group).

SMOKING

As in most countries, smoking is a major cause of health problems in Australia, although the number of smokers has steadily decreased over the last few decades and is now below 20 per cent of the population. Action on Smoking and Health (ASH) Australia (💻 www.ashaust.org.au) hopes to reduce the rate to just 10 per cent in the next decade. The dramatic reduction in smoking in recent years is due in part to the massive uptake of the anti-smoking drug Zyban, subsidised by the government since February 2001.

Smokers are increasingly under siege in Australia. Federal law bans smoking in all Commonwealth government buildings, on all public transport, in airports and on international and domestic flights. The National Health and Medical Research Council has recommended a statutory ban in all enclosed public spaces outside the home, but to date further bans have been the responsibility of individual states. Most states have banned smoking in all enclosed public places, including work places and licensed premises. Queensland has gone even further by banning smoking within 4m (15ft) of the entrance of any non-residential building (see also NSW below) and South Australia also bans smoking in vehicles carrying children. The Northern Territory, however, has no plans to ban smoking in licensed premises such as pubs and nightclubs.

In 2012, NSW announced plans to introduce the most extreme smoking bans in Australia, including public playgrounds within 10m (33ft) of children's play equipment, in open areas of public swimming pools, at major sports grounds and facilities, and within 4m of any building open to the public. Smoking will also be banned at public transport stops, including bus stops and taxi stands, and at railway and light-rail stations.

In recent years, there has been increasing concern about passive smoking (sometimes, clumsily, known as 'environmental tobacco smoke'). Although it hasn't generated the paranoia seen in the US, legal history was made in 2001 when a barmaid in NSW who contracted throat cancer as a result of inhaling smoke in the bar where she'd worked for eight years, was awarded over $300,000 in damages.

The anti-smoking group QUIT produces leaflets in 13 languages (National Quit Line 131848). There are also non-smoking clinics and self-help groups throughout Australia to assist those wishing to stop smoking. Contact your local health authority for information.

DEATHS

Deaths must be registered with the local state or territory Registrar of Births, Deaths and Marriages within a limited period, usually 21 days. The registrar is usually notified directly by the hospital authorities when a death occurs in a hospital. He decides whether to issue a death certificate after obtaining a medical certificate and other details concerning the deceased. If someone dies accidentally, suddenly, during an operation or in unusual circumstances, or the cause of death is unknown, the registrar notifies the police and/or a coroner, who decides whether an autopsy is necessary to determine the cause of death.

The registrar needs to know the personal details of the deceased, including his date and place of birth and death, marriage details (if applicable), and whether he was receiving a state pension or any welfare benefits. The registrar then issues a death certificate, which authorises the funeral to take place. The certificate must be given to a funeral director (or undertaker) to organise burial or cremation, or you can arrange for the body to be shipped to another country for burial. You may wish to announce a death in a local or national newspaper, giving the date, time and place of the funeral, and your wishes concerning flowers or contributions to a charity.

The death of a foreigner may also need to be reported to a consulate or embassy, e.g. to register the death in the deceased's home country. In the event of the death of an Australian resident, all interested parties must be notified (see **Chapter 20**). You need a number of copies of the death certificate, e.g. for financial institutions, insurance companies, pension claims and the proving of the will (probate). If you need to obtain a copy of a death certificate, the cheapest way is to apply to the registrar in the state or territory where it was registered.

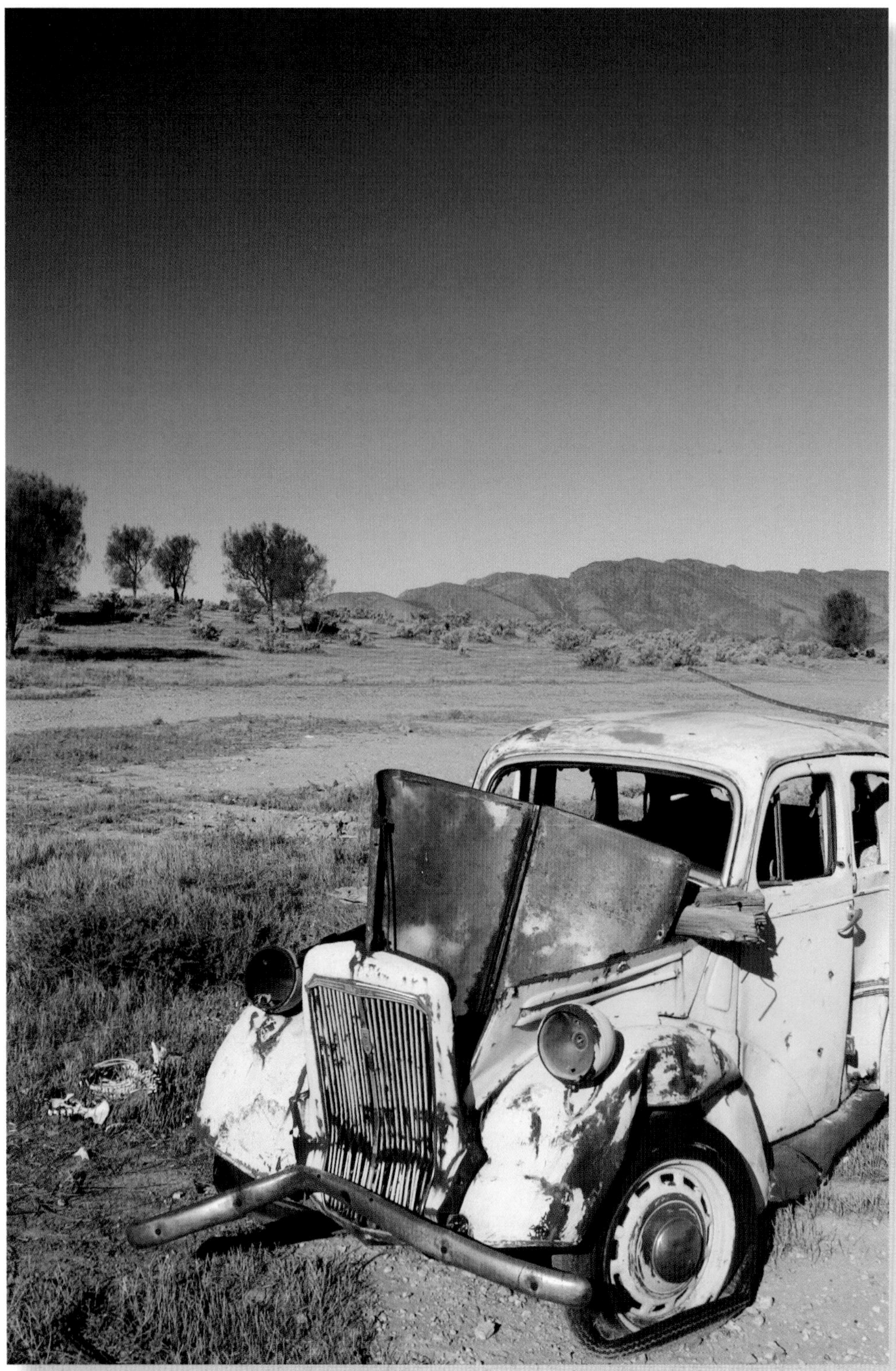

13. INSURANCE

Australia is a nation of gamblers, which is reflected in the relatively low level of insurance, even for basic contingencies. There are only a few cases in Australia where insurance for individuals is compulsory, including mortgage insurance (because lenders insist on it) and third party motor insurance, which is required by law. If you're an employee, you must also belong to a pension (superannuation) fund. You may also need third party and accident insurance for high-risk sports. Voluntary insurance includes accident, dental, home contents, income protection, legal expenses, life insurance, motor breakdown, personal liability, private health and travel. For information about motor breakdown insurance and car insurance, see pages 180 and 177 respectively; information about other kinds of insurance is included in this chapter.

The Australian government and Australian law stipulate various obligatory insurance and benefit schemes, including disability, health, sickness and work injuries insurance, state and private (superannuation) pensions, and maternity and unemployment benefit, some of which are the responsibility of the state (social security or 'welfare'), others of employers. Australia has one of the most comprehensive social security systems in the world in terms of the number of people eligible for benefits, which has engendered widespread welfare dependency, around a third of all Australians relying on welfare payments as their main source of income (half of them pensioners). However, benefits cover only the most basic needs.

Most Australians and foreign residents and their families receive health treatment under Medicare, the National Health Service (see page 196). If you don't qualify for Medicare, it's essential to have private health insurance, which is obligatory for some temporary residents. Many people who do qualify for Medicare have a policy to cover the expenses that aren't reimbursed under Medicare. You'd also be wise to ensure that your family has comprehensive health insurance during the period between leaving your last country of residence and arriving in Australia. This is particularly important if a private health insurance policy in your home country doesn't cover you overseas. One way is to take out a travel insurance policy. However, it's usually better to extend your present health insurance policy, if possible, particularly if you have existing health problems that may not be covered by a new policy.

It isn't necessary to spend half your income insuring yourself against every eventuality from the common cold to being sued for your last cent, but it's important to be covered for any event which could precipitate a major financial disaster (such as a serious accident or your house falling down). As with everything to do with finance, it's important to shop around when buying insurance. Just picking up a few brochures from insurance agents and making a few telephone calls can save you a lot of money. Regrettably, you cannot insure yourself against being uninsured or sue your insurance broker for giving you bad advice!

Information in this chapter is intended only as a guide, as the rules regarding insurance matters are constantly changing, particularly health insurance, social security and superannuation. You should therefore obtain the latest information from the appropriate authorities or an insurance company in Australia. It's your responsibility to ensure that your family is legally insured in Australia.

> **Caution**
>
> Australian law may be very different from that in your home country or your previous country of residence, and you should never assume that it's the same.

INSURANCE COMPANIES

There are numerous insurance companies in Australia, either providing a range of insurance services or specialising in certain fields only. You can buy insurance from many sources, including banks and other financial institutions, direct insurance companies (selling direct to the public instead of through brokers), internet agents and brokers, traditional insurance companies selling through independent agents (brokers), and motoring organisations (see page 190). In recent years, direct insurance companies have enabled consumers to make huge savings, particularly on car, building and home contents insurance. Direct selling companies give quotations over the telephone and often you aren't even required to complete a proposal form.

The major insurance companies have offices or brokers throughout Australia, including most large towns, and most of them provide a free analysis of your family or business insurance needs. If you choose a broker, you should use one who's independent and sells policies from a wide range of insurance companies. Some brokers or agents and most banks are tied to a particular insurance company and sell policies only from that company.

You can compare insurance premiums via a number of websites, including Captain Compare (💻 www.captaincompare.com.au) and Insurance Watch (💻 http://insurancewatch.com.au).

CONTRACTS

Most insurance policies run for a calendar year from the date on which you take them out. All premiums should be paid punctually, as late payment can affect your benefits or a claim, although if this is so it should be stated in your policy. Before signing an insurance contract, you should take a day or two to think it over, although with some insurance contracts you may have a 'cooling off' period during which you can cancel a policy without penalty.

Claims

Although insurance companies are keen to take your money, many aren't nearly so happy to settle claims. Like insurance companies everywhere, some Australian insurance companies will do almost anything to avoid paying out in the event of a claim and use any available loophole. For example, if you wish to make a claim, you must usually inform your insurance company in writing by registered letter within a number of days of the incident (possibly within 24 hours in the case of theft). Failure to do so may render a claim void. Don't send original bills or documents regarding a claim to your insurance company unless it's necessary (you can send certified copies). Keep a copy of all bills, correspondence and documents, and always send letters by registered post so that your insurance company cannot deny receipt.

When dealing with insurance companies, perseverance often pays. Don't bank a cheque received in settlement of a claim if you think it's insufficient, as you may be deemed to have accepted it as full and final settlement. Don't accept the first offer made, as many insurance companies try to get away with making a low settlement (if an insurer pays what you've claimed without a quibble, you probably claimed too little!). If you cannot reach agreement, you can contact the Insurance Ombudsman Service Limited (☎ 1300-780808, 💻 www.insuranceombudsman.com.au) for independent arbitration or take legal action.

SOCIAL SECURITY

Social security is the name given to state benefits paid to residents in Australia. It's non-contributory and financed from general taxation, although there's a specific levy for Medicare. Nevertheless, many people fail to apply for allowances and pensions to

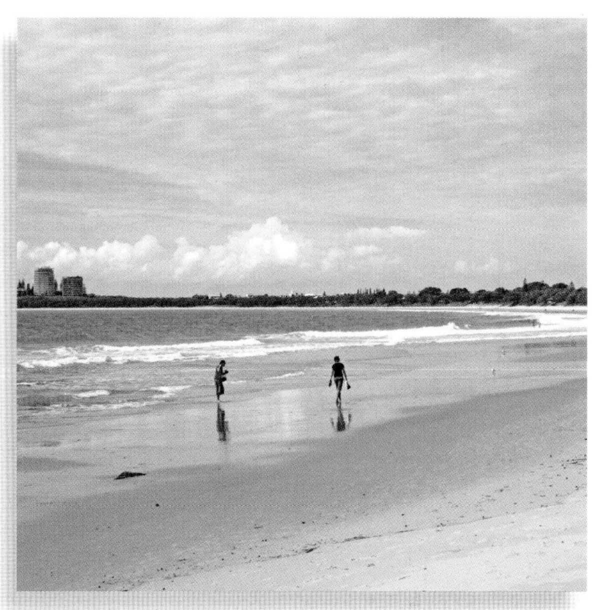

which they're entitled. If you apply and your application is rejected, you can ask for the decision to be reviewed by an Authorised Review Officer (ARO); if it's turned down again, you can appeal to the Social Security Appeals Tribunal, and finally to the Administrative Appeals Tribunal.

A range of publications detailing social security allowances, benefits and pensions is available from social security offices and community organisations. For more information, contact the Department of Families, Housing, Community Services and Indigenous Affairs (☎ 1300-653227, 💻 www.fahcsia.gov.au).

Eligibility

The main beneficiaries of social security are the aged; single parents; the unemployed; those who are disabled, sick or in special need; and families with children.

Eligibility for most social security benefits is subject to an income and/or means test. The poorest 10 per cent of Australians receive some 600 per cent more in government payments than the richest 10 per cent over their lifetime, and over 40 per cent of families receive more in handouts from the federal government than they pay in income tax.

Income from assets that are means tested include most investments (such as dividends from shares and income from investment property), but not superannuation pensions or belongings such as cars and antiques. Your assets don't include your principal family home or the land (up to two hectares) on which it's built, provided it's used for domestic purposes.

Migrants

Migrants must wait two years before they can claim most social security payments, although refugees and humanitarian migrants are exempt from the waiting period. Migrants can, however, claim Medicare benefits (💻 www.medicareaustralia.gov.au), the minimum rate of family tax benefit (see below) and, in exceptional circumstances, can claim a special benefit or a widow's allowance (see **Benefits** below) during the two-year waiting period. Some sponsors of migrants need to provide an Assurance of Support (see page 72), which makes them liable to repay the government if the migrant claims any welfare benefits during his first two years in Australia (ten years for children sponsoring a parent who's within ten years of retirement).

According to the Welfare Rights Centre (💻 www.welfarerights.org.au), the two-year waiting period for welfare has caused some migrants to become destitute and homeless, and there have been calls to have it suspended or cancelled, although these have so far been unsuccessful. Migrant service units monitor and review services to migrants and refugees, and liaise with ethnic and voluntary groups, and there are also migrant resource centres in the major towns and cities. Settlement support is provided for migrants with genuine financial problems.

Benefits

Social security benefits include a bereavement allowance, carer pension, child disability allowance, disability support pension, double orphan pension, family tax payment, health care card, 'baby bonus', mobility allowance, multiple birth payment (triplets or more), 'jobsearch' and 'newstart' allowances, parenting or guardian allowance (if a single parent), pharmaceutical allowance, rent assistance, sheltered employment and rehabilitation allowances, sickness allowance, widow's allowance and youth training allowance. The principal benefits of relevance to new residents are outlined below. A discretionary payment (called special benefit) may be paid to those who aren't eligible for other forms of assistance but are unable to support themselves.

The federal and state governments jointly fund a wide range of welfare services relating to home care for the elderly and disabled and their families. Some 1,500 nursing homes and around 1,000 hostels receive federal support to provide residential care for elderly people. A federal programme funds organisations to provide services which help people with disabilities maintain their independence and achieve their potential, and the Commonwealth Rehabilitation Service (💻 www.crsaustralia.gov.au) employs a number of specialists to work with disabled people to help them attain economic and social independence.

- **Family Tax Benefit:** administered by Human Services (💻 www.humanservices.gov.au), the family tax benefit is available to parents or guardians with dependent children, including those who are full-time students but aren't in receipt of an allowance or grant. The amount paid depends on the age and number of children in the family and the family's total income (see 💻 www.humanservices.gov.au for current benefits). A different scale of benefits (Benefit B) applies to single-parent families and those with only one earner. There's also a Large Family Supplement for those with three or more children. Payments are usually made fortnightly into the mother's bank account, although it's possible to receive the payment in a lump sum at the end of the financial year (July). Family tax benefits and other payments for children, e.g. child care benefit – see below, aren't taxable.
- **Child Care Benefit:** available to parents whose children are in registered or approved care while their parents are working, looking for work or studying. The benefit is also available for children in after-school care (between 20 and 50 hours per week), although only up to 85 per cent of the full amount. If your annual income is below a minimum figure you'll receive the full benefit, otherwise it's subject to an income test. For information, see 💻 www.humanservices.gov.au.

- **Baby Bonus:** is paid to families following the birth (including stillborn babies) or adoption of a child and recognises the extra costs incurred at the time of a new birth or adoption. Baby Bonus is indexed in July of each year and was $5,437 per eligible child (in a multiple birth) in July 2012, paid in 13 fortnightly instalments (you receive a first instalment of $879.77 followed by 12 fortnightly instalments of approximately $379.77). The baby bonus isn't classed as taxable income and also isn't considered income for Family Assistance or Social Security purposes. To be eligible, families need a combined Adjusted Taxable Income of $75,000 or less in the six months following the birth of a child or a child entering a family's care. Eligibility is also extended to families who adopt a child aged under 16. Families have 52 weeks in which to lodge a claim (see 💻 www.humanservices.gov.au). See also 💻 www.babybonus.com.au.
- **Unemployment Benefits:** Australia's unemployment benefit system takes the

form of 'jobsearch' and 'newstart' schemes. If you're unemployed, under 18 or have been registered as unemployed for less than one year and are a permanent resident, you must register for a jobsearch allowance and provide proof of identity and your tax file number. If you've been 'terminated' (sacked, made redundant, etc.) from a previous position, you need your Employment Separation Certificate, which states the reason you left work and your final wage. For immigrants there's a two-year waiting period before payments start.

If you remain unemployed for over a year, you must apply for a newstart allowance, for which you must be aged over 21, a permanent resident and unemployed, and have been registered as unemployed for over a year. Rates of payment depend on your circumstances, including your age, income, marital status and number of children.

Unemployed people aged 21 to 34 who have been receiving a newstart allowance for 6 to 12 months can be obliged to do work experience, mainly on local projects or in community service. For information, see the Human Services website (www.humanservices.gov.au).

State Pension

As in many other developed countries, there's a worsening crisis in state pension funding in Australia, where fewer and fewer workers must support an increasing number of pensioners. In 2010, 13.6 per cent of Australians were over the age of 65; by 2050, the figure is expected to double. The Commonwealth government spends around 3 per cent of the country's GDP on retirement benefits, which is expected to increase to around 5 per cent by 2050. As in many countries, there are plans to transfer the burden from the public to the private sector, which is why the mandatory Superannuation Guarantee Scheme was created in 1992 (see below).

However, despite the introduction of superannuation, some 75 per cent of people are still expected to be eligible for a full or part state pension (known as an Age Pension) for at least the next 25 years. In fact, the poor performance of super funds in recent years has meant that thousands of pensioners who previously didn't qualify for the pension can now claim it.

State retirement pensions are paid to men at 65 years of age and (currently) to women at 63.5. The pensionable age for women is gradually being increased to 65; the qualifying age was raised from 60 to 60.5 on 1st July 1995 and is being increased by six months at two-year intervals until 1st July 2013, when it will reach 65. From 1st July 2017, the qualifying age for the state (age) pension will increase from 65 to 65.5 years for both men and women, after which it will increase by six months every two years, until reaching 67 by 1st July 2023.

Pensions are pegged at 25 per cent of average male earnings. The full pension from 1st July 2010 was $695.30 a fortnight for a single person and $524.10 each for a married couple. State pensions are indexed twice a year (on 20th March and 20th September) in line with changes in the Consumer Price Index (CPI).

You generally need to have lived continuously in Australia for ten years to qualify for a state pension. A full pension is payable after 25 years' residence during your 'working' life (i.e. from the age of 16). However, Australia has reciprocal social security agreements with a number of countries (including Austria, Canada, Cyprus, Denmark, Ireland, Italy, Malta, the Netherlands, Portugal and Spain), which may enable newcomers to receive a pension as soon as they reach pensionable age, irrespective of their residence period. The UK no longer has a reciprocal social security agreement with Australia (see **British Pensioners** below).

If you've lived in Australia for less than 25 years and then go to live overseas, you receive an Australian pension proportionate to the number of years spent there, e.g. if you've spent 12.5 years in Australia, you receive half of the full retirement pension. Pensioners who delay their retirement become eligible for a cash bonus equal to 9.4 per cent of their pension entitlement for each year they continue working.

In addition to the basic retirement pension, various other pensions are paid in Australia, including pensions for bereaved people, carers, the disabled, double orphans (i.e. those whose parents are both deceased), single parents, widows and wives. All pensions are paid at the same rates. Other social security payments may be claimed in addition to a pension. The basic retirement pension is taxable, but on its own is below the tax threshold.

Australian pensioners are entitled to concessionary dental treatment, optometrist services and prescriptions, concessions on public transport fares in most states and territories, and various other benefits (which vary from state to state) which may include reduced council tax rates and utility costs (e.g. telephone rental and water rates), free post redirection and reduced registration fees for dogs.

Unlike state pensions in most countries, which are paid irrespective of a person's wealth or income, most Australian pensions are subject to taxable income and asset tests; the test which produces the lower rate of pension applies, although there's no asset test for those aged over 70. This is the case for all pensions except invalidity pensions for permanently blind people and pensions for war and defence widows. Around 25 per cent of Australians are considered too wealthy to receive a state pension.

You can choose the day on which you want your pension paid. Pensions are usually paid into a bank, building society or credit union account. Australian pensions can be paid overseas, although pensioners going overseas for longer than six months must obtain a pre-departure certificate from social security.

For more information about state pensions in Australia, see the Human Services website (💻 www.humanservices.gov.au) or contact or the Department of Families, Housing, Community Services & Indigenous Affairs (☎ 1300-653227, 💻 www.fahcsia.gov.au).

British Pensioners in Australia

British state pensions are frozen at the prevailing rate with no annual adjustments for inflation when the recipients move to certain Commonwealth countries, including Australia, Canada, New Zealand and South Africa. This affects over 350,000 British pensioners. There are some 250,000 British state pensioners in Australia with frozen British state pensions (which may be equivalent to just 'a few' $).

What's more, on 1st March 2001, Australia and the UK ceased their reciprocal social security agreement, whereby British pensioners could receive social security 'top-up' payments from the Australian government.

Those receiving top-up payments under the agreement on 1st March 2001 continue to receive payments, plus those who migrated to Australia on or before 1st March 2000 (the date on which Australia served notice of termination of the agreement on the UK) continue to have their British contributions recognised for grants of Australian pensions. Otherwise, you're eligible only for your frozen British pension.

There are a number of information websites and forums for British pensioners in Australia including the British Australia Pensioner Association (💻 www.britishpensions.org.au) and British Pensions in Australia (💻 http://youle.info/bpia-blog).

SUPERANNUATION

Superannuation (usually referred to simply as 'super') is the term commonly used in Australia for a private pension fund. As the number of retired workers has increased and the number of young workers has declined (due to a falling birth and rising unemployment rates), the pressure on government funds to pay state pensions has increased. In order to reduce the burden, the federal government introduced compulsory employer superannuation funds in 1992 under the Superannuation Guarantee Scheme.

Superannuation doesn't replace the state pension (which continues to be available, subject to eligibility) but is intended to supplement it to ensure an adequate income in retirement.

Since its introduction, superannuation has been extended to include part-time and casual workers and those who leave the workforce for up to two years. Self-employed and non-resident employees paid for work undertaken outside Australia aren't required to belong to a superannuation fund, and resident employees employed by non-resident employers and paid for work undertaken outside Australia also needn't be covered.

Generally, if you're aged over 18 and under 70 (proposed increase to 75 from 2013) and earn over $450 per month before tax (whether as a full- or part-time employee or a casual worker), your employer must make superannuation contributions for you. Some awards require employers to pay superannuation for employees earning less than $450 per month and those aged under 18 are also eligible if they work over 30 hours a week. Employees earning between $450 and $900 per month can choose, however, to receive their superannuation as additional salary.

Funds are non-contributory for employees, although voluntary contributions can be made. Employer contributions must be at least the minimum level laid down by the government, termed the Superannuation Guarantee. The minimum contribution employers must make for each employee is 9 per cent of their earnings base (excluding overtime rates but including bonuses, commissions, shift loading and casual loadings). The employers' contribution will increase from 9 to 12 per cent between 1st July 2013 and 1st July 2020.

You aren't obliged to join your employer's fund and may choose your own fund, but must do so within 28 days. You can also have a self-managed super fund (SMSF), also known as a DIY super. For independent advice see 💻 www.moneysmart.gov.au or www.ato.gov.au/superfunds. However, if you decide to go down this road, bear in mind that there are a lot of scams associated with fund advisers! In addition to DIY funds (which hold an increasing share of superannuation assets), there are also financial institution funds and industry funds. Banks, building societies, credit unions and life assurance companies can all provide superannuation funds in the form of Retirement Savings Accounts (RSAs). Repayment of all RSA deposits is guaranteed, but interest is usually modest.

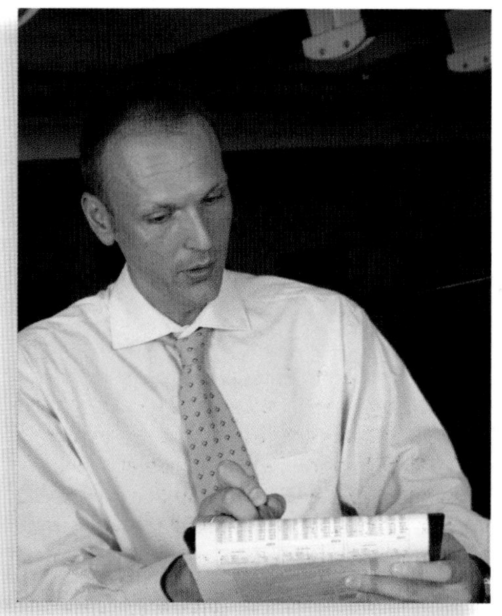

Your employer's contributions must be paid into a complying super fund or retirement saving account. Super funds are managed by trustees and each fund has its own rules, but must also follow government rules designed to ensure your super is properly managed. Funds that comply with these rules are called complying super funds. Retirement savings accounts offered by financial institutions aren't super funds but operate under similar rules. Just like complying super funds, they accept super contributions and provide benefits when you retire, become an invalid or pay benefits upon your death.

There's a huge difference between the best- and worst-performing superannuation funds, therefore it's wise to shop around and compare fund performance over a five- or ten-year period and also check the level of fees (smaller industry funds generally don't do as well as larger ones). One way to choose a fund is via a rating company such as SuperRatings (💻 www.superratings.com.au), an independent research centre.

Bank executives, postal workers and university staff are among those best placed for retirement, based on the long-term return performance of their superannuation funds. In contrast, higher-cost retail superannuation funds, including some operated by the nation's largest banks, have delivered some of the poorest investment returns.

In most cases, you would be foolish to turn down the opportunity to join an employer's fund, provided it's a good one, as it usually provides extra benefits. These may include free life and disability insurance, and insurance against loss of earnings due to injury or illness. Some funds offer members discounted home and personal loans and private health insurance. It's possible that in future employees will be able to use part of their superannuation funds to buy a home, although this is currently only possible if you have a self-managed super fund (SMSF).

Your superannuation payout may be related to your final salary, which is the best option. If it isn't, you should ensure that the fund is invested safely, as you could lose out if the share market or property prices collapse in the years just before retirement.

When you join a fund, you have a 14-day 'cooling-off' period, during which you may withdraw your membership. If you change employers or professions, your superannuation benefits can be transferred to another fund.

If you're aged under 55 you can only gain access to your super money in exceptional circumstances, for example, if you're suffering severe financial hardship or you're permanently disabled (for information see 💻 www.apra.gov.au). Temporary residents who leave Australia permanently can have their super funds reimbursed, but they will be taxed (see 💻 www.ato.gov.au); permanent residents, including New Zealand residents who leave permanently, cannot.

IMPORTANT

Superannuation is a complex subject – it's advisable to obtain expert advice before signing up to a fund and before making any major decisions regarding your super fund.

Since superannuation was introduced in 1992, it has become increasingly complicated and difficult for the layman (or anyone) to understand. Although successive governments have tinkered with the system (over 2,000 changes have been made), many analysts believe that it needs a complete overhaul.

The Association of Superannuation Funds of Australia (☎ 1800-812798 or +61-2-9264 9300 from abroad, 💻 www.superannuation.asn.au) publishes a number of useful information sheets, including *What Information You Should Receive from Your Superannuation Fund*. Information about changes to the superannuation system can be found on the

website of the Australian Taxation Office (💻 www.ato.gov.au) and general information from the Australian Bankers' Association (💻 www.smartersuper.com.au).

Tax & Surcharge

Superannuation is taxed at 15 per cent. This applies to both voluntary contributions to a superannuation fund and the income from it, although tax relief can be claimed against superannuation payments. Contributions to superannuation for high earners attract a surcharge.

In order to avoid being taxed on income at the top rate of 45 per cent, some employees negotiate higher superannuation contributions and a reduced salary (called 'salary sacrifice' arrangements). Since the surcharge was announced, many wealthy people have quit superannuation and made alternative investments (over 1.5m superannuation accounts have been closed). Nevertheless, superannuation remains attractive to lower earners.

Withdrawals & Payments

Superannuation fund payments can be taken in an annuity, a lump sum or a regular monthly income, e.g. an allocated or lifetime pension, or a combination of these. The age at which contributions may be withdrawn is called the preservation age, and depends on your date of birth, as follows:

Super Preservation Age

Date of Birth	Preservation Age
Before 1/7/60	55
1/7/60 to 30/6/61	56
1/7/61 to 30/6/62	57
1/7/62 to 30/6/63	58
1/7/63 to 30/6/64	59
From 1/7/64	60

Hence, by 2025, all Australian workers wishing to access their superannuation must be at least 60 years of age. Those aged over 55 are obliged to exhaust their superannuation funds before being entitled to unemployment benefit. If you leave Australia permanently, your superannuation benefits won't be released until you reach the required preservation age.

The maximum age for contributing to a superannuation fund is 70 (proposed increase to 75 in 2013), provided you work a minimum of ten hours per week; if you work beyond the age of 65, you should check whether you're still eligible for superannuation.

PRIVATE HEALTH INSURANCE

The Australian Medicare (see page 196) system provides free or subsidised medical treatment for all permanent residents. Anyone living or working in Australia (even temporarily) who isn't eligible for Medicare treatment and who isn't wealthy, should have private health insurance. If you're living or working in Australia and aren't covered by Medicare, it's risky or even foolhardy not to have private health insurance for you and your family. Whether you're covered by an Australian or foreign health insurance policy makes little difference (except perhaps in cost), provided you have the required level of cover, including international cover if necessary.

If your stay in Australia is short, you may be covered by a reciprocal healthcare agreement between your home country and Australia (currently includes Finland, Ireland, Italy, the Netherlands, New Zealand, Norway, Sweden and the UK – but check before travelling), or by a private health insurance scheme, although you should check exactly what this entitles you to. If you aren't adequately insured, you could be faced with some extremely high medical bills.

When changing employers or leaving Australia, you should make sure that you have continuous medical insurance. For example, if you and your family are covered by a company health fund, your insurance probably ceases after your last official day of employment. If you're planning to change your health insurance company, ensure that no important benefits are lost. When changing health insurance companies, you should inform your old insurance company if you have any outstanding bills for which they're liable.

Even if you're covered by Medicare, it 's advantageous to take out private health insurance, as Medicare doesn't cover all healthcare costs and there are waiting lists for many non-urgent procedures. Private insurance can also be used to cover private treatment, e.g. in order to circumvent Medicare waiting lists for specialist appointments and non-emergency hospital treatment (e.g. elective surgery). Medicare covers 75 per cent of the cost of private treatment, so this is an inexpensive way of obtaining private treatment. Private patients are also usually free to choose their own doctor and hospital.

Despite what insurance companies may say, the quality of private treatment is no better than that provided by Medicare, and you shouldn't assume that because a doctor (or any other medical practitioner) is in private practice, he's more competent than his Medicare counterpart. In fact, you're likely to see the same specialist or be treated by the same surgeon under Medicare as privately.

In Australia, private health insurance isn't 'risk-rated' (as, for example, in the US) like most forms of insurance. Private health insurers cannot refuse to insure any person and must charge everyone the same premium for the same level of cover, despite their risk profile and likelihood of using health services.

Most private health insurance in Australia is provided by health funds, which are regulated by the Commonwealth government and follow the principle of 'community rating' to determine premiums, i.e. premiums don't vary according to age, sex or your state of your health. This ensures that high-risk members such as the elderly and the chronically sick aren't required to pay astronomical premiums as in some other countries (e.g. the USA). However, most health funds are eroding this principle and in recent years have introduced a variety of conditions to exclude expensive treatment (called exclusion policies) and surgery such as joint replacements; there may also be financial limits. Many analysts believe this could be the thin end of the wedge and that insurance companies will abandon 'community rating' by stealth.

Types of Insurance

Health insurers offer two basic types of insurance: hospital and ancillary. Hospital cover contributes to the cost of inpatient treatment and accommodation as a private patient in a private or public hospital. Ancillary cover contributes to the cost of outpatient services which aren't covered by Medicare, such as acupuncture, chiropractic and other alternative therapies, dental treatment, physiotherapy, and spectacles or contact lenses. Ancillary insurance may also include ambulance cover, home nursing and other services, although there's usually no refund for X-rays or prescriptions. There are payment limits for ancillary cover – both per visit limits and annual limits. Some funds have a policy which pays for gym membership or sports equipment such as running shoes, on the basis that these improve your health and so reduce their costs.

Private health insurers are allowed to offer four categories of membership as follows:

- single person;
- couple;
- family, consisting of at least two adults and one or more other, which may include children and/or grandparents;
- single-parent, consisting of at least one adult (who's the contributor) and one or more dependent children.

 **Caution**

When taking out family or single-parent membership, always carefully check what constitutes a 'dependent' child, as your children may not be covered.

Insurance Providers

There are several private health insurers, the largest of which include the Hospital Contribution Fund (HCF), Medibank Private, the Medical Benefit Funds (MBF) and National Mutual Health Insurance. By far the largest insurer is Medibank Private (www.medibank.com.au), a non-profit health benefits organisation (established in 1976) operated by the state-run Health Insurance Commission, covering some 3m people (one-third of all those with private health insurance), with some 100 customer service centres throughout the country. Medibank Private also provides cover for temporary residents who aren't eligible for Medicare benefits.

It's possible to obtain health insurance from some banks, although they may insure only high earners. Compare the benefits and costs provided by a number of health insurers, most of which provide a choice of basic, intermediate and comprehensive cover.

If you're unable to resolve a complaint with your health insurer, you can contact the Private Health Insurance Ombudsman (1800-640695 or +61-2-8235 8777 from abroad, www.phio.org.au).

Premiums

Premiums vary considerably according to the state or territory, your income and the age of the oldest person on the policy (the latter two determine the level of government rebate, if applicable – see below). The average cost of the most comprehensive hospital plus ancillary cover for a family (no age loading and no excess) is around $3,500-5,000 per year or $300-400 per month, while a single person would pay around $2,000-2,750 or $150-225 per month. Premiums can usually be paid monthly, quarterly or annually – and a discount is given for annual payment. Alternatively, you can pay weekly or fortnightly through automatic salary deductions. You can compare premiums at www.iselect.com.au, www.privatehealth.gov.au or www.moneytime.com.au.

Health insurers have contracts with hospitals and doctors in order to assert some control over costs. You may need to choose a hospital and doctor contracted to your health insurer, otherwise you must pay the 'gap' between what the insurer pays and what your doctor or hospital charges. Some insurers have agreements with relatively few private hospitals, outside which you're limited to a private bed in a public hospital, and you may not be covered outside your home state. You should receive a written quotation for non-emergency hospital treatment, including all extra charges (see below).

The government is keen to encourage people to take out private health cover as Medicare is facing a funding crisis and its survival (at least in its present form) relies heavily on a strong private health sector. With this in mind, the government has introduced rebates (see below) for those with private health insurance.

Rebates

To encourage people to take out and maintain private health insurance the Australian Government introduced a 30 per cent rebate on private health insurance premiums in 2000. Under the scheme, anyone who pays hospital and/or ancillary premiums to a registered health fund can obtain a 10-30 per cent reduction on the cost of their health insurance. The rebate can be claimed in three ways: from your health fund as a straight premium reduction; from a Medicare office, which reimburses you the 30 per cent; or from the Tax Office on your annual income tax form. On 1st April 2005, new rebate amounts were introduced that applied to those aged 65 and over. Those aged from 65 to 69 are eligible to receive a 35 per cent rebate and people aged 70 and over are eligible to receive a 40 per cent rebate.

There are three tiers of Australian Government rebate, depending on your income and the age of the oldest person on the policy. Rebates vary from 10 to 40 per cent. To qualify for the maximum 40 per cent discount, families must earn less the $168,000 per year (singles $84,000) and one person covered must be aged 70 or older. If you're single and earning over $130,000 or a family earning over $260 000,you won't receive a rebate irrespective of age

As an added incentive, if you purchase hospital cover before the 1st July following your 31st birthday, you're exempt from paying the Lifetime Health Cover (LHC) loading on top of your premium, which increases annually from the age of 30.

See 💻 www.humanservices.gov.au and www.privatehealth.gov.au/healthinsurance/incentivessurcharges.

If you aren't covered by a private hospital insurance policy and you earn above a certain income threshold, you may have to pay the Medicare Levy Surcharge when you lodge your tax return.

Additional Costs

The benefits (rebates) provided by health insurers aren't usually 100 per cent and you usually need to make an extra payment or 'co-payment' towards fees, called 'out-of-pocket' costs. This can be very high and can run into hundreds or even thousands of dollars (and can increase at short notice). If you want your own doctor to treat you in a public hospital, you must pay a daily accommodation charge, and some insurers levy a fee per night (e.g. $80) for private hospital patients.

In addition to out-of-pocket costs, there may be an annual excess charge (deductible), which can be up to $2,000 for a family and may be applied per person for a couple. When you leave hospital, you're generally asked to pay the difference (if any) between your health insurer's refund and the hospital's fees. High additional costs are the main reason people have abandoned private health insurance in recent years.

Waiting Periods

All funds have waiting periods before new members are eligible to make a claim, e.g. a general two-month wait for all treatment, nine months for obstetrics (i.e. you cannot join when pregnant and claim for the costs associated with childbirth) and one year for existing conditions. This is to prevent you from making a claim directly after joining and then dropping your membership. However, accidents are covered from the day you join. Before changing funds, always check the waiting times before you can make a claim, particularly if you have existing health problems. If you already belong to a private health insurance scheme in another country, you may be able to transfer your membership to Australia, in which case you won't be subject to waiting lists. Some insurance companies offer a short-term scheme for people staying in Australia for only a few months.

Students

Overseas Student Health Cover (OSHC) is obligatory for foreign students and their dependants in Australia and must cover them for the duration of their visa or 12 months (whichever is shorter). It's offered by a number of insurance companies, including Medibank Private (💻 www.medibank.com.au). Your initial premium must be paid before you arrive in Australia and if your student visa is for more than 12 months, a further premium is payable after 12 months. If you're a government-sponsored student, e.g. by the Australian Agency for International Development/AusAID, the agency or department of the Australian government which is sponsoring you pays your premium to Medibank Private.

OSHC includes full or partial cover for the fees of doctors (including specialists) at a surgery, in your home or in hospital, and pathology services such as blood tests and X-rays. Payments are the same as for Medicare members, i.e. 85 per cent of the government schedule fee for outpatient treatment and 100 per cent of the schedule fee for hospital inpatient services and most GP services. If a doctor charges more than the schedule fee, you must pay the difference. If you choose to be treated in a private hospital, Medibank Private contributes towards the cost of treatment and accommodation, but you're responsible for paying the difference between the schedule fee and the actual fee charged. The services that aren't covered by OSHC are much the same as for Medicare (see page 196). If you wish to be covered for excluded services, you need additional private health insurance.

For more information about OSHC, see 💻 www.immi.gov.au/students/health-insurance.htm or www.studyinaustralia.gov.au/en/study-costs/oshc/overseas-student-health-cover.

Visitors

The cost of medical insurance for foreigners in Australia with a visitor's visa is much higher than for a resident, not least because private health premiums for residents are subject to official control and visitors' premiums aren't. This is a trap that has snared around 6,000 retired British expatriates in Australia, who came to the country on temporary visitors' visas (410) to join their adult emigrant children. The temporary visas have just 'rolled on' through the years and allow holders to own property, travel freely in and out of the country, and work for 20 hours a week.

Qualifying retired visitors are permitted to reside permanently in Australia on the condition that they don't become 'a burden on the state', which means comprehensive private medical cover is mandatory.

However, they are now trapped by rising health insurance costs, which are over $6,000 a year for a couple – almost twice as much as for a resident – with no cap on future increases. Consequently many British retirees are forced to leave Australia and return to Britain – if they can afford it.

International Health Policies

It's possible to take out an international health insurance policy, which may be of interest to people living in Australia temporarily, or those whose work involves a lot of travel or who work part of the time overseas. Companies usually offer a range of policies, from basic to comprehensive. All policies offer at least two fee scales, one covering the whole world, including North America (and possible other high-cost areas), the other excluding North America.

Most policies include a full refund of ambulance, emergency dental treatment, home nursing (usually for a limited period), hospital, outpatient and repatriation charges. All policies include an annual overall claims limit, usually from $200,000 to $2m (the higher the better, particularly for North America). Some comprehensive policies provide a fixed amount for general medical costs (including routine doctors' visits) and elective dental, maternity and optical expenses. If you don't require permanent international health insurance, you should consider a policy which provides limited or optional cover when you're overseas.

Premiums range from around $2,000 to over $5,000 per year, depending on your age, level of cover, health history and the areas covered (if North America is covered, premiums are much higher).

> **☑ SURVIVAL TIP**
>
> **All bills, particularly those received for treatment outside Australia, must include precise details of treatment received. Terms such as 'dental treatment' or 'consultation' are usually insufficient.**

DENTAL INSURANCE

Routine dental services aren't funded by Medicare, although it pays for 75 per cent of in-hospital medical procedures performed by an oral surgeon, and pensioners qualify for free general and emergency dental treatment under the Commonwealth Dental Health Program. Basic dental treatment is usually provided under a health insurer's ancillary policy (see **Private Health Insurance** above), and most international health insurance policies offer optional dental cover or extra dental cover for an additional premium, although there are many restrictions, and cosmetic treatment is excluded. Where applicable, the amount payable by a health insurance policy for a particular item of dental treatment is fixed and depends on your level of dental insurance. A list of specific refunds is available from insurance companies.

It's unusual to have full dental insurance in Australia as the cost is prohibitive, although some dentists offer a partial insurance scheme, which usually doesn't cover expensive items such as bridges, crowns and dentures. Patients must be 'dentally fit' and are graded according to the condition of their teeth. If you have healthy teeth and rarely pay for more than an annual check-up and a visit to a hygienist, dental insurance provides poor value for money.

BUILDING INSURANCE

When buying a home, you're usually responsible for insuring it (building insurance) before you even move in. If you take out a mortgage to buy a property, your lender will usually insist that your home (including most permanent structures on a property) has building insurance from the time you sign the contract and legally become the owner. Even when it isn't required by a lender, you'd be extremely unwise not to have building insurance. If you own a unit, building insurance is arranged and paid by the management company, with individual owners paying their share in their quarterly fees.

Building insurance usually includes loss or damage caused by aircraft or vehicles, animals, falling trees or aerials; theft, malicious damage or a riot; storm or lightning; subsidence or landslide; earthquake, explosion, fire or flood; oil leakage from a central heating system or water leakage from pipes or tanks; and may also include cover for temporary homelessness. Some insurance companies offer optional cover to include trees and shrubs damaged maliciously or by storms. The highest (and most expensive) level of cover usually includes damage to glass (e.g. windows and patio doors) and porcelain (e.g. baths, washbasins and WCs), although you may have to pay extra for accidental damage, e.g. when your son blasts a cricket ball through the patio window. Always ask your insurer what isn't covered and what it costs to include it (if required).

Building insurance must be renewed each year, and insurance companies are continually updating their policies, therefore you must ensure that a policy still provides the cover you require when you receive a renewal notice. Building insurance doesn't cover damage caused by structural faults that existed when you took out the policy, which is why it's important to have a survey carried out when you buy a property.

Lenders fix the initial level of cover when you first apply for a mortgage and usually offer to arrange the insurance for you, but you're usually free to make your own arrangements. If you arrange your own building insurance, your lender will insist that the level of cover is sufficient. Most people take the easy option and arrange insurance through their mortgage lender (premiums are usually added to your monthly mortgage payments), which is generally the most expensive option, e.g. some direct insurance companies guarantee to cut building insurance costs for the majority of homeowners insured through banks.

☑ SURVIVAL TIP

The amount for which your home must be insured isn't the current market value but the cost of rebuilding it if it's totally destroyed. However, bear in mind that the land value may far exceed the value of your home.

Most lenders provide index-linked building insurance, where premiums increase annually in line with inflation and building costs (although you need to be wary of this, as you could end up paying more than necessary). It's your responsibility, however, to ensure that your level of cover is adequate, particularly if you carry out improvements or extensions which substantially increase the value of your home. All lenders provide information and free advice. If your level of cover is too low, an insurance company is within its rights to reduce the amount it pays when a claim is made, in which case you may find you cannot afford to have your house rebuilt or repaired should disaster strike.

Premiums vary according to the type of property and the area as well as the level of cover – between around $3 to $4 per $1,000 of cover (per year) in an inexpensive area to $10 or more per $1,000 in the most expensive or high-risk areas. Therefore insurance on a property costing $150,000 to rebuild costs from around $450 to $1,500 per year. There's usually no deduction for wear and tear, and the cost of redecoration is usually met in full. Insurance for 'non-standard' homes, such as weatherboard and fibros (asbestos), is usually higher. In recent years, increased competition (particularly from direct insurers) has reduced premiums. The National Roads and Motoring Association (💻 www.mynrma.com.au) in New South Wales is the nation's largest insurer.

Premiums can usually be paid monthly (although there may be an extra charge) or annually. There may be an excess, e.g. $50 or $100, for some claims, which is intended to deter policyholders from making small claims. Some policies have an excess for certain claims only, e.g. subsidence or landslip (when your house disappears into a hole in the ground or over a cliff), which is usually $2,000 or $4,000. Not surprisingly, owners of houses vulnerable to subsidence and those living in flood-prone areas are likely to pay much higher premiums.

Many insurance companies provide emergency telephone numbers for policyholders requiring urgent advice. If you need to make emergency repairs, e.g. to weather-proof a damaged roof after a storm or other natural disaster, most insurance companies allow work up to a certain limit (e.g. $2,000) to be carried out without an estimate or approval from the insurance company, but check first.

Building insurance is often combined with home contents insurance (see below), when it's called home or household insurance, which is usually cheaper than taking out separate policies.

HOME CONTENTS INSURANCE

Home contents insurance is recommended for anyone who doesn't live in an empty house. Burglary is endemic in Australia, particularly in the major cities. Contents include everything that isn't part of the fixtures and fittings and which you could take with you if you were moving house. If you under-insure your contents, your claim may be reduced by the percentage by which you're under-insured.

A basic home contents policy covers your belongings against the same sort of 'natural disasters' as building insurance (see above). A basic policy doesn't usually include such items as bicycles, cash, credit cards (and their fraudulent use), jewellery, musical instruments, sports equipment and certain other valuables, for which you may need to take out extra cover. A basic policy doesn't usually include accidental damage caused by your family to your own property (e.g. putting your foot through the TV during a political broadcast) or your home freezer contents (in the event of a breakdown or power failure), although you may be able to add this for an extra premium. A basic policy may include garden contents, loss of heating oil and metered water, personal liability insurance (see below), replacement locks and temporary accommodation. If they aren't included, these items can usually be covered for an additional premium.

Some policies include legal expenses cover (e.g. up to $100,000) for disputes with employers, neighbours, shops, suppliers and anyone who provides you with a service, e.g. a plumber or builder. Most contents policies include public liability cover, e.g. up to $2m. Items such as computers and mobile telephones may need to be listed individually on your policy, and computers and other equipment used for business aren't usually covered (or may be covered only for a prohibitive extra payment). If you have friends or lodgers living in your home, their property won't be covered by your policy.

You can usually insure your property for its second-hand value (indemnity) or its full replacement value (new for old), which covers everything except clothes and linen (for which wear and tear is assessed) at the new cost price. Most Australians take out replacement value insurance, which should be index-linked so that the level of cover is automatically increased by a percentage or fixed amount each year.

Most policies have a maximum amount they will pay per item and/or a maximum amount per claim, e.g. $1,500 for each item of jewellery or work of art, or a total claim of $10,000.

Some insurance companies offer policies called 'no-sum' or 'fixed-sum', where you aren't required to value all your possessions but are covered for a fixed amount depending on the number of bedrooms in your home. With this type of policy the insurance company cannot scale down a claim because of under-insurance. However, the sums insured can be minimal, and you're usually better off calculating the value of the contents to be insured.

Premiums

Annual premiums start at around $400 per annum in a low-risk area, but can be several times this amount in a high-risk area. Even if you're willing to forgo theft insurance, insurance companies are reluctant to offer this option, as the risk of theft is a convenient excuse to load premiums. Your premium depends largely on where you live and your insurer. All insurance companies assess the risk by location, based on your postcode. Check before buying a home, as the difference between low-and high-risk areas can be considerable.

As with building insurance, it's important to shop around for the lowest premium, as premiums vary considerably with the insurer. If you're already insured, you may find that you can save money by changing insurers. However, look out for penalties when switching insurers. Combining your home contents insurance with your building insurance (see above) is a common practice, and is usually cheaper than insuring each separately. Having your building and contents insurance with the same company also avoids disputes over which company should pay what, which can arise if you have a fire or flood affecting both your home and its contents. Those aged over 50 or 55 (and possibly first-time homeowners) may be offered a discount, and some companies provide special policies for students in college accommodation or lodgings (ask an insurance broker).

Most insurers offer a no-claims discount or a discount (e.g. 5 or 10 per cent) for homes with burglar alarms and other high-security features. In high-risk areas, good security is usually a condition of insurance. Beware of the small print in policies, particularly those regarding security, which insurers often use to avoid paying claims. You forfeit all rights under your policy if you leave doors or windows open (or the keys under a mat or flower pot), particularly if you've claimed a discount for your home's impregnability. If there are no signs of forced entry, e.g. a broken window, you may be unable to claim for a theft (so break a window!). If you plan to leave your house empty for a long period, e.g. a month or longer, you may need to inform your insurer.

Claims

Claims should be made as soon as possible after loss or damage occurs, and policies may specify a maximum notification period. Some insurers provide a 24-hour emergency helpline for policyholders and assistance for repairs for domestic emergencies, such as a blocked drain or electrical failure, up to a maximum amount for each claim. Take care when completing a claim form, as insurers have tightened up on claims and few people receive a full settlement. Many insurers charge an excess of $50 to $100 per claim (check your policy).

You may need to wait months for a claim to be settled. Generally, the larger the claim, the longer you have to wait for your money, although in an emergency a company may make an interim payment. If you aren't satisfied with the final amount offered, don't accept it and try to negotiate a higher figure. If you still cannot reach agreement, you can contact the Insurance Ombudsman Service Limited (☏ 1300-780808, 💻 www.insurance ombudsman.com.au) for independent arbitration or take legal action.

PERSONAL LIABILITY INSURANCE

Personal (or legal) liability insurance covers individuals and their dependants against compensation claims for accidental damage, injury or death caused to third parties or their property. It usually covers anything from spilling wine on your neighbour's Persian carpet to your dog or child biting someone. Although common in Europe and North America, where people sue each other for $millions at the drop of a hat, personal liability insurance is unusual in Australia. However, home contents policies (see above) usually include personal liability insurance up to $2m against injury or damage to third parties in your home, and personal liability insurance outside your home may be included in a holiday or travel policy (see below).

HOLIDAY & TRAVEL INSURANCE

Holiday and travel insurance is recommended if you don't wish to risk having your holiday or trip ruined or to arrive home broke. As you know, anything can and something often does go wrong with a holiday, sometimes before you

even board the plane (particularly if you don't have insurance). Travel insurance is available from many sources, including airlines, banks, insurance brokers, motoring organisations, tour operators and travel agents.

When you pay for your travel costs with some credit cards, your family (possibly including children under the age of 25) are provided with free travel accident insurance (by the card issuer) up to a specified amount, e.g. $300,000. **Don't, however, rely on this insurance, as it usually covers only death and serious injury.**

Medical expenses are an important aspect of travel insurance and you shouldn't rely on reciprocal health agreements, cover provided by charge and credit card companies, or private medical insurance, none of which may provide the necessary cover. The minimum medical insurance recommended by experts is $500,000 for Europe and $2m for North America and the rest of the world. Personal liability should be at least $2m for Europe and $4m for the rest of the world.

Always check any exclusion clauses in contracts by obtaining a copy of the full policy document, as all relevant information isn't contained in insurance leaflets.

Cost

The cost of travel insurance varies considerably depending on your destination. Many companies have different rates for different areas, e.g. Australia, Europe, North America and worldwide (excluding North America). Generally, the longer the period covered, the cheaper the daily cost, although the maximum period may be limited, e.g. six months. Premiums for travel within Australia are around $30 to $40 per person for two weeks, European destinations are usually from $150 for two weeks, and North America (where medical treatment costs an arm and a leg) and a few other destinations cost from $200 for three weeks. The cheapest policies offer reduced cover which may not be adequate. Premiums may be higher for those aged over 65 or 70, and with some policies an excess (e.g. $50) must be paid for each claim.

Annual Policies

For people who travel overseas frequently, whether for business or pleasure, an annual travel policy is often an excellent idea, costing around $250 to $350 per year for worldwide cover for an unlimited number of trips. However, always check carefully exactly what's included and read the small print (some insist that travel is by air). Most annual policies don't cover you for travel within Australia and there's a maximum limit on the length of each separate trip, e.g. one to six months.

Claims

Although travel insurance companies quickly and gladly take your money, they aren't so keen to pay claims, and you may need to persevere before they pay up. Fraudulent claims against travel insurance are commonplace, so unless you can produce evidence to support your claim, insurers may assume that you're trying to cheat them. Always be persistent and make a claim irrespective of any small print, as this may be unreasonable and therefore invalid in law. Insurance companies usually require you to report any loss (or any incident for which you intend to make a claim) to the local police within 24 hours and to obtain a report. Failure to do this usually means that a claim won't be considered.

 **Caution**

Many travel and holiday insurance policies don't provide the level of cover that most people need.

14. FINANCE

Australia is one of the world's wealthiest 's countries with a per capita gross domestic product (GDP) of US$61,040 in 2011 (source *The Economist*). The country has the highest ratio of assets to population of any country in the world and its ratio of government debt to GDP is also one of the lowest among OECD countries. Australia's purchasing power parity (PPP) per capita is also one of the highest in the world, with around eight times more adults earning over $100,000 than the worldwide average. In 2011, the average middle-aged adult had a net worth of over $350,000. Sydney is Australia's most important financial market, home of the Australian Securities Exchange (■ www.asx.com.au), the country's leading stock market (although it's relatively small in international terms).

Competition for your money is fierce in Australia, where financial services are provided not only by Australian and foreign banks, but also by Australia Post, building societies, credit unions, insurance companies, investment brokers, mortgage providers, and even supermarkets and motoring organisations. As in most Western countries, personal finance in Australia is a minefield, and there are plenty of predators waiting to get their hands on your loot. Always shop around for financial services and never sign a contract unless you know exactly what the costs and implications are.

When you arrive in Australia to take up residence, ensure that you have sufficient cash, credit cards, gold nuggets, luncheon vouchers, coffee machine tokens, precious stones and silver dollars to last at least until your first pay day, which may be some time after your arrival. Don't, however, carry a lot of cash.

There are numerous books and magazines to help you manage your finances in Australia, and articles on personal finance are published in the financial pages of the Saturday and Sunday editions of major newspapers, which also contain 'best rate' tables for credit cards (plus balance transfer), mortgages, savings accounts, superannuation and loans. Independent financial advice is available from various websites including Money Buddy (■ www.moneybuddy.com.au) and Money Manager (■ http://moneymanager.com.au).

If you get into trouble with debt there are various free counselling services available, including the Citizens Advice Bureau and Financial Counselling Australia (■ www.financialcounsellingaustralia.org.au).

For information about the Medicare levy, pensions (including superannuation) and life insurance, see **Chapter 13**. See also **Economy** on page 17.

COST OF LIVING

No doubt you'd like to know how far your Australian dollars will stretch and how much money (if any) you'll have left after paying your bills. For many years, Australia was considered a relatively cheap country in which to live, but due to the increased cost of housing (and rents), energy, transport, health insurance, recreation, clothing and food (to name just a few things) in the last decade or so, it's now a relatively expensive country in which to live. **The cost of housing (see Chapter 5) is a critical issue for anyone planning to emigrate to Australia and needs to be**

researched thoroughly by prospective migrants.

The cost of living in Australia has increased considerably in the last decade, during which life for most people in 'middle Australia' has become much more expensive. Hardest hit are pensioners on a fixed income or receiving superannuation which has been decimated. It has been estimated that a couple needs an income of around $50,000 a year for a comfortable retirement and at least $30,000 for a modest retirement (the state pension for a couple is less than $25,000).

Australia's consumer price index (CPI), issued by the Australian Bureau of Statistics (www.abs.gov.au), gives an indication of how prices have risen (or fallen) over the past year (the inflation rate). The CPI, which sceptics believe stands for 'con people incessantly', is calculated from the cost of a basket of basic goods and services, including computer equipment, financial fees and higher education fees, but not mortgage interest rates. The inflation rate was 1.6 per cent in July 2012.

Manufactured goods tend to be expensive in Australia, particularly imported goods, including automobiles, clothes and other manufactured items, which are generally more expensive than in Europe or North America. Transport costs between major cities are high due to the large distances involved, although fuel is much cheaper than in Europe. The price of food is similar to Europe and North America. Approximately $800 should be sufficient to feed two adults for a month in most areas (excluding alcohol, caviar and fillet steak). The prices of staple foods in Australia is provided on the Yes Australia website (www.yesaustralia.com/estilo-custosing.htm) and a free online Property Value Guide is provided by the Commonwealth Bank of Australia (www.commbank.com.au/propertyvalueguide).

In the Mercer 2012 Cost of Living Survey (www.mercer.com/costofliving) of 214 cities worldwide, Sydney was Australia's most expensive city in 11th position, followed by Melbourne (15), Perth (19), Canberra (23), Brisbane (24) and Adelaide (27) – all much higher than previous years due to the sharp increase in the value of the A$ in recent years and the cost of accommodation. Tokyo, Luanda (Angola), Osaka, Moscow and Geneva had the dubious honour of holding the top five places. Selected other rankings were: Zurich and Singapore (equal 6), Hong Kong (9), Shanghai (16), London (25), New York (33 – the only US city in the top 50), Paris (37), Rome (42), Auckland (56), Amsterdam (57), Toronto (61), Vancouver (63), Los Angeles (68), Brussels (71), Dublin (72), Wellington (74), San Francisco (90), Washington DC (107), Miami and Chicago (110), Birmingham, UK (133), Aberdeen (144), Glasgow (161) and Belfast (165).

It's also possible to compare the cost of living between various cities, using websites such as the Economist Intelligence Unit (http://eiu.enumerate.com/asp/wcol_wcolhome.asp), for which a fee is payable. There are also websites that give you an idea of living costs in Australia, such as www.numbeo.com/cost-of-living/country_result.jsp?country=australia. The website Go Matilda (www.gomatilda.com/calculator/index.cfm) allows you to compare the cost of living between your home country and Australia, and between the State and Territory capitals of Australia. However, bear in mind that information should be taken with a pinch of salt, as it may not be up to date, and price comparisons with other countries are often wildly inaccurate (and often include irrelevant items which distort the results).

The fundamental flaw with most cost of living surveys is that they convert local prices into $US, which means that ranking positions are as much (or more) the result of currency fluctuations than price inflation. Therefore in the last few years, the Eurozone, Australia and New Zealand, with their harder currencies, have become more expensive in dollar terms, while the UK and the USA have become relatively cheaper (on paper).

It's difficult to estimate an average cost of living in Australia, as it depends on where you live as well as your lifestyle. The cost of living in rural areas is, not surprisingly, lower than in the major cities (particularly housing). If you live in Sydney, drive a BMW and dine in expensive restaurants, your cost of living will be much (much) higher than if you live in a rural area, drive a small Japanese car and eat mostly at home. You can live relatively inexpensively by buying Australian produce whenever possible and avoiding expensive imported goods.

AUSTRALIAN CURRENCY

The Australian unit of currency is the Australian dollar (A$), which fell to an 11-year low against the US$ in 1997 due to the turmoil in Asian money markets and collapsing Asian currencies. Although it took many years to recover, in recent years the A$ has been very strong and in September 2012 was stronger than the US$ (US$1 = A$0.97) and stood at $1.55 to the GB£ (see 💻 www.xe.com for the latest rates).

The Australian dollar is divided into 100 cents, and coins are minted in values of 5, 10, 20 and 50 cents (all silver-coloured cupronickel coins), and $1 and $2 (gold-coloured bronze coins with irregular milling on the edge). The $1 and $2 coins are smaller than the 20-cent coin, which can cause confusion. Although the smallest coin is 5 cents, prices are still shown in single cents but totals are rounded up or down to the nearest 5 cents when you pay. Australian banknotes have lurid designs and are printed in values of $5 (blue/mauve), $10 (blue/green/khaki), $20 (grey/red), $50 (blue/gold/orange) and $100 (green/orange). The $100 bills are treated with suspicion by some people and may not be accepted by small businesses, taxi drivers, etc., although $50 bills are in widespread use (and standard issue from ATMs).

Forgery used to be a problem in Australia, but it was the first country to have a complete set of plastic banknotes, which offer much greater security against counterfeiting and last four times as long as conventional paper notes (they are even unharmed when accidentally left in clothes in a washing machine – domestic money laundering!).

It's advisable to obtain some Australian banknotes (e.g. $100 in small bills) before arriving in Australia and to familiarise your family with them. This will save you having to change money on arrival at an Australian airport, where exchange rates are usually poor and there are usually long queues.

There's no limit to the amount of Australian or foreign currency that can be brought into Australia, but amounts of $10,000 or more (or the equivalent in foreign currency) must be declared on arrival (see below).

FOREIGN CURRENCY

Until recently, there were few restrictions on the amount of currency (i.e. banknotes) you could import and export. However, the Anti-Money Laundering & Counter-Terrorism Financing Act (which came into force in December 2006) imposed tighter restrictions and anyone importing large amounts of money must account for its provenance. Import and export declaration forms are available from customs officers at ports and airports. You must also declare whether you're carrying any 'bearer negotiable instruments', which include travellers' cheques, cheques, promissory notes, money orders and postal orders.

For more information contact the Australian Transaction Reports and Analysis Centre (☎ 1300-021037, 💻 www.austrac.gov.au).

Buying & Selling Currency

Most banks buy and sell foreign currency, although you usually need to order it a few days in advance, as only the major branches in capital cities keep foreign currency. Major Australian banks change most foreign banknotes (but not coins), but usually give a better exchange rate for cash obtained with a debit or credit card. *Bureaux de change* have longer opening hours than banks, including Saturdays and Sundays in tourist areas and large cities, but should be used sparingly, as they don't offer the best exchange rates and often charge a large commission (airports are the worst possible places to change money).

When buying or selling foreign currency in Australia, beware of excessive charges. Most banks have a wide margin (e.g. 5 to 10 per cent) between their buying and selling rates for foreign currencies. Apart from the difference in exchange rates, which are posted by all banks and bureaux de change, there may be a significant difference in charges. It pays to shop around for the best exchange rates and lowest charges, particularly when changing a lot of money. The standard A$ exchange rate against major international currencies is listed in banks and in the major daily newspapers, and on websites such as www.xe.com.

There isn't much difference in the cost between exchanging cash, buying and redeeming travellers' cheques and using a credit card to obtain cash in Australia. However, many people simply take cash when travelling overseas, which is asking for trouble, particularly if you have no way of obtaining more cash in Australia, e.g. with a credit or debit card.

One thing to bear in mind when travelling anywhere is never to rely on only one source of funds!

CREDIT RATING

Whether you're able to obtain credit (or how much) in Australia usually depends on your credit rating (or credit score), which is becoming increasingly important in today's credit-driven financial world. Most financial institutions use some kind of credit scoring system and request a credit reference agency report to find out whether you're 'worthy' of having money lent to you, i.e. can afford the exorbitant interest charges!

Caution

If you're a new arrival in Australia, a lender may request a report from an agency in your previous country of residence. You may be asked to provide written consent to having your credit rating checked.

Your credit rating depends on many factors, such as your age, occupation and marital status, how long you've held your current job, whether you're a homeowner, where you live, whether you're on the electoral roll, whether you have a telephone and, not least, your credit record. If you're refused credit because of a credit report, you're told and can ask to see the report and challenge anything that's incorrect.

If you have a bad credit rating it's almost impossible to obtain credit in Australia unless you're able to provide collateral, i.e. security such as a property. A life assurance policy can be used to provide collateral for a loan. If you're refused credit, look on the bright side: you cannot run up any debts!

You can check the credit rating of a company or person with whom you're planning to do business. Australia's main credit bureau is Veda Advantage (www.vedaadvantage.com), formerly Baycorp Advantage and before that the Credit Reference Association of Australia and Credit Advantage (perhaps it keeps changing its name to avoid its creditors?), which holds records on some 12m people and over 1m businesses.

BANKING

The Reserve Bank of Australia (www.rba.gov.au) conducts monetary policy, works to maintain a strong financial system, issues the country's banknotes and sets the bank lending rate (called the cash rate), which was 3.5 per cent in August 2012.

Australian banks made huge losses in the '80s and spent the first half of the '90s cost cutting and recovering. The second half of the '90s saw strong growth and

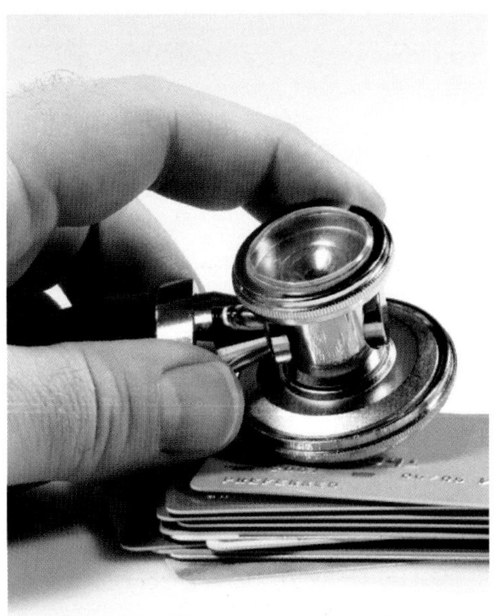

a stable credit environment, leading to higher profit margins. Australian banks are currently highly profitable and contribute more in company tax than any other industry. Nevertheless, many regional (bush or country) banks have closed in recent years (over 2,000 branches have closed in the last decade or so) as banks slimmed their branch networks. The proliferation of electronic banking (see below) has meant that banks require a much smaller workforce, and they've shed thousands of jobs (bank is a four-letter word with many people in Australia, where they're generally held in low esteem).

Consequently, many communities have been left without a local bank, although some towns have successfully fought closures by threatening to withdraw $millions in assets from a bank. In some areas credit unions have stepped in to fill the void, but in a small rural town or village there's likely to be a post office agency, but no bank branch. A post office account (or an account with one of the banks that allow withdrawals to be made from post offices) is handy for travellers in rural areas. The major banks have also established low-cost 'kiosk' branches in shopping centres operated by just one or two people and open seven days a week. For an independent review of the Australian financial sector, see 💻 www.banks.com.au.

In October 2008, the government announced a guarantee of deposits in all Australian-based financial institutions, prior to which there was no bank deposit guarantee scheme in Australia. The initial sum guaranteed per person per institution was £1m, but this was reduced to $250,000 in February 2012.

Banks

The major Australian banks with branches in cities and large towns throughout Australia are the Australia & New Zealand Bank (💻 www.anz.com.au), the Commonwealth Bank of Australia (💻 www.commbank.com.au), the National Australia Bank (💻 www.nab.com.au), and Westpac (💻 www.westpac.com.au), collectively referred to as 'the big four'. These banks also have the widest representation overseas. In addition to the national banks, there are many city, regional and state banks.

The major banks offer over 200 'products' (banks no longer provide services), ranging from current accounts (known as transaction accounts) and savings accounts, to home insurance and personal superannuation schemes. If you do a lot of travelling overseas, you may find the comprehensive range of travel and other services provided by the major banks advantageous. Banks are keen to attract migrants as customers and offer a range of services exclusively to newcomers. The major banks (e.g. the Commonwealth Bank of Australia) provide financial advice and assistance to migrants in a number of countries, and operate a network of Migrant Service Centres (💻 www.migrantservicecentres.org) in Australia's capital cities. Many services provided by Australian banks are also offered by credit unions and a few building societies.

GiroPost

GiroPost is a banking service offered at some 2,700 Australia Post outlets (see **Chapter 6**) shown by a bank@post sign – over 90 per cent of Australian households are within 5m (8km) of a GiroPost outlet. It's the largest agency banking network in Australia acting on behalf of over 70 financial institutions, although not all major banks are members. The only stipulation is that the account must be one which can be accessed by a credit or debit card and PIN.

GiroPost allows you to withdraw or deposit money, pay bills, check account balances and more – and there are no fees. For interstate travellers and tourists, it provides a nationwide agency banking when you're away from home.

For an independent review of the Australian financial sector, see 💻 www.banks.com.au.

Business Hours

Normal bank opening hours are from 9.30am until 4pm, Monday to Thursday, and from 9.30am until 5pm on Fridays, with no closure over the lunch period in cities and most towns. Some city branches open from 8am until 6pm, Monday to Thursday, and until 8pm on Fridays, while in rural areas banks may open on only one or two days a week. Some banks and building societies open on Saturday mornings, e.g. from 9am until noon. There are bank branches with extended opening hours at international airports and in an increasing number of shopping centres (some open seven days a week). All banks are closed on Public Holidays. Most banks and main post offices in Australia have 24-7 ATMs for cash deposits, withdrawals and statements.

MORTGAGES

The average home loan for first time buyers has risen from three times average annual income in 1996 to over six times average income in 2012. Around half of all Australian homeowners have a mortgage (home loan), although Australians make great efforts to pay off their mortgages – there's often no penalty for doing so – and most try to pay it off in 10 or 15 years.

Mortgages are available from literally dozens of sources, including banks, building societies, credit unions, finance and insurance companies, mortgage brokers (such as Aussie, 💻 www.aussie.com.au), motoring organisations and state housing authorities. Competition to lend you money is fierce and homebuyers in Australia have a wider variety of home loan finance than is available in many other countries, although the number of lenders and deals has diminished in the last few years.

In August 2012, interest rates for variable home loans were around 6 per cent (see 💻 www.interestrate.com.au). As in some other countries (e.g. the UK), banks increasingly fail to pass on rate cuts to borrowers (the official bank 'cash rate' was 3.5 per cent in August 2012).

The usual home loan period is 25 years, although it can be anything from 5 to 30 years (or up to the age at which a state pension is paid), while the maximum term for loans for the purchase of land is usually 20 years.

The Commonwealth and state governments provide funds for housing loans through the Commonwealth/State Housing Agreement. In most states, loans are also made through co-operative building societies. In some states housing commissions and state banks also provide loans, although eligibility is restricted to low and moderate income families and there are often long waiting lists.

Information about mortgages and the best deals is available from a number of publications and websites include *Your Mortgage* magazine (💻 www.yourmortgage.com.au), Mortgage Choice (💻 www.mortgagechoice.com.au), Australia's leading mortgage broker, and Mortgage Comparison Australia (💻 www.mortgagecomparisonaustralia.com.au).

For more information about mortgages, see our sister-publication, *Buying a Home in Australia*.

TAXATION

Taxes in Australia vary with the state or territory. They are levied at Commonwealth (federal), state and local government levels. For example, income tax and capital gains tax are levied at federal level. States and territories receive their income from stamp duty on commercial and legal documents (cheques, insurance policies, mortgage transactions, and receipts and transfers of land), payroll tax (a state tax imposed on an employer's payroll and the biggest source of income for state governments), taxes on land, spirits (liquor) and motor vehicles, and miscellaneous licence fees. (Since the high court's decision to outlaw state taxes on alcohol, petrol and tobacco, there has been an ongoing taxation war between state and federal governments.) The main form of local government tax is property tax, augmented by charges for services such as sewerage and water. There are no gift, inheritance or wealth taxes in Australia (it's the only OECD country not to have some form of inheritance tax).

The total of direct and indirect taxation is low by international standards, although the government is continually inventing new ways of taxing people, including fringe benefit tax, various taxes on superannuation (private pension) funds, a tax to pay for the public health service and a tax for not having private health insurance.

Among the various Australian eccentricities is the government's financial year, which runs from 1st July to 30th June.

Obtaining Help

Australia has Byzantine tax regulations (the Income Tax Act runs to over 3,000 pages!) and it's possible to receive conflicting information from different tax 'experts' and even from different branches of the Australian Tax Office (ATO). Taxpayers constantly complain of inconsistency in the way that the ATO makes its rulings and you should never trust the ATO to take only what it should or to credit you with all the allowances that you're entitled to; although the ATO won't cheat you deliberately, it does make mistakes.

Tax Help is a volunteer service to help certain people complete their tax returns, including Aborigines and Torres Strait Islanders, those on low incomes (including senior citizens), people from non-English-speaking backgrounds, and those with disabilities. The translating and interpreting service (TIS) helps non-English-speaking people with tax questions by setting up a three-way telephone conversation with an interpreter and the tax office (☎ 131450). The languages covered include Arabic, Chinese, Croatian, Greek, Indonesian, Italian, Japanese, Korean, Macedonian, Polish, Serbian, Spanish, Turkish and Vietnamese.

Most TAFE colleges (see page 147), in conjunction with the ATO, run a course explaining the tax system and how to complete tax returns. For general income tax enquiries, contact the ATO (☎ 132861). The ATO has a comprehensive – if complicated and cumbersome – website (💻 www.ato.gov.au), where most information is accessible, and a problem-resolution service (☎ 132870).

To help you complete your tax return, there are various computer tax programs, such as QuickTax (Reckon Intuit) and SmartTax (Mysterious Pursuit), although they're mainly for 'experts'. Another option is to join Taxpayers Australia (💻 www.taxpayer.com.au), a non-profit organisation which for an annual fee of $396 provides you with the latest tax information, a telephone helpline number and a booklet on the current year's tax return.

There are a number of books published about how to reduce your income tax bill, including the *Australian Master Tax Guide* (Longman) and the *Taxpayers Guide* by Tony Greco (John Wiley), although both are very expensive.

Using an Accountant

If your tax affairs are complicated and you aren't up to (or haven't time for) 'self-help', you should consider employing an accountant or tax agent (many banks also provide a personal tax service). This applies to most self-employed people, but very few who are on PAYG. Don't

choose an accountant simply by sticking a pin in the telephone book, but ask your colleagues or friends if they can recommend someone. If you're self-employed, you should choose an accountant who deals with people in your line of business and who knows exactly what you can and cannot claim.

Accountants' fees vary from around $100 to $400 per hour, so check in advance what the rates are (they're highest in the major cities). A good accountant may save you more than he charges in fees, but you can reduce these considerably by keeping itemised records of all your business expenses (preferably on a computer), rather than handing over a box of invoices and receipts at the end of each financial year.

Tax File Number

To receive an 'income' in Australia, you need a Tax File Number (TFN). Income includes wages or salary from a job, payments from the government, and money earned from investments including interest on savings accounts. Your tax file number (TFN) consists of nine digits and is probably the most important number you receive in Australia. Without it you're taxed at the maximum rate (45 per cent) on all your income (it's that important!).

You also need a TFN to claim sickness and unemployment benefits, to make any investment and to enrol in a fee-free course of higher education. It's required when completing your income tax return and when you start work or change jobs (there are both personal and business tax file numbers).

You can obtain an application form for a TFN from your local ATO office on production of identification, such as your birth certificate, driving licence or passport (with a valid residence visa); you should receive your TFN around two weeks after making an application. The ATO publishes a brochure, *Applying for Your Tax File Number*, which explains the application procedure. You can also apply online at 💻 www.ato.gov.au.

Withholding tax

When you earn interest income or receive dividends from shares or distributions from unit trust investments, you must ensure that you give your bank your TFN; it isn't compulsory, but Australian banks are required to deduct 'withholding' tax from residents at 45 per cent if you don't! Your bank is also required to report to the ATO the details of interest/dividend income earned and any withholding tax deducted. If you're a non-resident and don't have a TFN, you'll be charged withholding tax at 10 per cent. However, you may be entitled to a tax refund under double-taxation agreements, therefore you should include details of withholding tax payments on your tax form.

INCOME TAX

Federal income tax is levied under a two-tier system: the first class system applies to the self-employed and companies, and the second class system, called Pay-As-You-Go (PAYG), is for employees (see below). The self-employed pay their tax in arrears, whereas an employee's income tax is deducted at source from his salary by his employer. There's no state income tax in Australia. Changes in federal taxation are usually announced in the annual budget statement in May.

The income tax year in Australia runs from 1st July to 30th June (for reasons known only to the tax office), although in certain circumstances an accounting year beginning on a different date may be used for tax purposes.

Australian income tax law recognises the following general types of taxpayer: companies, individuals, partnerships and trusts. Specific provisions apply to certain businesses, minors and superannuation funds.

Domicile

Residents of Australia are taxed on their worldwide income and non-residents only on Australian income. You're considered to be resident in Australia for tax purposes if any of the following apply:

- you normally reside in Australia;
- you're domiciled in Australia and don't have a permanent place of abode outside the country;

♦ you spend at least 183 days in a financial year in Australia (unless you don't intend to take up Australian residence and have a usual place of abode outside Australia).

Double-taxation Agreements

Despite the name, double-taxation agreements are designed to prevent you paying taxes twice. Under double-taxation agreements, certain foreign residents are exempt from paying Australian tax. Australia has double-taxation agreements with many countries; for a list, see www.ato.gov.au/businesses/content.aspx?doc=/content/59547.htm. If part of your income is taxed in one of these countries, you won't be required to pay Australian tax on that income.

Foreign employees working in Australia for Australian companies or organisations are subject to Australian tax on their earnings. However, if your stay is for less than six months you're usually taxed at the (higher) rates applicable to non-residents (see below), although double-taxation agreements contain articles dealing with directors, entertainers, government services, professors and teachers, which may alter this. Income earned by residents from services performed overseas is exempt if you've been employed outside Australia for a continuous period of at least 91 days, provided the income has been taxed overseas.

Depending on your circumstances, you may be required to pay tax on part of your income in your home country and the remainder in Australia.

Citizens of most countries are exempt from paying taxes in their home country when they spend a minimum period overseas, e.g. a year. One exception is citizens of the US. American citizens can obtain a copy of a brochure entitled *Tax Guide for US Citizens and Resident Aliens Abroad* from American embassies (or see www.irs.gov/publications/p54/index.html). If you're in doubt about your tax liability in your home country, contact your embassy or consulate or your home country's tax office.

Taxable Income

Only a few types of income are exempt from tax, including defence and United Nations payments; education payments; certain pensions and social security allowances and payments; social security family payments; certain scholarships, bursaries and other educational allowances; and the income of certain non-profit organisations. The tax law makes a basic distinction between income and capital receipts, and generally only income is assessable. Capital gains made from the sale of assets acquired after 20th September 1985 are included in your taxable income (see **Capital Gains Tax** below). Taxable income also includes certain benefits, dividends and bonuses, foreign income, income from partnerships and trusts, interest, pensions, royalties, rental income, salary or wages, and termination payments.

Most government pensions are subject to tax, although a system of rebates ensures that no tax is paid by a pensioner who earns only a small amount of other income. Reductions or exemptions apply to certain other types of income, including lump-sum payments received on retirement, non-cash benefits, irregular income earned by artists, sportsmen, etc., and the income of farmers.

Those with irregular income are permitted to average their earnings out over five years; the tax payable is calculated according to a complicated formula, taking into account 'normal' income and adding this to one-fifth of your 'abnormal' income over a five-year period.

The profit earned in the operation of a business is added to any other income and you're taxed on the total. Each partner in a partnership is taxed individually on his share of partnership income.

Allowances & Rebates

All taxpayers can claim allowances from their taxable income and rebates, in addition to a credit for tax paid during the relevant financial year. Allowances reduce taxable income, but rebates (called credits in some other countries) are subtracted from the tax payable on your taxable income, i.e. rebates are 'worth' the same amount to all taxpayers, irrespective of their tax band.

Most allowances are occupation-specific and must be legitimate expenses incurred in earning your taxable income. They're commonly claimed by employees and include self-education, travel and work expenses. Allowances are also made for certain non-business expenses, such as gifts to approved charities. They must usually be substantiated by documentation, and strict requirements apply where expenses exceed $300 per year. There's a federal government taxation incentive for those who let a property for less than their mortgage repayments, when the loss can be offset against other income. You shouldn't hesitate to claim for anything that you believe is a legitimate business expense. The ATO will disallow them if it doesn't agree, but it won't grant you an allowance to which you're entitled but which you've forgotten to claim!

Rebates (also called tax offsets and tax relief) are essentially available only to Australian residents whose dependants also live in Australia. Rebates are made in respect of private health insurance premiums (at 30 per cent, provided the insurance is with a registered health fund; you may choose to claim the rebate as a reduction in your insurance premium) and net medical expenses (including dental, medical and optical aids) over $1,500 that aren't reclaimable from Medicare or private health insurance (at 20 per cent). Rebates don't reduce your Medicare levy.

Details of all allowances and rebates for individual taxpayers can be found on the ATO's website (www.ato.gov.au).

Tax Rates

Australia has different tax rates for residents and non-residents, as shown below.

Residents

Australia has four progressive income tax rates for resident taxpayers, which are as shown below for the 2012-13 tax year. Anyone who isn't resident in Australia for a whole financial year receives a pro rata portion of the tax-free allowance ($18,200 per year); for example, if you're resident in Australia for half the tax year, your tax-free allowance is $9,100. Different (usually higher) rates apply to those under the age of 18. There are no reductions for couples in Australia, where the same tax rates apply to married and single individuals.

Resident Income Tax Rates 2012-13

Taxable Income	Tax Rate (%)	Cumulative Tax
Up to $18,200	0	
$18,201 to $37,000	19	$3,572
$37,001 to $80,000	32.5	$17,547
$80,001 to $180,000	37	$54,547
Over $180,000	45	

The above rates don't include the Medicare levy of 1.5 per cent.

Non-residents

There's no tax-free allowance for non-residents (although they don't pay the Medicare levy) with business and trading income in Australia, who are taxed as shown below in the 2012-13 tax year. Note that non-residents must obtain a tax file number and give it to their employer, otherwise they will be taxed at the maximum rate of 45 per cent on all income.

Non-Resident Income Tax Rates 2012-13		
Taxable Income	**Tax Rate**	**Cumulative Tax**
Up to $80,000	32.5	$26,000
$80,001 to $180,000	37	$63,000
Over $180,000	45	

Pay-As-You-Go

The Pay-As-You-Go (PAYG) system of tax collection applies to salary and wage earners, and includes superannuation and termination payments. Under PAYG, an employee's tax is deducted from his gross salary at source by his employer, who pays it to the ATO. If you have no income apart from your salary or wages, PAYG covers your entire tax liability. Any additional income, e.g. part-time employment or income from investments or savings, whether tax is deducted at source or not, must be declared to the ATO. Nevertheless, you must lodge a tax return if you receive more than $18,200 in taxable income during the financial year. If you have non-salary income to declare, you'll receive a credit for your PAYG payments against any tax due.

You must give your employer your tax file number (see above), otherwise you could be taxed at the highest rate. If you want to receive your $18,200 tax-free allowance (and who doesn't?), you must lodge an *Employee Declaration Instalment Form* with your employer; otherwise tax is deducted from all your income.

The PAYG scheme is disadvantageous to employees, who in many cases would be entitled to claim larger and more allowances if they were classified as self-employed (they would also have the benefit of paying their tax in arrears). For this reason, many employees disguise themselves as self-employed contractors (the practice is estimated to cost the government at least $100m a year). However, companies are no longer able to pay employees as self-employed 'contractors' to avoid fringe benefit tax, the superannuation guarantee and workers' compensation payments.

If your most recent income tax assessment shows more than $2,000 of gross investment or business income or if your most recent income tax return resulted in a tax debt of over $500, you'll receive a letter from the Taxation Office advising you that you must pay PAYG instalments, i.e. advance payments against your next tax bill.

If you pay PAYG tax, make sure that the tax deducted is correct and never hesitate to dispute a tax bill with which you disagree.

Fringe Benefit tax

Fringe benefit tax (FBT) was introduced in 1986 in order to reduce the amount of non-cash, non-taxable benefits (or 'perks') offered to employees by employers as part of their salary package. FBT is payable by employees on various benefits, including children's private education, company cars for private use; free or subsidised accommodation; free holiday travel; low-interest or interest-free loans; private health insurance; airline transport provided free or at a discount to employees in the travel industry; discounted goods or services provided by an employer in excess of a specified threshold; entertainment expenses; payment or reimbursement of private expenses on behalf of employees; and the waiver of employee loans or debts.

Company cars are taxed at between 7 and 26 per cent, depending on the

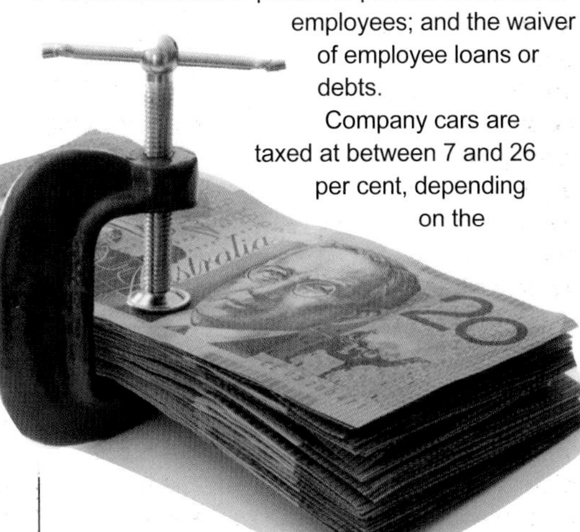

business 'mileage'. However, leases of luxury cars as part of executive salary packages are exempt. A portion of a 'living-away-from-home' allowance paid to employees may also be subject to FBT, although 'reasonable' costs for food and accommodation aren't. Staff canteens, employee share acquisition schemes and superannuation schemes are exempt from FBT. Frequent-flyer schemes aren't taxable, even when your employer pays the membership fees, and childcare provided on 'business premises' or a building controlled by your employer is also exempt (including employer-sponsored/leased places at childcare centres).

FBT is paid at the rate of 46.5 per cent. The FBT tax year is different from the financial year (just to confuse you even further) and runs from 1st April to 31st March. Payments must be made quarterly – by the 28th of July, October, January and April – each payment being equal to 25 per cent of the previous year's liability, the balance being payable when your annual tax return is filed. An employer must usually file an annual FBT return by 28th April each year and fringe benefits are recorded on an employee's payment summary (just in case you forget to declare any of them!).

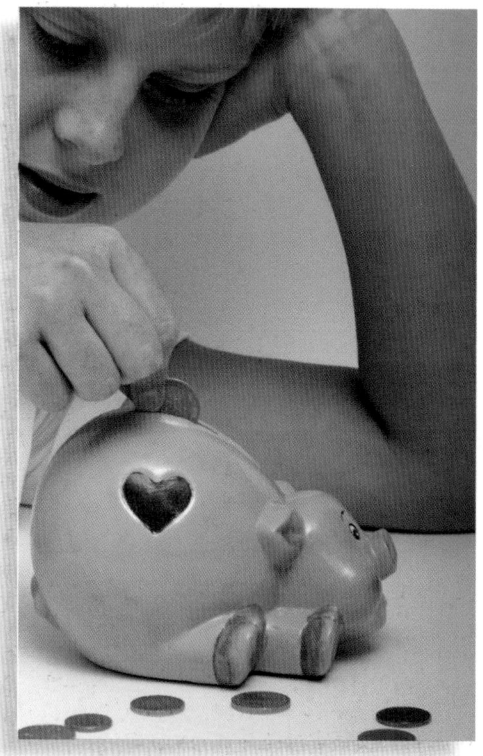

Self-employed

The business structure you choose when establishing a business in Australia is important in ensuring that you pay no more tax than is necessary (most family businesses operate a family trust in order to reduce taxes). The self-employed include sole traders and those in a partnership, but not a limited company or trust. If you have a limited company, you must pay corporate or company tax on your profits and will need the services of an accountant.

It's important to obtain expert legal advice before establishing a business or starting work as a self-employed person in Australia. Like everything to do with tax law, the regulations applying to the self-employed are complicated and time-consuming, and are estimated to cost some $7bn a year in lost time. Not surprisingly, some 90 per cent of the self-employed use a tax agent to complete their tax return.

From a tax point of view, you're generally better off being self-employed than employed, as you're eligible to claim more allowances in the form of business expenses, including telephone bills, travel to and from work, and work clothes or uniforms.

Another advantage for the self-employed is the delay between making profits (if they manage to do so) and paying tax on them, as the self-employed usually pay their tax in arrears. Recent court cases have declared that under the current tax laws airline pilots, bicycle/motorcycle couriers and taxi drivers are independent contractors, and are therefore entitled to be treated as self-employed. In the light of these decisions, the ATO sidelined proposals that would have re-classified thousands of self-employed contractors as employees subject to PAYG tax. Nevertheless, tens of thousands of 'employees' pose as self-employed in order to claim extra allowances.

Company Tax

For taxation purposes, companies include all bodies or associations (corporate and non-corporate), but not partnerships, where partners are taxed individually. In the 2010-11 financial year, companies were liable to pay tax on profits at a flat rate of 30 per cent. Employers are also liable for fringe benefit tax on non-cash benefits made available to employees (such as company cars and low-interest loans – see above). A company has its own tax file number and may also need a GST registration number (see above). The date for filing depends on the company's financial year; tax is usually paid in instalments in the year following the year of the tax liability, e.g. tax owed for 2012 income is paid in 2013.

Income Tax Returns

Even if you're an employee on PAYG and have no non-salary income, you must file a tax return in Australia if you receive over $6,000 in taxable income during the financial year. Returns must be lodged by 31st October for the previous tax year, e.g. the tax return for the 2012-13 tax year (ending 30th June 2013) must be lodged by 31st October 2013. If you're expecting a refund, the earlier you lodge your return the quicker you're likely to receive it. If you're unable to meet the deadline due to circumstances beyond your control, you should request permission to lodge at a later date in writing (and before the deadline) to the office where you last lodged.

The ATO provides a comprehensive free *TaxPack* for individual taxpayers, which is available from newsagents, post offices and tax offices. It contains tax return forms (including spare copies in case you make a mistake!) and instructions on how to complete them. The tax office where you must lodge your return is determined by your postcode; a list of offices and relevant postcodes is included in the *TaxPack*. You can post your tax return (to GPO Box 9845, in your state or territory's capital city) or lodge it personally in the box provided at any ATO office. You can also lodge your tax return online (as 2m people do) using 'E-tax', free tax return preparation software available via the ATO website (🖳 www.ato.gov.au – go to 'Online Services' on the right of the home page and click on 'E-tax Download now').

☑ SURVIVAL TIP

Keep a copy of your tax form and anything else you send to the ATO. This is useful if your tax form is lost in the post or there are any queries.

Also keep a copy of all documentation (invoices, receipts, statements, etc.) which substantiates claims made in your tax return. Records must be kept for three and a half years for salary and wage earners, and five years for the self-employed (seven years for vehicle- and travel-related expenses). Some tax returns are audited and you may be penalised if the information provided is found to be incorrect. As in most countries, the self-employed are much more likely to be audited than employees.

Although tax returns are relatively easy to follow and understand, only 30 per cent of taxpayers complete their own returns and many use a tax agent or accountant (see **Using an Accountant** above), the cost of which is tax deductible. A tax agent has the responsibility for completing your return correctly and is liable for any errors. He will (or should) also ensure that you claim for all the allowances and rebates to which you're entitled. A tax agent usually charges a few hundred dollars to complete a tax return for the 'average' taxpayer, although additional fees are charged for extra services; accountants are more expensive. Shop around and obtain a few quotations – some agents offer a free initial consultation.

Payment

After around eight weeks, you receive a *Notice of Assessment* from the ATO, which is an itemised account of the tax you owe. At the bottom of the assessment is your tax debt or, if you're due a refund, your refund cheque (lucky you!). Your notice of assessment gives the date when you must pay by in order to avoid incurring a penalty. If you don't agree with the ATO's assessment you can lodge an appeal.

If the amount owed is over $8,000, you can make the payment in quarterly instalments. Tax can be paid in person at a tax or post office or by post by cheque (payable to the Deputy Commissioner of Taxation), which must be sent with the bottom section of your notice of assessment. If you use a tax agent (see above) who lodges returns electronically, your tax bill (or refund) can be paid directly from (or into) a bank, building society or credit union account.

If you're unable to pay your bill on time, contact your tax office and ask for an extension. You need to give a reason for needing an extension and, if it's granted, you're charged interest at a daily rate (equal to 20 per cent per annum!) on the amount outstanding after the due date.

PROPERTY & LAND TAXES

Property Tax

Property tax (called council taxes or rates in Australia) is levied by councils on homeowners to pay for local services such as footpaths, health inspections, libraries, parks and recreational facilities, community and welfare services, roads, rubbish collection and disposal (which may be charged separately), and town planning and building control. In some states there's a swimming pool levy to ensure compliance with safety standards and fire service levies are payable in many areas.

Tax rates vary with the 'rateable value' of a property, officially called the 'unimproved capital value' (UCV) or the 'capital improved value' (CIV), which is reassessed every two to four years by the Valuer General's Department. When values are reassessed, rates cannot rise more than a certain amount, e.g. 50 per cent (a process known as 'capping') and the increase is usually spread over two or three years.

Rates are levied annually but are often paid (and quoted) quarterly. In some council areas, there's a rebate (e.g. 5 per cent) for prompt payment. Pensioners usually receive a reduction (concession), e.g. between 20 and 50 per cent.

Council rates vary hugely depending on the state and council, and tend to be higher in large cities, where there are more council services. For a home valued at $250,000, you can pay anything between $500 and $1,500 per year.

Land Tax

Land tax is levied on the ownership of property in all states and territories except the Northern Territory, although your principal home (and the land it occupies) is usually exempt provided you've lived in a property for at least six months. The calculation is based on the 'actual unimproved value' (AUV, known simply as the rate) of land – irrespective of whether anything is built on it – at a prescribed

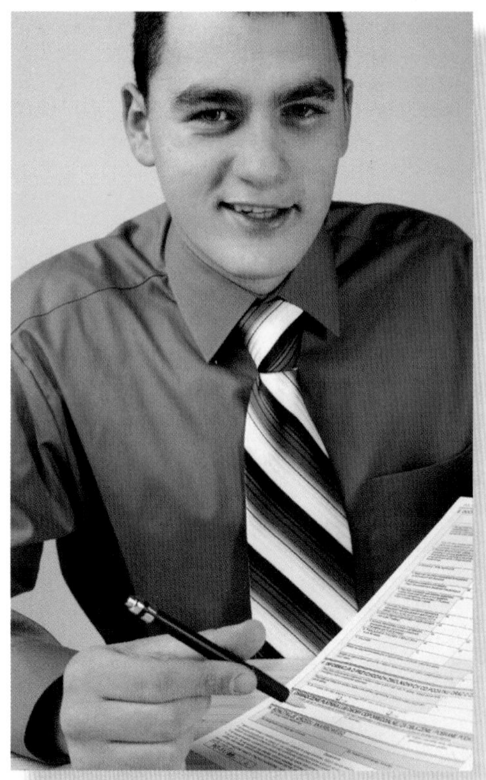

date, e.g. 31st December in NSW, which is determined by the state's Valuer General. Land tax is often high and regarded by many as an obstacle to second home ownership; the Real Estate Institute of Australia headed a national campaign in 2007 to persuade state governments to abolish all state property taxes, but with land tax revenue amounting to over $2m, states are understandably reluctant to scrap it. You can reduce your exposure to land tax by investing interstate, buying property in a variety of entities (names) and buying a unit instead of a house.

Payments are usually made quarterly, but most states offer the option of monthly payment. Many states have a threshold below which no land tax is payable.

Details of the land tax rates in each state can be found in our sister publication, *Buying a Home in Australia*.

CAPITAL GAINS TAX

Australia doesn't have a 'capital gains tax' (CGT), but profits made on certain assets are treated as income and subject to income tax at standard rates. The Capital Gains Tax system takes into account the staggered nature of capital gains. Often taxpayers will make large capital gains in a particular year, which increase their taxable income so that they fall into a higher tax bracket. The system deals with this issue by discounting capital gains made by individuals by 50 per cent, and gains made by superannuation funds by one-third, provided the taxpayer has held the asset for at least a year. If the asset is held by a company or is held by an individual or a super fund for less than a year, no capital gains tax discount applies.

Rollover provisions apply to some disposals, one of the most significant being transfers to beneficiaries on death, so that the CGT doesn't become a quasi death duty. A gift made by a living person is treated as a disposal at current market value, with the donor being taxed for a disposal at that value and the recipient using that as their cost base.

Profits on assets liable to tax include the sale of a business or a property other than your principal home, shares and trust distributions. What are termed 'listed personal use assets', such as works of art and antiques, are also taxable if the purchase price was over $10,000. Capital losses can be used to offset gains, either in the current year or in future years without a time limit, but cannot be used to offset other income. The sale of an asset that generates a capital gain or loss is known as a 'capital gains event' in Australia.

Your liability for tax depends on your residence status and there are different rules for permanent and temporary residents, as well as for Australians and foreigners. Foreign and temporary residents are liable for tax on certain assets only.

☑ SURVIVAL TIP

Given the complexity of the rules, you should take expert advice on your liability for CGT, particularly if you plan to change your residence status.

Further information about CGT can be obtained from the ATO (☎ 132861, 💻 www.ato.gov.au).

GOODS & SERVICES TAX

Goods and services tax (GST), which was introduced in 2000, is similar to value added tax (VAT) in European countries or sales tax in the US and is levied at a flat rate of 10 per cent on most goods and services. GST is included in most quoted prices, although some items are exempt, such as basic foods, cars for the disabled, and certain medical aids and appliances. There are also 'compensatory measures' such as the Educational Textbook Subsidy, which the government offered to students when they objected to the 10 per cent increase in the price of books.

Most businesses are required to register for GST and most must lodge a quarterly return to pay or reclaim GST, although if a company's annual turnover exceeds $20m, a monthly return must be made.

For information about duty and tax on imported vehicles, see **Importing a Vehicle** on page 169.

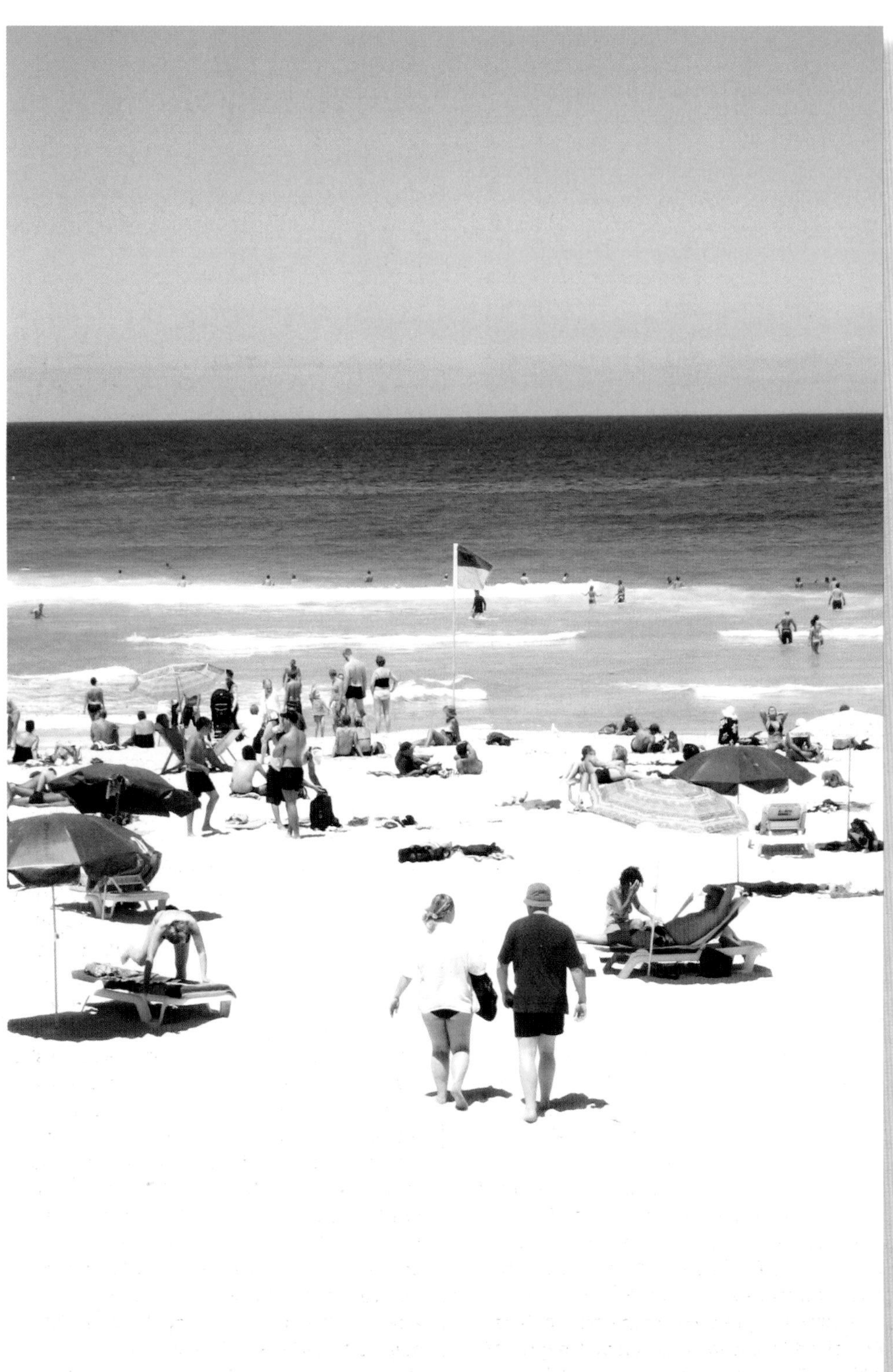

Bondi Beach, Sydney, NSW

15. LEISURE

Australia is one of the world's top tourist destinations, attracting around 6m visitors annually; the leisure and tourist industry earns some $35bn annually and provides direct or indirect employment for over 500,000 people. One of Australian tourism's biggest sources of income is 'frugal' backpackers – who spend an average of over $5,500 per head, although numbers have fallen dramatically in recent years due to the strong Australian dollar, worldwide recession and increasing competition. Sydney is one of the world's leading tourist destinations and is regularly listed among the world's top three tourist destinations outside Europe, along with Cape Town and San Francisco.

Australia is one of the world's most beautiful countries, with a wide range of attractions, including magnificent beaches, spectacular countryside and parks, mountains, waterways and the desolate beauty of the outback. It's a country of infinite variety, offering something for everyone: warm seas and raging rivers for watersports' enthusiasts, historic towns and bustling cosmopolitan cities for 'townies', a lively nightlife and club scene for ravers, fine wines and superb cuisine for gourmets, and a wealth of art and 'serious' music for culture vultures.

Until the '70s, Australia was (with some justification) considered to be a cultural desert, the only artistic tradition being the country's 60,000-year Aboriginal heritage. However, the arts have flourished since then and now match or surpass many 'old world' countries. Australia has a rich achievement in arts, including architecture, ballet, drama, film, literature, music, opera, painting and sculpture. The main funding for the arts comes from the Australia Council, and there are further contributions from state and local governments and corporate sponsorship. Nevertheless, Australians' appreciation of the arts still lags far behind their love of sport (see **Chapter 16**), which is the country's most popular leisure activity (whether taking part or spectating).

The most popular leisure activities (in addition to visiting show homes!) include visiting animal and marine parks, museums, art galleries and botanical gardens, cinema-going, dance shows, musicals, operas, plays and music concerts. There are modern performing arts centres in the main cities, many of which vie for the title 'arts capital of Australia', while cinemas, concert halls, galleries and theatres abound in the major towns and cities. In addition to the more formal events, a profusion of free concerts and entertainment is staged in public parks, shopping and entertainment centres, which include folk, jazz, opera, and rock and classical concerts, plus impromptu shows by an assortment of acrobats, buskers, dancers, fire-eaters, jugglers and mime artists.

A wealth of festivals and carnivals are held in Australia throughout the year and includes art, beer, folk, food, harvest, music and wine festivals, agricultural shows and surf carnivals. Australian cities stage a number of prestigious arts festivals, including the biennial Adelaide Festival (2012, 2014, etc.), which is modelled on the Edinburgh Festival and includes dance, musical and theatrical performances from around the world, plus a 'fringe' festival. Other major arts festivals include the Festival of Perth (February), the Melbourne International Comedy Festival (April), the Melbourne

International Festival (October) and the National Festival of Australian Theatre (Canberra, October).

Most states have a Royal Agricultural Show, usually in September or October (Sydney's Royal Easter Show is a notable exception), which are much more than 'simply' agricultural shows and include a wide range of displays and entertainment. One of the wackiest events is the Todd River Regatta held in Alice Springs in September, when the Todd River is dry!

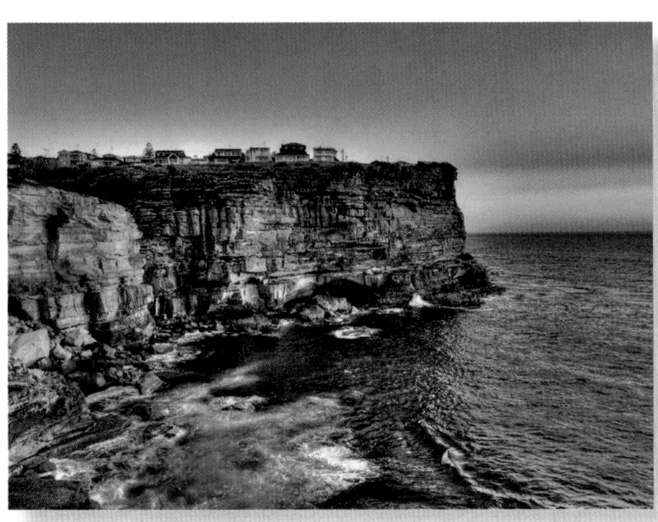

Vaucluse, Sydney, NSW

Tickets for most major entertainment and sporting events can be purchased from Bass (🖳 www.bass.net.au), Ticketek (🖳 http://premier.ticketek.com.au) and Ticketmaster (🖳 www.ticketmaster.com.au) ticket agencies, which have outlets in all the main towns and cities (there's a surcharge of around $5 per ticket).

Australia has an abundance of beautiful cities, many of which resemble large country towns. Sydney and Melbourne enjoy an intense rivalry for the title of Australia's premier city. Sydney (Australia's most sophisticated and exciting city) usually wins hands down, thanks largely to its peerless setting ('Venice of the 21st century'), although Melbourne is Australia's cultural and gastronomic capital (it hosts the Melbourne Food & Wine Festival in March – see 🖳 www.melbournefoodandwine.com.au), and its subtle charms tend to grow on you. The capital, Canberra, is home to the country's foremost art collections, although many people consider it a boring town with little charm. Other major cities include Adelaide, Brisbane, Darwin, Hobart and Perth, all of which have unique attractions.

However, despite the multifarious attractions of its lively cities, Australia's foremost and most enduring appeal is its immense natural beauty, which owes little to man's intervention. Getting away from it all isn't difficult in Australia, with its many lakes and rivers, miles of superb beaches, and areas of wilderness largeer than many countries. Australia is a country of endless contrasts and colour, with an amazing variety of environments, ranging from bleak, unearthly deserts to lush tropical rain-forests, from palm-fringed sandy beaches and stunning reefs to majestic snowfields, from sparkling blue seas and remote tropical islands to rugged mountains and spectacular rock formations, and rolling farmlands and vineyards to wild rivers and vast lakes.

Australia boasts a number of World Heritage Sites, including Ayers Rock (now 'officially' known by its Aboriginal name, Uluru), Bool Lagoon, the Dandenongs, the Flinders Ranges, the Grampians, the Great Barrier Reef (the world's most magnificent coral reef), Kakadu National Park, Katherine Gorge, the Murray River, the Naracoorte Caves, the Snowy Mountains, the Tasmanian Wilderness and the Yarra Valley, to name but a few. It's home to a plethora of unique and fascinating flora and fauna, including unusual or unique mammals such as the duck-billed platypus, kangaroos, koala bears, possums, wallabies and wombats.

If you're spending only a short time in Australia, bear in mind that it's a vast country, so don't try to see it all in a few weeks, which is impossible. If you rush through the outback by train or car, you'll see little and the country will appear to consist of a vast nothingness. However, if you take your time and do a bit of cycling or walking, you'll experience unexpected wonders. There are various organised tours, including 'soft-adventure' holidays (e.g. crocodile or shark watching, rather than a close encounter with the sharp end) and camel safaris.

TOURIST INFORMATION

There are tourist offices, travel centres, visitor centres and visitor information bureaux in all cities, large towns and resorts, although few organisations maintain information desks at airports or major railway stations. All states have Tourist Commissions that publish a wealth of information and also act as booking agencies for transport companies, hotels and other accommodation. They have offices in state capitals, on major highways at state borders and in some regional centres. Many smaller towns have tourist offices run by local councils and regional tourist associations.

There are no state-run tourist information offices in Queensland, where tourist offices are often privately operated and act as booking agents for hotels and travel and tour companies.

Tourist offices can provide you with a wealth of information about local accommodation, attractions, car hire, package holidays, public transport, restaurants, sporting events, sports facilities, tours and much more. Offices can provide information on a wide range of leisure activities and sports, so you should mention any special interests when making enquiries. The opening hours of city offices are usually from 9am until 5pm, Monday to Friday, from 9am to between 1 and 4pm on Saturdays, and from 10 or 11am until 4pm on Sundays.

Australia is promoted abroad by Tourism Australia (💻 www.tourism.australia.com or www.australia.com) and most Australian states also maintain tourist offices in a number of countries, including the UK and the US. Tourism Australia has offices in Auckland, Bangkok, Frankfurt, Hong Kong, Kuala Lumpur, London, Los Angeles, Seoul, Shanghai, Singapore, Taipei and Tokyo.

A plethora of travel guides are dedicated to Australia, including Lonely Planet's *Australia*, which is the most comprehensive guidebook, containing some 1,000 pages. Other leading guidebooks include the *Australia: DK Eyewitness Travel Guide*, the *Insight Guide to Australia, The Michelin Green Guide to Australia* and *The Rough Guide to Australia*. State motoring organisations (see page 190) also provide tourist and touring information, and leisure information is available on the internet via a wealth of websites – just Google the state or city that you're interested in.

Most cities and regions publish free entertainment magazines and newspapers (e.g. the *Sydney City Hub*) containing maps and a wealth of useful information about local attractions and events (distributed by hotels, information bureaux, tourist offices and transport companies), and many local councils publish a 'leisure directory'. Major newspapers publish weekly guides, and there's a variety of commercial entertainment magazines, such as the *Entertainment Guide* magazine in Melbourne.

A lot of information is published specifically for backpackers and budget travellers, such as the free *TNT Magazine* and *The Independent Travellers' Guide*, both published by TNT Magazine Pty Ltd. (☎ 02-8296 0252, 💻 www.tntdownunder.com).

ACCOMMODATION

The quality and standard of hotels and other accommodation in Australia varies considerably. It includes apartments, bed and breakfast accommodation, boutique and luxury hotels, budget hotels, farms, guesthouses, hostels, motels and resort hotels. Accommodation other than guesthouses, motels and private hotels must provide a public bar to serve alcohol (guesthouses don't have permits to serve alcohol).

Sydney has a huge range of accommodation, including a wide range of four- and five-star hotels. However, the widest choice of accommodation is to be found in Queensland, where tourism is the main industry and there's a wealth of apartments, hostels, luxury hotels and motels in all resort areas. In stark contrast to the major cities, in country and remote areas the choice of accommodation is severely restricted and it's wise to obtain recommendations unless you're prepared to put up with the most basic accommodation.

Motoring organisations (see page 190) publish guides to hotels, motels and other accommodation, including the *A-Z Australian Accommodation Guide*, the NRMA *Accommodation Directory* and *Weekends for Two*, an accommodation guide published bi-annually. The NRMA *Accommodation Directory* lists bed and breakfast accommodation, guesthouses, hotels, motels and serviced apartments throughout Australia. For general information, contact the Australian Hotels Association (☏ 02-6273 4007, 💻 www.aha.org.au).

There are accommodation information boards at airports and railway and bus stations in major cities with direct-dial free telephones where you can book rooms, although these are generally only up-market hotels. Tourist offices can also find you a room.

You can also book a hotel room via dozens of websites such as 💻 www.australiahotels.net, www.discoveraustralia.com.au and www.hotel.com.au.

Hotels

Major groups operating four- and five-star hotels in major cities include Accor, ANA, Beaufort, Hilton, Holiday Inn, Hyatt, InterContinental, Jewel Hotels and Resorts, Matson, Mirvac, Nikko, Parkroyal, Peppers, Radisson, Ramada, Regent, Ritz Carlton, Rydges, Select, Sheraton, Southern Pacific Hotels, Tradewinds, Vista, and Waratah Inns. Most top hotel chains have freecall (1800) booking numbers. Three- to four-star chains include All Seasons Resorts, Best Western, Centra, Country Comfort, Flag, Metro Inn, Quality Pacific and Travelodge. The term 'private hotel' is used to denote a hotel which doesn't serve alcohol. Other terms used for an unlicensed hotel are guesthouse, inn and lodge.

Breakfasts at private hotels are usually huge and excellent. You may come across 'boutique hotels', which are small hotels more like guesthouses, often stylish and aimed at up-market clients. There are old colonial-style hotels in country and outback areas, which include National Trust accommodation in pre-1901 buildings, full of character (the bar may also be full of characters) with eccentric owners and bizarre regulations.

Room rates usually vary with the season. The low season is generally from May to November (winter). However, in the centre and tropical north, winter is normally the best time to visit and is therefore the high season; in the summer, rates drop by up to 30 per cent. There's a lack of accommodation in some cities (such as Sydney, where many hotels average over 90 per cent occupancy), particularly budget accommodation, although prices remain reasonable by international standards.

The busiest period is between November and mid-May, beds being almost impossible to find from mid-December to late January in cities and resorts if you haven't booked. You can obtain discounts of up to 50 per cent for weekly bookings, stand-bys, weekend and low season stays. Travel agents who buy rooms in bulk may be able to offer you a better rate than you can obtain yourself, and motoring organisations also offer members' discounts.

The following table is a rough guide to per night room prices (prices are usually quoted per room and not per person):

Hotel Rates

Star Rating	Price Range
1	$50 to $75
2	$65 to $100
3	$95 to $175
4	$165 to $275
5	$265 to $500

Quoted prices generally include all taxes except goods and services tax (GST) at 10 per cent. There's also a 5 per cent accommodation tax in the Northern Territory. Some hotels close on Sundays and Public Holidays, as they cannot afford to pay staff the high overtime rates necessary.

Budget hotels are in short supply in Australia and, if you're looking for cheap accommodation, your best bet is a bed and breakfast, guesthouse, hostel or pub (all of which are described below). If you don't need to be in the middle of town, suburban hotels offer better value. The cheapest hotel rooms are usually from around $50 for a single and $75 for a double (some also have suites/ triples). Check whether breakfast is included.

Motels

There's a wide choice of modern, comfortable motels (also called motor hotels, motor inns and inns) throughout Australia. Motels are star-rated in the same way as hotels (see above). The major chains include A1, Best Western, Budget, Country Comfort, Flag International, Golden Chain, Metro Inns, and Quality Inns. In remote areas there are road stations (similar to motorway rest stops) with motel-type portable rooms called 'demountables'. (Rooms are also called apartments and units.) All motel chains will book you a room at another motel in the same chain free of charge, although you should note that not all motels within a chain are of the same standard.

Motel rooms have a private bath or shower, refrigerator, tea and coffee-making facilities, telephone and a TV. Some luxury motels have a swimming pool or spa. At smaller motels you can park outside your door. Most motels don't have bars, dining rooms or restaurants, although you can usually order breakfast in your room. Some motels have self-catering facilities (particularly in resort areas), although motel rooms may have only a small conventional or microwave oven.

Single rooms usually start from $75 per night and doubles from $100 (rising to $200 for a luxury motel). Lower rates are usually available if you're planning to stay for more than a few days. Prices in resort areas are around double those in small towns or country locations. Breakfast isn't usually included in the price.

Family rooms in motels are economical for a family or a group of three or four, and are popular with Australian families.

Pubs

Pubs used to be called pub hotels or simply hotels because they originally had to provide accommodation by law, but nowadays most pubs don't offer accommodation. Pubs in country areas, which may be called 'commercials' because guests were traditionally commercial travellers (salesmen), are more likely to offer accommodation than those in cities. Pub hotels are usually basic (so

don't expect a bidet or a trouser press) with a bar downstairs and rooms upstairs, and can be noisy (it's best to get a room at the top or rear of the building). Pub hotels in country areas generally charge from around $75 for a single room, usually with a shared bathroom. Check whether breakfast is included.

Bed & Breakfast

Bed and breakfast (B&B) accommodation consists of a room in a private house or on a university campus, and is found throughout Australia, from cities and large towns to small villages and outback stations. B&B accommodation is more informal than a hotel and often provides a friendly place to meet Australians in their own homes. It encompasses a huge variety of abodes, including conventional family homes, country homesteads, farms, historic houses and inner city townhouses.

B&Bs have become increasingly popular in the last decade or so, during which many more Australians have opened their homes to guests (a trend encouraged by the tourist authorities). However, it isn't an inexpensive option, with single rooms costing from around $75 and doubles from $100 to $200. B&Bs may not accept credit cards and most don't have a permit to serve alcohol. Bear in mind that some B&Bs have a minimum stay of two or three nights. If you're staying for more than one night, you may be expected to vacate your room for most of the day and to leave by noon (or earlier) on your last day.

There are a number of guide books to B&B accommodation in Australia, including the *Australian Bed & Breakfast Book*, by Carl Southern (Inn Australian) and the *Australian Bed & Breakfast Guide* by Elizabeth James (Pelican). There's also a wealth of online booking agents, including www.australianbedandbreakfast.com.au, www.bedandbreakfast.com.au and www.ozbedandbreakfast.com.

Self-catering

There's a wide choice of self-catering accommodation in Australia, usually consisting of apartments, although chalets, cottages, houses and mobile homes can also be rented in country and resort areas. An apartment is often a good choice for a family, as it's cheaper than an equivalent hotel room, provides more privacy and freedom, and allows you to prepare your own meals when you please. Standards, while generally high, are variable, and paying a high price doesn't always guarantee a well furnished or appointed apartment (most look wonderful in the brochure or online). Holiday apartments are generally found in tourist areas and serviced apartments in cities and large towns. Holiday apartments are usually rented on a weekly basis, and prices vary enormously according to the standard and location, as well as time of year. Serviced apartments, with one to three bedrooms, a bathroom, kitchen, laundry and living area, cost from around $150 to $250 per night (there may be discounts for stays of a week or more). There's usually no low season in major cities, where rates are constant throughout the year.

Holiday apartments are generally well equipped with cooking utensils, crockery and cutlery. However, small studios may have only an electric frying pan and a microwave oven for cooking, while larger apartments usually also have a stove. Check when booking, if you plan on cooking. You may need to provide your own linen and towels, although they can usually be hired for an additional fee. Prices vary considerably according to the location and season and may be higher during school and Public Holidays. Before booking self-catering accommodation, check the holiday changeover dates and times, what's included in the rent (e.g. cleaning, linen), whether cots or high chairs are provided and pets allowed, if a garden or parking is provided, access to public transport (if required), and anything you consider essential (such as air-conditioning, heating or a TV).

Self-catering accommodation is listed in guides such as the NRMA *Accommodation Guide* and lists are maintained by tourist offices. You can book self-catering accommodation via a wealth of websites, including www.ausvillagetaways.com, www.freedomaustralia.co.uk, www.holidayrentals.com.au and www.jasons.com/australia/accommodation-guide.

If you're seeking long term self-catering accommodation, see **Rented Accommodation** on page 90.

Hostels

One way to stretch limited financial resources is to stay in hostels, which include beach huts and tree houses in Queensland, mountain cabins in Tasmania, disused railway stations, historic renovated buildings and huge purpose-built developments. Some hostels call themselves 'resorts', although facilities remain firmly in the budget bracket. Modern 'chain' hostels generally provide the best facilities, although they lack character and atmosphere, and many people prefer the more intimate, smaller, owner-operated hostels. Standards vary enormously, even among hostels operated by the same organisation. One way to discover the best hostels is to ask other travellers.

The competition often leads to a range of extra services and perks being offered to those who turn up on spec, although it's advisable to book during the peak season and on Public Holidays. Note, however, that in some areas and cities, such as Perth, hostel accommodation is being increasingly occupied by workers (e.g. in the mining industry) and may be difficult to find and relatively expensive.

There are a number of online booking agencies, including 💻 www.hostelworld.com/hostels/australia, www.hostelbookers.com/hostels/australia and www.itchy-feet.com.au.

> **▲ Caution**
>
> If you don't book a hostel in advance, you may find it difficult to get a bed in cities and at popular tourist spots at any time.

Accommodation & Costs

Accommodation may include single and double rooms, family rooms and dormitories (sleeping up to 24). Most hostels have dormitories for between 4 and 12 people, either single sex or mixed (some hostels advertise separate dormitories but put men and women together!). Dormitories can be noisy and lack privacy.

The cost of a hostel is usually from around $25 per night for a bed in a dormitory up to $50 per person per night for a double room. Some hostels have two-bedroom, self-contained units where around six people share a bathroom, kitchen and lounge. Many hostels offer discounts for stays of at least four or five days, or weekly rates which usually save you a few dollars per night. Some hostels have limits on the length of stays during peak periods.

Youth Hostel Association

The Youth Hostel Association (YHA) has over 130 hostels in Australia, classified as simple, standard and superior, with a grading of one to five 'backpacks'. Guests don't have to be YHA members but, if you aren't a member there's an extra charge of around $3 per night. Annual membership is $32 for those aged under 26, $42 for those aged 26 and over and families. There are discounts for two- and three-year memberships and group membership is also available. Literally hundreds of discounts are offered to YHA members in Australia, including 10 per cent off Greyhound Pioneer Australia coach passes and up to 30 per cent off car hire.

There are few restrictions at YHA hostels, although the length of stays may be limited to a maximum of five to seven days. There are no age restrictions and no rules requiring early check-out.

Sheets and pillows are provided at all YHA hostels except for Wilderness Hostels (these can be purchased at hostels or hired for around $3 per night); unlined sleeping bags aren't permitted. Blankets are also provided.

The YHA has an international booking network where bookings can be made up to six months in advance (a fee of $2 may apply when booking in Australia). The YHA publishes a free annual *Accommodation and Discounts Guide* plus a free *Australia Visitors Map* showing the location of its hostels. For more information, contact the Australian Youth Hostel Association (💻 www.yha.com.au).

Publications & Information

There are many publications for hostellers and budget travellers, including the *Australia and New Zealand Travel Planner* (published by TNT Magazine (UK, ☎ 020-7373 3377, 💻 http://tntonline.co.uk), which provides invaluable advice for backpackers and travellers plus a complete hostel directory. The YHA publishes a free magazine, *The Hosteller*, available from YHA hostels. Other good books for backpackers include *BUG Australia: the Backpackers' Ultimate Guide* (Explore Australia, 💻 www.bugaustralia.com) and the *Backpacker's Bible* (Anova). There are numerous websites for hostellers, including, 💻 http://thebackpackerdirectory.com.au, www.backpackersworld.com.au, www.backpackingaround.com and www.hostelaustralia.com.

CARAVANNING & CAMPING

Australia is a great country for camping due to its generally mild climate and minimal camping restrictions. Campsites and caravan parks are common and are available in all major towns and tourist centres (many are near beaches). However, most campsites near major cities are well away from the centre, which means that you may need your own transport if you want to go sightseeing.

Campsite facilities vary but amenities usually include electricity hook-ups, hot and cold water, laundry facilities, showers and toilets. At large sites, there's usually a range of indoor recreation areas, lock-up storage for valuables, restaurants, shops and a wide variety of sports facilities, which may include boating, canoeing, cycling, fishing, swimming (i.e. a pool), table-tennis, tennis, trampolining and volleyball.

Rates are from around $30 to $40 per night for two people. A 'night' is usually from noon to noon. Some sites charge extra to use electricity, showers, sports facilities (such as tennis courts) and other amenities such as a freezer or iron. Outside peak periods you can usually find a campsite without difficulty on the spot, but don't leave it too late in the day when you're in a popular area (after noon is too late at some sites). It's important to book if you have a campervan or motor home and require an electricity hook-up.

Many campsites in Australia are primarily caravan parks, intended more for trailers and motor homes than for tents. Many have gravel surfaces (or hard ground) rather than turf, so pitching a tent can be hard work. Caravan parks may also have on-site cabins, caravans, holiday units and villas, which can be hired from around $50 to $100 per night. Linen and blankets can usually be hired,

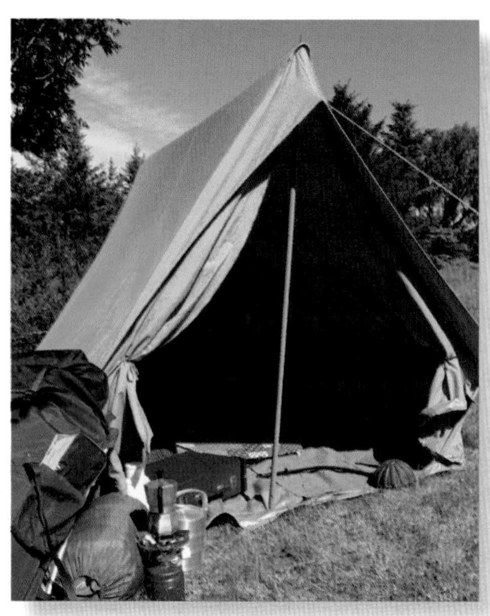

although a portable heater is useful in winter as many caravans and cabins are unheated.

In the outback you can pitch a tent virtually anywhere you please, although permission is required to camp on private property and in some areas there may be local regulations restricting camping. For example, in Western Australia, you aren't permitted to camp within 16km (10mi) of a campsite and it's illegal to camp on green areas outside a city centre. In Brisbane it's illegal to camp within a 22km (14mi) radius of the city centre, although short-term camping is allowed in roadside rest areas in most of the rest of Queensland.

In most national parks, camping is permitted only in designated areas, but you can camp in 'bush' areas in some of them.

Fees vary from park to park but are usually from around $10 per person per night (whether you camp in a designated area or not); you may need to book at popular campsites in national parks. When spending an extended period in a national park, you should let the park ranger know your route and when you expect to return. You mustn't 'interfere' with the flora and fauna; must observe all fire ban warnings (most camps don't permit open fires, so you'll need a portable stove); stick to existing camp sites where available rather than creating new ones; take no pets; take care not to desecrate Aboriginal sites; take your rubbish with you; use only fallen dead wood for fires (where permitted); and wash well away from lakes, rivers and streams – apart from which you can do what you like! All states publish information about camping in national parks.

A 'swag' is all you need when camping under the stars in the outback. Many different types are manufactured (e.g. by the Jolly Swag Company of Australia), the best of which include a blanket, mattress, pillow, sheet and down-filled sleeping bag inside a sturdy canvas bag. You can also buy a tarpaulin cover in case of rain. When camping wild, avoid dried-up river beds in the wet season due to the danger of flash floods.

Camping tours are popular and many companies offer organised tours in air-conditioned coaches or 4WD vehicles. You can buy or rent a campervan or mobile home throughout Australia; many people purchase a second-hand one from a departing visitor.

Interesting magazines for campers and caravanners include *Australian Geographic* (🖳 www.australiangeographic.com) *Outdoor Australia* and *Wild* (🖳 http://wild.com.au). Excellent guide books are available from automobile associations and include the *Camping and Caravan Directory*. For information about driving in the outback, see **Outback Roads** on page 186.

PARKS, GARDENS & ZOOS

There are some 2,000 national parks and reserves in Australia, covering a total area of over 40m hectares (100m acres – over 5 per cent of Australia's land area), plus a further 38m hectares (95m acres) of marine and estuarine protected areas. Australia has 16 World Heritage Sites, including Uluru-Kata Tjuta (Ayers Rock-Mount Olga), Fraser Island, the Great Barrier Reef, Kakadu National Park (Northern Territory, where *Crocodile Dundee* was filmed), the Queensland rainforests, and the Tasmanian Wilderness. National parks include every kind of habitat, and many are of great scientific interest. Australia was the second country to proclaim a national park, the Royal National Park in Sydney in 1879 (the first was Yellowstone Park in the USA).

Each state has its own national parks authority, most of which publish guides detailing park facilities. Some parks charge an entrance fee, e.g. between $10 and $25 for a car in New South Wales (less for motorbikes and pedestrians), although entry to smaller parks is often free and larger parks also allow free entry at weekends. All national parks have information or visitors' centres with leaflets, maps, films and slide shows, and guided tours are organised during peak periods. Some parks provide numbered pegs indicating points of interest, which can be cross-referenced with information sheets. Further information about national parks can be found on the website of the Department of the Environment and Water Resources (🖳 www.environment.gov.au) or the appropriate organisation in each state.

Australia has many excellent aquariums, wildlife parks and zoos. The most famous is the Royal Melbourne Zoological Gardens (Australia's oldest and the third-oldest in the world, dating from 1857), which houses around 4,000 species of animals and birds in 'natural' habitats. Taronga Zoo in Sydney is home to Australia's largest collection of native and exotic animals, and has a peerless setting beside Sydney Harbour (best visited by ferry from Circular Quay) and extensive breeding facilities, some of which are located at its 'sister' zoo (Western Plains Zoo in Dubbo).

Other top zoos and wildlife parks include Adelaide Zoo; the Australia Zoo (started by the late Steve Irwin) north of Brisbane, which houses a large collection of Australian wildlife; the Lone Pine Koala Sanctuary near Brisbane and the new Roma Street Parklands in the city; Perth Zoo (16 hectares/40 acres of exotic and native Australian fauna); and the Tidbinbilla Nature Reserve (west of Canberra). There are aquariums in many of Australia's major cities, e.g. Manly Oceanarium (Sydney), the Melbourne Aquarium, linked with the Yarra river, and the Sydney Aquarium, plus tourist resorts such as Sea World on the Gold Coast.

Australia's cities generally have an abundance of green spaces and wide boulevards, with both formal and informal ('native') parks in them or nearby.

All major cities have impressive botanical gardens, such as the Royal Botanic Gardens in Melbourne, the finest in Australia and home to some 12,000 plant species, and the City Botanic Gardens in Brisbane; the Mount Coottha Botanic Gardens, 12km (7mi) west of the city are also impressive. Sydney has its own Royal Botanic Gardens, located adjacent to the harbour and the Sydney Opera House, and an exquisite Chinese Garden (Darling Harbour), while Canberra is home to the National Botanic Gardens on Black Mountain, which contain over 6,000 native plants. Some cities, such as Melbourne, publish a *Parks and Gardens* brochure.

The National Trust of Australia (💻 www.nationaltrust.org.au) is dedicated to preserving historic buildings and parks throughout Australia, and owns a number of properties that are open to the public. Annual membership costs $100 for individuals and $130 for families (membership includes a $35 joining fee). There are local National Trust offices in each state.

Further information about aquariums, botanical gardens, national parks and zoos is available from Tourism Australia (💻 www.tourism.australia.com) or any good guide book. All tourist offices and visitors' centres provide information about local attractions.

MUSEUMS & GALLERIES

There are over 1,000 museums and galleries in Australia, visited by over 7m people annually, including federal and state museums, private galleries, privately-owned collections and regional exhibitions. The most important national collections are in Canberra and include the Australian War Memorial (which houses one of the best military museums in the world), the National Museum of Australia, the National Gallery of Australia, the National Portrait Gallery, the National Library, the National Film and Sound Archive (free admission), the National Science and Technology Centre, and the National Aquarium and Wildlife Sanctuary.

Elsewhere, major museums and galleries include the Art Gallery of NSW, the Australian Museum, the Museum of Contemporary Art, the National Maritime Museum and the Powerhouse Museum (science, decorative arts and social history) – all in Sydney – the National Museum of Melbourne, the Victorian Arts Centre (housing the National Gallery of Victoria), the Australian Gallery of Sport and Olympic Museum, and the Museum of Australian Art in Melbourne; the Art Gallery of South Australia and the South Australian Museum (both in Adelaide); the National Motor Museum (Birdwood, South Australia), the Western Australian Museum and the Art Gallery of Western Australia (Perth); the Queensland Museum and Queensland Art Gallery (Brisbane); the Tasmanian Museum and Art Gallery (Hobart); and the Northern Territory Museum of Arts and Sciences (Darwin), which houses one of the best collections of Aboriginal art in Australia. There are many reminders of Australia's past as a penal colony and many former prisons have been preserved as museums, notably the Old Melbourne Gaol, the Port Arthur penal colony in Tasmania and Hyde Park Barracks in Sydney.

Admission is usually between $10 and $20, and students normally pay half price. Most museums and galleries are open daily from around 9 or 10am until 5pm, although many have reduced opening hours on Sundays.

There's a strong market for contemporary Australian art, particularly Aboriginal art, which has become fashionable in recent years and can be seen in many galleries. It is, however, usually expensive (apart from mass-produced tourist artefacts), with prices running into many thousands of dollars. Nationally famous Australian painters include Sidney Nolan, Brett Whiteley and Fred Williams.

CINEMA

Cinema-going is the most popular leisure activity (apart from sport) among Australians, with ticket sales running to over 100m per year. Australian cinemas are split between mainstream ('first run') and 'arthouse' (which show classics, cult, experimental and foreign films). Mainstream cinema is dominated by four chains: Dendy (💻 www.dendy.com.au), Greater Union (💻 www.greaterunion.com.au), Hoyts (💻 www.hoyts.com.au) and Village Roadshow (💻 www.villagecinemas.com.au), which together account for over 50 per cent of screens (most in 'multiplexes') and some 60 per cent of tickets sold.

Independent operators (indies) control around 30 per cent of Australia's cinemas, although they're being hard hit by the multiplexes, which have as many as 30 screens (but usually between two and ten) and are often owned by the film distributors (film distribution rights are a constant battle for indies). Main cinemas usually have a number of shows a day, including late-night and all-night shows on Friday and Saturday evenings.

At the other extreme, small towns usually have just one single-screen cinema, many of which are ancient. There are private film clubs in the major cities and local film societies in all areas. Films are also shown by cultural organisations, at film festivals and at the State Film Centre (Melbourne). Major film festivals include the Melbourne International Film Festival (held in July) and the Sydney Film Festival (June). Cinema programmes are published in major national and local newspapers and online.

Some cinemas have giant screens employing IMAX 3-D technology. New centres have air-conditioned auditoriums, wide, comfortable seats and ample leg room, Dolby stereo or THX surround sound, and free parking. Many also have bars, cafés, games rooms and restaurants. Many cinemas (including all new cinemas) have facilities for wheelchair users. Smoking is prohibited in all cinemas.

A few open-air, drive-in cinemas remain in New South Wales, Queensland and Victoria. Most operate only in summer and some only on Saturday evenings, although a few open in winter (when you may be able to hire an in-car heater!). There's even a Deckchair Cinema in Darwin, where you can watch a film while reclining! The charge is usually per vehicle rather than per passenger.

All films on general release in Australia are given a classification, which denotes any age restrictions, as shown in the table opposite. Children (or adults) who look younger than their years may be asked for proof of age, e.g. a driving licence, school identity card or student card, for admission to age-restricted performances.

Cinema tickets cost from around $15 in cities (almost double the cost in the US), a little less in country areas. There are reduced prices for matinees, on Tuesday evenings and sometimes also on Mondays. Most cinemas offer reductions for children, pensioners and students, although you should check in

Film Classification

Classification	Signification	Age Restriction
G	General release	None
PG	Parental guidance	Children under 15 must be accompanied by an adult; not recommended for children under 12
M	Mature	Over 15s only
R	Restricted	Over 18s only

advance, as some reductions apply only to certain performances. Most chains provide discounted passes for multiple visits. Most cinemas accept telephone and internet bookings (major credit cards are accepted, although some cinemas charge a booking fee, e.g. $2 per ticket.

Australia has a thriving film industry which has produced many international hits in the last few decades, including such classics as *Babe, Crocodile Dundee, Gallipoli, Mad Max, Muriel's Wedding, The Piano, Picnic at Hanging Rock, Shine* and *The Year of Living Dangerously*. (The world's first feature film, *Soldiers of the Cross*, was also made in Australia in 1900 by the Salvation Army.) The Australian film industry is aided by the Australian Film Commission (AFC), established in 1975 to assist in the development of low budget, innovative film productions. In the industry's heyday, around 40 films per year were produced in Australia. However, state funding has been reduced in recent years and the Australian film industry faces an uncertain future.

Australian film stars include Bruce Beresford, Cate Blanchett, Toni Collette, Russell Crowe (claimed by Australia and New Zealand!), Mel Gibson (also claimed by the US!), Paul Hogan, Nicole Kidman and Jack Thompson; Errol Flynn and Chips Rafferty were also born in Australia. However, like most countries, Australia loses most of its talent to Hollywood.

PERFORMING ARTS

Dance, opera and theatre performance listings are provided in weekly and monthly entertainment guides, available from tourist offices in major cities, and many daily newspapers publish free guides such as the *Metro* on Fridays in the *Sydney Morning Herald* (which includes a theatre directory).

Theatre

Australian theatre is of a high standard and extremely varied, thanks to the country's cosmopolitan and multicultural cities, particularly Brisbane, Melbourne and Sydney. In addition to mainstream traditional theatre – classic plays and international musicals are performed to a very high standard – Australia has a thriving contemporary theatre scene where anything goes. Its wide-ranging performances include outrageous Australian comedy, experimental plays, image-based theatre, outdoor performances, and pub and coffee-shop theatre.

Melbourne has the most dynamic theatre scene in Australia and boasts over 70 theatres, including the George Fairfax Studio, Playhouse and State Theatre (all housed in the majestic Victorian Arts Centre), Athenaeum Theatre, Comedy Theatre, Her Majesty's, Princess Theatre and Russell Theatre (home of the Melbourne Theatre Company). Sydney's main theatres include the Belvoir Street Theatre, Griffin Theatre, New Theatre (boasting the oldest surviving theatre company in Australia – over 65 years old), Opera House, Pilgrim Theatre, Studio (at the Opera House), Seymour Theatre (at Sydney University), Wharf Theatre (home of the Sydney Theatre Company) and York Theatre. Other major Australian theatres include the Canberra Theatre Centre, the Lyric and Cremorne Theatres in Brisbane (within the Queensland Cultural Centre and Performing Arts Complex), and His Majesty's Theatre and the Subiaco Theatre Centre in Perth (home of the State Theatre Company of Western Australia).

Major international productions are regularly staged in Australia's major cities. Most plays performed in Australia have traditionally been written by American and British playwrights. However, Australian playwriting has blossomed in the last few decades and plays such as *The Removalist* (David Williams) and *Stretch of the Imagination* (Jack Hibbert) have become classics.

The Australians excel in comedy and love to send themselves (and everyone else) up. The most famous Australian comedy actor is Barry Humphries, whose larger-than-life characters include Dame Edna Everage, Barry McKenzie, Sir Les Patterson and Sandy Stone.

Melbourne is the comedy capital of Australia and stages the annual International Comedy Festival in April, while Sydney has the Comedy Store (💻 www.comedystore.com.au), which has a different show each night.

Tickets for most major productions vary considerably in price, but usually cost between $40 and $60, while performances at 'fringe' theatres cost from around $20. Half-price theatre tickets can be purchased on the day of a performance in Sydney from the Halifax kiosk in Martin Place (tickets must be purchased in person and be paid for in cash).

Online Australian theatre guides include 💻 www.aussietheatre.com, www.musictheatreaustralia.com.au and www.theatre.asn.au.

Opera

The Australian Opera was established in 1970 and is largely dependent on government subsidies and sponsorship. The Victoria State Opera and the Australian Opera (Sydney) were merged in 1996 to form a new integrated company, Opera Australia (💻 www.opera-australia.org.au), which performs at the State Theatre in Melbourne and the Sydney Opera House, and presents outdoor concerts such as 'Opera in the Park' in Sydney in January. There are small professional opera companies in some states. The standard of opera produced at Australia's main venues is among the highest in the world and international stars regularly perform there. Home-grown stars have included John Brownless, Peter Dawson, Joan Hammond, Yvonne Kenny, Dame Nellie Melba and Joan Sutherland.

The Sydney Opera House is one of the architectural landmarks of the 20th century and has become the symbol of the city since its completion in 1973 after 14 years and at a cost of $102m (it was scheduled to be completed in five years at a cost of $7m – an opera, *Eighth Wonder*, about the building process was even performed there!). In addition to the opera house itself, the building comprises two auditoriums (the larger, for orchestral concerts, seating 2,690, the smaller for song and ballet performances), a café, a drama theatre known as The Studio, a small playhouse and three restaurants. Despite its less than perfect acoustics, it's often ranked among the world's leading opera houses along with Covent Garden in London, La Scala in Milan and the New York Met. Most events at the Sydney Opera House are expensive, with tickets ranging from around $50 to $200.

Information can be obtained from the Box Office (☎ 02-9250 7111, 💻 www.sydneyoperahouse.com). The opera season runs from July to August and from November to December.

Dance

Ballet is the healthiest art form in Australia, surviving largely on box-office receipts, and the country has hundreds of ballet schools. The world-famous Australian Ballet (💻 www.australianballet.com.au) was founded in 1962 and has its headquarters in Melbourne, although it stages a summer and winter season at the Sydney Opera House and also tours Australia. Tickets cost from around $60.

Australia also has a number of contemporary dance companies, the most famous of which is the Sydney Dance Company (💻 www.sydneydancecompany.com), which performs at the Sydney Opera House.

MUSIC

In addition to the professional music scenes described below, there's a wide variety of amateur musicians in Australia, including barbershop singers, choral societies, military bands and orchestras, most of which are constantly on the lookout for new talent. Free music is provided by an army of buskers, some of whom are excellent.

Classical

Classical concerts, music festivals and solo concerts are regularly staged throughout Australia by Australian and foreign musicians and performers. Australia has eight professional orchestras: six symphony orchestras (one in each state capital) run by the Australian Broadcasting Corporation (ABC), the Australian Opera and Ballet Orchestra in Sydney, and the State Orchestra in Victoria (the last two perform with the Australian Opera and Australian Ballet).

A number of classical music festivals are staged, including the Melbourne Music Festival (February), the Sydney Festival (January) and the Sydney International Music Festival (July). The Sydney Symphony Orchestra (💻 www.sydneysymphony.com) performs outdoor concerts, e.g. during the 'Symphony in the Park' season in January. Musica Viva (Sydney) is the best known chamber music society (and the world's largest) and stages a concert series featuring international groups and artists. Regional companies (supported by state governments) perform in state capitals and provincial centres.

Pop

Pop music is an important part of the national culture and Australia, which has a thriving band scene, most of which perform in pubs, where the best of Australian music is found, and clubs, e.g. Returned Services League and working men's clubs – see **Social Clubs** below. Many amateur bands are surprisingly good (often performing their own songs), although some are excruciating. Australia is said to be among the hardest training grounds in the world for pop bands, where internationally famous bands and artists such as AC/DC, Air Supply, Nathalie Imbruglia, INXS, Men at Work, Mental as Anything and Kylie Minogue served their apprenticeships. There's usually an admission fee of $10 to $20 to clubs and pubs with live music, although many performances are free (you just need to buy drinks).

Major Australian cities, particularly Sydney, Melbourne and Brisbane, are on the itinerary of most international pop stars, many of whom perform in Australia during the Christmas (summer) season. In Sydney, the main venue for pop concerts is the Sydney Entertainment Centre (💻 www.sydentcent.com.au) and the Sydney Town Hall is also an important venue, while in Melbourne it's the Sport and Entertainment Centre (💻 www.mopt.com.au) on the banks of the Yarra River. Concerts are also held in Melbourne at the Kooyong Stadium, the Myer Music Bowl in Alexandra Gardens and Olympic Park. The big names also play at Brisbane's Entertainment Centre (💻 www.brisent.com.au), the 52,500-seat Suncorp Stadium and at the Perth Entertainment Centre. Free pop concerts are held on summer Sundays in some cities (if it's very hot and the band sounds a bit off key, it may be the result of high humidity, which causes instruments to go out of tune – or it may not!).

Concert and 'gig' guides are available in local newspapers, many of which publish a weekly entertainment guide (usually on Fridays). There are free weekly music publications in most cities, which are distributed via bottle shops, pubs and record stores. Gig guides are

also broadcast on local music radio stations. Popular music websites include 💻 http://themusic.com.au and www.take40.com.

Big Day Out (💻 www.bigdayout.com) is an Australia-wide, popular music festival featuring top bands, staged in January and February.

Jazz

Jazz has a lively following on the pub circuit, particularly in Sydney, where there are many regular venues (bands also perform in a variety of outdoor venues). A number of jazz festivals are staged in Australia, including the Montsalvat Jazz Festival (Eltham, VIC), held on the Australia Day weekend (January), and the York Jazz Festival in Western Australia in September.

Country & Folk Music

Australian country music has strong local themes and there are clubs in all major cities; many pubs also feature folk groups. Folk or bush music is popular, having its roots in English, Irish and Scottish folk music, where banjos, fiddles and tin whistles predominate along with a home-grown instrument called the 'lagerphone' (or zob stick), consisting of a wooden frame covered in metal bottle tops which is bashed on the ground, shaken or hit with a stick. The main festivals are the Australian Country Music Festival (see 💻 www.country.com.au for information) in Tamworth (NSW) in January featuring over 700 events, and the Land of the Beardies Bush Festival (which also includes a long beard competition!) at Glen Innes (NSW) in November.

Aboriginal Music

Few people forget the haunting sound of a didgeridoo, which is used in the bush to accompany tribal dances (called corroborees). Busking didgeridoo players (often non-Aboriginal) are common in the main cities, and performances are staged for tourists in northern regions, although they're a pale imitation of real corroborees. It's possible to hear the real thing at an Aboriginal cultural festival, and there are some contemporary Aboriginal bands such as Yothu Yindi, although few have had much commercial success. Other forms of native music are Koori, a cross between traditional Aboriginal music and country music, and 'gum-leaf', in which Aboriginal performers make 'music' by blowing on gum leaves.

SOCIAL CLUBS

If you want to become integrated into your local community or Australian society in general, one of the best ways is to join a social club (even better, join a number). There are numerous social clubs and organisations catering for both foreigners and Australians, including Ambassador clubs, Apex clubs, business clubs, church clubs and groups, the freemasons, international men's and women's clubs, Kiwani clubs, Lion and Lioness clubs, RSL clubs, Rotary clubs, Round Table clubs, ex-servicemen's clubs, sports clubs, women's clubs and working men's clubs. Many social clubs welcome visitors to have a drink or meal.

Leagues clubs (💻 www.lca.asn.au) are social clubs operated by the big rugby league clubs, such as Manly Sea Eagles and Penrith Panthers in NSW. They're an institution in NSW (where they have over 1m members) and Queensland and constitute the main social centre in many towns. Most have huge halls where shows are regularly staged, plus ballrooms, bars, discos, dozens of poker machines (pokies – which are the main source of income), pay TV and restaurants.

Expatriates from many countries run a variety of associations, clubs and organisations in major cities (ask at consulates for information). Many clubs organise events such as art and music classes, bridge and chess evenings, local history tours, sports activities, theatre and cinema outings, and whist drives.

There are singles' clubs in the major cities that organise a comprehensive range of activities on most days of the week. If you're retired you may find that your local council publishes a programme of recreational activities for the retired in your area.

Most councils publish a calendar of local sports and social events, and libraries provide information about local associations, clubs, groups and organisations.

NIGHTLIFE

There are discotheques (discos) and nightclubs in all cities and major towns in Australia. Other nightlife includes cabaret bars, casinos (see **Gambling** below), comedy clubs, dance clubs, karaoke clubs, pool halls and RSL clubs (see above). The differences between a bar, nightclub, pub and restaurant are often minimal in Australian cities, and some establishments are a combination of all four. There's a huge variety of gay clubs in some cities (such as Sydney), where information is published in the gay press such as the *Sydney Star Observer*, Australia's leading gay and lesbian newspaper.

Many nightclubs play a combination of live and recorded music. Admission to discos varies, but there's usually a $10 to $25 charge, which may include a 'free' drink, although venues with live music may charge as much as $20 for entry and $10 to $20 per drink. Some offer free entry for women on certain days (e.g. Wednesdays) and half-price drinks before 9pm (before the real 'action' starts) on some days. Drinks are usually expensive and even bottled water may cost from around $5 per glass. Some up-market discos and dance clubs allow admission only to couples.

The dress code is usually smart-casual, which normally excludes jeans, leather, T-shirts and trainers, although in some establishments these may be *de rigueur* (fashion usually dictates, depending on the venue). Dress may also be at the whim of the doorman (bouncer); if he doesn't like the look of you, you're out (or at least not in). Some nightclubs are for members only and have strict dress codes and high prices, which attract an older, more well-to-do clientele. Many discos are open until 3am or later, although some have variable closing times.

Brisbane, Melbourne and Sydney have the most cosmopolitan nightlife, with venues to suit every taste in atmosphere, fashion and music. Melbourne has some of the liveliest nightlife in Australia and a plethora of clubs, including the Metro, the largest nightclub in the southern hemisphere. Brisbane has many pubs and nightclubs and the Riverside area boasts dozens of restaurants, some with live entertainment. The main nightlife areas in Sydney are Oxford Street and the sleazy Kings Cross area, where drugs are freely available and violence is never far away.

In the cities, daily newspapers and free entertainment newspapers and information sheets provide comprehensive guides to entertainment venues and events.

GAMBLING

Gambling is one of Australia's favourite pastimes (for some people it's an occupation) and a $13bn industry, accounting for 1.5 per cent of annual GDP. It's estimated that 40 per cent of the population gamble regularly and that on average each person spends (i.e. loses) over $2,000 a year; the residents of NSW are among the heaviest gamblers, spending over $12m a day on lotteries alone. Gambling revenue is a favourite target of the tax man (around 30 to 40 per cent of the profit on poker machines alone), and tax raised from gambling accounts for almost 15 per cent of state and federal governments' revenue.

Gambling includes bingo (called housie); card games and roulette; football pools; horse, greyhound and camel racing; lotteries; poker machines ('pokies'); raffles; and two-up (see below). You can even bet on the results of general elections, public appointments, football matches and other sports events. Aussies are compulsive (and impulsive) gamblers and will bet on almost anything, even the proverbial two flies climbing a wall; in the outback (where you need to make your own entertainment) you can lose money on cane toad, cockroach, lizard and snail races!

An estimated 2 per cent of the population has a gambling problem (the percentage is lower than those addicted to nicotine or alcohol, but higher than the percentage of hard drug addicts). There are a huge number of Gamblers Anonymous groups, and also meetings for the relatives of compulsive gamblers to help them cope with their loved one's addiction. Compulsive gamblers can ban themselves from casinos under the Casino Control Act. However, you can now gamble at cyberspace casinos on the internet without leaving home.

Casinos

Most states have one or more casinos and there are now around 15 in Australia, including four in Queensland, two in Melbourne, two in Sydney, two in Tasmania (Hobart and Launceston) and one each in Adelaide, Alice Springs, Canberra, Darwin and Perth (for information, see 💻 www.worldcasinodirectory.com/australia). New casinos built in the last decade or so include the Sydney Star City and Sydney Harbour Casinos, the Conrad Treasury Casino in Brisbane and the Crown Casino in Melbourne (with 350 tables and 5,000 gaming machines). Games on offer include baccarat, blackjack, craps, keno, poker, roulette, Sic Bo and Pai Gow (Chinese card games), and two-up (see below).

Keno is similar to bingo except that you mark from one to 15 numbers out of 80 on your card and, if your numbers are among the 20 drawn, you win. Many casinos have a separate Totaliser Agency Board area (see **Racing** below), where you can place bets on horse and greyhound racing.

Casinos require 'smart-casual dress', which usually means a shirt with a collar and no shorts, sports shoes (trainers), T-shirts or flip-flops (thongs); jeans are usually acceptable but some casinos ban jeans and insist on a tie for men, so check in advance. Many casinos are open 24 hours a day. Games usually have a $2 minimum bet, although bets may start at $10 or more. Usually you must pay for drinks.

Most casinos publish a free Casino Gaming Guide, but don't expect any insider tips on how to break the bank!

Two-up

The national game of chance is called two-up, invented by soldiers in the First World War. It's illegal outside casinos (except on ANZAC Day) and a few licensed two-up schools (not that this discourages many Aussies). Not exactly the most sophisticated of games, it involves two coins being tossed together using a stick called a 'kip'. If one lands heads and the other tails, there's no result and all bets are held for the next throw. If both coins show the same, you win or lose depending on whether you chose heads or tails. Coins must spin when tossed or the arbitrator (called the 'spinner') calls the game void. Bets are placed with the 'boxer'. Casinos keep the stakes when there's a sequence of five identical results (unless you bet on this), which has around a 3 per cent chance.

Football Pools

Football (soccer) pools were traditionally the most common form of gambling in Australia, although they've been overtaken by lotteries and other forms of gambling in recent years. Operated by Australian Soccerpools, the pools offer huge cash prizes if you correctly forecast the results of football matches (Australian in the winter and British in the summer). The most popular bet (oddly known as a treble chance) is where you must guess which matches will be score draws (i.e. not 0-0). If you don't want to fill out a coupon each week, you can make a standing order using the same numbers.

Lotteries

The national lottery (or 'lotto') is popular in Australia, where you choose six numbers from one to 40. Numbers are drawn once or twice a week and those who select three or more correct numbers win a prize. The minimum stake is $1 and the first prize is usually in the $hundreds of thousands or $millions (the average payout is some 60 per cent of the amount staked). Results are published in the press and are also available via telephone information numbers. In recent years, instant lottery tickets, known as 'scratchies', have become one of the most popular (and addictive) forms of gambling.

Gaming Machines

Gaming or gambling machines ('pokies' – from poker machines) have spread like wildfire in Australia and are now seen almost everywhere (except Western Australia, where they're banned outside casinos), as state governments have rushed to cash in on the Australian gambling mania – machines now account for over half of all gambling revenue.

There are over 200,000 gambling machines in Australia, the world's second-highest per capita number; NSW leads the way with over 100,000.

Machines are common at leagues and other social clubs, where they're blamed for encouraging gambling among the elderly. Many can be played for as little as 20 cents and some boast jackpots of $25,000 (but not very often). In some states, e.g. Tasmania, there are limits on the amount that can be spent on gambling machines, and in others (e.g. Victoria) there has been a backlash against them, as they've encouraged gambling among the poor in disadvantaged areas.

Racing

Betting on animal racing is a popular form of gambling in Australia. Bets are placed on greyhound racing, harness racing (trotting) and horse racing. Gambling on horse and greyhound racing operates on the tote system (an Australian invention) operated by state Totaliser Agency Boards (TABs). TABs have outlets in all towns and cities (around 1,000 in Sydney alone), where offices (which also accept bets on the football pools) are open from around 11am until 6pm, Monday to Friday, and from 10am until 8pm on Saturdays. The TABs' annual turnover exceeds $4bn, including over $100m waged on the Melbourne Cup (💻 www.melbournecup.com) alone, Australia's premier horse race.

To place a bet, you simply write the name of your horse(s) or dog(s) and the race number on a betting slip and give it to the clerk with your stake. If you win, you can collect your winnings immediately after the race (provided you haven't lost your receipt). There are no off-course 'starting price' (SP) bookmakers in Australia, although there's on-course SP betting, where odds are given by bookmakers for each horse and you're given a fixed price. However, illegal telephone bookies flourish, and betting syndicates are active throughout Australia. Betting on harness racing is less organised and individual bookmakers set their own odds.

BARS & PUBS

It's hard to imagine it today, but some Australian states were originally temperance states. Australia is famous for its pubs (an abbreviation of public house), which are a tradition inherited from the British; they're usually referred to as hotels, although

Australian fast food includes crepes and pancakes, fish and chips, fried or grilled chicken, hamburgers, hot dogs, pies, sandwiches, sausages, seafood, stuffed potatoes and vegetarian snacks, and a huge variety of ethnic snacks such as bagels, calamari, couscous, dim sum, doner or shish kebab, felafel, filled croissants, focaccia, gyros, kosher food, pitta bread, pizza, samosa, sushi, tabouleh, tacos and tortillas. Many places also offer healthy food such as salads, skinless chicken, etc. However, the most popular Australian take-away remains the humble meat pie, which are typically served in cafés, milk bars and from mobile food vans (a common sight in major cities and tourist spots).

Common snack outlets include delicatessens, sandwich shops, and milk bars, which are shops selling meat pies, milkshakes, pasties, rolls, sandwiches, snacks and soft drinks. As in all developed (and many undeveloped) countries, American fast food outlets abound, and Hungry Jack's (trading as Burger King in other countries), Kentucky Fried Chicken, McDonald's and Pizza Hut can be found throughout the country. A popular budget restaurant chain is Sizzlers, an American-style restaurant serving chicken, fish and steak and a selection of desserts, pasta dishes and self-serve salads. Take-away barbecued chicken chains include Chicken Treat and Red Rooster. Some fast food outlets, such as the American-style Fast Eddy's, are open 24 hours a day. At most fast food restaurants you should expect to pay from around $10 for a filling meal.

Cafés

The Australians take after the British and drink a lot of tea and an increasing amount of coffee. Café society (and caffeine culture) is all the rage in Australian cities, where there's a huge variety of trendy and elegant cafés, the best of which are invariably Italian.

Coffee is served in a mind boggling variety in a plethora of coffee shops and cafés. If you just want a regular white coffee it's best to stick with an 'Americano' or a 'flat white'. Coffee also comes in various sizes including short (small – large enough for most people unless you want to swim in it) and long (large) and may be served in a cup (usually) or a glass. Philistines can also order decaf coffee (made with decaffeinated coffee beans), low-fat milk (skinny) or soya milk (soy). The more usual types of coffee offered in Australia include those in the table

Coffee Culture

Name	Description
Affogato	a single or double espresso poured over vanilla ice cream.
Americano	an espresso diluted with an equal portion of hot water (with milk).
Café au lait	coffee and heated milk in latte proportions, but using 'regular' coffee instead of espresso.
Cappuccino	a single shot of espresso with frothy milk, topped with a pinch of powdered chocolate.
Espresso	a black strong coffee prepared in the Italian way by forcing steam through dark-roast coffee beans – can be short (single shot, also called a short black) or long (double shot, also called a long black).
Filter	a method for brewing coffee which involves pouring water over coffee contained in a filter. Not considered real coffee (except by Americans) and may be left to stew in a jug. It may be available in caffeinated and decaffeinated (decaf) versions.
Flat White	made with one-third espresso and two-thirds steamed milk and similar to the ingredients in a latte. Can be a single or double (i.e. an extra shot).
Latte	an espresso with steamed milk and a cap of foam.
Long Black	a double-shot espresso topped with hot water.
Macchiato	a single espresso with a shot of cold or steamed milk (short macchiato) or a glass filled with hot frothed milk into which a double espresso is slowly dribbled (long macchiato).
Mocha	usually an espresso shot with steamed milk and chocolate.
Mochaccino	an espresso with hot chocolate milk.
Plunger	a one-person plunger or French press (cafetière) coffee.
Short Black	a single-shot espresso.
Vienna	a double shot espresso, laced with vanilla and topped with whipped cream.

above; the list isn't definitive and the names, descriptions and ingredients/style may vary depending on the establishment.

Most cafés serve food, although it's usually of the snack and fast food variety ('all-day breakfast' is common) rather than *à la carte* meals. Cafés may have printed menus or you check what's on the blackboard and order from the counter, where you also pay, take a number and display it at your table so that your order can be brought to you. Many people finish their meal in a café with coffee and a sweet (e.g. ice cream or pastries). Cafés in capital cities are often open until midnight or early morning and don't usually serve alcohol.

Prices

Eating out is inexpensive in Australia, where a good meal can be had from around $13 to $20 per head without wine. Expect to pay between $25 and $50 per head (plus wine) for three courses and coffee in a mid-range restaurant, while for top class restaurants the sky's the limit. If you're on a tight budget, some restaurants offer discounts to 'backpackers' (dress appropriately and preferably don't wash for a few days beforehand) and many employers operate canteens open to the public where food is served buffet-style and you can help yourself (not great food, but cheap and filling). Many restaurants offer lunches which are less expensive than the same meals served in the evening (lunch is a good time to eat in a classy restaurant). However, you should avoid tourist-trap restaurants in cities and resorts.

There are usually no additions for tax or service, although a 10 per cent surcharge may be levied at weekends and on public

holidays to pay extra staff costs. Few people tip in inexpensive restaurants, although many people leave 5 to 10 per cent in mid-range and top class restaurants. In a busy establishment, it's customary to leave the correct money on the table and leave rather than pay the waiter/waitress personally. Most restaurants accept payment by credit card, although you should check in advance at budget restaurants.

In a restaurant with an alcohol licence, wine usually starts at around $25 a bottle, although some restaurants sell wine at bottle shop (retail) prices. In wine-growing areas, there may be a wine tasting room, where you can choose from wines made on the property.

Opening Times

Australians are fairly inflexible about their meal times, and many restaurants have limited hours. For example, dinner (often called tea after the British working class habit) is often served as early as 6 or 7pm and last orders in restaurants may be as early as 9pm (the staff are packing up to go home by around 10pm). In small towns it's usually difficult to find anywhere serving food after 7.30 or 8pm other than a fast food outlet or a fish and chip shop (lunch may also be served for only one hour, e.g. from 12.30 to 1.30pm). However, in the major cities, many restaurants stay open late and may allow diners to circumvent local licensing laws. In order to drink legally at a restaurant outside official licensing hours, you must plan to dine, although you can order anything and aren't obliged to eat it (some places may provide a plate of free food to encourage drinkers!). The most common closing day for restaurants is Monday.

Bookings & Dress

Most restaurants accept bookings, and some top restaurants have a 'no show' penalty of around $10 (or 10 per cent of the average cost of a meal per head in more expensive venues) for those who don't bother to turn up or who cancel at short notice after booking a table, although many restaurants overbook to compensate for 'no-shows'.

> **▲ Caution**
>
> Some restaurants have dress rules, although smart-casual is usual, even for the most exclusive establishments, but many ban flip-flops (thongs) and shorts (unless perhaps when worn with shoes and socks – not a common habit in Australia).

There are many restaurant guides in Australia, including annual *Cheap Eats* guides to budget restaurants in Melbourne and Sydney (each listing over 500 restaurants) and the Lonely Planet *Out to Eat* series, which cover Melbourne and Sydney. Internet restaurant guides include www.bestrestaurants.com.au, www.restaurant.org.au, www.restaurantsofaustralia.com.au and www.yourrestaurants.com.au. Australia also has a number of excellent magazines for foodies including the *Australian Gourmet Traveller* (www.gourmettraveller.com.au) and *Good Taste* (www.taste.com.au/good+taste).

16. SPORTS

Australia is a sporting paradise, thanks largely to its generally mild climate. Sport is an integral part of the nation's culture and the favourite topic of conversation (people even call each other 'sport'!); to many Aussies it has the status of a religion. It's both a unifying and divisive pastime (competition is fierce between rival teams), although Australians are generally good sports and appreciate plucky opponents (unless they're Poms). Melbourne is the most sports-mad city (Sydney isn't far behind) and is home to Australia's unique brand of football, Australian Rules. Sports centres abound in all towns and cities and offer facilities for a wide range of sports.

Aerobics is Australia's favourite form of exercise among young people, followed by netball (played only by women but having larger participation than any other sport), basketball, swimming, cricket, soccer and Australian Rules football (the top spectator sport in the country). Other popular sports and activities (in no particular order) are cycling, golf, hiking, horse racing, jogging/running, lawn bowls, martial arts, motorsports, squash, tennis and tenpin bowling.

Australia is famous for its beach culture (80 per cent of Australians live within around 30km/18mi of the coast), and watersports are very popular. Australians like their sports tough and love endurance tests such as ironman competitions and triathlons (a 1,500m swim followed by a 40km/25mi bike ride and a 10km/6mi run). However, even these aren't tough enough for 'real' men, who recently invented the 'eco-challenge race', which consists of 500km/310mi of bushwalking, canoeing, climbing, cycling, horse-riding, kayaking, rafting and trekking in the outback, rainforests and reefs in northern Queensland.

In Australian schools, sport is incorporated into the normal school timetable and isn't only an extra-curricular activity, as in many other countries. Schools have a wide variety of teams for all sports and participate in inter-school and interstate competitions (most events are held on Saturdays, when parents are called upon to ferry their children around the country to compete). Children come under pressure from coaches, parents and teachers to perform at their highest level, and club scouts scour school sports meetings for talent. Two-thirds of Australian children join a sports club by the age of 11 and around half the population is registered to participate in sports (over 6m Australians take part in organised sport each year). Children who fail at sport can be made outcasts by their fellow pupils.

There's no such thing as just taking part or engaging in sport merely for fun in Australia, where winning is everything. Only the Americans devote more effort, money and time to sports perfection than Australians, who are consumed by sport (although more often than not it's only as gamblers or spectators).

The country has some 15 national leagues involving team sports – remarkable when you consider the vast distances involved. As a nation they excel at numerous sports, including cricket, cycling, golf, hockey, horse riding, lawn bowls, motorsports, netball, rowing, rugby, sailing, squash, surfing, swimming, tennis, triathlon and many others. Australians also compete successfully at the World and Olympic Games for the disabled.

The government and sports bodies promote sport with slogans such as 'sport for all' and 'life be in it'. Sporting talent is nurtured and given the best possible encouragement by the Australian Institute of Sport (www.ausport.gov.au/ais), founded in 1981 in Canberra, and centres of excellence such as the Australian Cricket Academy. There are over 130 national sporting organisations in Australia and thousands of state, regional, city and local club bodies. The government provides financial assistance and coaching for the disabled through the Aussie Able Program. The country received a huge sporting (and economic) boost from hosting the Olympics in the year 2000 in Sydney, where Australian competitors excelled, and Australian spectators will be remembered as among the best and most magnanimous ever. Melbourne hosted the Commonwealth Games in 2006.

However, despite the popular image of Australians as bronzed, muscular lifesavers and bathing beauties, many Australians are overweight and unfit, and the nearest they ever get to working up a sweat is jumping up and down in joy/anger while hurling abuse at TV sport. Fewer than a third of Australians participate in any form of physical activity (Sydneysiders are the biggest slobs).

Sports fans may be interested in visiting the Australian Gallery of Sport and Olympic Museum in Melbourne (open daily from 9.30am until 4.30pm). Tourism Australia (see **Tourist Information** on page 247) publishes a wealth of fact sheets on every conceivable sport and local municipal councils may publish a 'leisure directory' listing local sports centres and clubs. An annual *Sport Yearbook* (Gemkit Publishing) is available for those seeking an introduction to Australian sport. The federal government also runs a comprehensive website through the Australian Sports Commission (www.ausport.gov.au).

Sports results can be obtained in Australia by telephone or via the internet (see www.abc.net.au/sport).

AERIAL SPORTS

Most aerial sports have a wide following in Australia (which has an awful lot of airspace), particularly gliding, hang-gliding, hot-air ballooning, microlighting and paragliding. Hang-gliding has become increasingly popular in Australia in recent years, and there are hang-gliding schools in most areas. Tuition costs round $150 for half an hour to fly in tandem with an instructor; a full course to obtain a pilot's licence, which are issued by the Hang Gliding Federation of Australia (www.hgfa.asn.au), costs around $3,000 and can be undertaken in just ten days.

> **▲ Caution**
>
> Most aerial sports or private aviation are specifically excluded from many insurance policies, including, for example, health insurance and mortgage life assurance policies.

Hot-air ballooning has a small but dedicated band of followers in Australia, although participation is generally limited to the wealthy on account of the high cost of balloons. A flight in a balloon costs from around $400 ($300 for children) and is a spectacular way to see some of Australia's most stunning landscapes (e.g. Ayers Rock, where balloon operators offer 30-or 60-minute sunrise flights – including a 'champagne' breakfast). Alice Springs is the country's ballooning centre.

Aircraft and gliders (sailplanes) can be hired with an instructor or without (provided you have a pilot's licence) from many small airfields in Australia. There are many gliding clubs in Australia, and parachuting and free-fall parachuting (sky-diving) flights can be made from most private airfields. Schools offer tandem jumps for beginners (where you're strapped to an instructor), and a day's course costs around $600. You can take 'tourist' flights in a small aeroplane from most airfields, and seaplane flights are also offered in some areas, e.g. Sydney harbour. Microlight lessons are cheaper in Australia than in most European countries and similar to North America.

AUSTRALIAN RULES FOOTBALL

Australian rules football, officially known as Australian football (but called simply 'Aussie rules' by fans), is Australia's home-grown ball game, although it isn't the nation's leading sport – except in Melbourne. Fans and players of other football codes (and cricket) disparagingly refer to Aussie rules as aerial ballet or aerial ping-pong. Its rules were invented in 1858 and are unique, although it's believed to be based on Gaelic football (played in Ireland).

Aussie rules is an athletic, exciting, fast, skilful game, in which the score can change quickly and the outcome may hinge on the last kick. It's a gruelling, macho game and players are very fit and tough, most spurning any sort of protection (although some players do wear mouthguards, protective head gear and gloves to give them a better grip). They also wear tight shorts and sleeveless shirts to show off their muscles – not surprisingly, it's popular with women, who make up around half the spectators. Players cannot be sent off during a game and consequently there are often scraps on the field.

A match lasts for four quarters of 20 minutes each, but can extend to around three hours when breaks between quarters and stoppages for disputes, injuries and punch-ups are included (plus 'time on', i.e. time added by the umpire).

The goal consists of four tall, evenly-spaced posts, the outer pair of which are slightly shorter than the inner pair. Six points are awarded for kicking the ball between the two central posts (a 'goal') and one point for kicking it through the outer posts (a 'behind'). A typical point score for each team is between 70 and 120 points. The score (goals and behinds) is shown in newspapers for each quarter with the final points total shown in brackets.

The national professional league is the Australian Football League (🖳 www.afl.com.au) comprising 16 teams. Melbourne is the centre of Aussie rules and provides ten of the 16 teams in the AFL, the others coming from Adelaide, Brisbane, Fremantle, Perth, Port Adelaide and Sydney. Aussie rules is the number one sport in five states: the Northern Territory, South Australia, Tasmania, Victoria (where it's a religion) and Western Australia. Matches are played on Friday evenings and Saturday and Sunday afternoons throughout the winter. Crowds are noisy, but there's rarely any trouble. The Grand Final is played in September or October at the Melbourne Cricket Ground before 100,000 fans. It rivals the FA Cup Final in England or the American Super Bowl for atmosphere and passion.

Local, regional and state teams are listed in the phone book.

An excellent book on the history of Australian rules is *100 Years of Australian Rules Football* by Ross John.

CLIMBING & CAVING

Those who find walking a bit tame may like to try abseiling, caving, mountaineering, pot-holing (subterranean mountaineering) or rock-climbing. Australia doesn't offer much in the way of mountaineering (Mount Kosciusko in the Snowy Mountains, New South Wales (NSW) is the highest point, at 2,228m/7,307ft), although it has some of the best and most varied rock climbing in the world. Caving is particularly popular in Tasmania, which has some of the most spectacular caves in Australia. Some caves are open only to experienced cavers, including the Croesus caves, the Exit Cave and the Kubla Khan caves (permits are necessary to enter most caves, many of which are kept locked). There are caving (speleological) clubs and societies in all major cities.

If you're an inexperienced climber, you're advised to join a climbing club before heading for the hills (an eight-hour beginner's course costs from around $300). Contact the Australian School of Mountaineering (🖳 www.asmguides.com) for information. There are abseiling and climbing schools in all the major cities, many with indoor training apparatus (e.g. a climbing wall) for aspiring mountaineers. Ask about local clubs at climbing equipment stores.

CRICKET

There are some 500,000 registered cricket players in Australia, where there are leagues at all levels from tots to oldies, men and women, indoors and outdoors. Cricket, like footy, dominates its season (from October until March) and attracts big TV audiences. Half of all Australians watch cricket on TV and around 20 per cent go to matches, where tickets for top class games cost around $50 for a one-day match and up to $200 for a five-day test match. State cricket is played to a high standard (higher than the English county game), although it isn't a fully professional sport. The main national competition is the interstate Sheffield Shield (currently called the BUPA Sheffield Shield after its sponsor), in which matches are played over three or four days, and there's also high-quality district cricket.

Australia is the most successful country at international test cricket and also in the one-day World Cup, which they have won four times. It's also a top nation in women's cricket and they have won the women's World Cup five times (they were 4th in 2009 on home soil, when England won).

For more information, see 🖳 http://cricket.com.au.

CYCLING

Most people in Australia buy bicycles for getting around town rather than cycling purely for pleasure, exercise or sport, e.g. touring or racing. However, competitive cycling is also popular in Australia and includes bicycle motocross, bicycle polo, cross-country racing, cycle speedway, road and track racing, time-trial and touring. Australia has had considerable success in international cycle racing in recent years, particularly track racing at the Olympics and world championships, and is also becoming a major force in road racing.

Cycling is an excellent way to get around most Australian cities and most (except Sydney) have an extensive network of cycle paths and tracks (cycleways): Melbourne's cover 500km (310mi); cyclists in Canberra and Perth can legally ride on footpaths, and pedestrians can use cycle paths. There are children's off-road bicycle circuits in many cities and towns. In most cities, bicycles can be transported on suburban trains free of charge or for a small fee during off-peak times; during peak periods (e.g. 6 to 9am and 3 to 6pm on weekdays) it may not be permitted or a permit may be required. When transporting a bicycle on a plane or bus, you must usually dismantle and box it.

If you're cycling in Australia's cities you should note that fresh air may be in short supply and you would be wise to wear a face mask to insulate yourself from traffic pollution (although, according to some medical experts, they offer little or no protection against carbon monoxide).

The climate and topography (in most regions) of Australia lends itself to cycling, which is a good way to explore coastal areas. You can ride a long way in some regions without encountering any hills, although if you're looking for hills you're also well catered for.

A wide range of bicycles is available to suit all pockets and needs, ranging from a basic 'town' bicycle costing a few hundred dollars to a professional racing bike costing many thousands. In between these extremes are bicycles with folding frames, BMX bikes, mountain bikes, shopping bicycles, tandems, touring bicycles and tricycles. A new fifteen-speed touring or mountain bike costs from around $400 (you can pay up to $10,000!), a good second-hand one from around $150. If you're a visitor and need a bicycle for touring, it's cheaper to buy a second-hand bicycle and sell it when you no longer need it (some cycle shops buy back second-hand bicycles for a guaranteed price). Bicycle theft is common in Australia, therefore it's sensible to insure your bicycle if possible and buy a good lock.

Bicycles can be rented in all cities and large towns, and may include folding bicycles, tandems and tricycles. Ask at the local tourist office for information (see page 247). Touring and mountain bikes can be rented from around $35 per day, $50 for a weekend and around $100 per week. They can sometimes also be rented by the hour from around $5 (there may be lower rates for children). Usually a deposit is required or you must leave your passport or a credit card as security. Many hostels provide free bicycles for guests, although you should ensure that a rented or loan bicycle is insured against theft or damage.

> **▲ Caution**
>
> Cycling helmets are compulsory in all states and territories, and you can be fined on-the-spot (e.g. $25 to $50) for not wearing one.

Many books are published for cyclists in Australia, including *Cycling Australia: Bicycle Touring Throughout the Sunny Continent* by Ian Duckworth (Van der Plas Publishing), *Cycling Around Sydney*, *Seeing Sydney by Bicycle*, *Discovering Melbourne's Bike Paths* and a series of *Cycling The Bush* (Hill of Content) books by Sven Klinge, which cover a number of states, plus *Cycling The Bush – The Best Rides in Australia*. Free brochures such as *Canberra Cycleways* are also available from tourist offices. Local cycling guides and maps are published by councils and conservation and cycling groups in many areas; many of these organisations also publish safety booklets and brochures for children. Cycling maps are available in the major cities from bookshops and local cycling clubs and organisations (the best are the government series of 1:250,000 scale).

If you're interested in joining a cycling club, your library should have information about local clubs, or you can contact Cycling Australia (💻 www.cycling.org.au). There are cycling organisations in all states, such as Bicycle New South Wales (💻 www.bicyclensw.org.au) and Bicycle Network Victoria (💻 www.bicyclenetwork.com.au).

FISHING

Fishing (or angling) is one of the largest participant sports in the country. There's good fishing in Australian waters, both inland and offshore, where the main attraction is game fishing (see below). Tasmania's coastal waters are also rich fishing grounds (fishing is permitted all year), where bream, salmon and whiting can all be caught from the shore. Northern Australia is famed for its barramundi ('barra') fishing, found both offshore and inland. Fishing trips are organised from around $300 per day, usually between March and October, including accommodation, meals, bait, boat rental, equipment, guides and tackle. In the Northern Territory there are limits on catches of barramundi and mud crabs (contact the local fisheries management service for information). You should be wary of eating fish caught in inland waters, as many are polluted, despite $millions spent on cleaning them up (many rivers are used as waste disposal 'pipes' by industry).

Over-fishing of certain species is an increasing problem for Australia's fishing industry. There are bag and size limits in most areas for certain species of fish, e.g. Victoria limits trout catches to ten a day.

A licence may be required when fishing in inland waters. In Western Australia, for example, fishing licences cost around $40 for freshwater angling, marron, net fishing, rock lobster, and abalone; if you apply for more than one licence type in a single transaction, you're entitled to a 10 per cent discount. Tasmania (www.fishtas.com) has Australia's best freshwater fishing, including superb trout introduced in 1864 from England. Some species, such as clams, dugongs (sea cows), triton shells and turtles, are protected and may not be hunted in Australian waters. Licences are available from state and territory fishing authorities (see www.come-fishing-australia.com/fishing-license-australia.html).

 **Caution**

Take extra care when fishing from rocks, particularly when the sea is rough, as a number of anglers are swept out to sea and drowned each year – wearing a lifejacket may save their life!

The fishing season in most inland waters is from the Saturday nearest to 1st August until the Sunday closest to 30th April. However, there's a shorter season in many areas and in some waters (a *Fishing Code* brochure is available detailing the seasons).

Game Fishing

The main Australian game fishing industry is based in Townsville (Queensland), where game includes black and blue marlin (the prize catch), sailfish, saltfish, Spanish mackerel, tuna and wahoo. The Coral Sea off Cairns is one of the few places in the world where large black marlin are found. Other popular prey include brown trout, eel, English redfin, native blackfish and perch (off the west coast of Tasmania); Australian salmon, crayfish, giant crab, mulloway, shark, trevally and whiting (off South Australia); and bream, crayfish, herring, mulloway, salmon, samson fish, sea pike, Spanish mackerel, tailor and trevally (off the southern coast of Western Australia).

Black and blue marlin are protected by law and must be returned to the sea, whether dead or alive (often after being tagged) or you risk a fine of up to around $12,500! The main season is from June to November.

Good game fishing is also to be found in the waters off Broome (WA), where game includes bronze whale shark, kingfish, hammerhead shark, mackerel, yellowfin tuna, yellowtail and wahoo. There's also good game fishing off NSW (black marlin, marlin, mulloway and tailor fish), Victoria and Tasmania (Australian salmon, bluefin tuna and mulloway), South Australia (tuna), Perth (blue marlin) and Darwin (barracuda, barramundi, queenfish and Spanish mackerel). Fishing on the Great Barrier Reef is particularly popular, and fishing boats depart regularly from Cairns and Townsville for trips lasting 8 to 15 hours.

Game fishing competitions are regularly staged – one of the major events is the Gove Game Classic (NT), which attracts fishermen from all over the world. A game fishing boat for eight can be rented from around $1,000 per day, although marlin fishing can cost over $1,500 per day for four to six passengers. Bottom fishing boats (for those who like to catch bottom-dwelling fish) for up to 30 passengers are also available for hire.

There are a number of magazines published in Australia for anglers, including *Fishing World* (www.fishingworldmag.com.au), and there are also many websites, such as Sportsfish Australia (www.sportsfish.com.au). For more information contact the Australian National Sportfishing Association (www.ansa.com.au).

FOOTBALL (SOCCER)

Association football (which the Aussies call soccer) is a minor sport in Australia, where it's played mostly by immigrants (footy fans insultingly refer to it as 'wogball'). The majority of clubs in the National Soccer League (NSL) or A-League (www.footballaustralia.com.au/aleague) are dominated by Croatians, Dutch, Greeks, Italians, Macedonians, Maltese, Slavs and assorted other 'foreigners' (who represent the ethnic origins of the local populace). The

A-League attracts a small following (most fans prefer overseas football), although it's gaining in popularity thanks to the relative success of the national team (see below). The standard is on a par with top amateur teams in England and other European countries.

The national team (called the 'Socceroos') has improved beyond all recognition in recent years and qualified for the 2006 and 2010 World Cups, having only previously appeared once in the elite competition. Australian soccer looks set for a bright future with increasing sponsorship and $millions being invested in the game.

Further information can be found on the website of the Football Federation Australia (💻 www.footballaustralia.com.au).

GOLF

Golf was introduced to Australia in the 1820s and today there are over 1,400 clubs and around a million golfers, making it one of the most popular participant sports in the country. Melbourne has over 100 golf courses (it claims to have more than any other city in the world) and Sydney has nearly as many. There are beautiful and spectacularly sited courses throughout the country, many of which are open to the public, although the best courses are private. Most private courses allow non-members to play, although you may need to be invited by a member. Many private golf clubs are part of a larger country club or hotel sports complex, where facilities may include a bar, luxury hotel, restaurant, squash and tennis courts, swimming pool and other facilities.

Golf is a relatively expensive sport in Australia, where a round costs $60 to $100. Golf clubs can be hired for around $35. The best deals for non-members are evening rounds, which can cost as little as $25.

Many golf clubs have nets and covered driving ranges, and most also have professionals who give lessons. Separate driving ranges are also available in most areas and have all-weather, floodlit bays, and practice bunkers and greens. Crazy golf, miniature golf, pitch and putt, and putting greens (e.g. in public parks) are provided in most areas for those who set their sights a little lower than winning the Australian Open. You can also become a non-playing social member of a club for a small fee.

When not playing on the European or American circuits, Australia's top professionals play the ANZ PGA Tour of Australasia Order of Merit (💻 www.pgatour.com.au). The premier Australian event is the Australian Open (💻 www.australianopengolf.com.au), staged in November at the Metropolitan Golf Club in Melbourne and organised by Golf Australia (💻 www.golfaustralia.org.au).

GYMNASIUMS & HEALTH CLUBS

There are gymnasiums and health and fitness clubs in all cities and large towns in Australia, including multi-purpose fitness centres with aerobics, fitness machines and swimming pools. Many private health and fitness clubs organise aerobics and keep-fit classes, and may have a Jacuzzi, massage rooms, sauna, solarium and steam bath. Many top class hotels have health clubs and swimming pools, which may be open to the public, although access to facilities may be restricted to guests at certain times.

A good gymnasium or health club ensures that all members undergo a physical assessment, including a blood pressure test, fat distribution measurements and heart rate checks. All clubs should provide a free trial and

produce a personal training programme. Some gyms in major cities (e.g. Sydney) are open 24 hours a day from Monday to Friday.

The cost of membership varies considerably depending on the city or area, the facilities provided and the local competition. Note that there has been a spate of closures in recent years, which have left annual members out of pocket. This has led to a new law prohibiting gyms from offering annual membership specials that are much cheaper than a monthly payment scheme. Beware of fly-by-night outfits and choose a reputable, long-established club. Many gymnasiums can be used by non-members on payment of an admission fee, where a day ticket usually costs around $30 (monthly membership is also usually available). Some clubs offer reduced rates for couples and family membership.

HIKING

Australians tend to call hiking 'bushwalking', even when it's done far from the outback. Real bushwalking is serious, long-distance hiking in the outback, ranging from a day trip to a number of weeks. Australia has a wealth of beautiful, unspoiled hiking country in every state and territory. One of the major trails is the 5,330km (3,312mi) National Trail (🖳 www.nationaltrail.com.au) from Cooktown (north of Cairns) to Melbourne, following the old bush tracks, fire trails and stock routes. Around Sydney, there's the Blue Mountains, Snowy Mountains, Ku-ring-gai Chase National Park and the Royal National Park.

A 250km (150mi) trail links Sydney with the Hunter Valley, and in the west of the state the Hume and Hovell Track runs through the high country between Albury and Yass. The Snowy Mountains (part of the celebrated Kosciusko National Park in NSW and Victoria) are a Mecca for bushwalkers, and Thredbo is a popular summer hiking resort, with a chair-lift that takes you to the top of Mount Crackenback. One of NSW's most famous parks is the Warrumbungle National Park in the north of the state.

Victoria has some of the country's most spectacular and diverse walking country, including the Australian Alps Walking Track stretching for 655km (405mi) from Walhalla (145km/90mi east of Melbourne near Mount Baw Baw) to the Brindabella Ranges on the outskirts of Canberra. Other top walking areas in Victoria include the Coastal Walking Track, the Grampians National Park, the Great Dividing Range, Lederderg Gorge, the Little Desert National Park, Mount Bogong, the Snowy River National Park (where the film *The Man From Snowy River* was shot) and Wilsons Promontory National Park.

In South Australia, there's the Flinders Ranges and Mount Lofty, taking in the 1,500km (930mi) Heysen Trail, which crosses the state from Cape Jervis to Parachilna Gorge (in the Flinders Ranges). In Western Australia, the Porongurup National Park and the Stirling Range (both north of Albany) offer fine scenery, as do the Kalbarri, Karijini and Purnululu national parks. The 640km (400mi) Bibbulman Track runs between Perth and Walpole.

There are also many excellent bushwalking areas in Queensland, including Bellenden Ker south of Cairns, Cooloola north of the Sunshine Coast, Lamington in the southern Border Ranges and Main Range in the Great Divide, plus coastal islands such as Fraser and Hinchinbrook. The Northern Territory provides a wealth of walking areas, including Gregory National Park, Kakadu National Park, the Larapinta Trail in the Western MacDonnell Ranges (near Alice Springs), Trephina Gorge Nature Park in the Eastern MacDonnells and Watarrka (Kings Canyon).

Tasmania has some of the best bushwalking in Australia, including the famous Overland Track from Cradle Mountain to Lake St. Clair (85km/53mi). A seventh of Tasmania is occupied by national parks, although they're under constant threat from mining and logging interests.

There are marked trails in most national parks and state forests, although some offer tough walking and are only for the seriously fit, and there's generally a lack of marked long-distance trails. You require a national park permit to enter certain parks and reserves, costing from around $10 per day for a vehicle or $50 to $60 per year. Day/night permits are also available in some areas for campers. Tracks are usually marked by coloured triangles on posts, trees, etc. Before setting out on a walk in a national park, you should sign on in the ranger's log book and sign off when you return, so that searches are initiated if you don't return on time. When on a long walk, it's wise to let someone know your plans and when you expect to return. Some trails are closed in the summer due to fire risks.

It's important to be properly prepared and equipped when going on a long walk and staying out overnight. Many shops sell or rent bush clothing and equipment, and some hostels rent equipment. There are bushwalking associations in all states and territories, such as The Confederation of Bushwalking Clubs NSW (☎ 02-9294 6797, 🖳 www.bushwalking.org.au).

Orienteering is popular in Australia and is a combination of hiking and a treasure hunt, or competitive navigation on foot. It isn't necessary to be super fit and the only equipment that's required (in addition to suitable walking attire) is a good map and a compass. There are orienteering clubs in many areas and bushwalking clubs in most towns and regions. In many towns and country areas, guided walks are conducted throughout the year, ranging from sightseeing tours of towns to walks around local beauty spots, for which there may be a small fee. Walks are usually graded, e.g. easy, moderate or strenuous, and dogs can usually be taken unless otherwise stated. Many municipal councils provide local walking guides and there are short guided walks in the major cities. Ask for information at tourist information centres or local libraries.

A wealth of bushwalking books is published in Australia, including *Bushwalking in Australia* by John Chapman (Lonely Planet), *Sydney and Beyond* by Andrew Mevissen (Sandringham), and a series of bushwalking books by Tyrone T. Thomas detailing walks in most states and popular walking areas, including the *20 Best Walks in Australia* (Hill of Content). There are also a number of magazines published for hikers, including *Outdoor Australia* and *Wild*.

RACKET SPORTS

There are excellent facilities in Australia for most racket sports, including badminton,

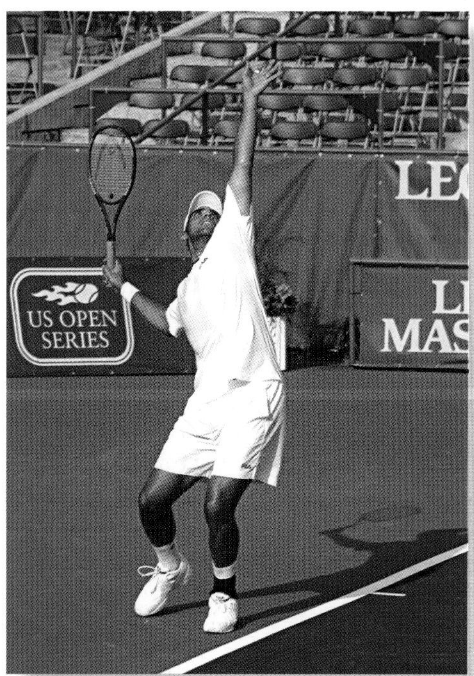

Mark Philippoussis

squash and tennis. Some racket clubs cater for both squash and tennis, a few also for badminton. Most private clubs have a resident or visiting coach, providing both individual and group lessons, and many sports clubs and resort hotels hold residential coaching courses and holidays throughout the year. To find the racket clubs in your local area look in the *Yellow Pages*, enquire at your local library or contact the appropriate national association.

Tennis

Tennis is the most popular racket sport in Australia and is played outdoors year round in most states. Public (council-owned) courts and those owned by local associations can be hired for around $15 to $20 per hour, although it can be difficult to book a court at popular times. Many hotels have tennis courts, and university courts can be hired during holiday periods for a small, e.g. from $5-10 an hour. Some companies and schools have their own courts. There are many private tennis clubs in Australia, although membership fees can be high and some have long waiting lists. Indoor courts are rare in Australia, where outdoor courts can be used year round in most regions.

Most courts in Australia are hard courts and there are few grass courts left.

The Australian Open Tennis Championships (💻 www.australianopen.com) are held in Melbourne at the National Tennis Centre at Flinders Park, where the main court is unique in that it has a roof which can be closed when it rains or during extreme heat (above 40ºC/104ºF). It's staged over two weeks in January and is the first of the world's four 'grand slam' tournaments (along with Wimbledon and the French and US Opens). Anyone can play at the National Tennis Centre (except when the Australian Open is being held) for around $30 per hour indoors and around $25 outdoors. Tours are also available. Further information about tennis in Australia can be found at 💻 www.tennisaustralia.com.au.

Squash & Racketball

Squash is a popular racket sport in Australia and there's an abundance of courts in the major cities and towns. The cost of hiring a court is around $15-20 per hour, and most clubs have club evenings when members can play for a few dollars. Rackets and balls can be hired. The club standard is among the highest in the world, and competitions are staged at all levels from club and state competitions to the Australian Open.

Australia is one of the world's top squash nations, although in the last few years squash has declined in popularity and the number of players has fallen. In some cities (e.g. Sydney), clubs have been closing in increasing numbers in recent years as the cost of maintaining or opening a club increases and property values rise (many former clubs have been redeveloped as apartments, office blocks and shops).

For information about playing squash in Australia, contact Squash Australia (☎ 07-3367 3200, 💻 www.squash.org.au).

Racketball – a variant of squash played on the same court but with slightly different rules, using shorter rackets and a larger, bouncier ball – is also played in Australia, and rackets and balls can be hired at some squash clubs.

Badminton & Table Tennis

Badminton is a popular sport, particularly among migrants from China, Indonesia, Malaysia and Singapore, although it lags behind tennis and squash. Most badminton facilities are provided by public sports centres and private clubs are rare. Table tennis is also quite popular and is played both as a serious competitive sport and as a pastime in social and youth clubs. If you want to play seriously, there are clubs in most areas. Costs vary, although it's an inexpensive sport with little equipment necessary.

RUGBY FOOTBALL

Both main codes of rugby football (usually referred to as 'footy'), rugby league and rugby union, are played in Australia. Rugby is the main football game in Canberra, NSW and Queensland, where rugby league is the most popular code. Most rugby league teams are based in Sydney, with others in Canberra, the Gold Coast of Queensland and Melbourne. Teams from New Zealand also compete in the Australian league (💻 www.australianrugbyleague.com.au). Sydney is the only major city in the world where rugby is more popular than soccer (it's estimated that some 80 per cent of the world's best league players live within 30km/18mi of central Sydney).

Australia is the world's leading rugby league nation (the Winfield Cup is the world's premier

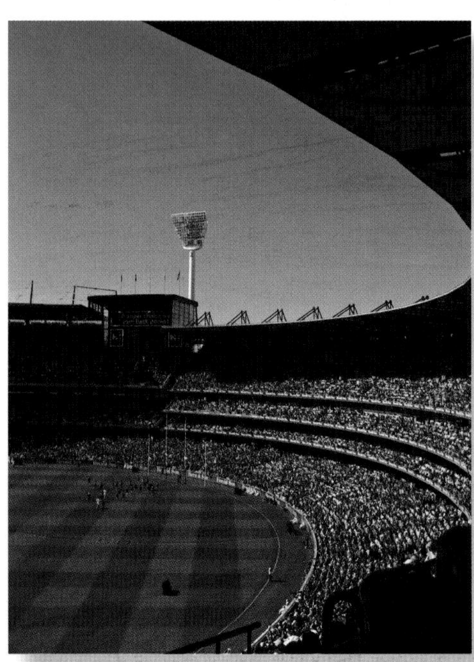

rugby league competition), usually easily beating the main opposition (England). The national rugby league team is known as the Kangaroos. National Rugby League (💻 www.nrl.com.au) matches are played on most Friday and Saturday evenings and Sunday afternoons between April and September. League is popular, although attendances are much lower than for NFL (Aussie rules) games. Its popularity has fallen sharply in recent years as a result of continual scandals on and off the pitch. The State-of-Origin series between the Australian states in May/June is the premier interstate competition, although it's poorly supported by the public.

Rugby union was once a strictly amateur code in Australia but is now fully professional at the top level. It's most popular in the Australian Capital Territory (ACT), NSW, Queensland and Western Australia. The national team (called the Wallabies) play around six internationals a year. The major competition is called the Rugby Super 15 (💻 www.superxv.com), with Australian state teams competing with teams from New Zealand and South Africa.

SKIING

Skiing in Australia dates back to the 1860s and is a popular sport, despite the fact that there's only one proper skiing area: the Australian Alps, straddling the NSW/Victoria border (see below). There are also some small snowfields in Tasmania, which has two minor resorts: Ben Lomond (60km/37mi from Launceston) and Mount Mawson (in Mount Field National Park). These are less developed and even less challenging than the major resorts in NSW and Victoria. However, they're also much cheaper, e.g. a day pass at Mount Field costs around $50 and at Ben Lomond it's around $25.

A lot of money has been spent on improving the infrastructure in recent years, and the facilities and lifts at the larger resorts now compare favourably with the best that Europe and North America have to offer. Australia has unreliable snowfall and in some years there's barely enough natural snow to cover even the highest slopes, and conditions can be hazardous for all but expert skiers. Many Australians ski in New Zealand, which has a reliable snow record and many more resorts. However, in the last decade snow cannons have been installed in most resorts, which can now guarantee at least some snow for part of the season. There are artificial snow slopes at Corin Forest Alpine Recreation Area 30 minutes from Canberra, where wheeled bobsleds achieve speeds of up to 80kph (50mph) on a stainless steel slide.

The (snow) skiing season normally begins in early June on the Queen's birthday weekend holiday and continues until around October. However, even in a good year there's usually adequate snow cover only in July, August and early September. Ski runs cater for all standards, from beginners to experts, although most long runs are relatively easy, while the more difficult runs are short. Snowboarding is increasingly popular in Australia (the major resorts have purpose-built runs and 'bowls') and equipment can be hired and lessons available. The conditions are usually excellent for cross-country skiing (also called Nordic or 'langlauf' in Australia) and telemark skiing.

The major resorts have ski schools and childcare centres. Ski lessons, including lift tickets cost around $80-100 per day (less for five or seven days) and the hire of boots and skis around $50 per day (costs are relatively high due to the short season). Major resorts have a reasonable choice of *après ski* entertainment and a selection of mountain restaurants, although there's little nightlife compared with most European and North American resorts.

Thredbo (💻 www.thredbo.com.au) in NSW is Australia's leading ski resort, which is popular with overseas skiers. It has 65 marked runs (including the longest in the country at 5km/3mi) and a specially designed snowboarding 'park'. A day ticket costs $110 and a five-day pass $362, although you get a 10 per cent discount on the latter by buying online.

The Perisher Blue resort (1,680m/5,500ft), previously named Blue Cow, is the largest ski resort in the southern hemisphere, with 506 acres of snow terrain, and includes Guthega, Mount Blue Cow, Perisher Valley and Smiggin Holes; it has 30 lifts, some floodlit runs for night skiing and special snowboarding runs.

Most accommodation is in nearby Jindabyne, which is cheaper as it's a 40-minute drive to the major resorts or a few minutes on the 'Skitube', which links it to various parts of the Perisher Blue resort. One of the advantages of staying in Jindabyne is that you can travel to whichever area has the best snow conditions each day. Other resorts include Lake Crackenback and Charlotte Pass (1,780m/5,850ft), which is the highest and oldest ski resort in Australia, and only reachable by snowcat from Perisher Valley (8km/5mi). Mount Selwyn (1,492m/4,900ft, 💻 www.selwynsnow.com.au) is a day resort (no accommodation) with 12 lifts and is ideal for beginners; a one-day lift pass costs $82 and a seven-day pass $367 (both peak season). The NSW snowfields are around four hours by road from Canberra.

Victoria is home to the vast High Country and the southern end of the Great Dividing Range and the Victorian Alps, where there are nine ski resorts. The best are Falls Creek, Mount Baw Baw, Mount Buffalo, Mount Buller, Mount Hotham and Lake Mountain. There's a resort entry fee in winter. Mount Buller is Australia's most popular resort, with 80km (50mi) of runs and an extensive lift system, within easy access of Melbourne's airport and rail and coach stations (from where buses take you directly to the resort). Falls Creek has 30km (18mi) of runs, 23 lifts and a vertical drop of 267m (875ft) – you can also ski directly from the village to the lifts and back; a recent merger with Mount Hotham has created a larger resort with improved facilities. There are also a number of cross-country ski centres in Victoria, e.g. Lake Mountain (💻 www.lakemountainresort.com.au), which is the closest resort to Melbourne (just 100km/62mi away) with around 40km (25mi) of trails. There's a $12 trail fee ($5.90 for children).

It's possible to travel to the Australian Alps from Sydney or Melbourne for a day's skiing, although it's more practical to ski for at least a weekend or a few days. You can fly to Cooma, from where it's a short trip by road to most resorts. If you drive, snow chains are compulsory (they can be hired) and there are heavy fines for motorists without them. Most resorts have a wide choice of accommodation, including hostel dormitories, luxury hotels and self-catering chalets and lodges, many of which are close to ski lifts and runs. The cheapest way to enjoy skiing is to rent a resort lodge or apartment with friends and bring most of your food and drink with you, as prices are high in resorts. Accommodation at a lodge in Thredbo or Perisher costs from around $100 to $500 per person, per day sharing a double room, depending on the season. Accommodation is cheaper in Cooma and Jindabyne, from where there's a bus service to the ski slopes.

For information about skiing in Australia, see 💻 http://ski.com.au, http://skicentral.com/australia.html and www.skiingaustralia.org.au.

SWIMMING

There's a wealth of public indoor and outdoor swimming pools in all towns in Australia, where the fee is usually around $5. There are also salt-water, tidal pools on many beaches and Olympic-size pools in all major cities. In the major cities and resorts, there are swimming centres with a number of heated pools, a diving area, solarium, sauna, spa and possibly a gymnasium. Many apartment complexes, hostels, hotels and motels have their own swimming pools. Outdoor pools may open only from around October until April in Melbourne and other southern cities.

Australian kids usually learn to swim 'before they can walk'. Children learn to swim at school and regularly swim in the school or local public pool (adult lessons are also given at most pools). Students are divided into classes according to age and swimming ability, and are taught the finer points of swimming by qualified coaches. Students can obtain swimming certificates from junior through intermediate and senior up to lifesaver qualifications (to gold medal standard). Private swimming clubs abound.

Under a law that came into effect in 1997, all private pools in Australia must have fences higher than 1.5m and be inspected by local councils. Legislation is designed to reduce the incidence of drowning among children aged under five, which is the most common cause of death for children in this age group (more than 300 people drown annually in Australia).

Sea Swimming

Australia has over 7,000 beaches (many of them long with white sand) and all Australian coastal cities have a number of beaches, all of which are open to the public. Sydney has miles of ocean beaches (48km/30mi in the Sydney metropolitan area alone) and also many along its harbour (e.g. Balmoral). Sydney's Bondi Beach is one of Australia's (and the world's) most famous beaches, particularly for surfing. Manly (11km/7mi from the city centre) is another famous Sydney beach resort and the TV programme *Home and Away* was filmed at Sydney's Palm Beach.

Topless bathing is prohibited on most beaches and at all swimming pools and leisure centres, although there are designated 'free' beaches (or sections of beaches) where topless or nude bathing is permitted in all states (South Australia was the first state to have a legal nudist beach). There are sunscreen patrols on many beaches to warn people of the need to protect their skin from the sun (especially if you're naked!).

Beach life led to the surf lifesaving movement (which is both a community service and a culture which began in 1906), the surf ski (a cross between a canoe and a waterski) and the surfboat. Australian beaches are among the best guarded and patrolled in the world. All public beaches are patrolled by lifesavers, who may be volunteers (over 50,000) or paid by the local council. They are on duty each day during the summer season and year round in some resorts. When swimming off a protected beach, it's important to stick to the patrolled 'flagged' areas. Protected beaches also have shark and jellyfish nets (Sydney has an 80km/50mi underwater shark net along its coast), although they aren't failsafe. If you get into trouble while swimming off a beach manned by lifesavers, you should raise one arm in the air to alert the lifesavers.

For a guide to Australian beaches, see www.wikiaustralia.com/articles/australias-best-beaches and www.australia.com/australian_beaches.aspx.

 **Caution**

Swimmers are urged by lifesaving associations never to swim outside patrolled areas, almost all beach drownings are on unpatrolled beaches.

Dangers

There are dangerous riptides (rips), shallow sandbanks and undertows off some beaches, which claim a number of lives each year (particularly on beaches which aren't patrolled by lifesavers).

Efforts are made to keep surfers apart from swimmers on protected beaches. On surfing beaches, swimmers must stay within the swimming area defined by red and yellow flags, which may be hoisted from around 6am until 6 or 7pm in summer (year round on some beaches). They're placed to indicate the safest swimming area in the prevailing conditions, and also indicate the area under closest scrutiny by lifesavers.

You should clear the water if a siren sounds, which may signal a shark sighting or a swarm of jellyfish. Shark attacks used to be rare in Australia (although widely reported) and, until recently, on average only one Australian per year was attacked by a shark. There's still little risk of being eaten alive, but the danger is increasing as a spate of deaths in the last five years has demonstrated. (The New South Wales government is considering new measures including the GPS monitoring of shark nets and an electronic tagging programme.)

Despite the recent increase in the number of shark attacks, the most common problem in Australian waters is jellyfish, particularly box jellyfish (known as sea wasps), whose sting can be fatal (another tiny jellyfish, irukandji, is almost as deadly). During the jellyfish season, warning signs are posted along the Queensland coast from Mackay northwards. However, it's sensible to stay out of the sea during the entire wet season (from October until May) in the Northern Territory and northern Queensland.

Saltwater crocodiles can be a danger near estuaries, and you should also keep a lookout for crocodiles if you're planning to swim in rivers in northern Queensland or the Northern Territory, or in swimming holes in the outback, where a number of people are taken by crocs each year. (Victims are even taken from the edge of lakes and waterways, e.g. fishermen.) You're apparently supposed to run away from a crocodile in a zig-zag pattern, as they cannot run that way (unless the croc's had a few beers, in which case you could be in trouble!). Other dangers include cone shells, poisonous coral, blue-ringed octopus, sea-snakes and stonefish, all of which can kill you.

The water off some Australian beaches is polluted, and many Australian rivers and lakes are too polluted to swim in. A survey by the Surfrider Foundation (💻 www.surfrider.org.au) showed that around 20 per cent of Australian beaches are within 5km (3mi) of a sewage outlet (over 3bn litres of raw sewage is pumped into the sea each day), a quarter have stormwater pipes draining onto beaches, almost three-quarters have developments within just 250m of the high-tide mark, and around 80 per cent are strewn with litter, including syringes left by drug addicts. If you're after clean sea and sand, go in search of a 'wilderness' beach (although they can be dangerous as they are unpatrolled).

Some resorts have a hotline where a recorded message updates callers on pollution from stormwater or sewer outfalls and warns of other hazards, such as stinging jellyfish and dangerous currents.

Daily beachwatch reports are published in newspapers (e.g. the *Sydney Morning Herald*) giving the location of sewage and stormwater pipes. Pollution warnings are posted on some beaches. For more information, see 💻 www.cleanup.org.au, who publish an annual 'Rubbish Report'.

WATERSPORTS

All watersports, including canoeing, parasailing, power boating, rowing, sailing, sub-aqua, surfing, waterskiing and windsurfing, are popular in Australia; hardly surprising considering it has numerous rivers and lakes as well as a coastline of 36,738km (22,826mi) – and 80 per cent of Australians live within 30km (18mi) of the coast. Boats and equipment can be rented at coastal resorts, lakes and rivers, and instruction is available for most watersports in holiday areas. Jet-skis and 'surf skis' can be hired (around $75 for half an hour) in many beach resorts and on some inland lakes.

Parasailing (or parascending/paraflying), where you're attached to a parachute pulled along by a motorboat and float off into the wide blue yonder, is possible in many beach resorts (it's less frightening than jumping out of a plane

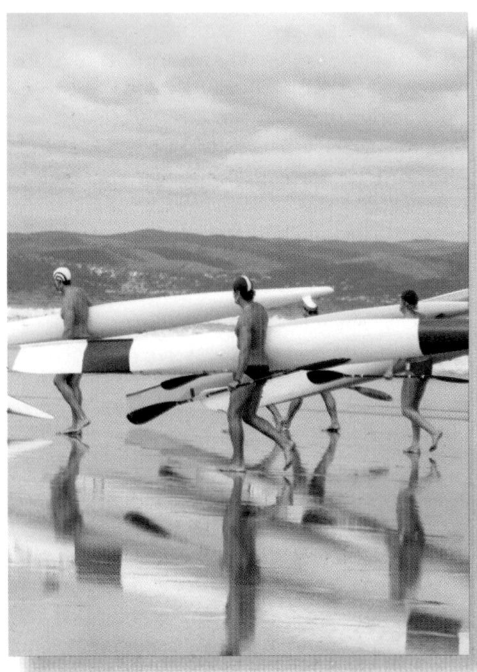

and you have a softer landing). A 10-15 minute 'flight' costs from around $125.

Every main beach resort stages a surf carnival in summer, in which individuals and teams compete for honours in board-paddling events, swimming and surfboat races, team lifesaving competitions and – the highlight – ironman/ironwoman competitions (a combination of swimming and surf ski riding). There's even a professional ironman circuit which tours Australia in the summer.

Sailing

Boat ownership is among the highest in the world, where boats of all shapes and sizes can be rented from coastal resorts throughout the country. A luxury yacht with up to eight berths costs around $750-1,000 per day (novices can charter a boat with a skipper) but a dinghy can be hired for around $50 per hour. Some companies offer flotilla trips, where you travel in a group with an experienced skipper. Sailing schools abound in resort areas and offer introductory lessons and courses for beginners up to racing standard. Airlie Beach and the Whitsunday Islands are the most popular sailing areas in Queensland, which is the centre of the yacht charter business. In many resorts it's possible to get a job or a free ride as a crew member on a yacht.

Yacht racing is popular in all areas, including 18-foot skiff (an Australian invention) races, which are staged in Sydney Harbour on most Saturdays during the summer. One of Australia's major sporting events is the Sydney to Hobart yacht race (run annually since 1945), which starts on 26th December. It's a handicap race over 630 nautical miles and attracts competitors from all over the world.

For more information, see 💻 www.yachting.org.au.

> **▲ Caution**
>
> There has been a spate of fatal boating and sailing accidents in recent years, many because the participants weren't wearing lifejackets, which are essential at all times, particularly for children. A book entitled *Go Boating Safely* is published by the Australian Government Publishing Service.

Scuba Diving & Snorkelling

Australia is a Mecca for scuba divers and snorkellers, particularly the Great Barrier Reef (see below), and diving shops abound in resort areas and the major cities. Divers in Australia need a Professional Association of Diving Instructors (PADI) certificate. To obtain one in Australia you usually require a doctor's certificate that you're fit to dive and must show that you can tread water for ten minutes and swim 200m to be accepted on a course. Tuition in Australia is among the cheapest available in tropical waters and a PADI certificate course lasts five days for beginners and costs between $500 and $1,000.

There are diving schools in many coastal towns in Queensland, among the most popular of which are Airlie Beach, Cairns and Townsville. Shop around and ask about courses and avoid cheap 'cowboy' operators, as beginners have occasionally died after receiving poor tuition from these. Some diving clubs offer free introductory lessons in a local pool. Not all courses offer good value and with the cheaper courses you're likely to spend most of the time in a classroom or pool. A good mix is two days in the classroom and pool, a day trip to the coast (ideally, the Great Barrier Reef), and perhaps a further two days at sea, spending the night on board.

Great Barrier Reef

The Great Barrier Reef (2,000km/1,240mi in length) offers some of the world's best diving and is one of the natural wonders of the world (a World Heritage Site), with some 400 different types of coral and around 1,500 species of fish. Experts enthuse about the diving on the outer reef wall and you can rent underwater photographic equipment. You can also wreck dive on the reef, which is the graveyard of over 500 ships.

Many diving boats operate out of Cairns and other towns on the northern Queensland coast (boats are licensed to operate from around 20 sites). A day trip from Cairns costs around $150 for snorkellers and $200 for scuba divers, which includes two tank dives. Full snorkelling gear can be hired for around $30 a day, although some day trip operators provide it for free. During the wet season (January to

March), however, floods can wash mud out into the ocean, seriously reducing viability. There are rules regarding where you can dive on the reef and what you can do, e.g. spearfishing is prohibited most places.

For information, see 💻 www.greatbarrierreef.org and www.gbrmpa.gov.au.

It isn't necessary to be a scuba diver or snorkeller to enjoy the Great Barrier Reef, which you can view from a glass-bottomed boat.

Other Locations

Although the Great Barrier Reef is the main destination for divers in Australia, there are interesting alternatives, including Fly Point at Port Stephens (north of Newcastle, NSW) and Ningaloo Marine Park (extending for 260km/160mi along the western side of the Northwest Cape in Western Australia), which is a smaller, more accessible version of the Great Barrier Reef (in places it's only a few hundred metres offshore). In some areas there are 18th-century wrecks (e.g. off Rottnest Island near Perth, WA) and Second World War wrecks, which make interesting dives.

Surfing & Windsurfing

Surfing is a way of life rather than just a sport in Australia, where surfers (variously known as seaweed munchers, shark-suckers, surfies and waxheads) are mocked for their fanaticism. A number of international surfing competitions are staged in Australia, which has many professional surfers (Australian Mark Richards, who won the world title four times from 1979 to 1982, is considered the greatest competitive surfer of all time).

There are surfing schools in all major (and many minor) surfing areas, which run beginners' courses usually lasting three to seven days. It's best to have a few lessons before buying your own board to see whether you take to it (surfboards can be hired for around $40 per hour and some resort hotels provide the free use of boards for guests). A wetsuit is usually necessary in winter. Some schools operate surfing 'safari' trips, where you camp in remote locations and learn how to surf, fish and look after yourself in the wild. Surfing variations include surf mats, surfoplanes and boogie boards (small boards that you lie on while learning to master a proper surfboard). Boogie board users comprise a large proportion of those rescued by lifesavers. Surfers must keep to the designated surfing areas off beaches; if you fail to comply, your board can be confiscated.

The best surfing is usually in NSW and Western Australia. The best beaches in Sydney are on the south shore, including Bondi, Coogee, Maroubra and Tamarama. Cronulla, south of Botany Bay, is also popular, and there are also many beaches between Manly and Palm Beach (such as North Narrabeen) on the North Shore. Byron Bay in northern NSW is considered one of Australia's best surfing areas. If you live in Canberra, the nearest good surfing beach is around 160km (100mi) away at Batemans Bay.

The best surfing close to Melbourne is found at Mornington peninsula on the Great Ocean Road. Anglesea, Bells Beach, Jan Juc, Lorne and Torquay are also popular surfing venues in Victoria. In South Australia you need to travel to Pondalowie for the state's most reliable and strongest waves. Tasmania has some good surfing beaches, the best of which is Marrawah on the west coast, although the sea is very cold. Surfing conditions are poor north of Brisbane and Surfers' Paradise doesn't live up to its name, although Coolangatta at the south end of the Gold Coast offers good surfing at Kirra beach. Cottesloe and Leighton are popular surfing venues in Perth, although the best surf is found at Yallingup further south. Surf carnivals are held in popular surfing resorts during the season (December to April).

The website Coast Watch (💻 www.coastalwatch.com/camera/cameraoverview.aspx) provides an online surfcam facility for the main surfing areas in Queensland, NSW, Victoria, South Australia and Western Australia, so you can check the actual conditions online.

Enthusiasts may wish to buy a copy of *Surfing Australia* by Mark Thornley (Periplus Publishing). There are a number of magazines for surfers, including *Surfing Life* (💻 www.surfinglife.com.au) and *Tracks* (💻 www.

tracksmag.com), plus a plethora of websites, including 💻 www.realsurf.com, www.surfingaustralia.com and www.surfinfo.com.au.

Windsurfing is popular throughout Australia, and schools abound in beach resorts and on inland lakes (you probably learn faster on an inland lake than on coastal waters). Tuition costs around $200 for two half-days with a wetsuit included; windsurfer hire costs around $75 per day.

Rowing, Canoeing & Rafting

Rowing is a serious sport in Australia, which is one of the most successful countries in world and Olympic competition (after the Poms!), and there are rowing clubs in all major cities and towns (see 💻 www.rowingaustralia.com.au for information). Canoeing is popular on rivers and lakes, where there are numerous clubs offering courses, equipment hire and tours (the *Canoeing Guide to NSW* is published by Australian Canoeing (💻 www.canoe.org.au), and Australia has a number of world champion canoeists.

White-water rafting is popular in Australia, with its many excellent rapid rivers graded from 1 (easy) to 6 (heeelp!!!!!). Among Australia's wildest rivers are the Franklin and Gordon in Tasmania. The Caltex Avon Descent is Australia's greatest (or, depending on your point of view, most scary) whitewater experience, covering 133km (83mi) on the Avon River in Western Australia from Northam to Perth.

Royal Arcade, Melbourne, VIC

17. SHOPPING

Australia isn't one of the world's great shopping countries, although the variety and quality of goods on offer has improved considerably in the last few decades and the major cities can now hold their own with most countries. There's a reasonable choice of chain, department and international stores in the major cities, and exclusive boutiques and chic stores abound in arcades and shopping centres.

The retail sector was badly hit by the credit crunch in the last few years, particularly shops selling designer goods – you know the economy isn't doing so well when the super-rich start cutting back! In recent years many Australians have become bargain hunters, deserting boutique and department stores for no-frills retailers and discount stores such as Big W (owned by Woolworths), Harris Scarfe, Kmart and Target. As in many other countries, High Street stores have suffered in recent years due to the onslaught of Internet shopping, where prices are generally much lower.

Consumers haven't always had the best deal in Australia, where cartels and protectionism has increased prices in the past, although things have improved considerably in the last decade or so. The price of many consumer goods such as cameras, computers, electrical apparatus, household appliances, and TV and stereo systems has fallen dramatically in recent years, although you may still be better off buying some items abroad and paying duty (e.g. books, CDs and DVDs – there's no GST on goods valued at below $1,000).

In stark contrast to the cities, small country towns are likely to have only a general store and a few other shops. Prices are also higher in rural areas due to freight costs, and most people who live in the country stock up on essentials and buy expensive items when visiting a city or large town, or shop by mail-order or via the internet.

There are many small, family-run stores in Australia, particularly in rural areas, small towns and the suburbs of major cities, although Australia's shopping scene has been transformed in the last few decades with the opening of numerous large shopping centres (malls) and vast supermarkets. Following the trend in most developed countries, there has been a drift away from town centres by retailers to out-of-town shopping malls, which has left some town centres run down and deserted. However, in some areas too many shopping malls were built for too few customers and some are now being redesigned, redeveloped, reinvented or even demolished. Towns are turning to 'street-scaping', i.e. reviving streets by landscaping, installing traffic 'calming' (speed bumps) or pedestrianising them. Australian cities have excellent shopping arcades, many housed in fine period buildings, and pedestrianised streets, although parking can be a nightmare.

There's generally no bargaining or bartering in Australia, although if you plan to spend a lot of money or buy something expensive, you shouldn't be reticent about asking for a discount (except in department and chain stores and supermarkets, where prices are fixed). Many shops will match any genuine advertised price, although often reluctantly. Taxes are usually included in advertised prices.

Always shop around before buying, but make sure that you're comparing similar goods or services, as it's easy to 'save' money by purchasing inferior products.

Goods made in Australia often have a green and gold symbol to distinguish them from less expensive (and supposedly inferior) goods made in Asia.

A wealth of quality arts and crafts are sold in Australia, including ceramics, embroidery, glassware, handbags, hand-woven and knitted woollen garments, hides and skins (particularly sheep- and lambskin products), jewellery (e.g. diamonds, gold, opals and pearls), leather goods, paintings, rugs, traditional Australian 'outback' clothing, and woodwork. Aboriginal art (of which there are many styles produced by different tribes) is popular and is best purchased direct from artists' cooperatives or Aborigine-owned shops rather than from tourist shops. It's cheapest in Alice Springs, Darwin and outback towns, although genuine Aboriginal art can be expensive. Aboriginal art can be purchase direct from Aboriginal owned cooperatives such as such as 💻 http://aboriginalart.com.au and www.aboriginalaustralia.com. Bear in mind that a lot of 'Aboriginal' artwork is mass-produced junk, and cheap 'fake' Aboriginal souvenirs are also made in Asia, therefore before buying anything always check where it was made and obtain a guarantee.

Most shops accept major credit and debit cards, although you may be asked for proof of identification. Personal cheques aren't usually accepted. Many retail outlets require customers to allow staff to search their bags (excluding small bags such as handbags) when paying or leaving a shop. This is usually shown by a sign; by entering a shop you consent to having your bags searched (no sign, no checks).

If you have any questions about your rights as a consumer, contact your local Citizens' Advice Bureau, consumer affairs office or fair trading bureau. Most retailers, particularly department and chain stores, exchange goods or give a refund without question, but smaller shops aren't so enthusiastic. The quality of service and assistance in shops ranges from excellent to poor, depending on the type of shop, although generally Australian stores aren't renowned for their service. See also **Consumer Rights** on page 304.

If you're looking for a particular item or anything unusual, the *Yellow Pages* (💻 www.yellowpages.com.au) can save you a lot of time and trouble (and shoe leather). You can also search for local business online via Local Direct (💻 www.localdirect.com.au) and there's also a number of shopping comparison websites where you can compare prices, including 💻 www.ausprices.com.au, www.getprice.com.au and www.shopbot.com.au.

SALES & BARGAIN SHOPPING

Most shops hold sales at various times of the year, the largest of which are in December/January and July. The most popular sales are the post-Christmas (or end-of-year) sales, which traditionally start on 26th December, when savings of over 50 per cent are possible. Some shops seem to have a permanent sale, although retailers aren't permitted to advertise goods as reduced when they've never been advertised or sold at a higher price.

A number of magazines are published for shoppers including *Bargain Shoppers Melbourne*, *Bargain Shoppers Sydney* and the *Sydney Factory Shopping Guide* (see 💻 www.universalmagazines.com.au). See also Bargain Shopper (💻 www.bargainshopper.com.au), Sydney and Melbourne's bargain outlet directory, Melbourne Shopping Tours (💻 www.melbourneshoppingtours.com.au) and the Discount Shopping Guide (💻 www.discountshoppingguide.com.au).

There's a lively second-hand market in Australia for almost everything, from antiques to motor cars, computers to photographic equipment. With such a large second-hand market there are often bargains to be found, particularly if you're quick off the mark. Many towns have a local second-hand or junk store and charity shops (e.g. Salvation Army or Vincent de Paul), selling new and secondhand articles for charity, where most of your money goes to help those in need.

There are a number of websites devoted to bargain hunters such as Ebay (💻 www.ebay.

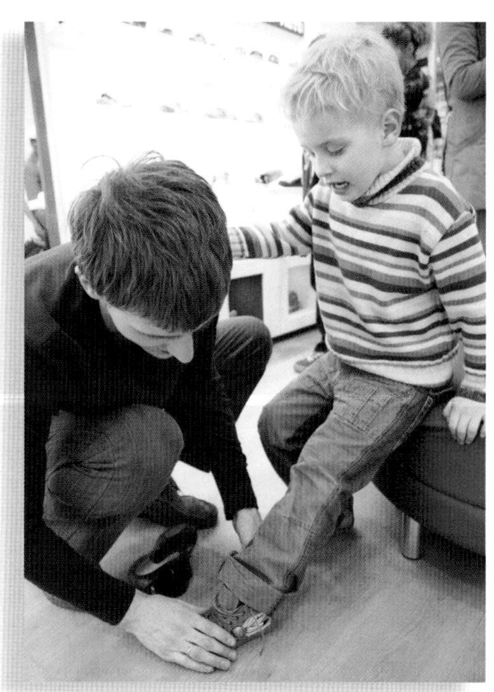

com.au) and Trading Post (💻 www.tradingpost.com.au).

Classified advertisements in local newspapers are also a good source of bargains, particularly for furniture and household appliances. Shopping centre (mall) and newsagent bulletin boards and company notice boards may also prove fruitful. Car boot (trunk) sales are gaining popularity in Australia, and garage sales, where people sell their surplus belongings at bargain prices, are also popular. Sales may be advertised in local newspapers and signposted on local roads (they're usually held at weekends).

Another place to pick up a bargain is at an auction, although it helps to have specialist knowledge about what you're buying (you'll be competing with experts). Auctions are held in Australia throughout the year for everything from antiques and paintings to motorcars and property. Local auctions are widely advertised in newspapers and via leaflets. There are antique shops and centres in most towns, and street markets (see below) and antique fairs are common in the major cities (where you can pick up interesting items – but you must get there early to beat the dealers to the best buys). For information about markets, ask at your local tourist office or library.

SHOPPING HOURS

Shopping hours in Australia vary with the city or town, the state or territory and the day of the week, but generally are among the most liberal in the world. Shopping hours have been extended in recent years, and in some states (e.g. Victoria) shops can now open 24 hours a day, seven days a week, apart from a few Public Holidays, e.g. before 1pm on ANZAC day, and at any time on Christmas Day and Good Friday. Most large stores and many smaller shops are open from 9am till 5 or 6pm on Sundays.

In the major cities, many shops are open for up to 12 hours a day (some are even open 24 hours) and on Sundays, and many remain open all day on Saturdays. Department stores may open on Sundays (e.g. from 10am to 4pm) and some open earlier on sales days, e.g. at 7.30 or 8am. City chemists, delicatessens and newsagents usually open on Sundays, e.g. from 8am until 8pm, and chemists may open up to 24 hours a day. There are Food Plus shops and 7–11 stores (modelled on the eponymous American stores) in the major cities which, despite their name, open 24 hours a day and may be 'attached' to a petrol station.

Harbourside shopping centres in Sydney (such as Darling Harbour) are open from 10am to 9pm, Monday to Saturday and from 10am to 6pm on Sundays. Many city bookshops are open during the evenings and throughout weekends. Even shops which aren't open all day and all night are usually open until 9 or 9.30pm one evening per week, generally Thursday or Friday.

In some areas, shops stay open an hour later in summer than in winter. Most shops in resorts such as the Gold and Sunshine Coasts are open at weekends and on Public Holidays as well as late at night. Normal shopping hours in country areas are usually from around 8.30 or 9am to between 5 and 6pm, Monday to Friday, and from 9am until noon on Saturday.

DEPARTMENT & CHAIN STORES

Australia has a number of excellent department and chain stores. A number of department stores are housed in beautiful art-deco or Victorian buildings and many are air-conditioned with a restaurant or caféteria, telephones and toilets. The floor at street level is designated the ground floor in Australia, the floor above the ground floor is the first floor and the floor below the ground floor is usually called the basement.

The major department store chains in Australia include Myer (www.myer.com.au) with 68 outlets and David Jones (www.davidjones.com.au) with 36 stores, both of which have branches in most major cities; David Jones boasts 12 stores in Sydney, one with an excellent international food hall. Department stores have struggled in recent years, under pressure from no-frills retailers, discount stores and internet retailers, although some have been revitalised and are making a comeback.

There are dozens of chain stores in Australia, selling everything from books and clothes to household goods and electronics (e.g. cameras, computers and mobile phones); typical of the latter are JB Hi-Fi (www.jbhifi.com.au), Dick Smith (www.dse.com.au) and Strathfield (www.strathfield.com). Australia's largest discount chain stores include Big W (www.bigw.com.au), Harris Scarfe (www.harrisscarfe.com.au), Kmart (www.kmart.com.au) and Target (www.target.com.au).

Many department and chain stores provide customer accounts and allow the account balance to be repaid over a period of time, although this isn't usually wise as interest rates are very high. Many department and chain stores offer gift vouchers. Department stores (and many smaller shops) provide a gift wrapping service, particularly at Christmas time, and deliver goods locally or send them by post/courier, both within Australia and worldwide.

SHOPPING CENTRES

In the last few decades, numerous vast indoor shopping centres (called malls after their American counterparts) have sprung up in out-of-town areas throughout Australia. Malls usually contain a huge selection of shops, including a large department store and many of the most popular chain stores, and are open seven days a week. The main attractions are one-stop shopping and free parking, which means you can simply wheel your trolley load of purchases to your car. The largest malls incorporate a wide range of leisure attractions, including children's play areas, cinemas, food halls, fun parks, games arcades, and a variety of cafés, pubs and restaurants.

Caution

Most towns and cities have covered shopping centres, although parking is often expensive and difficult in city and town centres, particularly on Saturdays, and parking areas may be located some distance from shops.

The largest developer and operator of shopping centres in Australia (and the world) is Westfield (http://westfield.com.au), which has vast shopping centres in all states and territories except for the Northern Territory and Tasmania. The largest shopping centres are Knox City Shopping Centre (www.knoxcity.com.au) at Wantirna South (Melbourne), which is the largest shopping centre in the southern hemisphere, and Westfield Fountain Gate in Narre Warren (Melbourne). Among the best downtown shopping centres are the vast Melbourne Central (www.melbournecentral.com.au) and The Galeries Victoria (www.tgv.com.au) and MLC Centre (www.mlccentre.com.au), both in Sydney.

Australia cities have a number of elegant Victorian arcades, including the Block and Royal Arcades (www.royalarcade.com.au) in Melbourne, and the Queen Victoria Building (www.qvb.com.au) and Strand Arcade (www.strandarcade.com.au) in Sydney. Many city malls are housed in restored period buildings (such as the converted GPO building in Sydney, now the New Mall), which are often connected by tunnels and walkways to other shops and centres.

MARKETS

Most small towns have markets on one or two days a week, and in major cities and towns there may be a market (or a number) on most days of the week. Markets are generally inexpensive (excluding farmers' markets), colourful and interesting, and are often a good place for shrewd shoppers to pick up bargains, although you need to be careful what you buy (beware of fakes). Items commonly for sale in markets include arts and crafts, books, clothes, fresh food, household wares and jewellery. Markets are the best place to buy fresh food, where the quality and variety rivals that of any country. Arts and craft markets are common in major cities and resort towns, where artisans can often be seen at work.

Flea markets are popular in the major cities and sell secondhand goods, including antiques, books, bric-a-brac, clothes and records. Some towns have permanent covered or indoor market places where markets are held from Monday to Saturday, and in some cities there are also popular outdoor Sunday markets. Check with your local council, library or tourist office for information (guides are available to markets in some states, e.g. Victoria).

For the latest information about Australian markets, obtain a copy of *Australian Markets & Fairs* magazine (💻 www.marketsandfairs.com.au).

FOOD

The quality and variety of food in Australia is generally excellent and the equal of any country. Food outlets include delicatessens (delis), ethnic food shops, general and corner shops, markets (where the freshest fish, meat and other produce are usually available) and, of course, supermarkets. There's a wealth of gourmet food shops in the major cities offering everything from bread and cheese to fruit and vegetables, from cakes and pastries to coffee and tea. You can buy almost any ethnic food and ingredients in the major cities, where there may also be shops specialising in imported American and British foods, although prices can be high. Many shops and supermarkets deliver groceries for a fee.

Australians have been eating more healthily in recent years, consuming less red meat, although they're still big meat eaters, and alcohol, and eating more fruit and vegetables (although you wouldn't think so from the size of many people!). Meat is reasonably priced and excellent quality, as is fresh fish and seafood (although it can be expensive). In recent years the marketeers have been trying to encourage Aussies to eat kangaroo, emu, crocodile – and even camel meat – but it's a hard slog. (Apparently over 1m camels now roam the outback inflicting major damage on desert ecosystems, so the latest jingle may become 'toss a camel on the barbie'!)

Most supermarkets sell good quality fruit and vegetables, although you should avoid packaged produce which may be over-ripe or in poor condition, e.g. rock hard as it's been poorly stored or frozen. Many supermarkets bake their own bread on the premises and most have cheese, fresh fish and meat counters, as well as delicatessens. Home cooking is one of the casualties of modern living and most Australians don't have sufficient time to shop and cook elaborate meals. Consequently, prepared, oven-ready meals, microwave food and take-away meals are increasingly popular, and all supermarkets cater for this lucrative growth market. Food prices in Australia vary according to the city, the shop and the season, but have risen sharply in recent years (see **Cost of Living** on page 229).

Australians buy most of their groceries in supermarkets, which are (not surprisingly) among Australia's most profitable retailers. However, despite increasing pressure from the major supermarket chains, independent grocers are surviving by providing locally-sourced products and personal service.

Supermarkets

The largest supermarket chains in Australia are Woolworths (🖳 www.woolworths.com.au) and Coles (🖳 www.coles.com.au), which together account for some 70 per cent of the market, the remainder being split between a few smaller players and independents. Woolworths has over 1,400 stores throughout Australia, including a chain of smaller Metro supermarkets, employing some 140,000 people (around one in every 100 Australians of working age). It was the first Australian supermarket to introduce food shopping via the internet (🖳 www2.woolworthsonline.com.au).

Coles has over 750 stores employing over 90,000 people. It also has smaller Coles Express stores in city centres stocking around 13,000 products and offering up-market deli products, gourmet take-home meals, a home catering service and personalised cakes, e.g. for office celebrations. Coles also offers online shopping and home deliveries (🖳 www.colesonline.com.au) for a fee, which depends on the delivery time. Coles also have over 600 petrol stations.

The latest entrant into the Australian food business is the German supermarket chain, Aldi (🖳 www.aldi.com.au), who entered the market in 2001 and now have over 200 stores in the ACT, New South Wales, Queensland and Victoria. Aldi are world-famous for their low prices and excellent value, and it's claimed that you can save up to 50 per cent on your groceries by shopping there.

Supermarkets may have in-store bank kiosks and petrol stations, and they also have plans to introduce news agencies and pharmacies. Major supermarkets open seven days a week and in some cities remain open until midnight or even 24/7. They provide trolleys, which may require a deposit; some stores insist that customers use a trolley or basket even when they're buying only a few items. Most supermarkets provide free plastic carrier bags and boxes, and provide staff to help pack your purchases.

All supermarkets use computerised (electronic point-of-sale) pricing systems where a bar code is included on the labels of goods and is read by a laser reader at the checkout. Always check your receipt carefully, as customers are frequently overcharged, particularly on special offer items. In most supermarkets, if an item is scanned at a higher price than advertised (or displayed), you're usually entitled to it free under the voluntary code of practice of the Australian Supermarket Institute.

Self-scanning, where customers scan their own goods, has been introduced in some supermarkets in recent years. Under this system, which reduces the time spent at checkouts, spot checks are made to deter cheats. In future, all supermarkets are expected to offer this option, although they won't do away with checkout staff (known as 'laser ladies') entirely.

ALCOHOL

The average Australian family spends around $25 to $50 a week on alcohol (liquor), which can only be purchased from licensed bottle shops (also called grog shops), pubs and restaurants; it isn't sold in food shops or supermarkets. There are drive-in bottle shops, possibly with 'express' and 'browse' lanes, in major cities, where the largest and cheapest chains include Dan Murphy's (🖳 www.danmurphys.com.au), who claim to beat any advertised price, and Liquorland (🖳 www.liquorland.com.au). Kemenys (🖳 www.kemenys.com.au), an online liquor shop, claims to be Australia's number one wine merchant. Note that some liquor stores charge for delivery, so take this into account when comparing prices. Grog shop opening hours vary with the state or territory, e.g. from 8.30am until 8.30pm, or 10am until 10pm, Monday to Saturday. There are reduced opening hours on Sundays.

Alcohol – and particularly wine – is increasingly sold online by a wealth of companies (in addition to those listed above), including Cellarmaster Wines (🖳 www.cellarmasters.com.au), Get Wines Direct (🖳 www.getwinesdirect.com) and Raffles Liquor Merchants (🖳 www.liquormerchant.com.au). Other major players include Woolworths,

Cracka Wines and Catch of the Day. Australians buy some 20 per cent of all bottled wines online, compared with less than 10 per cent in most other countries.

You must be aged over 18 to buy alcohol or consume it in a public place, which is now banned in most towns.

Wine

Although part of the 'new world', Australia isn't a newcomer when it comes to wine production; vines were first imported in 1788 and commercial production started in the 1820s in New South Wales (NSW) and Tasmania, and in the 1840s in South Australia, Victoria and Western Australia. Until 1960, some 80 per cent of Australian wine was fortified wine. Today, over 90 per cent is table wine and the country has some 2,500 wineries, although many are tiny. Only a dozen years ago, Australia imported more wine than it exported, although it's one of the country's fastest-growing exports; the country exports, worth over $2.5bn. Australia produces just 4 per cent of total world wine production, but is the fourth-largest exporter by volume after Italy, France and Spain.

The industry has an ambitious long-term strategy known as Vision 2025, by which date Australian wine is expected to be worth $4.5bn in annual sales and the industry to be the world's most profitable and influential. Exports are made to around 100 countries, the largest markets in the early 21st century being the UK, the US, Canada, New Zealand and China. However, while exports have soared, home sales have remained static in recent years, the average annual consumption per head being around 20 litres – Australians are increasingly choosing quality over quantity and drinking more premium wines (some of the best Australian wines rarely reaching foreign markets).

Australia makes good sparkling wines (both red and white), which are produced by the *méthode champenoise* (fermented in the bottle), although they cannot officially be called champagne. A reasonable sparkler can be purchased for $15 to $20. It's also noted for its fortified wines, although they aren't well known overseas. These include brandy, madeira, muscat, port (red and white), sherry and tokay (the last having little in common with the Hungarian wine after which it's named), the best of which are world-beaters. Port, which is made in Victoria, is particularly popular, the best vintages selling for $80 to $100 per bottle (and are a match for the best that Portugal has to offer), while a fair non-vintage, such as Hardy's Tall Ships Tawny Port, can be purchased for around $15.

Australian wines have earned an increasing international reputation in recent years, with their distinctive, deep fruity flavour, full-bodied character and consistency. In fact, they have been astounding judges and competitors at international wine exhibitions for over a century – one (apocryphal?) story tells of an Australian wine winning a competition in France in the 19th century and promptly losing it again when it was discovered where the wine was produced!

Australian winemakers have a pragmatic approach and are quick to introduce the latest technology; vineyards are noted for their high yields and low production costs. Producers aren't afraid to experiment; indeed, many go out of their way to introduce new grape varieties and create exciting new blends (they threw out the rule book decades ago). The climate, modern equipment, soil and techniques, allied to the Australians' freedom from tradition and love of experimentation, combine to produce some of the best and most original wines in the world. Australian wines are also noted for their high alcohol content, which for reds can be as high as 15 per cent.

Regions

South Australia produces over half of Australia's wine, NSW (including the ACT) 27 per cent, and Victoria 22 per cent, the remainder being shared between Tasmania, Western Australia and Queensland, with a small area of production around Alice Springs in the Northern Territory. The most famous wine regions are the Barossa Valley, Clare Valley and Coonawarra in South Australia; the Hunter Valley in New South Wales (famous for its white wines, particularly chardonnay); the Geelong area, Mornington Peninsula, Rutherglen/Milawa (port and muscat) and Yarra Valley, where sparkling wines are produced, in Victoria; and the Margaret River and Swan River Valley in Western Australia.

Although each region is noted for a particular style of wine and specific grape varieties (varietal wines – most famously from cabernet sauvignon, shiraz and chardonnay), there's also a lot of experimentation and blending of grapes between regions. In addition to the major producers, there are also numerous small independent producers, sometimes called boutique vineyards, making high-quality wines.

Australia has no national wine appellation or quality control system, and buyers need to rely on the reputation of individual producers, which is generally an excellent guide, as there's little year-on-year variation in quality.

Wineries

Many wine producers welcome visitors and provide tastings, although you may need to make an appointment at the smaller wineries, which are often more attractive than the larger, more commercialised establishments. Some wineries charge a fee of a few dollars, which is refunded if you buy. Wine at wineries isn't necessarily cheap, however, and can be much more expensive than at bottle shops. Some wineries have restaurants where you can sample excellent local food and wines at the same time. Most wine regions have a visitors' centre, e.g. the Barossa Valley Visitors' Centre, open from 9am to 5pm, Monday to Friday and from 10am to 4pm on weekends and Public Holidays.

Prices

The price of Australian wine has been increasing steadily over the years and the best are now among the more expensive in the world. Prices have increased due to a shortage of quality grapes, which has been exacerbated in recent years due to water shortages in some regions. A quaffable bottle of wine costs around \$10 to \$15, while \$20 to \$25 buys an excellent bottle. Imported wines are also available in Australia, but are expensive compared with similar quality local wines.

Australia invented the wine box ('chateau cardboard') in 1974; it consists of a plastic bag in a box with a built-in tap. Around half of all wine sold in Australia is sold in boxes (flatteringly referred to as casks). Wine boxes are good value, but no longer the bargain they once were, and cost from \$12 to \$18 for three or four litres, with up-market wines costing around \$16 for a two-litre box.

Information

There are many books about Australian wine, including James Halliday's *Australian Wine*

Companion (Hardie Grant), *The Penguin Good Australian Wine Guide* by Huon Hooke & Mark Shield, which contains ratings for all of Australia's premium wines, and *The Wine Atlas of Australia* by James Halliday (Mitchell Beazley). There are also a number of wine magazines, including *Gourmet Traveller Wine* (💻 www.gourmettravellerwine.com.au) and *Wine Estate* (💻 www.winestate.com.au), plus many websitessuch as 💻 www.southaustralianwines.com and www.wineaustralia.com.

Beer & Other Drinks

Before the Second World War, Australia was largely a beer-drinking country, and Australians still consume far more beer than wine – over 100 litres per head annually. Beer is sold in 375ml bottles (stubbies), 750ml bottles and 375ml cans. The cost of a dozen 750ml bottles is around $45 to $50. Most beer bottles have twist off caps, so no bottle-opener is required. Canned beer costs around $1.75 for single cans (375ml) reducing to around $1.35 per can when you buy a case of 24. 'No name' beers cost around 20 per cent less than the market leaders and don't taste significantly different.

Some companies give a refund (e.g. 10¢) on both bottles and cans for recycling. For more information about Australian beer, see **Bars & Pubs** on page 262.

Australians don't drink a lot of spirits such as whisky and gin (around a litre per head, per year). A bottle of 'cheap' Scotch whisky or London gin costs around $30 to $40.

Australia's most famous spirit is rum, of which the Bundaberg ('Bundy') brand is the national spirit (there are also 'over-proof' rums, which are lethal).

CLOTHES

Good quality clothes are expensive in Australia, although the mild climate for much of the year means that most people don't need an extensive wardrobe. It used to be said (with some justification) that fashions arrived in Australia a decade after they had swept Europe and North America, although this is certainly no longer the case. Today, Australian fashion shops offer a wide range of attire, from traditional made-to-measure clothing to the latest ready-to-wear fashions, with prices ranging from a few dollars to several thousand. Top quality and exclusive (i.e. expensive) international women's and men's fashion shops abound, and all the leading international labels are available in the major cities.

In addition to department and chain stores (see above), all towns and cities have a wealth of independent shops covering the whole fashion spectrum and all price brackets. Bush clothes (or 'bush chic') can be purchased at specialist shops, including R M Williams (💻 www.rmwilliams.com.au), whose clothing has achieved cult status, and the Thomas Cook Boot and Clothing Company in Sydney (💻 http://thomascookclothing.com.au). Bush clothes include leather belts, moleskins (trousers made of closely woven cotton), oilskin raincoats (e.g. Drizabone – 💻 www.drizabone.com.au), riding boots, sheepskin coats, wide-brimmed hats (e.g. Akubra – 💻 www.akubra.com.au) and work shirts.

Although Australia's once thriving clothing manufacturing industry has largely disappeared, the country has a number of celebrated designers, some of whom have received international acclaim, including Nicole Fendel, Nobody, Sass & Bide, Shakuhachi, Stylestalker and Zimmermann (see 💻 www.cultureandrecreation.gov.au/articles/fashion). Nowadays, most clothes are imported from Asia and many aren't of the high quality common in Europe and North America. However, although the quality of foreign-made clothes may occasionally be suspect, you usually get what you pay for.

> ☑ **SURVIVAL TIP**
>
> **Shopping malls and markets are the best place to shop for reasonably priced clothes, and mail-order fashion offers (in newspapers and magazines) usually provide good value.**

Reasonable clothes can also be purchased at huge savings from factory outlets, which also sell 'designer' clothes, although you should try them for size and check for faults. There are vintage and second-hand clothing shops and markets in most Australian cities, plus clothes hire shops, where you can hire anything from a ball gown to a wedding dress, a morning suit to an evening dress.

The sizing of clothes in Australia follows the American rather than the British system – i.e. 'medium' is usually on the large side. Women's clothing manufacturers usually base their sizes on the average size 12, and many women find it difficult to find fashionable clothes that fit. Most shops provide a tailoring or alteration service (for a small fee) and many also provide a made-to-measure service.

NEWSPAPERS, MAGAZINES & BOOKS

Australians read more newspapers per head than most other nationalities, including national, state, city, regional and suburban newspapers. In general, the Australian press is fairly parochial and provides scant coverage of foreign news (unless it's a major news item), and you shouldn't expect unbiased political reporting in Australian newspapers, which often reflect the political bias of their owners. Most major newspapers are owned by the News Corporation (run by Rupert Murdoch) or John Fairfax Holdings.

Daily and Sunday newspapers range from the broadsheet 'quality' newspapers for serious readers and the popular tabloids. There are just two national dailies, *The Australian* (including *The Weekend Australian* on Saturdays) and *The Australian Financial Review* (Monday to Friday only). *The Australian* is Australia's foremost newspaper, printed simultaneously at six sites around the country from Monday to Friday. Other major newspapers are either published state-wide or limited to one city. Those with the largest circulation are *The Herald-Sun* (Melbourne), *The Daily Telegraph* (Sydney), *The Sydney Morning Herald*, *The West Australian* (Perth), *The Courier Mail* (Brisbane), *The Age* (Melbourne) and *The Advertiser* (Adelaide). Most large regional cities have daily newspapers, and smaller towns publish weekly newspapers, (there are also suburban weeklies in capital cities).

Most dailies publish larger Saturday editions, which usually sell around 50 per cent more copies than the weekday editions and may include weekend supplements, e.g. *The Weekend Australian* and *The Sydney Morning Herald*. The major Sunday newspapers include *The Sunday Telegraph* (Sydney), *The Sunday Mail* (Brisbane), *The Sun-Herald* (Sydney), *The Sunday Herald-Sun* (Melbourne), *The Sunday Times* (Perth) and *The Sunday Mail* (Adelaide). Most Sunday newspapers are tabloids and aren't as good quality as the daily newspapers. Most cities also have evening newspapers.

> **☑ SURVIVAL TIP**
>
> **Most Australian newspapers can be accessed online, e.g. 💻 www.newspapers.com.au, which lists newspapers by state and territory, and 💻 www.onlinenewspapers.com/australi.htm.**

The circulation figures of Australian newspapers are relatively small by international standards, for example, around 130,000 for *The Australian* and over 670,000 for *The Sunday Telegraph*.

There's an active foreign-language press in Australia catering to immigrants of many different nationalities and producing around 150 publications in 40 languages. Foreign newspapers are also available from international news agencies in major cities but are expensive and usually a few days old when they arrive in Australia – better to read them online. They're also available in some (e.g. state) libraries.

Newspapers of particular interest to British expatriates include the weekly International Express and the Weekly Telegraph, which contain a summary of the week's most important news; they're available on subscription and from many newsagents in Australia.

Newsagents are open long hours in cities and also on Sundays. Prices are generally higher in remote areas and states other than where a newspaper is published, due to the high cost of distribution. Most cafés and tea rooms provide free newspapers for customers to read on the premises, and newspapers can also be read in public libraries and at newspaper offices.

Australians are avid magazine readers, and around 1,000 titles are published each month, plus a further 700 trade publications.

Foreign magazines are also popular and widely available in the major cities, particularly British and American magazines. Popular Australian political and business magazines include the *Business Review Weekly* and *My Business*. Women's magazines abound and include *Family Circle, Good Housekeeping, New Idea, The Australian Women's Weekly* (which is actually published monthly and sells around 1m copies) and *Woman's Day* (which is a weekly). There are also Australian editions of many international women's magazines, including *Cosmopolitan, Marie Claire* and *Vogue*. Magazines can be purchased on subscription direct from magazines and also from a number of websites, including 💻 www.bcl.com.au/magazines and www.isubscribe.com.au.

Books

Australian used to have a thriving book market, but in recent years many of the chains have disappeared or gone bust. The one remaining chain is Dymocks (over 75 stores, 💻 www.dymocks.com.au), who are represented in all major cities – their Sydney branch claims to be the largest bookshop in the southern hemisphere. Another excellent bookshop in Sydney is a branch of the Japanese chain, Kinokuniya (💻 www.kinokuniya.com/au). An Australian bookshop directory is available online at 💻 http://danny.oz.au/books/shops.

Many department stores and supermarkets also have book departments. Melbourne is reckoned to be the best city for bookshops, with Sydney not far behind. Many bookshops are open during the evening and at weekends in major cities. The major booksellers also provide websites where you can purchase books online. There are also a number of online only bookshops, which now include Angus & Robertson (💻 www.angusrobertson.com.au), previously Australia's largest chain of bookshops, and Booktopia (💻 www.booktopia.com.au). Many people also buy books overseas from websites such as Amazon.com.

There are specialist bookshops in major cities covering topics such as antiquarianism, art, backpacking, children's subjects, feminism, gay and lesbian interest, new age and travel. In many towns there are also 'remainder' or cut-price bookshops, and in the major cities there are second-hand bookshops for collectors and bargain hunters. Many large bookshops in cities also have a selection of foreign-language books, and there are ethnic bookshops in some areas. Government publications can be purchased at Commonwealth Government bookshops in the major cities or direct from the Australian Government (💻 http://australia.gov.au/publications).

Books aren't sold at fixed prices in Australia and books published locally are typically sold at a 10 per cent discount. However, imported books can be expensive and are usually marked up by 25 to 50 per cent.

Book tokens are sold and accepted by most bookshops. Many organisations and clubs run their own libraries or book exchanges and public libraries usually have an excellent selection of books.

FURNITURE

Furniture is usually good value in Australia, where there's a wide choice of modern and contemporary designs in every price range, although (as with most things) you generally get what you pay for. Exclusive imported furniture is available (with matching exclusive prices), which includes reasonably priced quality leather suites and a wide range of cane furniture from Asia. Among the largest furniture chain stores are Freedom Furniture (💻 www.freedom.com.au) and Harvey Norman (💻 www.harveynorman.com.au), plus online stores such as Furnish.com (💻 www.furnish.com.au).

The Swedish giant Ikea (💻 www.ikea.com/au) has five outlets in Australia in Brisbane (Logan), Melbourne (Richmond & Springvale) and Sydney (Homebush & Tempe). There are also many excellent stores for homewares, including Home Couture (🖳 www.homecouture.com.au), not forgetting the major department stores (see above), which offer a wide range of top quality Australian-made and imported furniture and home furnishings.

When ordering furniture, you may have to wait weeks or months for delivery. Try to find a shop that has what you want in stock or which can give you a guaranteed delivery date. A number of manufacturers sell direct to the public, although you shouldn't assume that this will result in huge savings and should compare prices and quality before buying. There are also shops specialising in beds, leather suites, reproduction and antique furniture, and a number of companies manufacture and install fitted bedrooms and kitchens. Fitted kitchens are a competitive business in Australia, although you should be wary of 'cowboy' companies specialising in shoddy workmanship.

It costs around $10,000 to furnish an average three-bedroom home, although second-hand furniture is widely available. Furniture can also be rented for around $250 to $300 per month for an average home. If you want reasonably priced, quality, modern furniture, there are a number of companies (e.g. Ikea, see above) selling furniture for home assembly (which helps keep down prices). Assembly instructions are generally easy to follow (although some people think Rubik's cube is easier) and some companies print instructions in a number of languages. Some shops offer a few hundred dollars for your old suite when you buy a new one from them, although this may not be much of a bargain (particularly if your suite is worth more than the amount offered) and you should shop around for the best price and quality.

Furniture and furnishings is a competitive business in Australia, and you can often reduce the price by some judicious haggling, particularly if you're spending a large amount of money. Some shops will match a competitor's price rather than lose a sale. Another way to save money is to wait for the sales. If you cannot wait and don't want to (or cannot afford to) pay cash, look for an interest-free credit deal. Check the advertisements in local newspapers and national home and design magazines such as *Australian Interiors, Better Homes and Gardens*, and *Home Beautiful*. See also *The Bargain Shoppers* guides to Melbourne and Sydney. All large furniture retailers publish catalogues, which may be distributed free to homes.

HOUSEHOLD GOODS

Large household appliances such as cookers and refrigerators are usually provided in furnished rented accommodation and may also be fitted in new homes. Many homeowners include fitted kitchen appliances when selling a house or apartment, although you may need to pay for them separately. Dishwashers are still something of a luxury item in Australia and aren't always found in rented accommodation. There's a wide range of household appliances available from both Australian and foreign manufacturers. Some appliances, e.g. refrigerators, cost twice as much to run as others (choose those with a high energy efficiency rating), and refrigerators/freezers in Australia are normally 'tropicised' or fan-assisted to cope with the high average temperatures.

If you wish to bring large appliances with you, such as a dishwasher or washing machine, note that the standard Australian unit width isn't the same as in other countries. Check the size and the latest Australian safety regulations before shipping these items to Australia, as they may need expensive modifications. On the other hand, if you already own small household appliances, it's worthwhile bringing them to Australia, as usually all that's required is a change of plug (but check first). If you're coming from a country with a 110/115V electricity supply (e.g. the US), you'll need a lot of expensive transformers (see **Electricity** on page 103).

A huge choice of home appliances is available in Australia, where smaller items such as electric irons, grills, toasters and vacuum cleaners are inexpensive and of good quality. It pays to shop around as prices, quality and reliability vary (the more expensive imported brands are usually the most reliable). Before buying household appliances, whether large or small, it pays to check the test reports in *Choice* magazine (see **Consumer Rights** on page 304) at your local library.

> **☑ SURVIVAL TIP**
>
> **If you need kitchen measuring equipment and cannot cope with decimal measures, you must bring your own cups (American and Australian recipe cups aren't the same size), jugs, measuring scales and thermometers. Australian pillows and duvets (called doonas in Oz) aren't the same size or shape as those in many other countries.**

HOME SHOPPING

Mail-order catalogue shopping has long been popular in Australia, particularly among those living in remote areas, and internet shopping (see below) has also soared in recent years. Direct retailing is fairly common in Australia, particularly for computers, financial and insurance services, and office equipment and supplies. It's big business in Australia and direct retailers and their suppliers employ over 600,000 people, according to the Australian Direct Marketing Association. In addition to dedicated mail-order companies, most major department stores also provide mail-order catalogues.

TV shopping is also becoming increasingly popular and products sold through 'infomercials' are popular. Shopping channels include TVSN, broadcasting 24 hours per day and offering an unconditional money-back guarantee and quick delivery.

Check that a mail-order company is a member of the Australian Direct Marketing Association (ADMA), which has a code of conduct and offers assistance to consumers (☎ 9277 5400, 💻 www.adma.com.au). The ADMA also offers extensive advice on e-commerce.

Internet Shopping

Internet shopping has rocketed in recent years and now accounts for an increasing share of purchases. Most Australia stores have a website where they offer online shopping and there are also online price comparison sites (such as 💻 www.getprice.com.au and www.shopbot.com.au) and a wealth of dedicated online shopping sites such as 💻 www.aussie-shopping.com, www.myshopping.com.au, www.oo.com.au and www.shopsafe.com.au. Ebay (💻 www.ebay.com.au) and the Trading Post (💻 www.tradingpost.com.au) are also popular online trading sites.

All prices on websites selling goods to domestic buyers must include GST. GST and duty must also be paid on imported goods, although some goods are exempt including items on which customs duty and taxes are $50 or less and items with a customs value of less than $1,000.

DUTY-FREE ALLOWANCES

Visitors and migrants are permitted to import the following goods duty free:

- 2.25 litres of alcoholic drinks, including beer, wine or spirits, per person over 18 years of age;
- 50g of tobacco products (for customs purposes, 50 cigarettes are equal to 50g) per person over 18 years of age (reduced from 250g on 1st September 2012);

- all personal clothing and footwear (excluding furs);
- articles for personal hygiene/grooming such as toiletries, but excluding perfume concentrate;
- articles taken out of Australia on departure, but excluding articles purchased duty and/or sales tax-free in Australia (any duty/tax-free goods are counted against your duty-free allowance);
- any other articles (except alcohol and tobacco) obtained overseas or duty and sales tax-free in Australia, up to a total purchase price of $900 per person aged 18 or over ($450 for under 18s), which includes goods intended as gifts or received as gifts, whether personal or carried on behalf of others.

Members of the same family travelling together may combine their individual duty-free allowances. Duty must be paid on any goods above the duty-free allowance, excess articles being valued for duty at the price paid for them, converted to Australian dollars. However, duty up to $50 is waived on goods in excess of duty-free concessions, provided they're declared and aren't for commercial purposes. If purchase receipts aren't available, alternative methods of valuation may be used. Some items (such as jewellery) are subject to high rates of duty. Payment of duty can be made in cash, by international credit card or by travellers' cheque (in A$). Information can be obtained from state customs offices (see **Appendix A**) or the Australian Customs Service (www.customs.gov.au).

As well as duty-free shops at Australian airports, there are city duty-free shops where you can buy duty-free goods (upon presentation of a valid international air ticket) before going to the airport to catch your flight. Check the prices here first as they're usually lower than at airports. Purchases must usually be taken from the shop in a sealed bag (marked 'Important – Duty-Free Goods in Possession') that must remain intact until you've boarded your flight. Alcohol, cigarettes, jewellery and perfume must be purchased within ten days of your departure and kept sealed until you've left Australia. However, some goods such as cameras, most electronic goods, film and watches can be used as soon as they're purchased.

Caution

The maximum permitted value of purchases is $900, and these are listed on your ticket and must be shown to customs officers at airports, so you must take them with you in your hand luggage when leaving the country.

One unusual feature at Australian airports is in-bound duty-free shops, where you can buy alcohol and tobacco products and a limited range of perfumes and cosmetics on arrival before you reach immigration and customs.

GST Refunds

A GST (goods and services tax levied at 10 per cent) refund on goods and services valued at over $300 is available to tourists leaving Australia, known as the tourist refund scheme or TRS. To obtain a refund, goods must be purchased at a registered shop or business and a tax invoice obtained, and they must be exported within 30 days of purchase. When you leave Australia you show the customs officer the tax invoice and you may also need to show your departure documents (e.g. airline ticket), passport and the goods.

If the amount refundable is less than $200, you usually receive it in cash. If it's more than $200 you'll need to complete a payment authorisation with instructions on how you wish the money to be repaid, e.g. by cheque, credit card or payment to an Australian bank account. GST refunds can be reclaimed only at airports or seaports with a TRS verification facility, and GST isn't refundable on duty-free goods.

For more information, see www.customs.gov.au/site/page4646.asp.

CONSUMER RIGHTS

If you buy something which is faulty, damaged or doesn't work or measure up to the manufacturer's or vendor's claims, you can return it and obtain a replacement or your money back. Extended warranties and money-back guarantees don't affect your statutory rights as a purchaser, although the legal status of a warranty may be unclear. Some shops offer an unconditional refund or exchange of goods, which isn't required by law, although this guarantee is usually only for a short period and goods must be returned unused and as new.

You have the right to a refund or replacement goods if you buy a faulty product (with the exception of goods purchased at auction). Signs such as 'all care but no responsibility taken', 'goods left for repair at your own risk', 'no refunds given' and 'no responsibility for loss or damage' are meaningless and unlawful under state and federal laws. All goods must be of 'merchantable' (reasonable) quality and fit for the purpose for which they were sold, and it's illegal for sellers to include a clause in the conditions of sale that exempts them from liability for defects, lack of care or product faults. Most traders back down once you show that you know the law and are determined to obtain your rights.

There are a number of consumers' organisations in Australia, including Citizens Advice Bureaux, consumer affairs bureaux, fair trading bureaux, ombudsmen and small claims tribunals (see also **Legal System & Advice** on page 318). A consumer affairs bureau provides general advice over the telephone, but won't usually take any action on a complaint unless it's made in writing or in person. If you make a complaint, the bureau gives you advice and writes to the trader concerned on your behalf, or may refer your complaint to another government or consumer body for investigation. However, callers are often given poor or incorrect advice.

If you're unable to resolve a dispute with a trader or tradesman, you can take a dispute to a small claims tribunal for a small fee, which are operated by individual states (see 💻 www.pinkinvestments.org/downloads/smallclaimstribunalsofaustralia.pdf). Claims are limited to between around $2,000 and $6,000, depending on the state.

You can also take a complaint to the Australian Competition and Consumer Commission (☎ 00-302502, 💻 www.accc.gov.au), which promotes competition and fair trade in the market place to benefit consumers, businesses and the community. Its primary responsibility is to ensure that individuals and businesses comply with the Commonwealth competition, fair trading and consumer protection laws.

The consumers' champion is the Australian Consumers' Association (ACA ☎ 02-9577 3333, 💻 www.choice.com.au), which publishes a number of magazines for consumers, including *Choice* (their general consumer magazine), *Choice Computer* and *Health Reader*. The ACA also publishes and distributes a wide range of consumer-oriented books. *Choice* contains independent tests of products and services and is essential reading when buying major household goods. Magazines are available only to members, either online and/or the printed version; membership costs from $7.65 to $11 per quarter. The ACA also provides a Consumer Information Service (☎ 1800-069552).

Drought

18. ODDS & ENDS

This chapter contains miscellaneous information, in alphabetical order. Although all topics aren't of vital importance, most are of general interest to anyone planning to live or work in Australia, including everything you ever wanted to know (but were afraid to ask) about tipping and toilets.

CITIZENSHIP

The residence requirements for Australian citizenship changed on 1st July 2010. Prior to this date you were required to have been living in Australia for two years as a permanent resident in the five years immediately prior to applying, including one year in the two years immediately before the application. Since 1st July 2010, in order to apply for citizenship, anyone aged 16 or over must have been living in Australia on a valid Australian visa for four years immediately before applying, including one year as a permanent resident. In addition, you mustn't have been absent from Australia for more than one year during the four-year period, including no more than 90 days in the year immediately before applying. There are certain exceptions to this rule.

Applicants must be aged at least 16 years; have a basic knowledge of the English language; be capable of understanding the nature of their citizenship application and understand the responsibilities and privileges of Australian citizenship; be of good character; and be likely to live permanently in Australia or maintain a close and continuing association with Australia. The ability to speak English doesn't apply to those aged over 50, and those aged over 60 aren't required to understand the responsibilities and privileges of Australian citizenship. There's an application fee of $260.

Prospective citizens must pass a 'citizenship test' in English, consisting of 20 questions drawn at random from a pool; to pass you must answer 75 per cent or 15 out of 20 questions correctly. You need to know and understand the information in the test section of the Australian citizenship test resource book, *Australian Citizenship: Our Common Bond*, which you can order or download from the Australian citizenship website (💻 www.citizenship.gov.au). The website also contains a practice citizenship test. The application fee covers the cost of the citizenship test and there's no extra charge for sitting the test again if you fail it the first time.

Most people born in Australia before 26th January 1949 automatically became Australian citizens on that day, and those born between 26th January 1949 and 20th August 1986 automatically became Australian citizens unless one of their parents was a foreign diplomatic or a consular official. Since 20th August 1986, citizenship has been acquired if, at the time of a person's birth in Australia, at least one parent was either an Australian citizen or a permanent resident. Those born overseas to an Australian citizen can apply for registration as an Australian citizen by descent provided they meet certain criteria. A child who's a permanent resident and legally adopted in Australia (after 22nd November 1994) automatically acquires Australian citizenship if at least one parent was an Australian citizen at the time of the adoption.

New citizens must make the following 'pledge of commitment': 'From this time forward, under God, I pledge my loyalty to Australia and its people, whose democratic beliefs I share, whose rights and liberties I respect, and whose laws I will uphold and obey.' The words 'under God' may be omitted.

The benefits of citizenship include the right to run for public office and to enlist in the defence and police forces, and undertake certain other public service jobs; the right to be protected under Australian diplomatic arrangements overseas; the right to claim full welfare benefits; and the right to register children born overseas as Australian citizens. They also have the right to vote, which is in fact an obligation, as Australian citizens are not only obliged to enrol on the electoral register, but obliged to vote in general elections as well! If you're granted Australian citizenship, you can retain your foreign passport (provided the country of issue permits dual nationality) and obtain an Australian passport. Once you're an Australian citizen, you must use your Australian passport to enter and leave Australia.

Over 70,000 people are granted citizenship each year, although only around 10 per cent of immigrants becomes Australian citizens, despite the fact that some 80 per cent of immigrants interviewed within six months of their arrival claim that they plan to become citizens. British immigrants are the least likely to become Australian citizens.

In 2001, the government launched a citizenship 'drive' (coinciding with the Federation Centenary Year) to try to persuade permanent residents to become citizens. For more information, consult the comprehensive Australian citizenship website (💻 www.citizenship.gov.au).

CLIMATE

The major attraction of Australia for many immigrants, particularly those from the northern hemisphere, is its temperate climate and the lifestyle it affords. Australia has climates to suit everyone, although it broadly has just two climatic zones. To those from the northern hemisphere, Australia is an 'upside down' country (weather-wise), with the warmest part (nearest the equator) at the top and the coldest at the bottom. Some 40 per cent of Australia lies in the tropical zone, while the remaining regions (south of the Tropic of Capricorn) are in the temperate zone. The tropical zone has two seasons: wet (November to April) and dry (May to October), while the temperate zones have four seasons: spring (September to November), summer (December to February), autumn (March to May) and winter (June to August).

Australia's seasons are also the opposite of those in the northern hemisphere, i.e. when it's summer in Europe it's winter in Australia and vice versa. Australia is less prone to climate extremes than other continents of comparable size because it's surrounded by oceans and has few high mountain masses. The most pleasant seasons in most of Australia are spring and autumn, with the exception of Tasmania where summer is the most enjoyable season.

The average hours of sunshine per day in Australia's capital cities ranges from five in Hobart to eight in Perth. January is the hottest month in most southern regions, while February is hottest in Tasmania and southern Victoria. Average summer temperatures in January range from around 17ºC (63ºF) in Hobart to 29ºC (84ºF) in Alice Springs and Darwin. Temperatures exceed 30ºC (86ºF) in most areas during summer, and temperatures occasionally soar to 45°C (113°F) or higher. The hottest place in Australia is Marble Bar (WA), where the temperature from October to March usually averages 40°C (104°F) or more. The highest recorded temperature in Australia is 53.1°C (127°F), measured at Cloncurry (QLD) in 1889. If you cannot stand extreme heat, you should choose to live in Adelaide, Hobart, Melbourne or Sydney rather than Brisbane, Darwin or Perth.

Australia has the lowest rainfall of any continent after Antarctica. Average annual rainfall for the capital cities varies from 1,536mm (60.4in) in Darwin, which is in the monsoon region, to 530mm (21in) in Adelaide. During the wet season in the north (particularly from January to March), roads can quickly become impassable as tracks turn into raging rivers after a downpour. In contrast, large arid inland areas get less than 250mm (10in) of rain per year. In winter temperatures can fall below 10°C (50°F) on winter nights in most regions, and sleet can fall on the urban areas of Hobart and even in Adelaide and Canberra. Snow is rare except in the Australian Alps, straddling the New South Wales/Victoria border, where it's possible to ski between June and October.

Approximate average daily maximum/minimum temperatures for Australia's major cities are shown below in centigrade and, in brackets, Fahrenheit.

The weather forecast is provided in daily newspapers, via the internet (e.g. www.weatherchannel.com.au and www.weatherzone.com.au), and on TV and radio broadcasts. Warnings of extreme weather conditions affecting motoring are broadcast regularly on ABC national and local radio stations. Many newspapers devote a full page (often in colour) to the weather, and news programmes on radio and TV are usually followed by detailed weather forecasts and analyses. Forecasts are usually accurate, not least because of Australia's generally stable weather patterns.

Extreme Weather

Australia is frequently hit by natural disasters, including bush fires, cyclones, droughts, floods and tropical storms, and occasionally by earthquakes. Periodic droughts are a way of life and a constant worry for farmers. In many rural areas, rivers are sucked almost dry by the demand for water for irrigation, causing many to slow to a trickle and the water to become polluted by toxic algae (rivers are also polluted by salt and some are dying). There are frequent (sometimes permanent) water restrictions in most regions of Australia, even in the major cities. Australian weather is periodically affected by *El Niño*, an ocean warming phenomenon where prevailing cold water currents along the west coast of South America become warmer, upsetting weather patterns and leading to floods in North and South America and droughts in Australia.

Average Temperature High/Low °C (°F)

City	Spring	Summer	Autumn	Winter
Adelaide	22/11 (72/52)	28/17 (82/63)	22/12 (72/54)	16/8 (61/46)
Alice Springs	30/14 (86/57)	35/21 (95/70)	18/13 (82/55)	20/7 (68/45)
Brisbane	26/16 (79/61)	29/21 (84/70)	26/16 (79/61)	21/10 (70/50)
Cairns	29/21 (84/70)	31/24 (88/75)	29/22 (84/72)	26/18 (79/64)
Canberra	19/6 (66/43)	27/12 (81/54)	20/7 (68/45)	12/1 (54/34)
Darwin	33/24 (91/75)	32/25 (90/77)	32/23 (90/73)	30/20 (86/68)
Hobart	17/8 (63/46)	21/12 (70/54)	17/9 (63/48)	12/5 (54/41)
Melbourne	20/9 (68/48)	25/14 (77/57)	20/11 (68/52)	14/7 (57/45)
Perth	22/12 (72/54)	29/17 (84/63)	24/14 (75/57)	18/9 (64/48)
Sydney	22/13 (72/55)	26/18 (79/64)	22/14 (72/57)	17/9 (63/48)

Drought: Until 2009 – when a ten-year drought (the worst in living memory) was broken – the water situation was dire in some parts of Australia, including two-thirds of NSW. One of the consequences was that the countries major water reserve, the Darling-Murray basin river system – which provides three-quarters of the water consumed nationally – was running dry. Farmers were devastated in many areas and forced to slaughter their livestock as they couldn't feed them and wildlife was also decimated. Water management remains one of the most serious issues facing Australia.

Bush fires: A constant threat in country areas (mainly in summer), bush fires are exacerbated by droughts. They often threaten country towns and occasionally major cities, and deaths among fire-fighters and homeowners are frequent (some people needlessly lose their lives by refusing to abandon their homes). Lighting fires in a bush fire zone is strictly forbidden; even where it's permitted, you must ensure that every spark is extinguished before leaving and must never throw cigarette butts out of car windows. In February 2009, bush fires in Victoria left 209 people dead – the most devastating fires ever and the worst natural disaster in Australia's history. Whole communities were wiped out and thousands more left homeless. The fires followed a heat wave, during which temperatures reached records of over 45°C (113°F) in both Adelaide and Melbourne.

Cyclones: Known as 'blows' in Australia, cyclones are fairly common in the summer months (between November and April) in the northern regions of Australia, from Western Australia to Queensland. In 1974, Cyclone Tracey flattened Darwin with gusts of up to 280kph (174mph). It killed 66 people and destroyed over 5,000 homes, leaving fewer than 500 intact. The city has since been completely rebuilt to 'withstand' cyclones. More recently, Exmouth in Western Australia was devastated by Cyclone Vance in 1999. Violent tropical and electrical storms are common in northern Australia, particularly northern Queensland. In January 1998, for example, torrential rains in Townsville caused widespread flooding when 500mm (20in) of rain fell in just 12 hours.

Earthquakes

Earthquakes are rare in Australia, although in 1989 one struck Newcastle (NSW), killing 13 people, injuring 160 and causing damage of $1.7bn.

Greenpeace Australia Pacific predicts that the Australian climate will become even more extreme in the 21st century. The average temperature of much of the country is expected to rise by up to 2°C by 2030 and by up to 6°C by 2070. Australia, already the world's second-driest continent (after Antarctica), is also expected to become even drier. High temperatures and the increasing dryness combined in 2003 to cause severe bushfires which burned for 59 days – a sign of what's to come. Rainfall in southwest Australia could decline by up to 60 per cent by 2070, and much of Australia can expect storms with greater maximum wind speeds and more sudden and extreme rainfall (but with a reduction of total rainfall).

Australian Capital Territory & Canberra

The Australian Capital Territory (ACT) has an average of seven hours sunshine per day and summer temperatures average around 27°C (81°F). Canberra has four distinct seasons, with hot, dry summers and cold winters. It's situated inland, therefore the climate isn't moderated by the ocean as in Australia's coastal cities. Canberra is the coldest capital city in winter, with temperatures plunging to around freezing at night, although it rarely snows. Winter mornings are frosty but most days are bright and sunny, temperatures averaging around 12°C (54°F). Annual rainfall is low at around 660mm (26in).

Canberra is noted for its clean air and isn't prone to pollution in summer.

New South Wales & Sydney

New South Wales (NSW) has a variety of weather, although it generally has an agreeable climate. Sydney's rainfall is higher than average for Australian cities at 1,140mm (45in), which is spread fairly evenly throughout the year, including summer. It rains on some 150 days a year in Sydney, the wettest months being April to June. It has mild winters, when daytime temperatures rarely fall below 10°C (50°F) and can reach 17°C (63°F). Summer temperatures average around 25°C (77°F), although the humidity sometimes makes the weather feel oppressive, particularly from January to March. Occasionally, the temperature in Sydney exceeds 40°C (104°F) and can still be 30°C (86°F) at midnight, although this is rare, as cool sea breezes help lower temperatures during heat waves. Sydney frequently has high pollution levels in summer.

Northern Territory, Darwin & Alice Springs

The Northern Territory has a tropical climate with just two seasons: wet from November to April (also known as the 'green' season) and dry for the remainder of the year. The weather is generally as hot as hell year round, with average daily temperatures between 20° and 33°C (68° and 91°F) and reaching over 40°C (104°F) for weeks on end in the central desert regions (and Alice Springs). Rainfall is almost non-existent from May to September, which is more than compensated for between December and March, when it's between 250 and 380mm (10 and 15in). The heat and humidity are often oppressive, with humidity as high as 95 per cent just before the start of the wet season. The Northern Territory is prone to cyclones and violent thunderstorms. Alice Springs has an average of 9.5 hours of sunshine a day, with warm winters and hot, dry summers. Summer evenings can be cool, while in winter the temperature often falls below freezing at night. Alice has low annual rainfall, with an average of around 40mm (1.5in) falling between December and February.

Queensland & Brisbane

Queensland has a sub-tropical climate in the south and is tropical in the north, with wet and dry seasons. Summer is the wet season, when rainfall averages around 1,000mm (40in), particularly in the north, where violent thunderstorms and floods are common. The state has the wettest town in Australia, Tully, with over 4,000mm (160in) of rain per year (four times that of Brisbane). Extremes of flood and drought are common in country areas. Brisbane is one of the sunnier cities in Australia, with an average of over 7.5 hours per day and mild, sunny winters. Average temperatures are between 10°C (50°F) and 21°C (70°F) in winter, and between 21°C (70°F) and 29°C (84°F) in summer. Summer temperatures can, however, exceed 38°C (100°F), and humidity can be very high, although it's usually tempered by cool sea breezes in coastal areas.

South Australia & Adelaide

South Australia is the driest state and its northern regions are mostly desert. The inhabited parts, however, have an almost Mediterranean climate, characterised by long, dry summers and short, mild winters, and are said to have the best year-round climate in Australia. Adelaide is noted for its low rainfall (the lowest of any state capital)

at just 530mm (21in), which falls mainly between April and October. It isn't too cold in winter, when average temperatures are between 8°C (46°F) and 16°C (61°F). There's an average of four hours sunshine per day in winter and seven hours in summer. Summers are hot with maximum temperatures averaging over 27°C (81°F), although nights aren't usually too hot and there's low humidity. It's very hot in the northern desert regions, where summer temperatures are frequently over 40°C (104°F). Adelaide experienced a heat wave in January 2009, when temperatures were over 40°C (104°F) for six days – the most prolonged heat wave on record – and the temperature soared to 45.7°C (114°F).

Sydney, NSW

Tasmania & Hobart

Tasmania has a temperate climate, with four distinct seasons, but is without the extremes of the mainland states. It's the coldest part of Australia and is occasionally hit by icy southerly winds from Antarctica, although it's still relatively mild by northern European standards. Nights can be cool throughout the year, although winters aren't as cold as in Canberra and Alice Springs. The average winter temperature in Hobart is between 5°C (41°F) and 12°C (54°F). It has around 620cm (25in) of rain per year (half that of Sydney and Brisbane), rain falling on around 180 days per year, mostly between July and October. In the west, rainfall is around four times that of Hobart. Hobart enjoys an average of around five hours of sunshine per day, maximum summer temperatures averaging around 21°C (70°F).

 **Caution**

Water temperatures are much lower than in the rest of Australia, and it's generally too cold for sea bathing.

Victoria & Melbourne

Victoria has a generally mild climate, somewhere between maritime and continental, although it can have very hot and cold periods. The weather in Melbourne can be extremely changeable, and it's said that you can experience all four seasons in one day. Melbourne experiences cold, wet and windy weather in autumn and winter, although temperatures rarely fall below 5°C (41°F), with highs of around 14°C (57°F).

Mountainous regions have snow in winter, when temperatures remain below freezing for long periods. Melbourne has low rainfall at around 660mm (26in), half that of Sydney and Brisbane, which is fairly evenly spread throughout the year (June and July are the wettest months). The city has mild autumns (the most pleasant season) and hot summers, when temperatures average 25°C (77°F) and occasionally soar to 40°C (104°F).

During a heat wave in January 2009, the temperature reached a record 46.4°C (115.5°F) in Melbourne, resulting in the death of many elderly people and culminating in the most devastating fires in Australia's history. The heat wave lasted six days and caused rail lines to buckle and a spate of power failures.

Western Australia & Perth

The southern areas of Western Australia enjoy a Mediterranean climate, while northern areas have a tropical climate with dry and wet seasons. Perth is the sunniest capital city in Australia with an average annual temperature of 18°C (64°F) and over eight hours' sunshine per day. Spring and autumn are the most pleasant seasons. The average rainfall is low at 914mm (36in) per year (although it's over 1,500mm/60in on the southwest coast), which falls mainly between April and October. The northern and eastern regions have very low rainfall and consist mostly of desert.

Winters in Perth are mild and sunny but wet, with average temperatures of between 9°C (48°F) and 18°C (64°F), although frost is common away from coastal areas. Summers are very hot, with daytime temperatures frequently between 30°C (86°F) and 40°C (104°F) and hot nights, although it's a dry rather than humid heat. The summer heat is mitigated by cool breezes that blow in off the sea from Fremantle (west of Perth); the breeze is called the Fremantle Doctor due to its soothing effect (some enterprising locals bottle it and sell it to tourists!).

CRIME

Australia is a safe country by international standards, however, it's important to take the usual safety precautions that you would in any country. Crime rates vary from state to state, city to city and suburb to suburb, and tend to be lower than the UK and US in most major categories and are falling. However, crime, and the fear of crime, consistently rate among the highest concerns of the Australian public and the Australian Institute of Criminology has estimated that crime costs Australia around $32bn per year.

Violent crime is below that of many other countries, although gun and knife crime remains a problem, with an increasing number of violent incidents fuelled by excessive alcohol. This has led the authorities to crack down on drinking and make many streets and beaches 'alcohol-free zones' (shown by signs). Australia has a relatively high rate of property crime, with burglary a serious problem in major cities; car crime is also widespread, although it's decreasing not least due to better security by manufacturers. Beware of pickpockets and opportunist thieves such as bag snatchers in major cities and crowded places, and keep a close eye on your belongings when travelling on public transport and when staying in hotels or hostels.

Most officials are honest, but there have been a number of high profile corruption scandals involving local politicians and police officers. Organised crime is also a problem in Australia's major cities and contributes to much of the country's serious crime (see 🖳 www.crimecommission.gov.au for information).

Although the states and territories have primary responsibility for the criminal justice system, since 1996 the Australian government has undertaken a range of substantial initiatives aimed at reducing the incidence of violence and other crime in Australia. Central government, local authorities, police forces and security companies all publish information and provide advice on crime prevention (see 🖳 www.crimeprevention.gov.au). Police forces have local crime prevention officers whose job is to provide free advice to businesses, homeowners and individuals.

Australia has a community 'crime prevention' scheme – similar to the UK's Neighbourhood Watch scheme – called Crime Stoppers (☏ 1800-333000, 🖳 http://crimestoppers.com.au), which encourages people to report crime anonymously.

Drugs

Illegal drug use and trafficking is a big problem in Australia – estimating to cost around $7bn annually – although most drug use involves so-called soft drugs. The authorities in some states have taken a more enlightened view of the use of 'soft' drugs such as cannabis and marijuana in recent years. Smoking cannabis and marijuana is widespread in Australia, where it's estimated that around a third of the adult population uses or has used the drugs, and growing cannabis/marijuana plants is a vast cottage industry. (The 2012 United Nations World Drug Report reported that

Australia and New Zealand contain the highest global prevalence of cannabis use.)

The law regarding their use varies considerably depending on the state or territory (see http://ncpic.org.au/ncpic/publications/factsheets/article/cannabis-and-the-law). However, unlike hard drugs, there's little crime associated with cannabis or marijuana use.

Hard drugs such as cocaine and heroin are directly or indirectly responsible for a large proportion of crime in Australia, including a high proportion of thefts in the major cities. It's also estimated that the trafficking of heroin and other hard drugs is involved in some 40 per cent of serious crime.

GEOGRAPHY

Australia is one of the world's oldest land masses (some of its rock was formed over 3bn years ago) and its largest island. Separated from other land masses, it evolved in partial isolation, resulting in its unique flora and fauna, and the development of the Aboriginal race, with a civilisation stretching back between 40,000 and 60,000 years. The country extends 3,200km (1,988mi) from north to south and 4,000km (2,485mi) from east to west, covering an area of 7,682,300km² (2,966,144mi²), including Tasmania, with a coastline of 36,738km (22,826mi). It's the world's sixth-largest country (after Russia, Canada, China, the USA and Brazil) and is around the same size as continental USA (minus Alaska), one and a half times the size of Europe (excluding Russia) and over 30 times the size of the UK.

Australia lies in the southern hemisphere, southeast of Asia and between the Indian and Pacific oceans. Its nearest neighbour is Papua New Guinea, which is some 200km (125mi) north of Cape York in the northwest. Bali and other Indonesian islands lie off the northwest coast, and the French island of New Caledonia is situated to the northeast. New Zealand is around 1,700km (1,050mi) from the southeast coast, while to the south lies Antarctica. Australia is surrounded by four seas (Arafura, Coral, Tasman and Timor) and three oceans (Indian, South Pacific and Southern). Almost 40 per cent of the country lies north of the Tropic of Capricorn.

Great Barrier Reef

The Great Barrier Reef lies between 50 and 300km (31 to 186mi) off the northeast coast and stretches from the Torres Strait to Gladstone. It's the largest coral reef in the world, extending some 2,000km (1,260mi) and encompassing an area of around 200,000km² (77,226mi²). The reef is the world's largest living entity and an important marine ecosystem containing many rare life forms (it has been declared a World Heritage site).

Australia is the world's flattest continent, with an average elevation of less than 500m (1,640ft) – the world's average is 700m (2,296ft) – and only around 5 per cent is more than 600m (1,968ft) above sea level. The Great Western Plateau covers most of Western Australia, a large part of the Northern Territory and South Australia, and part of Queensland. East of the plateau are the Central Eastern Lowlands, extending from the Gulf of Carpentaria in the north to eastern South Australia and the western Victorian coast. The Great Dividing Range (or Eastern Highlands) follows the east coast southwards from northern Queensland to southern Tasmania, separating a narrow fertile strip of land on the coast from the vast, flat, arid inland plain, which is broken only by a few low mountain ranges such as the Flinders and Macdonnell Ranges and the Olgas, and by Uluru (Ayers Rock).

Uluru is the largest rock on earth, 9.4km (5.8mi) in circumference; if you're tempted to climb it, bear in mind that it's Aboriginal sacred ground and a number of people have died of heart attacks in the attempt! Other mountain ranges include the Hamersley Range, the Kimberleys and the Stirling Range in Western Australia, and the Snowy Mountains (in the Australian Alps) in Victoria, where Mount Kosciusko is the highest point (2,230m/7,316ft) in Australia.

Australia has the lowest rainfall of any continent after Antarctica (see **Climate** above) and evaporation exceeds rainfall in 70 per cent of the country. Surface water is scarce and most lakes and rivers are dry most of the year (Lake Disappointment is appropriately named!). The country's longest rivers are the Murray, Darling, Ord and Swan.

The main river is the Murray which, along with the River Darling, has a catchment area covering NSW, Queensland and Victoria. Severe salting has occurred in recent years due to indiscriminate land clearing for agricultural use, which has reduced irrigation potential and lowered the quality of drinking water. The water table is also severely depleted. If nothing is done, many experts believe that the Murray-Darling basin could be dead within a few decades, with catastrophic consequences, although limits on the amount of water farmers and industry can take from the basin and the breaking of the drought has eased the situation in recent years.

Lush forests are found only on the east coast, particularly in the far north. Much of the centre and west of the country consists of barren terrain (some 1.5m km²/579,195mi²) – a third is desert or arid lands, around two-thirds semi-arid and shrub lands – and only around 6 per cent is cultivated for crops or used for grazing. Australia has three main deserts – the Great Sandy, the Great Victoria and the Gibson – and several smaller ones.

The country is divided into six states (New South Wales, Queensland, South Australia, Tasmania, Victoria and Western Australia) and two territories (the ACT and the Northern Territory). The island of Tasmania (also called the Apple Isle) is larger than Denmark or the Netherlands and was founded by the Dutchman Abel Tasman in 1642 and originally named Van Dieman's Land (changed to Tasmania in 1856). External territories include the Australian Antarctic Territory, Christmas Island, the Cocos (Keeling) Islands and Norfolk Island (the territory of Ashmore and Cartier Islands). Macquarie Island (around 1,600km/994mi southeast of Tasmania) is administered by Tasmania.

GOVERNMENT

The Commonwealth of Australia was formed on 1st January 1901 when the states gained their independence from Britain, prior to which each state was an independent colony. Australia has a parliamentary system of government based on the British system, while the (written) constitution and federal structure are based on the US model.

The powers of the Commonwealth parliament (the legislature) are laid down in the constitution, which can be amended only by a referendum carried by a majority of voters in a majority of the states, as well as an overall majority. The Australian constitution provides for a division of power between the Commonwealth and the states. The sovereign head of the Commonwealth of Australia is the UK sovereign (Queen Elizabeth II), who's represented in Australia by the Governor-General and state governors (see **Republic Debate** below). Australia has a three-tiered system of government: Commonwealth, state and local.

Commonwealth Government

Like Washington DC in the US, Canberra is a purpose-built capital city and capital of the Australian Capital Territory (ACT). In 1911, the ACT, located roughly half way between Sydney and Melbourne, was acquired from the NSW government. The Northern Territory was transferred from the state of South Australia to Commonwealth administration in the same

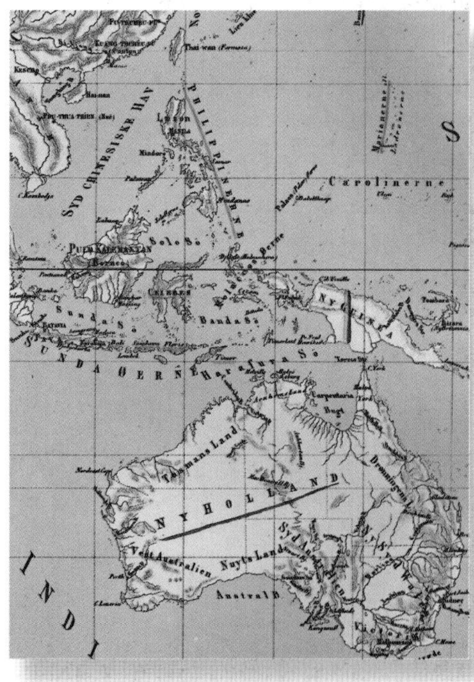

Parliament House, Canberra, ACT

year. The Commonwealth government first convened in Canberra in 1927, before which Melbourne was the seat of federal government. A new Parliament House was inaugurated in 1988 on Capitol Hill.

The ACT was created as a compromise when New South Wales (NSW) and Victoria couldn't decide between them whether Sydney or Melbourne should be the capital of Australia.

The Commonwealth government (💻 www.aph.gov.au) has constitutional power over Australian territories (the ACT and the Northern Territory) and can overturn laws made there, e.g. the controversial euthanasia law enacted in the Northern Territory in 1995. It's responsible for banking, currency, customs and excise, defence, foreign affairs, immigration, income and sales tax, intellectual property (copyright, patents and trademarks), international trade and commerce, postal services and communications, and social services. The Commonwealth government controls around 80 per cent of total government spending.

The Australian parliament is bicameral (consisting of two houses): the House of Representatives and the Senate (see below).

House of Representatives

The house of representatives (lower house), whose principal role is as legislator (maker of laws), is elected every three years (the next is due by 30th November 2013 at the latest) and its 150 members (MHRs) make up the government of the day. Each MHR is elected by (and therefore represents) a constituency with approximately the same population. The number of members allocated to each state and territory is proportionate to the number of residents, as follows: New South Wales (49), Victoria (37), Queensland (28), Western Australia (15), South Australia (11), Tasmania (5), the ACT (2) and the Northern Territory (2).

After the 2010 election, the Liberal Party (and its coalition partners) had 72 seats – an exact tie with the Labor Party, while the Australian Greens has one, the National Party (WA) one, with four independents.

Senate

The senate (upper house) represents state interests and reviews legislation passed by the lower house; its approval is required before proposed legislation can become law. The senate is composed of 12 senators from each state and two from each territory, making a total of 76. Senators are elected for a six-year term (except for the ACT and Northern Territory senators, who serve for three years) by a system of proportional representation. In senate elections (every three years) 40 seats are up for re-election (half the 72 six-year senators and the four three-year senators), when the whole state constitutes the electorate. After the 2010 election the state of the parties was: Labor 31, Liberal 29, Greens 9, National Party 5 and Democratic Labor Party one.

State & Territory Government

The state lower house is called the Legislative Assembly or the House of Assembly and is usually elected for four years, while the upper house is usually called the Legislative Council and elected for twice the period of the lower house. The ACT, the Northern Territory (self governing since 1978) and Queensland have a single house (the Legislative Assembly). The head of the largest party in the ACT and NT is called the chief minister, and the Queen's representative is called the administrator.

State governments have control over Aboriginal welfare, community services, conservation, education, forestry, health, housing, infrastructure, justice, mineral resources, police, roads, tourism, transport and water. The states receive the bulk of their funding from the Commonwealth government, although they also levy stamp duty and charges on banking and other financial transactions, plus various other duties and taxes. They're continually in conflict with the Commonwealth government over funding for services such as healthcare and law enforcement.

Each state has its own parliament with upper and lower houses, except for Queensland, which abolished its second house in 1922), a cabinet headed by a premier, a governor (who's the Queen's representative) and its own constitution.

State parliaments are generally elected under a preferential voting system for the lower house and by a variety of other systems for the upper house. Under the preferential voting system, voters must place number 1 against their first choice and 2, 3, etc. against the other candidates in order of preference. If nobody secures a majority from the first preference, the second is used. If nobody secures a majority from the second, the third is used, and so on.

State government was long noted for its corruption and nepotism, although this is generally considered to be no longer the case. Many state politicians do hardly anything, and in some states the upper house rarely sits (upper houses are essentially just a 'rubber stamp' for the lower house).

Local Government

Local government, which comprises various councils, is responsible for a number of services, including community services, the construction and maintenance of local roads and other infrastructure, libraries, parks and recreation grounds, public health, refuse (rubbish) collection, sports and community centres, swimming pools, town planning, water and sewerage, and weights and measures. Councils (including city, municipal, shire and town councils) provide services to their communities and control local matters, such as property zoning.

There are over 700 councils in Australia, whose powers and responsibilities vary from state to state, consisting largely of elected representatives who usually act in an honorary capacity. Although generally well run, some councils have built up huge debts, often through building and acquisition programmes. Councils are largely funded by business and property taxes (council rates), which are supplemented by federal and state funds. Local government departments and officials are listed in telephone directories under 'Local Government'.

Political Parties

Australia has four main political parties: the Australian Labor Party (ALP), the Liberal Party of Australia (Lib), the National Party (Nat), and the Australian Greens (GRN), plus a number of smaller parties that occasionally win a seat. Some parties are regional parties and stand in only one or two states, and Australia essentially has a two-party system, comprising the 'liberal' and 'national' parties (right wing), who traditionally form a coalition, and the ALP (left wing, but a much more moderate party than it was in the '60s and '70s). The party with a majority of seats in the House of Representatives generally forms the government (although, if it has no overall majority and cannot find coalition partners, it could find itself in opposition). The leader of the largest party (or the largest party in a coalition) becomes the Prime Minister (currently Julia Gillard), who presides over a cabinet of ministers.

The Labor Party held power from 1983 until 1996, when the Liberal/National coalition became the dominant force until November 2007, when the Labor Party was re-elected. The 2010 general election resulted in a 'hung' parliament with the Labor Party and the Liberal-National Coalition both having 72 seats; the incumbent Prime Minister Julia Gillard secured the support of four out of six Independent and Green Party crossbenchers and continued to govern.

All Australian citizens must vote in Commonwealth elections or face a fine (although there's a move to change to voluntary voting). Only Australian citizens over 18 years of age and British subjects who were resident in Australia and on the electoral roll on 25th January 1984 may vote.

Republic Debate

The sovereign head of the Commonwealth of Australia is Queen Elizabeth II, the Queen of England, who's represented in Australia by the governor-general (G-G) and the state governors.

The G-G is nominated by the Commonwealth government and appointed by the Queen, and acts on the advice of ministers in virtually all matters. However, this system led to a major political crisis in 1975, when the G-G dismissed the elected Labor government of Gough Whitlam and called a general election after the government failed to pass the budget bill (this has, in fact, occurred six times in Australia's parliamentary history).

There's a huge gulf between republicans and monarchists, and a referendum was held in November 1999. In spite of previous indications that the republicans would win, 55 per cent of Australians voted against a republic. Only the ACT and Victoria voted clearly for a republic. Therefore, for the time being, Queen Elizabeth II remains Australia's head of state.

LEGAL SYSTEM & ADVICE

Australian law is based on English common law, which it resembles closely. This is divided into statute law, enacted by legislature, and common law, which is developed by the courts, both of which continually evolve as a consequence of precedents set by the courts. There's also a clear distinction between criminal law (acts harmful to the community) and civil law (disputes between individuals). If there's a dispute between Commonwealth and state law, Commonwealth law takes precedence.

Less serious criminal cases are heard by magistrates or justices of the peace, while serious criminal and civil cases are heard before a judge and jury (e.g. in a district or county court) consisting of 12 people in criminal cases (fewer in civil cases). There's no capital punishment in Australia. Many minor offences incur fines, including drinking under age, littering, smoking where it's prohibited, taking alcohol on to Aboriginal lands, and topless and nude bathing (where prohibited) – laws regarding these and other activities differ from state to state.

Each state or territory has its own court system, consisting of magistrates' courts, intermediate district or county courts, and supreme courts. There are also state children's courts, courts of petty sessions, family courts (which handle divorce cases and the custody of children), industrial courts (which hear claims concerning industrial relations law) and small claims courts. Some disputes, such as family disputes and disputes between neighbours, can be resolved by mediation. Most criminal cases in Australia are heard in state or territory courts. There are huge delays in hearing cases, and local courts are hugely over-burdened, some magistrates courts processing up to 60 cases per hour! In serious cases, the accused are held in prison on remand for up to a year before their cases are heard; when the accused is on bail, cases can take up to 18 months to come to court.

A federal system exists to deal with matters over which the Commonwealth government has jurisdiction. The highest court in the land is the High Court of Australia (created in 1976), which is the country's final court of appeal from the states' supreme courts. It's presided over by the chief justice and six other justices, all of whom are political appointees. In recent years, there has been an acrimonious relationship between the High Court and politicians (at stake is the balance of power between the judiciary and the government). Other federal

courts include the Federal Court of Australia and the Family Court of Australia, both of which handle special cases involving federal law.

In 1986, Australia changed the constitution to prevent the UK making laws in Australia or having any government responsibility, thereby removing the ultimate legal appeal to the British Privy Council. At federal and state levels, the office of ombudsman deals with a variety of citizens' complaints against government administration. Administrative Appeals Tribunals hear appeals in cases involving freedom of information, immigration, pensions and tax.

If you're arrested, you aren't required to give your name or address and are permitted to contact a friend or lawyer (called solicitors in Australia) before answering any questions. The police provide an interpreter for those who are arrested and cannot speak English. It's best to say nothing until a lawyer is present and even then you have the right to remain silent. Your country's consulate or embassy in Australia (see **Appendix A**) can usually provide you with a list of local lawyers (if necessary someone speaking your native language). The police cal also provide a duty lawyer. In some states, interrogation is recorded on video. If you're charged with an offence, you may be released on bail (a surety) or remanded in custody; foreigners may have their passports confiscated to prevent them leaving the country. Each state has a legal aid commission and you may be able to obtain legal aid if you cannot afford a lawyer, although it's subject to a means test and is becoming increasingly difficult as a result of cuts; people are often refused help unless they're facing jail or a fine of over $1,000. Information about legal aid can be obtained from local courts (see also 💻 www.nla.aust.net.au).

☑ SURVIVAL TIP

Free legal advice is also available in all states and territories (there's a fee of $2 in Western Australia) from various organisations, including Citizens' Advice Bureaux (there's a fee of $25 for a consultation with a legal representative), community legal or justice centres and legal aid commissions.

As in most countries, civil liberties are constantly under threat, although Australia remains one of the most free and open societies in the world. For information regarding civil liberties, contact the Australian Civil Liberties Union (ACLU, ☎ 03-9347 8671, 💻 www.angelfire.com/folk/aclu), which publishes an annual booklet, *Your Rights*, containing information about your legal rights in various situations. The booklet is available from the ACLU and from newsagents. See also **Consumer Rights** on page 304.

MARRIAGE & DIVORCE

As in most developed countries, Australians are marrying later – on average around 28 years of age for women and 30 for men. Many people choose to remain single and there's an increasing number of single, childless women, although the annual number of marriages has increased slightly in recent years. Some 70 per cent of Australian adults are married, around 15 per cent are lone parents and some 8 per cent live in *de facto* marriages (an unmarried couple living together as husband and wife). *De facto* couples don't have the same inheritance rights as married couples and should therefore ensure that their wills reflect their wishes.

Weddings may take place anywhere, and an increasing number (currently around 45 per cent) don't take place in a church. Anyone planning to marry must complete a Notice of Intended Marriage form (see 💻 www.ag.gov.au) at least one month prior to the proposed wedding date and give it to the person (e.g. minister or civil marriage celebrant – see 💻 www.marriagecelebrants.org.au) who will conduct the marriage. Both parties must provide their birth certificates and a divorce decree or death certificate if they're divorced or widowed. A man must usually be 18 to marry and a woman 16, although anyone aged under 18 must have their parents' consent and permission from a judge or magistrate.

A marriage must be witnessed by two people aged over 18. A legal marriage that takes place overseas is almost always recognised in Australia. A woman usually takes her husband's surname when she marries, although it isn't obligatory and she can retain her maiden name.

Australia has one of the highest divorce rates in the world, marriages lasting an average of less than eight years (there's around one divorce for every two marriages). The year 2001 saw the highest number of divorces (55,300). Under the Family Law Act, the only grounds for divorce in Australia are the irretrievable breakdown of a marriage; 'fault' (e.g. adultery, cruelty or desertion) no longer constitutes grounds for divorce. Under the law, a marriage has irretrievably broken down if a couple has lived apart for one year and there's no reasonable likelihood of a reconciliation. It's also possible for these conditions to be met when a couple lives separately and apart in the matrimonial home, although it's difficult to prove.

If a couple have been married for less than two years, they must usually have considered reconciliation with the assistance of a marriage guidance counsellor before a court will hear divorce proceedings.

The average cost of a divorce in court fees alone (excluding your solicitor's fees) is around $4,000-5,000, with a fee of $577 (in a Federal Magistrates Court) simply to file an application. Extra fees apply to obtaining court orders regarding access to and custody of children and property orders. For more information, see the Family Court of Australia website (🖳 www.familycourt.gov.au).

One of the Family Court's main duties is to protect and promote the welfare and rights of dependent children. Both parents have joint custody of a child under Australian law, although one parent can ask for and be granted sole custody, in which case the wishes of the child are taken into consideration. Before maintenance is granted, the age, financial resources and obligations, and health of each party are taken into consideration (the same applies to the division of matrimonial property). Matters concerning the custody of children, division of property and maintenance must be decided before a divorce can be granted. After one month, a decree becomes absolute and the parties are free to re-marry. Although the law varies with the state, generally when a *de facto* marriage breaks up after two years, either party can apply for custody of children, division of property or maintenance, as if they were formally married.

MILITARY SERVICE

The Australian Defence Force (ADF – 🖳 www.defence.gov.au) comprises three services: the Australian Army, the Royal Australian Air Force and the Royal Australian Navy. The combined strength of the ADF (including reservists and civilians) is around 100,000 (59,000 permanent service personnel, 22,000 reservists and the remainder civilians). Some 15 per cent are women, who are eligible for most navy and air force positions and around two-thirds of army positions (women are banned from carrying combat arms). In recent years, there has been an exodus from the services, and the armed forces are finding it more difficult to recruit.

All soldiers initially enlist for a minimum of four years under the Open Ended Enlistment Scheme and after four years can apply for discharge by giving six months' notice. Applicants for the ADF must be Australian citizens or be eligible for grant of citizenship or must undertake to apply for citizenship when they become eligible. They must be aged at least 17 and under 35 (42 if they have a particular skill) and must be at least 152cm (5ft) tall. Reservists serve a minimum of 26 days a year (14 full-time). In recent years, a new form of reserve service has been introduced. Under the Ready Reserve programme, members serve full-time for 12 months and then train for 50 days a year for four years. Soldiers may also transfer from the regular army or army reserve to the Ready Reserve, in which case they're committed to five years' part-time training.

There's no conscription (draft) in Australia, where all members of the armed forces are volunteers.

Australia is a signatory to a number of defence treaties, including the Five Power Defence Arrangement (FPDA) with Malaysia, New Zealand, Singapore and the UK, and the ANZUS alliance with New Zealand and the US. The country also has a close military relationship with Indonesia, with whom it conducts combined exercises. Australian troops were deployed in East Timor in 1999 and 2000, and were responsible for most of the evacuation of UN personnel and the restoration of calm. Australia also sent around 2,000 troops to help with the invasion of Iraq in 2003 and has also deployed troops in Afghanistan in recent years.

Australia spent over $20bn a year on defence (1.8 per cent of GDP), although cuts of some $5.5bn are planned over the next four years.

PETS

Certain pets can be imported into Australia from most countries, although there are rigorous controls and it's expensive. The importation of birds and small mammals such as hamsters is also prohibited. Certain breeds of dog that are considered dangerous aren't eligible for importation, including American Pit Bull, Dogo Argentino, Fila Brazileiro, Japanese Tosa, Pit Bull Terrier and Presa Canario.

All imports are subject to quarantine (see below), and an import permit must be obtained before shipment. Applications should be made at least two months before the intended date of importation to the Australian Quarantine and Inspection Service (AQIS, 💻 www.daff.gov.au/aqis) in the state where you'll be living. The application fee is $325 for the first animal and $165 for a subsequent animal (although only one fee is charged if applications are received together and meet certain criteria). An import permit takes up to four weeks to be issued and is valid for two months. Imported dogs and cats must meet the following criteria:

- be aged at least 12 weeks at the time of export;
- be identified by a microchip;
- have been continuously resident for six months (or since their birth if less than six months old) in the country of origin immediately prior to their shipment to Australia;
- have not been in quarantine or under quarantine restrictions during the 30 days before export;
- have current vaccinations (see below).

Dogs must have vaccinations for canine parvovirus, distemper, infectious hepatitis, para-influenza, and bordetella bronchiseptica (kennel cough) and it's recommended that they aren't vaccinated against leptospira interrogans as this may interfere with the test results, causing dogs to be ineligible for export to Australia. Dogs must also test negative for canine brucellosis, ehrlichiosis (canine tropical pancytopenia), leishmaniosis and leptospirosis within 30 days of export.

Cats must have vaccinations for calicivirus, feline enteritis and rhinotracheitis. Vaccinations must have been given at least 14 days before shipment and not more than 12 months previously. All dogs and cats must be treated for internal parasites within 14 days of shipment and for external parasites within 96 hours of export, and must pass a clinical examination within 48 hours of shipment.

If dogs and cats exported to Australia don't meet all the pre-export and post-arrival testing, (and certification, health and vaccination requirements), they may need to be re-exported, treated or destroyed, or remain in quarantine until any disease concerns have been resolved.

From 1st January 2009, all cats and dogs being registered for the first time must be de-sexed from the age of three months; and (since 1st May 2007) must also have been microchipped (there are exemptions). All dogs aged over three months must be registered annually with the local council. Pets that are microchipped are automatically registered with the National Pet Register (💻 www.petregister.com.au).

Pets must be shipped by air to Australia in an International Air Transport Association (IATA) approved container, available from pet shipping agents such as Airpets Oceanic (UK ☎ 0800-371554 or 01753-685571, 💻 www.airpets.com) and Moving Abroad – Pet Shippers (UK ☎ 0845-408-0298 or 0113-239-7287, 💻 www.moggies.co.uk/services/pet_move.html) in the UK.

Animals are inspected at airports by a veterinary surgeon before shipment and can only arrive at the following airports in Australia: Kingsford Smith Airport (Sydney), Perth Airport and Tullamarine Airport (Melbourne). Other entry points require AQIS (see below) consent.

Quarantine

Dogs and cats from the Cocos (Keeling) Islands, New Zealand and Norfolk Island aren't required to undergo quarantine. Dogs and cats from approved rabies-free countries and territories, including Cyprus, Hawaii, Ireland, Japan, Malta, Norway, Singapore, Sweden, Taiwan and the UK, are quarantined for 30 days. Dogs and cats from countries and territories where rabies is considered to be well controlled (including Austria, Belgium, Canada, Denmark, Finland, France, Germany, Greece, Hong Kong, Israel, Italy, Luxembourg, Malaysia, the Netherlands, Portugal, Spain, Switzerland and the US) are quarantined for a minimum of 30 days and a maximum of 120.

Pets from certain other approved rabies-free countries (mostly Pacific islands) must spend 60 days in quarantine. The import of dogs and cats from countries and territories where dog-mediated rabies is endemic is permitted only indirectly via an approved country, where the animal must have been resident for at least six months prior to export to Australia.

On arrival in Australia, dogs and cats are quarantined in an approved animal quarantine station at Byford (Western Australia), Eastern Creek (NSW) or Spotswood (Victoria). Quarantine costs are around $15 per day for a cat and $20 for a dog; weekly visits are permitted during the quarantine period. Other charges include around $35/50 for document clearing, $70-80 for a veterinary examination and $95 or $120 for transport (depending on the time of day).

Many pet owners decide that the cost and strain of quarantine on their pets (and themselves) is too much to bear and find their pets new homes, acquiring new pets on arrival in Australia. For more information, contact the Australian Quarantine Inspection Service (AQIS, 💻 www.daff.gov.au/aqis), which publishes a leaflet, *The Importation of Dogs and Cats into Australia* (AQIS information sheet 2), as well as providing comprehensive information and forms online.

Licensing

There is no single national dog, cat or other pet register in Australia, where registration centres on the licensing of cat and dog ownership. Licences are issued by local government (e.g. municipal and shire councils) under state/territory legislation such as the Western Australian Dog Act 1976 and the South Australian Dog & Cat Management Act 1995. The cost of licences and the format of the licence tag vary across the country, as does the renewal of licences (usual every one or two years). Some states, such as Victoria, also require cat registration and microchipping.

Pet licensing provides revenue for the local governments and (in principle) ensures that owners can be held legally responsible for damages caused by their pets and reunited with lost animals. In practice, however, less than 60 per cent of pets are registered.

POLICE

Each state and the Northern Territory has an independent police force and there's also an Australian Federal Police (AFP – 💻 www.afp.gov.au) force, which is the Commonwealth government's primary law enforcement agency. The AFP is responsible for protecting federal property and enforcing federal laws such as those concerning counterfeiting, drug trafficking, fraud, illegal immigration, money laundering, organised crime and terrorism. The AFP also provides community police services in the ACT and in Australia's external territories. The Australian Crime Commission (www.crimecommission.gov.au) was established in 2003 to improve Australia's ability to meet the threats posed by nationally significant crime, including organised crime.

Most state police forces have special squads to handle VIP protection and specific crimes such as armed robbery, drug trafficking and use, fraud and homicide. There are also water police in cities and coastal areas.

All police in Australia are armed and in addition to guns carry other 'weapons' to pacify 'dangerous criminals', such as extendable batons and capsicum (pepper) sprays (used by NSW officers to disable armed attackers). Police officers in NSW have been issued with semi-automatic pistols (15-shot, .40 calibre) in order to confront armed gangs. General police policy if threatened is to shoot first and ask questions afterwards, although this is changing after a number of accidental deaths in recent years. There have been frequent incidents where police have shot dead unarmed assailants or even innocent bystanders (the Australian police shoot more innocent people than crooks). The number of deaths in custody has also risen alarmingly in recent years, including many Aboriginals – black people are around 20 times more likely to die in custody than white people.

Police in some states have stopped attending routine calls (such as security alarms, the vast majority of which are false) in an effort to redirect resources to fighting crime. In some areas they have considerably reduced the number of incidents they visit in order to cut their workload and allow more police to patrol the streets. Instead of sending a car, they may ask callers to report minor incidents by telephone or go to a police station. There are an increasing number of complaints by the public against the police in some states, and Australian police generally have a poor public image and are often seen as a law unto themselves.

There have been numerous police corruption scandals in recent decades, which, if the allegations are true, has some of the most corrupt police forces in the developed world. After investigations in NSW some years ago, for example, some 200 police officers were found to have criminal records. Corruption varies from minor infringements, such as accepting free food and drinks and tipping off repair companies in return for a commission, to assaults and sexual harassment, extortion, fabrication of evidence, involvement in organised crime, selling confiscated drugs, selling inside information to criminals, stealing goods and money, and taking bribes. Sexism and racism are widespread in Australia's police forces and female officers generally have poor promotion prospects compared with male officers.

Details of your rights regarding arrest, detention by the police, questioning and statements are explained in the ACLU publication *Your Rights* (see www.angelfire.com/folk/aclu). The police emergency number varies with the state – if in doubt, call the operator (1234) or the national emergency (000).

See also **Crime and Legal System & Advice** above.

POPULATION

The population of Australia is growing at around 1.4 per cent a year and reached 21m on 29th June 2007 and was 22.7m in August 2012. Australia's birth rate is slowly increasing (almost two births per woman), although women are generally choosing to marry later and have fewer children. Population projections by the Australian Bureau of Statistics (🖳 www.abs.gov.au) vary from 30.9m to 42.5m by 2056 and from 33.7 to 62.2m by 2101, based on a range of assumptions.

As in most other developed countries, the last 20 years have seen a huge rise in the number of people aged over 65 (who now account for almost 15 per cent of the population) and in particular those aged over 85. By 2020 the over 65s are expected to comprise around 16 per cent of the population. The average age in Australia is around 37 years.

The indigenous Aboriginal and Torres Strait Islander population of Australia is around 300,000, over half of whom live in NSW and Queensland. The Aboriginal population was estimated at between 200,000 and 750,000 when Australia was colonised by the English in 1788, although it was reduced dramatically in the 19th and early 20th centuries, since when it has recovered.

Australia is a country of immigrants and is the second most polyglot, multicultural nation in the world (after Israel), with large ethnic communities and migrants from over 125 nations. Before WWII, Australian migrants were predominantly from the UK and Ireland; even 40 years ago, when Australia would take virtually anyone and even offered a £10 assisted passage scheme, the UK dominated Australia's migrant intake and has provided over 2m migrants since 1945 and over 7m in total. However, in the last decade only some 10 per cent of new migrants have been British, although the UK remains the largest source of skilled migrants.

Since the war, there has been an influx of migrants from continental Europe, including large numbers of Greeks and Italians, plus Lebanese, Turks, Yugoslavs and various others. All major cities contain suburbs with predominantly 'foreign' communities,

including Chinese, Greek, Italian, Lebanese and Yugoslav. Sydney is home to more New Zealanders than most cities in New Zealand, and Melbourne's Greek population is the third largest in the world (after Athens and Thessalonica). Since the end of the official 'white Australia' policy in 1973, Australia has admitted large numbers of Asian immigrants, including many refugees from Indochina. There are also significant numbers of immigrants from Central and South America, the Middle East, the Pacific and South Africa. An estimated 90 per cent of the population is currently of European descent, 5 per cent Asian and 1.5 per cent Aboriginal. However, around 75 per cent of the population is Australian born.

In recent years, debate has centred on how migration affects employment, an increasing number of people believing that it increases unemployment (they claim that Australia's low unemployment rate would be even lower without immigrants). Some analysts see this as a knee-jerk reaction to make migrants the scapegoats for Australia's economic woes, and claim that no link has been established between migration and unemployment.

However, it isn't all one-way traffic. Around 5 to 10 per cent of Australians have emigrated to other countries, and over 30,000 people leave Australia each year. Many immigrants return home after a relatively short period.

Australia is a highly urbanised society: around 85 per cent of people live in urban areas (up from just over 60 per cent in 1921) and the population of the eight capital cities is growing faster than that of rural areas. Brisbane, Darwin and Perth are Australia's fastest-growing cities. Over 70 per cent of the population live in the major cities, which are situated on or near the coast, over 40 per cent in Sydney and Melbourne alone. Some 80 per cent of Australians live within 30km (20mi) of the coast, 35 per cent in NSW, where over 60 per cent of people live in Sydney and its suburbs.

The average population density in Australia, where vast areas are virtually uninhabited, is just two people per km² (compared with 85 people per km² in Asia). The capital, Canberra, has a density of just 20 people per km² or around a tenth of the population density of most European cities. Victoria is the most densely populated state. The population of states and territories (Dec 2011) and their capital cities (from 💻 www.abs.gov.au) is as follows:

State/Capital Populations

State	Population	Capital
ACT	0.37m	Canberra
NSW	7.2m	Sydney (4.6m)
NT	0.23m	Darwin (0.13m)
QLD	4.5m	Brisbane (2.1m)
SA	1.6m	Adelaide (1.3m)
TAS	0.5m	Hobart (0.22m)
VIC	5.6m	Melbourne (4.2m)
WA	2.4m	Perth (1.8m)

Within the next 50 years, around 25 per cent of Australia's population is likely to be of Asian origin. Today, Australia has a multicultural migration policy and settlers are encouraged to retain their ethnic artistic traditions, languages and lifestyles – although there's increasing pressure on them to learn English and 'integrate'. However, some Australians are alarmed about what they call the progressive 'Asianisation' of Australia's immigration

The long-term population shift away from the southeast to the west and the tropics has continued unabated in the early 21st century. Victoria has lost thousands of people to other states in the last decade or so, although by the late '90s the exodus had slowed to a trickle (most people move from Victoria to Queensland). South Australia and Tasmania have been losing the most people in recent years and the ACT is also losing residents at a high rate. In recent years, Australians have been fleeing the arid interior and clinging to the coast with more enthusiasm than ever.

Queensland is the fastest-growing state (most new arrivals are interstate migrants, many moving there on their retirement), although the flood of migrants, which increased by 30 per cent in the '90s, has slowed in recent years. Nevertheless, Queensland is expected to replace Victoria as the second most-populous state by around 2025. Rapid population growth in some areas of Queensland has placed a huge burden on the infrastructure such as hospitals, roads and schools, and is also having detrimental environmental and ecological consequences in some areas.

Some environmentalists believe that Australia already has more people than its natural resources (e.g. water!) can sustain, despite the huge size of the country and the low population density, while others argue that it can sustain a much larger population. The post-war slogan of 'populate or perish' has been changed to 'populate and perish' by those who would like to see immigration drastically reduced.

RELIGION

Australia has a tradition of religious tolerance, and residents have total freedom of religion without hindrance by the state or community. Australia is a secular society and has no official state religion, although around 64 per cent of the population are Christians, at least nominally, and 19 per cent claim to have no religion. Churches (particularly the Catholic Church)

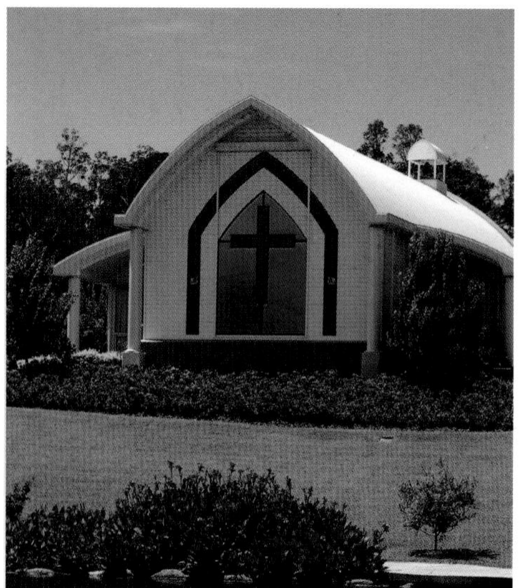
church, Hunter Valley, NSW

play an important role in education, most private schools being partly church-funded, although church attendance is low. In general, Australians are fairly laid-back about religion and there are few religious zealots and bible-thumpers, as are common in the US and some other countries.

Most Protestant churches have merged to become the Uniting Church, although the Anglican Church has remained independent. Roman Catholic (5.1m) and Anglican (3.7m) are the two main religions, followed by the Uniting Church (1.1m), Presbyterian (596,000), Orthodox (544,000), Baptist (316,000), Lutheran (251,000) and Pentecostal (219,000) churches. There are also sizeable Buddhist, Jewish and Muslim communities in the major cities. During the last decade, mainstream Christianity (apart from Catholicism) has declined (only the Orthodox Church thrives in Australia, particularly in Melbourne and Sydney), while 'nature-based' religions such as druidism, paganism and witchcraft have proliferated. Eastern and minority religions have also gained in popularity, including Japanese Mahikari, Shinto and Taoism. There's no recognised Aboriginal religion, although the Aboriginal people have many sacred sites throughout the country.

Every town and city has an Anglican and a Catholic church, and Uniting churches are also common. There are religious centres for all the world's major religions in the major cities – details of churches and religious services are published in local newspapers.

TIME DIFFERENCE

There are three different time zones in Australia (shown in the table below), which is one of the few countries in the world to have a zone that isn't a whole hour ahead of or behind its neighbours (CST).

To add to the confusion, all states and territories except the Northern Territory, Queensland and Western Australia operate 'daylight saving' in summer, when clocks are advanced one hour. All except Tasmania change their clocks at 2am on the last Sunday in October and the last Sunday in March. In Tasmania, daylight saving starts a month earlier and ends up to a month later! This creates no fewer than five different time zones in summer, e.g. when it's 9am in Western Australia, it's 10.30am in the Northern Territory; 11am in Queensland; 11.30am in South Australia; noon in the ACT, NSW and Victoria; and either 11am or noon (depending on the month) in Tasmania. Not surprisingly, attempts are being made to rationalise summer time zones. Time changes are announced in local newspapers and on radio and TV.

Australia doesn't use the 24-hour clock and times in many timetables are given using the 12-hour clock (i.e. am and pm), with before

Time Zones

Zone	GMT+	States/Territories
Western Standard Time (WST)	8 hours	WA
Central Standard Time (CST)	9.5 hours	NT, SA
Eastern Standard Time (EST)	10 hours	ACT, NSW, QLD, TAS, VIC

International Time Difference						
SYDNEY	**LONDON**	**CAPE TOWN**	MUMBAI	**TOKYO**	**LOS ANGELES**	**NEW YORK**
Noon	1am	3am	5.30am	10am	5pm*	8pm*

* previous day

noon times printed in light type and afternoon times printed in bold type.

In view of the huge time difference between Australia and many other continents (e.g. there are 10 or 11 hours' difference between Western Europe and EST), you should always check the local time when making international calls (one sure way to upset most people is to wake them at 3am). To check the time difference in major world cities, see 💻 www.timeanddate.com.

The table above shows the time in selected international cities when it's noon (in winter) in Sydney.

TIPPING

Tipping isn't a general practice in Australia (Americans please note!), although you may wish to leave a tip when you've had exceptional service or have received good value. However, tips are regarded by some Australians as patronising or even insulting. People almost never tip taxi drivers in Australia. However, it's common practice to round up taxi fares to the nearest dollar, although a cab driver may round the fare down rather than give you change.

Cloakroom attendants, garage staff (who clean your car's windscreen or check its oil or tyre pressures), hairdressers, hotel staff and porters (who usually have set charges) also don't expect to be tipped (but won't complain if they are). It isn't customary to tip a barman in a bar or pub, although many people leave their small change. Tipping in hotels depends where you're staying – it's unnecessary in tourist or medium class hotels, although staff in grand establishments are used to receiving tips from their wealthy clients. Otherwise, service charges aren't usually added to bills by hotels and restaurants.

One of the few exceptions to the 'no tipping' rule is top class restaurants, where it's customary to tip waiters up to 10 per cent of the bill for good service (although even here many Australians don't tip). Restaurant tips can be included in cheque or credit card payments or given as cash. The total on credit card counterfoils may be left blank to encourage you to leave a tip, so don't forget to fill in the total before signing it, or the waiter may enter his own 'tip'.

TOILETS

Public toilets in Australia are usually free and generally clean. They're commonly found in bus and train stations, council and tourist offices, department stores, parks and shopping centres. The most sanitary (even luxurious) toilets are found in department stores, hotels and restaurants, and are usually only for customers. Clean toilets are also found in airports, (near) beaches, car parks, museums and galleries, petrol stations, and public and private offices. Pub toilets vary from 'no-go areas' to spotless.

Australians don't use the terms bathroom, powder room or washroom when referring to a toilet, but use a variety of (often colourful) names, including ablutions, bog, crapper (after Thomas Crapper, who invented the WC), dunny (an outside toilet in country areas, often consisting of a wooden hut with an earth floor), ladies' or gents' (room), lavatory (lav), loo, privy, public convenience, thunder box, toot and WC (water closet).

Some toilets have nappy (diaper) changing facilities and facilities for nursing mothers, and there are also special toilets for the disabled at airports, bus and railway stations, and in shopping centres in major cities. Roadside pubs in country areas (roadhouses) have toilets and showers. When using a public toilet, make sure you use the correct one, as it's sometimes difficult to tell the difference between the stylish male and female signs.

19.

THE AUSTRALIANS

Who are the Australians? What are they like? Let us take a candid (and totally prejudiced) look at the Aussies, tongue firmly in cheek, and hope they forgive my flippancy or that they don't read this bit (which is why it's hidden away at the back of the book). The typical Aussie is amusing, an anarchist, a beach bum, boorish, brave, bronzed, a carnivore, casual, chauvinistic, classless, cosmopolitan, fiercely competitive, a cricket and footy fan, crude, delinquent, down to earth, eccentric, egotistical, a foreigner, frank (to the point of bluntness), friendly, a compulsive gambler, garrulous, generous, handsome, hedonistic, homophobic, honest, hospitable, idealistic, inebriated, informal, insular, irreverent, jingoistic, laid back, loud, macho, materialistic, matey, naïve, an 'ocker', open, optimistic, outspoken, parochial, a philistine, proud, relaxed, a republican, sincere, sociable, sophisticated, a surfie, tardy, tough, an inveterate traveller, unambitious, unpretentious, unreliable and xenophobic.

You may have noticed that the above list contains 'a few' contradictions (as does life in Australia), which is hardly surprising as there's no such thing as a typical Australian and few people conform to popular stereotypes. Australia is one of the most cosmopolitan and multicultural countries in the world and a nation of 'foreigners' (except for a few hundred thousand indigenous Aborigines), who have as much in common with each other as Icelanders with Africans or Tibetans with Maori. However, unlike the US, Australia isn't a universal melting pot, but a potpourri of ethnic splinter groups living separate lives with their own clubs, customs, neighbourhoods, newspapers, restaurants, shops, sports, and even TV and radio stations.

Australians pride themselves on their lack of class-consciousness and don't have the same prejudices and pretensions common in the 'old world', although Australia has never been an egalitarian society and is far from being classless. Status is as important here as it is anywhere else, although it's usually based on money and character rather than birthright. Australia generally has no 'old school tie' barriers to success and almost anyone, however humble his origins, can fight his way to the top of the heap (although colour barriers aren't so easy to overcome). Despite the fact that the vast majority of Australians are misplaced Britons and other Europeans on the wrong side of the world, modern Australia has more in common with the US in its ambitions, attitudes and lifestyle than with the UK and Europe.

Australians are noted for their insularity (which is hardly surprising when your nearest neighbours are thousands of miles away) and xenophobia – no doubt due to being inundated by foreigners, many of whom cannot (or won't) speak English. Nobody knows better than the Aussies that foreigners were created solely to be detested and loathed (Australians have a wealth of derogatory terms for immigrants), and transmit exotic diseases – which is why their planes are fumigated before they're allowed to set foot on Australian soil. Many Australians are prejudiced against all foreigners, who only come to Australia to steal their jobs and 'bludge' (scrounge) off the state, and they don't care much for anyone who isn't a dinky die

Aussie (newcomers are derisively called 'new Australians').

The culture gap is widest between Australians and Asians (the White Australia policy was officially abandoned in 1973 – but not in the nation's psyche), who are better educated, more industrious and often more intelligent – enough to incense anyone. However, for better or worse, the country has belatedly (and reluctantly) concluded that its future lies in trading with its Asian neighbours rather than maintaining its traditional ties with the UK.

▲ Caution

The natives have a particular abhorrence for the ubiquitous British (Poms) and New Zealanders (Kiwis), both of whom are the prime culprits in stealing Aussie jobs (when not dole bludging on Australian beaches).

Kiwis have free access to Australia and wash up on Australian shores in vast numbers (Bondi Beach is jokingly referred to as the 'home of the NZ government in exile'); not surprisingly they're the butt of many Australian jokes. However, Aussies reserve a special place in their hearts for the British, endearingly referred to as whinging Poms or Pommy bastards, to whom they're inexorably drawn by mutual antipathy. Making fun of the Poms (Pommy-bashing) is a popular pastime and has given rise to a surfeit of Pommy jokes, e.g. Q. What's the difference between a 747 and a Pom? A. When you switch off the engines, a 747 stops whining. Although most Pommy-bashing is good-natured, sometimes it's more malicious and it can get a bit wearing after a time (to deflect it you must give as good as you get).

The Aussies cannot bear to be constantly reminded of their convict ancestry, while the Poms are mortified that they gave the 'Aussies' free passage (admittedly brig class) to their land of sunshine and plenty while they stayed at home in the cold and rain. Aussies are an ungrateful shower and don't appreciate what the Poms have done for them, such as teaching them how to play cricket and rugby, introducing them to British culinary delights, and generally educating them on how to behave in polite society (admittedly this hasn't been an unqualified success – but what can you expect from 'Neanderthals' who live at the end of the earth, thousands of miles from civilisation?).

Australia is a hotbed of ethnic friction, although, apart from a small minority, most Australians aren't racist or even xenophobic – they just wish there were fewer foreigners! If it's any consolation to foreigners, Aussies don't get on too well with their fellow countrymen and delight in abusing their neighbours at every opportunity. All Australians look down on those from other states and love to make fun of them. The inhabitants of Australia's two major cities have a shared loathing for each other and the only thing that's (sometimes) worse than a whinging Pom to a Sydneysider is a Melbournite (and vice versa). Interstate rivalries, particularly between Victoria and New South Wales, were a brake on economic progress for decades.

To outsiders, Sydney is full of crooks, homosexuals (it's one of the gay capitals of the world), posers and yuppies; it's always raining in Melbourne (Bleak City), where the locals are staid and snobbish and consist mostly of Greeks and Italians (called Mexicans by those from NSW, as they're 'south of the border'); Queenslanders (banana benders) are red-necked fascists and uncivilised ockers; Canberra has been described as 'the ruination of a perfectly good sheep station' and is a deadly boring place (it's often likened to a cemetery) inhabited by civil servants and politicians (enough said) – if you develop a yearning to live in Canberra, you should seek immediate psychiatric help!

Adelaide is conservative and dull and inhabited by prudes and killjoys (wowsers) – South Australians are disparagingly termed crow-eaters after the eating habits of the early settlers; Western Australians (sandgropers) are aliens, backward and country bumpkins who inhabit a different planet (Perth is the most remote city in the world); Northern Territorians (topenders) are Crocodile Dundee types, drunks and primitives, who are either paid to stay or cannot afford to leave; and Tasmanians (taswegians) are dimwits (all that in-breeding), puritans and radical conservationists, descended from convicts and still living in the 19th century.

Being (relatively) intelligent people, Australians have a *laissez-faire* attitude to business and work, which lag well behind having a good time. They down tools at the drop of a spanner (Australia has traditionally had some of the most militant trade unions in the world) and think nothing of having a day off work (sickie) when they've something better to do, which is most of the time. If Australians worked as hard as they played (particularly at sport), they'd put even the Japanese to shame. Contrary to the widely held misconception that 'hard work never did anyone any harm', Aussies know only too well that hard 'yakka' is bad for your health and can prove fatal. They prefer to make (or more often lose) their fortune at gambling, the only acceptable way to get rich, and will bet on almost anything, including bingo, casinos, football pools, general elections, horse and greyhound racing, lotteries, poker machines (pokies), toad, cockroach and lizard races, which politician will get caught next with his hand in the till, or even (in desperation) two flies climbing a wall. Gambling on sporting events is a national obsession.

Australians are passionate about sport ('life be in it'), which is an integral part of Australian culture. The country is highly successful in international competition, particularly swimming, which isn't surprising as training includes trying to out-swim a shark! Australians can be found in their natural state on a beach or anywhere there's water (when not in a pub). However, with the exception of those who spend their time boxing kangaroos, racing water buffalo or wrestling crocodiles, the nearest most Australians get to working up a sweat is strolling from the TV to the fridge for a 'coldie' (smart Aussies have an esky by the sofa).

Despite the popular image of Australians as bronzed, muscular lifesavers and bathing beauties, many are overweight and unfit – a popular 'sport' in the outback is 'whammying', where fatties attempt to knock each other over with their beer bellies! Nevertheless, when achievements are measured against population, Australia is the foremost sporting nation in the world (but don't tell the Aussies – they're conceited enough as it is).

Australia has a fierce sporting rivalry with its neighbour New Zealand (particularly at rugby), although the most popular sport is Pommy-bashing, which reaches its peak in the biennial humiliation of the Poms at cricket – although in recent years the tables have been turned! However, although they're sports fanatics, Australians believe in fair play and love to support the underdog – unless it's the English, in which case they yearn to see them ground into the dust.

It's a common misconception among foreigners that Australians speak English – amazingly some people even go to Australia to learn English! However, don't expect Australians to speak British English or even American English (the Mad Max movies had to be dubbed for American audiences). The only people who speak proper English in Australia are the foreigners – apart, that is, from the million or so migrants who hardly speak a word of it. Australians converse in a secret language (slanguage) called 'strine', full of blasphemy, fun, profanity, rhyming slang, strange words and ungrammatical phonetic spelling (Aussies have some of the most colourful abuse in the world). Aussies routinely abbreviate everything, as it's usually too hot to say the whole word (and opening your mouth lets the flies in); most syllables are omitted to save energy – besides which, enunciating clearly is difficult when you're inebriated.

Which brings us to the Aussies' favourite pastime – boozing. The Aussies' natural habitat is a pub (preferably close to a beach), where they spend their waking hours between visits to the dole office and the meat pie van. Their favourite tipple is ice-cold beer, otherwise know as amber nectar, a cold one, neck oil, etc., or a glass of Chateau Chumbawumba for the wimps. Aussies are passionate about their local beers and aren't particularly complimentary about brands brewed in other states (outside Queensland, XXXX stands for CRAP). In truth, Aussies don't really care much for beer, which is just an excuse for a good vomit (big spit, chunder, kark, laugh at the ground, shout for Ruth, technicolor yawn, etc.). However, despite their awesome reputation as a nation of drunks, Aussies consume less alcohol per head than the inhabitants of many European countries (which is best not mentioned in your local hotel in Oz). Recent figures published by the World Health Organisation shows Australia languishing well down the table.

Australia has long been famous for its 'cultural cringe' and is still occasionally typecast as a land of mutton-eating philistines, although it's no longer the cultural desert some would have you believe. It may come as a surprise that not all Aussies are beer-swilling, loudmouthed, uncultured yobbos and some have even been known to visit theatres and listen to classical music (Australia even has an opera house!). Nowadays Australians export their culture in the guise of art, films, music and TV programmes, which are exported around the globe. It's even possible to take a degree in Australian studies, which lasts for a whole week and includes an in-depth study of barbies, the Bee Gees, the bush, Clive James, cricket, Crocodile Dundee, Dame Edna Everage, footy, Fosters, Germaine Greer, Kylie, Mad Max, Neighbours, Olivia Newton John, Rolf Harris, Skippy, surfing, and the Sydney Opera House.

> **▲ Caution**
>
> Although they have a sharp (crude) sense of humour, the Aussies are somewhat lacking in mirth when it comes to attacks on their culture, and newcomers should tread warily.

Aussies are infamous for their macho image and a peculiar Aussie male bonding called mateship (similar to American buddyship). Australian men are men's men, and mainstream males have no time for limp-wristed gays. However, rumour has it that Australian men are becoming more sensitive (heaven forbid!), that ockerism is dead and Aussie men are now new age guys – although anyone who believes that is a few snags short of a barbie (a sensitive Aussie is an oxymoron – or a foreigner). The former Australian lifestyle magazine *Ralph* (Responsible And Lovable Piss-Head) was much nearer the mark – it catered to the fun-loving Australian male who has a fine appreciation for the good looking women of the world, i.e. the ubiquitous politically incorrect bloke interested mainly in beer, boys' toys, humour, motors, sex, sport and trivia (not necessarily in that order – some Aussies actually prefer sex to beer, but most have a larger capacity for booze).

Aussie males are rampant chauvinists (not surprisingly, women's lib passed Australia by), and some of their more flattering terms for women include bush pigs, swamp hogs and maggots – a good looking Sheila is a 'glamour maggot' or 'glam mag'. Paradoxically, Australia was the one of the first countries in the world to give women the vote, although they were still banned from the pub (not that most women would have been seen dead in one). When attending social functions, men traditionally congregate at one end of the room (or garden), usually where the booze is, and the Sheilas at the other attending to the food.

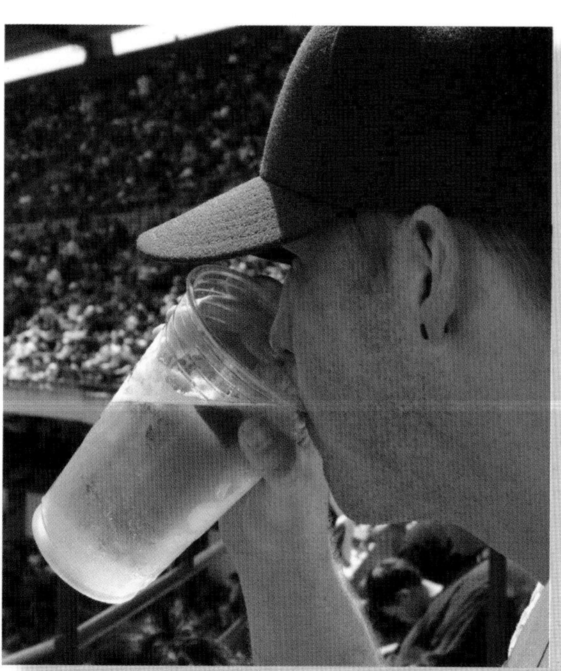

Despite their ocker image, many Australians are apparently (according to a recent 'survey') considerate lovers when sober, although they're also among the world's fastest performers (they don't want to waste valuable drinking time). To the average Aussie male, foreplay is 'hey Sheila, you wanna ****?' and sex drive is doing it in the back of a panel van.

Australian politicians (pollies) are world leaders in mismanagement and some of the most hilarious and entertaining in the world (you have to laugh, otherwise you'd cry). In a less liberal country they'd all be locked up, although this would deprive Aussies (not to mention a legion of broadcasters, cartoonists, journalists, etc.) of their best source of jokes. Whatever momentous events are happening elsewhere in the world, you can always rely on Aussie politics for some amusing diversions such as defections, lurks and perks, party infighting, rorts (scams), sackings and scandals, although strangely there are very few sex scandals – could they all be gay?

When not junketing around the world (or abusing their official credit cards, etc.), pollies spend their time (well at least a few days a year) hurling personal abuse at each other in parliament (not surprisingly, there are relatively few women politicians in Australia). Aussies have a healthy disrespect (contempt) for their politicians and need to be forced to vote under the threat of fines. The seat of government (Canberra) is appropriately located in the wilds of New South Wales – well away from civilisation and normal folk.

Immigration has undeniably made Australia a culturally richer, more diverse and infinitely more interesting country. However, today's Australia is closed to many of the immigrants who made it one of the best countries in the world. (First you were transported for free, then you had to pay £10 and now they won't even let you visit without a visa – if you want to stay, you need to be under 30, speak fluent English, and have a couple of university degrees and ten years' work experience – or a few million dollars). However, if you're rejected, try to look on the bright side. The Australian Dream isn't always what it's cracked up to be and surveys have found that many recently arrived migrants believe they were better off at home (admittedly most were unemployed and without access to social security).

Australia's problems include child poverty, drug abuse, a high divorce rate, relatively high suicide and crime rates, drought/bushfires, homelessness, pollution, welfare dependency and a poor record on 'preserving' its environment, animal life and indigenous peoples. As in many countries, the burgeoning number of single-parent families, low pay and spiralling prices (particularly rents) is increasingly creating two Australias: the haves and the have-nots.

Poverty is blamed for causing domestic violence, family breakdowns and lawlessness. Many Australians work too hard, travel too far to work, arrive home too late, and have kids who attend schools too far away from home. These problems are by no means unique to Australia in today's ever-competitive world and are shared by most developed countries. However, how Australia faces up to them and the other challenges of the 21st century will shape its future for generations to come.

Australians were profoundly shocked by the recession in the '90s, which destroyed the myth of economic security and eternal prosperity. They were under siege from all sides, with many of their traditional beliefs and values swept away by events largely beyond their control. However, the country has become a much more confident and prosperous society in the last decade or so, during which the economy has boomed and living standards soared. The country was hardly affected by the fallout from the worldwide credit crunch and recession in the last few years.

And now for the good news! Australia is one of the most liberal, open, stable and tolerant societies in the world. It has a strong economy, with abundant natural resources, political stability, a skilled workforce, steady population growth, and substantial domestic and foreign capital investment. It's renowned for its superb beaches, rugged beauty, wonderful climate, creativity, cultural diversity, freedom, outdoor lifestyle, excellent local government, friendly people, good food and excellent wines, open spaces, extensive sports facilities, good transportation and healthcare, and unique wildlife.

In the 2011 'Mercer Quality of Living Survey', Australian cities were highly rated with Sydney at number 11, Melbourne 18, Perth 21, Canberra 26, Adelaide 30 and Brisbane 37 (Australia was ranked lower than in previous years due to the higher cost of living) – all ahead of London (38) and New York (47). Australians rank among the world's most contented people and are generally happy with life, although paradoxically many people reckon that life is getting worse.

Australia is nothing if not a land of contradictions and, despite the gloomy predictions from some quarters, most Australians have remarkable faith in themselves and optimism for the future, although newcomers should be aware that 'she'll be right' is code for 'everything that can go wrong will', and 'no worries' means 'it's screwed up again'.

Newcomers should also avoid comparing Australia unfavourably with their home country (the worst sin is to say repeatedly, 'we do it like this/better at home').

However, if you really want to rile the Aussies, you could complain about their boring blue skies and tell them their beer's too cold and their wine's too warm, the sun's too hot (and gives you cancer), there are too many flies and bugs, their birds squawk instead of sing, much of the wildlife is out to eat or kill you, and everywhere you turn there are smiling, friendly Aussies!

Aussies are casual (relaxed to the point of stupor), informal and straight talkers ('tell it as it is'), and expect you to be open and friendly also. One of the things that endears Aussies to foreigners is their outrageous sense of humour and ability to poke fun at themselves and everyone else. Australians generally take people as they find them and if you're friendly and make an effort to adapt to their way of life, they may even take to you.

Although immigrants may criticise some aspects of Australian life, relatively few seriously consider leaving and most are proud to call themselves Aussies. In fact, immigrants from a vast range of backgrounds firmly believe that Australia is the best country in the world. Few other nations offer such an irrepressible and exciting lifestyle. For sheer vitality and *joie de vivre*, Australia has few equals and, for the fortunate few who are lucky enough to secure a residence visa, it's a land where you can turn your dreams into reality. Australia remains a country of great opportunity, although perhaps no longer the Lucky Country (if it ever was – you make your own luck in Oz through hard yakka). Provided you maintain a sense of humour about everything, you too may find that 'she will indeed be all right'!

Long Live Australia! God Save the Queen! Up the Republic!

20. MOVING HOUSE OR LEAVING AUSTRALIA

When you're moving house or leaving Australia, there are many things to be considered and a 'million' people to be informed. The checklists contained in this chapter are designed to make the task easier and with luck prevent an ulcer or a nervous breakdown, provided of course you don't leave everything to the last minute (only divorce and bereavement cause more stress than moving house). See also Moving House on page 88.

MOVING HOUSE

When moving house within Australia, you should consider the following:

- If you live in rented accommodation, you must give your landlord notice (the period depends on your contract). You may need to remain until a minimum period has elapsed and, if you don't give your landlord sufficient notice, you're required to pay the rent until the end of your contract or for the full notice period. This also applies if you have a separate contract for a garage or other rented property, e.g. a holiday home. If you're renting, make sure that your bond is returned.
- If you're a homeowner and are moving to a new council area, you should inform your present council when you move and re-register in your new council area after arrival. When moving to a new area or state, you may be entitled to a refund of a portion of your property taxes (council rates).
- If you have an Australian driving licence or an Australian registered car, give your local state traffic authority (see **Appendix A**) your new address as soon as possible after moving.
- Also inform the following:
  - your employer;
  - your utility (electricity, gas and water) companies;
  - your telephone company (or companies);
  - your accountant, bank or credit union, building society, businesses where you have accounts, credit and charge card companies, insurance companies (for example car, health and home), post office, solicitor, stockbroker and other financial institutions;
  - your family dentist, doctor and other health practitioners. Health records should be transferred to your new practitioners, if applicable.;
  - your children's schools. If applicable, arrange for schooling in your new area. Try to give a term's notice and obtain a copy of any relevant school reports or records from your children's current schools;
  - all regular correspondents, friends and relatives, professional and trade journals to which you subscribe, and social and sports clubs you belong to. Give or send them your new address and telephone number. Arrange to have your post redirected by Australia Post (see **Change of Address** on page 111);
  - your local consulate or embassy, if you're registered with it;

> ☑ **SURVIVAL TIP**
>
> **Terminate any outstanding hire purchase, lease or loan contracts and pay all outstanding bills (allow plenty of time, as some companies may be slow to respond).**

- Return any library books and anything else borrowed.
- Arrange removal of your furniture and belongings by booking a removal company well in advance. If you have only a few items of furniture to move, you may prefer to do your own move, in which case you may need to hire a van.
- Arrange for a cleaning company and/or decorating company for rented accommodation, if necessary.
- Cancel milk and newspaper deliveries.

LEAVING AUSTRALIA

Before leaving Australia permanently or for an indefinite period, the following items should be considered in addition to those listed under **Moving House** above:

- Give notice to your employer, if applicable.
- Check that your family's passports aren't out of date.
- Check whether any special requirements (e.g. inoculations, permits, visas) are necessary for entry into your country of destination by contacting the local embassy or consulate in Australia. An exit permit or visa isn't required to leave Australia.
- Book a removal company well in advance. International shipping companies usually provide a wealth of information and may also be able to advise you on various matters concerning your relocation. Find out the exact procedure for shipping your belongings to your country of destination from the relevant embassy in Australia (don't rely entirely on your shipping company). Forms may need to be completed before arrival. If you've been living in Australia for less than a year, you're required to re-export all personal effects, including furniture and vehicles that were imported tax and duty-free.
- Arrange to sell anything that you won't be taking with you, e.g. car, furniture and house. If you sell a second home in Australia, you may need to pay capital gains tax on any profit made on the sale.
- Claim a rebate on your tax payments, if applicable.
- If you're leaving Australia permanently and have been a member of a superannuation scheme, your benefits won't be paid until you reach the 'preservation' age. Contact your employer's personnel office or your superannuation company for information.
- If you have an Australian-registered car which you're exporting permanently, you should ask your local state traffic authority to de-register the vehicle, and register it in your new country of residence on arrival (as necessary).
- Depending on your destination, your pets may require inoculations or may need to go into quarantine for a period.
- Arrange health, travel and other insurance as necessary (see **Chapter 13**).
- Depending on your destination, you may wish to arrange dental and health checks for your family before leaving Australia. Obtain a copy of all your dental and health records and a statement from your health insurance company noting your present level of cover.
- Check whether you're entitled to a rebate on your car and other insurance. Obtain a letter from your Australian motor insurance company stating your number of years without a claim.
- If you aren't selling your property, arrange to let it through a friend or a letting agency (see **Chapter 5**).
- Check whether you need an international driving permit or a translation of your Australian or foreign driving licence for your country of destination.
- Give friends and business associates in Australia an email address, temporary address and/or telephone number where you can be contacted overseas.

- If you're travelling by air, allow plenty of time to get to the airport, register your luggage, and clear security and immigration.
- Buy a copy of the relevant *Living and Working* book before leaving Australia. If we haven't written it yet, drop us a line and we will get started on it right away!

Have a safe journey!

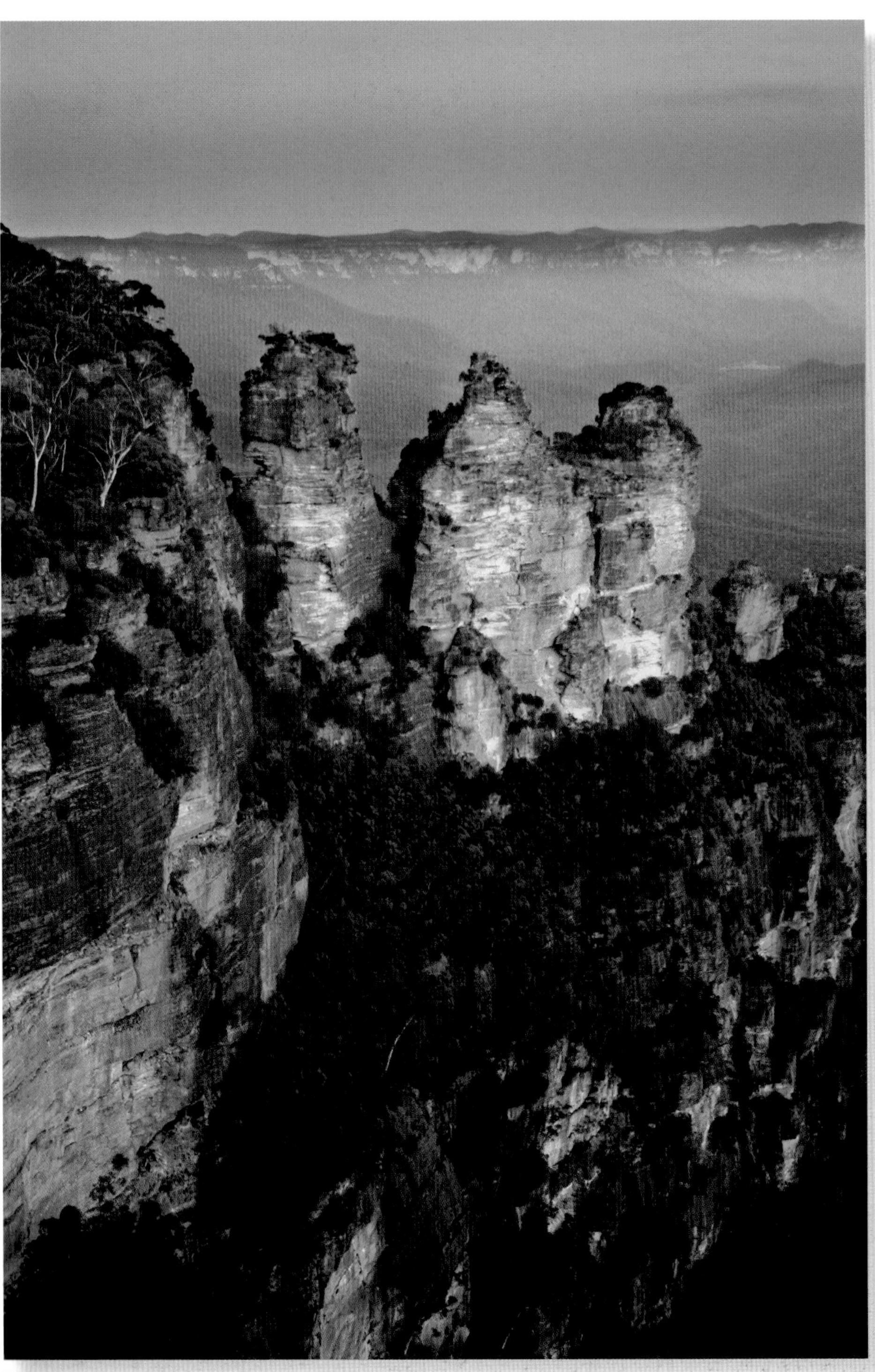

Three Sisters, Blue Mountains, NSW

APPENDICES

APPENDIX A: USEFUL ADDRESSES

Embassies & Consulates (Canberra)

A selection of embassies in Canberra is listed below. A full list of embassies and consulates in Australia is available from the Department of Foreign Affairs and Trade's website (💻 www.dfat.gov.au – go to 'Embassies'). Business hours vary considerably and all embassies close on their national holidays as well as on Australian Public Holidays. Always telephone to check the business hours before visiting.

Austria: 12 Talbot Street, Forrest, ACT 2603 (☎ 02-6295 1533, 💻 www.bmeia.gv.at/en/embassy/canberra.html).

Belgium: 19 Arkana Street, Yarralumla, ACT 2600 (☎ 02-6273 2501/02, 💻 www.diplomatie.be/canberra).

Bulgaria: 29 Pindari Crescent, O'Malley, ACT 2606 (☎ 02-6286 9700, 💻 www.bulgaria.org.au/en/index.htm).

Canada: Commonwealth Avenue, Canberra, ACT 2600 (☎ 02-6270 4000, 💻 www.canada.org.au).

China: 15 Coronation Drive, Yarralumla, ACT 2600 (☎ 02-6273 4780, 💻 http://au.china-embassy.org).

Czech Republic: 8 Culgoa Circuit, O'Malley, ACT 2606 (☎ 02-6290 1386, 💻 www.mzv.cz/canberra).

Denmark: 15 Hunter Street, Yarralumla, ACT 2600 (☎ 02-6270 5333, 💻 www.canberra.um.dk).

Finland: 12 Darwin Avenue, Yarralumla, ACT 2600 (☎ 02-6273 3800, 💻 www.finland.org.au/public/default.aspx).

France: 6 Perth Avenue, Yarralumla, ACT 2600 (☎ 02-6216 0100, 💻 www.ambafrance-au.org).

Germany: 119 Empire Circuit, Yarralumla, ACT 2600 (☎ 02-6270 1911, 💻 www.germanembassy.org.au).

Greece: 9 Turrana Street, Yarralumla, ACT 2600 (☎ 02-6273 3011, 💻 http://greece.visahq.com/embassy/australia).

Hungary: 17 Beale Crescent, Deakin, ACT 2600 (☎ 02-6282 3226, 💻 www.embassiesabroad.com/embassies-of/hungary).

India: 3-5 Moonah Place, Yarralumla, ACT 2600 (☎ 02-6273 3999, 💻 www.india-visa.com/canberra.htm).

Indonesia: 8 Darwin Avenue, Yarralumla, ACT 2600 (☎ 02-6250 8600, 🖳 www.kemlu.go.id/canberra).

Ireland: 20 Arkana Street, Yarralumla, ACT 2600 (☎ 02-6273 3022, 🖳 www.embassyofireland.au.com).

Israel: 6 Turrana Street, Yarralumla, ACT 2600 (☎ 02-6215 4500, 🖳 http://canberra.mfa.gov.il).

Italy: 12 Grey Street, Deakin, ACT 2600 (☎ 02-6273 3333, 🖳 www.ambcanberra.esteri.it).

Japan: 112 Empire Circuit, Yarralumla, ACT 2600 (☎ 02-6273 3244, 🖳 www.au.emb-japan.go.jp).

Malaysia: 7 Perth Avenue, Yarralumla, ACT 2600 (☎ 02-6120 0300, 🖳 www.malaysia.org.au/serv1.html).

Netherlands: 120 Empire Circuit, Yarralumla, ACT 2600 (☎ 02-6220 9400, www.netherlands.org.au).

New Zealand: Commonwealth Avenue, Canberra, ACT 2600 (☎ 02-6270 4211, 🖳 www.nzembassy.com/australia).

Norway: 17 Hunter Street, Yarralumla, ACT 2600 (☎ 02-6273 3444, 🖳 www.norway.org.au).

Papua New Guinea: 39-41 Forster Crescent, Yarralumla, ACT 2600 (☎ 02-6273 3322, 🖳 www.pngcanberra.org).

Philippines: 1 Moonah Place, Yarralumla, ACT 2600 (☎ 02-6273 2535/36, 🖳 www.philembassy.org.au).

Poland: 7 Turrana Street, Yarralumla, ACT 2600 (☎ 02-6272 1000, 🖳 www.canberra.polemb.net).

Portugal: 23 Culgoa Circuit, O'Malley, ACT 2606 (☎ 02-6290 1733, 🖳 www.consulportugal sydney.org.au).

Russia: 78 Canberra Avenue, Griffith, ACT 2603 (☎ 02-6295 9474, 🖳 www.australia.mid.ru).

Singapore: 17 Forster Crescent, Yarralumla, ACT 2600 (☎ 02-6271 2000, 🖳 www.mfa.gov.sg/canberra).

Slovakia: 47 Culgoa Circuit, O'Malley, ACT 2606 (☎ 02-6290 1516, 🖳 www.slovakemb-aust.org).

Slovenia: 26 Akame Circuit, O'Malley, ACT 2606 (☎ 02-6290 0000, 🖳 www.canberra.embassy.si/en).

South Africa: Corner State Circle and Rhodes Place, Yarralumla, ACT 2600 (☎ 02-6272 7300, 🖳 www.sahc.org.au).

Spain: 15 Arkana Street, Yarralumla, ACT 2600 (☎ 02-6273 3555, 🖳 www.maec.es/subwebs/embajadas/canberra).

Sweden: 5 Turrana Street, Yarralumla, ACT 2600 (☎ 02-6270 2700, 🖳 www.swedenabroad.com/canberra).

Switzerland: 7 Melbourne Avenue, Forrest, ACT 2603 (☎ 02-6162 8400, 🖳 www.eda.admin.ch/australia).

Thailand: 111 Empire Circuit, Yarralumla, ACT 2600 (☎ 02-6206 0100, 🖳 http://canberra.thaiembassy.org).

United Kingdom: Commonwealth Avenue, Canberra, ACT 2600 (☎ 02-6270 6666, 🖳 www.ukinaustralia.fco.gov.uk).

United States of America: Moonah Place, Yarralumla, ACT 2600 (☎ 02-6214 5600, 🖳 http://canberra.usembassy.gov).

Australian Customs Service

The Australian Customs Service has a nationwide telephone number (☎ 1300-363 263) and a website (💻 www.customs.gov.au) for general information. State and territory offices are as follows (not that 1300 numbers cannot be used from abroad):

ACT: Customs House, 5 Constitution Avenue, Canberra, ACT 2601 (☎ 1300-558 287).

NSW: 10 Cooks River Drive, Sydney International Airport, NSW 2020 (☎ 1300-558 287).

NT: 21 Lindsay Street, Darwin, NT 0800 (☎ 1300-558 287).

QLD: T20-22 The Circuit, Brisbane Airport, Brisbane 4007 (☎ 1300-558 287).

SA: 220 Commercial Road, Port Adelaide, SA 5015 (☎ 1300-558 287).

TAS: 1st Floor, MBF Building, 25 Argyle Street, Hobart, TAS 7001 (☎ 1300-558 287).

VIC: 1010 Latrobe Street, Melbourne Docklands, VIC 3001 (☎ 1300-558 287).

WA: Customs House, 2 Henry Street, Fremantle, WA 6160 (☎ 1300-558 287).

Consumer Affairs & Fair Trading

The government consumer service (💻 www.consumer.gov.au) provides general information, with state and territory services offering more comprehensive advice (not that 1300 numbers cannot be used from abroad):

ACT: Office of Fair Trading (☎ 02-6207 3000, 💻 www.ors.act.gov.au/community/fair_trading).

NSW: Office of Fair Trading (☎ 02-9895 0111, 💻 www.fairtrading.nsw.gov.au).

NT: Consumer Affairs (☎ 08-8999 1999, 💻 www.consumeraffairs.nt.gov.au).

QLD: Office of Fair Trading (☎ 07-3405 0985, 💻 www.fairtrading.qld.gov.au).

SA: Office of Consumer & Business Affairs (☎ 08-8204 9777, 💻 www.ocba.sa.gov.au).

TAS: Consumer Affairs & Fair Trading (☎ 1300-654 499, 💻 www.consumer.tas.gov.au).

VIC: Consumer Affairs (☎ 1300-558 181, 💻 www.consumer.vic.gov.au).

WA: Department of Consumer and Employment Protection (☎ 1300-304 054, 💻 www.docep.wa.gov.au).

Motor Vehicle Registration Authorities

ACT: Road Transport Authority, PO Box 582, Dickson, ACT 2602 (☎ 02-6207 7000, 💻 www.rego.act.gov.au).

NSW: Roads and Traffic Authority, 101 Miller Street North, Sydney, NSW 2060 (☎ 02-4920 4159, 💻 www.rta.nsw.gov.au).

NT: Motor Vehicle Registry, PO Box 530, Darwin, NT 0801 (☎ 1300-654 628, 💻 www.nt.gov.au/transport).

QLD: Queensland Transport, PO Box 673, Fortitude Valley, QLD 4006 (☎ 132380, 💻 www.transport.qld.gov.au).

SA: Vehicle Standards, Transport SA, PO Box 1, Walkerville, SA 5081 (☎ 08-8343 2222, 💻 www.transport.sa.gov.au).

TAS: Registrar of Motor Vehicles, PO Box 936, Hobart, TAS 7001 (1300-135513, www.transport.tas.gov.au).

VIC: Vic Roads, PO Box 1644, Melbourne, VIC 3001 (03-9854 2666, www.vicroads.vic.gov.au).

WA: Department of Transport, Licensing Division, PO Box R1290, Perth, WA 6844 (08-9427 6404, www.dpi.wa.gov.au/licensing).

Miscellaneous

Australia Travel & Tourism (www.australia.com).

Australian American Association, PO Box 869, Randwick, NSW 2031, Australia (www.americanaustralian.org).

Australian-Britain Society, National Office, 10 Canterbury Crescent, Deakin, ACT 2600, Australia (02-6273 3197, www.ausbrit.org).

Australian-British Chamber of Commerce, Suite 5, Level 9, 3 Spring Street, Sydney, NSW 2000, Australia (02-9247 6271, www.britishchamber.com).

Australian Bureau of Statistics (02-9268 4909, www.abs.gov.au).

Australian Embassy, 1601 Massachusetts Ave., NW, Washington, DC 20036, USA (202-797 3000, www.usa.embassy.gov.au).

Australian High Commission, Australia House, Strand, London WC2B 4LA, UK (020-7379 4334, www.uk.embassy.gov.au).

Australian Taxation Office, PO Box 9990 in the capital city of state or territory, Australia (132869, www.ato.gov.au).

Foreign Investment Review Board, Department of the Treasury, Langton Crescent, Parkes, ACT 2600, Australia (02-6263 2940, www.firb.gov.au). Provides information about buying property in Australia for non-residents and retirees.

APPENDIX B: FURTHER READING

Newspapers

The Advertiser (🖳 www.adelaidenow.com.au). Adelaide's leading daily newspaper.

The Age (🖳 www.theage.com.au). Melbourne's quality newspaper.

Australia & New Zealand magazine (🖳 www.getmedownunder.com). The UK's leading magazine for prospective migrants to Australia and New Zealand.

The Australian (🖳 www.theaustralian.news.com.au). Australia's only national and most respected newspaper.

The Australian Financial Review (🖳 http://afr.com). Australia's national daily financial newspaper.

The Canberra Times (🖳 http://canberra.yourguide.com.au). Canberra's leading daily.

The Courier Mail (🖳 www.thecouriermail.news.com.au). Brisbane's best-selling daily newspaper.

The Daily Telegraph (🖳 www.dailytelegraph.news.com.au). A leading Sydney newspaper.

The Herald-Sun (🖳 www.heraldsun.news.com.au). Melbourne's best-selling newspaper.

The Mercury (🖳 www.news.com.au/mercury). Tasmania's leading newspaper.

The Sydney Morning Herald (🖳 www.smh.com.au). Sydney's best-selling newspaper.

The West Australian (🖳 www.thewest.com.au). Western Australia's best-selling newspaper.

Books

There are many useful reference books for those seeking general information about Australia, including the *Year Book Australia* published annually by the Australian Bureau of Statistics (🖳 www.abs.gov.au). The Australia Government Publishing Service (🖳 www.publications.gov.au) publishes and distributes a wealth of useful publications for businessmen, prospective migrants and visitors.

A selection of books about Australia is listed below (the publication title is followed by the name of the author and the publisher's name in brackets). Some of the books listed are out of print, but you may still be able to find a copy in a library or bookshop.

Aboriginal Australia

Aboriginal Art, Wally Caruana (Thames & Hudson)

Aboriginal Art of Australia (Art Around the World), Carol Finley (Lerner)

Country of the Heart: An Australian Indigenous Homeland, Deborah Bird Rose (Aboriginal Studies Press)

Mutant Message Down Under, Marlo Morgan (Thorsons)

Stories from the Billabong, James Vance Marshall and Francis Firebrace (Frances Lincoln Children's Books)

Australians

Australians: Volume 1: Origins to Eureka, Thomas Keneally (Allen & Unwin)

Australians: Volume 2: Eureka to the Diggers, Thomas Keneally (Allen & Unwin)

From Strength to Strength, Sara Henderson (Thomas Dunne Books)

Unreliable Memoirs, Clive James (Picador)

Culture

Australian Language and Culture: No Worries!, Paul Smitz (Lonely Planet)

Australian Sport: Better by Design? (Routledge)

Culture Wise Australia, David Hampshire & Martin Kidd (Survival Books)

In the Vernacular: A Generation of Australia Culture and Controversy, Stuart Cunningham (ReadHowYouWant)

What Australia Means to Me, Bob Carr (Penguin)

Who We Are: A Snapshot of Australia Today, David Dale (Allen & Unwin)

Xenophobe's Guide to the Aussies, Ken Hunt & Mike Taylor (Oval)

The Great Outdoors

Cycling Australia, Nicola Wells (Lonely Planet)

Dangerous Creatures of Australia, Marty Robinson (New Holland)

Explore Australia's Outback 29th Edition, (Explore Australia)

Outback Australia (Lonely Planet)

Thumbs Up Australia: Hitchhiking the Outback, Tom Parry (Nicholas Brealey Publishing)

Travels in Outback Australia: Beyond the Black Stump, Andrew Stevenson (TravellersEye Ltd)

History

Australia, the People (Lands, Peoples & Cultures), Erinn Banting (Crabtree)

Australian History for Dummies, Alex McDermott (Wiley-Blackwell)

The Commonwealth of Thieves: The Story of the Founding of Australia, Thomas Keneally (Chatto & Windus)

A Concise History of Australia, Stuart Macintyre (Cambridge University Press)

Divided Nation: Indigenous Australians in Australian Political Culture, Tim Rowse & Murray Groot (Melbourne University Press)

The Oxford Companion to Australian History (OUP)

Terra Australis: Matthew Flinders' Great Adventures in the Circumnavigation of Australia, Matthew Flinders (The Text Publishing Co.)

Language

Australian Language & Culture, Paul Smitz (Lonely Planet)

Wordbook of Australian Idiom: Aussie Slang, Kerrin P. Rowe (Trafford)

Living & Working

At Home in Australia, Peter Conrad (Thames & Hudson)
Australia Gap Pack (Collins)
Buying a Home in Australia, David Hampshire & Joanna Styles (Survival Books)
Jump Down Under: True Stories of Relocating to Australia, Iain Ayres (Summertime)

Tourist Guides

Australia (Lonely Planet)
Australia by Rail, Colin Taylor (Trailblazer)
Australia: Eyewitness Travel (Dorling Kindersley)
Australia: Insight Guide (Insight Guides)
Berlitz Pocket Guide to Australia (Berlitz)
Globetrotter Australia, Bruce Elder (New Holland)
Sydney: Time Out Guide (Penguin)

Travel Literature

Australia: True Stories of Life Down Under (Traveler's Tales)
Bill Bryson: In a Sunburned Country, Bill Bryson (Broadway)
The Road from Coorain, Jill Kathryn Conway (Vintage)
Sean and David's Long Drive, Sean Condon (Lonely Planet)
Sydney, Jan Morris (Penguin)

Miscellaneous

1,000 Great Places to Explore in Australia (Explore Australia)
Australian Wildlife, Stella Martin (Bradt Travel Guides)
Australian Wine Companion 2013, James Halliday (Hardie Grant Books)
Cooking the Australian Way, Elizabeth Germaine (James Bennett Pty Ltd)
Explore Australia 2013 (Explore Australia)
The Slater Field Guide to Australian Birds, Peter Slater (Reed Natural History/New Holland (AUS)

APPENDIX C: USEFUL WEBSITES

Below is a list of useful websites, listed by subject, for readers wishing to learn more about Australia and Australians.

Commonwealth Government

Australian Bureau of Statistics (💻 www.abs.gov.au): A wide range of statistics on Australia's economy, environment and energy, industry, population and regions.

Australia Council for the Arts (💻 www.australiacouncil.gov.au): The Australian government's arts funding and advisory body.

Australian Customs (💻 www.customs.gov.au).

Australian Department of Foreign Affairs and Trade (💻 www.dfat.gov.au).

Australian Government (💻 www.australia.gov.au): Useful information for, among others, jobseekers, migrants, retirees, students and women.

Australian Trade Commission (💻 www.austrade.com).

Bureau of Meteorology (💻 www.bom.gov.au): Information about all aspects of Australia's climate and weather.

Department of Foreign Affairs and Trade (💻 www.dfat.gov.au/aib): Australia in brief.

Department of Immigration & Citizenship (💻 www.immi.gov.au): Everything you need to know about visas and immigration.

Office for Women (💻 www.fahcsia.gov.au/our-responsibilities/women/overview): The government website of the Office for Women.

Study in Australia (💻 www.study-in-australia.org): The official Australian government site for international students.

Culture

Australian War Memorial (💻 www.awm.gov.au): National museum commemorating the sacrifice of Australians in war.

Convict Creations (💻 www.convictcreations.com): The hidden story of Australia 's missing links.

Immigration Museum (💻 http://museumvictoria.com.au/immigrationmuseum): The history of Australian immigration from the 1800s to the present day.

Indigenous Australia (💻 www.dreamtime.net.au): Information about Australia's indigenous peoples.

National Gallery of Australia (💻 www.nga.gov.au): Details of collections, events and exhibitions.

National Library of Australia (💻 www.nla.gov.au): The website of Australia's largest reference library.

National Museum of Australia (💻 www.nma.gov.au): Details of collections, events and exhibitions.

Education

Adult Learning Australia (💻 www.ala.asn.au): A body concerned with adult education in Australia.

Australian Government Education Portal (💻 www.deewr.gov.au): Gateway to over 5,000 websites proving information about education and training in Australia.

The Australian National University (💻 www.anu.edu.au): The ANU (in Canberra) is one of the world's foremost research universities and attracts leading academics and outstanding students from Australia and across the world.

Study in Australia (💻 http://studyinaustralia.gov.au): A government site with advice on studying in Australia.

Expatriates

Adelaide Bound (💻 www.adelaidebound.com): Website dedicated to migrants in Adelaide.

American Australian Organization (💻 www.americanaustralian.org): Non-profit organization in the United States devoted to relations between the United States and Australia.

British-Australia Society (💻 www.britain-australia.org.uk): Society for Brits with branches throughout Australia.

British Balls Magazine (💻 http://bbmlive.com): Weekly guide for British expats.

British Expat Australia Forum (💻 www.britishexpat.com/expatforum/australia): Forum where you can read and post messages on Australia-related matters.

British Expats (💻 http://britishexpats.com): Forum for British expats in Australia.

Brits in Brisbane (💻 www.britsinbrisbane.com): Community forum for Brits in Brisbane.

Britz in Oz (💻 www.britzinoz.com): Website for British expats and migrants to Australia.

The Emigration Group (💻 www.emigrationgroup.co.uk): the website for The Emigration Group and Taylor & Associates, who together offer a comprehensive service for migrants to Australia and New Zealand.

Expat Australia (💻 www.expataustralia.com): Miscellaneous info for expats Immigrate

Melbourne Newcomers (💻 www.melbournenewcomers.com): Melbourne newcomers and friends' association.

Newcomers Network (💻 www.newcomersnetwork.com): Information and contact for migrants.

Perth (💻 www.immigrate-to-a-new-life-in-perth.com): Perth for migrants.

Pomigrate (💻 www.pomigrate.com): Life in Australia.

Poms in Oz (www.pomsinoz.com): Forum.

Poms in Perth (www.pomsinperth.com): Information and forum for Brits in Perth.

Sydney Newcomers (www.sydneynewcomers.com.au): Sydney newcomers club.

UK in Australia (http://ukinaustralia.fco.gov.uk/en): British government information website.

Victorian Australian-American Association (www.australianamerican.org).

Yanks Down Under (http://yanksdownunder.net/topic/460240/1): Forum for Americans in Oz.

Living & Working

About Australia (www.about-australia.com): One of Australia's longest established information portals containing information about business, lifestyle, towns and regions, and what's on.

Aussie Move (www.aussiemove.com): Information specifically aimed at new migrants.

City of Melbourne (www.melbourne.vic.gov.au): The official Melbourne local government website.

City of Sydney (www.cityofsydney.nsw.gov.au): The official Sydney local government website.

Come on Aussie (www.comeonaussie.com.au): Internet services directory.

Home I Own (www.homeiown.com): Aussie real estate blog.

Housing Institute of Australia (www.hia.com.au): Analysis and forecasting of Australia's housing industry.

Living in Australia (www.livingin-australia.com): Useful information for immigrants.

Media

Australian Newspapers Online (www.newspapers.com.au): Contains a complete directory of Australian publications by state and territory, with links to their websites.

The Australian (www.theaustralian.com.au): Australia's leading newspaper.

Australian Broadcasting Corporation (www.abc.net.au): Information about the government-owned television and radio stations.

ACP Magazines (www.acpmagazines.com.au): Australia's largest magazine publisher.

Crikey (www.crikey.com.au): Australia's leading independent online news service.

Radio Australia (www.radioaustralia.net.au/international).

Special Broadcasting Service (www.sbs.com.au): News website with more of a global than local outlook on news. Aims to reflect the multicultural nature of Australian society.

Sydney Morning Herald (www.smh.com.au): Sydney's leading newspaper; a useful source of Australian and international business, entertainment, news, sport and technology.

TNT Magazine (www.tntmagazine.co.uk). Free weekly magazine for expatriate Australians in the UK, but of interest to anyone planning to live in Australia.

Miscellaneous

Australia Institute (🖳 www.tai.org.au): develops and conducts research and policy analysis.

Best Restaurants of Australia (🖳 www.bestrestaurants.com.au): Search for restaurants by location, cuisine, price, features and more.

Charles Sturt University Guide to Australia (🖳 www.csu.edu.au/australia): A useful collection of links on many topics, including culture, education, geography, tourism, towns and cities, trade and commerce, and travel and communications.

Greenpeace Australia Pacific (🖳 www.greenpeace.org.au): Environmental information, news and resources.

National Wine Centre of Australia (🖳 www.wineaustralia.com.au): Part of the University of Adelaide, the NWCA provides information about winemaking and all aspects of Australia's vibrant wine industry.

National Womens Justice (🖳 http://nwjc.org.au/womensorgs.html): Promotes women's equality.

Ninemsn (🖳 http://ninemsn.com.au): A joint venture between Microsoft and Australia's leading media company, Publishing and Broadcasting Limited (PBL), ninemsn is Australia's number one interactive media company.

Online Opinion (🖳 www.onlineopinion.com.au): E-journal of social and political debate.

Relationships Australia (🖳 www.relationships.com.au): an organisation offering help to couples, families and individuals.

Wikipedia (🖳 http://en.wikipedia.org/wiki/portal:australia): The Australian encyclopaedia.

Wine Australia (🖳 www.wineaustralia.com and www.australianwines.com.au): Everything you need to know about Australian wines.

Yellow Pages (🖳 www.yellowpages.com.au): Online business telephone directory.

State Government Offices

ACT: Government of the Australian Capital Territory (🖳 www.act.gov.au).

NSW: New South Wales Government Trade and Investment Office (🖳 www.nsw.gov.au).

NT: Government of the Northern Territory (🖳 www.nt.gov.au).

QLD: Agent-General for Queensland (🖳 www.qld.gov.au).

SA: Agent-General for South Australia (🖳 www.sacentral.sa.gov.au).

TAS: Government of Tasmania (🖳 www.tas.gov.au).

VIC: Agent-General for Victoria (🖳 www.vic.gov.au).

WA: Government of Western Australia (🖳 www.wa.gov.au).

State Tourist Offices

Tourism Canberra (🖳 www.canberratourism.com.au).

Tourism New South Wales (🖳 www.visitnsw.com.au).

NT Tourist Commission (🖳 www.ntholidays.com).

Tourism Queensland (🖳 www.queenslandholidays.com.au).

SA Tourist Commission (🖳 www.southaustralia.com).

Tourism Tasmania (🖳 www.discovertasmania.com.au).

Tourism Victoria (🖳 www.tourism.vic.gov.au).

Tourism Western Australia (🖳 www.westernaustralia.com).

Travel & Tourism

About Australia (🖳 www.about-australia.com): Digests of each state and a wealth of information for travellers.

Austravel (🖳 www.austtravel.com.au): Australian travel emporium.

Flight Centre (🖳 www.flightcentre.com.au): A good website for flights, hotels and other travel arrangements, both in Oz and abroad.

Go Australia (🖳 http://goaustralia.about.com): Information for visitors.

Images Australia (🖳 www.imagesaustralia.com): Photographs and general information about Australia.

Melbourne Online (🖳 www.melbourne.com.au): What's on in Melbourne.

Picture Australia (🖳 www.pictureaustralia.org): A service hosted by the National Library of Australia, providing access to the digitised picture collections of a range of cultural institutions.

Smart Traveller (🖳 www.smartraveller.gov.au): The Australian government's travel advisory and consular assistance service.

Sydney Online (🖳 www.sydney.com.au): What's on in Sydney.

Tourism Australia (🖳 www.australia.com): The organisation responsible for marketing Australia, containing information about all aspects of visiting and living in the country.

Travel Australia (🖳 www.travelaustralia.com.au): Accommodation and travel in Australia.

Up From Australia (🖳 www.upfromaustralia.com/reallyaussie.html): Aussie browsing and shopping.

White Hat (🖳 www.whitehat.com.au): Information about Melbourne and Australia.

APPENDIX D: COMMUNICATIONS MAP

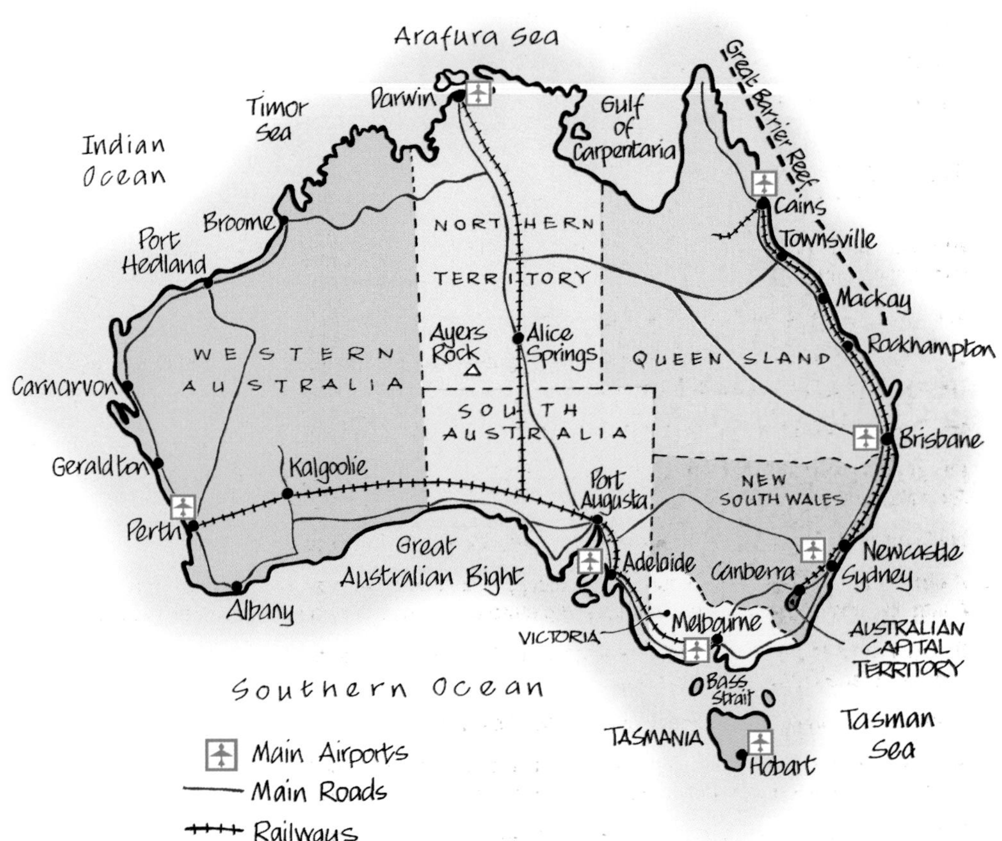

INDEX

A

B

C

D

U

V

W

Who Are We?

Survival Books was established in 1987 and by the mid-'90s was the leading publisher of books for people planning to live, work, buy property or retire abroad.

From the outset, our philosophy has been to provide the most comprehensive and up-to-date information available. Our titles routinely contain up to twice as much information as other books and are updated more frequently. All our books contain colour photographs and most are printed in full colour. They also contain original cartoons, illustrations and maps.

Survival Books are written by people with first-hand experience of the countries, cities and the people they describe, and therefore provide invaluable insights that cannot be obtained from official publications or websites, and information that is more reliable and objective than that provided by the majority of unofficial websites.

Survival Books are designed to be easy – and interesting – to read. They contain a comprehensive list of contents and index and many also have extensive appendices, including useful addresses, further reading and useful websites to help you obtain additional information, as well as other useful reference material.

Our primary goal is to provide you with the essential information necessary for a trouble-free life or property purchase and to save you time, trouble and money.

We believe our books are the best available – they are certainly the best-selling. But don't take our word for it – read what reviewers and readers have said about Survival Books at the front of this book.

Most of our books are available as Paperbacks, Kindle and eBooks.
Order your copies today by visiting
www.survivalbooks.net

WHO ARE WE?

OTHER SURVIVAL BOOKS

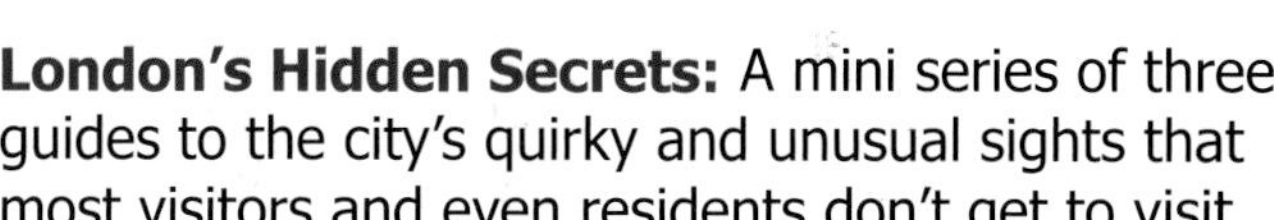

London's Hidden Secrets: A mini series of three guides to the city's quirky and unusual sights that most visitors and even residents don't get to visit.

London's Secret Walks: A walking book with a difference, taking you off the beaten track to visit London's hidden and 'secret' sights.

London's Secrets: a new series including Museums & Galleries, Parks & Gardens and Pubs & Bars, with more to come.

Retiring in France: Everything a prospective retiree needs to know about one of the world's most popular retirement destinations.

Running Gîtes and B&Bs in France: An essential guide for anyone planning to invest in a gîte or bed & breakfast business.

Shooting Caterpillars in Spain: The hilarious and compelling story of two innocents abroad in the depths of Andalusia in the late '80s.

Sketchbooks series: A series of beautiful sketchbooks with walks, including Cornwall, the Cotswolds, the Lake District and London.

Where to Live in London: The only book published to help newcomers choose the best area to live to suit both their lifestyle and pocket.

For a full list of our current titles, visit our website at www.survivalbooks.net

PHOTO CREDITS

www.dreamstime.com

Pages 14 © Chee-Onn Leong, 16 © Mikdam, 18 © Tashka, 20 © Phillip Minnis, 31 © Ximagination, 43 © Ximagination, 53 © Sintez, 64 © Kurhan, 69 © Showface, 70 © Siberia, 76 © Showface, 79 © Coleong, 83 © Alan Crosthwaite, 90 © Gurilla, 93 © Travelling-light, 98 © Jorgoman, 115 © Sportlibrary, 116 © Travelling-light, 127 © Solena 432, 128 © Iofoto, 135 © Hypedesk, 136 © Prebanac, 142 © Katseyephoto, 155 © Derind99, 156 © Gibbsterr, 160 © Rorem, 167 © Kiwirob, 175 © Litifeta, 176 © Terrasprite, 180 © Ta_Samaya, 185 © Actinicblue, 186 © Sinkers, 189 © Photographer, 191 © Innershadows, 195 © Igenkin, 202 © Amaviael, 206 © Negativex_digital_photography, 217 © Wonderwolf, 220 © Ximagination, 231 © Bamse008, 235 © Bmcent1, 236 © Lionandblue, 238 © Robynmac, 243 © Tmcnem, 247 © Nds_cgy, 249 © Budgetstockphoto, 250 © Jirsa, 252 © Redbaron, 257 © Araraadt, 259 © Bizaroo, 260 © Stormboy, 262 © Krystof, 265 © Jlye, 266 © Digitalkris, 269 © Klikk, 281 © G-image, 283 © Ptlee, 297 © NSP Images, 307 © Dreamphoto 1000, 325 © Yekorzh, 331 © Coleong, 332 © Oksanaphoto, 333 © Perrush, 341 © Chee-Onn Leong, 347 © Rosshipwell, 351 © China, 352 © Michaelmajor, 357 © Keeweeboy, 363 © Photooz, 364 © Gloria-leigh, 390 © Mollypix, 404 © Awcnz62, 404 © Erickn, 405 © Nsilcock, 405 © Elkeflorida

www.shutterstock.com

Pages 1 © Coleong &R. Gino Santa Maria, 13 © clearviewstock, 23 © Marten Czamanske, 25 © Dasilva, 27© Courtney Keating, 29 © Phillip Minnis, 32 © Rene Jansa, 34 © Glen Jones, 37 © Sandy Maya Matzen, 38 © Ximagination, 40 © Francois Etienne du Plessis, 44 © János Gehring, 46 © GeoM, 48 © Ingrid Balabanova, 51 © Pavel Bortel, 59 © Dimitrije Paunovic, 55 © Matthew J. Brown, 56 © Steven Reineck, 58 © John Austin, 61 © Francois Etienne du Plessis, 63 © Thorsten Rust, 67 © Lee Torrens, 80 © Pavel Losevsky, 84 © Anyka, 87 © Manuel, 88 © Chee-Onn Leong , 95 © Bob Denelzen, 97 © Colin & Linda McKie, 101 © Olivier Le Queinec, 102 © Gelpi, 104 © Rob Marmion, 107 © Christopher Meder, 108 © Pres Panayotov, 110 © Thomas M. Perkins, 113 © Stuart Taylor, 118 © Stephen Coburn, 121 © Max Blain, 122 © Christopher Meder, 125 © Andriy Rovenko, 131 © Ronen, 132 © Jason Stitt, 139 © Phil Morley, 140 © Alex Brosa, 144 © Leah-Anne Thompson, 147 © Buida Nikita Yourievich, 149 © Gelpi, 150 © Tijmen, 152 © Avalon Imaging, 158 © Tijmen, 163 © Gibsons, 164 © Milan Vasicek, 168 © GeoM, 170 © Lisa F. Young, 173 © Maarten Wagemans, 179 © Colin & Linda McKie, 182 © Stieglitz, 183 © Dudarev Mikhail, 192 © Tomasz Trojanowski, 201 © Ashley Whitworth, 204 © Iofoto, 209 © Marcin Balcerzak, 210 © Feng Yu, 213 © Olena Kucherenko, 214 © Beerkoff, 219 © Joan Kerrigan, 223 © Chee-Onn Leong, 224 © Leah-Anne Thompson, 227 © Sandra G, 232 © Stephen Coburn, 240 © Johnny Lye, 245 © Filaphoto, 254 © Robyn Mackenzie, 270 © Eric Isselée, 272 © Jenny Solomon, 275 © Aaron D. Settipane, 277 © Gregor Kervina, 278 © Carlos Sanchez Pereyra, 284 © Chee-Onn Leong, 286 © Photosbyjohn, 288 © Irina Tischenko, 290 © Sebastien Burel, 293 © Max Blain, 294 © Stephen Finn, 299 © John Barry de Nicola, 300 © Neale Cousland, 302 © Galina Barskaya, 304 © Lee Torrens, 308 © Graham Prentice, 311 © Pavel Losevsky, 313 © Maya Kruchankova, 315 © Andrey Armyagor, 319 © Volk 65, 321 © Carlos E. Santa Maria, 322 © Stuart Miles, 326 © Ben Heys, 328 © Vera Bogaerts, 335 © Elena Aliaga, 336 © (unknown), 339 © Matt Trommer, 342 © Robyn Mackenzie, 345 © Supri Suharjoto, 349 © Darrin Wassom, 355 © Neale Cousland, 359 © Max Earey, 360 © Creativa, 370 © Kwest, 404 © Dmitry Pichugin, 405 © Yury Zaporozhchenko